# Leaders & the Leadership Process

Readings, Self-Assessments, & Applications

# Leaders & the Leadership Process

Readings, Self-Assessments,
& Applications

*Third Edition*

Jon L. Pierce

John W. Newstrom

Boston   Burr Ridge, IL   Dubuque, IA   Madison, WI   New York
San Francisco   St. Louis   Bangkok   Bogotá   Caracas   Kuala Lumpur
Lisbon   London   Madrid   Mexico City   Milan   Montreal   New Delhi
Santiago   Seoul   Singapore   Sydney   Taipei   Toronto

*McGraw-Hill Higher Education*

*A Division of The McGraw-Hill Companies*

LEADERS & THE LEADERSHIP PROCESS:
READINGS, SELF-ASSESSMENTS & APPLICATIONS
Published by McGraw-Hill/Irwin, a business unit of The McGraw-Hill Companies, Inc.,
1221 Avenue of the Americas, New York, NY, 10020. Copyright © 2003, 2000, 1995 by
The McGraw-Hill Companies, Inc. All rights reserved. No part of this publication may be
reproduced or distributed in any form or by any means, or stored in a database or retrieval
system, without the prior written consent of The McGraw-Hill Companies, Inc.,
including, but not limited to, in any network or other electronic storage or transmission,
or broadcast for distance learning.

Some ancillaries, including electronic and print components, may not be available to customers
outside the United States.

This book is printed on acid-free paper.

3 4 5 6 7 8 9 0 QPD/QPD 9 0 9 8 7 6 5 4

ISBN 0-07-248256-7

Publisher: *John E. Biernat*
Senior editor: *John Weimeister*
Editorial coordinator: *Trina Hauger*
Senior marketing manager: *Ellen Cleary*
Producer, Media technology: *Mark Molsky*
Project manager: *Natalie J. Ruffatto*
Production supervisor: *Debra R. Sylvester*
Designer: *Adam Rooke*
Supplement producer: *Betty Hadala*
Senior digital content specialist: *Brian Nacik*
Cover and Interior design: *Adam Rooke*
Typeface: *10 / 12 New Century Schoolbook*
Compositor: *Shepherd Incorporated*
Printer: *Quebecor World / Dubuque*

**Library of Congress Cataloging-in-Publication Data**

Pierce, Jon L. (Jon Lepley)
  Leaders & the leadership process : readings, self-assessments & applications / Jon L.
Pierce, John W. Newstrom.—3rd ed.
    p. cm
  Includes bibliographical references and index.
    ISBN 0-07-248256-7 (alk. paper)
    1. Leadership.  2. Leadership—Case studies.  3. Leadership—Problems, exercises, etc.  I.
Title: Leaders and the leadership process.  II. Newstrom, John W.  III. Title.
HM 1261 .P54 2003
303.3'4—dc21                                                          2002070137

www.mhhe.com

To our colleagues in the Department of Management Studies: Thank you for enriching the qualify of our work life. To our students: Thank you for helping us sustain our commitment to the intellectual growth and development of others.

*Jon L. Pierce*
*John W. Newstrom*

# Preface

## THE BOOK: LEADERS AND THE LEADERSHIP PROCESS

Several years ago the management and organization faculty at the University of Minnesota Duluth decided that the undergraduate curriculum needed a course in leadership. Claims that many of our organizations were "over managed and under led" and that the crisis facing American organizations was in large part a function of "bad management and inept leadership" led us to believe that it was important for our students to explore the subject of leadership in greater depth and to begin thinking about and looking at themselves within the leadership context. A course in leadership might serve as an important catalyst in fulfilling this objective.

As part of the design process, we consulted several leading leadership scholars around the country, asking for assistance with the construction of a reading list for our new course. We informed these individuals of our decision to conduct an undergraduate seminar in leadership and asked them to help identify important material from the leadership literature. After compiling this list we offered our first course. During the past several years this course has been offered on several occasions and continually refined. It has proven to be extremely popular with our students.

Mary Fischer, John Weimeister, and Bill Schoof of The Austen Press encouraged us to take our undergraduate course materials in leadership and put them into book form. Their interest in our leadership class led to the creation of this book.

## PURPOSE OF THE BOOK

Few management and organization topics have generated as much interest and research activity as leadership. "Fads" in the corporate world find their roots in practitioners' fancy for and belief in "quick fixes" for organizational woes and consultants' desire to make a quick buck. Thus, the corporate desire to search continually for "new bottles for old wine," coupled with academicians' inclination to study and think about what inspires them, creates all the ingredients for a short-lived interest in leadership and the leadership process. However, this has not been the case. Instead, widespread interest in leadership has spanned more than six decades with significant historical roots stemming from the works of many ancient Greek, Roman, Chinese, and Egyptian philosophers.

Thousands of pages in academic books and journals have been devoted to the topic of leadership. During the past several years, the popular press has published and sold millions of copies of several dozen books written on the topic of leaders and leadership. Organizations frantically search for the magical leader who can pull the firm together and place it back on the competitive path. We frequently hear stories about important historical leaders; we attribute organizational successes and failures to the things that our leaders did or failed to do; and at the national level we commonly resurrect dreams of the way it was when certain charismatic leaders were at the nation's helm.

It is evident that there is a strong interest in leadership. Our university, along with a large number of other institutions of higher education, has in recent years instituted courses in leadership.

This book's development reflects that interest and the obvious need for a greater number of individuals to take the issue of organizational leadership more seriously. *The primary purpose of this book is to serve as a catalyst for the student of leadership's thinking and dialogue about leaders and the leadership process.* This book is intended to give the student a feel for the breadth and richness of this study. This set of readings aims to provide the student with a sense of the complexity associated with organizational leadership as well as an important understanding of some of the pieces that serve to define this complex mosaic called leadership.

## WHAT THE BOOK IS AND IS NOT

This book of readings cannot provide the reader with thorough and complete coverage of the leadership literature. During the past six-plus decades, those leadership scholars who have chosen to observe, study, think, and write about leadership have produced literally thousands of pages of theory and empirical observation. For obvious reasons, this text provides but a sampling of this literature.

While this book does touch on many of the major themes that have characterized the work done in the realm of leadership, there are many important authors and contributions that could not be included. This omission is not intended to downplay the importance of the scholarship that they have given to our understanding of this very important topic.

While this book does include some of the classic and seminal articles on leadership, there are many classical pieces that could not be included. Once again, this is not intended to suggest that they are less important than the pieces that we ultimately chose to include.

## THE LEADERSHIP MOSAIC

Before we embark upon our study of leadership, we would like to share a metaphor with you. The metaphor is that of a mosaic. Your authors live and work at the University of Minnesota located in Duluth, Minnesota, a community located along the north shore of Lake Superior. On the city's boardwalk there are many beautiful views of the "big lake" (Lake Gitchi Gummi, as named by the native Americans who lived in this part of the world) and the hilled city rising several hundred feet above the lake and named after the explorer Daniel Greysolon Sieur du-Luth.

As one walks along Duluth's boardwalk you come upon an extremely large, blue and white mosaic that depicts many scenes from the city's long maritime history. This mosaic is made up of literally thousands and thousands of $1 \times 1$ inch tile squares.

As we worked to prepare our school's undergraduate leadership class and the readings contained in this book we were confronted by an extremely rich, complex, and extensive literature. This is a literature whose contemporary history dates back to the early 1900s, a literature given to us by those who have led and those who have followed, a literature given to us by a number of philosophers, and a literature that has stemmed from the careful and systematic application of the scientific method. Not only have there been hundreds of books written about leadership, there have been thousands and thousands of journal pages devoted to an exploration of the concept and its myriad of themes.

The study of leadership that you are about to embark upon reminds us of a mosaic. There are dozens and dozens of concepts, perspectives, themes, hypotheses, and theories. Each represents a small piece of the overall mosaic. It is impossible to see and therefore appreciate the mosaic that captures images of the tall ships and whale-back boats that once sailed Lake Superior by looking at a single tile. In a similar way, you will not come to understand leadership by reading the work of a single author or by becoming familiar with a single concept, definition of leadership, or one of the many midrange leadership theories.

We invite you to read carefully the many authors who share with us their views and observations on leadership. No one singularly paints a full and complete picture for us. We encourage you to examine the concepts, propositions, perspectives, and theories one at a time, and then use each as a tile for the construction of your own leadership mosaic.

## THE BOOK'S ORGANIZATION

This book is organized into two parts. Part One, divided into 15 chapters, presents a set of readings that will help students understand leaders and the leadership process. The majority of the readings are taken from academic journals. Our editing has streamlined several readings by removing complex sections, thus making the material more "reader friendly" and appropriate for diverse audiences.

- Chapter 1 looks at the definition of leadership, suggests that leadership is a process, and provides some insight into the role played by leaders.

- Chapter 2 inquires about the leader–follower relationship. Fairness, trust and ethical behavior are three important dimensions that define this relationship.

- Chapter 3 suggests that effective leaders are individuals who possess the "right stuff." The traits associated with effective leadership are reviewed.

- Chapter 4 continues the theme of leader traits and looks specifically at the role of sex and gender in the leadership equation.

- Chapter 5 asks the question, How do people come to be leaders? The dynamics associated with leader emergence are explored.

- Chapter 6 builds upon the suggestion that leadership is an influence process. The bases of power and forms of influence that leaders use in order to move followers are examined.

- Chapter 7 explores the suggestion that effective leadership is in part a function of what leaders do. The behaviors that can be used to describe effective leadership are examined.

- Chapter 8 suggests that different situations call for different leader behaviors. One leadership style simply does not serve all individuals (followers), nor does it serve all situations within which leaders and their followers find themselves embedded.

- Chapter 9 continues the theme that "it all depends upon the situation," or "every situation is different." This chapter asks if leadership style and effectiveness are bound by cultural dissimilarities.

- Chapter 10 reinforces the notion that the follower plays a powerful role in the leadership process. The follower is not a passive part of the leadership formula and, in fact, the attributes and behaviors of the follower frequently serve to shape the leadership process.

- Chapter 11 explores the long-standing interest in participative leadership. Issues surrounding the theoretical reasons for the use of participative leadership and insight into the relationship between participation and leader effectiveness are explored.

- Chapter 12 suggests that there are "substitutes" for leadership. While it is easy to conclude that leadership is always necessary, the readings in this chapter suggest that there are situational factors that can serve as substitutes for, neutralizers of, and enhancers of leaders and their behaviors.

- Chapter 13 provides insight into the nature and character of the charismatic and transformational leader—the leadership style that today's business world appears to be frantically searching for.

- Chapter 14 asks us to recognize that leadership is not always a positive force. The readings in this chapter suggest that there are a number of potentially dysfunctional aspects associated with leadership.

- Chapter 15 asks the seemingly strange question, Does leadership really make a difference? The readings in this chapter address both sides of the debate. *Point:* Leadership does *not* make a difference; it is simply the product of a societal love affair and romantic notions that surround leaders. *Counterpoint:* Leadership *does* make a difference in the level of organizational performance; it is not simply a socially constructed organizational reality.

## SELF-ASSESSMENTS

Many of the chapters include self-assessment exercises, which give readers the opportunity to profile themselves along several different dimensions associated with leaders and the leadership process. These self-assessments provide readers with an opportunity to take a look at themselves and further understand how they fit within the realm of this complex mosaic of leadership.

You are encouraged to use the grid that follows to record your score on each of the self-assessments and interpret your score.

## PART TWO: BEYOND THE THEORY AND INTO THE PRACTICE OF LEADERSHIP

Part Two provides readers with additional opportunities to explore leaders and the leadership process. This section of the book is intended to move students beyond the theory of leadership and closer to the world of practice and application.

To facilitate students' ability to apply their understanding of the leadership literature and work on the development of analytical and problem-solving skills, we have included several incidents, case studies, and exercises. We firmly believe that active learning contributes more to the overall learning process than passive learning. We therefore encourage students to read, think about, discuss, debate, observe, experiment with, analyze, and solve issues that define leadership and the leadership process. The cases, incidents, and exercises are intended to supplement the conceptual material and help readers come to understand leaders and the leadership process more fully.

# Self-Assessment Summary Record

*Instructions:* You are encouraged to record each of your "self-assessment" scores below. Accompanying each score you should also provide a brief interpretation of what that score means to you and/or an action plan for change. You might find it interesting to return to this self-assessment in one, three, and five years to monitor changes (or consistency) in your profile.

| | Score | Interpretation |
|---|---|---|
| *Self-confidence* | | |
| *Leader–Member Exchange* | | |
| *Justice* | | |
| *Procedural justice* | | |
| *Distributive justice* | | |
| *Interpersonal justice* | | |
| *Informational justice* | | |
| *Trust in Leadership* | | |
| *Affect* | | |
| *Positive* | | |
| *High positive* | | |
| *Negative* | | |
| *High negative* | | |
| *Emotional Intelligence* | | |
| *Leadership Motivation* | | |
| *Masculinity–Femininity* | | |
| *Masculinity* | | |
| *Femininity* | | |
| *Androgyny* | | |
| *Self-monitoring* | | |
| *Influence Tactics* | | |
| *Rational persuasion* | | |
| *Others:* | | |
| *Pressure* | | |
| *Upward appeal* | | |
| *Exchange* | | |
| *Ingratiation* | | |
| *Coalition* | | |
| *Inspirational appeal* | | |
| *Consultation* | | |
| *Personal Power Profile* | | |
| *Reward power* | | |
| *Coercive power* | | |
| *Legitimate power* | | |
| *Referent power* | | |
| *Expert power* | | |
| *Michigan Organizational Assessment* | | |
| *Personal support* | | |

| | Score | Interpretation |
|---|---|---|
| Goal emphasis | | |
| Work facilitation | | |
| *Initiating Structure* | | |
| *Consideration* | | |
| *Least Preferred Co-worker* | | |
| *Individualism–Collectivism* | | |
| *Participatory Leadership Attitudes* | | |
| Person's capacity | | |
| Information sharing | | |
| Participation | | |
| Supervisory control | | |
| *Substitutes for Leadership* | | |
| Ability, experience, training, and knowledge | | |
| Professional orientation | | |
| Indifference toward organizational rewards | | |
| Unambiguous, routine, and methodologically invariant tasks | | |
| Task-provided feedback concerning accomplishments | | |
| Intrinsically satisfying tasks | | |
| Organizational formalization | | |
| Organizational inflexibility | | |
| Advisory and staff functions | | |
| Closely knit, cohesive, interdependent work group | | |
| Rewards not within the leader's control | | |
| Spatial distance between superior and subordinate | | |
| Subordinate need for independence | | |
| *Group Cohesiveness* | | |
| *Organization-based Self-esteem* | | |
| *Transformational and Charismatic Leadership* | | |
| Articulate vision | | |
| Role model | | |
| Foster goal acceptance | | |
| Performance expectations | | |
| Individual support | | |
| Intellectual stimulation | | |
| Transactional leader behaviors | | |
| *Machiavellianism* | | |

# Acknowledgments

There are many individuals whom we would like to acknowledge for their role in assisting us with the creation of this book. First, there are many organization scholars who have worked hard at developing the theory of leadership and providing scientific observations of leaders and the leadership process. We thank them for providing us with an understanding of and insight into this very important organizational phenomenon.

Robert J. House, Craig Lundberg, Jerry Hunt, Chet Schreisheim, Warren Bennis, Henry P. Sims, Jr., Peter Frost, Jane M. Howell, Alan C. Filley, Charles C. Manz, Kimberly Boal, Larry L. Cummings, and Bernard M. Bass each provided us with ideas pertaining to important pieces of leadership literature, case studies, and exercises/incidents that could be employed to help communicate the many lessons of leadership.

Several individuals, including Edwin Hollander, Brian P. Niehoff, Albert A. Vicere, Morgan McCall, and Martin Schatz, reviewed, critiqued, and offered very helpful suggestions that aided us in strengthening the breadth, inclusiveness, thoroughness, and quality of our edited work. We want to say "thank you" for your assistance.

A special form of recognition must go to the undergraduate and graduate students who took the leadership course from us here at the University of Minnesota Duluth. Your passionate interest in leadership and the understanding of leaders and the leadership process that you derived from this set of readings encouraged us to assemble this book. Consequently, other students can now benefit from this interesting collection of materials taken from the leadership literature.

We benefited greatly from the many hours of assistance that we received from two individuals here at the University of Minnesota Duluth. Jackie Johnson, thank you very much for your assistance. Connie Johnson, thank you for your help with the myriad tasks associated with the preparation of our manuscript. Your patience and ever-willingness to help is appreciated.

We would like to extend our appreciation to Mary Fischer and Bill Schoof of Austen Press. We sincerely appreciate your encouragement, which led to the creation and publication of this book. Finally, we would like to thank John Weimeister for his encouragement and assistance in bringing about this third edition.

*Jon L. Pierce*

*John W. Newstrom*

# Table of Contents

# Prologue

Where should a systematic study of leadership begin? The contemporary study of leaders and the leadership process finds its most recent roots stemming from social psychology, sociology, psychology, and organizational behavior. Several noted group and organizational scholars, among them Kurt Lewin, Ronald Lippitt, Ralph White, J. Dowd, Ralph Stogdill, Edwin Fleishman, and G. Spiller, launched their inquiries into leadership during the 1930s and 1940s, yet many leadership studies were published during the earlier part of the 1900s.

It is, however, possible to start the study of leadership by turning to the classics. Homer's *Iliad* and the *Odyssey* provide detailed biographies of great leaders. Plutarch's *Lives* provides insight into what makes great leaders act the way that they do, while Sophocles's plays, *Ajax* and *Antigone,* depict the psychology of leadership. Shakespeare, in *Othello,* provides a look into the role of intuition and *King Lear* provides clues into the difference that leadership makes by examining the role of succession. *The Republic,* by Plato, examines and expresses reservations about democratic management and leadership, while John Stuart Mill, in his essay *On Liberty,* constructs his arguments for participative management.[1]

Fred A. Kramer (1992), author of the first reading, launches our study of leadership with his "Perspectives on Leadership from Homer's *Odyssey*." We concur with his conclusion that "each of us should evaluate our own journey into self-awareness and self-understanding." We hope that the wide variety of readings and other materials in this collection will stimulate you to begin that search into your understanding of leaders and the leadership process. We invite you to study the classic, recent, and emerging perspectives on leadership and reflect on their implications for you, organizations, and our rapidly emerging global community.

---

[1] For the reader interested in the "classic touch" to the subject of leadership, we recommend John K. Clemens and Douglas F. Mayer's *The Classic Touch: Lessons in Leadership from Homer to Hemingway* (Homewood, IL: Dow Jones-Irwin, 1987).

This is the first of several self-assessment exercises that you will be given the opportunity to complete as you read *Leaders and the Leadership Process*. This self-assessment highlights one of Homer's leadership lessons—the importance of self-confidence. As you will see, Chapter 3 (Leaders and the Role of Personal Traits) also emphasizes the importance of self-confidence as a part of leader emergence and leader effectiveness. We encourage you to return to this particular self-assessment in conjunction with your reading and reflection upon the material in Chapter 3 and the question, Who is a leader and what are his/her distinguishing personal traits?

**Instructions:** For each of the following statements, indicate the degree to which you *agree* or *disagree* with the statement.

| | Strongly Disagree | Disagree | Slightly Disagree | Neither Agree nor Disagree | Slightly Agree | Agree | Strongly Agree |
|---|---|---|---|---|---|---|---|
| 1. When I make plans, I am certain I can make them work. | 1 X | 2 | 3 | 4 | 5 | 6 | (7) |
| 2. One of my problems is that I cannot get down to work when I should. | 1 | (2) | 3 | 4 | 5 | 6 | 7 |
| 3. If I can't do a job the first time, I keep trying until I can. | 1 | 2 | 3 | 4 | 5 | 6 | (7) |
| 4. When I set important goals for myself, I rarely achieve them. | (1) | 2 | 3 | 4 | 5 | 6 | 7 |
| 5. I give up on things before completing them. | (1) | 2 | 3 | 4 | 5 | 6 | 7 |
| 6. I avoid facing difficulties. | 1 | (2) | 3 | 4 | 5 | 6 | 7 |
| 7. If something looks too complicated, I will not even bother to try it. | (1) | 2 | 3 | 4 | 5 | 6 | 7 |
| 8. When I have something unpleasant to do, I stick to it until I finish it. | 1 | 2 | 3 | 4 | 5 | 6 | (7) |
| 9. When I decide to do something, I go right to work on it. | 1 | 2 | 3 | 4 | 5 | 6 | (7) |
| 10. When trying to learn something new, I soon give up if I am not initially successful. | (1) | 2 | 3 | 4 | 5 | 6 | 7 |
| 11. When unexpected problems occur, I don't handle them well. | 1 | 2 | 3 | 4 | (5) | 6 | 7 |
| 12. I avoid trying to learn new things when they look too difficult for me. | (1) | 2 | 3 | 4 | 5 | 6 | 7 |
| 13. Failure just makes me try harder. | 1 | 2 | 3 | 4 | 5 | 6 | (7) |
| 14. I feel insecure about my ability to do things. | (1) | 2 | 3 | 4 | 5 | 6 | 7 |
| 15. I am a self-reliant person. | 1 | 2 | 3 | 4 | 5 | 6 | (7) |
| 16. I give up easily. | (1) | 2 | 3 | 4 | 5 | 6 | 7 |
| 17. I do not seem capable of dealing with most problems that come up in life. | 1 | (2) | 3 | 4 | 5 | 6 | 7 |

*(continued)*

**Scoring:** Subtract each of your scores to questions 2, 4, 5, 6, 7, 10, 11, 12, 14, 16, and 17 from 8. Next, employing your adjusted scores, sum your score for each of the 17 questions, then divide by 17, and enter your score here: _____.

**Interpretation:** Mowday (1979) notes that self-confidence can be viewed as a belief in one's ability to successfully influence an outcome—that is, a belief that one's efforts can produce results.[1] Thus, it might be suggested that an individual with high self-confidence possesses a strong generalized self-efficacy. Homer (in the *Odyssey*) suggests to us that self-confidence (i.e., a belief in one's self) is a precursor to strong and effective leadership. In addition, it is suggested that Mentor's sense of confidence and vision was contagious, empowering Telemachus to become, himself, an effective leader. The higher your score the stronger your expressed sense of generalized self-efficacy, and the lower your score the weaker the assessment of your generalized self-efficacy. A score of greater than 6 would reflect a strong sense of self-efficacy—confidence that one believes that one has the capacity to succeed when confronted with achievement situations in general. A score of 2 or less would suggest a weak sense of self-efficacy—possessing doubt as to one's capacity to succeed when confronted with achievement situations.

Source: M. Sherer, J. E. Maddux, B. Mercadante, S. Prentice-Dunn, B. Jacobs, and R. W. Rogers, "The Self-efficacy Scale: Construction and Validation," *Psychological Reports* 53 (1982), pp. 899–902. Reprinted with permission.

[1] R. T. Mowday, "Leader Characteristics, Self-confidence, and Methods of Upward Influence in Organizational Decision Making," *Academy of Management Journal* 22, (1979), pp. 709–725.

## Reading 1

# Perspectives on Leadership from Homer's *Odyssey*

**Fred A. Kramer**
University of Massachusetts–Amherst

Business and public-administration education and practice can be a harrowing experience. As Warren Bennis has suggested, "The more our work makes us specialists, the more we must strive to remain or become generalists in other matters, to perceive the interconnections among science, esthetics, and ethics, to avoid becoming lopsided. All of humanity's pursuits are connected, after all, and we remain ignorant of those connections at our peril."[1] Classic works of literature can help us overcome parochial tendencies, so we can better deal with our immediate problems and look beyond them.

Homer's epic poem, the *Odyssey,* illuminates truths that have value today. Many of us may look back to our high-school introduction to the *Odyssey* and recall a series of stories that may surface from the mists of our memories. Maybe our memories of the *Odyssey* support Edgar Allen Poe's view of epic poems. To Poe, epic was "the art of being dull in verse."[2] But the *Odyssey* need not be dull if read by more mature minds than the average teenager's. It may even be relevant. Surely modern leaders are not going to confront a Cyclops in a cave or see some of our trusted lieutenants turned into swine by the magical powers of Circe. But on some level, similar things happen in the course of coping with administrative demands today.

There are two levels on which the modern manager who aspires to improve his or her leadership abilities may engage the story of Odysseus. The deeper level is the intensely personal psychological journey toward self-awareness and self-development. As Cedric H. Whitman suggests, "The nature of myth, or folk tale, is to reflect in external form the psyche's subconscious exploration of itself and its experience."[3] In the chang-

ing environment of modern business and government, leaders are expected to embark on journeys into the unknown. Perhaps the successful completion of these journeys depends on notions of self-discovery similar to the ones that Odysseus went through.

To deal with this personal level of the *Odyssey,* one must read the tales and reflect deeply on how Homer's metaphors enhance one's personal growth.

On another level, however, one can reinterpret the stories that we first encountered in high school with a special relevance to management or leadership problems. The purpose of this paper is to show the relevance of some of Homer's insights into management with the hope that some readers will be inspired to read more of Homer to develop the arguments on a deeper, more personal level. We will see that many of Homer's key insights on leadership and management are relevant today, but, more important, we will see that thinking metaphorically can enhance our own development.

The *Odyssey* is, in part, the story of one man's adventures after the Trojan War. After the successful sack of Troy, Odysseus embarked with several ships and many followers to return to his native Ithaca, off the western coast of the Peloponesian peninsula. In what should have been a fairly standard trip—there was the usual side trip to sack and pillage Lauchachia en route just to keep certain that standard operating procedures honed by years of planning and maneuvers remained in good order—Odysseus incurred the wrath of Poseidon, the god of earth and sea. Despite Odysseus's efforts to meet his goal on time and within budget, events beyond his control intervened. Instead of a few weeks, Odysseus was gone for 10 more years.

During this time, his wife, Penelope, steadfastly remained loyal to him. Although pursued by several dozen suitors from all over the Greek world, she remained virtuous. She also was faced with some budgetary difficulties. In the manner of the times, the suitors who wanted to replace Odysseus in Penelope's bed as well as lay claim to Odysseus's kingdom hung around the palace

**Source:** Edited and reprinted with permission from *Business and the Contemporary World* (Summer 1992), pp. 168–173.

At the time this article was written, Fred A. Kramer was a professor of political science and director of the MPA Program at the University of Massachusetts—Amherst. He is the author of *Dynamics of Public Bureaucracy* and a variety of articles that have appeared in professional journals. Author affiliation may have changed since article was first published.

drinking and feasting—at Penelope's expense. This drain on Ithaca's coffers did not escape the gods. Athena, in particular, took pity on Penelope and successfully argued that the gods should allow Odysseus to return. As part of her plan, she told Telemachus, Odysseus's son, who was a baby when Odysseus went off to war but who was not full grown, to outfit a ship and go looking for his father.

Fed up with the actions of the suitors, who had virtually taken over his father's palace, Telemachus embarked on what he felt would be an impossible mission. He was helped in this effort by the man Odysseus left behind to look after the palace and grounds, Mentor. Athena assumed Mentor's appearance and accompanied Telemachus on the journey. Along the way, "Mentor" gave him encouragement—the encouragement that he needed to develop into a fully functioning, responsible adult. Telemachus was relieved to be doing something. He was a man of action even though he perceived that the odds were against him.

Like all good mentors, Athena imbued Telemachus with a sense of responsibility. In seeking to master his challenging assignment, Telemachus discovered his inner strength. The babbling teenager became an articulate, courageous adult who impressed others with his leadership potential. With his mentor's help and support, Telemachus gained confidence and achieved a degree of success that he had not previously thought possible. In short, under a mentor's guidance, Telemachus showed leadership qualities similar to those his father had displayed during the Trojan War.

Mentor meets each of the leadership criteria suggested by a current observer of leadership problems, Warren Bennis. In *Why Leaders Can't Lead,* Bennis suggests four "competencies" that leaders must show. These are: management of attention through vision; management of meaning through communication; management of trust through reliability and constancy; and management of self through knowing one's skills and deploying them effectively.[4]

The first three competencies are closely related. To Bennis, having a vision is absolutely essential to leadership. The leader's vision provides a focus and sets the agenda for the organization. Having a clear vision brings about confidence in the followers. To engender confidence in the followers, the leader must be able to communicate that vision. A leader organizes meaning for the members of the organization. "Leadership creates a new audience for its ideas because it alters the shape of understanding by transmitting information in such a way that it 'fixes' and secures tradition. Leadership, by communicating meaning, creates a commonwealth of learning, and that, in turn, is what effective organizations are."[5] The management of trust implies accountability, predictability, and reliability and is based on the kinds of positions that a leader takes.[6] These positions are based on the leader's vision for the organization, which must be clear, attractive, and attainable. According to Bennis and Burt Nanus, his collaborator on an earlier book, vision and position stand in the same relationship to each other as do thought and action.[7]

The management of self is another order of skill—one that may have to precede the others. Deployment of self is based largely on positive self-regard. To Bennis, positive self-regard is not "narcissistic character." Instead, leaders know their worth; they trust themselves without letting their ego or image get in the way.[8] They do this in several ways. First, they recognize their strengths and compensate for their weaknesses. Second, they nurture their own skills with discipline by working on and developing their own talents. And third, leaders have the capacity to discern the fit between their perceived skills and what the job requires. According to Bennis and Nanus, the self-regard that leaders show is "contagious." It empowers subordinates throughout the organization to bring their own skills to bear on issues that affect the organization within the context of the leader's vision.[9]

In the *Odyssey,* Mentor provides a vision—Telemachus must search for his father. Mentor communicates that vision clearly and takes positions that indicate to Telemachus that he, in fact, can succeed in his task. This is possible because, as one of the immortals (remember that Mentor was really Athena, Zeus's daughter), Mentor had a strong sense of self. What is more important for us, however, is the impact that Mentor has on Telemachus. Mentor's sense of confidence and vision was contagious. This confidence and vision empowered Telemachus to become a leader in his own right.

Not only did Athena get the gods' consent to serve as mentor and protector of Telemachus in his search for his father, but she convinced Zeus to intervene directly with Calypso, the beautiful nymph, who had kept Odysseus prisoner on her island for seven years. Even though Calypso was disappointed at the prospect of losing Odysseus, she helped him build and stock a raft for his sea journey back to Ithaca. All was smooth sailing for Odysseus until his old Nemesis, Poseidon, spotted his raft. Poseidon had not been a party to the gods' discussion about Odysseus. Athena had broached the idea of allowing Odysseus to return to Ithaca at a meeting that took place on Olympus while Poseidon was finishing up a project in Ethiopia. Even though the gods had made a decision regarding the Odysseus matter, Poseidon felt that his interests had not been adequately treated in the deliberations. Upon spotting Odysseus, the "mighty Earthshaker" waved his trident to start an incredible storm. Unanticipated changes in the political environment can upset stated goals.

With some supernatural help, Odysseus managed to swim to shore in the land of the Phaeacians. The Phaeacians were a neutral, peace loving, seafaring people. Because the ruler, Alcinous, claimed to be a direct descendent of Poseidon, Odysseus wisely did not relate the story of his adventures. Initially Odysseus was mistakenly thought to be an immortal, but, without revealing his identity, he convinced his host that he was just an ordinary guy who wanted to get home. Although Odysseus struck a modest, humble pose, he was goaded into participating in some athletic games. Naturally, the self-effacing stranger beat his adversaries at their own games. But Odysseus was a gracious winner, and Alcinous agreed to help him get back to Ithaca. Odysseus, at this point, shows virtually all the aspects that Bennis attributes to leaders.[10] He shows integrity, dedication, magnanimity, humility, and creativity. No wonder he was mistaken for an immortal.

At a feast that preceded his departure, Odysseus, upon hearing a song about his exploits during the Trojan War, broke into tears and admitted that he was the long-suffering subject of the bard's song. He then related his story, which is a metaphoric journey into self-awareness—a journey essential for all leaders.

A brief recapitulation of a few stories will show how interesting and relevant Odysseus's adventures are for today's managers. Odysseus had an early encounter in the land of the lotus-eaters. The lotus-eaters were a peaceful people. They were different from Odysseus and his men, who were the aggressive sackers of cities. What made the lotus-eaters so different was their food—lotus flowers. Bread and meat were the staples of Odysseus and his band. The lotus flowers induced a feeling of well-being in anyone who ate them. Odysseus discovered this when some of his men

who were sent out to serve as ambassadors to these people accepted some lotus flower snacks. Perhaps they should have just said, "No." The effect of their tasting the lotus was to deflect them from group goals. One taste and they lost sight of the objective of returning to Ithaca and desired only to "go native"—to stay happily in the land of the lotus-eaters. Odysseus exercised a classical Theory X management technique to cope with this insubordination. He ordered these men dragged back to the ships by force and kept under tight control until the effects of the lotus flowers dissipated. We can interpret this action as a solely managerial, as opposed to a leadership, response. There is no attempt to broaden vision or incorporate new goals or learn from new experiences. Dragging those spaced-out comrades back to the boat was efficient, but was it really the right thing to do?

After the interlude with the lotus-eaters, Odysseus and his band rowed on to the land of the Cyclopes, who are described as having had no stable laws, and, by implication, no lawyers. Odysseus, like many modern public and business leaders, was curious as to how such a system could operate. He and a group of 12 followers set off to explore the environment. Their curiosity drew them to the care of Polyphemus, the one-eyed giant who imprisoned them. Of course, the monster did take a couple of men for dinner and breakfast, summarily dashing their heads on the rocks in the cave and devouring them. Clearly Odysseus's leadership was put to the test.

Analyzing the situation and the materials available to him, Odysseus developed a plan while the monster was out tending his flocks of sheep and goats. Essentially it entailed getting the Cyclops drunk and poking his eye out with a burning stake while he slept under the influence of some fortified wine, which Odysseus just happened to have brought with him. While Odysseus gave Polyphemus the wine, he referred to himself as "Nobody." Odysseus, evidently, had a passion for anonymity. This ruse had immediate benefits for Odysseus, because the monster agreed that he would eat Nobody last. Carrying out the plan was dangerous, but Odysseus rallied his men and they successfully blinded Polyphemus.

The pain of the blinding, however, woke the giant and he called for his fellow Cyclopes, who gathered at the mouth of his cave. Polyphemus told his fellows, "Nobody is murdering me by craft." They were puzzled. "If nobody harms you . . . ," they responded before going about their own business. Odysseus managed to get his men out of the angry monster's cave and back to the ships.

Once aboard his ship, Odysseus could not refrain from deriding the blind, miserable monster. Far from keeping in the background and practicing anonymity, Odysseus boasted of his cleverness. Despite the wise words of those in his crew who advised him to keep quiet and get on with the journey, Odysseus continued to make fun of the blinded Cyclops and told Polyphemus his name. Even a vanquished foe may have some power resources that can be brought to bear on future issues. In Polyphemus's case, he prayed to his father Poseidon to make life difficult for Odysseus. His prayers were answered, but perhaps Odysseus became a better person, and leader, because of the trials set up by Poseidon.

This story brings out some leadership attributes of Odysseus as well as some drawbacks. Bennis would applaud the curiosity and vision that took Odysseus and his band to the cave. Although Bennis sees a difference between leadership and problem-solving, the clever way in which Odysseus leads his men to freedom is a positive aspect of leadership potential. Once back on his ship, however, Odysseus shows us that he is not really a true leader yet. His boasting almost brings disaster immediately. Surely there is little of the magnanimity and humility that Bennis found in some modern leaders.

The adventures of Odysseus go on and on. The story of this journey becomes increasingly metaphorical at ever-deepening levels until he reaches a state of self-awareness that is a key to successful leadership. But we need not get into all the details of Odysseus's adventures on his eventual return to Ithaca and reunion with his wife and son. There are enough interesting stories—the sailors breaking into the bag of winds while Odysseus slept, the dilemma of Scylla and Charybdis, the Sirens' song, and many more—to keep a modern manager engaged with the plot so that he or she may encounter the deeper metaphors that might inspire more creative thinking. If one reacquaints oneself with the rich metaphors of the epic, one will think. One will grow.

Public and business leaders should be beyond literal thinking. Although they certainly have to be concerned with real-world problems, perhaps the solutions to these problems can be found through more creative responses than are routinely tried in both the public and private sectors.

Rosabeth Moss Kanter has admonished her readers to "think across boundaries."[11] A fundamental challenge to leaders in this turbulent world is to expand their own, and others', thinking. They must also engage in integrative, holistic thinking. As Kanter puts it:

> To see problems and opportunities integratively is to see them as wholes related to larger wholes, rather than dividing information and experience into discrete bits assigned to distinct, separate categories that never touch one another. Blurring the boundaries and challenging the categories permit new possibilities to emerge, like twisting a kaleidoscope to see the endless patterns that can be created from the same set of fragments.[12]

Think of that metaphor of the kaleidoscope. Those are the same fragments. They have simply been rearranged. Can we train our minds to rearrange the fragments that we work with in business and public-policy problems?

The modern reader generally sees myths to be misconceptions or lies. Indeed, Bennis and Nanus present several leadership "myths" and then dispel them.[13] Myth to Homer, however, is a metaphor for the truth. The teachings about leadership that come from Homer are distilled from myths as metaphors. From these metaphors we find that such attributes as vision, dedication, communication, delegation, openness, creativity, magnanimity, and integrity are important components of leadership. But most important, Homer teaches us that a person should grow and develop. A person should learn from experience.

The main lesson of the *Odyssey* is that each of us should undertake our own journeys into self-awareness and self-understanding. By so doing we can develop our own leadership potential if we so choose. Although Homer does not tell us exactly how to go about our search for self-understanding, a deep reflection on his metaphors might illuminate that search for some people because thinking metaphorically can help us see things in new ways.

## Notes

[1] Warren Bennis, *Why Leaders Can't Lead* (San Francisco: Jossey-Bass, 1989), 119.

[2] Quoted in Cedric H. Whitman, *Homer and the Heroic Tradition* (Cambridge, MA: Harvard University Press, 1958), 15.

[3] Ibid., 297.

[4] Bennis, 19–21.

[5] Warren Bennis and Burt Nanus, *Leaders: The Strategies for Taking Charge* (New York: Harper & Row, 1985), 42.

6 Ibid., 43.

7 Ibid., 154.

8 Bennis, 57–58.

9 Bennis and Nanus, 58–60.

10 Bennis, 118–20.

11 Rosabeth Moss Kanter, "Thinking Across Boundaries," *Harvard Business Review* 68 (November–December 1990), 9.

12 Ibid.

13 Bennis and Nanus, 222–25.

# Part One

# Readings

# Chapter **One**

# Introduction to Leadership

This journey through the leadership literature starts with a set of readings that helps define leadership. On the surface, leadership would appear to have a simple definition. In fact, arriving at a definition is more complex because of the variety of ways that leadership has been envisioned.

In the first reading in this chapter, Jon L. Pierce and John W. Newstrom provide us with a perspective on the meaning of leadership. The ancient Greeks, Egyptians, and Chinese tended to focus on some of the key qualities possessed by the leader. For example, Taoism suggests that leaders need to act such that others come to believe that their success was due to their own efforts and not that of the leader. Lao Tzu said, "A leader is best when people barely know he exists, Not so good when people obey and acclaim him, Worse when they despise him. But of a good leader, who talks little, When his task is done, his aim fulfilled, They will all say, We did it ourselves." The Greeks believed that leaders possessed justice and judgment, wisdom and counsel, shrewdness and cunning, and valor and activism. Drawing upon the Egyptians, Bernard Bass (1990) suggests that the leadership context consists of the leader and follower.[1] He goes on to note that there are nearly as many definitions given to leadership as there have been authors who have written about the concept. Based upon an extensive review of the leadership literature, Bass provides us with an overview to the meaning of leadership by organizing the myriad of definitions around 13 different approaches. Pierce and Newstrom provide an overview of Bass's review. Among some of the interesting concepts that have been linked to the definition of leadership has been its role as "the focus of group processes, as a personality attribute, as the art of inducing compliance, as an exercise of influence, as a particular kind of act, as a form of persuasion, as a power relation, as an instrument in the attainment of goals, as an effect of interaction, as a differentiated role, and as the initiation of structure" (Bass, 1990, 20). To these many roles many contemporary writers are suggesting that leaders also coach, facilitate, and nurture. Finally, Pierce and Newstrom comment upon several alternative perspectives (e.g., self, symbolic, team, and organizational) as leadership.

According to Albert Murphy (1941), the author of the second reading, leadership is not a psychological phenomenon (something embedded in the traits of the individual); instead, leadership is essentially *sociological* in nature. Situations in

---

[1] Bernard Bass, "Concepts of Leadership" in *Bass & Stogdill's Handbook of Leadership* (New York: Free Press, 1990, pp. 13–20.)

which people find themselves create needs, and it is the nature of these demands that serves to define the type of leadership needed and thus who will lead. Leadership, according to Murphy, is said to be a function of the whole situation and not something that resides in a person. Murphy views leadership as a function of an interaction between the person and the situation, where the situation consists of the follower(s) and the context confronting them. $L = f$ [(Person) (Group) (Context)].

Leadership, when viewed from a sociological perspective, is framed as an interplay and relationship between two or more actors (i.e., leader and followers) within a particular context. This interplay and relationship between the situation, the needs that it creates for people, and the individual is defined as the leadership process, and it is this process that serves to define who is the leader, group effectiveness, future group (social) needs, and once again who serves as the group's next leader. Thus, the leadership process is fluid and not static in nature.

Edwin P. Hollander and James W. Julian (1969), in the third reading, provide us with insight into several dimensions of leadership. Among their observations is that leadership is: a process, an influence relationship, a leader–follower transaction, a differentiated role, an element of the situation in which the follower finds him/herself, and an exchange relationship.

Today, in the popular world of leadership, the word *vision* is at center stage. The country and many organizations find themselves suffering from a leadership void. As a consequence there is a search for those who have a vision that can unite people in the social system, providing them with a sense of purpose, unity, and a common direction. The third selection in this opening chapter provides a perspective on the leadership phenomenon of *vision*.

Linda Smircich and Gareth Morgan (1982) define the phenomenon of leadership from the perspective of what it is that leaders do for the groups that they are a part of. Leaders, according to Smircich and Morgan, assign meaning to events for others. Some individuals emerge as leaders because they "frame experience in a way that provides a viable basis for action . . ." (258). They are individuals who are capable of taking ambiguous situations, interpreting these situations, and framing for the follower an understanding of the situation and what needs to be done in order to move forward. Smircich and Morgan reinforce Murphy's notion that leadership is a sociological process that is characterized by an interplay between the leader, the followers, and their common situation (context). Finally, their work implies a power and dependency relationship. Followers surrender their power to interpret and define reality, while simultaneously granting this power to someone else. The second chapter of this book takes a closer look at the role of power and influence as a part of the leadership process.

An implicit message derived from this set of readings is that leadership can sometimes be differentiated from management and headship. Leadership therefore can be cast as either a formal role, wherein someone is a group's designated leader, or an informal role, as in the case of an emergent leader arising from a set of dynamics that are transpiring between members of a group and the context within which they are embedded. For those interested in pursuing the manager/leader distinction further, we encourage you to read the following: "What Leaders Really Do," by John P. Kotter, appearing in the *Harvard Business Review* (May–June 1990), p. 103–111; and "The Manager's Job: Folklore and Fact," by Henry Mintzberg, also appearing in the *Harvard Business Review* (July–August 1975), p. 49–61.

Figure 1.1 provides a visual and conceptual framework around which you can organize your understanding of leadership and the leadership process.

The leadership process can be envisioned as a complex and dynamic exchange. There are four key components involved in this interactive process (i.e.,

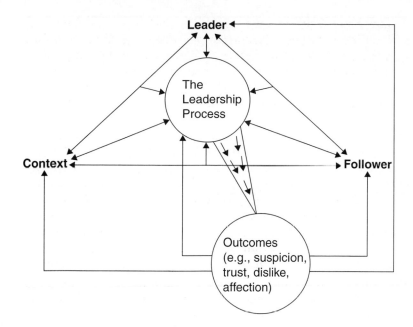

**FIGURE 1.1**
**The Leadership Process**

Source: R. B. Dunham and J. L. Pierce, *Management* (Glenview, IL: Scott, Foresman, 1989), p. 556.

leader, follower[s], the context, and the resulting by-product) that can be employed to articulate the meaning of leadership and the leadership process:

- The *leader* is the person who takes charge and guides the performance or activity.

- The *follower(s)* is a person who performs under the guidance and instructions of a leader.

- The *context* is the situation—formal or informal, social or work, dynamic or static, emergency or routine, complex or simple, and so on—surrounding a leader–follower relationship.

- *Outcomes* can include nearly anything arising from interplay between the leader–follower and leader–situation, such as respect for an able leader's decisions, goal attainment, customer satisfaction, high-quality products, or animosity resulting from a punitive leader's actions.

The leadership process is both interactive and dynamic. Leaders influence followers, followers influence leaders, and all parties are influenced by the context in which the exchange takes place. In turn, the outcomes that stem from a leader–follower exchange can influence future interactions as they may produce a change in the context, in the followers, and/or in the leader.

According to this model, understanding of leadership and the leadership process necessitates developing an understanding of the leader, the follower(s), the context, the influence processes (e.g., follower → leader; situation → follower; situation → leader; leader → situation; leader → follower), and the resulting consequences. The figure reveals that leadership (according to Murphy, 1941) is a sociological phenomenon and that it is dynamic (fluid) in nature. As suggested by Murphy (1941), Hollander and Julian (1969), and Smircich and Morgan (1982), leadership is a social influence relationship, interactive between two or more people dependent upon one another for the attainment of certain mutual goals, bound together within a group situation. It is a dynamic and working relationship, built over time, involving an exchange between leader and follower in which leadership is a resource embedded in the situation, providing direction for goal attainment.

## Reading 2

# On the Meaning of Leadership

**Jon L. Pierce and John W. Newstrom**
University of Minnesota Duluth

Leaders and leadership permeate the context of contemporary society, in much the same way that they have throughout the history of civilization. Mythical characters, such as those in Homer's *Odyssey* and the *Iliad,* have been used to portray great leaders and great feats of leadership, as well as to carry messages of leader character to succeeding generations. In Homer's *Odyssey,* for example, we learn about the importance of self-confidence in successful leadership.

In addition to finding leadership lessons in the Latin, Greek, and Roman classics, Chinese classics from as early as the sixth century B.C. illustrate an interest in leaders and feats of leadership. Confucian writings emphasized the importance of setting a moral example and using rewards and punishment as leadership tools for molding moral behavior. In addition, Taoism emphasized that effective leaders maintain a low profile and work through others:

> A leader is best, When people barely know he [she] exists, Not so good when people obey him [her], Worse when they despise him [her]. But of a good leader, who talks little, When his [her] task is done, his aim fulfilled, They will say: We did it ourselves.

Stories from the Old and New Testament provide more recent evidence of a long-standing interest in leadership. The Book of Exodus, for example, presents an interesting story about the leadership challenges confronting Moses in his attempt to lead the Israelites out of Egypt.

Scholars writing during the twentieth century maintained this long-standing interest in leaders and the leadership process. During the twentieth century, there were few if any organizational concepts that have received as much scholarly attention for as long a period of time as the concept of leadership. Stogdill's review of the leadership literature, published in 1948, examined studies of leadership dating back to 1904. He cited more than 100 authors who provided insight into the nature of leaders and their personality traits. In 1974, he published a second review of 163 studies which were published between 1949 and 1970. Today there are journals such as *Leadership*

*Quarterly* and the *Journal of Leadership Studies* that exclusively focus on leadership. In addition, each of the major management and organization journals (e.g., *Academy of Management Journal, Academy of Management Review, Journal of Applied Psychology, Journal of Management,* and *Administrative Science Quarterly*) routinely publish leadership articles, and virtually every organizational behavior and management textbook devotes a chapter to the topic. Finally, the last two decades have witnessed the publication of dozens of popular leadership books (e.g., Covey's *The 7 Habits of Highly Effective People,* Bennis's *Why Leaders Can't Lead,* and Daft and Lengel's *Fusion Leadership*), which are sold in most of the major airports in North America as well as neighborhood bookstores (e.g., Barnes & Noble and B. Dalton). Many of these books have sold literally thousands upon thousands of copies.

Scholars interested in leadership have approached the development of an understanding of leadership from a variety of perspectives. Starting with the "Great Person Theory of Leadership," which posited that great leaders such as Julius Caesar, Joan of Arc, Catherine II the Great, Napoleon, Mao Tse-tung, Churchill, and Franklin Delano Roosevelt were "born" with a set of personal qualities that destined them to be "great leaders." Much of the leadership scholarship conducted during the first half of the twentieth century was focused on the identification of the personal traits (attributes) that characterized those individuals who emerged as leaders and those who came to be highly effective leaders. Following the study of leaders and personal traits, the focus turned to a variety of themes, such as leader behaviors, the conditions under which certain leader behaviors were effective, the nature of the relationship between leaders and followers, and the forms of influence that were associated with effective leadership.

In this lead reading for *Leaders and the Leadership Process,* we will address the question, What does the concept of leadership mean? We recommend that you read an outstanding piece on the "Concepts of Leadership" by Bernard M. Bass (Chapter One in *Bass & Stogdill's Hand-*

*book of Leadership: Theory, Research, and Management Applications*). Bass provides a detailed review of the diversity of perspectives that have been taken by scholars as they have attempted to wrestle with the leadership phenomenon.

## ON THE MEANING OF LEADERSHIP

A review of the leadership literature quickly reveals that there are multiple definitions that have been given to the leadership construct. This diversity of definitions reveals, in part, the complexity of the construct. Some authors have chosen to treat leadership as a psychological phenomenon (i.e., the leader is a person who possesses certain desirable personality and demographic traits), while others see it as a sociological phenomenon (i.e., the leader is the result of a confluence of a person, a group, and the needs arising from a situation faced by each).

Bass (1990), in the introductory chapter to *Bass & Stogdill's Handbook of Leadership*, focuses on the concept of leadership. He suggests that there are several different approaches to the definition. Specifically, he identifies the following:

- *Leadership as a focus of group processes.* This set of definitions positions the leader as the hub, nucleus, and/or pivotal point for group activity as might be illustrated with Chapin's (1924) definition of leadership as "a point of polarization for group cooperation."

- *Leadership as personality and its effects.* This set of definitions tends to define leadership in terms of the personality attributes or the strength of character of the leader himself. Of leadership, Bernard (1926), said that "Any person who is more than ordinarily efficient in carrying psychosocial stimuli to others and is thus effective in conditioning collective responses may be called a leader."

- *Leadership as an act or behavior.* There was a tradition in leadership research that focused upon the acts of leadership, attempting to answer the question, What do leaders do? This set of definitions can be illustrated by Shartle's (1956) suggestion that the act of leadership is "one which results in others acting or responding in a shared direction."

- *Leadership as an instrument of goal achievement.* This set of definitions ascribes an instrumental value to the act of leadership. A leader, according to Cowley (1928), "is a person who has a program and is moving toward an objective with his group in a definite manner," while Davis (1942) defines leadership as "the principal dynamic force that motivates and coordinates the organization in the accomplishment of its objectives."

- *Leadership as an emerging effect of interaction.* There is a set of definitions of leadership that casts it as an "effect or outgrowth" of group interaction. It is not seen as the "cause" of group action, but something which emerges as a result of interactions within and among members of the group. Bogardus (1929) suggests that it is a social process "which causes a number of people to set out toward an old goal with new zest or a new goal with hopeful courage . . ."

- *Leadership as a differentiated role.* Emerging out of role theory and its perspective that members of social systems occupy different roles that are needed to advance the system, leadership is but one of several well-defined, needed, and differentiated roles. Different members of a social system (group) might be seen as making different contributions to the attainment of the group's goals. These roles, according to Sherif and Sherif (1956) come to be defined in terms of stable expectations that group members develop for themselves and other members of the group. From this perspective, leadership might be seen as that role which integrates the other roles to advance the cause of the social system.

- *Leadership as the initiation of structure.* A continuation of the "role theme" to the definition of leadership, those who view leadership as the "initiation of structure" see a unique role as defining leadership. Stogdill (1959) took this approach, when he defined leadership as "the initiation and maintenance of structure in expectation and interaction."

There appear to be several approaches to the definition of leadership that revolve around, for example, such concepts as: influence, power, and securing compliance. For example:

- *Leadership as the art of inducing compliance.* This set of definitions tends to cast leadership in terms of the molding of the group around the will, intentions, and/or wishes of the leader. Leadership is, therefore, cast from an induction-compliance perspective and influence is exercised from a single direction—leader to follower—without regard to the follower's wishes. Allport's (1924) definition of leadership as "personal social control" and

Bundel's (1930) definition of leadership as "the art of inducing others to do what one wants them to do" are illustrative of the inducing compliance approach to the definition of leadership.

- *Leadership as the exercise of influence.* There is a set of definitions of leadership that appears to employ the concept of "influence" as separate and distinct from dominance, control, or the forcing of compliance. Such definitions might range from Gandhi's emphasis upon leading by example (he states, "Clean examples have a curious method of multiplying themselves"), to the statement "follow me," (cf., Bass, 1990), to attempts to move others through speech and the communication process (cf. Tannenbaum, Weschler, & Massarik, 1961), to the movement of others through the production of an effect on followers' perceptions (cf., Ferris & Rowland, 1981). Some of the definitions simply employ the word "influencing," such as Tannenbaum, et al.'s (1961) suggestion that it is "interpersonal influence," and Tead's (1935) observation that it is "the activity of influencing people to cooperate toward some goal which they come to find desirable."

- *Leadership as a form of persuasion.* Some definitions of leadership reflect the movement of others through strongly held convictions and/or reason. A former U.S. president, Dwight Eisenhower, built his definition of leadership around the concept of persuasion. For Eisenhower, "leadership is the ability to decide what is to be done, and to get others to want to do it" (cf., Larson, 1968, p. 21). Lippmann (1922) employed the same conceptualization, "the final test of a leader is that he leaves behind him in other men the conviction and the will to carry on."

- *Leadership as a power relationship.* This set of definitions focuses on the key role played by power. French and Raven (1959) defined leadership from the perspective of the differences in power relationships among members of a group. Similarly, Janda (1960) saw leadership in terms of a "group member's perception that another group member has the right to prescribe behavior patterns for the former regarding his activity as a member of a particular group."

Finally, Bass (1990) observes that there are a number of conceptualizations of leadership that employ a combination of elements. Leadership as a combination of elements was illustrated by Dupuy and Dupuy (1959), who make reference to obedience, confidence, respect, and loyal cooperation in their definition.

Bass (1990) employs the following definition of leadership in *Bass and Stogdill's Handbook of Leadership:*

> Leadership is an interaction between two or more members of a group that often involves a structuring or restructuring of the situation and the perceptions and expectations of the members (p. 19).

He goes on to suggest that leaders are "agents of change," "persons whose acts affect other people more than other people's acts affect them," and that "leadership occurs when one group member modifies the motivation or competencies of others in the group" (pp. 19–20).

Joseph Rost (1991) in *Leadership for the Twenty-First Century* reviewed 221 definitions of leadership, which emphasizes the point that there are "many definitions." After reviewing many of the different definitions of leadership, Ciculla (1995) notes that "one can detect a family resemblance between the different definitions. All of them talk about leadership as some kind of process, act, or influence that in some way gets people to do something" (p. 12). She suggests that if the authors of these 221 definitions were assembled in a room each would understand one another and they would be able to understand the individual who spoke of leadership as the process of influencing the movement of a group toward the attainment of a particular outcome. The major differences, Ciculla notes, are to be found in aspects of the relationship that exists between the leader and follower, and in terms of "how" leaders get people to do things.

Yukl (1998), commenting upon the variety of definitions of leadership, states "The differences are not just a case of scholarly nitpicking. They reflect deep disagreement about identification of leaders and leadership processes" (p. 3). We, too, have come to believe that it is unlikely that there will ever be a single definition. The complexity of the phenomena, the fact that it manifests itself in so many different ways in so many different contexts, and the different purposes to which it gets put call for a variety of defining features. It appears to us that most students of leadership see it as *a sociological phenomenon (a process) involving the intentional exercise of influence exercised by one person over one or more other individuals, in an effort to guide activities toward the attainment of some mutual goal.*

# ALTERNATIVE CONCEPTUALIZATIONS

We would like to note that there are additional conceptualizations and uses of the leadership construct. Among them are self-leadership, team leadership, strategic leadership, symbolic leadership, servant, and organization (and nation) leadership.

## SELF-LEADERSHIP

The self-leadership concept is frequently employed in reference to the "self leading the self" (cf., Manz, 1986). Self-leading individuals are described as self-starters, those who provide themselves with self-direction and motivation, providing themselves with feedback, rewarding personal accomplishment and chastising personal failure.

## TEAM LEADERSHIP

The year 1998 saw the merger of Travelers Insurance and Citicorp (a large banking institution) into Citigroup. Accompanying the merger, Citigroup formed the "office of the CEO" and John Reed and Sandy Weill (the CEOs of Citicorp and Travelers, respectively) became co-CEOs of the newly formed organization.[1] They envisioned that through their coleadership (i.e., team leadership) the megacorporation that they formed would be a major player in the financial services industry of the twenty-first century. Several years ago, when Louis V. Gerstner, Jr., left RJR Nabisco to lead IBM, RJR moved two of its executive vice presidents to their newly created "office of the chairman." They were to jointly operate as the chief executive and chairman.

In essence, the concept of team leadership, as employed here, makes reference to several individuals who, as a team, share in the leadership function. Acting collectively as one, they attempt to exercise the influence necessary to move a larger group toward the achievement of a common goal.

## STRATEGIC LEADERSHIP

Hambrick (1989) focuses on the people who have overall responsibility for an organization. The term "strategic leadership," according to Hambrick, connotes management of the overall enterprise. It makes reference to those individuals who

[1]R. Charan, "Two on Top," *Fortune* (May 25, 1998), pp. 193–197.

occupy positions of power operating out of the organization's upper echelon.

## SYMBOLIC LEADERSHIP

Smircich and Morgan (1982) observe that the symbols, slogans, rituals, stories, and myths are among the "tools of leadership" (cf. Pfeffer, 1981; Pondy, Frost, Morgan, & Dandridge, 1982). Over time the use of these tools can become institutionalized in their ability to exercise a "leadership role." Many individuals (e.g., Buddha, Jesus Christ, Mohammad) have been able to sustain their role of leadership in absentia. In part, their leadership has been exercised through these various tools (instruments) of leadership.

## SERVANT LEADERSHIP

Robert K. Greenleaf (1977) provides us with the concept *servant leader,* a normative theory of leadership, in his book *Servant Leadership: A Journey into the Nature of Legitimate Power and Greatness.* As a normative theory of leadership, Greenleaf presents a perspective on how leadership "ought to" unfold. Herman Hesse (1991), in his book *Journey to the East,* provides an insight into the servant leader through a story about a spiritual journey to the East.

Among the distinguishing characteristics of the servant leader are service to others and perceptions of trust. According to Greenleaf, the servant leader leads because s/he wants to serve others. He also suggests that people follow servant leaders, accepting their influence because of a high level of trust that gets placed in the leader by their followers.

## ORGANIZATIONAL (NATION) LEADERSHIP

Which of today's business corporations is foremost in leading us into the twenty-first century? Which nation will emerge as the world "leader" in the twenty-first century? Through the decades, various gurus in the business community (e.g., Peter Drucker, Tom Peters, Stephen Covey, Warren Bennis, Noel Tichy, Rosabeth Moss Kanter) have made reference to the dominant leadership role played by such organizations as Microsoft, Intel, and General Electric. All of these organizations have, at one time or another, been identified as major leaders in one context or another. American politicians are quick to highlight their perception that the United States of America is the "leader" among the free nations of the world, especially when it comes to military action and democracy.

While each of these perspectives and uses of the term is a legitimate use of the construct of leadership, each reflects a different conceptualization than that which traditionally has been employed. Each of these alternative perspectives on the concept of leadership is different from that which is focused on by this collection of readings. Throughout the remainder of this set of readings, leadership will be seen as a sociological phenomenon, arising out of and operating within a group context. The term leadership will generally be cast as a dynamic (fluid), interactive, working relationship between a leader and one or more followers, operating within the framework of a group context for the accomplishment of some collective goal. Efforts to address self, team, strategic, symbolic, organizational, and nation leadership will not be undertaken in this collection of readings.

## EMERGING ROLES

Finally, several of the readings in this collection will provide insight into the role and meaning of leadership by answering the question, What do leaders do? Smircich and Morgan (1982), in the last reading in this chapter, for example, suggest that leaders provide meaning by framing reality for others, and Stogdill (1948) in Chapter 2 (Reading 6) suggests that leaders orchestrate group activity.

There are some contemporary writers who suggest that there may be a new role for leaders in organizations of the twenty-first century. Manz and Sims (1991), for example, talk about *SuperLeadership*. This type of leader will represent the transformation from the "follow me leader" to the leader who engages in "leading others to lead themselves" and thus the attainment of self-leadership.

Senge (1990) suggests that accompanying the emergence of the learning organization, a new leadership role emerges. The role of the leader of a learning organization will be that of designer, teacher, and steward. This new leader role brings with it the need for a new set of leadership skills and tools of leadership.

We also note that an increasing number of management gurus are suggesting that many of today's organizations are "over managed and under led." Increasingly, organizations are modifying the role of yesterday's manager, changing the role to that of a leader charged with the responsibility to gain follower recognition and acceptance and become a facilitator and orchestrator of group activity, while also serving as coach and cheerleader. It is feasible that many of these roles (e.g., servant, teacher, coach, cheerleader) will become a common part of the conceptualization of leader and leadership as the twenty-first century continues to unfold.

## References

Allport, F. H. (1924). *Social Psychology*. Boston: Houghton Mifflin.

Bass, B. M. (1990). "Concepts of Leadership" (Chapter One). *Bass & Stogdill's Handbook of Leadership: Theory, Research, & Managerial Applications* (3rd edition). New York: Free Press.

Bernard, L. L. (1926). *An Introduction to Social Psychology*. New York: Holt.

Bogardus, E. S. (1929). "Leadership and Attitudes." *Sociology and Social Research* 13, pp. 377–387.

Bundel, C. M. (1930). "Is Leadership Losing Its Importance?" *Infantry Journal* 36, pp. 339–349.

Chapin, F. S. (1924). "Leadership and Group Activity." *Journal of Applied Psychology* 8, pp. 141–145.

Ciculla, J. B. (1995). "Leadership Ethics: Mapping the Territory." *Business Ethics Quarterly* 5, 1, 5–28.

Cowley, W. H. (1928). Three distinctions in the study of leaders. *Journal of Abnormal and Social Psychology* 23, 144–157.

Davis, R. C. (1942). *The Fundamentals of Top Management*. New York: Harper.

Dupuy, R. E., & Dupuy, T. N. (1959). *Brave Men and Great Captains*. New York: Harper & Row.

Ferris, G. R., & Rowland, K. M. (1981). "Leadership, Job Perceptions, and Influence: A Conceptual Integration." *Human Relations* 34, pp. 1069–1077.

French, J. R. P., Jr., & Raven, B. (1959). "The Bases of Social Power." In D. Cartwright (ed.), *Studies in Social Power*. Ann Arbor, MI: Institute for Social Research, University of Michigan.

Greenleaf, R. K. (1977). *Servant Leadership*. New York: Paulist Press.

Hambrick, D. C. (1989). "Putting Top Managers Back in the Strategy Picture." *Strategic Management Journal* 10, pp. 5–15.

Hesse, H. (1991). *Journey to the East*. New York: Farrar Straus and Giroux.

Janda, K. F. (1960). "Towards the Explication of the Concept of Leadership in Terms of the Concept of Power." *Human Relations* 13, pp. 345–363.

Larson, A. (1968). *Eisenhower: The President Nobody Knew*. New York: Popular Library.

Lippmann, W. (1922). *Public Opinion*. New York: Harcourt, Brace.

Manz, C. C. (1986). "Self-leadership: Toward an Expanded Theory of Self-influence Processes in Organizations." *Academy of Management Review* 11, pp. 585–600.

Manz, C. C., & Sims, H. J., Jr. (1991). "SuperLeadership: Beyond the Myth of Heroic Leadership." *Organizational Dynamics* 32, p. 1.

Pfeffer, J. (1981). "Management as Symbolic Action: The Creation and Maintenance of Organizational Paradigms." *Research in Organizational Behavior* 3, pp. 1–52.

Pondy, L. R., Frost, P., Morgan, G., & Dandridge, T. (eds.). (1982). *Organizational Symbolism.* Greenwich, CT: JAI Press.

Rost, J. (1991). *Leadership for the Twenty-First Century.* New York: Praeger.

Senge, P. M. (1990). "The Leader's New Work: Building Learning Organizations." *Sloan Management Review* 32, p. 1.

Shartle, C. L. (1956). *Executive Performance and Leadership.* Englewood Cliffs, NJ: Prentice-Hall.

Sherif, M., & Sherif, C. W. (1956). *An Outline of Social Psychology.* New York: Harper.

Smircich, L., & Morgan, G. (1982). "Leadership: The Management of Meaning." *Journal of Applied Behavioral Science* 18, 3, pp. 257–273.

Stogdill, R. M. (1959). *Individual Behavior and Group Achievement.* New York: Oxford University Press.

Tannenbaum, R., Weschler, I. R., & Massarik, F. (1961). *Leadership and Organization.* New York: McGraw-Hill.

Tead, O. (1935). *The Art of Leadership.* New York: McGraw-Hill.

Yukl, G. (1998). *Leadership in Organizations.* Englewood Cliffs, NJ: Prentice-Hall.

## Reading 3

# A Study of the Leadership Process

**Albert J. Murphy**
New York University

A fault of most leadership studies is emphasis upon the "individual" rather than upon the individual as a factor in a social situation. Such studies seek to determine the qualities of a person which distinguish him as a leader. They imply that these somehow can be abstracted. Difficulties immediately appear. It is discovered that leadership takes protean forms, that it is unstable, that the qualities necessary at one time are unnecessary at other times, that leaders rise and fall as situations change, that the same individual alternates between leading and following. Consequently, leadership becomes a slippery, ill-defined concept. These are commonplaces, but in spite of them, the authors usually fail to sense the root difficulty, viz., the inadequacy of the personality concept as a means of understanding the problem. Leadership is not a psychologically simple concept.

Leadership study calls for a situational approach; this is fundamentally sociological, not psychological. Leadership does not reside in a person. It is a function of the whole situation. The situation calls for certain types of action; the leader does not inject leadership but is the instrumental factor through which the situation is brought to a solution. The emphasis in the title of this paper is not on "leadership qualities" but on the "leadership process." The word *process* calls attention to the interplay of factors in a total situation. The situation is fundamental and in all cases makes the leader. This is obvious in everyday life and in history. The Hitlers and the Mussolinis are made by situations, and they can be understood only in terms of those situations. Their characteristics are indicative of the times in which they live and the situations of which they are a part. Groups do not act because they have leaders, but they secure leaders to help them to act. In other words, the leader meets a critical need just as a dentist meets a critical need. We go to a dentist because we have a toothache, not the other way around. Skills and abilities of all kinds have a functional relation to the needs of the situation, and these needs are always primary. Leadership comes into being when an individual meets certain social needs, when he releases in the social situation of which he is a part certain ideas and tendencies which are accepted by the group because they indicate solutions of needs which are dimly sensed. Leadership is best understood when it is looked at impersonally as that quality of a complex situation which, when lifted into a place of prominence, composes its conflicts and creates a new and more desirable situation.

The concept of process is important also in that it calls attention to the fluidity of the leadership situation. Leadership is not a static thing; it is an immutable aspect of personality. Many of the components of leadership, such as self-confidence and the confidence of the group, which are so essential, change with the situation. The self-confidence of a work leader or of a boys' gang leader usually disappears as soon as these individuals are put into a parlor. Ascendance, also a leadership component, increases when training is given in handling the materials of a situation. While leadership, self-confidence, ascendancy, and other so-called traits and attitudes, apparently carry over from one situation to another, it is only because the situations have practically identical elements. They are not fixed qualities of a person in any sense, nor are they fixed in the relation of two people, but are functions of a three-cornered relation—between the persons concerned and the job. Shyness often becomes dominance when the situation includes elements in which the individual's skill counts. So-called traits are names of processes; they are fluid; in no strict sense are they "attached" to anybody as "innate" or "acquired" characteristics. While studies of leadership make it appear that leaders usually have certain characteristics which combine under the term leadership ability, this generalization is misleading. Such factors as knowledge, forcefulness, tone of voice, and size are effective components in the solution of many social situations and are, therefore, generally regarded as leadership qualities, especially in unorganized group

**Source:** Edited and reprinted with permission from *American Sociological Review* 6 (1941), pp. 674–687. Author affiliation may have changed since article was first published.

situations like gangs, but the variety of possible factors is endless. Leadership qualities, so-called, vary indefinitely as the needs of groups vary indefinitely.

A few illustrations will make it obvious that the choice of leaders is dictated by group needs. A group lost in the woods would immediately follow the man who, no matter what his personal qualities, had a knowledge of the woods and the way out. A social group whose needs are conviviality and the pleasant interplay of personalities will be most stimulated by a person who is lively and sociable. The leader of an organization which integrates the functions of other organizations will be a person through whom the leadership drives of others may function; such a person becomes a leader through releasing, channelizing, and integrating the abilities of others. A discussion group leader will be self-effacing, tolerant, critical, and interested in the contributions of others. In the case of the group in the woods, personality, height, weight, and voice count for nothing: The only qualification is a knowledge of the way out. In the case of the social gathering, a personality characterized by pleasing vivacity is of major importance. In the third case, the essential characteristic of the leader is ability to release the activities and ambitions of others in a way which will promote the interest of all the groups concerned; in this case, height, weight, and voice would be irrelevant and forcefulness might even be disastrous. In the case of the discussion group, where leadership is of a highly integrative type, dominance and self-assertiveness, usually thought of as leadership traits, would be fatal. When the great variety of possible groups is considered, leadership appears clearly as a function of the situation. When the situation is simple, as in the case of the group lost in the woods, the demands on leadership are simple, but in complex situations the demands on leadership are multiple.

In order to bring out the meaning of leadership in terms of the situational processes, we may take a case from the study of leaders in work camps. In response to the request that members of work crews describe the characteristics of leaders whom they regarded as successful, the men mentioned things like these: he gets the work done; he explains things to you and doesn't yell at you; he plays no favorites but treats all men alike; he isn't so easy that you can step all over him; he watches out for the safety of the men in his crew.

These are modes of behavior. They are called for by the situation and are, in fact, responses to it. The young men who mentioned these desirable activities were not thinking of traits. So-called traits are derived by grouping these activities which are responses to the situation under classificatory labels or trait names. The first activity, "He gets the work done," is called the trait of efficiency. The second is called reasonableness; the third is called justice; the fourth is called strictness; the fifth, carefulness. Obviously, the leader is reacting to a total situation which embraces these elements as well as others. The qualities mentioned are simply names for types of activity which meet the needs of a group, which incorporate and make effective the important factors of the situation, emotional and otherwise. The group takes pride in doing a reasonable amount of work; it desires reasonable explanations; it desires fair play in work assignments; it appreciates the need of necessary strictness; it appreciates care for its safety. Does the leader have these traits? The abstractions mentioned and imputed to the leader as qualities are really descriptions of what most of the members of the work gang desire. The names of the appropriate activities are imputed to him as his characteristics. In short, what has happened is this: (1) the group has certain needs, practical and emotional; (2) the leader responds to the situation as a whole with appropriate activities; (3) those responses are classified and labeled with trait names; (4) these names which are abstractions and summational fictions are imputed to the leader as causal psychological entities.

Confusion in the study of leadership results from endowing abstractions with reality and imputing character qualities to the person who brings the element of control into the situation. We have failed to see the leadership process as an interplay of forces, as an integrative activity. Of course, when types of a leader's integrative activities become habitual, we may call them traits provided we understand that they are activities, and we may try to develop them because these habits of conduct are useful in a large number of situations.

In summary, leadership is the process of securing direction in social activity which otherwise would be blind and disorderly. Leadership activities are resultants of the interplay of the factors which emerge out of a situation and reenter it as controls. Emphasis on so-called traits of personality, which have been shown to be hypostatized summational fictions, therefore, gives way to a study of the integrative factors in the situation. The personality does not stand alone but is a changing element in a total situation. The situation is a concept embracing many elements: the leader with his abilities and drives, the group (including potential leaders), material resources, viewpoints, desires, and needs, and a condition of readiness for leadership. This situational whole is a continuous series of influences and changes. Relativity characterizes every factor. Leading alternates with following. Solutions are new stages in the situation preparing the way for other solutions which in turn call for new types of leadership to secure new ends. Leadership may be defined as *that element in a group situation which, when made conscious and controlling, brings about a new situation that is more satisfying to the group as a whole.* . . .

## Reading 4

# Contemporary Trends in the Analysis of Leadership Processes

**Edwin P. Hollander and James W. Julian**
State University of New York at Buffalo

The history of leadership research is a fitful one. Certainly as much, and perhaps more than other social phenomena, conceptions and inquiry about leadership have shifted about. The psychological study of leadership in this century began with a primary focus on the personality characteristics which made a person a leader. But the yield from this approach was fairly meager and often confused, as Stogdill (1948) and Mann (1959), among others, documented in their surveys of this literature. In the 1930s, Kurt Lewin and his coworkers (Lewin, Lippitt, & White, 1939) turned attention to the "social climates" created by several styles of leadership, that is, authoritarian, democratic, or laissez-faire. Together with developments in the sociometric study of leader–follower relations (e.g., Jennings, 1943), this work marked a significant break with the past.

Two residues left by Lewin's approach fed importantly into later efforts, even with the limited nature of the original study. One was the concern with "leader style," which still persists, especially in the work on administrative or managerial leadership (see, e.g., McGregor, 1960, 1966; Preston & Heintz, 1949). The other was the movement toward a view of the differential contexts of leadership, ultimately evolving into the situational approach which took firm hold of the field by the 1950s (cf. Gouldner, 1950).

For the most part, the situational movement was spurred by the growing recognition that there were specialized demands made upon leadership, depending upon the nature of the group task and other aspects of the situation. Clearly, a deficiency in the older approach was its acceptance of "leader" as a relatively homogeneous role, independent of the variations in leader–follower relationships across situations. The disordered state in which the trait approach left the study of leadership was amply revealed by Stogdill in his 1948 survey, which marked a point of departure for the developing situational emphasis. The publication in 1949 of Hemphill's *Situational Factors in Leadership* contributed a further push in this direction.

The main focus of the situational approach was the study of leaders in different settings, defined especially in terms of different group tasks and group structure. Mainly, though not entirely, through laboratory experimentation, such matters as the continuity in leadership across situations with variable tasks was studied (e.g., Carter, Haythorn, Meirowitz, & Lanzetta, 1951; Carter & Nixon, 1949; Gibb, 1947). The findings of this research substantially supported the contention that who became a leader depended in some degree upon the nature of the task. With this movement, however, there came a corresponding deemphasis on the personality characteristics of leaders or other group members. . . .

Within the present era, characterized by a greater sensitivity to the social processes of interaction and exchange, it becomes clearer that the two research emphases represented by the trait and situational approaches afforded a far too glib view of reality. Indeed, in a true sense, neither approach ever represented its own philosophical underpinning very well, and each resulted in a caricature. The purpose here is to attempt a rectification of the distortion that these traditions represented, and to point out the increasing signs of movement toward a fuller analysis of leadership as a social influence process, and not as a fixed state of being.

## AN OVERVIEW

By way of beginning, it seems useful to make a number of observations to serve as an overview. First, several general points which grow out of current research and thought on leadership are established. Thereafter, some of the directions in which these developments appear to be heading are indicated, as well as those areas which require further attention.

One overriding impression conveyed by surveying the literature of the 1960s, in contrast to the preceding two decades, is the redirection of interest

**Source:** Edited and reprinted with permission of *Psychological Bulletin* 71, 5 (1969), pp. 387–397. Copyright (1969) American Psychological Association.

in leadership toward processes such as power and authority relationships (e.g., Blau, 1964; Emerson, 1962; Janda, 1960; Raven, 1965). The tendency now is to attach far greater significance to the interrelationship between the leader, the followers, and the situation (see, e.g., Fiedler, 1964, 1965, 1967; Hollander, 1964; Hollander & Julian, 1968; Steiner, 1964). In consequence, the problem of studying leadership and understanding these relationships is recognized as a more formidable one than was earlier supposed (cf. Cartwright & Zander, 1968). Several of the particulars which signalize this changing emphasis may be summarized under four points, as follows:

1. An early element of confusion in the study of *leadership* was the failure to distinguish it as a process from the *leader* as a person who occupies a central role in that process. Leadership constitutes an influence relationship between two, or usually more, persons who depend upon one another for the attainment of certain mutual goals within a group situation. This situation not only involves the task but also comprises the group's size, structure, resources, and history, among other variables.

2. This relationship between leader and led is built *over time,* and involves an exchange or *transaction* between leaders and followers in which the leader both gives something and gets something. The leader provides a *resource* in terms of adequate role behavior directed toward the group's goal attainment, and in return receives greater influence associated with status, recognition, and esteem. These contribute to his "legitimacy" in making influence assertions, and in having them accepted.

3. There are differential tasks or functions attached to being a leader. While the image of the leader frequently follows Hemphill's (1961) view of one who "initiates structure," the leader is expected to function too as a mediator within the group, as a group spokesman outside it, and very often also as the decision maker who sets goals and priorities. Personality characteristics which may fit a person to be a leader are determined by the perceptions held by followers, in the sense of the particular role expectancies and satisfactions, rather than by the traits measured via personality scale scores.

4. Despite the persisting view that leadership traits do not generalize across situations, leader effectiveness can and should be studied as it bears on the group's achievement of desired outputs (see Katz & Kahn, 1966). An approach to the study of leader effectiveness as a feature of the group's success, in system terms, offers a clear alternative to the older concern with what the leader did do or did not do.

A richer, more interactive conception of leadership processes would entertain these considerations as points of departure for further study. Some evidence for a trend toward this development is considered in what follows.

## WHITHER THE "SITUATIONAL APPROACH"?

What was the essential thrust of the situational approach, after all? Mainly, it was to recognize that the qualities of the leader were variously elicited, valued, and reacted to as a function of differential group settings and their demands. Hemphill (1949a) capped the point in saying "there are no absolute leaders, since successful leadership must always take into account the specific requirements imposed by the nature of the group which is to be led, requirements as diverse in nature and degree as are the organizations in which persons band together" [p. 225].

Though leadership events were seen as outcomes of a relationship that implicates the leader, the led, and their shared situation, studies conducted within the situational approach, usually left the *process* of leadership unattended. . . .

But even more importantly, the situational view made it appear that the leader and the situation were quite separate. Though they may be separable for analytic purposes, they also impinge on one another in the perceptions of followers. Thus, the leader, from the follower's vantage point, is an element in the situation, and one who shapes it as well. As an active agent of influence he communicates to other group members by his words and his actions, implying demands which are reacted to in turn. In exercising influence, therefore, the leader may set the stage and create expectations regarding what he should do and what he will do. Rather than standing apart from the leader, the situation perceived to exist may be his creation.

It is now possible to see that the trait and situational approaches merely emphasize parts of a process which are by no means separable. One kind of melding of the trait and situational approaches, for example, is found in the work of Fiedler. His essential point, sustained by an extensive program of research (see 1958, 1964, 1965, 1967), is that the leader's effectiveness in the group depends upon the structural properties of the group and the situation, including interpersonal perceptions of both leader and led. He finds, for example, that the willingness of group members to be influenced by the leader is conditioned by leader characteristics, but that the quality and direction of this influence is contingent on the group relations and task structure (1967). This work will be discussed further in due course. . . .

A leader, therefore, sets the basis for relationships within the group, and thereby can affect outcomes. As Hemphill (1961) suggested, the leader initiates structure. But more than just structure in a concrete sense, he affects the process which occurs within that structure. Along with other neglected aspects of process in the study of leadership is the goal-setting activity of the leader. Its importance appears considerable, though few studies give it attention. In one of these, involving discussion groups, Burke (1966) found that the leader's failure to provide goal orientations within the group led to antagonism, tension, and absenteeism. This effect was most acute when there was clear agreement within the group regarding who was to act as the leader. Though such expectations about the leader undoubtedly are pervasive in groups studied in research on leadership, they are noted only infrequently.

## LEGITIMACY AND SOCIAL EXCHANGE IN LEADERSHIP

Among the more substantial features of the leader's role is his perceived legitimacy—how he attains it and sustains it. One way to understand the process by which the leader's role is legitimated is to view it as an exchange of rewards operating to signalize the acceptance of his position and influence.

In social exchange terms, the person in the role of leader who fulfills expectations and achieves group goals provides rewards for others which are reciprocated in the form of status, esteem, and heightened influence. Because leadership embodies a two-way influence relationship, recipients of influence assertions may respond by asserting influence in return, that is, by making demands on the leader. The very sustenance of the relationship depends upon some yielding to influence on both sides. As Homans (1961) put it, "Influence over others is purchased at the price of allowing

one's self to be influenced by others" [p. 286]. To be influential, authority depends upon esteem; he said. By granting esteem itself, or symbolic manifestations of it, one may in turn activate leadership, in terms of a person taking on the leader role. . . .

The "idiosyncrasy credit" concept (Hollander, 1958) suggests that a person's potential to be influential arises out of the positive dispositions others hold toward him. In simplest terms, competence in helping the group achieve its goals, and early conformity to its normative expectations for members, provide the potential for acting as a leader and being perceived as such. Then, assertions of influence which were not tolerated before are more likely to be acceptable. This concept applies in an especially important way to leadership succession, since it affords the basis for understanding how a new leader becomes legitimized in the perceptions of his peers. Further work on succession phenomena appears, in general, to be another area of fruitful study. There are many intriguing issues here, such as the question of the relative importance in legitimacy of factors such as "knowledge" and "office," in Max Weber's terms, which deserve further consideration (see, e.g., Evan & Zelditch, 1961). . . .

## EFFECTIVENESS OF THE LEADER

By now it is clear that an entire interpersonal system is implicated in answering the question of the leader's effectiveness. The leader is not effective merely by being influential, without regard to the processes at work and the ends achieved. Stressing this point, Selznick (1957) said that, "far more than the capacity to mobilize personal support . . . (or) the maintenance of equilibrium through the routine solution of everyday problems," the leader's function is "to define the ends of group existence, to design an enterprise distinctively adapted to these ends, and to see that the design becomes a living reality" [p. 37].

As Katz and Kahn (1966) observed, any group operates with a set of resources to produce certain outputs. Within this system, an interchange of inputs for outputs occurs, and this is facilitated by leadership functions which, among other things, direct the enterprise. The leader's contribution and its consequences vary with system demands, in terms of what Selznick referred to as "distinctive competence." Taken by itself, therefore, the typical conception of leadership as one person directing others can be misleading, as already indicated. Though the leader provides a valued resource, the group's resources are not the leader's alone. Together, such resources provide the basis for functions fulfilled in the successful attainment of group goals, or, in other terms, group outputs.

Given the fact that a group must work within the set of available resources, its effectiveness is gauged in several ways. Stogdill (1959), for one, distinguished these in terms of the group's performance, integration, and member satisfaction as group outputs of a leadership process involving the use of the group's resources. Thus, the leader and his characteristics constitute a set of resources contributing to the effective utilization of other resources. A person who occupies the central role of leader has the task of contributing to this enterprise, within the circumstances broadly confronting the group. . . .

## IDENTIFICATION WITH THE LEADER

For any leader, the factors of favorability and effectiveness depend upon the perceptions of followers. Their identification with him implicates significant psychological ties which may affect materially his ability to be influential. Yet the study of identification is passé in leadership research. Though there is a recurring theme in the literature of social science, harking back to Weber (see 1947), about the so-called "charismatic leader," this quality has a history of imprecise usage; furthermore, its tie with identification processes is by no means clear. Putting the study of the sources and consequences of identification with the leader on a stronger footing seems overdue and entirely feasible.

Several lines of work in social psychology appear to converge on identification processes. The distinction made by Kelman (1961) regarding identification, internalization, and compliance, for example, has obvious relevance to the relationship between the leader and his followers. This typology might be applied to the further investigation of leadership processes. The work of Sears (1960) and of Bandura and Walters (1963), concerning the identification of children with adult models, also has implications for such study.

One point which is clear, though the dynamics require far more attention, is that the followers' identification with their leader can provide them with social reality, in the sense of a shared outlook. . . .

## SOME CONCLUSIONS AND IMPLICATIONS

The present selective review and discussion touches upon a range of potential issues for the further study of leadership. The discussion is by no means exhaustive in providing details beyond noting suggestive developments. It is evident, however, that a new set of conceptions about leadership is beginning to emerge after a period of relative quiescence. . . .

Then, too, there is a need to consider the two-way nature of the influence process, with greater attention paid to the expectations of followers within the system. As reiterated here, the key to an understanding of leadership rests in seeing it as an influence process, involving an implicit exchange relationship over time.

No less important as a general point is the need for a greater recognition of the system represented by the group and its enterprise. This recognition provides a vehicle by which to surmount the misleading dichotomy of the leader and the situation which so long has prevailed. By adopting a systems approach, the leader, the led, and the situation defined broadly, are seen as interdependent inputs variously engaged toward the production of desired outputs.

Some release is needed from the highly static, positional view of leadership if we are to analyze its processes. A focus on leadership maintenance has weighted the balance against a more thorough probe of emerging leadership and succession phenomena. Investigators should be more aware of their choice and the differential implications, as between emerging and ongoing leadership. In this regard, the significance of the legitimacy of leadership, its sources, and effects requires greater attention in future investigations.

In studying the effectiveness of the leader, more emphasis should be placed on the outcomes for the total system, including the fulfillment of expectations held by followers. The long-standing overconcern with outcome, often stated only in terms of the leader's ability to influence, should yield to a richer conception of relationships geared to mutual goals. Not irrelevantly, the perception of the leader held by followers, including their identification with him, needs closer scrutiny. In this way, one may approach a recognition of stylistic elements allowing given persons to be effective leaders.

Finally, it seems plain that research on task-oriented groups must attend more to the organizational frameworks within which these groups are imbedded. Whether these frameworks are industrial, educational, governmental, or whatever, they are implicated in such crucial matters as goal-setting, legitimacy of authority, and leader succession. Though not always explicit, it is the organizational context which recruits and engages members in particular kinds of tasks, role relationships, and the rewards of participation. This context deserves more explicitness in attempts at understanding leadership processes.

# References

Anderson, L. R., & Fiedler, F. E. The effect of participatory and supervisory leadership on group creativity. *Journal of Applied Psychology,* 1964, 48, 227–236.

Bandura, A., & Walters, R. H. *Social learning and personality development.* New York: Holt, Rinehart & Winston, 1963.

Banta, T. J., & Nelson, C. Experimental analysis of resource location in problem-solving groups. *Sociometry,* 1964, 27, 488–501.

Bavelas, A. Leadership: Man and function. *Administrative Science Quarterly,* 1960, 4, 491–498.

Bavelas, A., Hastorf, A. H., Gross, A. E., & Kite, W. R. Experiments on the alteration of group structure. *Journal of Experimental Social Psychology,* 1965, 1, 55–70.

Berkowitz, L. Personality and group position. *Sociometry,* 1956, 19, 210–222.

Blau, P. *Exchange and power in social life.* New York: Wiley, 1964.

Brown, J. F. *Psychology and the social order.* New York: McGraw-Hill, 1936.

Burke, P. J. Authority relations and descriptive behavior in small discussion groups. *Sociometry,* 1966, 29, 237–250.

Carter, L. F., Haythorn, W., Meirowitz, B., & Lanzetta, J. The relation of categorizations and ratings in the observation of group behavior. *Human Relations,* 1951, 4, 239–253.

Carter, L. F., & Nixon, M. An investigation of the relationship between four criteria of leadership ability for three different tasks. *Journal of Psychology,* 1949, 27, 245–261.

Cartwright, D. C., & Zander, A. (eds.) *Group dynamics: Research and theory.* (3rd ed.) New York: Harper & Row, 1968.

Clifford, C., & Cohen, T. S. The relationship between leadership and personality attributes perceived by followers. *Journal of Social Psychology,* 1964, 64, 57–64.

Cohen, A. M., & Bennis, W. G. Continuity of leadership in communication networks. *Human Relations,* 1961, 14, 351–367.

Dittes, J. E., & Kelley, H. H. Effects of different conditions of acceptance upon conformity to group norms. *Journal of Abnormal and Social Psychology,* 1956, 53, 100–107.

Dubno, P. Leadership, group effectiveness, and speed of decision. *Journal of Social Psychology,* 1965, 65, 351–360.

Emerson, R. M. Power-dependence relations. *American Sociological Review,* 1962, 27, 31–41.

Evan, W. M., & Zelditch, M. A laboratory experiment on bureaucratic authority. *American Sociological Review,* 1961, 26, 883–893.

Fiedler, F. E. *Leader attitudes and group effectiveness.* Urbana: University of Illinois Press, 1958.

Fiedler, F. E. A contingency model of leadership effectiveness. In L. Berkowitz (ed.), *Advances in experimental social psychology.* Vol. 1. New York: Academic Press, 1964.

Fiedler, F. E. The contingency model: A theory of leadership effectiveness. In H. Proshansky & B. Seidenberg (eds.), *Basic studies in social psychology.* New York: Holt, Rinehart & Winston, 1965.

Fiedler, F. E. The effect of leadership and cultural heterogeneity on group performance: A test of a contingency model. *Journal of Experimental Social Psychology,* 1966, 2, 237–264.

Fiedler, F. E. *A theory of leadership effectiveness.* New York: McGraw-Hill, 1967.

Freud, S. *Group psychology and the analysis of the ego.* London & Vienna: International Psychoanalytic Press, 1922.

Gibb, C. A. The principles and traits of leadership. *Journal of Abnormal and Social Psychology,* 1947, 42, 267–284.

Goldman, M., & Fraas, L. A. The effects of leader selection on group performance. *Sociometry,* 1965, 28, 82–88.

Gordon, L. V. & Medland, F. F. Leadership aspiration and leadership ability. *Psychological Reports,* 1965, 17, 388–390.

Gouldner, A. W. (ed.) *Studies in leadership.* New York: Harper, 1950.

Haythorn, W., Couch, A., Haefner, D., Langham, P., & Carter, L. F. The effects of varying combinations of authoritarian and equalitarian leaders and followers. *Journal of Abnormal and Social Psychology,* 1956, 53, 210–219.

Hemphill, J. K. The leader and his group. *Education Research Bulletin,* 1949, 28, 225–229, 245–246. (a)

Hemphill, J. K. *Situational factors in leadership,* Columbus: Ohio State University, Bureau of Educational Research, 1949. (b)

Hemphill, J. K. Why people attempt to lead. In L. Petrullo & B.M. Bass (eds.), *Leadership and interpersonal behavior,* New York: Holt, Rinehart & Winston, 1961.

Hollander, E. P. Authoritarianism and leadership choice in a military setting. *Journal of Abnormal and Social Psychology,* 1954, 49, 365–370.

Hollander, E. P. Conformity, status, and idiosyncrasy credit. *Psychological Review,* 1958, 65, 117–127.

Hollander, E. P. Competence and conformity in the acceptance of influence. *Journal of Abnormal and Social Psychology,* 1960, 61, 365–369.

Hollander, E. P. Emergent leadership and social influence. In L. Petrullo & B. M. Bass (eds.), *Leadership and interpersonal behavior.* New York: Holt, Rinehart & Winston, 1961.

Hollander, E. P. The "pull" of international issues in the 1962 election. In S. B. Withey (Chm.), Voter attitudes and the war–peace issue. Symposium presented at the American Psychological Association, Philadelphia, August 1963.

Hollander, E. P. *Leaders, groups, and influence.* New York: Oxford University Press, 1964.

Hollander, E. P., & Julian, J. W. Leadership. In E. F. Borgatta & W. W. Lambert (eds.), *Handbook of personality theory and research.* Chicago: Rand McNally, 1968.

Homans, G. C. *Social behavior: Its elementary forms.* New York: Harcourt, Brace & World, 1961.

Hunt, J. McV. Traditional personality theory in the light of recent evidence. *American Scientist,* 1965, 53, 80–96.

Janda, K. F. Towards the explication of the concept of leadership in terms of the concept of power. *Human Relations,* 1960, 13, 345–363.

Jennings, H. H. *Leadership and isolation.* New York: Longmans, 1943.

Julian, J. W., & Hollander, E. P. A study of some role dimensions of leader–follower relations. Technical Report No. 3, April 1966, State University of New York at Buffalo, Department of Psychology, Contract 4679, Office of Naval Research.

Julian, J. W., Hollander, E. P., & Regula, C. R. Endorsement of the group spokesman as a function of his source of authority, competence, and success. *Journal of Personality and Social Psychology,* 1969, 11, 42–49.

Katz, D., & Kahn, R. *The social psychology of organizations.* New York: Wiley, 1966.

Kelman, H. C. Processes of opinion change. *Public Opinion Quarterly,* 1961, 25, 57–78.

Kirkhart, R. O. Minority group identification and group leadership. *Journal of Social Psychology,* 1963, 59, 111–117.

Lewin, K., Lippitt, R., & White, R. K. Patterns of aggressive behavior in experimentally created "social climates." *Journal of Social Psychology,* 1939, 10, 271–299.

Maier, N. R., & Hoffman, L. R. Acceptance and quality of solutions as related to leader's attitudes toward disagreement in group problem solving. *Journal of Applied Behavioral Science,* 1965, 1, 373–386.

Mann, R. D. A review of the relationships between personality and performance in small groups. *Psychological Bulletin,* 1959, 56, 241–270.

Marak, G. E. The evolution of leadership structure. *Sociometry,* 1964, 27, 174–182.

McGrath, J. E., & Altman, I. *Small group research: A critique and synthesis of the field.* New York: Holt, Rinehart & Winston, 1966.

McGregor, D. *The human side of enterprise.* New York: McGraw-Hill, 1960.

McGregor, D. *Leadership and motivation.* (Essays edited by W. G. Bennis & E. H. Schein.) Cambridge, Mass.: M.I.T. Press, 1966.

Nelson, P. D. Similarities and differences among leaders and followers, *Journal of Social Psychology,* 1964, 63, 161–167.

Pepinsky, P. N., Hemphill, J. K., & Shevitz, R. N. Attempts to lead, group productivity, and morale under conditions of acceptance and rejection. *Journal of Abnormal and Social Psychology,* 1958, 57, 47–54.

Preston, M. G., & Heintz, R. K. Effects of participatory versus supervisory leadership on group judgment. *Journal of Abnormal and Social Psychology,* 1949, 44, 345–355.

Pryer, M. W., Flint, A. W., & Bass, B. M. Group effectiveness and consistency of leadership. *Sociometry,* 1962, 25, 391–397.

Raven, B. Social influence and power. In I. D. Steiner & M. Fishbein (eds.), *Current studies in social psychology.* New York: Holt, Rinehart & Winston, 1965.

Riecken, H.W. The effect of talkativeness on ability to influence group solutions to problems. *Sociometry,* 1958, 21, 309–321.

Rosen, S., Levinger, G., & Lippitt, R. Perceived sources of social power. *Journal of Abnormal and Social Psychology,* 1961, 62, 439–441.

Rudraswamy, V. An investigation of the relationship between perceptions of status and leadership attempts. *Journal of the Indian Academy of Applied Psychology,* 1964, 1, 12–19.

Scodell, A., & Mussen, P. Social perception of authoritarians and nonauthoritarians. *Journal of Abnormal and Social Psychology,* 1953, 48, 181–184.

Sears, R. R. The 1958 summer research project on identification. *Journal of Nursery Education,* 1960, 16, (2).

Secord, P. F., & Beckman, C. W. Personality theory and the problem of stability and change in individual behavior: An interpersonal approach. *Psychological Review,* 1961, 68, 21–33.

Selznick, P. *Leadership in administration.* Evanston: Row, Peterson, 1957.

Shaw, M. E. A comparison of two types of leadership in various communication nets. *Journal of Abnormal and Social Psychology,* 1955, 50, 127–134.

Shaw, M. E., & Blum, J. M. Effects of leadership style upon group performance as a function of task structure. *Journal of Personality and Social Psychology,* 1966, 3, 238–242.

Slater, P. E., & Bennis, W. G. Democracy is inevitable, *Harvard Business Review,* 1964, 42(2), 51–59.

Steiner, I. Group dynamics. *Annual review of psychology,* 1964, 15, 421–446.

Stogdill, R. M. Personal factors associated with leadership: A survey of the literature. *Journal of Psychology,* 1948, 25, 35–71.

Stogdill, R. M. *Individual behavior and group achievement.* New York: Oxford University Press, 1959.

Weber, M. *The theory of social and economic organization.* (Trans. and ed. by T. Parsons & A. M. Henderson.) New York: Oxford University Press, 1947.

Zoep, S. M., & Oakes, W. I. Reinforcement of leadership behavior in group discussion. *Journal of Experimental Social Psychology,* 1967, 3, 310–370.

## Reading 5

# Leadership: The Management of Meaning

**Linda Smircich**
University of Massachusetts–Amherst

**Gareth Morgan**
York University

The concept of leadership permeates and structures the theory and practice of organizations and hence the way we shape and understand the nature of organized action, and its possibilities. In fact, the concept and practice of leadership, and variant forms of direction and control, are so powerfully ingrained into popular thought that the absence of leadership is often seen as an absence of organization. Many organizations are paralyzed by situations in which people appeal for direction, feeling immobilized and disorganized by the sense that they are not being led. Yet other organizations are plagued by the opposite situation characterized in organizational vernacular as one of "all chiefs, no Indians"—the situation where the majority aspire to lead and few to follow. Thus, successful acts of organization are often seen to rest in the synchrony between the initiation of action and the appeal for direction; between the actions of leaders and the receptivity and responsiveness of followers. . . .

## THE PHENOMENON OF LEADERSHIP

Leadership is realized in the process whereby one or more individuals succeeds in attempting to frame and define the reality of others. Indeed, leadership situations may be conceived as those in which there exists an *obligation* or a perceived *right* on the part of certain individuals to define the reality of others.

This process is most evident in unstructured group situations where leadership emerges in a natural and spontaneous manner. After periods of interaction, unstructured leaderless groups typically evolve common modes of interpretation and shared understandings of experience that allow them to develop into a social organization (Bennis & Shepard, 1965). Individuals in groups that evolve this way attribute leadership to those members who structure experience in meaningful ways. Certain individuals, as a result of personal inclination or the emergent expectations of others, find themselves adopting or being obliged to take a leadership role by virtue of the part they play in the definition of the situation. They emerge as leaders because of their role in framing experience in a way that provides a viable basis for action, e.g., by mobilizing meaning, articulating and defining what has previously remained implicit or unsaid, by inventing images and meanings that provide a focus for new attention, and by consolidating, confronting, or changing prevailing wisdom (Peters, 1978; Pondy, 1976). Through these diverse means, individual actions can frame and change situations, and in so doing enact a system of shared meaning that provides a basis for organized action. The leader exists as a formal leader only when he or she achieves a situation in which an obligation, expectation, or right to frame experience is presumed, or offered and accepted by others.

Leadership, like other social phenomena, is socially constructed through interaction (Berger & Luckmann, 1966), emerging as a result of the constructions and actions of both leaders and led. It involves a complicity or process of negotiation through which certain individuals, implicitly or explicitly, surrender their power to define the nature of their experience to others. Indeed, leadership depends on the existence of individuals willing, as a result of inclination or pressure, to surrender, at least in part, the powers to shape and define their own reality. If a group situation embodies competing definitions of reality, strongly held, no clear pattern of leadership evolves. Often, such situations are characterized by struggles among those who aspire to define the situation. Such groups remain loosely coupled networks of interaction, with members often feeling that they are "disorganized" because they do not share a common way of making sense of their experience.

**Source:** Edited and reprinted with permission from NTL Institute, "Leadership: The Management of Meaning" by L. Smircich and G. Morgan, pp. 257–273, *Journal of Applied Behavioral Science* 18, 3, copyright 1982. Author affiliation may have changed since article was first published.

Leadership lies in large part in generating a point of reference, against which a feeling of organization and direction can emerge. While in certain circumstances the leader's image of reality may be hegemonic, as in the case of charismatic or totalitarian leaders who mesmerize their followers, this is by no means always the case. For the phenomenon of leadership in being interactive is by nature dialectical. It is shaped through the interaction of at least two points of reference, i.e., of leaders and of led.

This dialectic is often the source of powerful internal tensions within leadership situations. These manifest themselves in the conflicting definitions of those who aspire to define reality and in the fact that while the leader of a group may forge a unified pattern of meaning, that very same pattern often provides a point of reference for the negation of leadership (Sennett, 1980). While individuals may look to a leader to frame and concretize their reality, they may also react against, reject, or change the reality thus defined. While leadership often emerges as a result of expectations projected on the emergent leader by the led, the surrender of power involved provides the basis for negation of the situation thus created. Much of the tension in leadership situations stems from this source. Although leaders draw their power from their ability to define the reality of others, their inability to control completely provides seeds of disorganization in the organization of meaning they provide.

The emergence of leadership in unstructured situations thus points toward at least four important aspects of leadership as a phenomenon. First, leadership is essentially a social process defined through interaction. Second, leadership involves a process of defining reality in ways that are sensible to the led. Third, leadership involves a dependency relationship in which individuals surrender their powers to interpret and define reality to others.[1] Fourth, the emergence of formal leadership roles represents an additional stage of institutionalization, in which rights and obligations to define the nature of experience and activity are recognized and formalized.

## LEADERSHIP IN FORMALIZED SETTINGS

The main distinguishing feature of formal organization is that the way in which experience is to be structured and defined is built into a stock of taken-for-granted meanings, or "typifications" in use (Schutz, 1967) that underlie the everyday def-inition and reality of the organization. In particular, a formal organization is premised upon shared meanings that define roles and authority relationships that institutionalize a pattern of leadership. In essence, formal organization truncates the leadership process observed in natural settings, concretizing its characteristics as a mode of social organization into sets of predetermined roles, relationships, and practices, providing a blueprint of how the experience of organizational members is to be structured.

Roles, for example, institutionalize the interactions and definitions that shape the reality of organizational life. Rules, conventions, and work practices present ready-made typifications through which experience is to be made sensible. Authority relationships legitimize the pattern of dependency relations that characterize the process of leadership, specifying who is to define organizational reality, and in what circumstances. Authority relationships institutionalize a hierarchical pattern of interaction in which certain individuals are expected to define the experience of others—to lead, and others to have their experience defined—to follow. So powerful is this process of institutionalized leadership and the expectation that someone has the right and obligation to define reality, that leaders are held to account if they do not lead "effectively.". . .

## LEADERSHIP AS THE MANAGEMENT OF MEANING

A focus on the way meaning in organized settings is created, sustained, and changed provides a powerful means of understanding the fundamental nature of leadership as a social process. In understanding the way leadership actions attempt to shape and interpret situations to guide organizational members into a common interpretation of reality, we are able to understand how leadership works to create an important foundation for organized activity. This process can be most easily conceptualized in terms of a relationship between figure and ground. Leadership action involves a moving figure—a flow of actions and utterances (i.e., what leaders do) within the context of a moving ground—the actions, utterances, and general flow of experience that constitute the situation being managed. Leadership as a phenomenon is identifiable within its wider context as a form of action that seeks to shape its context.

Leadership works by influencing the relationship between figure and ground, and hence the meaning and definition of the context as a whole.

The actions and utterances of leaders guide the attention of those involved in a situation in ways that are consciously or unconsciously designed to shape the meaning of the situation. The actions and utterances draw attention to particular aspects of the overall flow of experience, transforming what may be complex and ambiguous into something more discrete and vested with a specific pattern of meaning. This is what Schutz (1967) has referred to as a "bracketing" of experience, and Goffman (1974) as a "framing" of experience, and Bateson (1972) and Weick (1979) as the "punctuation of contexts." The actions and utterances of leaders frame and shape the context of action in such a way that the members of that context are able to use the meaning thus created as a point of reference for their own action and understanding of the situation.

This process can be represented schematically in terms of the model presented in Figure 1. When leaders act, they punctuate contexts in ways that provide a focus for the creation of meaning. Their action isolates an element of experience, which can be interpreted in terms of the context in which it is set. Indeed, its meaning is embedded in its relationship with its context. Consider, for example, the simple situation in which someone in a leadership role loses his or her temper over the failure of an employee to complete a job on time. For the leader this action embodies a meaning that links the event to context in a significant way—e.g., "This employee has been asking for a reprimand for a long time"; "This was an important job"; "This office is falling apart." For the employees in the office, the event may be interpreted in similar terms, or a range of different constructions placed upon the situation—e.g., "Don't worry about it; he always loses his temper from time to time"; "She's been under pressure lately because of problems at home."

The leader's action may generate a variety of interpretations that set the basis for meaningful action. It may serve to redefine the context into a situation where the meeting of deadlines assumes greater significance, or merely serves as a brief interruption in daily routine, soon forgotten. As discussed earlier, organized situations are often characterized by complex patterns of meaning, based on rival interpretations of the situation. Different members may make sense of situations with the aid of different interpretive schemes, establishing "counterrealities," a source of tension in the group situation that may set the basis for change of an innovative or disintegrative kind. These counterrealities underwrite much of the

---

**FIGURE 1   Leadership: A Figure-Ground Relationship Which Creates Figure-Ground Relationships**

| Framing Experience $\longrightarrow$ | Interpretation $\longrightarrow$ | Meaning and Action |
|---|---|---|
| Leadership action creates a focus of attention within the ongoing stream of experience which characterizes the total situation. Such action "brackets" and "frames" an element of experience for interpretation and meaningful action. | The action assumes significance, i.e., is interpreted within its wider context. The leader has a specific figure-ground relation in mind in engaging in action; other members of the situation construct their own interpretation of this action. | Action is grounded in the interpretive process which links figure and ground. |

---

political activities within organizations, typified by the leader's loyal lieutenants—the "yes men" accepting and reinforcing the leader's definition of the situation and the "rebels" or "out" groups forging and sustaining alternative views.

Effective leadership depends upon the extent to which the leader's definition of the situation (e.g., "People in this office are not working hard enough") serves as a basis for action by others. It is in this sense that effective leadership rests heavily on the framing of the experience of others, so that action can be guided by common conceptions as to what should occur. The key challenge for a leader is to manage meaning in such a way that individuals orient themselves to the achievement of desirable ends. In this endeavor the use of language, ritual, drama, stories, myths, and symbolic construction of all kinds may play an important role (Pfeffer, 1981; Pondy, Frost, Morgan & Dandridge, 1982; Smircich, 1982). They constitute important tools in the management of meaning. Through words and images, symbolic actions and gestures, leaders can structure attention and evoke patterns of meaning that give them considerable control over the situation being managed. These tools can be used to forge particular kinds of figure-ground relations that serve to create appropriate modes of organized action. Leadership rests as much in these symbolic modes of action as in those instrumental modes of management, direction, and control that define the substance of the leader's formal organizational role. . . .

## IMPLICATIONS FOR THE THEORY AND PRACTICE OF CONTEMPORARY ORGANIZATION

. . . Leaders symbolize the organized situation in which they lead. Their actions and utterances project and shape imagery in the minds of the led, which is influential one way or another in shaping actions within the setting as a whole. This is not to deny the importance of the voluntary nature of the enactments and sense-making activities initiated by members of the situation being managed. Rather, it is to recognize and emphasize the special and important position accorded to the leader's view of the situation in the frame of reference of others. Leaders, by nature of their leadership role, are provided with a distinctive opportunity to influence the sense making of others. Our case study illustrates the importance of the leader recognizing the nature of his or her influence and managing the meaning of situations in a constructive way. At a minimum this involves that he or she (a) attempt to deal with the equivocality that permeates many interactive situations; (b) attend to the interpretive schemes of those involved; and (c) embody, through use of appropriate language, rituals, and other forms of symbolic discourse, the meanings and values conducive to desired modes of organized action. A focus on leadership as the management of meaning encourages us to develop a theory for the practice of leadership in which these three generalizations are accorded a central role.

Our analysis also draws attention to the role of power as a defining feature of the leadership process. We see the way the power relations embedded in a leadership role oblige others to take particular note of the sense-making activities emanating from that role. We have characterized this in terms of a dependency relation between leaders and led, in which the leader's sense-making activities assume priority over the sense-making activities of others.

The existence of leadership depends on and fosters this dependency, for insofar as the leader is expected to define the situation, others are expected to surrender that right. As we have noted, leadership as a phenomenon depends upon the existence of people who are prepared to surrender their ability to define their reality to others. Situations of formal leadership institutionalize this pattern into a system of rights and obligations whereby the leader has the prerogative to define reality, and the led to accept that definition as a frame of reference for orienting their own activity.

Organized action in formal settings constitutes a process of enactment and sense making on the part of those involved, but one shaped in important ways by the power relations embedded in the situation as a whole. Leadership and the organizational forms to which it gives rise enact a reality that expresses a power relationship. An understanding of the power relationship embedded in all enactment processes is thus fundamental for understanding the nature of organization as an enacted social form, for enactments express power relationships.

Thus our analysis of the leadership process tells us much about the nature of organization as a hierarchical phenomenon. Most patterns of formal organization institutionalize the emergent characteristics of leadership into roles, rules, and relations that give tangible and enduring form to relationships between leaders and led. Our analysis of leadership as a social phenomenon based on interaction, sense making, and dependency implies a view of much modern organization in which these factors are seen as defining features. To see leadership as the management of meaning is to see organizations as networks of managed meanings, resulting from those interactive processes through which people have sought to make sense of situations.

This view of leadership and organization provides a framework for reconsidering the way leadership has been treated in organizational research. By viewing leadership as a relationship between traits, roles, and behaviors and the situations in which they are found, or as a transactional process involving the exchange of rewards and influence, most leadership research has focused upon the dynamics and surface features of leadership as a tangible social process. The way leadership as a phenomenon involves the structuring and transformation of reality has with notable exceptions (e.g., Burns, 1978), been ignored, or at best approached tangentially. The focus on the exchange of influence and rewards has rarely penetrated to reveal the way these processes are embedded in, and reflect a deeper structure of power-based meaning and action. Leadership is not simply a process of acting or behaving, or a process of manipulating rewards. It is a process of power-based reality construction and needs to be understood in these terms.

The concept of leadership is a central building block of the conventional wisdom of organization and management. For the most part the idea that good organization embodies effective leadership practice passes unquestioned. Our analysis here leads us to question this wisdom and points toward the unintended consequences that leadership situations often generate.

The most important of these stem from the dependency relations that arise when individuals surrender their power and control over the definition of reality to others. Leaders may create situations in which individuals are crippled by purposelessness and inaction when left to guide efforts on their own account. Leadership may actually work against the development of self-responsibility, self-initiative, and self-control, in a manner that parallels Argyris's (1957) analysis of the way the characteristics of bureaucratic organization block potentialities for full human development. These blocks arise whenever leadership actions divert individuals from the process of defining and taking responsibility for their own action and experience.

Leadership situations may generate a condition of "trained inaction" in the led, a variant form of Veblen's (1904) "trained incapacity," observed by Merton (1968) as a dominant characteristic of the bureaucratic personality. . . .

The conventional wisdom that organization and leadership are by definition intertwined has structured the way we see and judge alternative modes of organized action. Approaching this subject from a perspective that treats organization as a phenomenon based on the management of meaning, we can begin to see and understand the importance of developing and encouraging alternative means through which organized action can be generated and sustained.

## Notes

[1] A minor qualification is appropriate here in that certain charismatic leaders may inspire others to restructure their reality in creative ways. The dependency relation is evident, however, in that the individual takes the charismatic leader as a point of reference in this process.

## References

Argyris, C. *Personality and organization.* New York: Harper, 1957.

Barnard, C. *The functions of the executive.* Cambridge, Mass.: Harvard University Press, 1938.

Bateson, G. *Steps to an ecology of mind.* New York: Ballantine Books, 1972.

Bennis, W. G., & Shepard, H. A. A theory of group development. *Human Relations,* 1965, 9, 415–457.

Berger, P., & Luckmann, T. *The social construction of reality.* New York: Anchor Books, 1966.

Bogdan, R., & Taylor, S. J. *Introduction to qualitative methods.* New York: Wiley, 1975.

Burns, J. M. *Leadership.* New York: Harper & Row, 1978.

Emery, F. E., & Trist, E. L. *Towards a social ecology.* Harmondsworth: Penguin, 1973.

Fiedler, F. E. *A theory of leadership effectiveness.* New York: McGraw-Hill, 1967.

Goffman, E. *Frame analysis.* New York: Harper Colophon Books, 1974.

Jacobs, T. O. *Leadership and exchange in formal organizations.* Alexandria, Va.: Human Resources Organization, 1971.

Katz, D., & Kahn, R. L. *The social psychology of organizations.* New York: Wiley, 1966.

Mann, R. D. A review of the relationships between personality and performance in small groups. *Psychological Bulletin,* 1959, 56, 241–270.

Merton, R. K. *Social theory and social structure.* (enlarged ed.). New York: Free Press, 1968.

Mintzberg, H. *The nature of managerial work.* Englewood Cliffs, NJ: Prentice-Hall, 1973.

Peters, T. J. Symbols, patterns and settings: An optimistic case for getting things done. *Organizational Dynamics,* 1978, 3–22.

Pfeffer, J. Management as symbolic action: The creation and maintenance of organizational paradigms. *Research in Organizational Behavior,* 1981, 3, 1–52.

Pondy, L. R. Leadership is a language game. In M. McCall & M. Lombardo (eds.), *Leadership: Where else can we go?* Durham, N.C.: Duke University Press, 1976.

Pondy, L. R., Frost, P., Morgan, G., & Dandridge, T. (eds.). *Organizational symbolism.* Greenwich, Conn.: JAI Press, 1982.

Quinn, J. B. *Strategies for change.* New York: Irwin, 1980.

Roethlisberger, F. J., & Dickson, W. J. *Management and the worker.* Cambridge, Mass.: Harvard University Press, 1939.

Schatzman, L., & Strauss, A. *Fieldwork.* Englewood Cliffs, N.J.: Prentice-Hall, 1973.

Schutz, A. *Collected papers I: The problem of social reality.* (2nd ed.). The Hague: Martinus Nijhoff, 1967.

Selznick, P. *Leadership in administration.* New York: Harper & Row, 1957.

Sennett, R. *Authority.* New York: Knopf, 1980.

Smircich, L. Organizations as shared meanings. In Pondy, L. R., Frost, P., Morgan, G., & Dandridge, T. (eds.), *Organizational symbolism*. Greenwich, Conn.: JAI Press, 1982.

Stogdill, R. M. *Handbook of leadership: A survey of theory and research*. New York: The Free Press, 1974.

Veblen, T. *The theory of business enterprise*. Clifton, N.J.: Augustus M. Kelly, 1975 (originally published 1904).

Weick, K. *The social psychology of organizing*. Reading, Mass.: Addison-Wesley, 1979.

# Chapter Two

# The Leader–Follower Relationship:
## Fairness, Trust, and Ethical Behavior

After conducting an extensive review of the leadership literature in an attempt to gain insight into the role of personal traits, Ralph Stogdill in 1948 offered the observation that leadership is a *relationship*.[1] Specifically, he wrote that the findings from his literature review "suggest that leadership is not a matter of passive status, or of the mere possession of some combination of traits. It appears rather to be a *working relationship* [emphasis added] among members of a group, in which the leader acquires status through active participation and demonstration of his [her] capacity for carrying cooperative tasks through to completion" (p. 70).

The conceptualization of leadership as a relationship has been taken by a large number of leadership scholars. The close connection between leader and follower manifests itself in a number of diverse ways. In addition to seeing leadership as a working relationship where two or more people in differentiated roles work to accomplish a goal held in common, leadership is often cast in terms of a power or influence relationship. As we saw in Chapter 1, for example, Pierce and Newstrom observed that there are several approaches to the definition of leadership that revolve around the concepts of influence, power, persuasion, and securing compliance. In addition, we observed that Hollander and Julian (1969) see leadership as a "social influence process." Leadership, they note, "constitutes an influence relationship between two, or usually more, persons who depend upon one another for the attainment of certain mutual goals."[2]

In this chapter we continue to explore the central question raised in the last chapter: What does the concept of leadership mean? In this chapter we conceptualize leadership as a *relationship*. The relationship (i.e., connection) that develops between a leader and follower is often complex and multidimensional in nature. It is filled with perception, cognition, affect, behavioral tendencies, and actual behavior. A full and complete examination of the concept of leadership

[1] R. M. Stogdill. Personal factors associated with leadership: A survey of the literature. *Journal of Psychology* 28 (1948), pp. 35–71.
[2] E. P. Hollander, & J. W. Julian. Contemporary trends in the analysis of leadership processes. *Psychological Bulletin* 7, 5 (1969), pp. 387–397.

from a relational perspective necessitates an exploration of each of these areas, a task well beyond the scope of this chapter. While there are many dimensions to a relationship (e.g., identification, loyalty, possessiveness, affect, commitment/ attachment), three aspects of this relationship (i.e., fairness, trust, and ethical behavior) will be illuminated by the readings contained in this chapter.

One of the most extensive elaborations of leadership as a relationship is the Leader–Member Exchange (LMX) Theory. Developed during the mid-1970s with subsequent articulations (cf. Dansereau, Graen, & Haga, 1975; Graen & Cashman, 1975; Graen, 1976; Graen & Uhl-Bien, 1995),[3] LMX describes how leaders, over time, develop different exchange relationships with their various followers.

A basic premise of LMX theory notes that leaders develop separate exchange relationships with each of their followers. Two very different types of relationships develop. One relationship that the leader develops is with a small group of followers that constitutes an "in-group," while with the majority of the followers an "out-group" relationship emerges. Selection of those who will come to be a part of the leader's in-group is based, in large part, on personal compatibility, perceptions of subordinate competence, and dependability. This relationship identifies a trusted subset of one's followers, those with whom the leader has a very special relationship. With regard to the personal compatibility, Phillips and Bedeian (1994) observed a significant relationship between leader perceptions of leader-follower attitudinal similarity and the quality of the leader–member exchange relationship. This observation supports a basic tenet of LMX Theory—attitudinal similarity is an important influence on leader-follower interactions, being a major cause of a successful and ongoing relationship. Phillips and Bedeian (1994) also observed a positive relationship between follower extroversion and the quality of the leader–member exchange relationship.[4] These two observations suggest that attributes of the follower play a role shaping the nature of the relationship that develops between the leader and follower. (Chapter 10 provides additional insight into the follower as a part of the leadership equation.)

The relationships that develop between the leader and his/her followers vary in terms of the "quality of their exchange relationship" (e.g., How well does your leader understand your job problems and needs? Would your leader "bail you out" at his/her own expense?). The self-assessment presented at the end of these introductory comments to Chapter 2 provides you with the opportunity to assess the quality of your relationship with one of your leaders. According to the theory, the quality of the relationship that develops between a leader and a follower is predictive of the outcomes that will be attained (e.g., commitment, member satisfaction, member and group performance, member competence, and turnover intentions) and ultimately leader effectiveness.[5]

In addition to the quality of the relationship being different for in- and out-group followers significant differences emerge in the exchanges that take place

---

[3] G. Dansereau, G. B. Graen, & W. Haga. The role of affect and ability in initial exchange quality perceptions. *Group & Organization Management* 17 (1975), pp. 388–397; G. B. Graen, & J. Cashman. A role-making model of leadership in formal organizations: A developmental approach. In J. G. Hunt & L. L. Larson (Eds.), *Leadership Frontiers* (pp. 143–166). Kent, OH: Kent State University Press, 1975; G. B. Graen. Role making processes within complex organizations. In M. D. Dunnette (Ed.), *Handbook of Industrial and Organizational Psychology*, (pp. 1201–1245). Chicago: Rand-McNally, 1976; G. B. Graen, & M. Uhl-Bien. Relationship-based approach to leadership: Development of leader–member exchange (LMX) theory of leadership over 25 years: Applying a multi-level multi-domain approach. *Leadership Quarterly* 6 (1995), pp. 219–247.

[4] A. S. Phillips, & A. G. Bedeian. Leader–follower exchange quality: The role of personal and interpersonal attributes. *Academy of Management Journal* 37 (1994), pp. 990–1001.

[5] For a recent review of the correlates of the quality of the leader-follower relationship literature see: C. R. Gerstner & D. V. Day. Meta-analytic review of Leader–Member Exchange Theory: Correlates and construct issuer. *Journal of Applied Psychology* 82 (1997), pp. 827–844.

between the leader and followers, differences in terms of their roles, expectations, rights, and responsibilities. In-group members may be given more interesting and desirable task assignments, they are likely to be communicated with more frequently and completely, they are likely to participate more frequently and therefore exercise more influence/control over group activities and receive more support and recognition, and their tangible rewards are often greater than that received by out-group members. There is a price to be paid for this differential in relationship, however. The leader commonly expects more from in-group members. They are often expected to work harder, make more sacrifices, assume greater risk, accept more responsibility, be more loyal and committed, and give more personal time to the satisfaction of the leader needs and to the attainment of the group's goals.

As shown by this brief overview of LMX theory, it is evident that the idea of leadership as a relationship can be extremely complex and multidimensional in nature. As illustrated in Figure 2.1, any attempt to understand leadership as a relationship identifies for us a number of domains (i.e., the leader, the follower, their "relationship," and the context in which the leader, the follower(s), and their relationship is forged).

In the first reading, Terri A. Scandura (1999) employs Leader–Member Exchange (LMX) Theory to explore one dimension of the leader–follower relationship. Scandura introduces us to the concept of "organizational justice." She employs and expands LMX Theory to explore the social comparison processes that operate within groups. The construct of organizational justice reflects the notion that group members engage in social comparisons, and one result of these comparisons is the experience of "fairness"—fairness, for example, in terms of the distribution of outcomes (e.g., rewards) among group members. The second self-assessment in this chapter provides you with an opportunity to reflect upon your experiences with organizational justice in one of your leader–follower relationships.

In the second reading Kurt T. Dirks introduces us to another very important dimension of the leader–follower relationship—trust. [Before you read the article by Dirks, we encourage you to complete the third self-assessment in this introduction to Chapter 2.]

Dirks explored the relationship between leadership, trust, and team performance. Dirks studied this relationship inside 30 different basketball teams that

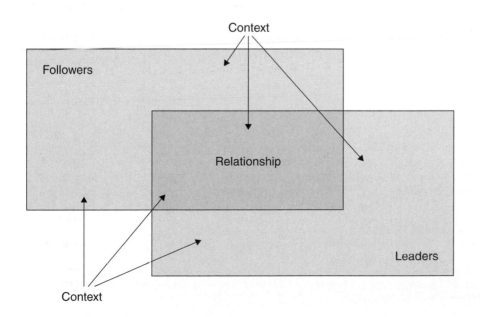

**FIGURE 2.1**
**Leadership**
**Domains**

are members of the National Collegiate Athletic Association. Dirks conceptualizes trust as "an expectation or belief that the team can rely on the leader's actions or words and that the leader has good intentions toward the team" (p. 1004). His work gives us the opportunity to reflect upon several very important questions, among them: What is trust (distrust)? Where does it come from? Why is it important? What role does trust play in the leader–follower relationship? Is a high level of trust always important in the leader–follower relationship, or is it more important under some circumstances? What are the implications of the lack of trust in a leader–follower relationship?

The "ethics" of leadership can be examined from a number of perspectives, among them "the moral character of the leader; the ethical legitimacy of the values embedded in the leader's vision, articulation, and program which followers either embrace or reject; and the morality of the processes of social ethical choice and action that the leaders and followers engage in and collectively pursue" (Bass & Steidlmeier, 1999, p. 182).[6] Reflection upon Mahatma Gandhi contrasted with Osama bin Laden, or Mother Theresa contrasted with Saddam Hussein provides us with the opportunity to draw rich and interesting contrasts among these leaders along each of these three dimensions.

The third and final reading in this chapter invites us to think about the leader–follower relationship from the perspective of ethics and the leader's ethical challenge. Jill W. Graham explores the relationship between several different styles of leadership (e.g., autocratic, servant, transformational), levels of moral development, and follower contributions to organizational success and acts of good organizational citizenship.

[6] B. M. Bass, & P. Steidlmeier. Ethics, character, and authentic transformational leadership behavior. *Leadership Quarterly* 10 (1995), pp. 181–217.

**Leader–Member Exchange**

**EXERCISE**
*Self-Assessment*

**Instructions:** Think about a situation in which you are a follower (subordinate) in a group (team) situation, and for which you have a leader (manager, supervisor). Indicate the degree to which you *agree* or *disagree* with each of the following statements.

1 = Strongly disagree
2 = Disagree
3 = Slightly disagree
4 = Neither agree nor disagree
5 = Slightly agree
6 = Agree
7 = Strongly agree

| | | | | | | | |
|---|---|---|---|---|---|---|---|
| 1. I usually know where I stand with my leader. | 1 | 2 | 3 | 4 | 5 | 6 | 7 |
| 2. My leader has enough confidence in me that he/she would defend and justify my decisions if I was not present to do so. | 1 | 2 | 3 | 4 | 5 | 6 | 7 |
| 3. My working relationship with my leader is effective. | 1 | 2 | 3 | 4 | 5 | 6 | 7 |
| 4. My leader understands my problems and needs. | 1 | 2 | 3 | 4 | 5 | 6 | 7 |
| 5. I can count on my leader to "bail me out," even at his or her own expense, when I really need it. | 1 | 2 | 3 | 4 | 5 | 6 | 7 |
| 6. My leader recognizes my potential. | 1 | 2 | 3 | 4 | 5 | 6 | 7 |
| 7. Regardless of how much power my leader has built into his/her position, my leader would be personally inclined to use his/her power to help me solve problems in my work. | 1 | 2 | 3 | 4 | 5 | 6 | 7 |

**Scoring:** Sum your answers to questions 1 through 7 and divide by 7.

My leader–member exchange relationship score is: _____.

**Interpretation:** A high score (6 and greater) suggests that you have a high-quality leader–member exchange relationship with your leader. A low score (2 or less) suggests that you have a low-quality leader–member exchange relationship with your leader. Recent research evidence (cf., Wayne, Shore, & Liden, 1997)[1] suggests that followers who experience a high-quality leader–member exchange relationship may help their leader by carrying out their required role activities and by engaging in good citizenship behaviors (i.e., going above and beyond expected role requirements) in exchange for the benefits provided by the leader in the exchange process.

**Source:** Reprinted with the permission of the author, T. A. Scandura: T. A. Scandura and G. B Graen, "Moderating Effects of Initial Leader–Member Exchange Status on the Effects of a Leadership Intervention," *Journal of Applied Psychology* 69 (1984), pp. 428–436.

[1]S. J. Wayne, S. M. Shore, and R. C. Liden, "Perceived Organizational Support and Leader–Member Exchange: A Social Exchange Perspective," *Academy of Management Journal* 40 (1997), pp. 92–111.

| **EXERCISE** | **Justice** |
| --- | --- |
| *Self-Assessment* | **Instructions:** The following set of questions ask that you think about one of your most recent class-based team assignments. As a normal part of your work as students your performance is evaluated and you are assigned a grade. This is typically the case even when you work on team (group) assignments. |

The following questions refer to the *procedures used* to arrive at your grade. Employing the following response scale, please answer this first set of questions:

To a Small Extent     1 ------- 2 ------- 3 ------- 4 ------- 5  To a Large Extent

To what extent:

_____ 1. Have you been able to express your views and feelings during those procedures?
_____ 2. Have you had influence over the outcomes arrived at by those procedures?
_____ 3. Have those procedures been applied consistently?
_____ 4. Have those procedures been free of bias?
_____ 5. Have those procedures been based on accurate information?
_____ 6. Have you been able to appeal the outcome arrived at by those procedures?
_____ 7. Have those procedures upheld ethical and moral standards?

The following questions refer to your *grade*. Employing the same response scale (1 = to a small extent to 5 = to a large extent), please answer the following four questions.

To what extent:

_____ 8. Does your grade reflect the effort you have put into your work?
_____ 9. Is your grade appropriate for the work you have completed?
_____ 10. Does your grade reflect what you have contributed to the organization?
_____ 11. Is your grade justified, given your performance?

The following questions refer to how you were treated. Employing the same response scale (1 = to a small extent to 5 = to a large extent), please answer the following four questions.

To what extent:

_____ 12. Has s/he treated you in a polite manner?
_____ 13. Has s/he treated you with dignity?
_____ 14. Has s/he treated you with respect?
_____ 15. Has s/he refrained from improper remarks or comments?

The following questions refer to the way you were communicated with. Employing the same response scale (1 = to a small extent to 5 = to a large extent), please answer the following five questions.

To what extent:

_____ 16. Has s/he been candid in his/her communications with you?
_____ 17. Has s/she explained the procedures thoroughly?
_____ 18. Were his/her explanations regarding the procedures reasonable?
_____ 19. Has s/he communicated details in a timely manner?
_____ 20. Has s/he seemed to tailor his/her communications to individuals' specific needs?

**Scoring:** You will construct four scores, one for each set of questions.

Sum your score for questions 1 through 7, and divide by 7.

   My procedural justice score is: _____

Now sum your score for questions 8 through 11, and divide by 4.

   My distributive justice score is: _____

Next sum your scores for questions 12 through 15, and divide by 4.

   My interpersonal justice score is. _____

Finally, sum your scores for questions 16 through 20, and divide by 5.

   My informational justice score is: _____

*(continued)*

**Interpretation:** The concept of "Organizational Justice" is concerned with the notion of "fairness" or "justice" within the context of an individual's relationship with an organization. Organizational justice has been conceptualized from a number of different dimensions (e.g., distributive justice, procedural justice, and interactional justice). Interactional justice is evident when decision makers treat people with respect and sensitivity. In addition, they attempt to explain thoroughly the rationale for the decisions that they make. Some justice scholars have broken interactional justice into two additional dimensions—interpersonal justice (I have been treated in a polite manner; I have been treated with dignity) and informational justice (S/he has been candid in his/her communication with me; S/he communicated with me in a timely manner).

The first set of questions and your first score reflects **procedural justice.** Procedural justice reflects experienced "fairness" in terms of the *procedures* that were employed to make a decision, such as the allocation of pay increases, promotions, and the assignment of grades. The higher your score, the greater the level of fairness or justice experienced. A score of 4 and greater suggests a high level of experienced fairness in the procedures employed to assign your grade. A score of 2 or less suggests that you experienced a lack of fairness (justice) in the way that the grading decision was made.

The second set of questions and your second score reflects **distributive justice.** Distributive justice reflects experienced "fairness" in terms of the *outcomes* that were administered, such as the size of the pay increase, the promotion (or lack of promotion), and the grade received. The higher your score, the greater the level of fairness or justice experienced. A score of 4 and greater suggests a high level of experienced fairness in the outcome received. A score of 2 or less suggests that you experienced the lack of fairness (justice) in the grade received.

The third and fourth set of questions reflect **interpersonal justice** and **informational justice.** These two dimensions of justice reflects experienced "fairness" in terms of how they were treated interpersonally and the manner in which they were communicated with. The higher your score, the greater the level of fairness or justice experienced. A score of 4 and greater suggests a high level of experienced fairness. A score of 2 or less suggests that you experienced the lack of fairness (justice) in the way you were personally treated and/or the way with which you were communicated.

**Source:** J. A. Colquitt. On the dimensionality of organizational justice: A construct validation of a measure. *Journal of Applied Psychology* 86 (2000), p. 389. Copyright 2001. American Psychological Association, reprinted with permission.

**EXERCISE**
*Self-Assessment*

**Trust in Leadership**

**Instructions:** In responding to the following set of questions, please think about your team leader. To what extent do you *agree* or *disagree* with each of the following statements.

1 = Strongly disagree
2 = Disagree
3 = Slightly disagree
4 = Neither agree nor disagree
5 = Slightly agree
6 = Agree
7 = Strongly agree

_____ 1. Most team members trust and respect our leader.

_____ 2. I can talk freely to the team leader about difficulties I am having on the team and know that s/he will want to listen.

_____ 3. If I shared my problems with the team leader, I know s/he would respond constructively and caringly.

_____ 4. I have a sharing relationship with the team leader; I can freely share my ideas, feelings, and hopes with him/her.

_____ 5. I would feel a sense of loss if the team leader left to take a job elsewhere.

_____ 6. The team leader approaches his/her job with professionalism and dedication.

_____ 7. Given the team leader's past performance, I see no reason to doubt his/her competence.

_____ 8. I can rely upon the team leader not to make my job more difficult by poor coaching.

_____ 9. Others consider the team leader to be trustworthy.

**Scoring:** You now have a score of 1 to 7 for each question. Sum your scores across the 9 questions and divide by 9.

**Interpretation:** The higher your score, the more trust you place in your team leader. A score of 6 and greater reflects a very high level of trust. The lower your score, the less you trust your team leader. A score of 2 and less reflects a very low level of trust.

**Source:** K. T. Dirks. Trust in leadership and team performance: Evidence from NCAA basketball. *Journal of Applied Psychology* 85 (2000), p. 1012. Copyright 2000, American Psychological Association. Reprinted with permission along with an edited version of the Dirks 2000 article.

**Reading 6**

# Rethinking Leader–Member Exchange: An Organizational Justice Perspective

**Terri A. Scandura**
University of Miami

## INTRODUCTION

Relationships between leaders and members have been researched for over 25 years (Graen & Uhl-Bien, 1995), beginning with studies of the socialization of organizational newcomers indicating the importance of supervisors' attention to new role incumbents (Dansereau, Graen, & Haga, 1975). In these studies, some leaders treated their subordinates in different ways. Some were treated as "trusted assistants" (in-group members) and others as "hired hands" (out-group members) (Dansereau, Graen, & Haga, 1975). In-group members have better relationships with leaders and receive more work-related benefits in comparison to out-group members. This "Vertical Dyad Linkage" (VDL) concept includes characteristics of leaders, members, and the relationships between leaders and members (Dansereau, Yammarino, & Markham, 1995). This concept was later measured differently and labelled Leader–Member Exchange, or LMX (Graen, Liden, & Hoel, 1982a; Graen, Novak, & Sommerkamp, 1982b). LMX has recently been defined as the unique relationship-based social exchange between leaders and members (Graen & Uhl-Bien, 1995). However, this new emphasis on the relationship may obscure important exchange-based issues (including economic exchange such as performance ratings and pay increases) that take place in leader–member dyads. It is perhaps necessary to rethink the LMX concept, considering what constitutes "fair exchange in leadership" (Hollander, 1978, p. 71).

Dyadic relationships that emerge between leaders and followers in organizations are an important aspect of leadership theory and research (Bass, 1990; Graen & Uhl-Bien, 1995; Yukl, 1994). Moreover, measures of LMX have been re-lated in some studies to a number of important outcome variables in organizational research including job satisfaction and performance ratings (Graen, Novak, & Sommerkamp, 1982b), turnover (Graen, Liden, & Hoel, 1982a; Ferris, 1985), subordinate decision influence (Scandura, Graen, & Novak, 1986), and career progress of managers (Wakabayashi & Graen, 1984; Scandura & Schriesheim, 1994). Yet, other studies do not find such conclusive evidence for the relationship between LMX and productivity (cf., Vecchio & Gobdel, 1984; Duarte, Goodson, & Klich, 1994) nor turnover (Vecchio, 1985). Such discrepancies in empirical studies conducted suggest that there might be mediator variables that account for some of the differences reported across studies of LMX. One possible explanation for discrepant findings across studies is the relationship between LMX and organizational justice, which delves into complex issues of the exchange aspect of LMX relationships. Yet, these issues have received scant theoretical and empirical attention in the LMX literature.

The purpose of this review is to extend LMX theory to consider issues of organizational justice. Despite numerous empirical investigations of LMX, some authors have commented that there has been limited theoretical development of the concept (Dansereau et al., 1995; Dienesch & Liden, 1986; Miner, 1980; Vecchio & Gobdel, 1984). It seems useful to re-examine some underlying assumptions in the literature on LMX, reintroducing relevant exchange theory concepts and treating LMX development from a justice perspective. This article briefly reviews the LMX literature and introduces relevant concepts from literature on organizational justice to reconcile some theoretical concerns regarding the usefulness of the model. Next, a model of the role of organizational justice in the formation of in-groups and out-groups is offered and new research propositions are developed.

Edited and reprinted with permission, *Leadership Quarterly*, 10, 1 (1999), 25–40. Copyright 1999, Elsevier Science.

# REVIEW

## WORK GROUP DIFFERENTIATION PROCESS

Dansereau et al. (1975) presented a descriptive model of how work groups become differentiated into in-groups and out-groups based upon the quality of leader–member relationships that emerge between immediate supervisors and members of work groups. Despite the clear indication that work group differentiation occurs (Graen & Cashman, 1975; Vecchio, 1997), the idea that some subordinates are treated better than others is inconsistent with norms of equality (cf., Kabanoff, 1991; Meindl, 1989). However, empirical research studies continue to document differences in the quality of relationships and more benefits for in-group members [cf. (Graen & Uhl-Bien, 1995) for review]. For example, Lagace, Castleberry and Ridnour (1993) found that in-group members (with higher quality LMX relationships) were higher on motivational factors and evaluations of their bosses and experienced less role-related stress (role overload, role insufficiency, role ambiguity and conflict). The literature has indicated, in some studies, that in-group members (i.e., those with higher quality LMX) receive more attention and support from the leader than out-group members (those with lower quality LMX) (cf., Graen et al., 1982b). Also, out-group members (with lower LMX) are more likely to file grievances (Cleyman, Jex, & Love, 1993). These results seem relevant to the concept of organizational justice since out-group members might see their leader as treating them unfairly. A careful review of the literature indicates that the LMX literature has referenced issues related to the fair treatment of members.

Dansereau, Alutto, and Yammarino (1984) presented a general model of exchange theory discussing the role of equity perceptions in the development of leader–member relationships. They defined investments as ". . . what one party gives to another party" (p. 98) and returns as ". . . what one party gets back from another" (p. 98). Their formulation suggests that investments trigger returns and vice versa and that, over time, stable patterns of exchange emerge between leaders and members, based on the ratios of investments to returns by both parties. Equity is thus maintained by changes in either what is invested or returned to attain an overall optimal level for both parties. Relationship development,

over time, was proposed to be a function of these investment-return cycles.

As an illustrative example of the use of multiple levels of analysis in theory-building, Dansereau et al. (1984) then elaborated their model to include multiple-relationships which invokes the concept of social comparisons between work group members. Investment-return cycles were compared for two different hypothetical work group members, noting that equity can be maintained at different levels of investments and returns. Social comparison processes emerge as one member compares his/her investments and returns to a comparison other in the work group. However, as long as the leader attends to the appropriate level of returns for investments, feelings of inequity should not emerge for the member receiving lower returns. This theoretical example presented by Dansereau and his colleagues captures the complexity (and also the necessity) of examining issues of organizational justice in studies of LMX.

As noted by Graen and Scandura (1987), one of the requirements for the development of high quality leader–member exchanges in organizations is that ". . . each party must see the exchange as reasonably equitable or fair" (p. 182). Yet, current theoretical approaches may limit the potential of LMX theory, because they place too much emphasis on social exchange and do not develop aspects of economic exchange (Graen & Uhl-Bien, 1995). Both social and economic exchange should perhaps be given more weight in future studies. It seems that exchange can involve both social aspects (such as availability and support) and economic aspects (such as pay raises).

Most studies of work group differentiation into in-groups and out-groups are descriptive, and not intended to instruct managers on how to manage their work groups. This differs from prescriptive or normative theory where guidelines for managerial practice are developed. Without concerns for organizational justice, LMX may have limited contributions in terms of normative theory, because perceptions of organizational justice are necessary for the leadership process. From an organizational justice perspective, the LMX model might be criticized as reinforcing the special treatment of some work group members over others (Vecchio, 1997). Hence, supervisors may be reluctant to discuss the work group differentiation process; concern for organizational justice may explain lower variance in some supervisor reports of LMX (Scandura et al., 1986).

Lack of attention to theoretical concerns related to organizational justice have perhaps limited the theoretical development of LMX. Yet, the empirical literature on LMX is expanding (cf., Graen & Uhl-Bien, 1995). Several researchers have employed longitudinal research designs (cf., Liden, Wayne, & Stilwell, 1993), which have illuminated the development of LMX relationships over time. These studies support the premise that in-group members receive more benefits compared to out-group members, yet the question of whether or not this results in deprecation of team-level outcomes remains. This study reviews the literature on organizational justice to further explain the "fair exchange" aspect of LMX development (Dansereau et al., 1984; Graen & Scandura, 1987; Hollander, 1978) by revisiting important exchange-based issues in LMX (including economic exchange) that may be lost in current treatments of LMX as relationship-based and predominantly grounded in relationship-based social exchange (Graen & Uhl-Bien, 1995).

## ORGANIZATIONAL JUSTICE: A BRIEF REVIEW OF RELEVANT CONCEPTS

Cropanzano and Folger (1991) present a two-component model of justice, which includes distributive and procedural forms of justice. Distributive justice is defined as the individual's perception that the outcomes that they receive are fair (Adams, 1965; Greenberg, 1990). Examples of distributive outcomes are pay increases, promotions, and challenging work assignments. Procedural justice is defined as an employee's perception that the procedures followed by the organization in determining who receives benefits are fair (Folger & Greenberg, 1985; Greenberg, 1987; Lind & Tyler, 1988). Examples of procedural justice are the degree of voice the person has in decision making and whether or not consistent rules are followed in making decisions.

Research on justice has indicated that a decision will be accepted by subordinates if procedural justice is followed, even if the distributive outcome is less that what an individual desires (Tyler, 1986). For example, a low pay raise would still be accepted if the organization's procedures of performance appraisal and rewards are seen as being followed in the determination of the raise. Also, communications about what is fair to organizational members, labelled interactional justice, has been proposed as a third aspect of justice at the workplace (Bies & Moag, 1986; Moorman,

1991). Interactional justice involves the manner in which organizational justice is communicated by supervisors to followers. Moorman (1991) demonstrated that distributive, procedural, and interactional justice are correlated, but distinct aspects of organizational justice. Following this conceptualization, organizational justice is defined as distributive, procedural, and interactional justice.

Members of work groups often interpret the behavior of their immediate supervisor in terms of organizational justice. Studies of procedural and distributive justice indicate that leaders who are perceived as procedurally fair are rated favorably by subordinates even when resource allocation is unequal (Folger & Konovsky, 1989; Tyler, 1986; Tyler, 1989; Tyler & Caine, 1981: Tyler & Lind, 1992). Organizational justice has implications for LMX theory since the focus of LMX is on the development of differentiated (in-group/out-group) leader–member relationships.

Despite suggestions by Hollander (1978), Dansereau et al. (1984) and Graen and Scandura (1987) that equity matters for LMX development, the issue has received little empirical attention. Notable exceptions are studies by Vecchio, Griffeth, and Hom (1986) and Manogran, Stauffer, and Conlon (1994). These studies suggest LMX is significantly related to perceptions of organizational justice by subordinates. Vecchio et al. (1986) showed a relationship between LMX and distributive justice. Those who had high quality relationships with their immediate supervisor viewed the workplace as being more fair than those with low quality relationships with their boss. Manogran et al. (1994) showed positive and significant correlations between LMX and procedural and interactional justice, in addition to distributive justice, using measures developed by Moorman (1991). These empirical findings are intriguing, yet it is unclear whether the correlations reported between LMX and organizational justice variables reflect that organizational justice is a tangential outcome to the LMX process or a more central element in the development of LMX relationships. A theoretical framework is needed to further elucidate the role of organizational justice in the LMX development process.

## LMX AND ORGANIZATIONAL JUSTICE

Hollander (1978) noted that a "psychological contract" (p. 73) emerges between leaders and followers that depends upon expectations and actions of both parties to the dyad. He noted that equitable treatment of subordinates is often one of the most valued behaviors of a leader, since social comparison processes are so fundamental to human nature (Festinger, 1957). Hollander's (1978) treatment of leadership and exchange focused mostly on issues of distributive justice, ensuring that reward distribution is fair. Meindl (1989) contrasted equity with parity, noting that equity refers to ". . . entitlement based on relative contributions" (p. 254). He also noted that the most frequently used alternative to equity is parity (also referred to as equality). Yet, equal distribution of rewards would not totally avoid inequity perceptions, since those whose investments are high might feel that they are not receiving appropriate (i.e., higher) levels of returns in comparison to others (Dansereau et al., 1984). Equal reward distribution may harm those who are the hardest workers in the group.

Now we come to the crux of the argument: can we have work group differentiation and organizational justice as well? LMX and work group differentiation may be perceived very differently, based upon whether norms of equity or parity (equality) are operating in the leader's decisions regarding allocation of work group resources. Viewing LMX from an organizational justice perspective expands the model, in that LMX must be viewed as a system of interdependent relationships rather than as a set of independent dyads (Graen & Scandura, 1987). Social comparison processes operate at the unit, team, or network level. Although it makes the model more complex, justice in LMX is a theoretically rich framework through which the distribution of benefits (both economic and social) within the LMX process may be studied. Understanding role development within complex systems of interlocked roles ne-

cessitates incorporation of multiple levels of analysis (Dansereau et al., 1984). For example, social comparison processes between work group members (i.e., between dyads) must be addressed. At the group level of analysis, we must also consider the interdependencies between subordinate and subordinate in addition to leader–member interdependencies.

The differentiation process of in-groups and out-groups is not discrepant with the concept of organizational justice. Procedural justice suggests that as long as a leader is perceived as fair by all work unit members (fair procedures for allocating rewards are followed), then a fair exchange of inputs to rewards might be maintained for all members of the work unit. Also, interactional justice seems to play a role in member's perceptions of the reasons for reward distribution in the work group as these are communicated to them by the leader.

In the development of work group perceptions of organizational justice, it is necessary to consider whether fair procedures are followed (procedural justice) and how this is communicated to members (interactional justice). Although it makes the model more complex, viewing LMX through a broad justice perspective (distributive, procedural, and interactional) provides a rich theoretical framework from which some interesting and non-obvious hypotheses can be generated. First, distributive justice enables us to understand how leaders distribute both economic and social benefits. Second, procedural justice and interactional justice provide an understanding as to how employees in the in-group and the out-group react to the distribution of benefits.

Figure 1 suggests how organizational justice issues may affect the LMX development process over time. This time-based model suggests the

**FIGURE 1**
**The Role of Organizational Justice in In-Group/ Out-Group Differentiation**

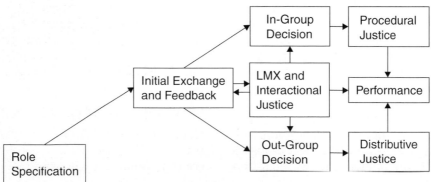

points at which organizational justice concepts become relevant to the development of LMX and performance (other possible outcomes will be discussed later). Time in this model specifically refers to the tenure of the leader–member relationship. Once leader and member begin to interact, a process unfolds which results in the differentiation of the member into an in-group or an out-group member.

### Role Specification

Early in the LMX development process, leaders send roles to members and members respond to these sets of expectations. Specifically, the leader specifies the tasks to be performed by the member. Issues of organizational justice may emerge in this early phase, since the leader and member are essentially strangers and levels of trust are probably low (Graen & Uhl-Bien, 1995). Distributive justice may become a concern, for example, if a member is asked to perform a task that he/she feels is beyond the formal job description. The member may feel that his/her level of compensation is too low for the task and that they are being asked to perform work that is more appropriate to a higher job classification. This involves issues of procedural justice, because if the member's perceptions are correct, then the formal procedures of the organization for assigning work have been violated. These early perceptions of roles develop into patterns of initial exchange as the member provides feedback to the leader regarding whether or not roles are accepted.

### Initial Exchange and Feedback

As the leader makes requests and the member responds, the leader begins to form a perception of the member based upon his/her responses to requests. Dansereau et al. (1984) referred to these exchange patterns as investment-return cycles. In the above example in which the leader asks the member to perform an extra-role behavior (i.e., a task that is outside of the formal job description), the member can provide different forms of feedback to the leader. In response to the request the member can (a) complete the task without questions, but expect a reward (a distributive justice response), (b) not do the task or do it poorly because it is not in the job description and he/she is not compensated for it (another variation on the distributive justice theme), (c) file a grievance because the leader has asked for an inappropriate task for his/her level (a procedural justice response), or (d) ask the leader for an explanation regarding why he/she has been asked

to perform the task (an interactional justice response). These responses have clear implications for the next step, which is the emergence of a leader–member relationship of either an in-group or out-group type. It is important to note that this decision is not necessarily the sole judgement of the leader; it is, in part, based upon the feedback provided to the leader by the member. As Vecchio (1997) notes, some group members may want to be in the out-group. Some members may not want to invest extra effort in their work, and out-group status is perceived as equitable.

### LMX and Interactional Justice

Aspects of interactional justice such as honesty (Bies & Moag, 1986) are important in the development of LMX. In Figure 1, LMX and interactional justice are included in the same box because they represent aspects of the leader–member relationship. The leader must be consistent, and not hide things from members—even those with low LMX. This is critical to the process of LMX development, since the first test of the leader by the member will often be his/her honesty in dealing with the member. For example, if the leader promises a reward, the leader must come through or else the member may perceive the leader as dishonest. Interactional justice pervades the LMX-organizational justice process because communication is such an integral part of LMX relationships (Fairhurst & Chandler, 1989; Schiemann, 1977), and the construction of meaning regarding what constitutes fair exchange (Sias & Jablin, 1995).

While interactional justice is a distinct concept from LMX, it is expected that they will be positively and significantly correlated (Manogran et al., 1994). LMX and interactional justice are variables that measure aspects of the quality of the leader–member relationship. Based upon the quality of the relationship that emerges, a decision is made regarding each member's in-group/out-group status in the work group, as shown in Figure 1. This process is described in detail by Vecchio (1997):

> The boss tries out each new employee by offering small but challenging assignments. The subordinate's reaction to these additional responsibilities is then closely watched. If the employee reacts negatively (by saying, "It's not *my* job") or positively (by replying, "I'm happy to help"), then a cycle of trust or distrust is begun. In short, supervisors learn quickly who is reliable and who is not (p. 275).

In this manner, members in a work group are sorted into in-group or out-group members.

It is important to note that LMX and interactional justice are measured along a continuum (Dienesch & Liden, 1986), and some work group members' status may therefore be ambiguous (maybe in-group or out-group). As depicted in Figure 1, the LMX and interactional justice process have not yet resulted in an in-group or out-group decision, and the exchange and feedback processes continue (this is shown as recursive arrows between the initial exchange and feedback box and the LMX/interactional justice box).

### In-Group/Out-Group Decisions

Dansereau et al. (1975) presented a descriptive model of how units become differentiated into in-groups and out-groups based upon the degree of negotiating latitude offered by the immediate supervisor to members of their work groups. From a distributive justice perspective, LMX is equity-based. From procedural and interactional justice perspectives, in-groups and out-groups may peacefully coexist, if the leader maintains fairness in procedures and interactions with all work group members (Tyler, 1986). Research has indicated that if a leader is procedurally fair, his/her resource allocation decisions will be accepted by all work group members, even the out-group (Tyler & Caine, 1981).

In-group members are more likely to understand procedural justice issues due to the higher quality LMX and communication with supervisors. In-group members perform at higher levels, based upon perceptions that their leader is being procedurally just and explains decisions (interactional justice). Out-group members may be more likely to focus on distributive justice and perform at the level that is appropriate to the rewards they receive based upon the formal employment agreement (Graen & Scandura, 1987). This does not mean that procedural justice is irrelevant for out-group members, however, because their performance may be more related to reward distribution (distributive justice).

### Performance and Other Outcomes

Since LMX has been linked to a number of outcome variables in organizational research [cf. (Graen & Uhl-Bien)], it can be expected that job satisfaction, organizational commitment, and extra-role behavior (such as organizational citizenship) would have similar relationships to organizational justice. Also, decision influence and delegation (Scandura et al., 1986; Schriesheim, Neider, & Scandura, 1998) would be outcomes of the LMX-organizational justice model. Also, ab-senteeism and turnover might be negatively related to LMX and organizational justice variables, since those who perceive their leader as being fair may be less likely to psychologically and/or physically withdraw from work. Role conflict and role ambiguity might be lower, since the process of why the work group has become differentiated might be better understood by work group members. For simplification, the model and research propositions refer to performance as an outcome. However, propositions with the additional outcome variables noted above as dependent variables can be tested as well. . . .

## IMPLICATIONS FOR PRACTICE

Perceptions of organizational justice within work groups must be maintained throughout the LMX development process. For example, a critical incident in which the leader or the member perceives the other's action as violating the norms that have emerged, justice may be questioned. The idea that attributions of leaders (or members) may bound the process of leader–member exchanges has been proposed by Dienesch and Liden (1986). For example, a leader may fail to come through on a promised reward (a distributive justice concern), without appropriately communicating the reasons to the member (interactional justice). Without communications about organizational justice, the member begins to question the leader's actions, which over time destroys the established norms of procedural justice. These perceptions may send the relationship back to the role-specification phase (see Figure 1).

A second implication of the model outlined in this review is that leaders should offer in-group relationships to all work group members initially. Also, out-group members should be re-tested periodically by the leader making offers of in-group roles. Work group differentiation should not be based on factors other than performance (such as race, sex, or handicap status). The assumption should be made that all members can become in-group members if given the opportunity to contribute to the work group and the research base on LMX supports this (Scandura & Graen, 1984). Thus, the leaders' offering of in-group tasks and benefits to all members has clear ethical (and perhaps legal) implications. Thus, the integration of organizational justice and LMX moves LMX theory in the direction of normative theory which provides clearer guidelines for leaders in the management of work groups. Access must be provided to the leadership process for all members and out-group status should be based upon members' decisions not to participate and/or performance and not other factors.

Failure to recognize the important role that organizational justice plays in LMX can help explain why some high quality LMXs disintegrate over time. Recognition of distributive, procedural, and interactional justice is necessary to maintain long-term LMX relationships. Key issues for future empirical study are attribution processes and interactional justice variables (such as perceptions of honesty) in the process of communicating justice issues to members (Lind & Lissak, 1985). Perceptions of justice may operate at multiple levels of analysis—both between unit members as they compare their inputs to rewards, but also within the dyad as individuals compare their current level of outcomes with previous outcomes from the LMX relationship (Dansereau, et al., 1984; Klein. et al., 1994).

## Summary

Issues of organizational justice appear central to further refinement of the LMX model. A conceptual framework was offered in this review that integrates LMX and organizational justice theories. This framework highlighted some multiple level research propositions that might be pursued in future research on LMX and organizational justice. The empirical examination of some research questions regarding LMX and justice requires multiple levels of analysis perspective because a leader may have an overall approach to justice (between unit) and may also develop unique justice norms with members one-on-one through the LMX development process (within unit). Also, the collection of data from multiple perspectives to determine the degree of agreement between leaders and members is encouraged. The LMX model is perhaps one of the more promising developments in leadership research. Grounded in initial descriptive studies of work group differentiation (Dansereau et al., 1975), the model has been integrated with a number of other theories and variables in organizational research over the past 25 years (Graen & Uhl-Bien, 1995). Although the importance of equity was noted by some leadership theorists [cf. (Dansereau et al., 1984)], research on this aspect of LMX has been sparse. This review hopefully addresses this deficiency in the literature by further developing a conceptualization of LMX and organizational justice.

## References

Adams, J. S. (1965). Inequity in social exchange. In L. Berkowitz (Ed.), *Advances in experimental social psychology, 2,* 267–300.

Baron, R. B., & Kenny, D. A. (1986). The moderator-mediator variable distinction in social psychological research: Conceptual, strategic and statistical considerations. *Journal of Personality and Social Psychology, 51,* 1173–1182.

Bass, B. M. (1990). *Bass and Stogdill's handbook of leadership,* 3rd. ed. New York, NY: Free Press.

Bies, R. J., & Moag, J. S. (1986). Interactional Justice: Communication criteria of effectiveness. In R. J. Lewicki, B. H. Sheppard, & B. H. Bazerman (Eds.), *Negotiation in Organizations,* 1, 43–55, Greenwich, CT: JAI Press.

Cleyman, K. L., Jex, S. M., & Love, K. G. (1993). *Employee grievances: An application of the leader–member exchange model.* Paper presented at the 9th Annual Meeting of the Society for Industrial and Organizational Psychology, Nashville, TN.

Cropanzano, R., & Folger, R. (1991). Procedural justice and worker motivation. In R. M. Steers and L. W. Porter (Eds.), *Motivation and work behavior.* New York. NY: McGraw-Hill.

Dansereau, F., Alutto, J. A., & Yammarino, F. J. (1984). *Theory testing in organizational behavior: The varient approach.* Englewood Cliffs, NJ: Prentice-Hall.

Dansereau, F., Graen, G., & Haga, W. J. (1975). A vertical dyad linkage approach to leadership within formal organizations: A longitudinal investigation of the role making process. *Organizational Behavior and Human Performance, 13,* 46–78.

Dansereau, F., Yammarino, F. J., & Markham, S. E. (1995). Leadership: The multiple-level approaches. *Leadership Quarterly, 6,* 97–109.

Dienesch, R. M., & Liden, R. C. (1986). Leader–member exchange model of leadership: A critique and further development. *Academy of Management Review, 11,* 618–634.

Duarte, N. T., Goodson, J. R., & Klich, N. R. (1994). Effects of dyadic quality and duration on performance appraisal. *Academy of Management Journal, 37,* 499–521.

Fairhurst, G. T., & Chandler, T. (1989). Social structure in leader–member interaction. *Communication Monographs, 56,* 215–239.

Ferris, G. R. (1985). Role of leadership in the employee withdrawal process: A constructive replication. *Journal of Applied Psychology, 70,* 777–781.

Festinger, L. (1957). *A theory of cognitive dissonance.* Evanston, IL: Row, Peterson.

Folger, R., & Greenberg, J. (1985). Procedural justice: An interpretive analysis of personnel systems. In

K. Rowland & G. Ferris (Eds.), *Research in personnel and human resources management,* Vol. 3 (pp. 141–183). Greenwich, CT: JAI Press.

Folger, R., & Konovsky, M. A. (1989). Effects of procedural and distributive justice on reactions to pay raise decisions. *Academy of Management Journal, 32,* 115–130.

Graen, G., & Cashman, J. (1975). A role-making model of leadership in formal organizations: A developmental approach. In J. G. Hunt & L. L. Larson (Eds.), *Leaderships frontiers,* Kent, OH: Kent State University Press.

Graen, G., Ginsburgh, S., & Schiemann, W. (1977). Effects of linking-pin quality on the quality of working life of lower participants. *Administrative Science Quarterly, 22,* 491–504.

Graen, G., Liden, R., & Hoel, W. (1982a). Role of leadership in the employee withdrawal process. *Journal of Applied Psychology, 67,* 868–872.

Graen, G., Novak, M., & Sommerkamp, P. (1982b). The effects of leader–member exchange and job design on productivity and satisfaction: Testing a dual attachment model, *Organizational Behavior and Human Performance, 30,* 109–131.

Graen, G. B., & Scandura, T. A. (1986). A theory of dyadic career reality. In G. Ferris and K. Rowland (Eds.), *Research in Personnel and Human Resource Management,* 4: 147–181.

Graen, G. B., & Scandura, T. A. (1987). Toward a psychology of dyadic organizing. In L. L. Cummings, & B. Staw (Eds), *Research in Organizational Behavior,* 9: 175–208.

Graen, G. B., & Uhl-Bien, M. (1995). Relationship-based approach to leadership: Development of Leader–member exchange (LMX) theory of leadership over 25 years: Applying a multi-level-multi-domain perspective. *Leadership Quarterly, 6,* 219–247.

Greenberg, J. (1987). A taxonomy of organizational justice theories. *Academy of Management Review, 12,* 9–22.

Greenberg, J. (1990). Organizational justice: Yesterday, today and tomorrow. *Journal of Management, 16,* 399–432.

Greenberg, J., & Folger, R. (1983). Procedural justice, participation, and the fair process effect in groups and organizations. In P. B. Paulus (Ed.), *Basic group processes* (pp. 235–256). New York, NY: Springer-Verlag.

Hollander, E. P. (1978). *Leadership dynamics: A practical guide to effective relationships,* New York, NY: Free Press.

Kabanoff, B. (1991). Equity, equality, power, and conflict. *Academy of Management Review, 16,* 416–441.

Klein, K. J., Dansereau, F., & Hall, R. J. (1994). Levels issues in theory development, data collection, and analysis. *Academy of Management Review, 19,* 195–229.

Lagace, R. R., Castleberry, S. B., & Ridnour, R. E. (1993). An exploratory salesforce study of the relationship between leader–member exchange and motivation, role stress, and manager evaluation. *Journal of Applied Business Research, 9,* 110–119.

Liden, R. C., Wayne, S. J., & Stilwell, D. (1993). A longitudinal study on the early development of leader–member exchanges. *Journal of Applied Psychology, 78,* 662–674.

Lind, E. A., & Lissak, R. I. (1985). Apparent impropriety and procedural fairness judgements. *Journal of Experimental Social Psychology, 21,* 19–29.

Lind, E. A., & Tyler, T. R. (1988). *The social psychology of procedural justice.* New York, NY: Plenum Press.

Manogran, P., Stauffer, J., & Conlon, E. J. (1994). *Leader–member exchange as a key mediating variable between employees' perceptions of fairness and organizational citizenship behavior.* National Academy of Management meeting proceedings, Dallas, TX.

Meindl, J. R. (1989). Managing to be fair: An exploration of values, motives, and leadership, *Administrative Science Quarterly, 34,* 252–276.

Miner, J. B. (1980). *Theories of organizational behavior.* Hinsdale, IL: Dryen Press.

Moorman, R. H. (1991). Relationship between organizational justice and organizational citizenship behavior: Do fairness perceptions influence employee citizenship? *Journal of Applied Psychology, 76,* 845–855.

Scandura, T. A., & Graen, G. B. (1984). Moderating effects of initial leader–member exchange status on the effects of a leadership intervention. *Journal of Applied Psychology, 69,* 428–436.

Scandura, T. A., Graen, G. B., & Novak, M. A. (1986). When managers decide not to decide autocratically: An investigation of leader–member exchange and decision influence. *Journal of Applied Psychology, 71,* 579–584.

Scandura, T. A., & Schriesheim, C. A. (1994). Leader–member exchange and supervisor career mentoring as complementary concepts in leadership research. *Academy of Management Journal, 37,* 1588–1602.

Schiemann, W. A. (1977). *Structural and interpersonal effects on patterns of managerial communications: A longitudinal investigation* (Ph.D. dissertation) University of Illinois, Urbana-Champaign, IL.

Schriesheim, C. A., Neider, L. L., & Scandura, T. A. (1998). A within- and between-groups analysis of leader–member exchange as a correlate of delegation and a moderator of delegation relationships with performance and satisfaction. *Academy of Management Journal, 41,* 298–318.

Sias, P. M., & Jablin, F. M. (1995). Differential superior-subordinate relations, perceptions of fairness, and coworker communication. *Human Communication Research, 22,* 5–38.

Tyler, T. R. (1986). The psychology of leadership evaluation. In H. W. Bierhoff, R. L. Cohen, & J. Greenberg (Eds.), *Justice in social relations.* New York. NY: Plenum.

Tyler, T. R. (1989). The psychology of procedural justice: A test of the group-value model. *Journal of Personality and Social Psychology, 57,* 830–838.

Tyler, T. R., & Caine, A. (1981). The role of distributive and procedural fairness in the endorsement of formal leaders. *Journal of Personality and Social Psychology, 41,* 643–655.

Tyler, T. R., & Lind, E. A. (1992). A relational model of authority in groups. In M. P. Zanna (Ed.), *Advances in experimental social psychology, 25,* 115–191.

Vecchio, R. P. (1985). Predicting employee turnover from leader–member exchange: A failure to replicate. *Academy of Management Journal, 28,* 478–485.

Vecchio, R. P. (1997). Are you in or out with your boss? In R. P. Vecchio (Ed.), *Leadership: Understanding the dynamics of power and influence in organizations.* Notre Dame, IN: University of Notre Dame Press.

Vecchio, R. P., & Gobdel, B. C. (1984). The vertical dyad linkage model of leadership: Problems and prospects. *Organizational Behavior and Human Performance, 34,* 5–20.

Vecchio, R. P., Griffith, R. W., & Hom, P. W. (1986). The predictive utility of the vertical dyad linkage approach. *Journal of Applied Psychology, 126,* 617–625.

Wakabayashi, M., & Graen, G. (1984). The Japanese career progress study: A 7-year follow up. *Journal of Applied Psychology, 69,* 603–614.

Yukl, G. (1994). *Leadership in organizations,* 3rd ed. Englewood Cliffs, NJ: Prentice-Hall.

## Reading 7

# Trust in Leadership and Team Performance: Evidence from NCAA Basketball

**Kurt T. Dirks**
Simon Fraser University

In the past 3 decades, research from several literatures in applied psychology, as well as writings in the popular press, has implied that a higher level of trust in a leader results in higher team (or organizational) performance (e.g., Bennis & Nanus, 1985; Fairholm, 1994; Golembiewski & McConkie, 1975; Kouzes & Posner, 1987; Likert, 1967; McGregor, 1967; Zand, 1972, 1997). This proposition has served as the basis for the claim that trust is an important variable in applied settings and therefore deserves further research. The proposition also provides a justification for the importance of management practices such as leadership development and team building.

Despite its importance for research and practice, the relationship between trust in leadership and team performance has been the subject of little empirical research. The purpose of this article is to address two specific issues. First, does trust in a leader affect team performance? At this point, there is no empirical evidence to directly substantiate the proposition that a higher level of trust in a leader results in higher team performance. It is dangerous to use this untested assumption as a basis for research and practice—particularly given that related studies on the main effects of trust in teammates on team performance have provided very inconsistent results (Dirks & Ferrin, in press). Second, this study explores a more complex and dynamic relationship between trust and team performance. Specifically, the study examines whether trust in leadership mediates the relationship between past and future team performance. This idea advances prior research that has focused on a unidirectional relationship (trust → team performance) by examining how trust is both an important product and a determinant of team performance.

In addressing the preceding issues, this research is intended to contribute to the growing literature on the role of trust in applied settings

(Kramer, 1999), as well as to the more established literatures on leadership and group performance. Given the frequency of the use of teams in applied settings, understanding the role of trust in leadership within teams is particularly important for research and practice.

## THEORY AND HYPOTHESES

### TRUST

It is clear that trust has been defined in multiple ways in the literature. Although each researcher has used slight variations, most empirical studies seem to conceptualize and measure trust as an expectation or belief that one can rely on another person's actions and words and/or that the person has good intentions toward oneself (e.g., Cook & Wall, 1980; Cummings & Bromiley, 1996; Dirks, 1999; McAllister, 1995; Robinson, 1996). As Mayer, Davis, and Schoorman (1995) and Rousseau, Sitkin, Burt, and Camerer (1998) have noted, trust is most meaningful in situations in which one party is at risk or vulnerable to another party.

In this study, the focal referent of the belief or expectation is the leader of the team. Specifically, the study conceptualizes trust as an expectation or belief that the team can rely on the leader's actions or words and that the leader has good intentions toward the team. Trust in leadership is a meaningful concept in many teams, because the leader typically has the most formal power on the team (Bass, 1990), causing others to be vulnerable to him or her. As I discuss later, I also take into account the extent to which team members trust each other, because they are also vulnerable to each other, given their interdependence.

### THE EFFECT OF TRUST IN LEADERSHIP ON TEAM PERFORMANCE

The idea that trust can have an important influence on team performance can be found in several literatures, as well as in management practices. In the early literature on organizational psychology,

Argyris (1962), McGregor (1967), and Likert (1967) professed the significance of trust in leadership for effective teams and organizations. Consistent with these ideas, more current researchers studying trust have suggested that it is an important element of effective work groups (e.g., Golembiewski & McConkie, 1975; Larson & LaFasto, 1989). Other researchers have begun to examine empirically the effects of trust in leadership on workplace outcomes, including organizational citizenship behavior, information sharing, goal acceptance, and task performance (Oldham, 1975; O'Reilly & Roberts, 1974; Podsakoff, MacKenzie, Moorman, & Fetter, 1990; Rich, 1997). Multiple theories of leadership have also cited the critical role of trust. For example, theories have suggested that charismatic leaders build trust in their followers (Kirkpatrick & Locke, 1996; Shamir, Zakay, Breinen, & Popper, 1998), that integrity or trustworthiness is an important trait of leaders (Bass, 1990), that trust is a core basis of effective leadership (Bennis & Nanus, 1985; Fairholm, 1994; Zand, 1997), and that trust is central in subordinates' perceptions of effective leadership (Hogan, Curphy, & Hogan, 1994). Lastly, a number of management practices, such as leadership development programs, recognize the importance of trust to varying degrees (e.g., Conger, 1992; Peterson & Hicks, 1996). To date, however, the idea that a team's trust in its leader has a main effect on team performance has not yet directly been examined or validated empirically.

The studies previously cited share a common theory as to why trust in leadership is assumed to be an important determinant of team performance. In short, trust in leadership is important in that it allows the team to be willing to accept the leader's activities, goals, and decisions and work hard to achieve them. The leader's role typically involves a number of activities related to team performance, such as determining team member roles, distributing rewards and motivating employees, developing team members, and setting the team's goals and strategies. When the team feels that it cannot rely on the leader or that the leader does not have the team's interests at heart, team members are unlikely to carry out the roles specified by the leader or to work toward the performance-related objectives and strategies set by the leader. This makes it difficult for the team to work together effectively and perform at a high level.

Although elements of this idea can be found in several domains of leadership research, the literature on transformational and charismatic leadership provides perhaps the best case in point. Trust in leadership is cited as one means by which transformational leadership operates (Yukl, 1998).[1] Podsakoff et al. (1990) empirically examined how trust mediated the effect of transformational leadership on whether subordinates worked beyond role expectations. Other researchers have suggested that trust is important if followers are to accept the goals, beliefs, or vision of the leader (Bennis & Nanus, 1985; House, 1977). One might hypothesize that these effects are particularly important under conditions of perceived uncertainty (Waldman & Yammarino, 1999). For instance, under high levels of perceived uncertainty, trust in the leader may be crucial for getting individuals to buy into a common goal and work toward it as a unit. Given little trust in the leader, team members are unlikely to be willing to sacrifice their interests for the team or its goals in a context of uncertainty.

*Hypothesis 1:* Trust in leadership has a positive effect on team performance.

It is important to note that the effect of trust in leadership is distinct from the potential effect of another form of trust within a team that has received attention in the literature: trust in teammates (work partners). Prior empirical research examining the role of trust in teams has focused on the proposition that a higher level of trust between team members results in higher team performance (e.g., Dirks, 1999; Klimoski & Karol, 1976), although the results have been mixed (Dirks & Ferrin, in press). This proposition is built on the logic that trust increases the ability of group members to work together, which in turn increases team performance (Larson & LaFasto, 1989). Although the distinction between trust in the leader and trust in teammates is implicit in the literature, it has not been clarified, nor has it

---

[1] The meaningful role of trust in transformational leadership is recognized by the conceptualization of the charismatic component (Bass, 1985) and its measurement (at least 3 of the 19 items in the charismatic component of the Multifactor Leadership Questionnaire are related to trust building). To the extent that the charismatic component does involve some trust-building behaviors, there exists indirect evidence of a relationship between trust in leadership and leader effectiveness or unit performance (see the results of the meta-analysis by Lowe, Kroeck, & Sivasubramaniam, 1996). Nevertheless, the qualities or behaviors of leaders are distinct from the outcomes (e.g., trust, motivation, identification) they produce. Several recent studies have provided evidence that it is useful to distinguish between behaviors of transformational or charismatic leaders and the level of trust that followers have in them (Kirkpatrick & Locke, 1996; Podsakoff et al., 1990; Shamir et al., 1998). Hence, the present study provides evidence relevant to, but not directly overlapping with, existing research on transformational leadership.

been used empirically. In this study, I empirically control for the potential effects of trust in team members when examining the impact of trust in leadership on team performance.

## TRUST AS MEDIATING THE EFFECTS OF PAST PERFORMANCE ON FUTURE PERFORMANCE

The logic in the prior section, as well as in existing research, has been focused on a relationship between trust and team performance that is unidirectional—that is, trust affects team performance. In this section, I examine a more complex relationship between trust and team performance, whereby trust mediates the relationship between past and future team performance. Examining this connection may help advance understanding of trust from a simple unidirectional relationship to a more sophisticated and dynamic relationship. The foundation for this argument is derived by combining theories of trust with attributional theories of leadership.

The idea that trust has multidirectional relationships with other variables has a precedent in research that has theorized that trust is interrelated with risk-taking behaviors (Butler, 1995; Golembiewski & McConkie, 1975; Mayer et al., 1995). To date, however, research has not discussed such a relationship between trust and group performance. A multidirectional relationship between trust and performance may, however, be derived from Bhattacharya, Devinney, and Pillutla's (1998) proposition that trust involves expectations about outcomes associated with another party under uncertainty. From this definition, one can argue that expectations about future outcomes in situations of uncertainty are likely to be created by observing past outcomes produced by the party. In other words, observations of past outcomes (e.g., performance) are likely to shape those expectations, particularly in an uncertain environment.

Although the preceding idea helps explain why past performance of a team might influence trust, it does not speak to why the belief might be transferred to the leader. Attributional theories of leadership provide the explanation. According to Lord and Maher (1991), "people tend to assume that a major function of leaders is to produce good performance outcomes, and they infer leadership from knowledge of successful task or organizational performance" (p. 55). Studies have suggested that because of the ambiguity involved in team or organizational performance, individuals tend to make inferences about the leader on the basis of information about past performance (Lord & Maher, 1991; Meindl, Ehrlich, & Dukerich, 1985). Positive qualities tend to be inferred from high team performance, and negative qualities tend to be inferred from poor team performance (Staw, 1975).[2]

Hence, in the present case, the team would perceive a team's past performance and would be likely to attribute (correctly or incorrectly) that performance to the team's leader. After attributing the performance to the team's leader, team members may come to form expectations about team outcomes from those attributions—and hence may be more or less willing to trust the leader. Perceiving low performance may cause the team to expect low team performance in the future and make them unwilling to trust the leader and unwilling to "put themselves in the leader's hands." In contrast, perceiving high team performance in the past may cause the team to expect high team performance in the future and make them willing to trust the leader and put themselves in his or her hands. In summary, trust in the leader seems to be a viable cognitive process through which past performance is translated into future performance.

*Hypothesis 2:* Trust in leadership mediates the relationship between past team performance and future team performance.

## METHOD

### SAMPLE

I examine the previous questions using a sample of men's college basketball teams that are members of the National Collegiate Athletic Association (NCAA). Head coaches of teams were identified using the NCAA directory and were contacted either by mail or by telephone. Teams from Division I and Division III were contacted to obtain maximum variation in teams within the NCAA. Thirty-four teams originally agreed to participate by completing surveys; data were eventually received from 31 teams. One team was subsequently dropped from the analysis when it was determined that the coach was new, leaving a total of 30 teams (11 Division I and 19 Division III). The 30 teams are members of 12 different

---

[2] Following the social information processing perspective (Salancik & Pfeffer, 1978), the process is likely to involve numerous social processes (discussion among team members) and symbols (e.g., ceremonies, newspaper articles), particularly in a team context that would foster a common perception on the team.

conferences located in the Midwestern and Western United States. In these 30 teams, 355 individuals completed surveys.

College basketball teams are an attractive setting, both empirically and theoretically, for studying the relationship between trust and team performance. Empirically, the setting provides a reliable and valid measure of team performance that is independent of team members' perceptions (which are the source of measure of trust). In addition, the setting provides access to reliable and objective measures of control variables. Lastly, each team operates under the same guidelines (NCAA rules) and has the same performance objectives. Because these issues typically present problems in collecting data on teams, the present sample is attractive. Theoretically, basketball teams provide a setting in which trust in the leader and trust in teammates are likely to be meaningful. Teams are highly vulnerable to the coach, because he or she controls many resources (e.g., playing time, key decisions) that are valuable to the team. In addition, given the interdependence on the team, basketball teams provide a setting in which players are highly vulnerable to each other. Lastly, there is significant uncertainty (actual and perceived) for players on important issues, including the likelihood that a coach can help a team win, the performance of one's own team and opposing teams throughout the season, and the amount of playing time one will receive. As I noted earlier, perceived vulnerability, interdependence, and uncertainty are likely to be important factors for trust in leadership.[3] . . .

[3] As a reviewer pointed out, although all teams face perceived uncertainty, vulnerability, and interdependence, there is likely to be some variation between teams. Although highly restricted, this variation may impact the relationship between trust and team performance.

## RESULTS

Descriptive statistics are provided in Table 1. . . . The data provide support for Hypothesis 1. After controlling for several potential determinants of performance, trust in the coach had a significant effect on winning percentage ($\beta = .44$, $p < .05$).

Because trust had a significant effect on winning percentage, mediation can be examined. In the first two equations, the preconditions for mediation are fulfilled: Past performance does have a significant effect on trust ($\beta = .61$, $p < .01$) and an effect on winning percentage ($\beta = .44$, $p < .05$), after controlling for other variables. When trust was added in the third equation ($\beta = .44$, $p < .05$), the coefficient for past performance decreased in magnitude ($\beta = .20$) and became statistically insignificant. Hence, the pattern of results from these three equations provides support for trust mediating the relationship between past performance and future performance.

Trust in leadership and the control variables accounted for a substantial portion of the variance in team performance ($R^2_{adj} = .66$). Variables other than trust in leadership that demonstrated significant bivariate correlations with team performance include team talent, past team performance, preconference performance, coach record (but not coach experience), and trust in teammates.

## DISCUSSION

Much of the current interest in trust arguably stems from its assumed (and relatively empirically unvalidated) impact on the performance of various social units. The present study examines the significance of trust by exploring potential relationships between trust in leadership and team performance. The study provides several notewor-

## TABLE 1   Means, Standard Deviations, and Correlations for Study Variables

| Variable | M | SD | 1 | 2 | 3 | 4 | 5 | 6 | 7 | 8 | 9 |
|---|---|---|---|---|---|---|---|---|---|---|---|
| 1. Team performance_Future | 0.59 | 0.23 | | | | | | | | | |
| 2. Trust_Leader | 51.01 | 6.56 | .57** | — | | | | | | | |
| 3. Team performance_Prior | 0.51 | 0.21 | .62** | .60** | — | | | | | | |
| 4. Trust_Teammates | 48.77 | 5.40 | .37* | .64** | .23 | — | | | | | |
| 5. Team Talent | 0.15 | 0.11 | .72** | .27 | .54** | .24 | — | | | | |
| 6. Coach record | 0.45 | 0.18 | .39* | .18 | .44** | −.06 | .26 | — | | | |
| 7. Experience | 305.27 | 218.42 | .19 | −.11 | −.08 | −.14 | .06 | .71** | — | | |
| 8. Preconference | 0.67 | 0.28 | .41* | .10 | .25 | .13 | .45* | −.05 | .21 | — | |
| 9. Player tenure | 2.14 | 0.42 | .18 | −.04 | .08 | .04 | −.02 | .36* | .50** | .16 | — |

Note. $N = 30$.
* $p < .05$. ** $p < .01$.

thy findings. First, the finding that trust in the leader has an effect on team performance has significance for theory and practice. This evidence validates an idea that is fundamental to theories of trust and leadership and provides a basis for management practices. Although prior research has focused on the effects of trust in leadership on various behaviors and attitudes, this is the first study to directly examine its effects on performance—arguably the most important criterion. The findings suggest that the effects of trust on team performance are not only important theoretically but also substantial in practical terms. For example, after I took into account a number of alternative determinants of team performance, trust in the coach accounted for a significant amount of variance ($\Delta R^2_{adj} = .07$). A qualitative examination of the data illustrates the substance of this difference. The 2 teams reporting the highest levels of trust in their coach early in the season excelled: 1 team was ranked as the Number 1 team in the nation for the latter part of the season, before being upset in the NCAA tournament, and the other team ended up playing in the championship game for the national title. In contrast, the team with the lowest level of trust in its coach won approximately 10% of its conference games, and the coach was fired at the end of the season.

The effect of trust in leadership is particularly interesting when compared with the effect of another frequently cited determinant of team performance—trust in teammates. Although the effect of trust in leadership was substantial and significant, trust in teammates was not significant after controlling for other variables, despite the fact that it was studied in a context that theoretically should have allowed both variables to be important. Although some may consider this to be surprising, they should note that other researchers have also found that trust in a partner does not have a main effect on the performance of the group or dyad (e.g., Dirks, 1999; Kimmel, Pruitt, Magenau, Konar-Goldband, & Carnevale, 1980). The relative importance of trust in these two different referents for group outcomes provides an interesting direction for future research. Researchers might, for example, examine whether the relative importance of trust in the leader versus trust in the team differs by the type of task the team performs. For instance, would the relative importance of the two referents differ if the team was engaging in a problem-solving task (e.g., creating a new product or idea), as opposed to performing a physical task that requires

carrying out a strategy (particularly in situations in which the leader champions the strategy)? To date, there is not enough research on trust to address this question.

The results of the current study provide initial evidence that trust in leadership is critical to team effectiveness in some situations. Building on the theory discussed earlier, one might speculate that trust in leadership is particularly important because the decisions are of great importance to the team and must be embraced by followers for the team to perform well. Exploratory interviews with coaches and players provide some tentative support for this idea. According to one coach, trust "allows players to be willing to accept their role, so that they can do what it takes to win" and to "be willing to do things that we ask of them that are unpleasant or hard but are necessary to win" (personal communication, April 1998). Likewise, a player commented that

> once we developed trust in Coach __, the progress we made increased tremendously because we were no longer asking questions or were apprehensive. Instead, we were buying in and believing that if we worked our hardest, we were going to get there. (personal communication, April 1998)[4]

Hence, trust in leadership allows the team members to suspend their questions, doubts, and personal motives and instead throw themselves into working toward team goals. Future research might explore these ideas empirically.

Whereas past research on trust has focused on the effects of trust on team performance, this study suggests that a more complex relationship may exist than has been previously theorized. Specifically, the study provides theory and evidence that trust mediates the relationship between past performance and future performance. This provides several interesting implications. One implication of this idea is that trust in the leader is not only a determinant of team performance but also a product of it. Although researchers have suggested that trust might have such a relationship with behaviors (e.g., Mayer et al., 1995), they have not yet examined theoretically, let alone empirically within a single study, this idea with regard to performance.

On the basis of the findings of the mediating role of trust, one might speculate that trust in a

---

[4] Personal communications are taken from interviews that were conducted with the promise of anonymity.

leader plays a crucial role in helping translate past performance of a team into future performance. Prior research by Hackman (1990) "found considerable evidence to support the dictum, that, over time the rich get richer and the poor get poorer" (p. 481). Whereas existing research on this topic appears to be focused on team efficacy (e.g., Lindsley, Brass, & Thomas, 1995), this study suggests that one of the reasons that the inertia in performance can be sustained is because performance affects the team's trust in its leader, which in turn affects team performance. For example, low levels of past performance may be translated into low levels of future performance, because the team does not trust the leader and is unwilling to accept his or her decisions, goals, and strategies. Future research might consider the significant role trust might play in this phenomenon.

The more complex relationship just noted was derived by combining theories from the trust and leadership literatures to explain why past performance influenced a team's trust in its leader. The data suggest that this effect was quite strong. This evidence suggests that researchers should consider trust as having the potential to be both an outcome and a determinant of organizational outcomes. The finding also suggests that future research on the determinants of trust in a leader clearly should take past performance of a relationship into account.

## IMPLICATIONS FOR PRACTICE

The increasing use of work teams makes the findings of this study important for practice. This is particularly the case because much of the existing research on trust has been focused on individuals. Given some evidence that trust in leadership can affect team performance, one can begin to speculate about the implications for selecting, evaluating, training, and retaining leaders for teams. On the basis of the present study, trust, whatever its origins, appears be a valid criterion for these decisions, as it can have performance implications.

Given that trust is important, leaders may consider existing research on how trust can be built through their actions. For example, research suggests that leaders can build trust by engaging in transformational leadership behaviors such as role modeling (Podsakoff et al., 1990; Rich, 1997), by creating fair processes (Korsgaard, Schweiger, & Sapienza, 1995), and by allowing followers to participate in decision making (Magner, Welker, & Johnson, 1996).

Lastly, the data from this study highlight the fact that there are many determinants of team performance, of which trust is only one. For example, team talent appeared to be the single greatest determinant of team success in this sample. Clearly, leaders need to attend to many of these factors to create successful teams.

## LIMITATIONS AND DIRECTIONS FOR FUTURE RESEARCH

This study has several limitations that provide opportunities for future research. First, the correlational design of the study does not completely rule out all plausible relationships between trust and team performance. For example, despite the statistical support for mediating the relationship between past performance and future performance and statistically controlling for other key constructs, the design cannot completely rule out the possibility that trust co-occurs with group performance, as opposed to affecting it directly. This idea needs to be ruled out using an experimental method.

Second, this study provides data from a single setting—men's college basketball teams. Although the teams in this sample share numerous attributes (e.g., performance objectives, ongoing relationships, existing roles and norms) common to most types of teams that are of interest to applied psychologists, it is important to highlight differentiating attributes. One of the most common attributes used to differentiate groups is their task (McGrath, 1984). The task of the teams in this sample primarily involved the execution of manual or psychomotor tasks, as opposed to intellective tasks. As McGrath (1984) noted, these type of tasks arguably constitute much of the work of groups in organizations but are often overlooked in research. A second factor to note is that I intentionally chose teams with hierarchical leader–member relations (i.e., "manager-led teams"—see Hackman, 1990) and high levels of interdependence to create high levels of actual vulnerability. Vulnerability is likely to help maximize the magnitude of the effects of trust; therefore, the magnitude of the effect in the present sample may be higher than in samples of less hierarchical teams. Even if the effect was smaller in other contexts, trust in leadership would, however, still be likely to be important, given the magnitude of the effect in the present study.

Lastly, as I discussed earlier, higher levels of perceived vulnerability (Rousseau et al., 1998) or perceived uncertainty (Waldman & Yammarino, 1999) may increase the impact of trust in leadership on team performance. Although they are not assessed in this study, these factors are likely to vary between teams for a variety of reasons (e.g., higher levels of player turnover, autocratic leadership styles). Future research directed at examining the potential moderating effect of perceived vulnerability and perceived uncertainty (and the factors creating them) may advance knowledge of the conditions under which trust in leadership is more or less critical to team success.

# References

Argyris, C. (1962). *Interpersonal competence and organizational effectiveness.* Homewood, IL: Dorsey.

Baron, R. M., & Kenny, D. A. (1986). The moderator–mediator variable distinction in social psychological research: Conceptual, strategic, and statistical considerations. *Journal of Personality and Social Psychology, 51,* 1173–1182.

Bass, B. (1985). *Leadership and performance beyond expectations.* New York: Free Press.

Bass, B. (1990). *Bass & Stodgill's handbook of leadership.* New York: Free Press.

Bennis, W., & Nanus, B. (1985). *Leaders: The strategies for taking charge.* New York: Harper & Row.

Bhattacharya, R., Devinney, T., & Pillutla, M. (1998). A formal model of trust based on outcomes. *Academy of Management Review, 23,* 459–472.

Butler, J. K. (1995). Behaviors, trust, and goal achievement in a win–win negotiating role play. *Group & Organization Management, 20,* 486–501.

Conger, J. (1992). *Learning to lead: The art of transforming managers into leaders.* San Francisco: Jossey-Bass.

Cook, J., & Wall, T. (1980). New work attitude measures of trust, organizational commitment, and personal need fulfillment. *Journal of Occupational Psychology, 53,* 39–52.

Cummings, L., & Bromiley, P. (1996). The organizational trust inventory (OTI): Development and validation. In R. Kramer & T. Tyler (Eds.), *Trust in organizations* (pp. 302–330). Thousand Oaks, CA: Sage.

Dirks, K. T. (1999). The effects of interpersonal trust on work group performance. *Journal of Applied Psychology, 84,* 445–455.

Dirks, K. T., & Ferrin, D. L. (in press). The role of trust in organizational settings. *Organization Science.*

Fairholm, G. (1994). *Leadership and the culture of trust.* Westport, CT: Praeger.

Georgopolous, D. B. (1986). *Organizational structure, problem solving, and effectiveness.* San Francisco: Jossey-Bass.

Golembiewski, R., & McConkie, M. (1975). The centrality of interpersonal trust in group process. In C. Cooper (Ed.), *Theories of group process* (pp. 131–185). New York: Wiley.

Hackman, J. R. (Ed.). (1990). *Groups that work (and those that don't).* San Francisco: Jossey-Bass.

Hogan, R., Curphy, G., & Hogan, J. (1994). What we know about leadership: Effectiveness and personality. *American Psychologist, 49,* 493–504.

House, R. (1977). A 1976 theory of charismatic leadership. In J. Hunt & L. Larson (Eds.), *Leadership: The cutting edge* (pp. 189–207). Carbondale, IL: Southern Illinois University Press.

James, L., Demaree, R., & Wolf, G. (1984). Estimating within-group interrater reliability with and without response bias. *Journal of Applied Psychology, 69,* 85–98.

Jehn, K., & Shah, P. (1997). Interpersonal relationships and task performance: An examination of mediating processes in friendship and acquaintance groups. *Journal of Personality and Social Psychology, 72,* 775–790.

Jones, M. (1974). Regressing group on individual effectiveness. *Organizational Behavior and Human Performance, 11,* 426–451.

Kimmel, M., Pruitt, D., Magenau, J., Konar-Goldband, E., & Carnevale, P. (1980). Effects of trust, aspiration, and gender on negotiation tactics. *Journal of Personality and Social Psychology, 38,* 9–22.

Kirkpatrick, S., & Locke, E. (1996). Direct and indirect effects of three core charismatic leadership components on performance and attitudes. *Journal of Applied Psychology, 81,* 36–51.

Klimoski, R. J., & Karol, B. L. (1976). The impact of trust on creative problem solving groups. *Journal of Applied Psychology, 61,* 630–633.

Korsgaard, M. A., Schweiger, D., & Sapienza, H. (1995). Building commitment, attachment, and trust in strategic decision-making teams: The role of procedural justice. *Academy of Management Journal, 38,* 60–84.

Kouzes, J., & Posner, B. (1987). *The leadership challenge: How to get extraordinary things done in organizations.* San Francisco: Jossey-Bass.

Kramer, R. (1999). Trust and distrust in organizations: Emerging perspectives, enduring questions. *Annual Review of Psychology, 50,* 569–598.

Larson, C., & LaFasto, F. (1989). *Teamwork.* Newbury Park, CA: Sage.

Likert, R. (1967). *The human organization.* New York: McGraw-Hill.

Lindsley, D., Brass, D., & Thomas, J. (1995). Efficacy-performance spirals: A multi-level perspective. *Academy of Management Review, 20,* 645–678.

Lord, R., & Maher, K. (1991). *Leadership and information processing: Linking perceptions and performance.* Boston: Unwin Hyman.

Lowe, K., Kroeck, K. G., & Sivasubramaniam, N. (1996). Effectiveness correlates of transformational and transactional leadership: A metaanalytic review of the MLQ literature. *Leadership Quarterly, 7,* 385–425.

Magner, N., Welker, R., & Johnson, G. (1996). The interactive effects of participation and outcome favorability on turnover intentions and evaluations of supervisors. *Journal of Occupational and Organizational Psychology, 69,* 135–143.

Mayer, R. C., Davis, J. H., & Schoorman, F. D. (1995). An integrative model of organizational trust. *Academy of Management Review, 20,* 709–734.

McAllister, D. (1995). Affect- and cognition-based trust as foundations for interpersonal cooperation in organizations. *Academy of Management Journal, 38,* 24–59.

McGrath, J. (1984). *Groups: Interaction and performance.* Englewood Cliffs, NJ: Prentice-Hall.

McGregor, D. (1967). *The professional manager.* New York: McGraw-Hill.

Meindl, J., Ehrlich, S., & Dukerich, J. (1985). The romance of leadership, *Administrative Science Quarterly, 30,* 78–102.

Neter, J., Wasserman, W., & Kunter, M. (1990). *Applied linear statistical models* (3rd ed.). Homewood, IL: Irwin.

Oldham, G. (1975). The impact of supervisory characteristics on goal acceptance. *Academy of Management Journal, 18,* 461–475.

O'Reilly, C. A., & Roberts, K. H. (1974). Information filtration in organizations: Three experiments. *Organizational Behavior and Human Performance, 11,* 253–265.

Peterson, D., & Hicks, M. D. (1996). *Leader as coach.* Minneapolis, MN: Personnel Decisions International.

Podsakoff, P., MacKenzie, S., Moorman, R., & Fetter, R. (1990). Transformational leader behaviors and their effects on followers' trust in leader, satisfaction, and organizational citizenship behaviors. *Leadership Quarterly, 1,* 107–142.

Pollock, T. (1998). *Risk, reputation, and interdependence in the market for initial public offerings: Embedded networks and the construction of organization value.* Unpublished doctoral dissertation, University of Illinois at Urbana–Champaign.

Rich, G. (1997). The sales manager as a role model: Effects of trust, job satisfaction, and performance of salespeople. *Journal of Academy of Marketing Science, 25,* 319–328.

Robinson, S. (1996). Trust and the breach of the psychological contract. *Administrative Science Quarterly, 41,* 574–599.

Rousseau, D. (1985). Issues of level in organizational research: Multi-level and cross-level perspectives. In L. L. Cummings & B. Staw (Eds.), *Research in organizational behavior* (pp. 1–37). Greenwich, CT: JAI Press.

Rousseau, D., Sitkin, S., Burt, R., & Camerer, C. (1998). Not so different after all: A cross-discipline view of trust. *Academy of Management Review, 23,* 387–392.

Salancik, G. J., & Pfeffer, J. (1978). A social information processing approach to job attitudes and task design. *Administrative Science Quarterly, 23,* 224–253.

Shamir, B., Zakay, E., Breinen, E., & Popper, M. (1998). Correlates of charismatic leader behavior in military units: Subordinates' attitudes, unit characteristics, and superiors' appraisals of leader performance. *Academy of Management Journal, 41,* 387–409.

Staw, B. (1975). Attribution of the 'causes' of performance: A general alternative interpretation of cross-sectional research on organizations. *Organizational Behavior and Human Performance, 13,* 414–432.

Waldman, D., & Yammarino, F. (1999). CEO charismatic leadership: Levels-of-management and levels-of-analysis effects. *Academy of Management Review, 24,* 266–285.

Yukl, G. (1998). *Leadership in organizations* (4th ed.). Upper Saddle River, NJ: Prentice Hall.

Zand, D. (1972). Trust and managerial problem solving. *Administrative Science Quarterly, 17,* 229–239.

Zand, D. (1997). *The leadership triad: Knowledge, trust, and power.* New York: Oxford University Press.

## Reading 8

# Leadership, Moral Development, and Citizenship Behavior

**Jill W. Graham**
Loyola University

Inducing constructive contributions from participants in collective entities and enterprises has long been a concern of political philosophers and organizational scholars. The role leaders potentially play in inspiring or otherwise motivating the behavior of followers has received special attention. Building on the observations of Burns (1978) and Greenleaf (1977) that leaders have the potential of enhancing the moral development of followers, this paper proposes theoretical linkages between a range of well-known styles of leadership behavior, three paradigmatic levels of moral reasoning, and three forms of participant contribution, also called organizational citizenship behavior (OCB).

The first section of the paper offers brief overviews of research on varieties of OCB and levels of moral development. In the second section these typologies are related to each other and also to a range of styles of leadership. The paper concludes with an assessment of the contradictory potential of charismatic leadership.

## THEORETICAL BACKGROUND

### VARIETIES OF PARTICIPANT CONTRIBUTION

Over the long term, successful organizations benefit from a variety of forms of participant contribution which vary in motivational impetus (Katz, 1964; Organ, 1990). Three distinctive types of contribution—displayed in Figure 1—are dependable task accomplishment, work group collaboration, and civic virtue (Graham, 1991a).

Dependable task accomplishment includes the basics of regular on-time attendance, reliable effort expended on both quality and quantity of output, efficient use of resources, and common-sense handling of unforeseen contingencies. All these behaviors concern individual task performance and are familiar indicators of the hard-working employee who is attentive to detail and responsive to instruction.

**FIGURE 1 Varieties of Participant Contribution to Organizational Success: Organizational Citizenship Behavior**

**Dependable Task Accomplishment**
- Regular on-time attendance
- Reliable effort expended on both quality and quantity of output
- Efficient use of resources
- Compliance with rules and instructions
- Common sense handling of unforeseen contingencies

**Work Group Collaboration**
- Sharing information, tools, and other resources
- Helping to train and socialize newcomers
- Assisting those with heavy workloads
- Responding flexibly to disruption
- Representing the group favorably to outsiders

**Civic Virtue: Constructive Participation in Organizational Governance**
- Keeping informed about current (and potential) issues of organizational importance
- Attending nonrequired meetings
- Giving decision makers timely information and input about organizational policy or practice
- Providing reasoned arguments for proposed changes
- Listening to other points of view

Sources: Adapted from Graham (1991a), "An Essay on Organizational Citizenship Behavior," and Organ (1988), *Organizational Citizenship Behavior: The Good Soldier Syndrome.*

A second category of contribution—work group collaboration—differs from the first by focusing on interpersonal cooperation in the workplace (Kohn, 1986). Illustrative behaviors include sharing information, tools and other resources with others, helping newcomers and those with heavy workloads, representing the group favorably to outsiders, and responding flexibly to inconveniences occasioned by others' mistakes. These cooperative behaviors reflect a generosity of spirit and loyalty to the group as a whole. While theoretically distinct from the task-focused behaviors in the first category, work group collaboration presumes that the individual's assigned task is also performed reliably.

Edited and reprinted with permission from: *Business Ethics Quarterly,* Volume 5, Issue 1. pp. 43–54. Copyright 1995, Philosophy Documentation Center.

Dependable task accomplishment as well as work group collaboration have long been identified as examples of participant contributions necessary for organizational success (Katz, 1964), and about a decade ago began to be termed "organizational citizenship behavior" (Bateman & Organ, 1983; Smith, Organ, & Near, 1983). Reference to the term "citizenship," however, also suggests a third form of contribution, civic virtue, or constructive participation in organizational governance (Graham, 1986). This form of OCB is less obvious and more controversial than the other two (Graham, 1991a), but also has been described as the most admirable form (Organ, 1988:13). It includes keeping informed about issues of organizational importance, attending nonrequired meetings, giving decision-makers timely information and input about organizational policies and practices, providing reasoned arguments for proposed changes, and listening to other points of view. Such behaviors assume a capacity for independent critical analysis and may require moral courage to deliver bad news or defend a minority point of view.

The three categories of participant contribution are theoretically distinct, and in general each builds on the previous one. However, conflicts are conceivable between civic virtue and the other forms of contribution. For example, if a worker feels that a work instruction is unwise or unethical, s/he may refuse to comply with it while appealing to a higher authority for clarification and/or correction of the order. Thus, while responsible participation in governance has long been recognized as a vital contribution of active citizens (Inkeles, 1969), and can also play an important role in helping organizations to stay up-to-date and avoid wrongdoing, it may be seen as inconvenient or even threatening by those who put a premium on individual task accomplishment and/or smooth-running group collaboration. As a result of ambivalent or even hostile attitudes toward civic virtue, motivating participants to contribute in that particular way may pose the greatest challenge.

## VARIETIES OF NORMATIVE MOTIVATION

The motivation to contribute to organizational success varies across persons, situations, and types of contribution, but has long been analyzed in terms of the rewards (or inducements) associated with specific forms of contribution (e.g., Simon, 1952). One way to broaden the discussion of motivation is to rephrase the question, "What makes a behavior worth doing?" to "What makes the behavior good?" This normative approach to motivation does not ignore the traditional rewards-centered approach; but rather situates the logic of pay-offs along a continuum of cognitive moral development.

Developmental psychologists have identified several levels of moral reasoning (e.g., Gilligan, 1982; Kohlberg, 1969, 1976), and all have limits. A summary of the logic used at each level is shown in Figure 2.

At the earliest level of development—preconventional morality—morality is defined solely in terms of what an unquestioned authority figure (e.g., parent, teacher, soldier, boss) declares to be right and wrong. Right action is that which buys favor from the authority figure, thereby protecting or enhancing self-interest. This makes preconventional morality essentially instrumental in character. As such, it contains no restraint on unbridled egotism, on the one hand; and, on the other, no basis for independently assessing the morality of authoritative pronouncements. For a pre-conventional moral reasoner, "I was just following orders" is an adequate moral defense for any behavior, no matter how outrageous.

---

### FIGURE 2   Stages of Moral Development

**Level 1: Pre-conventional**

Stage 1: Uncritical obedience to rules set by an external authority who controls rewards and punishments.

Stage 2: Instrumental performance of explicit exchange agreements if nonperformance would adversely affect self-interest.

**Level 2: Conventional**

Stage 3: Fulfilling role obligations arising from specific interpersonal relationships.

Stage 4: Fulfilling fixed social duties arising from membership in a specific group, institution, or society.

**Level 3: Post-conventional**

Stage 5: Utilitarian calculus taking all stakeholders' interests into account.

Stage 6: Utilization of self-chosen, universal ethical principles to seek creative solutions to ethical dilemmas that serve the common good while respecting the individual rights of all interested parties (including self).

Sources: Adapted from Carol Gilligan (1982), *In a Different Voice: Psychological Theory and Women's Development,* and Lawrence Kohlberg (1969), "Stage and Sequence: The Cognitive-Developmental Approach to Socialization," and (1976), "Moral Stages and Moralization: The Cognitive-Developmental Approach."

The second level—conventional morality—moves away from individual authority figures to social systems of rules and responsibilities. The focus of moral concern broadens from protection of personal interests to performance of social duties. While these obligations may be articulated by individual spokes-people, they have authoritative force because the hearer takes seriously his or her identity as a member of a social group with cultural traditions and normative expectations; the member is loyal to the group. Such loyalty, however, can give rise to groupthink, the uncritical acceptance of majority opinion (Janis, 1972). Gilligan's (1982) analysis of female moral development identifies another danger of conventional morality: the potential for imbalance caused by an abdication of self-interest by those who devote themselves entirely to the needs and interests of others.

Both the first and second levels of moral reasoning have the advantage of simplifying moral decisions by relying on external authorities to distinguish right from wrong. The third level—post-conventional morality—moves from external definitions of morality (be they determined by individual authority figures or social convention) to independently arrived at principled beliefs that are used creatively in the analysis and resolution of moral dilemmas. When an individual moves from the relative passivity of levels one and two to become an active subject at level three, the limitations of the other levels of moral reasoning are overcome: respect for and careful balancing of all interests avoids both excessive attention to or abdication of self-interests; and independent analysis and moral courage counteract the threats posed by uncritical reliance on a single authority and/or groupthink. Such efforts are complex and time-consuming, however, and presuppose a mature and well-balanced personality. Some leadership styles have what Burns (1978: 41) describes as an "elevating power" that may both provide a model for and help to nurture the personal development of followers that is necessary to post-conventional morality.

## CLUSTERS OF LEADERSHIP, NORMATIVE MOTIVATION, AND OCB

While leadership surely is not the only determinant of the moral reasoning capacity of followers, the example that leaders set, the encouragement they provide, and the inspiration they offer arguably can influence followers' moral development in a variety of ways. In this section of the paper, a range of well-known leadership styles is related to the levels of moral reasoning and OCB that were described earlier. An overview of the proposed relationships is provided in Figure 3.

**FIGURE 3    Leadership Styles Encouraging Various Levels of Moral Development and OCB among Organizational Members**

| Leadership Style | Level of Moral Development | Moral Referent(s) | Additional Form of OCB |
|---|---|---|---|
| | **Pre-Conventional** | | |
| Autocratic or Coercive Leadership | Uncritical obedience to external authority | Authoritative rules and instructions | Dependable task accomplishment |
| Path-Goal or Transactional Leadership | Instrumental compliance with exchange agreements | Enforcible contracts and job descriptions | |
| | **Conventional** | | |
| Leader–Member Exchange and Consideration | Meet interpersonal role obligations | Personal relationship with supervisor | Work group collaboration |
| Institutional Leadership | Fulfill social duties from group membership | Cultural expectations | |
| | **Post-Conventional** | | |
| Transforming | Utilitarian calculus | Costs and benefits for all stakeholders | Constructive participation in organizational governance |
| or | | | |
| Servant Leadership | Discern and apply universal principles | Principles of justice | |

*Cluster I:* Dependable task performance can be induced by incentives and the instrumental moral imperative of pre-conventional moral reasoning. Leadership that assists followers in understanding the connection between their contributions to the organization and the personal consequences of their acts will strengthen followers' normative motivation to perform the specifics of their assigned tasks. Leaders can not only clarify but also enforce these connections. If the emphasis is on positive outcomes of subordinate action, such leadership can be described as clarifying path-goal relationships (House, 1971). If the emphasis is on negative outcomes of subordinate (in)action, such leadership can be described as autocratic or coercive (Greenleaf, 1978). Neutral terms include initiating structure (Stogdill & Coons, 1957) and transactional leadership (Bass, 1985). These leadership styles all have in common an emphasis on influencing subordinate behavior by connecting it to specific rewards and/or punishments. They are based on an operant conditioning (or perhaps expectancy) model of behavioral psychology (Sims, 1977).

Command and control leadership is likely to be most effective for subordinate behaviors that are concrete and specifiable in advance, such as regular on-time attendance, reliable effort expended on quantity and quality of output, and compliance with work rules—all examples of dependable task accomplishment. While convenient for management in the short run, such ready obedience provides no check on the possibility of unethical rules or instructions; authority is obeyed without question.

*Cluster II:* Work group collaboration—helpfulness, generosity, and cooperation—is less amenable to command and control methods of leadership than dependable task performance because the description and timing of desired behaviors are difficult to specify in advance. Since cooperative behavior is more a way of life than a set of discrete acts capable of assignment, monitoring and reward, leadership that establishes and nurtures ongoing interpersonal relationships and their related social roles is likely to be important for work group collaboration. For example, leader consideration (Stogdill & Coons, 1957; Bass, 1985) and cultivation of vertical dyadic exchange between leaders and favored subordinates (Dansereau, Graen & Haga, 1975) may engender interpersonal loyalty and a moral obligation to fulfill or exceed role expectations above and beyond the promised payoffs for dependable task performance. On a more impersonal basis, institutional leadership or "organizational statesmanship" (Selznick, 1957) may help to create and sustain an organizational culture with strong norms of role performance and supererogatory contribution. Several OCB studies have found evidence connecting leader attributes such as trustworthiness and fairness with subordinate altruism/cooperation, but a different set of causal factors for obedience-type OCBs (e.g., Farh, Podsakoff, & Organ, 1990; Podsakoff, MacKenzie, Moorman, & Fetter, 1990; Smith et al., 1983). In these studies it appears that leadership helps create strong interpersonal and/or social relationships that broaden self-interest to include service to a dyad or group, thereby giving rise to social norms that favor cooperation as well as personal industry.

The dedication to duty and generosity engendered by conventional moral reasoning is less self-serving than the instrumental ethic of preconventional morality, yet it too has its limits. While Gilligan's (1982) analysis of conventional morality focuses on women and family relationships, an analogous imbalance is conceivable within organizations: the organization man's [sic] workaholism, for example, may entail sacrificing self-interest to organizational goals to an extent that is not only generous but potentially self-destructive.

*Cluster III:* Constructive participation in organizational governance avoids the extremes of both chronic complainers agitating exclusively for selfish interests (operating from a pre-conventional morality) and docile acquiescence to groupthink or unhealthy altruism (operating out of conventional morality). Selfishness and naive gullibility are both lessened when people are empowered to engage in high level moral reasoning that assesses and balances interests of all stakeholders in terms of universal moral principles. Leadership that models and encourages post-conventional moral reasoning has been termed "transforming" (Burns, 1978) and "servant leadership" (Greenleaf, 1977). Burns describes transforming leaders as "rais[ing] the level of human conduct and ethical aspiration of both leader and led" (Burns, 1978: 20) in terms of "near-universal ethical principles of justice such as equality of human rights and respect for individual dignity" (p. 42). Greenleaf (1977) describes servant leadership as focusing on the highest priority needs of those being served, both within and outside an organization. As a practical test for this form of leadership, Greenleaf asks:

. . . do those served grow as persons; do they, *while being served,* become healthier, wiser, freer, more autonomous, more likely themselves to become servants? *And,* what is the effect on the least privileged in society; will he benefit, or, at least, will he not be further deprived? (Greenleaf, 1977: 13–14)

Drake and Baasten (1990, pp. 4–6) identify three things leaders can do to elevate moral dialogue. First, they can legitimate it by engaging in it themselves, making it clear they are open to conversations about the ethics of their own, as well as organizational, policies and practices. Second, leaders can demonstrate concern for a wide range of stakeholders of the organization. At a moral minimum, this requires that organizational actions benefit, or at least not harm, all stakeholder groups. Finally, leaders can encourage diversity and dissent to "prevent complacency and encourage continued learning by all parties" (Drake & Baasten, 1990, p. 5). By these means leaders can nurture high level moral reasoning and the practice of civic virtue in the workplace.

*Charismatic leadership:* Until recently, organizational scholars writing about charismatic leadership and its variants have emphasized its capacity to motivate performance beyond expectations (e.g., Avolio & Bass, 1988; Bass, 1985, 1988; Conger & Kanungo, 1987, 1988). Its inspirational quality has been associated with follower trust in the correctness of the leader's beliefs, unquestioning acceptance of the leader, willing obedience to the leader, and emulation of the leader (House, 1977). What is troublesome is that such a perspective on charismatic leadership neglects the moral hazards involved when "people abdicate responsibility for any consistent, tough-minded evaluation of the outcomes of specific policies" (Katz & Kahn, 1978: 545). It would appear that charismatic leadership, as traditionally understood, encourages pre-conventional moral reasoning with its blind faith in the authority of the (charismatic) leader. It is not surprising, then, that Bass (1985: 20) counts Hitler among history's most charismatic/transformational leaders.

Happily, several recent articles on charismatic leadership (e.g., Graham, 1988 & 1991b; Howell, 1988; Howell & Avolio, 1992) have addressed questions such as, "What safeguards the morality of the ends and means advocated by a charismatic leader?" (Graham, 1991b: 105). Howell & Avolio (1992) distinguish between "ethical charismatics" and "unethical charismatics." The former are inspiring leaders who

> develop creative, critical thinking in their followers, provide opportunities for them to develop,

welcome positive and negative feedback, recognize contributions of others, share information with followers, and have moral standards that emphasize collective interests of the group, organization, or society. (Howell & Avolio, 1992: 44).

Howell & Avolio's (1992) ethical charismatics, Burns' (1978) "transforming leaders," and Greenleaf's (1977) "servant leaders" all describe leader-follower relationships that focus on the ideals of service and growth. In servant-led organizations, serving the needs and interests of all participants is part of the purpose and normal functioning of the enterprise, and opportunities for wide participation in discussions about policies and practices provide the means for that end. The consequence of such organizational ends and means is an ethically elevating climate that frees participants from the need to guard self-interest without regard for the cost to others (in the manner of pre-conventional morality), or to subordinate self-interest entirely to group interests or organizational goals (as is possible with conventional morality). Instead participants, encouraged by servant leaders, are responsible both for informing others of their own needs and interests, *and* for inquiring about those of others—the object being to serve in a balanced way all those needs and interests that do not violate moral injunctions such as not harming others. Integrative solutions are devised to resolve conflicts—for example, by applying universal moral principles behind a Rawlsian (1971) veil of ignorance (of which interests are one's own)—so that some interests are not systematically favored over others. The role of the transforming/servant leader is to envision, espouse, facilitate, and model this process.

## CONCLUSION

That servant leaders encourage others to engage in high level moral reasoning is significant for several reasons. First, impartial application of universal principles to resolve moral conflicts and dilemmas balances self-interest with equal concern for others' interests. This has the effect of calling forth reserves of emotional and physical energy to serve the common good.

But that is not all. For who determines what the common good is? Should leaders—even servant leaders—presume to have infallible insight into what best serves the common good of all? If that position be accepted, where are the safeguards against leaders who would disguise their personal interests in the attractive garb of the common interest, thereby neglecting, or even harming, the interests of other stakeholders? It is here that the second significant role of post-conventional moral reasoning and the civic virtue associated with it are critical. Followers are encouraged to do their own thinking, not to accept the moral definitions espoused by powerful or otherwise appealing authority figures. Selfishness and gullibility are both lessened when people are empowered to engage in high level moral reasoning. Servant leaders serve their followers best when they model and also encourage others not only to engage in independent moral reasoning, but also to follow it up with constructive participation in organizational governance.

# Bibliography

Avolio, B. J., & Bass, B. M. (1988). Transformational Leadership, Charisma, and Beyond. In Hunt, J. G., Baliga, B. R., Dachler, H. P. & Schriesheim, C. A. (Eds.), *Emerging Leadership Vistas,* 29–49. Lexington, MA: Lexington Books.

Bass, B. M. (1988). Evolving Perspectives on Charismatic Leadership. In Conger, J. A., Kanungo, R. N., & Associates (Eds.), *Charismatic Leadership: The Elusive Factor in Organizational Effectiveness,* 40–77. San Francisco: Jossey-Bass.

Bass, B. M. (1985). *Leadership and Performance: Beyond Expectations.* New York: Free Press.

Bateman, T. S., & Organ, D. W. (1983). Job Satisfaction and the Good Soldier: The Relationship Between Affect and 'Citizenship.' *Academy of Management Journal, 26*(4), 587–595.

Burns, J. M. (1978). *Leadership.* New York: Harper and Row.

Conger, J. A., & Kanungo, R. N. (1987). Toward a Behavioral Theory of Charismatic Leadership in Organizational Settings. *Academy of Management Journal, 12*(4), 637–647.

Conger, J. A., Kanungo, R. N., & Associates. (1988). *Charismatic Leadership: The Elusive Factor in Organizational Effectiveness.* San Francisco: Jossey-Bass.

Dansereau, F., Graen, G., & Haga, W. J. (1975). A Vertical Dyad Linkage Approach to Leadership in Formal Organizations. *Organizational Behavior and Human Performance, 13,* 46–78.

Drake, B., & Baasten, M. (1990). Facilitating Moral Dialogue and Debate: A New Leadership Dimension. Paper presented at the Western Academy of Management, Shizuoka, Japan, June.

Farh, J-L., Podsakoff, P. M., & Organ, D. W. (1990). Accounting for Organizational Citizenship Behavior: Leader Fairness and Task Scope versus Satisfaction. *Journal of Management, 16*(4), 705–721.

Gilligan, C. (1982). *In a Different Voice: Psychological Theory and Women's Development.* Cambridge, MA: Harvard University Press.

Graham, J. W. (1991a). An Essay on Organizational Citizenship Behavior. *Employee Responsibilities and Rights Journal, 4*(4), 249–270.

Graham, J. W. (1986). Organizational Citizenship Informed by Political Theory. Paper presented at the Annual Meeting of the Academy of Management, Chicago, IL, August.

Graham, J. W. (1991b). Servant-leadership in Organizations: Inspirational and Moral. *Leadership Quarterly* 2(2), 105–119.

Graham, J. W. (1988). Transformational Leadership: Fostering Follower Autonomy, not Automatic Followership. In Hunt, J. G., Baliga, B. R., Dachler, H. P., & Schriesheim, C. A. (Eds.), *Emerging Leadership Vistas,* 73–79. Lexington, MA: Lexington Books.

Greenleaf, R. K. (1978). *The Leadership Crisis: A Message for College and University Faculty.* Indianapolis, IN: The Robert K. Greenleaf Center.

Greenleaf, R. K. (1977). *Servant Leadership: A Journey into the Nature of Legitimate Power and Greatness.* New York: Paulist Press.

House, R. J. (1977). A 1976 Theory of Charismatic Leadership. In Hunt, J. G., & Larson, L. L. (Eds.), *Leadership: The Cutting Edge,* 189–207. Carbondale: Southern Illinois University Press.

House, R. J. (1971). A Path-Goal Theory of Leader Effectiveness. *Administrative Science Quarterly, 16,* 321–338.

Howell, J. M. (1988). Two Faces of Charisma: Socialized and Personalized Leadership in Organizations. In Conger, J. A., Kanungo, R. N., & Associates (Eds.), *Charismatic Leadership: The Elusive Factor in Organizational Effectiveness,* 213–236. San Francisco: Jossey-Bass.

Howell, J. M., & Avolio, B. J. (1992). The Ethics of Charismatic Leadership: Submission or Liberation? *Academy of Management Executive* 6(2), 43–54.

Inkeles, A. (1969). Participant Citizenship in Six Developing Countries. *American Political Science Review, 63*(4), 1120–1141.

Janis, I. L. (1972). *Victims of Groupthink: A Psychological Study of Foreign-Policy Decisions and Fiascoes.* Boston: Houghton Mifflin.

Katz, D. (1964). The Motivational Basis of Organizational Behavior. *Behavioral Science, 9,* 131–146.

Katz, D., & Kahn, R. L. (1978). *The Social Psychology of Organizations,* 2nd ed., New York: John Wiley & Sons.

Kohlberg, L. (1976). Moral Stages and Moralization: The Cognitive-Developmental Approach. In T. Lickona (Ed.), *Moral Development and Behavior.* New York: Holt, Rinehart & Winston.

Kohlberg, L. (1969). Stage and Sequence: The Cognitive-Developmental Approach to Socialization. In D. Goslin (Ed.), *Handbook of Socialization Theory and Research,* 347–480. Chicago: Rand McNally.

Kohn, A. (1986). *No Contest: The Case Against Competition.* Boston: Houghton Mifflin.

Organ, D. W. (1988). *Organizational Citizenship Behavior: The 'Good Soldier' Syndrome.* Lexington, MA: Lexington Books.

Organ, D. W. (1990). The Motivational Basis of Organizational Citizenship Behavior. In B. M. Staw & L. L. Cummings (Eds.), *Research in Organizational Behavior, 12:* 43–72. Greenwich, CT: JAI Press.

Podsakoff, P. M., MacKenzie, S. B., Moorman, R. H., & Fetter, R. (1990). Transformational Leader Behaviors and Their Effects on Followers' Trust in Leader, Satisfaction, and Organizational Citizenship Behaviors. *Leadership Quarterly, 1*(2), 107–142.

Rawls, J. (1971). *A Theory of Justice.* Cambridge, MA: Harvard University Press.

Selznick, P. (1957). *Leadership in Administration.* New York: Harper & Row.

Simon, H. A. (1952). Inducements and Incentives in Bureaucracy. In R. K. Merton, A. P. Gray, B. Hockey, & H. C. Selven (Eds.), *Reader in Bureaucracy,* 327–333. Glencoe: The Free Press.

Sims, H. P. (1977). The Leader as a Manager of Reinforcement Contingencies: An Empirical Example and a Model. In J. G. Hunt and L. L. Larson (Eds.), *Leadership: The Cutting Edge,* 121–137. Carbondale, IL: Southern Illinois University Press.

Smith, C. A., Organ, D. W., & Near, J. P. (1983). Organizational Citizenship Behavior: Its Nature and Antecedents. *Journal of Applied Psychology, 68*(4), 653–663.

Stogdill, R., & Coons, A. F. (1957). *Leader Behavior: Its Description and Measurement.* Monograph 88, Bureau of Business Research, Ohio State University.

# Chapter **Three**

# Leaders and the Role of Personal Traits

At one point in time "great person" theories of leadership were popular. It was commonly assumed that certain individuals, when born, were destined to lead. Julius Caesar, Joan of Arc, Catherine II the Great, and Napoleon are cited as naturally great leaders, individuals supposedly born with a set of personal qualities that enabled them to be effective leaders.

Early in the twentieth century, students of leadership raised a critical question assumed by the great person theories. Do leaders tend to possess a set of traits (i.e., physical, demographic, intellective, and personality characteristics) that equip them to be leaders? For some, leadership began to be seen as a psychological phenomenon, with individuals inherently possessing capacities, motives, and patterns of behavior that distinguished them from others (i.e., nonleaders).

Ralph Stogdill (1948) conducted an extensive review of the literature and attempted to identify and summarize the personal factors that are associated with leadership.[1] His review produced an identification of several categories of important leader traits. Among them are:

- Capacity (intelligence, alertness, verbal facility, originality, judgment).

- Achievement (scholarship, knowledge, athletic accomplishments).

- Responsibility (dependability, initiative, persistence, aggressiveness, self-confidence, desire to excel).

- Participation (activity, sociability, cooperation, adaptability, humor).

- Status (socioeconomic position, popularity).

Stogdill's most consistent observation pertained to the relationship between intelligence and leadership (Lord, DeVader, & Alliger, 1986).[2] Stogdill's (1948) literature review and the review conducted by Mann (1959)[3] produce the observation that there is a fairly strong relationship between personality and leadership perceptions (who is the leader).

---

[1] R. M. Stogdill. Personal factors with leadership: A survey of the literature. *The Journal of Psychology,* 28, 35–71.

[2] R. G. Lord, C. L. DeVader, & G. M. Alliger. A meta-analysis of the relation between personality traits and leadership perceptions: An application of validity generalization procedures. *Journal of Applied Psychology* 71, 3 (1986), pp. 402–410.

[3] R. D. Mann. A review of the relationships between personality and performance in small groups. *Psychological Bulletin* 56 (1959), pp. 241–270.

Stogdill's work also provided additional insight into the process of leadership. He suggested that leadership is a relationship; that it is associated with the attainment of group objectives, implying that leadership is an activity, consisting of movement and getting work accomplished; and that it is evolutionary and interactive in nature.

Again in 1974 Stogdill reviewed 163 studies published between 1949 and 1970 that provided additional insight into leader traits. This body of evidence reinforced the observations that he drew in 1948 and identified some additional traits and skills. Stogdill (1974) provided the following trait profile of the successful leader:

> The leader is characterized by a strong drive for responsibility and task completion, vigor and persistence in pursuit of goals, venturesomeness and originality in problem solving, drive to exercise initiative in social situations, self-confidence and sense of personal identity, willingness to accept consequences of decision and action, readiness to absorb interpersonal stress, willingness to tolerate frustration and delay, ability to influence other persons' behavior, and capacity to structure social interaction systems to the purpose at hand (p. 81).[4]

Certain individuals (i.e., those possessing a unique configuration of personal factors—ideas, initiative, persistence, knowledge of how to get things done, responsibility, status—relative to the other members of the group) come to occupy a special position in the group. Through their orchestration of group activity (e.g., providing meaning, information, judgment, activity), they emerge as leaders, and in this capacity they continue to provide orchestration to group activities. Reference to the orchestration of group activity suggests that leadership can be seen as a working relationship among members of a group. Through this working and interactive process, the leader makes contributions that are important to the group, acquires a status within the group, and comes to fulfill a leadership role. Verbal fluency, popularity, cooperativeness, self-confidence, initiative, and persistence, for example, tend to contribute to the individual's emergence into this leadership role and subsequently tend to reinforce the person's legitimacy as the group's leader.

Stogdill also highlighted the importance of the situation. He notes that a person does not emerge as a leader simply by possessing these key traits. The pattern of traits possessed must achieve some semblance of fit with the situation in which the followers find themselves as well as the characteristics, goals, and activities of the followers. Thus, according to Stogdill, the person who is a leader in one group may not be a leader in the next situation.

Between the mid-1940s and the early 1990s, there has been a continued interest in the role of individual traits in the leadership equation. Edwin A. Locke and several of his students conducted an extensive review of the leadership trait literature, resulting in the publication of *The Essence of Leadership* (1991). Part of their work is summarized in the second reading in this chapter. Shelley A. Kirkpatrick and Edwin A. Locke (1991) provide a contemporary answer to the question, Do leadership traits really matter?

According to Kirkpatrick and Locke, there appears to be a set of traits that endows an individual with "the right stuff" to be an effective leader. These traits are important "preconditions" giving an individual the *potential* to be an effective leader. Possessing these traits, however, does not guarantee leadership success. Among the key traits that appear to differentiate leaders from nonleaders, according to Kirkpatrick and Locke, are drive, the desire to lead, honesty/integrity, self-confidence, cognitive ability, and knowledge of the business. Several other traits identified as possible characteristics of effective leaders included charisma, creativity/originality, and flexibility/adaptiveness. In their ar-

---

[4] R. M. Stogdill. *Handbook of leadership: A survey of the literature* (New York: Free Press, 1974).

ticle the authors provide us with insight into the meaning of and leadership role played by each of these attributes.

Energy and drive as it characterizes an individual's disposition has been the focus of recent research. Evidence suggests that individuals whose personality can be characterized by positive affectivity (i.e., a positive mood state, high levels of energy and drive) tend to be more competent interpersonally and contribute more to group activities; therefore they are able to function more effectively in their leadership role.[5] By virtue of their energetic personalities, these individuals infuse excitement and energy into group activity. The self-assessments presented at the end of this chapter opener provides you with an opportunity to profile your own level of positive and negative affectivity, as well as your "readiness" for this leadership role.

According to Kirkpatrick and Locke, people who possess these traits are more likely to engage in the behaviors associated with effective leadership. These traits help leaders acquire the necessary skills (i.e., capacities for action such as decision making and problem solving) needed for effective leadership. In addition, they have the ability to create vision, and they possess the capacity to design a strategy that leads to vision implementation (e.g., structure activities, motivate others, manage information, build teams, and promote change and innovation). Those who possess these traits are simply more likely to engage in the behaviors associated with effective leadership than individuals who are not endowed with these characteristics.

Jennifer M. George suggests that feelings (i.e., moods and emotions) play an important role in the leadership process. She builds upon the notion that moods and emotions affect the way people think, their motivation, the decisions that are made, and behaviors engaged in. George suggests that it is important to consider the role that feelings and emotions play in leadership.

Several years ago the concept "emotional intelligence" was introduced into both the popular and psychology (personality) literature. Emotional intelligence refers to the ability to both understand and manage moods and emotions in the self and in others. (The third self-assessment in this chapter provides you with the opportunity to profile your emotional intelligence.) George suggests that leader effectiveness is affected by the strength of the emotional intelligence possessed by the leader. She explores four major aspects of emotional intelligence—the appraisal and expression of emotion, the use of emotion to enhance cognitive processes and decision making, knowledge about emotions, and management of emotions—and the relationship between each and several dimensions of leader effectiveness.

Returning to our leadership process model (see Figure 3.1), the discussion of traits provides further insight into the leadership process through an expanded understanding of the leader.

In the first two readings presented in this chapter, Stogdill suggests that leadership unfolds in a working relationship, and Kirkpatrick and Locke conclude that those with the key leadership traits are more likely to engage in the behaviors associated with effective leadership. This leads to a new question—What are the behaviors associated with effective leadership? The readings in Chapter 7 look at what it is that effective leaders "do."

---

[5] B. M. Staw and S. G. Barsade, "Affect and Managerial Performance: A Test of the Sadder-but-Wiser vs. Happier-and-Smarter Hypothesis, "*Administrative Science Quarterly* 38 (1993), 304–331.

**FIGURE 3.1**
**The Leadership Process: Leader Traits**

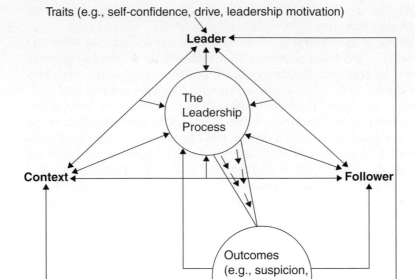

Traits (e.g., self-confidence, drive, leadership motivation)

**EXERCISE**
*Self-Assessment*

**Positive and Negative Affect**

**Instructions:** For each of the following items, please indicate how you felt at work during the past week.

| | | Very Slightly or Not at All | | | | Very Much |
|---|---|---|---|---|---|---|
| 1. | Active | 1 | 2 | 3 | 4 | 5 |
| 2. | Calm | 1 | 2 | 3 | 4 | 5 |
| 3. | Distressed | 1 | 2 | 3 | 4 | 5 |
| 4. | Sleepy | 1 | 2 | 3 | 4 | 5 |
| 5. | Strong | 1 | 2 | 3 | 4 | 5 |
| 6. | Excited | 1 | 2 | 3 | 4 | 5 |
| 7. | Scornful | 1 | 2 | 3 | 4 | 5 |
| 8. | Hostile | 1 | 2 | 3 | 4 | 5 |
| 9. | Enthusiastic | 1 | 2 | 3 | 4 | 5 |
| 10. | Dull | 1 | 2 | 3 | 4 | 5 |
| 11. | Fearful | 1 | 2 | 3 | 4 | 5 |
| 12. | Relaxed | 1 | 2 | 3 | 4 | 5 |
| 13. | Peppy | 1 | 2 | 3 | 4 | 5 |
| 14. | At rest | 1 | 2 | 3 | 4 | 5 |
| 15. | Nervous | 1 | 2 | 3 | 4 | 5 |
| 16. | Drowsy | 1 | 2 | 3 | 4 | 5 |
| 17. | Elated | 1 | 2 | 3 | 4 | 5 |
| 18. | Placid | 1 | 2 | 3 | 4 | 5 |
| 19. | Jittery | 1 | 2 | 3 | 4 | 5 |
| 20. | Sluggish | 1 | 2 | 3 | 4 | 5 |

**Scoring:**

1. Subtract your response to each of the following items from 6: 2 (calm), 4 (sleepy), 10 (dull), 12 (relaxed), 14 (at rest), 16 (drowsy), 18 (placid), and 20 (sluggish).
2. *Positive affect* is reflected with two scores, the first signaling general and positive affect and the second denoting "high positive affect."
   a. Positive affect—Where appropriate, employing your adjusted response scores, sum your response scores to the following items: 1, 4, 5, 6, 9, 10, 13, 16, 17, and 20; divide by 10; and enter that score here _____.
   b. High positive affect—Where appropriate, employing your adjusted response scores, sum your response scores to the following items: 1, 5, 6, 9, 13, and 17; divide by 6; and enter that score here _____.
3. *Negative affect* is reflected with two scores, the first signaling general and negative affect and the second denoting "high negative affect."
   a. Negative affect—Where appropriate, employing your adjusted response scores, sum your response scores to the following items: 2, 3, 7, 8, 11, 12, 14, 15, 18, and 19; divide by 10; and enter that score here _____.
   b. High negative affect—Where appropriate, employing your adjusted response scores, sum your response scores to the following items: 3, 7, 8, 11, 15, and 19; divide by 6; and enter that score here _____.

**Interpretation:** The positive and negative affect test is designed to measure "mood at work"—that is, how people felt at work, while on the job, during the past week. A high score (4 and greater) implies a high level of affect (i.e., positive, negative, high positive and high negative). A low score (2 or less) implies a low level of affect (i.e., positive, negative, high positive, and high negative).

Mood at work, as assessed here, is a state-based condition. As a state-based condition, people can express different moods, depending upon the state to which they are exposed.

*(continued)*

Mood can, however, be relatively stable across states and across time. It has been noted that some people have a "sunny" disposition—seeing the glass as almost full as opposed to almost empty. Others nearly always appear gloomy. Affectivity (to be distinguished from affect as measured by this instrument) essentially reflects an individual's *pervasive mood.* Negative affectivity and high negative affectivity reflect negative emotionality. Those people are distressed, scornful, hostile, fearful, nervous, and jittery. Positive affectivity and high positive affectivity reflect positive emotionality. These individuals tend to feel active, excited, enthusiastic, peppy, and strong. Leaders who have strong positive affect (and/or affectivity) are characterized as possessing an air of confidence, competency, and optimism. They tend to transfer their energy to others and to be characterized as leaders of cohesive, productive work groups.

Source: M. J. Burke, A. P. Brief, J. M. George, L. Roberson, and J. Webster, Measuring Affect at Work: Confirmatory Analyses of Competing Mood Structures with Conceptual Linkage to Cortical Regulatory Systems, *Journal of Personality and Social Psychology* 57 (1989), 1091–1102. Copyright 1989, American Psychological Association, adopted with permission of publisher and A. P. Brief.

**EXERCISE**

*Self-Assessment*

**Leadership Motivation**

**Instructions:** Indicate the extent to which you agree with each of the following statements, using the following scale: 1 = strongly disagree; 2 = disagree; 3 = neither agree nor disagree; 4 = agree; and 5 = strongly agree.

1. I am energized when people count on me for ideas. _____
2. As a practice, I ask people provocative questions when we are working on projects together. _____
3. I take delight in complimenting people that I work with when progress is made. _____
4. I find it easy to be the cheerleader for others, when times are good and when times are bad. _____
5. Team accomplishment is more important to me than my own personal accomplishments. _____
6. People often take my ideas and run with them. _____
7. When involved in group projects, building team cohesiveness is important to me. _____
8. When involved in group projects, coaching others is an activity that I gravitate toward. _____
9. I find pleasure in recognizing and celebrating the accomplishments of others. _____
10. When involved in group projects, my team members' problems are my problems. _____
11. Resolving interpersonal conflict is an activity that I enjoy. _____
12. When involved in group projects, I frequently find myself to be an "idea generator." _____
13. When involved in group projects, I am inclined to let my ideas be known. _____
14. I find pleasure in being a convincing person. _____

**Scoring and Interpretation:** Sum your responses to the 14 questions and then divide that number by 14. Your score should fall between a low of 1 and a high of 5. A tentative interpretation of your scoring is as follows:

> 4.25 and greater implies a high motivation for leadership.
> ~3.0 implies uncertainty about your motivation for leadership.
> 1.75 and less implies a low motivation for leadership.

**My leadership motivation (readiness) score is:** _____.

Source: This set of questions was constructed for this self-assessment and for illustrative purposes only. No *a priori* validation work has been conducted that enables us to address the construct validity of this assessment. This self-assessment was patterned after that of A. J. DuBrin in *Leadership: Research Findings, Practice and Skills* (2nd edition) (Boston: Houghton Mifflin Co., 1998), pp.10–11.

## EXERCISE
*Self-Assessment*

**Emotional Intelligence**

**Instructions:** For each of the following questions, please indicate the degree to which each statement characterizes you.

For each item, assign yourself:

1 if—Never like me.
2 If—Occasionally like me.
3 if—Sometimes like me.
4 if—Frequently like me.
5 if—Always like me.

_____ 1. I sympathize with other people when they have problems.
_____ 2. I go out of my way to help someone in need.
_____ 3. Most people feel comfortable talking to me about their personal feelings.
_____ 4. People enjoy spending time with me.
_____ 5. It is easy for me to openly express warm and loving feelings toward others.
_____ 6. When someone is annoying me, I stop to think about the other person's situation rather than losing my temper.
_____ 7. In most cases I give people a second chance.
_____ 8. I think about how I can improve my relationships with those people with whom I don't get along.
_____ 9. I think why I don't like a person.
_____ 10. When someone makes me uncomfortable, I think why I am uncomfortable.
_____ 11. I can be assertive and forceful in situations where others are trying to take advantage of me.
_____ 12. I can delay gratification in pursuit of my goals.
_____ 13. When I am anxious about a challenge, I still can prepare for it.
_____ 14. I am able to stay motivated when things do not go well.
_____ 15. I keep myself focused on my goals.
_____ 16. Overt human suffering makes me feel uncomfortable.
_____ 17. Criticism is difficult for me to accept.
_____ 18. Having car trouble makes me feel stressed.
_____ 19. I lose control when I do not win in a sporting contest.
_____ 20. Traffic jams cause me to lose control.

**Scoring:** Sum your score for questions 1–5, and divide by 5.
My "perception, appraisal, and expression of emotions" score is: _____.

Sum your score for questions 6–10, and divide by 5.
My "emotional facilitation of thinking" score is: _____.

Sum your score for questions 11–15, and divide by 5.
My "understanding and analyzing emotions, and employing emotional knowledge" score is: _____.

For questions 17–20, reverse score each item by subtracting your score from 6. Next sum your new scores for these four questions, and add in your score to question 16, then divide by 5.
My "reflective regulation of emotions" score is: _____.

Finally, sum your four scores together and divide by 4.
My overall (global) emotional intelligence score is: _____.

**Interpretation:** Thorndike (1920) provided an intelligence framework that identified three types of intelligence—social, concrete, and abstract. Thorndike's conceptualization of social intelligence is the underpinning for the contemporary reference to emotional intelligence (EI). EI "involves the ability to perceive emotions, to access and generate emotions to assist thought, to understand emotions and emotional knowledge, and to regulate emotions reflectively to promote emotional and intellectual growth" (Tapia, p. 353). This definition links

*(continued)*

intelligence and emotion and promotes the dual ideas that emotion can make thinking more intelligent and that one can think intelligently about emotions.

According to Tapia (pp. 354–355), your first score reflects your ability to appraise emotions in yourself and appraise emotions in others (empathy). The second score deals with emotions when thinking is prioritized by directing attention to important information. (Are your emotions sufficiently vivid and available so they can be used as aids to judgment and memory concerning feelings?) Your third score deals with your ability to label emotions and to understand complex feelings. Your fourth and final score concerns the ability to stay open to feelings (both those that are pleasant and unpleasant). Overall, the global scale for emotional intelligence attempts to assess the perception, assimilation, understanding, and management of emotion.

A high score on each of the four dimensions is reflective of a high level of emotional intelligence on that particular score. A score equal to or greater than 4 on each dimension and on the global assessment suggests a high level of emotional intelligence. A score equal to or less than 2 on each dimension and on the global assessment suggests a low level of emotional intelligence.

---

Source: Reproduced with permission of author and publisher from: M. Tapia. Measuring Emotional Intelligence. *Psychological Reports*, 88 (2001) pp. 353–364. © Psychological Reports 2001. These 20 items reflect a subset of the Tapia (2001) and Tapia & Burry-Stock (1998) instrument for the measurement of emotional intelligence, and are shown here to illustrate the measure and highlight the construct's meaning. Tapia and Burry-Stock's 41-item measure can be found in: M. Tapia & J. Burry-Stock. 1998. *Emotional Intelligence Inventory,* Tuscaloosa, AL: The University of Alabama.

## Reading 9

# Personal Factors Associated with Leadership: A Survey of the Literature[1]

**R. M. Stogdill**
Ohio State University

Smith and Krueger (100) have surveyed the literature on leadership to 1933. Recent developments in leadership methodology, as related especially to military situations, were reviewed in 1947 by Jenkins (54). The present survey is concerned only with those studies in which some attempt has been made to determine the traits and characteristics of leaders. In many of the studies surveyed, leadership was not defined. In others the methods used in the investigation appeared to have little relationship to the problem as stated. An attempt has been made to include all studies bearing on the problem of traits and personal factors associated with leadership. In all except four cases, the original book or article has been read and abstracted in detail. The data from one American and three German publications have been derived from competent abstracts.

The present survey lists only those factors which were studied by three or more investigators. Evidence reported by fewer investigators has not been regarded as providing a satisfactory basis for evaluation. It is realized that the number of investigations in which a factor was studied is not necessarily indicative of the importance of the factor. However, the frequency with which a factor was found to be significant appears to be the most satisfactory single criterion for evaluating the data accumulated in this survey, but other criteria, such as the competency of the experimental methods employed and the adequacy

of the statistical treatment of data, have also been regarded in evaluating the results of a particular study.

In analyzing data obtained from various groups and by various methods, the question arises as to the extent to which results may be influenced by differences in social composition of the groups, differences in methodology, and differences in leadership criteria. There is no assurance, for example, that the investigator who analyzes the biographies of great men is studying the same kind of leadership behavior that is revealed through observation of children's leadership activities in group situations. It is of interest, however, that some of the studies employing the two different methods yield remarkably similar results. On the other hand, there are some factors that appear only in certain age and social groups or only when certain methods are employed. . . .

## Summary

1. The following conclusions are supported by uniformly positive evidence from 15 or more of the studies surveyed:
   a. The average person who occupies a position of leadership exceeds the average member of his group in the following respects: (1) intelligence, (2) scholarship, (3) dependability in exercising responsibilities, (4) activity and social participation, and (5) socioeconomic status.
   b. The qualities, characteristics, and skills required in a leader are determined to a large extent by the demands of the situation in which he is to function as a leader.
2. The following conclusions are supported by uniformly positive evidence from 10 or more of the studies surveyed:
   a. The average person who occupies a position of leadership exceeds the average member of his group to some degree in the following respects: (1) sociability, (2) initiative, (3) persistence, (4) knowing how to get things done,

**Source:** *The Journal of Psychology* 28, 35–71, 1948. Edited and reprinted with permission of the Helen Dwight Reid Educational Foundation. Published by Heldref Publications, 1319 Eighteenth St., N.W. Washington, D.C. 20036-1802. Copyright 1948. Author affiliation may have changed since article was first published.

[1] Received in the Editorial Office on September 1, 1947, and published immediately at Provincetown, Massachusetts. Copyright by The Journal Press, a cooperative contribution of the U.S. Navy, Office of Naval Research, and the Ohio State University Research Foundation. This study represents one aspect of a program of research on leadership being conducted by the Personnel Research Board of the Ohio State University, under the direction of Dr. C. L. Shartle. The opinions expressed herein are not to be regarded as representing the opinion of, or having the endorsement of, the Navy Department.

(5) self-confidence, (6) alertness to, and insight into, situations, (7) cooperativeness, (8) popularity, (9) adaptability, and (10) verbal facility.

3. In addition to the above, a number of factors have been found which are specific to well-defined groups. For example, athletic ability and physical prowess have been found to be characteristics of leaders in boys' gangs and play groups. Intellectual fortitude and integrity are traits found to be associated with eminent leadership in maturity.

4. The items with the highest overall correlation with leadership are originality, popularity, sociability, judgment, aggressiveness, desire to excel, humor, cooperativeness, liveliness, and athletic ability, in approximate order of magnitude of average correlation coefficient.

5. In spite of considerable negative evidence, the general trend of results suggests a low positive correlation between leadership and such variables as chronological age, height, weight, physique, energy, appearance, dominance, and mood control. The evidence is about evenly divided concerning the relation to leadership of such traits as introversion-extroversion, self-sufficiency, and emotional control.

6. The evidence available suggests that leadership exhibited in various school situations may persist into college and into later vocational and community life. However, knowledge of the facts relating to the transferability of leadership is very meager and obscure.

7. The most fruitful studies, from the point of view of understanding leadership, have been those in which leadership behavior was described and analyzed on the basis of direct observation or analysis of biographical and case history data.

## DISCUSSION

The factors which have been found to be associated with leadership could probably all be classified under the general headings of *capacity, achievement, responsibility, participation,* and *status:*

1. *Capacity* (intelligence, alertness, verbal facility, originality, judgment).

2. *Achievement* (scholarship, knowledge, athletic accomplishments).

3. *Responsibility* (dependability, initiative, persistence, aggressiveness, self-confidence, desire to excel).

4. *Participation* (activity, sociability, cooperation, adaptability, humor).

5. *Status* (socioeconomic position, popularity).

These findings are not surprising. It is primarily by virtue of participating in group activities and demonstrating his capacity for expediting the work of the group that a person becomes endowed with leadership status. A number of investigators have been careful to distinguish between the leader and the figure-head, and to point out that leadership is always associated with the attainment of group objectives. Leadership implies activity, movement, getting work done. The leader is a person who occupies a position of responsibility in coordinating the activities of the members of the group in their task of attaining a common goal. This leads to consideration of another significant factor.

6. *Situation* (mental level, status, skills, needs and interests of followers, objectives to be achieved, etc.).

A person does not become a leader by virtue of the possession of some combination of traits, but the pattern of personal characteristics of the leader must bear some relevant relationship to the characteristics, activities, and goals of the followers. Thus, leadership must be conceived in terms of the interaction of variables which are in constant flux and change. The factor of change is especially characteristic of the situation, which may be radically altered by the addition or loss of members, changes in interpersonal relationships, changes in goals, competition of extra-group influences, and the like. The personal characteristics of leader and of the followers are, in comparison, highly stable. The persistence of individual patterns of human behavior in the face of constant situational change appears to be a primary obstacle encountered not only in the practice of leadership, but in the selection and placement of leaders. It is not especially difficult to find persons who are leaders. It is quite another matter to place these persons in different situations where they will be able to function as leaders. It becomes clear that an adequate analysis of leadership involves not only a study of leaders, but also of situations.

The evidence suggests that leadership is a relation that exists between persons in a social situation and that persons who are leaders in one situation may not necessarily be leaders in other situations. Must it then be assumed that leadership is entirely incidental, haphazard, and unpredictable? Not at all. The very studies which provide the strongest arguments for the situational nature of leadership also supply the strongest evidence indicating that leadership patterns as well as nonleadership patterns of behavior are persistent and relatively stable. Jennings (55) observes that "the individual's choice behavior, in contrast to his social expansiveness, appears as an expression of needs which are, so to speak, so 'central' to his personality that he must strive to fulfill them whether or not the possibility of fulfilling them is at hand." A somewhat similar observation is made by Newstetter, Feldstein, and Newcomb (78), who report that:

> Being accepted or rejected is not determined by the cordiality or antagonism of the individual's treatment of his fellows, nor evidently is the individual's treatment of his fellows much affected by the degree to which he is already being accepted or rejected by them. Their treatment of him is related to their acceptance or rejection of him. Their treatment of him is, of course, a reaction to some or all of his behaviors, but we have been completely unsuccessful in attempting to measure what these behaviors are.

The authors conclude that these findings provide "devastating evidence" against the concept of the operation of measurable traits in determining social interactions. The findings of Newstetter and his associates do not appear to provide direct evidence either for or against a theory of traits, but they do indicate that the complex of factors that determines an individual's status in a group is most difficult to isolate and evaluate.

The findings of Jennings and Newstetter suggest that the problem of selecting leaders should be much less difficult than that of training nonleaders to become leaders. The clinician or group worker who has observed the fruitless efforts of socially isolated individuals to gain group acceptance or leadership status is aware of the real nature of the phenomena described by Jennings and Newstetter. Some individuals are isolates in almost any group in which they find themselves, while others are readily accepted in most of their social contacts.

A most pertinent observation on this point is made by Ackerson (1), who reports that "the correlation for 'leaders' and 'follower' are not of opposite sign and similar magnitude as would be expected of traits supposed to be antithetical." These may not be the opposite poles of a single underlying trait. "It may be that the true antithesis of 'leader' is not 'followers,' but 'indifference,' i.e., the incapacity or unwillingness either to lead or to follow. Thus it may be that some individuals who under one situation are leaders may under other conditions take the role of follower, while the true 'opposite' is represented by the child who neither leads nor follows."

The findings suggest that leadership is not a matter of passive status, or of the mere possession of some combination of traits. It appears rather to be a working relationship among members of a group, in which the leader acquires status through active participation and demonstration of his capacity for carrying cooperative tasks through to completion. Significant aspects of this capacity for organizing and expediting cooperative effort appear to be intelligence, alertness to the needs and motives of others, and insight into situations, further reinforced by such habits as responsibility, initiative, persistence, and self-confidence. The studies surveyed offer little information as to the basic nature of these personal qualifications. Cattell's (19) studies suggest that they may be founded to some degree on basic intelligence, but Cattell and others also suggest that they are socially conditioned to a high degree. Problems which appear to be in need of thorough investigation are those relating to factors which condition social participation, insight into situations, mood control, responsibility, and transferability of leadership from one situation to another. Answers to these questions seem basic not only to any adequate understanding of the personal qualifications of leaders, but also to any effective training for leadership.

# References

[1] Ackerson, L. *Children's Behavior Problems: Relative Importance and Intercorrelation among Traits.* Chicago: Univ. Chicago Press, 1942.

[2] Arrington, R. E. Time sampling in studies of social behavior: A critical review of techniques and results with research suggestions. *Psychol. Bull.,* 1943, 40, 81–124.

[3] Baldwin, L. E. A study of factors usually associated with high school male leadership. Unpublished master's thesis, Ohio State Univ., 1932.

[4] Barker, R. G. The social interrelations of strangers and acquaintances. *Sociometry,* 1942, 5, 169–179.

[5] Bellingrath, G. C. Qualities associated with leadership in extra-curricular activities of the high school. *Teach. Coll. Contr. Educ.,* 1930, No. 399.

[6] Bernard, J. Political leadership among North American Indians. *Amer. J. Sociol.,* 1928, 34, 296–315.

[7] Bonney, M. E. The constancy of sociometric scores and their relationship to teacher judgments of social

success and to personality self-ratings. *Sociometry,* 1943, 6, 409–424.

8 Bowden, A. O. A study of the personality of student leaders in colleges in the United States. *J. Abn. & Soc. Psychol.,* 1926, 21, 149–160.

9 Brogden, H. E., & Thomas, W. F. The primary traits in personality items purporting to measure sociability. *J. of Psychol.,* 1943, 16, 85–97.

10 Broich, H. Führeranforderungen in der Kindergruppe. *Z. angew. Psychol.,* 1929, 32, 164–212.

11 Brown, M. Leadership among high school pupils. *Teach. Coll. Contr. Educ.,* 1933, No. 559.

12——. Leadership among high school pupils. *Teach. Coll. Rec.,* 1934, 35, 324–326.

13 Brown, S. C. Some case studies of delinquent girls described as leaders. *Brit. J. Educ. Psychol.,* 1931, 1, 162–179.

14 Burks, F. W. Some factors related to social success in college. *J. Soc. Psychol.,* 1938, 9, 125–140.

15 Buttgereit, H. Führergestalten in der Schulklass. *Z. angew. Psychol.,* 1932, 43, 369–413.

16 Caldwell, O. W. Some factors in training for leadership. *Nat. Ass. Sec. Sch. Prin., Fourth Yearb.,* 1920, 2–13.

17 Caldwell, O. W., & Wellman, B. Characteristics of school leaders. *J. Educ. Res.,* 1926, 14, 1–15.

18 Carlson, H. B., & Harrell, W. An analysis of Life's "Ablest Congressman" poll. *J. Soc. Psychol.,* 1942, 15, 153–158.

19 Cattell, R. B. *Description and Measurement of Personality.* New York: World Book, 1946.

20 Chapin, F. S. *Community Leadership and Opinion in Red Wing.* Minneapolis: Univ. Minnesota Press, 1945.

21 Chapple, E. D., & Donald, G., Jr. A method of evaluating supervisory personnel. *Harvard Bus. Rev.,* 1946, 24, 197–214.

22 Chevaleva-Ianovskaia, E., & Sylla, D. Essai d'une étude sur les enfants meneurs. *J. de Psychol.,* 1929, 26, 604–612.

23 Clem, O. M., & Dodge, S. B. The relation of high school leadership and scholarship to post-school success. *Peabody J. Educ.* 1933, 10, 321–329.

24 Courtenay, M. E. Persistence of leadership. *Sch. Rev.,* 1938, 46, 97–107.

25 Cowley, W. H. Three distinctions in the study of leaders. *J. Abn. & Soc. Psychol.,* 1928, 23, 144–157.

26——. Traits of face-to-face leaders. *J. Abn. & Soc. Psychol.,* 1931, 26, 304–313.

27 Cox, C. M. The Early Mental Traits of Three Hundred Geniuses. Stanford University: Stanford Univ. Press, 1926.

28 Crawford, A. B. Extra-curriculum activities and academic work. *Person, J.,* 1928, 7, 121–129.

29 Dashiell, J. F. Personality traits and the different professions. *J. Appl. Psychol.,* 1930, 14, 197–201.

30 Davis, J. A study of one hundred sixty-three outstanding communist leaders. *Publ. Amer. Sociol. Soc.,* 1930, 24, 42–55.

31 Detroit Teachers College. How Children Choose Friends. Detroit: Detroit Teachers College, 1929.

32 Drake, R. M. A study of leadership. *Charac. & Pers.,* 1944, 12, 285–289.

33 Dunkerley, M. D. A statistical study of leadership among college women. *Stud. Psychol. & Psychiat.,* 1940, 4, 1–65.

34 Eichler, G. A. Studies in student leadership. *Penn. St. Coll. Stud. Educ.,* 1934, No. 10.

35 Fauquier, W., & Gilchrist, T. Some aspects of leadership in an institution. *Child Devel.,* 1942, 13, 55–64.

36 Fay, P. J., & Middleton, W. C. Judgment of leadership from the transmitted voice. *J. Soc. Psychol.,* 1943, 17, 99–102.

37 Finch, F. H., & Carroll, H. A. Gifted children as high school leaders. *J. Genet. Psychol.,* 1932, 41, 476–481.

38 Flemming, E. G. A factor analysis of the personality of high school leaders. *J. Appl. Psychol.,* 1935, 19, 596–605.

39 Garrison, K. C. A study of some factors related to leadership in high school. *Peabody J. Educ.,* 1935, 11, 11–17.

40 Goodenough, F. L. Inter-relationships in the behavior of young children. *Child Devel.,* 1930, 1, 29–48.

41 Gowin, E. B. The Executive and His Control of Men. New York: Macmillan, 1915.

42——. The Selection and Training of the Business Executive. New York: Macmillan, 1918.

43 Guilford, J. P., & Guilford, R. B. Personality factors, D, R, T, and A. *J. Abn. & Soc. Psychol.,* 1939, 34, 21–36.

44 Hanawalt, N. G., Hamilton, C. E., & Morris, M. L. Level of aspiration in college leaders and nonleaders. *J. Abn. & Soc. Psychol.,* 1934, 38, 545–548.

45 Hanawalt, N. G., Richardson, H. M., & Hamilton, R. J. Leadership as related to Bernreuter personality measures: II. An item analysis of responses of college leaders and nonleaders. *J. Soc. Psychol.,* 1943, 17, 251–267.

46 Hanawalt, N. G., & Richardson, H. M. Leadership as related to the Bernreuter personality measures: IV. An item analysis of responses of adult leaders and nonleaders. *J. Appl. Psychol.,* 1944, 28, 397–411.

47 Hanfmann, E. Social structure of a group of kindergarten children. *Amer. J. Orthopsychiat.,* 1935, 5, 407–410.

48 Heath, C. W., & Gregory, L. W. What it takes to be an officer. *Infantry J.,* 1946, 58, 44–45.

49 Henning, H. Ziele und Möglichkeiten der experimentellen charakterüfung *Jarbuch d. Charakterol.,* 1929, 6, 213–273.

50 Hollingworth, L. S. *Gifted Children.* New York: Macmillan, 1926.

51 Hooker, E. R. Leaders in village communities. *Soc. For.,* 1928, 6, 605–614.

52 Howell, C. E. Measurement of leadership. *Sociometry,* 1942, 5, 163–168.

53 Hunter, E. C., & Jordan, A. M. An analysis of qualities associated with leadership among college students. *J. Educ. Psychol.,* 1939, 30, 497–509.

54 Jenkins, W. O. A review of leadership studies with particular reference to military problems. *Psychol. Bull.,* 1947, 44, 54–79.

55 Jennings, H. H. *Leadership and Isolation.* New York: Longmans Green, 1943.

56 Jones, A. J. *The Education of Youth for Leadership.* New York: McGraw-Hill, 1938.

57 Kohs, S. C., & Irle, K. W. Prophesying Army promotion. *J. Appl. Psychol.,* 1920, 4, 73–87.

58 Lehman, H. C. The creative years in science and literature. *Sci. Mon.,* 1937, 45, 65–75.

59———. Optimum ages for eminent leadership. *Sci. Mon.,* 1942, 54, 162–175.

60 Leib, A. Vorstellungen und Urteile von Schülern über Fuhrer in der Schulklasse. *Z. angew. Psychol.,* 1928, 30, 241–646.

61 Levi, I. J. Student leadership in elementary and junior high school, and its transfer into senior high school. *J. Educ. Res.,* 1930, 22, 135–139.

62 Link, H. C. The definition of social effectiveness and leadership through measurement. *Educ. & Psychol. Meas.,* 1944, 4, 57–67.

63 Luithlen, W. F. Zur Psychologie der Initiative und der Führereigenschaften. *Z. angew. Psychol.,* 1931, 39, 56–122.

64 Maller, J. B. Cooperation and competition: An experimental study in motivation. *Teach. Coll. Contr. Educ.,* 1925, No. 384.

65 Malloy, H. Study of some of the factors underlying the establishment of successful social contacts at the college level. *J. Soc. Psychol.,* 1936, 7, 205–228.

66 McCandless, B. R. Changing relationships between dominance and social acceptability during group democratization. *Amer. J. Orthopsychiat.,* 1942, 12, 529–535.

67 McCuen, T. L. Leadership and intelligence. *Education,* 1929, 50, 89–95.

68 McGahan, F. E. Factors associated with leadership ability. *Texas Outlook,* 1941, 25, 37–38.

69 Merriam, C. E. *Four American Party Leaders.* New York: Macmillan, 1926.

70 Merriam, C. E., & Gosnell, H. E. *The American Party System.* New York: Macmillan, 1929.

71 Michels, R. *Political Parties.* New York: Macmillan, 1915.

72 Middleton, W. C. Personality qualities predominant in campus leaders. *J. Soc. Psychol.,* 1941, 13, 199–201.

73 Miller, N. E., & Dollard, J. *Social Learning and Imitation.* New Haven: Yale Univ. Press, 1941.

74 Moore, L. H. Leadership traits of college women. *Sociol. & Soc. Res.,* 1932, 17, 44–54.

75———. Leadership traits of college women. *Sociol. & Soc. Res.,* 1935, 20, 136–139.

76 Nafe, R. W. A psychological description of leadership. *J. Soc. Psychol.,* 1930, 1, 248–266.

77 Newcomb, T. M. *Personality and Social Change.* New York: Dryden Press, 1943.

78 Newstetter, W. I., Feldstein, M. J., & Newcomb, T. M. *Group Adjustment: A Study in Experimental Sociology.* Cleveland: Western Reserve Univ., 1938.

79 Nutting, R. L. Some characteristics of leadership. *Sch. & Soc.,* 1923, 18, 387–390.

80 Page, D. P. Measurement and prediction of leadership. *Amer. J. Sociol.,* 1935, 41, 31–43.

81 Parten, M. B. Leadership among preschool children. *J. Abn. & Soc. Psychol.,* 1933, 27, 430–440.

82 Partridge, E. D. Leadership among adolescent boys. *Teach. Coll. Contr. Educ.,* 1934, No. 608.

83 Peck, E. M. A study of the personalities of five eminent men. *J. Abn. & Soc. Psychol.,* 1931, 26, 37–57.

84 Pigors, P. Leadership and domination among children. *Sociologus,* 1933, 9, 140–157.

85 Pinard, J. W. Tests of perseveration. *Brit. J. Psychol.,* 1932, 32, 5–19.

86 Prosh, F. The basis on which students choose their leaders. *Amer. Phys. Educ. Rev.,* 1928, 33, 265–267.

87 Puffer, J. A. Boys gangs. *Ped. Sem.,* 1905, 12, 175–213.

88 Reals, W. H. Leadership in the high school. *Sch. Rev.,* 1938, 46, 523–531.

89 Reininger, K. Das soziale Verhalten von Schulneulingen. *Wien Arb. pädag. Psychol.,* 1927, 7, 14.

90 Remmelin, M. K. Analysis of leaders among high school seniors. *J. Exp. Educ.,* 1938, 6, 413–422.

91 Reynolds, F. J. Factors of leadership among seniors of Central High School, Tulsa, Oklahoma. *J. Educ. Res.,* 1944, 37, 356–361.

92 Richardson, H. M., & Hanawalt, N. G. Leadership as related to Bernreuter personality measures: I. College leadership in extra-curricular activities. *J. Soc. Psychol.,* 1943, 17, 237–249.

93———. Leadership as related to the Bernreuter personality measures: III. Leadership among adult men in vocational and social activities. *J. Appl. Psychol.*, 1944, 28, 308–317.

94 Roslow, S. Nation-wide and local validation of the *PQ* or Personality Quotient test. *J. Appl. Psychol.*, 1940, 24, 529–539.

95 Schuler, E. A. A study of the consistency of dominant and submissive behavior in adolescent boys. *J. Genet. Psychol.*, 1935, 46, 403–432.

96 Shannon, J. R. The post-school careers of high school leaders and high school scholars. *Sch. Rev.*, 1929, 37, 656–665.

97 Sheldon, W. H. Social traits and morphologic type. *Person. J.*, 1927, 6, 47–55.

98 Simpson, R. H. A study of those who influence and of those who are influenced in discussion. *Teach. Coll. Contr. Educ.*, 1938, No. 748.

99 Smith, C. Social selection in community leadership. *Soc. For.*, 1937, 15, 530–545.

100 Smith, H. L., & Krueger, L. M. A brief summary of literature on leadership. *Bull. Sch. Educ., Indiana Univ.*, 1933, 9, No. 4.

101 Smith, M. Comparative study of Indian student leaders and followers. *Soc. For.*, 1935, 13, 418–426.

102 Smith, M., & Nystrom, W. C. A study of social participation and of leisure time of leaders and nonleaders. *J. Appl. Psychol.*, 1937, 21, 251–259.

103 Sorokin, P. A. *Social Mobility*. New York: Harper, 1927.

104——. Leaders of labor and radical movements in the United States and foreign countries. *Amer. J. Sociol.*, 1927, 33, 382–411.

105 Sorokin, P. A., & Zimmerman, C. C. Farmer leaders in the United States. *Soc. For.*, 1928, 7, 33–46.

106 Spaulding, C. B. Types of junior college leaders. *Sociol. & Soc. Res.*, 1934, 18, 164–168.

107 Starch, D. *How to Develop Your Executive Ability*. New York: Harper, 1943.

108 Stray, H. F. Leadership traits of girls in girls' camps. *Sociol. & Soc. Res.*, 1934, 18, 241–250.

109 Sward, K. Temperament and direction of achievement. *J. Soc. Psychol.*, 1933, 4, 406–429.

110 Swigart, J. S. A study of the qualities of leadership and administrative qualifications of thirty-eight women executives. Master's thesis, Ohio State Univ., 1936.

111 Taussig, F. W., & Joslyn, C. S. American Business Leaders. New York: Macmillan, 1932.

112 Terman, L. M. A preliminary study in the psychology and pedagogy of leadership. *Ped. Sem.*, 1904, 11, 413–451.

113 Terman, L. M., et al. *Genetic Studies of Genius: I. Mental and Physical Traits of a Thousand Gifted Children*. Stanford: Stanford Univ. Press, 1925.

114 Thorndike, E. L. The relation between intellect and morality in rulers. *Amer. J. Sociol.*, 1936, 42, 321–334.

115 Thrasher, F. *The Gang: A Study of 1,313 Gangs in Chicago*. Chicago: Univ. Chicago Press, 1927.

116 Thurstone, L. L. A *Factorial Study of Perception*. Chicago: Univ. Chicago Press, 1944.

117 Tryon, C. M. Evaluations of adolescent personality by adolescents. *Monog. Soc. Res. Child Devel.*, 1939, 4, No. 4.

118 Warner, M. L. Influence of mental level in the formation of boys' gangs. *J. Appl. Psychol.*, 1923, 7, 224–236.

119 Webb, U. Character and intelligence. *Brit. J. Psychol. Monog.*, 1915, No. 20.

120 Wetzel, W. A. Characteristics of pupil leaders. *Sch. Rev.*, 1932, 40, 532–534.

121 Wilkins, E. H. On the distribution of extracurricular activities. *Sch. & Soc.*, 1940, 51, 651–656.

122 Winston, S. Studies in negro leadership: Age and occupational distribution of 1,608 negro leaders. *Amer. J. Sociol.*, 1932, 37, 595–602.

123 Winston, S. Biosocial characteristics of American inventors. *Amer. Soc. Rev.*, 1937, 2, 837–849.

124 Zeleny, L. Characteristics of group leaders. *Sociol. & Soc. Res.*, 1939, 24, 140–149.

## Reading 10

# Leadership: Do Traits Matter?

**S. A. Kirkpatrick and E. A. Locke**
University of Maryland

Few issues have a more controversial history than leadership traits and characteristics. In the nineteenth and early twentieth centuries, "great man" leadership theories were highly popular. These theories asserted that leadership qualities were inherited, especially by people from the upper class. Great men were born, not made (in those days, virtually all business leaders were men). Today, great man theories are a popular foil for so-called superior models. To make the new models plausible, the "great men" are endowed with negative as well as positive traits. In a recent issue of the *Harvard Business Review,* for example, Slater and Bennis write,

> The passing years have . . . given the coup de grace to another force that has retarded democratization—the "great man" who with brilliance and farsightedness could preside with dictatorial powers as the head of a growing organization.[1]

Such great men, argue Slater and Bennis, become "outmoded" and dead hands on "the flexibility and growth of the organization." Under the new democratic model, they argue, "the individual *is* of relatively little significance."

Early in the twentieth century, the great man theories evolved into trait theories. ("Trait" is used broadly here to refer to people's general characteristics, including capacities, motives, or patterns of behavior.) Trait theories did not make assumptions about whether leadership traits were inherited or acquired. They simply asserted that leaders' characteristics are different from nonleaders'. Traits such as height, weight, and physique are heavily dependent on heredity, whereas others such as knowledge of the industry are dependent on experience and learning.

The trait view was brought into question during the mid-century when a prominent theorist, Ralph Stogdill, after a thorough review of the literature concluded that "a person does not become a leader by virtue of the possession of some combination of traits."[2] Stogdill believed this because

**Source:** Edited and reprinted with permission from Copyright Clearance Center, *Academy of Management Executive* 5, 2 (1991), pp. 48–60. Author affiliation may have changed since article was first published.

the research showed that no traits were universally associated with effective leadership and that situational factors were also influential. For example, military leaders do not have traits identical to those of business leaders.

Since Stogdill's early review, trait theory has made a comeback, though in altered form. Recent research, using a variety of methods, has made it clear that successful leaders are not like other people. The evidence indicates that there are certain core traits which significantly contribute to business leaders' success.

Traits *alone,* however, are not sufficient for successful business leadership—they are only a precondition. Leaders who possess the requisite traits must take certain *actions* to be successful (e.g. formulating a vision, role modeling, setting goals). Possessing the appropriate traits only makes it more likely that such actions will be taken and be successful. After summarizing the core leadership traits, we will discuss these important actions and the managerial implications.

## THE EVIDENCE: TRAITS DO MATTER

The evidence shows that traits do matter. Six traits on which leaders differ from nonleaders include drive, the desire to lead, honesty/integrity, self-confidence, cognitive ability, and knowledge of the business.[3]

### DRIVE

The first trait is labeled "drive," which is not to be confused with physical need deprivation. We use the term to refer to a constellation of traits and motives reflecting a high-effort level. Five aspects of drive include achievement motivation, ambition, energy, tenacity, and initiative.

#### *Achievement*

Leaders have a relatively high desire for achievement. The need for achievement is an important motive among effective leaders and even more important among successful entrepreneurs. High achievers obtain satisfaction from successfully completing challenging tasks, attaining standards of excellence, and developing better ways of doing things. To work their way up to the top of the organization, leaders must have a desire to complete challenging assignments and projects. This also allows the leader to gain technical expertise, both through education and work experience, and to initiate and follow through with organizational changes. . . .

### Ambition

Leaders are very ambitious about their work and careers and have a desire to get ahead. To advance, leaders actively take steps to demonstrate their drive and determination. Ambition impels leaders to set hard, challenging goals for themselves and their organizations. Walt Disney, founder of Walt Disney Productions, had a "dogged determination to succeed," and C. E. Woolman of Delta Air Lines had "inexhaustible ambition."

Effective leaders are more ambitious than nonleaders. In their 20-year study, psychologists Ann Howard and Douglas Bray found that among a sample of managers at AT&T, ambition, specifically the desire for advancement, was the strongest predictor of success 20 years later. . . .

### Energy

To sustain a high achievement drive and get ahead, leaders must have a lot of energy. Working long, intense work weeks (and many weekends) for many years requires an individual to have physical, mental, and emotional vitality.

Leaders are more likely than nonleaders to have a high level of energy and stamina and to be generally active, lively, and often restless. Leaders have been characterized as "electric, vigorous, active, full of life" as well as possessing the "physical vitality to maintain a steadily productive work pace."[4] Even at age 70, Sam Walton, founder of Wal-Mart discount stores, still attended Wal-Mart's Saturday morning meeting, a whoop-it-up 7:30 A.M. sales pep rally for 300 managers.

The need for energy is even greater today than in the past, because more companies are expecting all employees, including executives, to spend more time on the road visiting the organization's other locations, customers, and suppliers.

### Tenacity

Leaders are better at overcoming obstacles than nonleaders. They have the "capacity to work with distant objects in view" and have a "degree of strength of will or perseverance."[5] Leaders must be tirelessly persistent in their activities and follow through with their programs. Most organizational change programs take several months to establish and can take many years before the benefits are seen. Leaders must have the drive to stick with these programs, and persistence is needed to ensure that changes are institutionalized. . . .

Persistence, of course, must be used intelligently. Dogged pursuit of an inappropriate strategy can ruin an organization. It is important to persist in the right things. But what are the right things? In today's business climate, they may include the following: satisfying the customer, growth, cost control, innovation, fast response time, and quality, or, in Tom Peters's terms, a constant striving to improve just about everything.

### Initiative

Effective leaders are proactive. They make choices and take action that leads to change instead of just reacting to events or waiting for things to happen; that is, they show a high level of initiative. . . .

Instead of sitting "idly by or [waiting] for fate to smile upon them," leaders need to "challenge the process."

Leaders are achievement-oriented, ambitious, energetic, tenacious, and proactive. These same qualities, however, may result in a manager who tries to accomplish everything alone, thereby failing to develop subordinate commitment and responsibility. Effective leaders must not only be full of drive and ambition, they must *want to lead others.*

## LEADERSHIP MOTIVATION

Studies show that leaders have a strong desire to lead. Leadership motivation involves the desire to influence and lead others and is often equated with the need for power. People with high leadership motivation think a lot about influencing other people, winning an argument, or being the greater authority. They prefer to be in a leadership rather than subordinate role. The willingness to assume responsibility, which seems to coincide with leadership motivation, is frequently found in leaders. . . .

Sears psychologist Jon Bentz describes successful Sears executives as those who have a "powerful competitive drive for a position of . . . authority . . . [and] the need to be recognized as men of influence."[6] Astronauts John Glenn and Frank

Borman built political and business careers out of their early feats as space explorers, while other astronauts did not. Clearly, all astronauts possessed the same opportunities, but it was their personal makeup that caused Glenn and Borman to pursue their ambitions and take on leadership roles.

Psychologist Warren Bennis and colleague Burt Nanus state that power is a leader's currency, or the primary means through which the leader gets things done in the organization. A leader must want to gain the power to exercise influence over others. Also, power is an "expandable pie," not a fixed sum; effective leaders give power to others as a means of increasing their own power. Effective leaders do not see power as something that is competed for but rather as something that can be created and distributed to followers without detracting from their own power. . . .

A manager who was not as successful completed the sentence fragment "Taking orders . . ." with the ending "is easy, for it removes the danger of a bad decision."

Successful leaders must be willing to exercise power over subordinates, tell them what to do, and make appropriate use of positive and negative sanctions. Previous studies have shown inconsistent results regarding dominance as a leadership trait. According to Harvard psychologist David McClelland, this may be because there are two different types of dominance: a personalized power motive, or power lust, and a socialized power motive, or the desire to lead.[7]

### Personalized Power Motive

Although a need for power is desirable, the leader's effectiveness depends on what is behind it. A leader with a personalized power motive seeks power as an end in itself. These individuals have little self-control, are often impulsive, and focus on collecting symbols of personal prestige. Acquiring power solely for the sake of dominating others may be based on profound self-doubt. The personalized power motive is concerned with domination of others and leads to dependent, submissive followers.

### Socialized Power Motive

In contrast, a leader with a socialized power motive uses power as a means to achieve desired goals, or a vision. Its use is expressed as the ability to develop networks and coalitions, gain cooperation from others, resolve conflicts in a constructive manner, and use role modeling to influence others.

Individuals with a socialized power motive are more emotionally mature than those with a personalized power motive. They exercise power more for the benefit of the whole organization and are less likely to use it for manipulation. These leaders are also less defensive, more willing to take advice from experts, and have a longer-range view. They use their power to build up their organization and make it successful. The socialized power motive takes account of followers' needs and results in empowered, independent followers.

## HONESTY AND INTEGRITY

Honesty and integrity are virtues in all individuals but have special significance for leaders. Without these qualities, leadership is undermined. Integrity is the correspondence between word and deed, and honesty refers to being truthful or nondeceitful. The two form the foundation of a trusting relationship between leader and followers.

In his comprehensive review of leadership, psychologist Bernard Bass found that student leaders were rated as more trustworthy and reliable in carrying out responsibilities than followers. Similarly, British organizational psychologists Charles Cox and Cary Cooper's "high flying" (successful) managers preferred to have an open style of management, where they truthfully informed workers about happenings in the company. Morgan McCall and Michael Lombardo of the Center for Creative Leadership found that managers who reached the top were more likely to follow the following formula: "I will do exactly what I say I will do when I say I will do it. If I change my mind, I will tell you well in advance so you will not be harmed by my actions."[8]

Successful leaders are open with their followers, but also discreet and do not violate confidences or carelessly divulge potentially harmful information. One subordinate in a study by Harvard's John Gabarro made the following remark about his new president: "He was so consistent in what he said and did, it was easy to trust him." Another subordinate remarked about an unsuccessful leader, "How can I rely on him if I can't count on him consistently?"[9]

Professors James Kouzes, Barry Posner, and W. H. Schmidt asked 1,500 managers "What values do you look for and admire in your supervisors?" Integrity (being truthful and trustworthy, and having character and conviction) was the most frequently mentioned characteristic. Kouzes and Posner conclude:

Honesty is absolutely essential to leadership. After all, if we are willing to follow someone, whether it be into battle or into the boardroom, we first want to assure ourselves that the person is worthy of our trust. We want to know that he or she is being truthful, ethical, and principled. We want to be fully confident in the integrity of our leaders.

Effective leaders are credible, with excellent reputations, and high levels of integrity. The following description (from Gabarro's study) by one subordinate of his boss exemplifies the concept of integrity: "By integrity, I don't mean whether he'll rob a bank, or steal from the till. You don't work with people like that. It's whether you sense a person has some basic principles and is willing to stand by them."

Bennis and Nanus warn that today credibility is at a premium, especially since people are better informed, more cautious, and wary of authority and power. Leaders can gain trust by being predictable, consistent, and persistent and by making competent decisions. An honest leader may even be able to overcome lack of expertise, as a subordinate in Gabarro's study illustrates in the following description of his superior: "I don't like a lot of the things he does, but he's basically honest. He's a genuine article and you'll forgive a lot of things because of that. That goes a long way in how much I trust him."

## SELF-CONFIDENCE

There are many reasons why a leader needs self-confidence. Being a leader is a very difficult job. A great deal of information must be gathered and processed. A constant series of problems must be solved and decisions made. Followers have to be convinced to pursue specific courses of action. Setbacks have to be overcome. Competing interests have to be satisfied. Risks have to be taken in the face of uncertainty. A person riddled with self-doubt would never be able to take the necessary actions nor command the respect of others.

Self-confidence plays an important role in decision making and in gaining others' trust. Obviously, if the leader is not sure of what decision to make, or expresses a high degree of doubt, then the followers are less likely to trust the leader and be committed to the vision.

Not only is the leader's self-confidence important, but so is others' perception of it. Often, leaders engage in impression management to bolster their image of competence; by projecting self-confidence they arouse followers' self-confidence. Self-confident leaders are also more likely to be assertive and decisive, which gains others' confidence in the decision. This is crucial for effective implementation of the decision. Even when the decision turns out to be a poor one, the self-confident leader admits the mistake and uses it as a learning opportunity, often building trust in the process. . . .

### *Emotional Stability*

Self-confidence helps effective leaders remain even-tempered. They do get excited, such as when delivering an emotionally charged pep talk, but generally do not become angry or enraged. For the most part, as long as the employee did his/her homework, leaders remain composed upon hearing that an employee made a costly mistake. For example, at PepsiCo, an employee who makes a mistake is "safe . . . as long as it's a calculated risk."

Emotional stability is especially important when resolving interpersonal conflicts and when representing the organization. A top executive who impulsively flies off the handle will not foster as much trust and teamwork as an executive who retains emotional control. Describing a superior, one employee in Gabarro's study stated, "He's impulsive and I'm never sure when he'll change signals on me."

Researchers at the Center for Creative Leadership found that leaders are more likely to "derail" if they lack emotional stability and composure. Leaders who derail are less able to handle pressure and more prone to moodiness, angry outbursts, and inconsistent behavior, which undermines their interpersonal relationships with subordinates, peers, and superiors. In contrast, they found the successful leaders to be calm, confident, and predictable during crisis.

Psychologically hardy, self-confident individuals consider stressful events interesting, as opportunities for development, and believe that they can influence the outcome. K. Labich in *Fortune* magazine argued that "By demonstrating grace under pressure, the best leaders inspire those around them to stay calm and act intelligently."[10]

## COGNITIVE ABILITY

Leaders must gather, integrate, and interpret enormous amounts of information. These demands are greater than ever today because of rapid technological change. Thus, it is not surprising that leaders need to be intelligent enough to formulate suitable strategies, solve problems, and make correct decisions.

Leaders have often been characterized as being intelligent, but not necessarily brilliant and as being conceptually skilled. Kotter states that a "keen mind" (i.e., strong analytical ability, good judgment, and the capacity to think strategically and multidimensionally) is necessary for effective leadership, and that leadership effectiveness requires "above average intelligence," rather than genius.

An individual's intelligence and the perception of his or her intelligence are two highly related factors. Professors Lord, DeVader, and Alliger concluded that "intelligence is a key characteristic in predicting leadership perceptions."[11] Howard and Bray found that cognitive ability predicted managerial success 20 years later in their AT&T study. Effective managers have been shown to display greater ability to reason both inductively and deductively than ineffective managers.

Intelligence may be a trait that followers look for in a leader. If someone is going to lead, followers want that person to be more capable in *some* respects than they are. Therefore, the follower's perception of cognitive ability in a leader is a source of authority in the leadership relationship.

## KNOWLEDGE OF THE BUSINESS

Effective leaders have a high degree of knowledge about the company, industry, and technical matters. For example, Jack Welch, president of GE, has a PhD in engineering; George Hatsopolous of Thermo Electron Corporation, in the years preceding the OPEC boycott, had both the business knowledge of the impending need for energy-efficient appliances and the technical knowledge of thermodynamics to create more efficient gas furnaces. Technical expertise enables the leader to understand the concerns of subordinates regarding technical issues. Harvard Professor John Kotter argues that expertise is more important than formal education.

Effective leaders gather extensive information about the company and the industry. Most of the successful general managers studied by Harvard's Kotter spent their careers in the same industry, while less successful managers lacked industry-specific experiences. Although cognitive ability is needed to gain a thorough understanding of the business, formal education is not a requirement. Only 40 percent of the business leaders studied by Bennis and Nanus had business degrees. In-depth knowledge of the organization and industry allows effective leaders to make well-informed decisions and to understand the implications of those decisions.

## OTHER TRAITS

Charisma, creativity/originality, and flexibility are three traits with less clear-cut evidence of their importance to leadership.[12] Effective leaders may have charisma; however, this trait may only be important for political leaders. Effective leaders also may be more creative than nonleaders, but there is no consistent research demonstrating this. Flexibility or adaptiveness may be important traits for a leader in today's turbulent environment. Leaders must be able to make decisions and solve problems quickly and initiate and foster change.

There may be other important traits needed for effective leadership; however, we believe that the first six that we discussed are the core traits. . . .

## MANAGEMENT IMPLICATIONS

Individuals can be *selected* either from outside the organization or from within non- or lower-managerial ranks based on their possession of traits that are less changeable or trainable. Cognitive ability (not to be confused with knowledge) is probably the least trainable of the six traits. Drive is fairly constant over time although it can change; it is observable in employees assuming they are given enough autonomy and responsibility to show what they can do. The desire to lead is more difficult to judge in new hires who may have had little opportunity for leadership early in life. It can be observed at lower levels of management and by observing people in assessment center exercises.

Two other traits can be developed through experience and *training*. Knowledge of the industry and technical knowledge come from formal training, job experience, and a mentally active approach toward new opportunities for learning. Planned job rotation can facilitate such growth. Self-confidence is both general and task-specific. People differ in their general confidence in mastering life's challenges, but task-specific self-confidence comes from mastering the various skills that leadership requires as well as the technical and strategic challenges of the industry. Such confidence parallels the individual's growth in knowledge.

Honesty does not require skill building; it is a virtue one achieves or rejects by choice. Organizations should look with extreme skepticism at any employee who behaves dishonestly or lacks integrity, and should certainly not reward dishonesty in any form, especially not with a promotion. The key role models for honest behavior are those at the top. On this issue, organizations get what they model, not what they preach.

## CONCLUSIONS

Regardless of whether leaders are born or made or some combination of both, it is unequivocally clear that *leaders are not like other people.* Leaders do not have to be great men or women by being intellectual geniuses or omniscient prophets to succeed, but they do need to have the "right stuff," and this stuff is not equally present in all people. Leadership is a demanding, unrelenting job with enormous pressures and grave responsibilities. It would be a profound disservice to leaders to suggest that they are ordinary people who happened to be in the right place at the right time. Maybe the place matters, but it takes a special kind of person to master the challenges of opportunity. Let us not only give credit, but also use the knowledge we have to select and train our future leaders effectively. We believe that in the realm of leadership (and in every other realm), the individual *does* matter.

## Notes

1. P. Slater and W. G. Bennis, "Democracy is Inevitable," *Harvard Business Review,* Sept–Oct, 1990, 170 and 171. For a summary of trait theories, see R. M. Stogdill's *Handbook of Leadership* (New York: Free Press, 1974). For reviews and studies of leadership traits, see R. E. Boyatzis, *The Competent Manager* (New York: Wiley & Sons, 1982); C. J. Cox and C. L. Cooper, *High Flyers: An Anatomy of Managerial Success* (Oxford: Basil Blackwell); G. A. Yukl, *Leadership in Organizations* (Englewood Cliffs, NJ: Prentice Hall, 1989), Chapter 9.

2. R. M. Stogdill, "Personal Factors Associated with Leadership: A Survey of the Literature," *Journal of Psychology,* 1948, 25, 64.

3. See the following sources for evidence and further information concerning each trait: 1) drive: B. M. Bass's *Handbook of Leadership* (New York: The Free Press, 1990); K. G. Smith and J. K. Harrison, "In Search of Excellent Leaders" (in W. D. Guth's *The Handbook of Strategy,* New York: Warren, Gorham, & Lamont, 1986). 2) desire to lead: V. J. Bentz, "The Sears Experience in the Investigation Description, and Prediction of Executive Behavior," (In F. R. Wickert and D. E. McFarland's *Measuring Executive Effectiveness* (New York: Appleton-Century-Crofts, 1967); J. B.

Miner, "Twenty Years of Research on Role-Motivation Theory of Managerial Effectiveness," *Personnel Psychology,* 1978, 31, 739–760. 3) honesty/integrity: Bass, op cit.; W. G. Bennis and B. Nanus, *Leaders: The Strategies for Taking Charge* (New York: Harper & Row, 1985); J. M. Kouzes and B. Z. Posner, *The Leadership Challenge: How to Get Things Done in Organizations* (San Francisco: Jossey-Bass); T. Peters, *Thriving on Chaos* (New York: Harper & Row, 1987); A. Rand, *For the New Intellectual* (New York: Signet, 1961). 4) self-confidence: Bass, op cit. and A. Bandura, *Social Foundations of Thought and Action: A Social Cognitive Theory,* (Englewood Cliffs, NJ: Prentice-Hall). Psychological hardiness is discussed by S. R. Maddi and S. C. Kobasa, *The Hardy Executive: Health under Stress* (Chicago: Dorsey Professional Books, 1984); M. W. McCall, Jr., and M. M. Lombardo, *Off the Track: Why and How Successful Executives get Derailed* (Technical Report No. 21, Greensboro, NC: Center for Creative Leadership, 1983). 5) cognitive ability: R. G. Lord, C. L. DeVader, and G. M. Alliger, "A Meta-Analysis of the Relation between Personality Traits and Leadership Perceptions: An Application of Validity Generalization Procedures," *Journal of Applied Psychology,* 1986; 61, 402–410; A. Howard and D. W. Bray, *Managerial Lives in Transition: Advancing Age and Changing Times* (New York: Guilford Press, 198). 6) knowledge of the business: Bennis and Nanus, op. cit.; J. P. Kotter, *The General Managers* (New York: MacMillan); Smith and Harrison, op. cit.

4. From Kouzes and Posner, op. cit., pp. 122 and V. J. Bentz, op cit. The Sam Walton quote is from J. Huey, "Wal-Mart: Will it take over the world?" *Fortune,* January 30, 1989, 52–59.

5. From Bass, op. cit.

6. From Bentz, op. cit.

7. The distinction between a personalized and a socialized power motive is made by D. C. McClelland, "N-achievement and entrepreneurship: A longitudinal study," *Journal of Personality and Social Psychology,* 1965, 1, 389–392. These two power motives are discussed further by Kouzes and Posner, op. cit.

8. From McCall and Lombardo, op. cit.

9. From Gabarro, op. cit.

10. From K. Labich, "The Seven Keys to Business Leadership," *Fortune,* October 24, 1988, 58–66.

11. From Lord, DeVader, and Alliger, op. cit.

12. For research on charisma, see Bass, op. cit., and R. J. House, W. D. Spangler, and J. Woycke, "Personality and charisma in the U.S. presidency: A psychological theory of leadership effectiveness (Wharton School, University of Pennsylvania, 1989, unpublished manuscript), on creativity/originality, see Howard and Bray, op. cit., and A. Zaleznik, *The Managerial Mystique* (New York: Harper and Row, 1989); on flexibility, see Smith and Harrison, op. cit.

## Reading 11

# Emotions and Leadership: The Role of Emotional Intelligence

**Jennifer M. George**
Rice University

By all counts, leadership ranks among the most researched and debated topics in the organizational sciences. A wide diversity of approaches to leadership has been proposed—researchers have analyzed what leaders are like, what they do, how they motivate their followers, how their styles interact with situational conditions, and how they can make major changes in their organizations, for example (for reviews of the leadership literature see Bass, 1990; Fiedler & House, 1994; Yukl, 1998; Yukl & Van Fleet, 1992). Researchers have also explored when leadership might not be important and some leadership experts have proposed that leadership is more a creation in the minds of followers than a characteristic of those who occupy leadership roles (e.g. Meindl, 1990). While we have learned much about leadership from this diversity of approaches, it still remains somewhat of an enigma. While research has been conducted which supports (and sometimes fails to support) currently popular theories, and these theories have increased our understanding of leadership, how and why leaders have (or fail to have) positive influences on their followers and organizations is still a compelling question for leadership researchers.

While existing studies detail what leaders are like, what they do, and how they make decisions, the effects of leaders' feelings or their moods and emotions and, more generally, the role of emotions in the leadership process, are often not explicitly considered in the leadership literature, with the notable exception of work on charisma (e.g. Conger & Kanungo, 1998; Lindholm, 1990). This relative neglect is not surprising as the organizational literature has been dominated by a cognitive orientation (Ilgen & Klein, 1989), with feelings being ignored or being seen as something that gets in the way of rationality and effective decision making (Albrow, 1992). Just as motivation theory and research have ignored how workers' moods and emotions influence their choice of work activities, levels of effort, and levels of per-

sistence in the face of obstacles (George & Brief, 1996), leadership theory and research have not adequately considered how leaders' moods and emotions influence their effectiveness as leaders. Two preliminary studies suggest that leaders' feelings may play an important role in leadership. George and Bettenhausen (1990) found that the extent to which leaders of existing work groups experienced positive moods was positively related to levels of prosocial behavior performed by group members and negatively related to group turnover rates, George (1995) found that work groups led by sales managers who tended to experience positive moods at work provided higher quality customer service than groups led by managers who did not tend to experience positive moods at work. While these two studies help to fill a gap in the leadership literature, in and of themselves, they do not illuminate the role of moods and emotions in the leadership process per se but rather suggest that feelings may be an important factor to consider.

The growing body of literature exploring the role of moods and emotions in human and organizational affairs (e.g. Fineman, 1993; Forgas, 1995) suggests that, rather than being simply an additional factor to consider, feelings play a much more central role in the leadership process. The purpose of this paper is to present a framework describing what the role might be. First, however, it is useful to sample the literature and research findings attesting to the central role of feelings in human affairs.

## THE ROLE OF FEELINGS IN HUMAN AFFAIRS

A growing body of literature suggests that moods and emotions play a central role in cognitive processes and behavior. What distinguishes moods from emotions is their intensity. Moods are pervasive and generalized feeling states that are not tied to the events or circumstances which may have caused the mood in the first place (Morris, 1989). Moods are relatively low intensity feelings which do not interrupt ongoing activities

**Source:** Edited and reprinted with permission from Sage Publications, Ltd., *Human Relations,* 2000, 53, 8, pp. 1027–1055, Copyright 2000.

(Forgas, 1992a). Emotions are high intensity feelings that are triggered by specific stimuli (either internal or external to the individual), demand attention, and interrupt cognitive processes and behaviors (Forgas, 1992a; Morris, 1989; Simon, 1982). Emotions tend to be more fleeting than moods because of their intensity. Emotions often feed into moods so that, once the intensity of an emotion subsides because the individual has cognitively or behaviorally dealt with its cause, the emotion lingers on in the form of a less intense feeling or mood. Hence, for example, the intense anger that a leader might experience upon learning that he or she was deceived by a follower resulting in a lost opportunity subsides once the leader has recovered from the shock and decides how to deal with the situation. However, the anger lives on for the rest of the day in the form of a negative mood which colors the leader's interactions and thought processes.

Feelings have been shown to influence the judgments that people make, material recalled from memory, attributions for success and failure, creativity, and inductive and deductive reasoning. When people are in positive moods, for example, their perceptions and evaluations are likely to be more favorable, they are more prone to remember positive information, they are more self-assured, they are more likely to take credit for successes and avoid blame for failures, and they are more helpful to others (e.g. Bower, 1981; Cunningham et al., 1980; Forgas et al., 1984, 1990; George, 1991; Isen et al., 1976, 1978; Rosenhan et al., 1981). Positive moods have been found to enhance flexibility on categorization tasks and facilitate creativity and inductive reasoning (Isen et al., 1985, 1987). Conversely, negative moods may foster deductive reasoning and more critical and comprehensive evaluations (Salovey et al., 1993; Sinclair & Mark, 1992).

While a stereotype of the "rational" decision maker is a person who can set aside their personal feelings and coolly calculate the best course of action to deal with a problem or opportunity, neurological findings suggest that feelings are necessary to make good decisions (Damasio, 1994; Goleman, 1995). Neurological research on patients who have had brain tumors removed and subsequent damage to sectors of the brain responsible for moods and emotions has yielded a perplexing pattern of results. Some of these patients show no deficits in memory, intelligence, verbal ability, and numerical ability. Given the nature of their injuries, however, they tend to be emotionally flat. For example, they don't seem upset when recounting their own personal injury, problems, and disappointments or when viewing pictures that induce negative feelings in people without any brain injuries. Elliot, a former attorney, seen by neurologist Damasio, was one such patient. After removal of his brain tumor, Elliot continued to score either at average or above-average levels on measures of intelligence and other cognitive abilities. However, his life fell apart after his injury. He had trouble regularly attending work, when at work had a hard time getting things done, and eventually lost his job and got divorced. After much research and analysis and comparison with other patients with similar kinds of injuries, Damasio concluded that Elliot's lack of feeling left him unable to make decisions. On problem-solving tasks, for example, Elliot could come up with multiple viable solutions and the pros and cons for each, yet could not choose among them. Feelings help us to make choices and decide among options and, once devoid of feelings, people can "rationally" assess pros and cons of choices ranging from what's the best time to schedule a doctor's appointment to what type of career to pursue, yet may never be able to make a wise choice from the alternatives generated (Damasio, 1994; Goleman, 1995). While very intense emotions can certainly interfere with effective decision making, as Damasio (1994: 53) suggests, "reduction in emotion may constitute an equally important source of irrational behavior."

This brief sampling of findings is indicative of a wider body of literature which, though in diverse areas such as neuropsychology, social psychology, and organizational behavior, point to a consistent conclusion: feelings are intimately connected to the human experience. Feelings are intricately bound up in the ways that people think, behave, and make decisions.

In this regard, Forgas' (1995) affect infusion model (AIM) provides a useful framework for understanding the conditions under which affect is most likely to influence cognition, judgment, and decision making. More specifically and counterintuitively, the AIM suggests that affect is particularly likely to influence judgments during substantive processing. Substantive processing occurs when decision makers are faced with a complex task in need of extensive and constructive information processing, and when ambiguity and uncertainty exist, new information needs to be assimilated, and decision makers desire to make accurate judgments and good decisions (Fiedler, 1991; Forgas, 1992b, 1993, 1994, 1995).

Affect priming is an important mechanism through which affect infuses judgments during substantive processing. Affect priming refers to the selective attention to, encoding, and retrieval of information congruent with one's current affective state as well as the tendency to make mood-congruent interpretations and associations (e.g. Bower, 1981, 1991; Clark & Waddell, 1983; Forgas, 1995; Forgas & Bower, 1987; Isen, 1984, 1987; Singer & Salovey, 1988).

Additionally, the AIM model suggests that affect is likely to influence judgments when decision makers resort to a heuristic processing strategy. Heuristic processing tends to take place when decision makers are making judgments that are simple or commonplace and not very personally relevant, there is little pressure to be detailed or accurate, and there are other demands on current information processing (Forgas, 1995). Under these conditions, one's current affective state may be used as a heuristic such that decision makers deduce their judgment from their current affective state or how they feel at the time the judgment is being made (Clore & Parrott, 1991; Forgas, 1995; Schwarz & Bless, 1991).

## FEELINGS AND LEADERSHIP

The literature briefly described above is representative of a much wider body of knowledge which suggests that feelings serve multiple purposes in human affairs. As will be demonstrated below, it is likely that feelings play an important role in leadership. While George and Bettenhausen (1990) and George (1995) investigated some of the potential beneficial consequences of leader positive mood, it is likely that a diversity of feelings (both emotions and moods) influences leadership effectiveness. Negative moods, for example, foster systematic and careful information processing (Sinclair, 1988; Sinclair & Mark, 1992) and may be advantageous when leaders are dealing with complex problems in which errors carry high risk. As another example, relatively intense negative emotions may appropriately redirect a leader's attention to an issue in need of immediate attention (Frigda, 1988). For example, a leader who experiences anger upon learning of a pattern of covert sexual harassment in a department might be well served by this emotional response. The anger signals to the leader (Frigda, 1988) that his or her attention must be redirected from new product development to confronting the sexual harassment problem and improving the organization's efforts to eliminate harassment.

By now, it may be apparent that it is not too difficult to construct scenarios in which leaders would be well served by the experience of a variety of types of moods and emotions. Moreover, one can also construct scenarios in which a leader's effectiveness may be hampered by the experience of certain moods and emotions. Leaders who experience anger frequently may have a difficult time building good relationships with followers and engendering their trust (Jones & George, 1998). Similarly, a leader who frequently experiences positive moods on the job may fail to notice and attend to performance shortfalls that are less than apparent.

Hence, this inquiry into the role of feelings in leadership is not bent on determining the "right" or "effective" moods and emotions that facilitate leadership effectiveness. Leaders are obviously human beings with the full range of moods and emotions potentially available to them. Both positive and negative moods and emotions serve numerous functions in people's lives. Likewise, both positive and negative moods and emotions can sometimes be the cause of human dysfunctions.

This paper does seek to explore, however, whether effective leaders possess certain emotional capabilities just as they may possess certain cognitive capabilities (Bass, 1990; Kirkpatrick & Locke, 1991; Yukl, 1998). Moods and emotions play an extensive role in thought processes and behavior (Bower, 1981; Bower & Cohen, 1982; Clark & Isen, 1982; Forgas, 1995; George & Brief, 1992; Isen & Baron, 1991; Isen & Shalker, 1982; Isen et al., 1978; Leventhal & Tomarken, 1986; Rosenhan et al., 1981; Teasdale & Fogarty, 1979) and the same moods and emotions can result in both improved or impaired effectiveness depending upon multiple factors including the index of effectiveness (for example, a quick, heuristic-based response vs. a careful consideration of alternatives) (Salovey et al., 1993; Sinclair & Mark, 1992). Moreover, research suggests that people can and do take steps to manage their own and others' moods and emotions (Mayer et al., 1991; Salovey & Mayer, 1989–90). Might it be that some leaders have superior mood/emotion capabilities which allow them to use and benefit from the variety of feelings they experience on the job? Might it also be that these capabilities enable leaders to influence, and develop effective interpersonal relationships with, their followers? Interpersonal relationships are laden with moods and emotions as is effective social influence.

These mood/emotion capabilities have been addressed by emotional intelligence theory and research. In the next section, I briefly describe emotional intelligence, and the theory and research which support its role in human affairs. Next, I describe how emotional intelligence may be a key contributor to leadership effectiveness and outline how different aspects of emotional intelligence facilitate the varied activities central to effective leadership. While emotional intelligence has been linked previously to specific leader behaviors (Megerian & Sosik, 1996), this paper adopts a broader approach and explores the multitude of ways in which emotional intelligence may contribute to leadership effectiveness.

Additionally, I would like to point out that earlier leadership approaches, and in particular the trait approach, also have described certain leadership skills or traits that may either be subsumed under or may partially overlap with emotional intelligence (for reviews, see Bass, 1990; Yukl, 1998). Moreover, while the term "emotional intelligence" has been coined relatively recently, it bears some resemblance and partially overlaps with earlier concepts such as social intelligence (Legree, 1995; Sternberg & Smith, 1985; Wong et al., 1995). However, as Mayer, Salovey and Caruso (in press) suggest, emotional intelligence is theoretically preferable to earlier constructs such as social intelligence because it is more focused on affect per se. Emotional intelligence includes internal, private feelings that influence functioning which may not necessarily be linked to social skills and also focuses exclusively on emotional skills rather than confounding them with social or political knowledge (Mayer et al., in press). Hence, as will become clearer below, emotional intelligence captures capabilities and skills in the emotion domain to a greater extent than prior constructs.

# EMOTIONAL INTELLIGENCE

Emotional intelligence is "the ability to perceive emotions, to access and generate emotions so as to assist thought, to understand emotions and emotional knowledge, and to reflectively regulate emotions so as to promote emotional and intellectual growth" (Mayer & Salovey, 1997: 5). Prior to continuing, it should be pointed out that the term "emotional" in emotional intelligence is used broadly to refer to moods as well as emotions. So as to be consistent with the emotional intelligence literature, in the remainder of this paper, "emotions" will be used to refer to both emotions and moods.

Emotional intelligence essentially describes the ability to effectively join emotions and reasoning, using emotions to facilitate reasoning and reasoning intelligently about emotions (Mayer & Salovey, 1997). In other words, emotional intelligence taps into the extent to which people's cognitive capabilities are informed by emotions and the extent to which emotions are cognitively managed. Additionally, it should be pointed out that emotional intelligence is distinct from predispositions to experience certain kinds of emotions captured by the personality traits of positive and negative affectivity (George, 1996; Tellegen, 1985).

There are at least four major aspects of emotional intelligence: the appraisal and expression of emotion, the use of emotion to enhance cognitive processes and decision making, knowledge about emotions, and management of emotions (Table 1 on page 86). While each of these aspects of emotional intelligence is quite involved, here I provide you with a brief overview of some of their key elements. This discussion draws from the work of Mayer, Salovey, and their colleagues (e.g. Mayer & Salovey, 1993, 1995, 1997; Mayer et al., 1990; Salovey & Mayer, 1989–90, 1994; Salovey et al., 1993, 1995).

## THE APPRAISAL AND EXPRESSION OF EMOTION

Appraisal and expression of emotion pertain to both the self and other people. People differ in terms of the degree to which they are aware of the emotions they experience and the degree to which they can verbally and nonverbally express these emotions to others. Accurately appraising emotions facilitates the use of emotional input in forming judgments and making decisions. The accurate expression of emotion ensures that people are able to effectively communicate with others to meet their needs and accomplish their goals or objectives.

Some people are actually reluctant or ambivalent about expressing emotions. Two types of ambivalence have been identified (King & Emmons, 1991). Some ambivalent people actually want to express their emotions, agonize over doing it, and fail to (Emmons & Colby, 1995). Others do express their emotions but then regret doing so. Both types of ambivalence have been linked to anxiety, depression, some psychiatric disorders, lower well-being, and less social support (Emmons & Colby, 1995; Katz & Campbell, 1994;

**TABLE 1**   Aspects of Emotional Intelligence

| Appraisal and Expression of Emotion | Use of Emotions to Enhance Cognitive Processes and Decision Making | Knowledge about Emotions | Management of Emotions |
| --- | --- | --- | --- |
| Aware of own emotions | Emotions direct attention and signal focus of attention | Knowing the causes of emotions | Meta-regulation of mood (reflection on the causes, appropriateness, and changeability of emotions) |
| Can accurately express own emotions | Emotions facilitate making choices | Knowing the consequences of emotions | Positive mood maintenance |
| Aware of others' emotions | Use of specific emotions to enhance certain kinds of cognitive processes | Knowing how emotions progress over time | Negative mood repair or improvement. |
| Can accurately express others' emotions | Use of shifts in emotions to promote flexibility | | Management of others' emotions |
| Empathy | | | |

Based on the work of Mayer, Salovey, and colleagues (e.g., Mayer et al., 1990; Mayer & Salovey, 1993, 1995, 1997; Salovey & Mayer, 1989–90, 1994; Salovey et al., 1993,1995).

King & Emmons, 1990, 1991). At a general level, ambivalence over expression of emotions can hamper an individual from developing beneficial interpersonal relationships in life.

People also differ in terms of their ability to accurately express emotions. Some people, referred to as alexithymics, cannot appraise their own emotions and are unable to communicate their feelings using language (Apfel & Sifneos, 1979; Krystal et al., 1986; Sifneos, 1972, 1973; Taylor, 1984; Thayer-Singer, 1977). Alexithymics are vulnerable to a variety of psychological problems which may result from their inability to express their feelings (Salovey et al., 1993). Individuals also differ in their ability to express emotions nonverbally with facial expressions and body language (Buck, 1979, 1984; Friedman et al., 1980).

Appraising and expressing the emotions of others is the ability to accurately determine the emotions other people are experiencing and the ability to accurately convey or communicate these feelings. Much of the appraisal of emotion in others comes from nonverbal cues. When people tell each other how they are feeling, appraisal is relatively straightforward. However, sometimes the emotions people claim to have are not actually the ones they are experiencing and at other times people are reluctant to express their emotions. People differ in the extent to which they can accurately appraise emotions in others, particularly from facial expressions (Buck, 1984; Campbell et al., 1971).

Related to the appraisal and expression of emotion in others is the concept of empathy, the ability to understand and experience another person's feelings or emotions (Mehrabian & Epstein, 1972; Wispe, 1986). Empathy, a contributor to emotional intelligence, is an important skill which enables people to provide useful social support and maintain positive interpersonal relationships (Batson, 1987; Kessler et al., 1985; Thoits, 1986).

## THE USE OF EMOTION TO ENHANCE COGNITIVE PROCESSES AND DECISION MAKING

Emotional intelligence does not only entail being aware of one's own emotions, but also using these emotions in functional ways. First, emotions can be useful in terms of directing attention to pressing concerns and signalling what should be the focus of attention (Frigda, 1988; George & Brief, 1996). Second, emotions can be used in choosing among options and making decisions; being able to anticipate how one would feel if certain events took place can help decision makers choose among multiple options (Damasio, 1994). Third, emotions can be used to facilitate certain kinds of cognitive processes. As mentioned earlier, positive moods can facilitate creativity, integrative thinking, and inductive reasoning, and negative moods can facilitate attention to detail, detection of errors and problems, and careful information processing (Isen et al., 1985, 1987; Salovey et al., 1993; Sinclair & Mark, 1992). Finally, shifts in emotions can lead to more flexible planning, the generation of multiple alternatives, and a broadened perspective on problems (Mayer, 1986; Salovey & Mayer, 1989–90). When people are in positive moods, for example, they tend to be more optimistic and perceive that positive events are more likely and negative events are less likely; when people are in negative moods they tend to be more pessimistic and perceive that positive events are less likely and negative events are more likely (Bower, 1981; Salovey & Birnbaum, 1989). People in positive moods also tend to have heightened perceptions of their future success and self-efficacy (Forgas et al., 1990; Kavanagh & Bower, 1985). By evaluating the same opportunities and problems in varying mood states, a broad range of options will be brought to mind and considered. And, as you will see below, emotional intelligence entails using emotions for these purposes.

## KNOWLEDGE ABOUT EMOTIONS

Emotional knowledge is concerned with understanding both the determinants and consequences of moods and emotions, and how they evolve and change over time. People differ in their awareness and understanding of how different situations, events, people, and other stimuli generate emotions. A leader who is surprised when followers' initial reaction to an announced restructuring (even with a guarantee of no layoffs) is fear and anxiety is not knowledgeable about the determinants of emotions. Over time, emotions and moods change—fear and anxiety might evolve into a negative mood and then to apathy or to a more intense state of agitation. While emotions can progress in different ways—enthusiasm can lead to further levels of excitation or to a less intense sense of general wellbeing—some people are especially attuned to these kinds of progressions and their causes.

Appreciation of the consequences of moods and emotions also varies across individuals. Some people have a rudimentary understanding of how they (and other people) are influenced by feelings and use this knowledge in functional ways. A leader in a negative mood who decides to delay meeting with followers to discuss upcoming changes in need of their support until they are feeling better intuitively realizes how their ability to enthusiastically communicate information about the changes and garner their followers' support is influenced by their current feelings. Similarly, a home buyer in a positive mood who sees a house they really like but forestalls making a final decision until they return to the house in a couple of days in a different "frame of mind"

possesses an understanding of how their appraisal of the house may be colored by their good mood. On the other hand, some people are oblivious to the effects of feelings. A stereotype of obliviousness to the effects of feelings is the family member who has had a hard day at work, comes home in a bad mood, and proceeds to get into arguments with spouse and children. This family member, however, never realizes how their bad mood is contributing to the disagreements and, instead, berates everyone else for their presumed failings, intensifying their own bad mood as well as the disagreements.

## MANAGEMENT OF EMOTIONS

Emotional intelligence also includes a more proactive dimension with regards to feelings: the management of one's own and other people's moods and emotions. Research has found that people strive to maintain positive moods and alleviate negative moods (e.g. Clark & Isen, 1982; Isen & Levin, 1972; Mayer et al., 1991; Mischel et al., 1973; Morris & Reilly, 1987); emotional intelligence captures individual differences in the extent to which one is able to successfully manage moods and emotions in these ways. Management of one's own moods and emotions also relies on knowledge and consideration of the determinants, appropriateness, and malleability of moods and emotions. This regulation entails a reflective process, which has been referred to as the meta-regulation of mood (Mayer & Salovey, 1997). Essentially, emotional intelligence encompasses individual differences in the ability to accurately reflect on one's moods and manage them (Salovey et al., 1995).

Emotional intelligence entails not just being able to manage one's own feelings, but also being able to manage the moods and emotions of others. Being able to excite and enthuse other people or make them feel cautious and wary is an important interpersonal skill and vehicle of social influence (Wasielewski, 1985). In order to be able to manage the moods and emotions of others, people must be able to appraise and express emotions, effectively use emotions, and be knowledgeable about emotions. Hence, the other three dimensions of emotional intelligence described above contribute to leaders being able to influence and manage the emotions of their followers.

## RECAP

These four aspects of emotional intelligence are related. For example, as mentioned above, awareness of emotions is necessary for their management. As another example, empathy may contribute to being able to manage emotions in others. Consistent with this reasoning, preliminary research suggests that the four aspects of emotional intelligence are positively correlated with each other (e.g. Mayer et al., 1990, in press; Mayer & Geher, 1996; Mayer & Salovey, 1997). Additionally, and as mentioned earlier, while emotional intelligence is a relatively new construct, it has roots in other constructs such as social intelligence which have a relatively long history (Ford & Tisak, 1983; Sternberg & Smith, 1985; Walker & Foley, 1973). However, emotional intelligence captures more of the essence of the active and purposeful integration of feelings and thoughts for effective functioning than these earlier constructs.

## EMOTIONAL INTELLIGENCE AND EFFECTIVE LEADERSHIP

While emotional intelligence can lead to enhanced functioning in a variety of aspects of life such as achievement and close relationships (Goleman, 1995 Salovey & Mayer, 1989–90), I propose that it may play a particularly important role in leadership effectiveness. To clarify this role, I propose how these four aspects of emotional intelligence described above—appraisal and expression of emotion, use of emotion to enhance cognitive processing and decision making, knowledge about emotions, and management of emotions—contribute to effective leadership.

In order to explore the implications of emotional intelligence for effective leadership, it is necessary to identify the fundamental nature of effective leadership. This is no easy task given the plethora of leadership theories, approaches, and empirical findings. Fortunately, several recent syntheses of the leadership literature have been offered which are consistent in terms of their descriptions of effective leadership. Based on the syntheses of Yukl (1998), Locke (1991), and Conger and Kanungo (1998), as well as the large leadership literature, specific elements of leadership effectiveness can be identified. Note that, while no specific theory of leadership is entailed in those elements, the elements themselves have roots in a variety of theoretical traditions. As described by these authors (i.e. Conger & Kanungo, 1998; Locke 1991; Yukl, 1998), effective leadership includes the following essential elements.

- development of a collective sense of goals and objectives and how to go about achieving them;

- instilling in others knowledge and appreciation of the importance of work activities and behaviors;

- generating and maintaining excitement, enthusiasm, confidence, and optimism in an organization as well as cooperation and trust;

- encouraging flexibility in decision making and change;

- establishing and maintaining a meaningful identity for an organization.

Below, I consider how emotional intelligence may help leaders carry out those activities and therefore contribute to leader's effectiveness.

## DEVELOPMENT OF A COLLECTIVE SENSE OF GOALS AND OBJECTIVES AND HOW TO GO ABOUT ACHIEVING THEM

The goals and objectives considered here are major, overarching goals that are commonly referred to as the leader's vision for the organization (e.g., Conger & Kanungo, 1998; Locke, 1991). Emotional intelligence may contribute to leaders developing a compelling vision for their groups or organizations in a number of ways. First, leaders may use their emotions to enhance their information processing of the challenges, threats, issues, and opportunities facing their organizations. Leaders are often faced with a large amount of information characterized by uncertainty and ambiguity; out of this information, they need to chart a course for their groups or organizations. In terms of the AIM model (Forgas, 1995), leaders are likely to engage in substantive processing as they seek to determine the direction for their organizations. They are dealing with complex information with high uncertainty and the desire to be accurate. Recall that the AIM model suggests that current affective state is likely to influence judgments resulting from substantive processing through the mechanism of affect priming.

Research linking positive moods to creativity suggests that when leaders are in positive moods they may be more creative (Isen et al., 1987) and, hence, more likely to come up with a compelling vision that contrasts with existing conditions. For example, people in positive moods have been found to be more integrative, use broader categories, and approach problems and categorization more flexibly (Isen & Baron, 1991; Isen & Daubman, 1984; Isen et al., 1985; Murray et al., 1990). Creating a compelling vision for an organization can be an exercise in creativity, positive thinking, and flexibility and such an exercise will be facilitated by positive moods (Isen et al., 1985; Murray et al., 1990). Leaders who are high on emotional intelligence will be better able to take advantage of and use their positive moods and emotions to envision major improvements in their organizations' functioning.

Leaders high on emotional intelligence also are likely to have knowledge about the fact that their positive moods may cause them to be overly optimistic. Hence, in order to ensure that they are being realistic and appropriately critical, they may be more likely to revisit their judgments when in a more neutral or negative mood to ensure a careful consideration of all the issues involved. Such leaders also are likely to be better able to repair negative moods arising from any number of sources that may limit flexibility and creativity, and, more generally, use meta-mood processes to manage their moods and emotions in functional ways (Mayer et al., 1991).

Importantly, leaders need not only to come up with a compelling vision, but also to effectively communicate it throughout the organization in such a way that it does come to be shared and is "collective." By accurately appraising how their followers currently feel, relying on their knowledge of emotions to understand why they feel this way, and influencing followers' emotions so that they are receptive to and supportive of the leader's goals or objectives for the organization and proposed ways to achieve them, leaders may help to ensure that their vision is shared or collective. For example, a leader who is high on emotional intelligence may act on emotional knowledge which suggests that followers are more likely to experience positive emotions and be supportive of the leader's goals and objectives when the leader expresses confidence in followers and serves to elevate their levels of self-efficacy (Gardner & Avolio, 1998).

## INSTILLING IN OTHERS KNOWLEDGE AND APPRECIATION OF THE IMPORTANCE OF WORK ACTIVITIES AND BEHAVIORS

In order to instill in others an appreciation of the importance of work activities, leaders need to ensure that followers are aware of problems and major issues facing an organization as well as potential opportunities while at the same time raising their confidence in their own abilities to successfully overcome problems, meet challenges, and seize opportunities. Leaders need to understand and influence followers' emotions such that

they are aware of the serious nature of problems yet, given the leader's vision, are enthusiastic about resolving the problems and feel optimistic about personal contributions. Leaders who are high on emotional intelligence are more knowledgeable of, and adept at managing, emotions in these subtle kinds of ways. Moreover, they are more likely to intuitively possess and act on meta-mood regulation knowledge such as the fact that people feel better when gains or positive events are presented in terms of improvements over previous conditions (Aronson & Linder, 1965; Salovey et al., 1993).

## GENERATING AND MAINTAINING EXCITEMENT, ENTHUSIASM, CONFIDENCE, AND OPTIMISM IN AN ORGANIZATION AS WELL AS COOPERATION AND TRUST

In order for leaders to generate and maintain excitement and enthusiasm, they must be able to appraise how their followers feel, and be knowledgeable about how to influence these feelings. They must also be able to anticipate how followers will react to different circumstances, events, and charges, and effectively manage these reactions. Leaders need to manage emotions such that followers are aware of problems yet, given the collective vision, are confident about resolving problems and feel optimistic about the efficacy of their personal contributions.

Moreover, leaders need to be able to distinguish between the emotions their followers are actually experiencing, their "real" feelings, and the emotions they express. Research on the expression of emotion has documented that people often deliberately control their expressed emotions for a variety of reasons including the existence of display rules (Ekman, 1973) which dictate which emotions should and should not be expressed in a given social context (Hochschild, 1983; Rafaeli & Sutton, 1987, 1989). Effective leaders need to be able to distinguish between, for example, excitement and enthusiasm that are faked versus excitement an enthusiasm that are genuinely felt. When the excitement and enthusiasm are faked, a leader needs to determine why as well as try to instill real feelings of excitement and enthusiasm. Through their ability to appraise other people's emotions, their knowledge of emotions, and their ability to manage emotions, leaders who are high on emotional intelligence are likely to be better able to decipher when expressed emotions are genuine, understand why they may be faked, and influence followers to experience genuine excitement, enthusiasm, confidence, and optimism rather than fake these feelings.

Leadership positions in organizations often entail a very hectic work pace with multiple and changing demands and high levels of stress (Kanter, 1983; Mintzberg, 1973). Not only do leaders have to meet these multiple demands, but they also have to constructively resolve conflicts, and generate and maintain a sense of cooperation and trust. Emotional intelligence contributes to what Epstein and colleagues refer to as constructive thinking or the ability to solve problems with a minimum of stress (Epstein, 1990; Katz & Epstein, 1991). While constructive thinking may facilitate problem solving in the workplace in general (Epstein & Meier, 1989), it may be especially important for leaders. Constructive thinking can lead to the generation of creative ideas to settle disagreements, arrive at win-win solutions to problems, and ensure cooperation and trust throughout an organization. Because leaders who are high on emotional intelligence are better able to understand and manage their own emotions, they may be more likely to engage in constructive thinking to build and maintain high levels of cooperation and trust.

Finally, leaders who are high on emotional intelligence may instill in their organizations a sense of enthusiasm, excitement, and optimism as well as an atmosphere of cooperation and trust through their being able to develop high quality interpersonal relationships with their followers. High quality interpersonal relationships between leaders and their followers have been documented to produce numerous advantages for organizations, leaders, and followers (Gerstner & Day, 1997; Graen & Uhl-Bien, 1995). Recognizing, appropriately responding to, and influencing followers' emotions is necessary for leaders to develop high quality interpersonal relationships with them (Salovey & Mayer, 1989–90) and positive affect is a critical ingredient for high levels of trust (Jones & George, 1998).

## ENCOURAGING FLEXIBILITY IN DECISION MAKING AND CHANGE

When leaders know and manage their emotions, they may be able to use them to improve their decision making. First, they can use them as signals to direct their attention to pressing concerns in need of immediate attention, given the many demands they face (Easterbook, 1959; Frigda, 1988; Mandler, 1975; Simon, 1982). Emotions (linked to their causes) can serve as important information

to use in prioritizing these demands. Moreover, when a leader realizes that emotions generated by low priority demands are interfering with more pressing demands, the leader's ability to actively manage the emotions (part of emotional intelligence) will also facilitate effective decision making.

Second, emotions can provide leaders with information about problems and opportunities (Schwarz, 1990; Schwarz & Clore, 1988). Leaders who accurately perceive their emotions and can determine their causes can determine when emotions are linked to opportunities, problems, or proposed courses of action, and use those emotions as information in the process of making decisions (Schwarz, 1990; Schwarz & Clore, 1988). By knowing their emotions and their roots, leaders can effectively use emotional input in decision making. Additionally, when a leader identifies an experienced emotion as irrelevant to a decision, they can take steps to discount and manage the emotion so that it will not be a source of error in decision making. Emotional intelligence, therefore, enables leaders to both effectively use emotions in decision making and manage emotions which interfere with effective decision making.

When leaders know and manage their emotions, they may be better able to flexibly approach problems, consider alternative scenarios, and avoid rigidity effects in decision making. Intuitively, and through meta-mood regulation, they may realize that different moods and emotions cause them to view issues differently and consider different types of options or alternatives. As mentioned earlier, the generation of multiple points of view and options can be aided by changes in moods and emotions (Mayer, 1986). When leaders are experiencing positive moods and emotions, their cognitive processes and considered alternatives will be different than when they are experiencing negative moods and emotions. For example, when leaders realize, through meta-mood regulation (Salovey et al., 1995), that a current negative mood is causing them to be overly pessimistic, they may deliberately revisit a proposed course of action in a more positive mood state to gain a richer, more flexible point of view. Similarly, meta-mood regulation may cause leaders who are optimistic and excited about a course of action due, in part, to a more pervasive positive mood state, to reconsider the course of action in a more neutral or negative mood state to more critically evaluate its pros and cons.

This increased flexibility deriving from emotional intelligence may also contribute to effective leadership in another way. Effective leaders are able to identify relationships among the many issues they are confronted with (Yukl & Van Fleet, 1992), enabling them to respond to multiple issues simultaneously (Isenberg, 1984; McCall & Kaplan, 1985; Yukl & Van Fleet, 1992). Flexible thinking arising out of emotional intelligence facilitates seeing connections among divergent information, and thus may help leaders see how issues are interrelated.

Additionally, emotional intelligence may contribute to a leader's ability to successfully implement changes in an organization. As Wasielewski (1985: 213) suggests, when leaders understand and are able to influence their followers' emotions, they may be able:

> to get followers to reassess the feelings they experience and the manner in which they display them. Based on the ability to do this, a leader may then be able to substitute an alternative view of the world that resolves this emotional ambiguity; for example, a leader may point out that anger is not an adequate emotional response to existing injustices if the group is interested in affecting real change. The leader might then propose an alternative view of the present situation, along with an appropriate set of alternative emotions more suitable to achieving the desired goal.

Emotional intelligence in general, and the extent to which a leader accurately perceives and is able to influence followers' emotions in particular, captures the emotion-related abilities or skills which Wasielewski (1985) suggests result in a leader's ability to make major changes. Some people have a difficult time determining how other people feel. Other people have a difficult time appropriately responding to others' feelings. Both types of people would be very unlikely to be able to spearhead major changes in an organization. On the other hand, people who can accurately assess how others feel and respond to, and sometimes alter, these feelings in productive ways are much more likely to be able to effectively overcome resistance to change and transform an organization in significant ways. Responding to and altering others' emotions necessitates that leaders possess accurate knowledge about the causes of emotions and their change over time, an important aspect of emotional intelligence.

## ESTABLISHING AND MAINTAINING A MEANINGFUL IDENTITY FOR AN ORGANIZATION

An organization's identity derives from and is a consequence of its culture (Trice & Beyer, 1993). Through an organization's culture, organizational members develop a collective identity embodied with meaning. In this regard, an increasingly important leadership activity pertains to the development and expression of organizational culture (e.g. Alvesson, 1992; Trice & Beyer, 1993). Organizational culture is embodied in relatively shared ideologies containing important beliefs, norms, and values (Trice & Beyer, 1993). Ongoing technological advances suggest that work, in general, will become less routine in the future (House, 1995). Less routine work is harder to monitor and control directly and, hence, organizations may be increasingly dependent upon culture as a mechanism of influence. The development and expression of culture and organizational identity is, thus, likely to only increase in importance for effective leadership.

Values, and to a lesser extent norms and beliefs, are emotion-laden. As conceptions of what is desirable or sought after (Rokeach, 1973), values evoke and appeal to emotions. As described earlier, it is difficult, if not impossible, to determine what is desired or preferred in an emotional vacuum (Damasio, 1994; Goleman, 1995). Norms, especially internalized norms, are also value-laden in that positive feelings accompany conformity and negative feelings accompany deviance. Reaffirmations of norms also evoke emotions stemming from a feeling of "rightness" of behavior. Beliefs above how things are also are intimately connected to emotions in that it is impossible to separate feelings from beliefs and both have the potential to influence each other. Firmly held beliefs are often firmly held because of their emotional content and appeal. Consistent with this analysis, Trice and Beyer (1993: 33) suggest that the content or substance of organizational culture resides in ideologies which are "shared, relatively coherently interrelated sets of emotionally charged beliefs, values, and norms that bind some people together and help them to make sense of their worlds."

Trice and Beyer (1993) suggest that cultures are infused with emotions and the allegiance to and identification with cultures stem from people's emotional needs rather than from a more "rational" or instrumental perspective. Violation of norms and values in a culture results in strong emotional reactions and cultures actually provide organizational members with socially acceptable ways to express their emotions.

Management of organizational culture is thus, in a sense, management of emotions (Van Maanen & Kunda, 1989). It necessitates that leaders are able to instill in followers a collective sense of an organization's important norms and values. In order to identify these norms and values, leaders must be attuned to their own and their followers' feelings, and express and embrace norms and values in a way that will appeal to and generate strong feelings. Norms and values must be infused with feelings and emotions that support them, and leaders can be instrumental in this process for their own motivation and sensemaking, for the motivation and sensemaking of their followers, and to build and maintain a meaningful collective identity for the organization.

Some of the major ways that culture is manifested in organizations is through cultural forms including symbols, language, narratives, and practices (Trice & Beyer, 1993). Cultural forms help organizational members to make sense of and identify with organizational reality, and to manage and regulate their emotions (Trice & Beyer, 1993). Cultural forms also are a means of expressing emotions in organizations and the effective use of cultural forms hinges on their ability to generate emotions (Ashforth & Humphrey, 1995; Harris & Sutton, 1986). As Ashforth and Humphrey (1995: 111) suggest, "the success of symbolic management is largely dependent upon the evocation of emotion."

Leaders' effective use of cultural forms is contingent upon many of the aforementioned aspects of emotional intelligence—being aware of feelings, knowing the causes of feelings and how they change over time, being able to express feelings, being able to induce feelings in others, and even having the tacit knowledge of how and why emotions are tied up with cultural forms. Whether in drama and literature or in organizations, symbols and stories appeal to and often operate through emotions.

## CONCLUSIONS

The present analysis suggests that, at a minimum, emotions and emotional intelligence are worthy of consideration in the leadership domain. Emotional intelligence has the potential to contribute to effective leadership in multiple ways, some of which have been illuminated in this paper. At this point, a skeptic might ask, "But why is this so relevant to leadership per se?" The special relevance to leadership revolves around the fact that leadership is an emotion-laden process, both from a leader and a follower perspective.

Clearly, what is needed now is empirical research which tests the ideas proposed in this paper. Given the complexities of the issues involved, both qualitative and quantitative methodologies hold promise for exploring the ways in which emotional intelligence may contribute to leader effectiveness, as theorized in this paper. Meaningful quantitative investigations could take place in both field and laboratory settings as well as through the use of management simulations. Additionally, given the stage of development of theorizing and research on emotional intelligence, I would like to point out that there are several measures of emotional intelligence that have been developed and could be used to measure the emotional intelligence levels of research participants (e.g. Mayer et al., 1997; Salovey et al., 1995).

A caveat concerning the current analysis is that it has focused primarily on leaders and it has been argued that leadership theory and research would benefit from consideration of a more follower-centered approach (e.g. Meindl, 1990, 1993; Meindl et al., 1985). In this regard, the study of emotional intelligence and leadership would benefit from the consideration of emotional intelligence in followers and its effects on the leadership process. Additionally, and from a symbolic interactionist perspective, it would be interesting to explore how interactions between leaders and followers result in the creation and management of emotions in a work setting.

All in all, investigating how leaders' capabilities in the emotion domain or their emotional intelligence contribute to their effectiveness certainly seems worthy of future empirical research and theorizing. Hopefully, the current analysis has provided researchers with some guidance in this regard.

## References

Albrow, M. Sine ira et studio—or do organizations have feelings? *Organization Studies,* 1992, *13,* 313–29.

Alvesson, M. Leadership as social integrative action: A study of a computer consultancy company. *Organization Studies,* 1992, *13,* 185–209.

Apfel, R. J. & Sifneos, P. E Alexithymia: Concept and measurement. *Psychotherapy and Psychosomatics,* 1979, *32,* 180–90.

Aronson, E. & Linder, D. Gain and loss of esteem as determinants of interpersonal attractiveness. *Journal of Experimental Social Psychology,* 1965 *1,* 156–71.

Ashforth, B. E. & Humphrey, R. H. Emotion in the workplace: A reappraisal. *Human Relations,* 1995, *48,* 97–125.

Bass, B. M. *Bass and Stogdill's handbook of leadership: Theory, research, and managerial applications* (3rd ed.). New York: Free Press, 1990.

Batson, C. D. Prosocial motivation: Is it ever truly altruistic? In L. Berkowitz (Ed.), *Advances in experimental social psychology*. Vol. 20. New York: Academic Press, 1987, pp. 65–122.

Bower, G. H. Mood and memory. *American Psychologist,* 1981, *36,* 129–48.

Bower, G. H. Mood congruity of social judgments. In J.P. Forgas (Ed.), *Emotion and social judgments*. Elmsford, NY: Pergamon Press, 1991, pp. 31–53.

Bower, G. H. & Cohen, P. R. Emotional influences in memory and thinking: Data and theory. In M. S. Clark and S. T. Fiske (Eds), *Affect and cognition: The Seventeenth Annual Carnegie Symposium on Cognition.* Hillsdale, NJ: Erlbaum, 1982, pp. 291–331.

Buck, R. Individual differences in nonverbal sending accuracy and electrodermal responding: The externalizing-internalizing dimension. In R. Rosenthal (Ed.), *Skill in nonverbal communication: Individual differences.*

Cambridge, MA: Olegeshlager, Gunn, & Hain, 1979, pp. 140–70.

Buck, R. *The communication of emotion.* New York: Guilford Press, 1984.

Campbell, R. J., Kagan, N. I. & Krathwohl, D. R. The development and validation of a scale to measure affective sensitivity (empathy). *Journal of Counseling Psychology,* 1971, *18,* 407–12.

Clark, M. S. & Isen, A. M. Toward understanding the relationship between feeling states and social behavior. In A. Hastorf and A. M. Isen (Eds), *Cognitive social psychology*. New York: Elsevier, 1982, pp. 73–108.

Clark, M. S. & Waddell, B. A. Effects of moods on thoughts about helping, attraction and information acquisition. *Social Psychology Quarterly,* 1983, *46,* 31–5.

Clore, G.L. & Parrott, G. Moods and their vicissitudes: Thoughts and feelings as information. In J. P. Forgas (Ed.), *Emotion and social judgments*. Elmsford, NY: Pergamon Press, 1991, pp. 107–23.

Conger, J. A. & Kanungo, R. N. *Charismatic leadership in organizations*. Thousand Oaks, CA: Sage, 1998.

Cunningham, M. R., Steinberg, J. & Grev, R. Wanting to and having to help: Separate motivations for positive mood and guilt-induced helping. *Journal of Personality and Social Psychology,* 1980, *38,* 181–92.

Damasio, A. R. *Descartes' error*. New York: G. P. Putnam's Sons, 1994.

Esterbrook, J. A. The effects of emotion on cue utilization and the organization of behavior. *Psychological Review,* 1959, *66,* 183–200.

Ekman, P. Cross culture studies of facial expression. In P. Ekman (Ed.) *Darwin and facial expression: A century of research in review.* New York: Academic Press, 1973, pp. 169–222.

Emmons, R. A. & Colby, P. M. Emotional conflict and well-being: Relation to perceived availability, daily utilization, and observer reports of social support. *Journal of Personality and Social Psychology,* 1995, *68,* 947–59.

Epstein, S. Cognitive-experiential self-theory. In L. Pervin (Ed.), *Handbook of personality theory and research.* New York: Guilford Press, 1990, pp. 165–91.

Epstein, S. & Meier, P. Constructive thinking: A broad coping variable with specific components. *Journal of Personality and Social Psychology,* 1989, *57,* 332–50.

Fiedler, K. On the task, the measures and the mood in research on affect and social cognition. In J. P. Forgas (Ed.), *Emotion and social judgments*. Elmsford, NY: Pergamon Press, 1991, pp. 83–104.

Fiedler, F. E. & House, R. J. Leadership theory and research: A report of progress. In C. L. Cooper and I. T. Robertson (Eds), *Key reviews in managerial psychology*. New York: John Wiley & Sons, 1994, pp. 97–116.

Fineman, S. (Ed.) *Emotion in organizations*. London: Sage, 1993.

Ford, M. E. & Tisak, M. S. A further search for social intelligence. *Journal of Educational Psychology,* 1983, *75,* 196–206.

Forgas, J. P. Affect in social judgments and decisions: A multi-process model. In M. Zanna (Ed.), *Advances in experimental and social psychology,* Vol. 25. San Diego, CA: Academic Press, 1992a, pp. 227–75.

Forgas, J. P. On bad mood and peculiar people: Affect and person typicality in impression formation. *Journal of Personality and Social Psychology,* 1992b, *62,* 863–75.

Forgas, J. P. On making sense of odd couples: Mood effects on the perception of mismatched relationships. *Personality and Social Psychology Bulletin,* 1993, *19,* 59–71.

Forgas, J.P. Sad and guilty? Affective influences on the explanation of conflict episodes. *Journal of Personality and Social Psychology,* 1994, *66,* 56–68.

Forgas, J. P. Mood and judgment: The affect infusion model. *Psychological Bulletin,* 1995, *117,* 39–66.

Forgas, J. P. & Bower, G. H. Mood effects on person perception judgments. *Journal of Personality and Social Psychology,* 1987, *53,* 53–60.

Forgas, J. P., Bower, G. H. & Krantz, S. E. The influence of mood on perceptions of social interactions. *Journal of Experimental Social Psychology,* 1984, *20,* 497–513.

Forgas, J. P., Bower, G. H. & Moylan, S. J. Praise or blame? Affective influences on attributions for achievement. *Journal of Personality and Social Psychology,* 1990, *59,* 809–19.

Friedman, H. S., Prince, L. M., Riggio, R. E. & Dimatteo, M. R. Understanding and assessing nonverbal expressiveness: The affective communication test. *Journal of Personality and Social Psychology,* 1980, *39,* 333–51.

Frigda, N. H. The laws of emotion. *American Psychologist,* 1988, *43,*349–58.

Gardner, W. L. & Avolio, B. J. The charismatic relationship: A dramaturgical perspective. *Academy of Management Review,* 1998, *23,* 32–58.

George, J. M. State or trait: Effects of positive mood on prosocial behaviors at work. *Journal of Applied Psychology,* 1991, *76,* 299–307.

George, J. M. Leader positive mood and group performance: The case of customer service. *Journal of Applied Social Psychology,* 1995, *25,* 778–94.

George, J. M. Trait and state affect. In K. R. Murphy (Ed.), *Individual differences and behavior in organizations.* San Francisco, CA: Jossey-Bass, 1996, pp. 145–71.

George, J. M. & Bettenhausen, K. Understanding prosocial behavior, sales performance, and turnover: A group level analysis in a service context. *Journal of Applied Psychology,* 1990, *75,* 698–709.

George, J. M. & Brief, A. P. Feeling good—doing good: A conceptual analysis of the mood at work—organizational spontaneity relationship. *Psychological Bulletin,* 1992, *112,* 310–29.

George, J.M. & Brief, A.P. Motivational agendas in the workplace: The effects of feelings on focus of attention and work motivation. In B.M. Staw and L.L. Cummings (Eds), *Research in organizational behavior,* Vol. 18. Greenwich, CT: JAI Press, 1996, pp. 75–109.

Gerstner, C. R. & Day, D. V. Meta-analytic review of leader-member exchange theory: Correlates and construct issues. *Journal of Applied Psychology,* 1997, *82,* 827–44.

Goleman, D. *Emotional intelligence.* New York: Bantam Books, 1995.

Graen, G. B. & Uhl-Bien, M. Relationship-based approach to leadership: Development of leader–member exchange (LMX) theory over 25 years: Applying a multi-level multi-domain perspective. *Leadership Quarterly,* 1995, *6,* 219–47.

Harris, S. G. & Sutton, R. I. Functions of parting ceremonies in dying organizations. *Academy of Management Journal,* 1986, *29,* 5–30.

Hochschild, A. R. *The managed heart: The commercialization of human feeling.* Berkeley, CA: University of California Press, 1983.

House, R. J. Leadership in the twenty-first century. In A. Howard (Ed.), *The changing nature of work.* San Francisco: Jossey-Bass, 1995, pp. 411–555.

Ilgen, D. R. & Klein, H. J. Organizational behavior. In M.R. Rosenzweig & L.W. Porter (Ed), *Annual Review of Psychology,* Vol. 40. Palo Alto, CA: Annual Reviews, 1989, pp. 327–51.

Isen, A. M. Towards understanding the role of affect in cognition. In R. S. Wyer and T. K. Srull (Eds), *Handbook of social cognition,* Vol. 3. Hillsdale, NJ: Erlbaum 1984, pp. 179–236.

Isen, A. M. Positive affect, cognitive processes and social behavior. In L. Berkowitz (Ed.), *Advances in experimental social psychology,* Vol. 20. San Diego, CA: Academic Press, 1987, pp. 203–53.

Isen, A. M. & Baron, R. A. Positive affect as a factor in organizational behavior. In B. M. Staw and L. L. Cummings (Eds), *Research in organizational behavior,* Vol. 13. Greenwich, CT: JAI Press, 1991, pp. 1–54.

Isen, A. M. & Daubman, K. A. The influence of affect on categorization. *Journal of Personality and Social Psychology,* 1984, *47,* 1206–17.

Isen, A. M. & Levin, P. F. The effect of feeling good on helping: Cookies and kindness. *Journal of Personality and Social Psychology,* 1972, *21,* 384–88.

Isen, A. M. & Shalker, T. E. The influence of mood state on evaluation of positive, neutral, and negative stimuli. *Social Psychology Quarterly,* 1982, *45,* 58–63.

Isen, A. M., Clark, M. & Schwartz, M. F. Duration of the effect of good mood on helping: 'Footprints on the sands of time'. *Journal of Personality and Social Psychology,* 1976, *34,* 385–93.

Isen, A. M., Daubman, K. A. & Nowicki, G. P. Positive affect facilitates creative problem solving. *Journal of Personality and Social Psychology,* 1987, *52,* 1122–31.

Isen, A.M., Johnson, M.M.S., Mertz, E & Robinson, G.F. The influence of positive affect on the unusualness of word associations. *Journal of Personality and Social Psychology,* 1985, *48,* 1413–26.

Isen, A. M., Shalker, T. E., Clark, M. Karp, L. Affect, accessibility of material in memory, and behavior: A cognitive loop? *Journal of Personality and Social Psychology,* 1978, *36,* 1–12.

Isenberg, D. J. How senior managers think. *Harvard Business Review,* 1984, November–December, 81–90.

Jones, G. R. & George, J. M. The experience and evolution of trust: Implications for cooperation and teamwork. *Academy of Management Review,* 1998, *23,* 531–46.

Kanter, R. M. *The change masters.* New York: Simon & Schuster, 1983.

Katz, I. M. & Campbell, J. D. Ambivalence over emotional expression and well-being: Nomothetic and idiographic tests of the stress-buffering hypothesis. *Journal of Personality and Social Psychology,* 1994, *67,* 513–24.

Katz, L. & Epstein, S. Constructive thinking and coping with laboratory-induced stress. *Journal of Personality and Social Psychology,* 1991, *61,* 789–800.

Kavanagh, D. J. & Bower, G. H. Mood and self-efficacy: Impact of joy and sadness on perceived capabilities. *Cognitive Therapy and Research,* 1985, *9,* 507–25.

Kessler, R. C., Price, R. H. & Wortman, C. B. Social factors in psychopathology: Stress, social support, and coping processes. *Annual Review of Psychology,* 1985, *36,* 531–72.

King, L. A. & Emmons, R. A. Conflict over emotional expression: Psychological and physical correlates. *Journal of Personality and Social Psychology,* 1990, *58,* 864–77.

King, L. A. & Emmons, R. A. Psychological, physical, and interpersonal correlates of emotional expressiveness, conflict and control. *European Journal of Personality,* 1991, *5,* 131–50.

Kirkpatrick, S. A. & Locke, E. A. Leadership: Do traits matter? *Academy of Management Executive,* 1991, *5*(2), 48–60.

Krystal, J. H., Giller, E. L. & Cicchetti, D. V. Assessment of alexithymia in post-traumatic stress disorder and somatic illness: Introduction of a reliable measure. *Psychosomatic Medicine,* 1986, *48,* 84–91.

Legree, P. J. Evidence for an oblique social intelligence factor established with a Likert-based testing procedure. *Intelligence,* 1995, *21,* 247–66.

Leventhal, H. & Tomarken, A. J. Emotion: Today's problem. *Annual Review of Psychology,* 1986, *37,* 565–610.

Lindholm, C. *Charisma.* Cambridge, MA: Basil Blackwell, 1990.

Locke, E. A. *The essence of leadership.* New York: Lexington Books, 1991.

McCall, M. W. & Kaplan, R. E. *Whatever it takes: Decision makers at work.* Englewood Cliffs, NJ: Prentice-Hall, 1985.

Mandler, G. *Mind and emotion.* New York: Wiley, 1975.

Mayer, J. D. How mood influences cognition. In N. E. Sharkey (Ed.), *Advances in cognitive science,* Vol. 1. Chichester: Ellis Horwood, 1986, pp. 290–314.

Mayer, J. D. & Geher, G. Emotional intelligence and the identification of emotion. *Intelligence,* 1996, *22,* 89–113.

Mayer, J. D. & Salovey, P. The intelligence of emotional intelligence. *Intelligence,* 1993, *17,* 433–42.

Mayer, J. D. & Salovey, P. Emotional intelligence and the construction and regulation of feelings. *Applied and Preventive Psychology,* 1995, *4,* 197–208.

Mayer, J. D. & Salovey, P. What is emotional intelligence: Implications for educators. In P. Salovey and D. Sluyter (Eds), *Emotional development, emotional literacy, and emotional intelligence.* New York: Basic Books, 1997, pp. 3–31.

Mayer, J. D., DiPaolo, M. & Salovey, P. Perceiving affective content in ambiguous visual stimuli: A component of emotional intelligence. *Journal of Personality Assessment,* 1990, *54,* 772–81.

Mayer, J. D., Salovey, P. & Caruso, D. R. Multifactor Emotional Intelligence Scale. New Caanan, CT: Unpublished manuscript, 1997.

Mayer, J. D., Salovey, P. & Caruso, D. Competing models of emotional intelligence. In R. J. Sternberg (Ed.), *Handbook of human intelligence.* New York: Cambridge, in press.

Mayer, J. D., Salovey, P., Gomberg-Kaufman, S. & Blainey, K. A broader conception of mood experience. *Journal of Personality and Social Psychology,* 1991, *60,* 100–11.

Megerian, L. E. & Sosik, J. J. An affair of the heart: Emotional intelligence and transformational leadership. *Journal of Leadership Studies,* 1996, *3*(3), 31–48.

Mehrabian, A. & Epstein, N. A measure of emotional empathy. *Journal of Personality,* 1972, *40,* 525–43.

Meindl, J. R. On leadership: An alternative to the conventional wisdom. In B. M. Staw and L. L. Cummings (Eds), *Research in organizational behavior,* Vol. 12. Greenwich, CT: JAI Press, 1990, pp. 159–203.

Meindl, J. R. Reinventing leadership: A radical social psychological approach. In J. K. Murnighan (Ed.), *Social psychology in organizations.* Englewood Cliffs, NJ: Prentice Hall, 1993, pp. 89–118.

Meindl, J. R., Ehrlich S. B. & Dukerich, J. M. The romance of leadership. *Administrative Science Quarterly,* 1985, 30, 78–102.

Mintzberg, H. *The nature of managerial work.* New York: Harper & Row, 1973.

Mischel, W., Ebbesen, E. & Zeiss, A. Selective attention to the self: Situational and dispositional determinants. *Journal of Personality and Social Psychology,* 1973, *27,* 204–18.

Morris, W. N. *Mood: The frame of mind.* New York: Springer-Verlag, 1989.

Morris, W. N. & Reilly, N. P. Toward the self-regulation of mood: Theory and research. *Motivation and Emotion,* 1987, *11,* 215–49.

Murray, N., Sujan, H., Hirt, E. R. & Sujan, M. The influence of mood on categorization: A cognitive flexibility interpretation. *Journal of Personality and Social Psychology,* 1990, *59,* 411–25.

Rafaeli, A. & Sutton, R. I. Expression of emotion as part of the work role. *Academy of Management Review,* 1987, *12,* 23–37.

Rafaeli, A. & Sutton, R. I. The expression of emotion in organizational life. In B. M. Staw and L. L. Cummings (Eds), *Research in organizational behavior,* Vol. 11. Greenwich, CT: JAI Press, 1989, pp. 1–42.

Rokeach, M. *The nature of human values.* New York: Free Press, 1973.

Rosenhan, D. L., Salovey, P. & Hargis, K. The joys of helping: Focus of attention mediates the impact of positive affect on altruism. *Journal of Personality and Social Psychology,* 1981, *40,* 899–905.

Salovey, P. & Birnbaum, D. Influence of mood on health-relevant cognitions. *Journal of Personality and Social Psychology,* 1989, *57,* 539–51.

Salovey, P. & Mayer, J. D. Emotional intelligence. *Imagination, Cognition, and Personality,* 1989–90, *9,* 185–211.

Salovey, P. & Mayer, J. D. Some final thoughts about personality and intelligence. In R.J. Sternberg and P. Ruzgis (Eds), *Personality and intelligence.* Cambridge, UK: Cambridge University Press, 1994, pp. 303–18.

Salovey, P., Hsee, C. K. & Mayer, J. D. Emotional intelligence and the self-regulation of affect. In D. M. Wegner and J. W. Pennebaker (Eds), *Handbook of mental control.* Englewood Cliffs, NJ: Prentice Hall, 1993, pp. 258–77.

Salovey, P., Mayer, J. D., Goldman, S. L., Turvey, C. & Palfai, T. P. Emotional attention, clarity, and repair: Exploring emotional intelligence using the trait meta-mood scale. In J. W. Pennebaker (Ed.), *Emotion, disclosure, and health.* Washington, DC: American Psychological Association, 1995, pp. 125–54.

Schwarz, N. Feelings as information: Informational and motivational functions of affective states. In E. T. Higgins and R. M. Sorrentino (Eds), *Handbook of motivation and cognition: Foundations of social behavior,* Vol. 2. New York: Guilford Press, 1990, pp. 527–61.

Schwarz, N. & Bless, H. Happy and mindless, but sad and smart? The impact of affective states on analytic reasoning. In J. P. Forgas (Ed.), *Emotion and social judgements.* Elmsford, NY: Pergamon Press, 1991, pp. 55–71.

Schwarz, N. & Clore, G. L. How do I feel about it? The informative function of affective states. In K. Fiedler and J. Forgas (Eds), *Affect, cognition and social behavior.* Lewiston, NY: C. J. Hogrefe, 1988, pp. 44–62.

Sifneos, P. E. The presence of 'alexithymic' characteristics in psychosomatic patients. *Psychotherapy and Psychosomatics,* 1973, *22,* 225–62.

Simon, H. A. Comments. In M. S. Clark and S. T. Fiske (Eds), *Affect and cognition.* Hillsdale, NJ: Erlbaum, 1982, pp. 333–42.

Sinclair, R. C. Mood, categorization breadth, and performance appraisal: The effects of order of information acquisition and effective state on halo, accuracy, information retrieval, and evaluations. *Organizational Behavior and Human Decision Processes,* 1988, *42,* 22–46.

Sinclair, R. C. & Mark, M. M. The influence of mood state on judgement and action: Effects on persuasion, categorization, social justice, person perception, and judgmental accuracy. In L. L. Martin and A. Tesser (Eds), *The construction of social judgment.* Hillsdale, NJ: Erlbaum, 1992, pp. 165–93.

Singer, J. A. & Salovey, P. Mood and memory: Evaluating the network theory of affect. *Clinical Psychology Review,* 1988, *8,* 211–51.

Sternberg, R. L. & Smith, C. Social intelligence and decoding skills in nonverbal communication. *Social Cognition,* 1985, *3,* 168–92.

Taylor, G. J. Alexithymia: Concept, measurement, and implications for treatment. *American Journal of Psychiatry,* 1984, *141,* 725–32.

Teasdale, J. D. & Fogarty, S. J. Differential effect of induced mood on retrieval of pleasant and unpleasant events from episodic memory. *Journal of Abnormal Psychology,* 1979, *88,* 248–57.

Tellegen, A. Structures of mood and personality and their relevance to assessing anxiety, with an emphasis on self-report. In A. H. Tuma and J. D. Maser (Eds), *Anxiety and the anxiety disorders.* Hillsdale, NJ: Erlbaum, 1985, pp. 681–706.

Thayer-Singer, M. Psychological dimensions in psychosomatic patients. *Psychotherapy and Psychosomatics,* 1977, *28,* 13–27.

Thoits, P. Social support as coping assistance. *Journal of Consulting and Clinical Psychology,* 1986, *54,* 416–23.

Trice, H. M. & Beyer, J. M. *The cultures of work organizations.* Englewood Cliffs, NJ: Prentice Hall, 1993.

Van Maanen, J. & Kunda, G. 'Real feelings': Emotional expression and organizational culture. In B. M. Staw and L. L. Cummings (Eds), *Research in Organizational Behavior,* Vol. 11. Greenwich, CT: JAI Press, 1989, pp. 43–103.

Walker, R. E. & Foley, J. M. Social intelligence: Its history and measurement. *Psychological Reports,* 1973, *33,* 839–64.

Wasielewski, P. L. The emotional basis of charisma. *Symbolic Interactionism,* 1985, *8,* 207–22.

Wispe, L. G. The distinction between sympathy and empathy: To call forth a concept, a word is needed. *Journal of Personality and Social Psychology,* 1986, *50,* 314–21.

Wong, C. T., Day, J. D., Maxwell, S. E. & Meara, N. M. A multitrait-multimethod study of academic and social intelligence in college students. *Journal of Educational Psychology,* 1995, *87,* 117–33.

Yukl, G. *Leadership in organizations* (4th ed.) Upper Saddle River, NJ: Prentice Hall, 1998.

Yukl, G. & Van Fleet, D. D. Theory and research on leadership in organizations. In M. D. Dunnette and L. M. Hough (Eds), *Handbook of Industrial and Organizational Psychology,* Vol. 3. Palo Alto, CA: Consulting Psychologists Press, 1992, pp. 147–97.

# Chapter **Four**

# Leadership and the Role of Gender

The past two decades have been characterized by significant increases in the number of women in business and other professional careers such as law and medicine. Accompanying this trend there has been an increase in the number of women occupying leadership positions as well as managerial (administrative) positions in work organizations.

In recent years, leadership scholars have attempted to address the issue of sex-based and gender role differences within the context of leadership. There has been an interest, for example, in the effects of sex and gender role in terms of leader emergence, leadership style, uses of power, and effectiveness.

The first reading in this chapter by Russell L. Kent and Sherry E. Moss (1994) examines the effects of sex and gender role on leader emergence. They note that whereas prior research revealed that men were more likely to emerge as leaders than women, the results from their study show that women are slightly more likely to emerge as leaders than men. Stronger effects, however, were produced for gender role than for biologically-based sex differences. Individuals characterized by androgynous and/or masculine attributes were more likely to emerge as leaders than those with feminine attributes. The self-assessment exercise appearing at the end of this chapter opener provides you with an opportunity to profile your gender characteristics.

Alice H. Eagly and Blair T. Johnson (1990), in the second reading, review the arguments given for expecting an absence (and presence) of sex differences in leadership style. They also conduct a statistical (meta) analysis of a number of research studies that have attempted to address the question, Is there a difference in the leadership style of men and women? Although this study uncovers gender-related leadership style patterns, it is yet unclear whether the behaviors observed are primarily caused by different sex-based traits, perceived role requirements, or other task and environmental factors.

Returning to our leadership process model (see Figure 4.1), the discussion of gender, together with our discussion of traits presented in Chapter 3 provides further insight into the leadership process through an expanded understanding of "the leader."

In the next chapter, we will address the issue of leader emergence. While we will not discuss the role of gender per se in that discussion, it will be important to keep in mind what you have learned regarding the role of gender.

**FIGURE 4.1**
**The Leadership**
**Process: Gender**

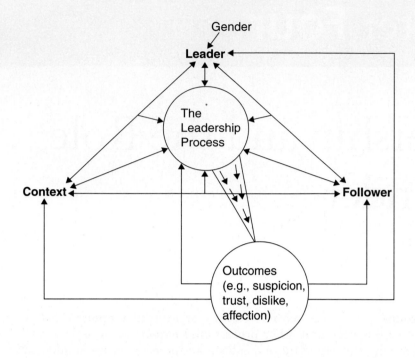

**EXERCISE**
*Self-Assessment*

**Masculinity-Femininity**

**Instructions:** Please indicate how well each of the characteristics presented below describes you.

|  | Never, or Almost Never True | | | | | Always, or Almost Always True | |
|---|---|---|---|---|---|---|---|
| 1. Defends own beliefs | 1 | 2 | 3 | 4 | 5 | 6 | 7 |
| 2. Cheerful | 1 | 2 | 3 | 4 | 5 | 6 | 7 |
| 3. Controlling | 1 | 2 | 3 | 4 | 5 | 6 | 7 |
| 4. Affectionate | 1 | 2 | 3 | 4 | 5 | 6 | 7 |
| 5. Assertive | 1 | 2 | 3 | 4 | 5 | 6 | 7 |
| 6. Intuitive | 1 | 2 | 3 | 4 | 5 | 6 | 7 |
| 7. Loyal | 1 | 2 | 3 | 4 | 5 | 6 | 7 |
| 8. Analytical | 1 | 2 | 3 | 4 | 5 | 6 | 7 |
| 9. Winning | 1 | 2 | 3 | 4 | 5 | 6 | 7 |
| 10. Sympathetic | 1 | 2 | 3 | 4 | 5 | 6 | 7 |
| 11. Willing to take risks | 1 | 2 | 3 | 4 | 5 | 6 | 7 |
| 12. Empathic | 1 | 2 | 3 | 4 | 5 | 6 | 7 |
| 13. Sensitive to the needs of others | 1 | 2 | 3 | 4 | 5 | 6 | 7 |
| 14. Understanding | 1 | 2 | 3 | 4 | 5 | 6 | 7 |
| 15. Rational | 1 | 2 | 3 | 4 | 5 | 6 | 7 |
| 16. Makes decisions easily | 1 | 2 | 3 | 4 | 5 | 6 | 7 |
| 17. Aggressive | 1 | 2 | 3 | 4 | 5 | 6 | 7 |
| 18. Collaborative | 1 | 2 | 3 | 4 | 5 | 6 | 7 |
| 19. Gullible | 1 | 2 | 3 | 4 | 5 | 6 | 7 |
| 20. Competitive | 1 | 2 | 3 | 4 | 5 | 6 | 7 |
| 21. Willing to take a stand | 1 | 2 | 3 | 4 | 5 | 6 | 7 |
| 22. Gentle | 1 | 2 | 3 | 4 | 5 | 6 | 7 |

**Scoring:** The Bem Sex-Role Inventory (BSRI) provides three (3) scores—masculinity, femininity, and androgyny. (What follows reflects a modification of the scoring instructions for the BSRI, employed here for the ease of in-class assessment and utilization.)

*Masculinity* consists of the following items: 1, 5, 8, 11, 16, 17, 20, and 21.
   Sum your response to each of these 8 items for your *masculinity* score.
   My masculinity score is _____.

*Femininity* consists of the following items: 2, 4, 7, 10, 13, 14, 19, and 22.
   Sum your response to each of these 8 items for your *femininity* score.
   My femininity score is _____.

The following are neutral items: 3, 6, 9, 12, 15, and 18. You do not need to sum your responses to these items.

Your *androgyny* score is the arithmetic difference between your masculinity score and your femininity score.
   My androgyny score is _____.

**Interpretation:** The masculinity and femininity scores indicate the extent to which a person employs masculine and feminine personality characteristics as self-descriptive. Your scores do *not* have any known connection to your biological sex, nor are your scores intended to reflect something that is "right or wrong," "good or bad." Instead, masculinity is characterized by (*a*) a high score reflecting the endorsement of the masculine attributes, and (*b*) a low score reflecting the simultaneous rejection of the feminine attributes. Similarly, femininity is reflected by (*a*) a high score endorsing the feminine attributes as self-descriptive, and (*b*) a low score reflecting the simultaneous rejection of the masculine attributes. Finally, the closer the true androgyny score (without regard to sign) is to zero, the more the person is androgynous. Lower androgyny scores reflect the equal endorsement of both masculine and feminine attributes.

*(continued)*

A person is "sex-typed"—masculine or feminine—to the extent that the difference score is large, and androgynous, to the extent that the difference score is low. Your masculinity and femininity scores may range from a low of 8 to a high of 56. Your difference scores can range from a low of 0 to a high of 48. The closer your difference score is to 0, the more your orientation is assessed as androgynous. The closer your difference score is to 48, the more you are assessed as endorsing either masculine or feminine attributes (the masculine versus feminine distinction is determined by the higher of the two masculine/feminine assessments). A difference score of 40 and greater might be seen as reflecting a strong masculine or feminine self-description, while a difference score of 8 or less might be seen as reflecting a strong androgynous self-description.

My sex-type orientation is _____.

Unlike many, who see masculinity and femininity as bipolar ends of a single dimension, such that a person is either masculine or feminine in orientation, Bem (1974) suggests that people can be androgynous. Androgynous individuals are both masculine and feminine in orientation—both assertive and yielding, both instrumental and expressive, dependent upon the situational appropriateness of a particular behavior. Bem's measure of "psychological androgyny" characterizes a person as either masculine, feminine, or androgynous as a function of one's endorsement of masculine and feminine personality characteristics as self-descriptive.

The reading in this chapter by Kent and Moss (1994) reports on the effects of sex and gender role on leader emergence. Based upon their North American study conducted in the early 1990s, they report that "androgynous and masculine subjects were the most likely to emerge as leaders" (p.1335).

---

Source: The eight masculinity and eight femininity items are presented here for illustrative purposes. They are a subset of the full instrument. The response scale and scoring instructions are reflective of the procedure employed in the Bem Sex-Role Inventory to assess masculinity, femininity, and androgyny.

Reproduced by special permission of the Distributor, MIND GARDEN, INC., 1600 Woodside Road #202, Redwood City, CA 94061 USA www.mindgarden.com from the Bem Six Role Inventory by Sandra Bem. Copyright 1978, 1981 by Consulting Psychologists Press, Inc. All rights reserved. Further reproduction is prohibited without the Distributor's written consent.

Original source: S. L. Bem. (1974). The measurement of psychological androgyny. *Journal of Consulting and Clinical Psychology* 42, 2, pp. 155–162.

Items 3, 6, 9, 12, 15, and 18 derive from M. Loden's (1985) description of characteristics which describe "masculine and feminine leadership." They were employed here as neutral items in our illustration of Bem's Sex-Role Inventory. M. Loden. *Feminine Leadership or How to Succeed in Business without Being One of the Boys.* New York: Random House, Inc.

**Reading 12**

# Effects of Sex and Gender Role on Leader Emergence

**Russell L. Kent**
Georgia Southern University

**Sherry E. Moss**
Florida International University

A considerable amount of research has been devoted to understanding the factors associated with individuals emerging as leaders in groups (see Bass [1990] for a review). Two of these characteristics are biological sex and gender role (Goktepe & Schneier, 1989). Past research has consistently shown that men more often emerge as leaders than women (Carbonell, 1984; Megargee, 1969). This phenomenon has been attributed to internal (Terborg, 1977; Wentworth & Anderson, 1984; White, DeSanctis, & Crino, 1981) and external (Ahrons, 1976; Bowman, Worthy, & Greyson, 1965; Goodale & Hall, 1976; Powell, 1993; Weisman, Morlock, Sack, & Levine, 1976) barriers limiting women's leader emergence. However, recent evidence suggests that there have been shifts in societal acceptance of women as leaders (Sutton & Moore, 1985) and that some of the barriers that prevented women from emerging as leaders may be coming down (Brenner, Tomkiewicz, & Schein, 1989; Chusmir & Koberg, 1991).

Changes also appear to be occurring in perceptions of the importance of stereotypically masculine and feminine characteristics for leaders. Past research has overwhelmingly associated masculine characteristics with leader emergence (Fagenson, 1990; Goktepe & Schneier, 1989), but recent studies present somewhat different views. For example, Brenner and colleagues (1989) found that female managers described the "successful middle manager" as possessing both stereotypically masculine and feminine characteristics. Other studies suggest that an androgynous leadership style may help women overcome stereotypes that have prevented them from being viewed as leaders in the past (e.g., Korabik, 1990).

Given what appear to be changing perceptions of leaders, a reexamination of the characteristics of emergent leaders is appropriate. Thus, the purpose of this study was to reexamine the relationships between leader emergence and the characteristics of sex and gender role. Specifically, this study had three objectives: (1) to determine whether men are still more likely to emerge as leaders in group situations, (2) to further investigate the effects of gender role on leader emergence, and (3) to determine whether sex or gender role better predicts leader emergence.

## SEX EFFECTS

Over the past three decades, many studies of sex and leader emergence have been conducted. A classic study by Megargee (1969) examined the effects of dominance and sex on leader emergence. In what Megargee intended to be a gender-neutral task, subjects rated high on dominance, as measured by the dominance scale on the California Personality Inventory, (Gough, 1957), and working in same-sex dyads emerged as leaders 69 percent of the time. In mixed-sex dyads with high-dominance men and low-dominance women, the men emerged as leaders 88 percent of the time. However, in mixed-sex dyads with high-dominance women and low-dominance men, the women emerged as leaders only 25 percent of the time. A similar pattern of results was produced when a masculine task was used.

There have been several replications of the original Megargee (1969) study. Anticipating that shifts in societal gender-role expectations would affect the frequency of women's leader emergence, Nyquist and Spence (1986) used what they thought to be a more gender-neutral task and found similar results. In Carbonell's (1984) replication study, only 30 percent of the high-dominance women in mixed-sex pairs became leaders when a masculine task was used. Women were somewhat more likely to emerge as leaders when a feminine task was used, but not more likely than men.

A study by Wentworth and Anderson (1984) included masculine, neutral, and feminine tasks.

**Source:** Edited and reprinted with permission from the Copyright Clearance Center, *Academy of Management Journal* 37, 5 (1994), pp. 1335–1346. Copyright (1994) Academy of Management.

Using only low-dominance subjects, they found that men emerged as leaders in the masculine and neutral tasks and women emerged in the feminine tasks. Interestingly, those authors attributed women's leader emergence in the feminine tasks to task expertise but attributed men's emergence in the masculine and neutral tasks to role expectations. Thus, the researchers concluded that women must be seen as experts to be perceived as leaders, whereas men become leaders when there are no female experts because it is expected.

Fleisher and Chertkoff (1986) conducted the most recent replication of the Megargee study, using a gender-neutral task. In the critical groups pairing high-dominance women and low-dominance men, women emerged as leaders 50 percent of the time. An additional feature in this study was that half the subjects in the high-dominance female—low-dominance male dyads received feedback that the women had performed better than the men on a task-related pretest. Results indicated that the men who received this information were significantly more willing to have a female leader than those who did not receive the information. The results of Fleischer and Chertkoff (1986), Wentworth and Anderson (1984), and Carbonell (1984) suggest that women may have been slightly more likely to emerge as leaders in the 1980s than in the 1960s, but their chances of doing so were best when they were perceived as experts.

Finally, Dobbins, Long, Dedrick, and Clemons (1990), using a different research method, asked groups consisting of four subjects to work on a task that allowed them to interact for longer than was allowed in the Megargee paradigm. Upon task completion, subjects were asked to (1) choose one leader and (2) to rate each group member on the extent to which they would like him or her to be leader. Men were rated higher and chosen more often as leaders than women. Thus, even though recent research shows that barriers to female leader emergence are being lowered (Brenner et al, 1989; Chusmir & Koberg, 1991), most research supports the notion that men are still more likely to emerge as leaders than women.

## GENDER-ROLE EFFECTS

Because of traditional gender stereotypes, it appears that the possession of feminine characteristics is detrimental to leader emergence, and the possession of masculine characteristics is beneficial (Fagenson, 1990). However, with the women's movement of recent decades, the mass entrance of women into the work force, the increasing number of female managers (Powell, Posner, & Schmidt, 1984), and the societal shifts in gender-role perceptions (Helmreich, Spence, & Gibson, 1982), the formerly clear, unambiguous roles of the sexes have been blurred. In principle, the concepts of masculinity and femininity are not necessarily precise correlates of biological sex (Bem, 1974). Thus, a man or a woman may possess either masculine or feminine characteristics, or both. Given the changes in societal perceptions of the role of women and the advancement of some women into leadership positions, it is possible that women today possess more masculine characteristics than they have at any time in the past. Several studies support this contention. For example, Powell and Butterfield (1979) found that female master's in business administration (MBA) students rated themselves higher in masculinity than in femininity. Additionally, women who have chosen traditionally masculine or managerial careers have very likely rejected customary gender stereotypes (Brenner et al., 1989), are more likely to have been raised in families with full-time working mothers (Almquist, 1974), and possess attitudes uncorrelated with interest in traditional feminine professions (Tipton, 1976).

Several studies have shown masculinity to be associated with leader emergence. In a study by Goktepe and Schneier (1989), college students performed gender-neutral tasks over the course of a semester. The effects of both sex and gender role on leader emergence were assessed. The results indicated that sex had no effect on leader emergence, but gender role did. Specifically, regardless of sex, masculine subjects were more likely to emerge as leaders than feminine, androgynous, and undifferentiated individuals.

A field study by Fagenson (1990) produced similar results. Men and women in this study who were high in an organizational hierarchy were significantly higher on measures of masculinity than were lower-level workers. These significant findings emerged after the researcher had controlled for several important demographic variables.

In view of these findings, we predicted that gender identity would better explain leader emergence than sex.

Hypothesis 1: Men will more often emerge as leaders in group situations than women.

Hypothesis 2: Group members high in masculinity will emerge as leaders more frequently than those low in masculinity.

Hypothesis 3: Gender identity will account for more variance in leader emergence than biological sex.

An additional feature of our study was an attempt to further assess the relationship between gender role and leader emergence. To do this, we followed Bem's (1974) method of classifying individuals on the basis of their levels of both masculinity and femininity, since these are considered to be independent dimensions. Thus, individuals were classified as (1) masculine when they rated high on items assessing masculinity and low on those assessing femininity; (2) feminine, low masculinity, and high femininity; (3) androgynous, high masculinity, and high femininity, or (4) undifferentiated, low masculinity, and low femininity. In view of the research overwhelmingly concluding that masculinity is related to leader emergence, we hypothesized

Hypothesis 4: Individuals classified as masculine or androgynous will emerge as leaders more frequently than individuals classified as feminine or undifferentiated.

However, it was not clear whether having feminine characteristics would strengthen or weaken the prospects of leader emergence for those high in masculinity. Thus, an exploratory aspect of this study was to identify potential differences in leader emergence between masculine and androgynous subjects. . . .

## DISCUSSION

The most significant result of this study, that androgynous individuals have the same chances of emerging as leader as masculine individuals, has three important implications. First, consistent with previous studies and in support of Hypothesis 2, it is clear that masculinity is still an important predictor of leader emergence. In the correlational analysis, participants' masculinity scores were the only variables significantly associated with either measure of leader emergence. Second, contrary to previous findings, the emergence of androgynous leaders suggests that the possession of feminine characteristics does not decrease an individual's chances of emerging as a leader as long as the individual also possesses masculine characteristics. Third, as an extension, if women in other contexts are more likely to be androgynous than masculine, as they were in our study, they may have better chances of rising to leadership status. Of course, verification of this finding depends upon whether future studies find androgyny to be related to leader emergence in other settings.

The second important finding of the study, contrary to Hypothesis 1, was that women were slightly more likely than men to be perceived as leaders by group members when the percentage of women per group was controlled statistically. This finding is significantly different from the results of all other studies linking sex to leader emergence. Although some recent studies have found maleness to be less predictive of leader emergence than it has been in the past (e.g., Goktepe & Schneier, 1989), no study has found women more likely to emerge as leaders than men. However, we feel that this finding should be regarded with some caution because of the unequal distribution of women in the student groups studied here and the small amount of variance explained by sex. Future studies should control for the sex composition of subject groups in order to better assess the current status of women with respect to emergent leadership. Even though the current finding is tentative, we should consider alternatives explaining why group members were slightly more likely to perceive women than men as leaders. It is possible that female participants were perceived as leaders because they tended to be more grade conscious than men (Hornaday, Wheatley, & Hunt, 1989) and may have pushed for higher levels of group performance. Alternatively, Eagly's (1987) gender-role theory may provide some insight. Eagly suggested, and a subsequent meta-analysis confirmed, that men are more likely to emerge as leaders in task-oriented groups, but women are more likely to emerge as leaders in socially oriented groups (Eagly & Karau, 1991). Though the groups in this study were initially task-oriented, they may have developed a social component because this study allowed for extensive interaction time between group members, unlike previous studies in which group members only interacted for a few minutes. As a result, group members may have perceived the women as having considerable influence over the social components of the group. Finally, another possible explanation for this nonconvergent finding is that women are exerting their leadership abilities more today than ever before and group members are becoming more accepting of female leaders.

A third important finding was that gender role is a better predictor of leader emergence than sex. Though women were slightly more likely to be perceived by the groups as leaders, gender role explained more variance in leader emergence.

Future studies may need to focus more on gender role than on sex.

Finally, the results of self-perceptions of leadership emergence are interesting. Comparing the effects of gender role on the self- and group perceptions makes it clear that those classified as masculine and androgynous were not only more likely than feminine and undifferentiated subjects to be perceived by their groups as leaders, but were also more likely to perceive themselves as leaders. Also notable was the nonsignificant effect of sex on self-perceptions of leadership emergence, which suggests that women were as likely as men to perceive themselves as leaders. In general, it appears that those whom others perceive as leaders also perceive themselves as leaders. . . .

In summary, the results of this study suggest that androgynous individuals and women may be more likely than they were in the past to emerge as leaders in business school settings, where becoming a leader is fairly important. Although we must be cautious in generalizing our results to present business people, we feel that these changes in a college setting mean that future business people may be more accepting of female and androgynous leaders than their counterparts have been in the past. This acceptance could affect the probabilities of emergent leadership for future female and androgynous business people.

---

# References

Ahrons, C. R. 1976. Counselor's perceptions of career images of women. *Journal of Vocational Behavior,* 8: 197–207.

Almquist, E. M. 1974. Sex stereotypes in occupational choice: The case for college women. *Journal of Vocational Behavior,* 5: 13–21.

Bass, B. M. 1981. *Stogdill's handbook of leadership.* New York: Free Press.

Bass, B. M. 1990. *Handbook of leadership.* New York: Free Press.

Bem, S. L. 1974. The measurement of psychological androgyny. *Journal of Consulting and Clinical Psychology,* 42: 155–162.

Bowman, G. W., Worthy, N. B., & Greyson, S. A. 1965. Problems in review: Are women executives people? *Harvard Business Review,* 43 (4): 52–67.

Brenner, O. C., Tomkiewicz, J., & Schein, V. 1989. The relationship between sex-role stereotypes and requisite management characteristics revisited. *Academy of Management Journal,* 32: 662–669.

Carbonell, J. L. 1984. Sex roles and leadership revisited. *Journal of Applied Psychology,* 69: 44–49.

Chusmir, L. H., & Koberg, C. S. 1991. Relationship between self-confidence and sex role identity among managerial women and men. *Journal of Social Psychology,* 161: 781–790.

Dobbins, G. H., Long, W. S., Dedrick, E. J., & Clemons, T. C. 1990. The role of self-monitoring and gender on leader emergence: A laboratory and field study. *Journal of Management,* 16: 609–618.

Eagly, A. H. 1987. *Sex differences in social behavior: A social-role interpretation.* Hillsdale, NJ: Erlbaum.

Eagly, A. H., & Karau, S. J. 1991. Gender and the emergence of leaders: A meta-analysis. *Journal of Personality and Social Psychology,* 60: 685–710.

Fagenson, E. A. 1990. Perceived masculine and feminine attributes examined as a function of individuals' sex and level in the organizational power hierarchy: A test of four theoretical perspectives. *Journal of Applied Psychology,* 75: 204–211.

Fleischer, R. A., & Chertkoff, J. M. 1986. Effects of dominance and sex on leader selection in dyadic work groups. *Journal of Personality and Social Psychology,* 50: 94–99.

Goktepe, J. R., & Schneier, C. E. 1989. Role of sex, gender roles, and attraction in predicting emergent leaders. *Journal of Applied Psychology,* 74: 165–167.

Goodale, J. G., & Hall, D. T. 1976. Inheriting a career: The influence of sex, values, and parents. *Journal of Vocational Behavior,* 8: 19–30.

Gough, H. G. 1957. *Manual for the California Psychological Inventory.* Palo Alto, CA: Consulting Psychologists Press.

Helmreich, R. L., Spence, J. T., & Gibson, R. H. 1982. Sex role attitudes: 1972–1980. *Personality and Social Psychology Bulletin,* 8: 656–663.

Hornaday, R. W., Wheatley, W. J., & Hunt, T. G. 1989. Differences in performance between male and female business students. *Journal of Education for Business,* 64(6): 259–264.

Kent, R. L., & Moss, S. E. 1990. Self-monitoring as a predictor of leader emergence. *Psychological Reports,* 66: 875–881.

Korabik, K. 1990. Androgyny and leadership style. *Journal of Business Ethics,* 9: 283–292.

Megargee, E. I. 1969. Influence of sex roles on the manifestation of leadership. *Journal of Applied Psychology,* 53: 377–382.

Moss, S. E., & Kent, R. L. 1994. *The effects of self-monitoring, sex, and gender role on leader emergence.* Working paper. Florida International University, Miami.

Nyquist, L. V., & Spence, J. T. 1986. Effects of dispositional dominance and sex role expectations on leadership behaviors. *Journal of Personality and Social Psychology,* 50: 87–93.

Podsakoff, P. M., & Organ, D. W. 1986. Self-reports in organizational research: Problems and prospects. *Journal of Management,* 12: 531–544.

Powell, G. N. 1993. *Women and men in management* (2d. ed). Newbury Park, CA: Sage.

Powell, G. N., & Butterfield, D. A. 1979. The "good manager": Masculine or androgynous? *Academy of Management Journal,* 22: 395–403.

Powell, G. N., Posner, B. Z., & Schmidt, W. H. 1984. Sex effects on managerial value systems. *Human Relations,* 37: 909–921.

Sutton, C. D., & Moore, K. K. 1985. Executive women—20 years later. *Harvard Business Review,* 63(5): 43–66.

Terborg, J. R. 1977. Women in management: A research review. *Journal of Applied Psychology,* 62: 647–664.

Tipton, R. M. 1976. Attitudes towards women's roles in society and vocational interests. *Journal of Vocational Behavior,* 8: 155–165.

Weisman, C. S., Morlock, L. L., Sack, D. G., & Levine, D. M. 1976. Sex differences in response to a blocked career pathway among unaccepted medical school applicants. *Sociology of Work and Occupations,* 3: 187–208.

Wentworth, D. K., & Anderson, L. R. 1984. Emergent leadership as a function of sex and task type. *Sex Roles,* 11: 513–523.

White, M. C., DeSanctis, G., & Crino, M. D. 1981. Achievement, self-confidence, personality traits, and leadership ability: A review of literature on sex differences. *Psychological Reports,* 48: 547–569.

## Reading 13

# Gender and Leadership Style: A Meta-analysis

**Alice H. Eagly and Blair T. Johnson**
Purdue University

In recent years many social scientists, management consultants, and other writers have addressed the topic of gender and leadership style. Some authors with extensive experience in organizations who write nontechnical books for management audiences and the general public have argued for the presence of sex differences in leadership style. For example, Loden (1985) maintained that there is a masculine mode of management characterized by qualities such as competitiveness, hierarchical authority, high control for the leader, and unemotional and analytic problem solving. Loden argued that women prefer and tend to behave in terms of an alternative feminine leadership model characterized by cooperativeness, collaboration of managers and subordinates, lower control for the leader, and problem solving based on intuition and empathy as well as rationality. Loden's writing echoes the androgynous manager theme developed earlier by Sargent (1981), who accepted the idea that women and men, including those who are managers in organizations, behave stereotypically to some extent. Sargent advocated that managers of each sex adopt "the best" of the other sex's qualities to become more effective, androgynous managers. In a somewhat different rendition of this sex-difference theme, Hennig and Jardin (1977) also acknowledged sex-differentiated managerial behavior, which they ascribed to personality traits acquired in early socialization, particularly through differing male and female resolutions of the Oedipus complex.

**Source:** Edited and reprinted with permission from *Psychological Bulletin* 108 (1990), 233–256. Copyright (1990) by the American Psychological Association. Author affiliation may have changed since article was first published. Author A. H. Eagly made some additional modifications to the original article for this student audience.

This research was supported by National Science Foundation Grants BNS–8605256 and BNS–8807495. Preliminary reports of this research were presented at the Annual Meetings of the Eastern Psychological Association, April 1988; the Midwestern Psychological Association, April 1988; the International Congress of Psychology, September 1988; and the American Psychological Association, August 1989. A table showing the effect sizes and study characteristics for each study included in the meta-analysis is available from the first author.

In contrast to these generalizations about gender-stereotypic leadership styles promulgated in books written primarily for practicing managers and the general public, social scientists have generally maintained that there are in fact no reliable differences in the ways that women and men lead. Although a few social scientists have acknowledged that there is some evidence for sex differences in leadership style among research participants who have not been selected for occupancy of leadership roles in natural settings (e.g., Brown, 1979; Hollander, 1985), most have agreed that women and men who occupy leadership roles in organizations do not differ (but see Shakeshaft, 1987, for a contrasting opinion). Illustrating this consensus among social scientists are the following representative statements summarizing research comparing the styles of female and male leaders: "The preponderance of available evidence is that no consistently clear pattern of differences can be discerned in the supervisory style of female as compared to male leaders" (Bass, 1981, p. 499); "Contrary to notions about sex specialization in leadership styles, women leaders appear to behave in similar fashion to their male colleagues" (Nieva & Gutek, 1981, p. 91); "There is as yet no research evidence that makes a case for sex differences in either leadership aptitude or style" (Kanter, 1977a, p. 199); "In general, comparative research indicates that there are few differences in the leadership styles of female and male designated leaders" (Bartol & Martin, 1986, p. 278).

Underlying this divergence in the opinions voiced in popular and social scientific writings is the fact that authors in these two camps have based their conclusions on quite different kinds of data. Authors such as Loden (1985) who have written books for managers and the general public based their conclusions primarily on their own experience in organizations as well as on the impressions they gleaned from interviews with practicing managers. Social scientists typically based their conclusions on more formal studies of managerial behavior in which data were gathered via questionnaires or behavioral observations and then analyzed quantitatively. In view of these contrasting methods, it is tempting for social scientists to dismiss the generalizations that are based on personal experience and interviews and to accept as valid only those conclusions that stem from more formal empirical research on leadership. However, the generalizations that social scientists appear to have accepted in this area, which stem from reviews of empirical research (e.g., Bartol & Martin, 1986), are quite vulnerable to error because of the relatively informal methods by which reviewers have drawn conclusions from the available research. With only one exception,[1] these reviews were traditional, narrative reviews and, therefore, were not based on any clear rules about how one derives conclusions from research findings. Moreover, none of the existing reviews was based on more than a small proportion of the available studies. For example, both Bartol and Martin (1986) and Dobbins and Platz (1986) based their generalizations on eight studies that compared the leadership styles of men and women, yet we located 162 studies pertaining only to the four types of leadership style we included in our meta-analysis (see *Method*). Moreover, prior reviewers did not state the criteria by which they selected their small samples of studies. As we became aware of these selection problems and of the severe underuse of available research on gender and leadership style, we decided that a thorough survey of this domain was long overdue. Our meta-analysis thus provides a systematic, quantitative integration of the available research in which the leadership styles of men and women were compared and statistical analyses were performed on the resulting data.

## THEORETICAL ANALYSIS OF SEX DIFFERENCES IN LEADERSHIP STYLES

Leaving aside the claims of both the social scientists and the management experts who have written about gender and leadership style, we face a topic of considerable complexity that we analyze from several perspectives. One of our perspectives takes into account existing knowledge about sex differences in social behaviors such as aggression, helping, and conformity as well as numerous nonverbal and communicative behaviors. Large numbers of laboratory and field studies have been performed on such behaviors, primarily by social psychologists, and in many of these studies female and male behavior has been compared. Quantitative reviews of this research have established the presence rather than the absence of overall sex differences (see overviews by Eagly, 1987; Eagly & Wood, in press; Hall, 1984). These differences, although typically not large, tend to be comparable in magnitude to most other findings reported in social psychological research. On the average, sex appears to be a variable that has neither especially impactful nor especially weak effects on social behavior and that produces findings consistent with laypeople's ideas about how the sexes differ (see Eagly, 1987).

## REASONS TO EXPECT THE ABSENCE OF SEX DIFFERENCES IN LEADERSHIP STYLE

Despite the gender-stereotypic findings generally produced in studies of social behavior, similar results would not necessarily be obtained for leaders and managers because of important differences between leadership research and typical research in social psychology. In particular, the majority of leadership studies have been performed in organizations. In contrast, most social psychological research has been carried out in experimental laboratories and to a lesser extent in field settings not embedded within organizations (e.g., on street corners). In such environments, subjects interact with strangers on a short-term basis, and the constraints of organizational and familial roles are generally minimal or absent. Consequently, there is often considerable ambiguity about how one should behave, and people may react in terms of quite global and readily observable attributes of themselves and others (e.g., sex, age, race, and general physical appearance). In situations of this type, gender roles, which are rules about how one should behave as a male or female, may provide more guidance than they otherwise would and thus produce gender-stereotypic behavior.

Behavior may be less stereotypic when women and men who occupy the same managerial role are compared because these organizational leadership roles, which typically are paid jobs, usually provide fairly clear guidelines about the conduct of behavior. Managers become socialized into their roles in the early stages of their experience in an organization (see Feldman, 1976; Graen, 1976; Terborg, 1977; Wanous, 1977). In addition, male and female managers have presumably been selected by organizations (and have selected themselves into these roles) according to the same set of organizationally relevant criteria, further decreasing the likelihood that the men and women who occupy these roles differ substantially in their style. Thus, reasonable assumptions about socialization into leadership roles and selection for these roles suggest that male and female leaders *who occupy the same organizational role* should differ very little. Managers of both sexes are presumably more concerned about managing effectively than about representing sex-differentiated features of societal gender roles.

This argument that organizational roles should override gender roles is consistent with Kanter's (1977a) structural interpretation of organizational behavior. Kanter argued that apparent sex differences in the behavior of organizational leaders are in fact a product of the differing structural positions of the sexes within organizations. Because women are more often in positions of little power or opportunity for advancement, they behave in ways that reflect their lack of power. Kanter's reasoning thus suggests that women and men who are equivalent in terms of status and power would behave similarly, even though sex differences may appear to be substantial when women and men are compared without control of their organizational status.

## REASONS TO EXPECT THE PRESENCE OF SEX DIFFERENCES IN LEADERSHIP STYLE

Despite these reasons for arguing that differences between female and male organizational leaders should be minimal, other perspectives suggest that sex differences may be common, especially in some types of leadership research. As our reasoning has already implied, the social structural rationale for the absence of differences between occupants of the same managerial role within organizations is fully consistent with the presence of differences in leadership studies that compare women and men in other circumstances. In the leadership literature, there are two major types of studies that did not examine organizational leaders—namely, laboratory experiments, usually conducted with college students, and assessment studies, which we defined as research assessing the styles of people who were not selected for occupancy of leadership positions. Because the social structural rationale for the absence of differences between women and men in the same organizational role is not relevant to studies of these two types, sex-differentiated leadership styles are likely to be prevalent in such research, just as gender-stereotypic behav-

ior is commonly found in social psychological research more generally.

There are, in addition, several reasons to suggest that male and female organizational leaders, even those who occupy the same positions, may differ to some extent in their leadership style despite the structural forces for minimizing differences that we have already noted. One such reason acknowledges the possibility of ingrained sex differences in personality traits and behavioral tendencies, differences that are not nullified by organizational selection or socialization. For example, some psychologists have maintained that sex differences in adult social behavior are in part a product of biological influences such as the greater prenatal androgynization of males (e.g., Money & Ehrhardt, 1972). Other psychologists have emphasized the importance of childhood events that are different for the sexes such as experiences that occur in sex-segregated play groups in which girls and boys play in different styles and use different methods of influencing one another (Maccoby, 1988). Thus, it is possible that biological sex differences and sex-differentiated prior experiences cause men and women to be somewhat different kinds of people, even if they do occupy the same managerial role. It may not be possible to find men and women who are so nearly equivalent that trait-level differences disappear entirely, even though sex differences in the behavior of organizational leaders may be smaller than those in the general population. In particular, men and women may come to managerial roles with a somewhat different set of skills. Especially relevant is the evidence meta-analyses have provided for women's social skills: Women as a group, when compared with men as a group, can be described as friendly, pleasant, interested in other people, expressive, and socially sensitive (see Eagly, 1987; Hall, 1984). To the extent that such findings reflect ingrained sex differences that are not leveled by organizational selection or socialization, male and female managers may behave differently, despite structural forces toward sameness.

Another perspective suggesting that leader behavior may be somewhat sex differentiated in organizations postulates *gender-role spillover,* which is "a carryover into the workplace of gender-based expectations for behavior" (Gutek & Morasch, 1982, p. 58; see also Nieva & Gutek, 1981). The spillover concept suggests that gender roles may contaminate organizational roles to some extent and cause people to have different expectations for female and male managers. In support of this idea, Russell, Rush, and Herd (1988) found that university women described an effective female (vs. male) leader as exhibiting higher levels of both the interpersonally oriented and the task-oriented aspects of leadership (i.e., higher in consideration and initiation of structure, see discussion of these variables in next subsection).[2]

Consistent with the idea that gender roles spill over to organizational roles, several social scientists have claimed that female leaders and managers experience conflict between their gender role and their leadership role (see Bass, 1981; Bayes & Newton, 1978; Kruse & Wintermantel, 1986; O'Leary, 1974). This conflict arises for female leaders because the stereotype of manager and the normative expectations associated with being a good manager include more masculine than feminine qualities (see Powell, 1988). The idea that women are subjected to incompatible expectations from the managerial and the female role thus presumes that gender roles are important within organizations.

Another manifestation of the spillover of gender roles onto organizational roles is that people who hold positions in organizations tend to have negative attitudes about women occupying managerial roles. Reflecting the subordinate status of women in the society, numerous studies have shown that people are often reluctant to have a female supervisor and think that women are somewhat less qualified for leadership and that female managers would have negative effects on morale (see reviews by O'Leary, 1974; Riger & Galligan, 1980; Terborg, 1977). Because these attitudes and beliefs raise questions about women's competence, ability to lead, and potential for advancement, female managers often face a less supportive environment than male managers. Sex differences in leadership style might result from this aspect of gender-role spillover as well as from the other aspects we have noted.

Finally, some of the fine-grained features of the structural interpretation of organizational behavior suggest other possible sources of sex differences in the behavior of organizational leaders. One such consideration is that, as Kanter (1977b) pointed out, women in managerial roles often have the status of *token* because of their rarity in such positions. Thus, female managers commonly are members of a numerically small minority, whereas their male counterparts are members of a majority group. As Kanter and others argued, token status increases one's visibility (Taylor, Fiske, Etcoff, & Ruderman, 1978) and can have a

number of negative implications for how one is perceived and treated, especially when the token is a woman (Crocker & McGraw, 1984; Ott, 1989; Yoder & Sinnett, 1985). In addition, even those female and male leaders who occupy the same organizational role may differ systematically in seniority, salary, the availability of mentoring and informal collegial support, and other characteristics that convey some of the subtleties of organizational status. Women, especially as relative newcomers in many managerial roles, tend to have less status in these ways, and this difference may be reflected in their behavior.

In summary, ingrained sex differences in traits and behavioral tendencies, a spillover of gender roles onto organizational roles, and subtle differences in the structural position of women and men could cause leadership behavior to be somewhat sex-differentiated even when occupants of the same organizational role are compared. Therefore, some evidence of sex differences in leadership style in organizational studies would not be surprising. Nonetheless, our reasoning that organizational roles are more important than gender roles led us to predict that differences between men and women occupying the same leadership role in organizations would be smaller than differences between men and women observed in other types of leadership research, namely laboratory experiments and assessment studies.

## DESIGN OF THE META-ANALYSIS

### TYPES OF LEADERSHIP STYLE

The fact that investigators have examined many facets of leadership style (see Bass, 1981) requires that reviewers decide which facets to include and how to organize them into types. In examining this issue, we found that the majority of the studies had assessed the extent to which leaders or managers were concerned with two aspects of their work. The first of these aspects we termed *task accomplishment* (or, for brevity, task style)—that is, organizing activities to perform assigned tasks. The second aspect we termed *maintenance of interpersonal relationships* (or, for brevity, interpersonal style)—that is, tending to the morale and welfare of the people in the setting.

This distinction between task and interpersonal styles was first represented in leadership research by Bales (1950), who proposed two categories of leaders, those with an orientation to task accomplishment and those with a socioemotional orientation indicative of concern for morale and relationships among group members. This distinction was developed further in the Ohio State studies on leadership (e.g., Halpin, 1957; Halpin & Winer, 1957; Hemphill & Coons, 1957; Stogdill, 1963). In this research, task orientation, labeled *initiation of structure,* included behavior such as having subordinates follow rules and procedures, maintaining high standards for performance, and making leader and subordinate roles explicit. Interpersonal orientation, labeled *consideration,* included behavior such as helping and doing favors for subordinates, looking out for their welfare, explaining procedures, and being friendly and available. Task and interpersonal orientations are typically regarded as separate, relatively orthogonal dimensions (e.g., in the Leader Behavior Description Questionnaire [LBDQ] constructed by the Ohio State researchers; Halpin & Winer, 1957). Less commonly, these orientations are treated as two ends of a single continuum (e.g., in the Least Preferred Co-Worker [LPC] instruments; Fiedler, 1967).[3]

Task and interpersonal styles in leadership research are obviously relevant to gender because of the stereotypes people have about sex differences in these aspects of behavior (see Ashmore, Del Boca, & Wohlers, 1986; Eagly & Steffen, 1984). Men are believed to be more self-assertive and motivated to master their environment (e.g., more aggressive, independent, self-sufficient, forceful, dominant). In contrast, women are believed to be more selfless and concerned with others (e.g., more kind, helpful, understanding, warm, sympathetic, aware of others' feelings). In research on gender, these two orientations have been labeled *masculine* and *feminine, instrumental* and *expressive,* and *agentic* and *communal.* Although the task and interpersonal dimensions studied in leadership research are not as broad as these very general tendencies examined in gender stereotype research, the ideas are quite similar. Therefore, leadership research provides an excellent opportunity to determine whether the behavior of leaders is gender stereotypic.

The only other aspect of leadership style studied frequently enough to allow us to represent it in our meta-analysis is the extent to which leaders (a) behave democratically and allow subordinates to participate in decision making, or (b) behave autocratically and discourage subordinates from participating in decision making.[4] The dimension of *democratic* versus *autocratic* leadership (or *participative* versus *directive* leadership) follows from early experimental studies of leadership style (e.g., Lewin & Lippitt, 1938) and has been developed since that time by a number of researchers (e.g., Likert, 1961; Vroom & Yetton, 1973). Although democratic versus autocratic style is a different (and narrower) aspect of leader behavior than task-oriented and interpersonally oriented styles (see Bass, 1981), the democratic–autocratic dimension also relates to gender stereotypes, because one component of the agentic or instrumental aspect of these stereotypes is that men are relatively dominant and controlling (i.e., more autocratic and directive than women).

## METHODS OF ASSESSING LEADERSHIP STYLE

The diversity of the methods that have been used to assess style complicates the task of integrating research in this area. Moreover, a substantial methodological literature criticizes and compares these measures (see Bass, 1981). Because the methodological issues that have been raised remain largely unresolved by leadership researchers, we did not attempt to settle these issues in order to base our meta-analytic generalizations on only those measures that we or other investigators might regard as most valid. Instead, we included all measures that researchers regarded as assessing task-oriented and interpersonally oriented styles or autocratic versus democratic style. We coded our studies on a number of these measures' features, many of which may be regarded as having implications for the quality of the measures. For example, measures differed in how directly or indirectly they assessed leadership style; the most direct measures were based on observers' coding of ongoing leadership behavior, and the most indirect measures were based on leaders' responses to questionnaire measures of attitudes or personality. Representing such features in our coding scheme (see *Method*) allowed us to determine whether they covaried with sex differences in leadership style.

## CONGENIALITY OF LEADERSHIP ROLES FOR MEN AND WOMEN

When we thought about gender in relation to the available studies of leadership style, we were struck by the variation in the extent to which the leadership roles investigated in this research (e.g., elementary school principal, nursing supervisor, military officer) would be perceived as congenial mainly for women or men. For leadership roles that are typically regarded as especially suitable for women, negative attitudes toward female leaders presumably would not be prevalent, nor would conflict between the female and the leader role be an issue. Presumably women would be under less pressure to adopt male-stereotypic styles of leadership in such positions.

To enable us to take account of the gender congeniality of leadership roles, we conducted a questionnaire study to obtain judgments of each role and analyzed these judgments to estimate the extent to which women or men were more interested in each role and believed themselves more competent to perform it. In addition, because people associate task-oriented qualities with men and interpersonally oriented qualities with women, we also determined the extent to which each role was judged to require each set of these gender-stereotypic qualities. These features of our meta-analysis allowed us to determine whether the ascription of gender-stereotypic qualities to leadership roles related to sex differences in the styles by which people carry out these roles.

## PREDICTIONS FOR META-ANALYSIS

As we have already stated, our major prediction is that gender-stereotypic sex differences in leadership style are less pronounced in organizational studies comparing occupants of the same managerial role than in leadership studies of other types. Beyond this prediction, our purposes as reviewers are primarily descriptive and exploratory, even though other predictions might follow from the issues we have discussed. For example, if, as we suggested, female managers often face a less supportive environment than do male managers, these women might strive so hard to overcome antifemale prejudices that they behave counterstereotypically as a result. Additional complexities enter if we reason that ratings of leaders' behavior could produce findings that are more stereotypic than those produced by measures grounded more firmly in behavior. Rather than set forth a series of speculative hypotheses that take these and other considerations into account, we prefer to present our review and to discuss such issues as they become relevant to interpreting our meta-analytic findings. . . .

## SUMMARY OF METHOD[5]

The method used in this project was meta-analysis. The task of meta-analyzing requires the following steps: (a) locating relevant studies and deciding whether they are appropriate for inclusion, (b) coding the studies to represent their attributes, (c) computing effect sizes to represent the studies' findings, and (d) performing statistical analyses on the effect sizes. One type of statistical analysis in this meta-analysis consisted of averaging the effect sizes to determine what the overall findings were in the studies that had compared the leadership styles of men and women. A second type of analysis consisted of using the attributes of the studies to predict the effect sizes; the point of these analyses was to find out if studies with different attributes produced different results.

Locating the studies was accomplished primarily by performing keyword searches in databases such as PsycINFO, *Dissertation Abstracts International,* and ABI/INFORM. Other studies were located by scrutinizing existing reviews in articles and books and searching through the reference lists of all of the studies that were located. We then developed decision rules for including studies, and many studies were excluded by them. For example, studies that assessed participants' *ideas* about ideal leadership styles were omitted because we were interested only in actual leadership style.

The coding of the studies was carried out by the two authors working independently. The results of their coding were then compared to assess inter-rater reliability and to catch any errors that either person made. Many features were coded, including characteristics of the report (e.g., publication date); type of study (organizational, assessment, or laboratory); level of leadership (line, middle, or higher); percentage of men among leaders and subordinates; and type of style assessed (interpersonal, task, interpersonal versus task, or democratic versus autocratic). It was also important to keep track of the identity of the raters whose data provided the measure of leadership style: The main variants were that people rated themselves, supervisors rated the leaders, subordinates rated the leaders, peers rated the leaders, or judges not related organizationally to the leaders rated the leaders. What was rated to produce a measure of leadership style also differed across the studies: The main types of ratings were responses to attitude or personality scales, responses to hypothetical leadership situations, presumed observation of a leader's behavior (e.g., subordinates rating how their supervisor typically behaved), and actual observation of a leader's behavior based on behaviors made available during the study itself.

Another important part of the method consisted of having student judges rate each leadership role that appeared in the studies of leadership style.

These ratings provided an assessment of the perceived gender congeniality of the roles—that is, whether women or men would be more comfortable in the role and more attracted to it. The means of the ratings of the role were attached to each study in the meta-analytic data set as additional characteristics of the studies. These rated variables thus provided a numerical representation of the extent to which the role in each study was more congenial to men (e.g., military officer) or more congenial to women (e.g., nursing supervisor).

For this rating task, the student judges each received a questionnaire in which leadership roles were briefly described—for example, "principal of an elementary school," "manager in the communications division of a company," "director of intercollegiate athletics in a major university," and "leader of a laboratory group trying to decide which items to take along in order to survive in a desert." Ratings were made in response to the following questions: (a) How competent would you be as a [role description given]? (b) How interested would you be in becoming a [role description given]? (c) How interested would the *average woman* be in becoming a [role description given]? (d) How interested would the *average man* be in becoming a [role description given]? (e) How much *ability to cooperate and get along with other people* is needed to be an effective [role description given]? (f) How much *ability to direct and control people* is needed to be an effective [role description given]? For the competence and interest questions, role congeniality was represented by differencing the ratings of the male and female judges. The responses to the questions about the average woman and average man were analyzed by subtracting the average woman rating from the average man rating to yield a stereotypic sex difference. The question on cooperation and getting along with others and the question on directing and controlling were used separately to estimate how much interpersonal ability and task ability each leadership role was perceived to require.

The authors calculated an effect size for each study to represent the sex difference in leadership style. If more than one type of style was assessed, more than one effect size was computed. Each effect size consisted of the difference in the leadership style of the men and women on whatever measure was used, divided by the pooled standard deviation. A positive sign was given to stereotypic differences (i.e., women more interpersonally oriented, men more task-oriented, women more democratic and less autocratic), and a negative sign to counterstereotypic differences.

## SUMMARY OF RESULTS

One component of the results consisted of a presentation of frequency distributions classifying the studies on all of the study characteristics, to display the kinds of studies that were typical or atypical of this research literature. This display showed, for example, that the majority of the studies were doctoral dissertations rather than journal articles, that most studies were organizational, that middle managers were usually examined, and that most leadership measures required people to rate themselves or subordinates to rate their supervisors. Also displayed in the results were the specific measures of leadership style used, many of which were standard, well-validated instruments.

Another component of the results consisted of averages of the effect sizes across all of the studies for each type of leadership style that had been studied. These mean sex differences showed little evidence that men and women differed in their interpersonal style or task style. However, on measures that assessed tendencies to be democratic versus autocratic or participative versus directive, men were more autocratic or directive than women, and women were more democratic or participative than men.

Because averaging effect sizes over all of the studies can obscure important results that are limited to subgroups of studies, we divided the studies into the three main types of studies that we had identified: organizational, assessment, and laboratory. We found that the absence of sex differences for task and interpersonal style that appeared in our analysis averaged over all of the studies was limited to the organizational studies. In contrast, in the laboratory studies, and to some extent in the assessment studies, men and women did have stereotypic styles, with men appearing more task-oriented and women more interpersonally oriented. However, the tendency for women to be more participative and democratic than men was intact in all three classes of studies, including the organizational. This sex difference on democratic–autocratic styles was thus quite robust. Yet, another analysis showed that in studies in which women were rare as leaders (i.e., they were numerical tokens), the tendency for them to be more participative and democratic than men eroded.

One of the most provocative findings showed the influence of the gender congeniality of the leadership roles. These are the variables that we constructed from judges' ratings of the roles.

Gender congeniality influenced sex differences in task style. If the leadership role was more congenial to men than women, men were more task-oriented than women. If the role was more congenial to women than men, women were more task-oriented than men.

## DISCUSSION

### INTERPERSONAL AND TASK STYLES

Our major hypothesis was that stereotypic sex differences would be less pronounced in organizational studies than in assessment or laboratory studies. Indeed, this hypothesis was confirmed for both interpersonal and task styles. These findings support our arguments that the criteria organizations use for selecting managers and the forces they maintain for socializing managers into their roles minimize tendencies for the sexes to lead or manage in a stereotypic manner. Yet these data also suggest that people not selected or trained for leadership roles do manifest stereotypic leadership behavior when placed in these roles, as shown by the data from the assessment and the laboratory studies. Moreover, our claim that selection criteria lessen sex differences is strengthened by the finding that those few laboratory leaders who gained their positions through emergence did not manifest the stereotypic styles of laboratory leaders who were appointed. Evidently sex differences were leveled even by the implicit leader selection criteria of initially leaderless groups.

When we ignored whether the sex comparisons were from organizational, assessment, or laboratory studies, sex differences in interpersonal and task styles were quite small, with overall trends toward women being more concerned about both maintenance of interpersonal relationships and task accomplishment. In view of these trends, it is not surprising that measures placing interpersonal and task orientation on the ends of a single dimension produced no sex difference in any of the overall summaries. On such bipolar measures, the stereotypic interpersonal sex difference and the counterstereotypic task difference would cancel one another, resulting in no difference.

Given the variety of settings, roles, and measures encountered in this research, the sex comparisons for the task and interpersonal styles were expected to be inconsistent across the studies. Yet the removal of relatively small numbers of the effect sizes (10 percent to 13 percent) produced homogeneous sets of effect sizes consistent with description in terms of single means. This aspect of the findings lends some confidence to our statements that if we take the entire research literature into account, women's leadership styles emphasize both interpersonal relations and task accomplishment to a slightly greater extent than men's styles.

### DEMOCRATIC VERSUS AUTOCRATIC STYLE

The strongest evidence we obtained for a sex difference in leadership style occurred on the tendency for women to adopt a more democratic or participative style and for men to adopt a more autocratic or directive style. Moreover, this sex difference did *not* become smaller in the organizational studies, as did the differences in the interpersonal and task styles. Although the overall mean weighted effect size ($d_+ = 0.22$) was not large, the mean became larger once outliers were removed ($d_+ = 0.27$), and 92 percent of the available comparisons went in the direction of more democratic behavior from women than men. Despite this impressive consistency in the direction of the sex difference, the effect sizes themselves were quite heterogeneous, requiring the removal of 22 percent to obtain a set that did not reject the hypothesis of homogeneity. Yet substantial inconsistency across the studies is not unexpected for this type of style in view of the tendency for investigators to construct unique measures and not to rely on standard instruments, as did most investigators of the other types of leadership style that we reviewed.

Our interpretation of the sex difference in the extent to which leaders behave democratically versus autocratically is necessarily speculative, but follows from some of the considerations that we presented early in this article (see *Reasons to Expect the Presence of Sex Differences in Leadership Style*). We thus argued that women and men recruited into leadership roles in organizations may not be equivalent in personality and behavioral tendencies, even though they satisfy the same selection criteria. In particular, we noted that women's social skills might enable them to perform managerial roles differently than men. Interpersonal behavior that is skillful (e.g., in terms of understanding others' feelings and intentions) should facilitate a managerial style that is democratic and participative. Making decisions in a collaborative style requires not only the soliciting of suggestions from one's peers and subordinates, but also the preservation of good relationships with them when evaluating and perhaps rejecting their ideas. The give-and-take of collaborative decision making introduces interpersonal complexity not encountered by leaders who behave in an autocratic or directive manner. This interpretation is supported by research showing that teachers who lacked social skills, as indexed by their relative inability to decode nonverbal cues, had more autocratic attitudes and were generally more dogmatic (Rosenthal, Hall, DiMatteo, Rogers, & Archer, 1979).

Another perspective on the democratic–autocratic sex difference acknowledges the attitudinal bias against female leaders that we considered in the beginning of the article. The skepticism that many people have expressed concerning women's capabilities in managerial and leadership roles may be exacerbated by any tendency for women in these roles to take charge in an especially authoritative manner. Placating subordinates and peers so that they accept a woman's leadership may to some extent require that she give them input into her decisions and allow some degree of control over these decisions. Moreover, to the extent that women leaders have internalized to some degree the culture's reservations about their capability for leadership, they may gain confidence as leaders by making collaborative decisions that they can determine are in line with their associates' expectations. Thus, proceeding in a participative and collaborative mode may enable many female leaders to win acceptance from others, gain self-confidence, and thereby be effective. Because men are not so constrained by attitudinal bias, they are freer to lead in an autocratic and nonparticipative manner should they so desire.[6]

## THE IMPACT OF GENDER CONGENIALITY OF LEADERSHIP ROLES AND SEX DISTRIBUTION OF ROLE OCCUPANTS

Our findings suggested that leaders of each sex emphasized task accomplishment when they were in a leadership role regarded as congruent with their gender. Thus, only the sex differences in task style were significantly correlated with the tendency for the leadership roles to be regarded as more congenial for men or women, as indexed by our questionnaire respondents' judgments. Male leaders tended to be more task oriented than female leaders to the extent that a leadership role was more congenial to men; female leaders tended to be more task oriented than male leaders to the extent that a leadership

role was more congenial to women. Furthermore, women tended to be more task oriented than men in leadership roles that are feminine in the sense that our respondents judged they require considerable interpersonal ability.[7]

These findings suggest that being out of role in gender-relevant terms has its costs for leaders in terms of some decline in their tendency to organize activities to accomplish relevant tasks. Because our meta-analytic data are not informative concerning the mediation of these effects, these provocative findings should be explored in primary research. Perhaps people who are out of role lack (or are perceived to lack) the skills necessary to organize the task-relevant aspects of their environment. Out-of-role leaders may be somewhat deficient in the knowledge and authority required to organize people and resources to accomplish task-relevant goals.

The extent to which leadership roles were male dominated numerically also related to sex differences in leadership style. Specifically, the tendencies for female leaders to be more interpersonally oriented and more democratic than male leaders weakened to the extent that a role was male dominated. Thus, when women were quite rare in leadership roles and therefore tended to have the status of token in organizations or groups, they abandoned stereotypically feminine styles characterized by concern for the morale and welfare of people in the work setting and consideration of these people's views when making decisions. These findings suggest that women may tend to lose authority if they adopt distinctively feminine styles of leadership in extremely male-dominated roles. Women who survive in such roles probably have to adopt the styles typical of male role occupants.

## CONCLUSION

The view, widely accepted by social scientists expert on leadership, that women and men lead in the same way should be very substantially revised. Similarly, the view, proclaimed in some popular books on management, that female and male leaders have distinctive, gender-stereotypic styles also requires revision. Our quantitative review has established a more complex set of findings. Although these findings require further scrutiny before they should be taken as definitive, the agreement of these findings with our role theory framework substantiates our interpretation of them. Thus, consistent with research on sex differences in numerous social behaviors (Eagly,

1987; Hall, 1984), we have established that leadership style findings generated in experimental settings tend to be gender stereotypic. Indeed, these findings concur with the generalizations of those narrative reviewers who noted that male and female leaders often differ in laboratory experiments (Brown, 1979; Hollander, 1985). In such settings, people interact as strangers without the constraints of long-term role relationships. Gender roles are moderately important influences on behavior in such contexts and tend to produce gender-stereotypic behavior (see Eagly, 1987). In addition, somewhat smaller stereotypic sex differences were obtained in assessment studies, in which people not selected for leadership responded to instruments assessing their leadership styles. Because respondents not under the constraints of managerial roles completed questionnaires in these studies, some tendency for leadership styles to appear stereotypic was expected from the perspective of our social role framework.

When social behavior is regulated by other, less diffuse social roles, as it is in organizational settings, behavior should primarily reflect the influence of these other roles and therefore lose much of its gender-stereotypic character. Indeed, the findings of this meta-analysis for interpersonal and task styles support this logic. Nonetheless, women's leadership styles were more democratic than men's even in organizational settings. This sex difference may reflect underlying differences in female and male personality or skills (e.g., women's superior social skills) or subtle differences in the status of women and men who occupy the same organizational role. Deciding among the various causes that we have discussed would require primary research targeted to this issue.

The magnitude of the aggregate effect sizes we obtained in this meta-analysis deserves comment. When interpreting effect sizes, reviewers should take the methods of the studies into account, and, as Glass, McGaw, and Smith (1981) argued, they should avoid applying numerical guidelines to identify effect sizes as small or large. One feature of research on leadership style that is especially relevant to interpreting the magnitude of our aggregate effect sizes is that investigators face many barriers to achieving well-controlled studies. In organizational studies, the environments in which managers carry out their roles are quite diverse, even within a single organization. Because managers' leadership styles are evaluated either by themselves or by their associates, the various managers in a study are not necessarily evaluated by the same standard. Although more control of environmental influences can be achieved in laboratory studies of leadership (e.g., all leaders can be observed in a similar social setting), even these studies are relatively uncontrolled because each leader interacts with a unique group of followers. Counterbalancing the greater control of environmental factors in laboratory than organizational studies is the less rigorous selection of research participants for laboratory research and the resulting greater variability of leadership style within each sex. In general, uncontrolled variability in both organizational and laboratory studies of leadership would inflate the standard deviations that are the denominators of the effect sizes and thereby decrease the magnitude of these effect sizes. As a consequence, neither sex nor other variables would ordinarily produce large effect sizes in studies of leadership style. Therefore, we believe that effect sizes of the magnitude we obtained are considerably more consequential than effect sizes of the same magnitude obtained in more controlled forms of research.

Our review has not considered the extent to which the sex differences in leadership style that we have documented might produce differences in the effectiveness of leaders. Whether men or women are more effective leaders as a consequence of their differing styles is a complex question that could be addressed meta-analytically only by taking measures of group and organizational outcomes into account along with measures of leadership style. Because experts on leader effectiveness ordinarily maintain that the effectiveness of leadership styles is contingent on features of the group or organizational environment (e.g., Fiedler, 1967; Vroom & Yetton, 1973), we are unwilling to argue that women's relatively democratic and participative style is either an advantage or disadvantage. No doubt a relatively democratic style enhances a leader's effectiveness under some circumstances.[8] Nonetheless, we note that in recent years many management and organizational consultants have criticized traditional management practices for what they believe are overly hierarchical and rigidly bureaucratic forms (Foy, 1980; Heller & Van Til, 1986; Kanter, 1983; Naisbett, 1982; Ouchi, 1981; Peters & Waterman, 1982). Moreover, it is consistent with many feminist theorists' descriptions of hierarchy and domination (e.g., Elshtain, 1981; Miller, 1976) to argue that employment would be less alienating if forms of interaction in the workplace were less hierarchical and instead characterized by cooperation and collaboration between collegial groups of coworkers. Indeed, both consultants and feminists have advocated organizational change toward the more democratic and participative leadership styles that our meta-analysis suggests are more prevalent among women than men.

## Notes

1. The one available quantitative review of sex differences in leadership style (Dobbins & Platz, 1986) unfortunately included studies with designs not suited for examining these differences. These inappropriate studies investigated bias in subjects' perceptions of leaders by equalizing the behavior of male and female leaders and varying only the leader's sex (Butterfield & Powell, 1981; Lee & Alvares, 1977). Because equivalence of male and female behavior was ensured in these studies, they cannot be regarded as assessing sex differences in leadership style.

2. Whereas the belief that effective female managers are especially concerned about relationships may reflect stereotypic beliefs about women in general, the belief that effective female managers are especially concerned about task accomplishment may reflect a more complex theory about women having to perform extremely well to succeed as managers.

3. Although the Least Preferred Co-Worker Scale has been given a variety of interpretations, the view that low-LPC people are task oriented and high-LPC people are relationship oriented seems to be the most widely accepted of these interpretations (see Rice, 1978).

4. Although Bass (1981) distinguished between (a) democratic versus autocratic leadership and (b) participative versus directive leadership, we treated these measures as a single class because we found this distinction difficult to maintain when categorizing measures. We refer to this single class as *democratic versus autocratic* style. Researchers have treated this style as a single, bipolar dimension because democratic and autocratic styles presumably are incompatible. In contrast, interpersonal and task styles apparently are not incompatible, as suggested by the preference of most researchers for treating these styles as separate, relatively orthogonal dimensions.

5. The "Summary of Method" and "Summary of Results" sections were prepared by Professor Alice Eagly exclusively for this edited version of the original publication. We sincerely appreciate her time, effort, and contribution to our work.

6. A subsequent meta-analysis by Eagly, Makhijani, and Klonsky (1990) showed that subjects evaluate autocratic behavior by female leaders more negatively than they evaluate the equivalent behavior by male leaders. An additional consideration in interpreting the democratic–autocratic sex difference is that measures of this type were based primarily on leaders' self-reports, and, at least for task and interpersonal styles, leaders' self-reports were more stereotypic than subordinates' reports on leaders (see *Results*). Thus, it is possible that the tendency for women to be more democratic than men was exaggerated somewhat by the reliance on leaders' self-reports in these studies. Yet, because the sex comparisons for the democratic versus autocratic style were more stereotypic than the subset of sex comparisons for the interpersonal and task styles that were based on self-reports, it is very unlikely that this methodological feature of the democratic–autocratic studies fully accounts for the sex difference in this type of style.

7. We explored whether a tendency for laboratory leadership roles to be more congenial for men might have contributed to the more stereotypic task styles found in laboratory (vs. organizational) studies. Indeed, our questionnaire respondents judged the laboratory (vs. organizational) roles as somewhat more congenial to men on the measures of sex differences in competence and interest and on the measure of stereotypic sex differences in interest ($ps<.05$ or smaller). In addition, the laboratory roles were judged to require less interpersonal ability than organizational roles but, contrary to the idea that the laboratory roles were relatively masculine, they were also judged to require less task ability ($ps<.001$). Thus, there was some degree of confounding between the type of study and the gender congeniality of the roles. Nonetheless, the significant relations between the congeniality measures and sex differences in task style remained significant when examined within the set of organizational studies.

8. Consistent with the position that effectiveness of leadership styles depends on a group's task and other considerations, Wood (1987) argued, based on her meta-analysis of sex differences in group performance, that women's distinctive style of social interaction facilitated group performance at tasks requiring positive social activities such as cooperation but lacked this facilitative effect for other types of tasks.

## References

Alpren, M. (1954). The development and validation of an instrument used to ascertain a school principal's pattern of behavior (Doctoral dissertation, University of Florida). *Dissertation Abstracts International 33,* 1579A.

Arcy, J. A. B. (1980). Self-perceptions of leader behavior of male and female elementary school principals in selected school districts in the midwest United States (Doctoral dissertation, Iowa State University, 1979). *Dissertation Abstracts International 40,* 3638A.

Ashmore, R. D., Del Boca, F. K., & Wohlers, A. J. (1986). Gender stereotypes. In R. D. Ashmore & F. K. Del Boca (eds.), *The social psychology of female–male relations: A critical analysis of central concepts* (pp. 69–119). Orlando, FL: Academic Press.

Bales, R. F. (1950). *Interaction process analysis: A method for the study of small groups*. Reading, MA: Addison-Wesley.

Barone, F. J. (1982). A comparative study of Theory X–Theory Y attitudes among managers and OD agents. *Dissertation Abstracts International* 42, 4260A. (University Microfilms No. 82–07, 156)

Bartol, K. M., & Martin, D. C. (1986). Women and men in task groups. In R. D. Ashmore & F. K. Del Boca (eds.), *The social psychology of female–male relations: A critical analysis of central concepts* (pp. 259–310). Orlando, FL: Academic Press.

Bass, B. M. (1981). *Stogdill's handbook of leadership: A survey of theory and research* (rev. ed.). New York: Free Press.

Baugher, S. L. (1983). Sex-typed characteristics and leadership dimensions of vocational education administrators in a midwest region of the United States (Doctoral dissertation, University of Missouri–Columbia, 1982). *Dissertation Abstracts International* 44, 22A.

Bayes, M., & Newton, P. M. (1978). Women in authority: A sociopsychological analysis. *Journal of Applied Behavioral Science* 14, 7–20.

Birdsall, P. (1980). A comparative analysis of male and female managerial communication style in two organizations. *Journal of Vocational Behavior* 16, 183–196.

Blake, R. R., & Mouton, J. S. (1964). *The managerial grid*. Houston, TX: Gulf.

Blake, R. R., & Mouton, J. S. (1978). *The new managerial grid*. Houston, TX: Gulf.

Brown, S. M. (1979). Male versus female leaders: A comparison of empirical studies. *Sex Roles* 5, 595–611.

Butterfield, D. A., & Powell, G. N. (1981). Effect of group performance, leader sex, and rater sex on ratings of leader behavior. *Organizational Behavior and Human Performance* 28, 129–141.

Carli, L. L. (1989). Gender differences in interaction style and influence. *Journal of Personality and Social Psychology* 56, 565–576.

Coleman, D. G. (1979). *Barnard's effectiveness and efficiency applied to a leader style model*. Unpublished manuscript, Northeast Missouri State University, Kirksville, MO.

Crocker, J., & McGraw, K. M. (1984). What's good for the goose is not good for the gander: Solo status as an obstacle to occupational achievement for males and females. *American Behavioral Scientist* 27, 357–369.

Crudge, J. (1983). The effect of leadership styles on the rehabilitation training of student-workers (Doctoral dissertation, United States International University, 1982). *Dissertation Abstracts International* 43, 3300A.

Dobbins, G. H. (1986). Equity vs. equality: Sex differences in leadership. *Sex Roles* 15, 513–525.

Dobbins, G. H., Pence, E. C., Orban, J. A., & Sgro, J. A. (1983). The effects of sex of the leader and sex of the subordinate on the use of organizational control policy. *Organizational Behavior and Human Performance* 32, 325–343.

Dobbins, G. H., & Platz, S. J. (1986). Sex differences in leadership: How real are they? *Academy of Management Review* 11, 118–127.

Eagly, A. H. (1987). *Sex differences in social behavior: A social-role interpretation*. Hillsdale, NJ: Erlbaum.

Eagly, A. H., & Carli, L. L. (1981). Sex of researchers and sex-typed communications as determinants of sex differences in influence-ability: A meta-analysis of social influence studies. *Psychological Bulletin* 90, 1–20.

Eagly, A. H., Makhijani, M. G., & Klonsky, B. G. (1990). *Gender and the evaluation of leaders: A meta-analysis*. Manuscript submitted for publication.

Eagly, A. H., & Steffen, V. J. (1984). Gender stereotypes stem from the distribution of women and men into social roles. *Journal of Personality and Social Psychology* 46, 735–754.

Eagly, A. H., & Wood, W. (in press). Explaining sex differences in social behavior: A meta-analytic perspective. *Personality and Social Psychology Bulletin*.

Elshtain, J. (1981). *Public man, private woman: Women in social and political thought*. Princeton, NJ: Princeton University Press.

Feldman, D. C. (1976). A contingency theory of socialization. *Administrative Science Quarterly* 21, 433–452.

Fiedler, F. E. (1967). *A theory of leadership effectiveness*. New York: McGraw-Hill.

Fleishman, E. A. (1953). The management of leadership attitudes in industry. *Journal of Applied Psychology* 36, 153–158.

Fleishman, E. A. (1957). The Leadership Opinion Questionnaire. In R. M. Stogdill & A. E. Coons (eds.), *Leader behavior: Its description and measurement* (pp. 120–133). Columbus, OH: Bureau of Business Research, Ohio State University.

Fleishman, E. A. (1960). *Manual for the Leadership Opinion Questionnaire*. Chicago: Science Research Associates.

Fleishman, E. A. (1970). *Manual for the Supervisory Behavior Description Questionnaire*. Washington, DC: American Institutes for Research.

Foy, N. (1980). *The yin and yang of organizations*. New York: Morrow.

Ghiselli, E. E. (1964). *Theory of psychological measurement*. New York: McGraw-Hill.

Glass, G. V., McGaw, B., & Smith, M. L. (1981). *Meta-analysis in social research*. Beverly Hills, CA: Sage.

Graen, G. (1976). Role-making processes within complex organizations. In M. D. Dunnette (ed.), *Handbook of industrial and organizational psychology* (pp. 1201–1245). Chicago: Rand McNally.

Grobman, H., & Hines, V.A. (1956). What makes a good principal? *National Association of Secondary School Principals Bulletin* 40, 5–16.

Gupta, N., Jenkins, G. D., Jr., & Beehr, T. A. (1983). Employee gender, gender similarity, and supervisor-subordinate cross-evaluations. *Psychology of Women Quarterly* 8, 174–184.

Gustafson, L.C. (1982). The leadership role of the public elementary school media librarian as perceived by the principal and its relationship to the factors of the sex, educational background, and the work experience of the media librarian (Doctoral dissertation, University of Maryland). *Dissertation Abstracts International* 43, 2206A.

Gutek, B. A., & Morasch, B. (1982). Sex-ratios, sex-role spillover, and sexual harassment of women at work. *Journal of Social Issues* 38, 55–74.

Hall, A. H. (1983). The influence of a personal planning workshop on attitudes toward managerial style (Doctoral dissertation, University of Maryland, 1983). *Dissertation Abstracts International* 44, 2953A.

Hall, J. A. (1984). *Nonverbal sex differences: Communication accuracy and expressive style.* Baltimore, MD: Johns Hopkins University Press.

Halpin, A. W. (1957). *Manual for the Leader Behavior Description Questionnaire.* Columbus, OH: Bureau of Business Research, Ohio State University.

Halpin, A. W. (1966). *Theory and research in administration.* New York: Macmillan.

Halpin, A. W., & Winer, B. J. (1957). A factorial study of the leader behavior descriptions. In R. M. Stogdill & A. E. Coons (eds.), *Leader behavior: Its description and measurement* (pp. 39–51). Columbus, OH: Bureau of Business Research, Ohio State University.

Hedges, L. V. (1981). Distribution theory for Glass's estimator of effect size and related estimators. *Journal of Educational Statistics* 6, 107–128.

Hedges, L. V. (1982a). Fitting categorical models to effect sizes from a series of experiments. *Journal of Educational Statistics* 7, 119–137.

Hedges, L. V. (1982b). Fitting continuous models to effect size data. *Journal of Educational Statistics* 7, 245–270.

Hedges, L. V. (1987). How hard is hard science, how soft is soft science? The empirical cumulativeness of research. *American Psychologist* 42, 443–455.

Hedges, L. V., & Becker, B. J. (1986). Statistical methods in the meta-analysis of research on gender differences. In J. S. Hyde & M. C. Linn (eds.), *The psychology of gender: Advances through meta-analysis* (pp. 14–50). Baltimore, MD: Johns Hopkins University Press.

Hedges, L. V., & Olkin, I. (1985). *Statistical methods for meta-analysis.* Orlando, FL: Academic Press.

Heft, M., & Deni, R. (1984). Altering preferences for leadership style of men and women undergraduate residence advisors through leadership training. *Psychological Reports* 54, 463–466.

Heller, T., & Van Til, J. (1986). Leadership and followership: Some summary propositions. In T. Heller, J. Van Til, & L. A. Zurcher (eds.), *Contemporary studies in applied behavioral science: Vol. 4. Leaders and followers: Challenges for the future* (pp. 251–263). Greenwich, CT: JAI Press.

Hemphill, J. K., & Coons, A. E. (1957). Development of the Leader Behavior Description Questionnaire. In R. M. Stogdill & A. E. Coons (eds.), *Leader behavior: Its description and measurement* (pp. 6–38). Columbus, OH: Bureau of Business Research, Ohio State University.

Hennig, M., & Jardin, A. (1977). *The managerial woman.* New York: Anchor Press.

Hersey, P., & Blanchard, K. H. (1977). *Management of organizational behavior: Utilizing human resources* (3rd ed.). Englewood Cliffs, NJ: Prentice-Hall.

Hersey, P., & Blanchard, K. H. (1982). *Management of organizational behavior: Utilizing human resources* (4th ed.). Englewood Cliffs, NJ: Prentice-Hall.

Hollander, E. P. (1985). Leadership and power. In G. Lindzey & E. Aronson (eds.), *Handbook of social psychology* (3rd ed., Vol. 2, pp. 485–537). New York: Random House.

Hughes, H., Jr., Copeland, D. R., Ford, L. H., & Heidt, E. A. (1983). *Leadership and management education and training (LMET) course requirements for recruit company and "A" school instructors* (Tech. Rep. No. 154, Report No. AD-A137306). Orlando, FL: Department of the Navy.

Hurst, A. G., Stein, K. B., Korchin, S. J., & Soskin, W. F. (1978). Leadership style determinants of cohesiveness in adolescent groups. *International Journal of Group Psychotherapy* 28, 263–277.

Jacoby, J., & Terborg, J. R. (1975). *Managerial Philosophies Scale.* Conroe, TX: Teleometrics International.

Kanter, R. M. (1977a). *Men and women of the corporation.* New York: Basic Books.

Kanter, R. M. (1977b). Some effects of proportions on group life: Skewed sex ratios and responses to token women. *American Journal of Sociology* 82, 965–990.

Kanter, R. M. (1983). *The change masters: Innovations for productivity in the American corporation.* New York: Simon and Schuster.

Koberg, C. S. (1985). Sex and situational influences on the use of power: A follow-up study. *Sex Roles* 13, 625–639.

Kruse, L., & Wintermantel, M. (1986). Leadership Ms.-qualified: I. The gender bias in everyday and scientific thinking. In C. F. Graumann & S. Moscovici (eds.),

*Changing conceptions of leadership* (pp. 171–197). New York: Springer-Verlag.

Lanning, G. E., Jr. (1982). A study of relationships and differences between management styles and staff morale as perceived by personnel in the colleges of the Ventura County community district. *Dissertation Abstracts International* 43, 996A. (University Microfilms No. 82–20, 739).

Lee, D. M., & Alvares, K. M. (1977). Effects of sex on descriptions and evaluations of supervisory behavior in a simulated industrial setting. *Journal of Applied Psychology* 62, 405–410.

Lewin, K., & Lippitt, R. (1938). An experimental approach to the study of autocracy and democracy: A preliminary note. *Sociometry* 1, 292–300.

Likert, R. (1961). *New patterns of management.* New York: McGraw-Hill.

Loden, M. (1985). *Feminine leadership or how to succeed in business without being one of the boys.* New York: Times Books.

Maccoby, E. E. (1988). Gender as a social category. *Developmental Psychology* 24, 755–765.

Marnani, E. B. (1982). Comparison of preferred leadership styles, potential leadership effectiveness, and managerial attitudes among black and white, female and male management students (Doctoral dissertation, United States International University, 1981). *Dissertation Abstracts International* 43, 1271A.

Martinez, M. R. (1982). A comparative study on the relationship of self-perceptions of leadership styles between Chicano and Anglo teachers (Doctoral dissertation, Bowling Green State University). *Dissertation Abstracts International* 43, 766A.

McGregor, D. (1960). *The human side of enterprise.* New York: McGraw-Hill.

McNemar, Q. (1962). *Psychological statistics* (3rd ed.). New York: Wiley.

Miller, J. B. (1976). *Toward a new psychology of women.* Boston: Beacon Press.

Money, J., & Ehrhardt, A. A. (1972). *Man & woman, boy & girl.* Baltimore, MD: Johns Hopkins University Press.

Moore, S. F., Shaffer, L., Goodsell, D. A., & Baringoldz, G. (1983). Gender or situationally determined spoken language differences? The case of the leadership situation. *International Journal of Women's Studies* 6, 44–53.

Myers, M. S. (1970). *Every employee a manager.* New York: McGraw-Hill.

Naisbitt, J. (1982). *Megatrends: Ten new directions transforming our lives.* New York: Warner Books.

Nieva, V. F., & Gutek, B. A. (1981). *Women and work: A psychological perspective.* New York: Praeger.

O'Leary, V. E. (1974). Some attitudinal barriers to occupational aspirations in women. *Psychological Bulletin* 81, 809–826.

Ott, E. M. (1989). Effects of the male-female ratio at work: Policewomen and male nurses. *Psychology of Women Quarterly* 13, 41–57.

Ouchi, W. G. (1981). *Theory Z: How American business can meet the Japanese challenge.* Reading, MA: Addison-Wesley.

Peters, T. J., & Waterman, R. H., Jr. (1982). *In search of excellence: Lessons from America's best-run companies.* New York: Harper & Row.

Powell, G. N. (1988). *Women & men in management.* Newbury Park, CA: Sage.

Reddin, W. J., & Reddin, M. K. (1979). *Educational Administrative Style Diagnosis Test (EASDT).* Fredericton, New Brunswick, Canada: Organizational Tests.

Renwick, P. A. (1977). The effects of sex differences on the perception and management of superior–subordinate conflict: An exploratory study. *Organizational Behavior and Human Performance* 19, 403–415.

Rice, R. W. (1978). Construct validity of the Least Preferred Co-Worker score. *Psychological Bulletin* 85, 1199–1237.

Rice, R. W., Instone, D., & Adams, J. (1984). Leader sex, leader success, and leadership process: Two field studies. *Journal of Applied Psychology* 69, 12–31.

Riger, S., & Galligan, P. (1980). Women in management: An exploration of competing paradigms. *American Psychologist* 35, 902–910.

Rosenthal, R., Hall, J. A., DiMatteo, M. R., Rogers, P. L., & Archer, D. (1979). *Sensitivity to nonverbal communication: The PONS test.* Baltimore, MD: Johns Hopkins University Press.

Rosenthal, R., & Rubin, D. B. (1986). Meta-analytic procedures for combining studies with multiple effect sizes. *Psychological Bulletin* 99, 400–406.

Russell, J. E. A., Rush, M. C., & Herd, A. M. (1988). An exploration of women's expectations of effective male and female leadership. *Sex Roles* 18, 279–287.

Sargent, A. G. (1981). *The androgynous manager.* New York: Amacom.

Sargent, J. F., & Miller, G. R. (1971). Some differences in certain communication behaviors of autocratic and democratic group leaders. *Journal of Communication* 21, 233–252.

Shakeshaft, C. (1987). *Women in educational administration.* Newbury Park, CA: Sage.

Sirianni-Brantley, K. (1985). The effect of sex role orientation and training on leadership style (Doctoral dissertation, University of Florida, 1984). *Dissertation Abstracts International* 45, 3106B.

Stake, J. E. (1981). Promoting leadership behaviors in low performance–self-esteem women in task-oriented mixed-sex dyads. *Journal of Personality* 49, 401–414.

Stogdill, R. M. (1963). *Manual for the Leader Behavior Description Questionnaire-Form XII*. Columbus, OH: Bureau of Business Research, Ohio State University.

Stogdill, R. M., Goode, O. S., & Day, D. R. (1962). New leader behavior description subscales. *Journal of Psychology* 54, 259–269.

Tanner, J. R. (1982). Effects of leadership, climate and demographic factors on school effectiveness: An action research project in leadership development (Doctoral dissertation, Case Western Reserve University, 1981). *Dissertation Abstracts International* 43, 333A.

Taylor, S. E., Fiske, S. T., Etcoff, N., & Ruderman, A. (1978). The categorical and contextual bases of person memory and stereotyping. *Journal of Personality and Social Psychology* 36, 778–793.

Terborg, J. R. (1977). Women in management: A research review. *Journal of Applied Psychology* 62, 647–664.

Van Aken, E. W. (1954). An analysis of the methods of operation of principals to determine working patterns (Doctoral dissertation, University of Florida). *Dissertation Abstracts International* 14, 1983.

Vroom, V. H., & Yetton, P. W. (1973). *Leadership and decision-making*. Pittsburgh, PA: University of Pittsburgh Press.

Wanous, J. P. (1977). Organizational entry: Newcomers moving from outside to inside. *Psychological Bulletin* 84, 601–618.

Wood, W. (1987). Meta-analytic review of sex differences in group performance. *Psychological Bulletin* 102, 53–71.

Yoder, J. D., & Sinnett, L. M. (1985). It is all in the numbers? A case study of tokenism. *Psychology of Women Quarterly* 9, 413–418.

# Chapter **Five**

# Leader Emergence

In this chapter, we ask the question, How do people become leaders? This question represents a continuation of the theme addressed in an earlier chapter. There we learned that the "great person" theory of leadership, while not necessarily accurate in its literal suggestion that some people are "born to lead," may have been accurate in suggesting that leaders are those individuals who generally possess the "right stuff." This "right stuff," as Kirkpatrick and Locke (1991) refer to it, may help identify who will be an effective leader as well as who will emerge as "the" leader.

Scholars interested in the processes associated with the emergence of a leader provide us with several different perspectives. Some have attempted to look at group dynamics and leader emergence (cf., Hollander, 1961), others have looked to the role played by personality traits (cf., Kirkpatrick & Locke, 1991; Mann, 1959; Stogdill, 1948), while others have suggested that power provides us with an explanation (cf., Salancik & Pfeffer, 1977).

Our earlier readings provided a glimpse into the dynamics and processes that are associated with leadership. Bass's (1990) reference to figureheads clearly suggests that in many organizational situations people come to positions of leadership as a result of forces outside of the group per se. These individuals can be referred to as "designated leaders." They are not the focus of this chapter. Our focus in Chapter 5 is centered on emergent processes and what we will refer to as "emergent leaders." This means that there are forces at work within the group that play a role in the leader-emergent process.

Murphy (1941) suggests that there are situational needs that "call for" certain knowledge, skills, and abilities. Emergent leadership results from an interaction between the situational needs for certain knowledge, skills, and abilities, and the individual's knowledge, skills, and abilities. Within this context, Smircich and Morgan (1982) suggest that, as individuals confront ambiguous situations, certain individuals surrender their power to define reality to others and it is through this surrendering process that a leader emerges.

Stogdill (1948) and Kirkpatrick and Locke (1991) provide a similar perspective on leader emergence. Leadership is a relational process (i.e., a working relationship). As individuals and group members attempt to work with situational demands, individuals who possess certain traits are more likely to engage in efforts directed toward the orchestration of group activity. Simultaneously, group members are more likely to turn to (i.e., accept the orchestration attempts of) individuals possessing the "right stuff" (e.g., self-confidence, drive, trustability) as opposed to allowing themselves to be directed by individuals who are not endowed with the right mix of individual traits.

Hollander's (1961) *idiosyncrasy credit theory* provides insight into leader emergence.[1] According to the idiosyncrasy model, group members evaluate other members in terms of the degree to which they conform to expectations and help the group move toward goal attainment. The result of these evaluations serves to define an individual's status and role in the group. Group status is defined in terms of idiosyncrasy credits, which represent the accumulation of positive impressions that others hold toward members of the group. These credits allow a group member to deviate from the group's norms of accepted behavior. For an individual to emerge as a group leader, he/she must deviate from expected member behavior, and, in the process, display behaviors that are both unique and perceived as helping the group move toward the attainment of its goals.

The first reading in this chapter is by Hollander (1964). In this reading he provides us with some insight into social influence and emergent leadership. As suggested by Hollander's reference to idiosyncrasy credits and the emergence of a group leader, power does not automatically flow to just anyone, nor is one guaranteed that, once received, that power will be retained. In the second reading in this chapter, Salancik and Pfeffer (1977) provide an interesting insight into two questions—who gets power and how do they hold on to it.[2] The answer to these two questions provides an additional insight into who is the group's leader, leader influence, and the leadership process.

Power—according to Salancik and Pfeffer—derives from activities rather than individuals, and the power possessed by a leader is never absolute. As the situation in which a leader and his or her followers are embedded changes, so too may the amount of power held by the leader change as well as the person in the leadership position.

As the situation facing a group of individuals (e.g., a project team, work group, organization) changes, so too do the "critical" issues facing the group. Power in social systems tends to flow to those individuals who possess the resources, especially if those resources that the group needs to solve its critical issues are scarce. The individual in a group, therefore, who is capable of contributing the scarce resources needed by the group to solve its most pressing problems tends to define leadership, the nature of the leader's power, and the amount of influence that he or she is capable of exercising.

The final reading in this chapter focuses attention on the role of personality and the actions of individuals that serve to influence their emergence as leaders. Before reading the article by Dobbins, Long, Dedrick, and Clemons (1990), we encourage you to complete the self-monitoring self-assessment that follows this chapter opener.

Dobbins and his colleagues look into the role that self-monitoring and gender play in the emergence of a leader. They claim that there is evidence to support the continued examination of the role of personal traits in the leadership process. Toward this end they suggest that group members who are high self-monitors are more "attentive to the attitudes, needs, and desires of group members" (p. 611); therefore, they are more likely to exhibit the behaviors that will result in their emergence as leaders.

---

[1] E. P. Hollander, "Emergent Leadership and Social Influence." In L. Petrullo and J. C. Brengelmann, eds., *Leadership and Interpersonal Behavior* (New York: Holt, Rinehart, & Winston, 1961), pp. 30–47.
[2] G. R. Salancik & J. Pfeffer, "Who Gets Power—And How They Hold on to It: A Strategic Contingency Model of Power," *Organizational Dynamics* (Winter 1977), pp. 3–21.

**Self-Monitoring**

**Instructions:** The statements below concern your personal reaction to a number of different situations. No two statements are exactly alike, so consider each statement carefully before answering. If a statement is *True* or *Mostly True* as applied to you, circle the "T". If a statement is *False* or *Not Usually True* as applied to you, circle the "F".

   It is important that you answer as frankly and as honestly as you can.

|  | True, or Mostly True | False, or Not Usually True |
|---|---|---|
| 1. I find it hard to imitate the behavior of other people. | T | F |
| 2. My behavior is usually an expression of my true inner feelings, attitudes, and beliefs. | T | F |
| 3. At parties and social gatherings, I do not attempt to do or say things that others will like. | T | F |
| 4. I can only argue for ideas which I already believe. | T | F |
| 5. I can make impromptu speeches even on topics about which I have almost no information. | T | F |
| 6. I guess I put on a show to impress or entertain people. | T | F |
| 7. When I am uncertain how to act in a social situation, I look to the behavior of others for cues. | T | F |
| 8. I would probably make a good actor. | T | F |
| 9. I rarely need the advice of my friends to choose movies, books, or music. | T | F |
| 10. I sometimes appear to others to be experiencing deeper emotions than I actually am. | T | F |
| 11. I laugh more when I watch a comedy with others than when alone. | T | F |
| 12. In a group of people I am rarely the center of attention. | T | F |
| 13. In different situations and with different people, I often act like very different persons. | T | F |
| 14. I am not particularly good at making other people like me. | T | F |
| 15. Even if I am not enjoying myself, I often pretend to be having a good time. | T | F |
| 16. I'm not always the person I appear to be. | T | F |
| 17. I would not change my opinions (or the way I do things) in order to please someone else or win their favor. | T | F |
| 18. I have considered being an entertainer. | T | F |
| 19. In order to get along and be liked, I tend to be what people expect me to be rather than anything else. | T | F |
| 20. I have never been good at games like charades or improvisational acting. | T | F |
| 21. I have trouble changing my behavior to suit different people and different situations. | T | F |
| 22. At a party I let others keep the jokes and stories going. | T | F |
| 23. I feel a bit awkward in company and do not show up quite so well as I should. | T | F |
| 24. I can look anyone in the eye and tell a lie with a straight face (if for a right end). | T | F |
| 25. I may deceive people by being friendly when I really dislike them. | T | F |

**Scoring:** Assign yourself one (1) point if you answered True, or Mostly True (i.e., you circled T) for each of the following questions: 5, 6, 7, 8, 10, 11, 13, 15, 16, 18, 19, 24, and 25, and assign yourself one (1) point if you answered False, or Not Usually True (i.e., you circled F) for each of the following questions: 1, 2, 3, 4, 9, 12, 14, 17, 20, 21, 22, and 23.

My self-monitoring score is: _____.

**Interpretation:** Snyder (1974) provides the following description of the self-monitoring individual: "The self-monitoring individual is one who, out of a concern for social appropriateness, is particularly sensitive to the expression and self-presentation of others in social situations and uses these cues as guidelines for monitoring his (her) own self-presentation" (Snyder, 1974, p.528). Your score on this self-assessment could range from zero (0) to twenty-five (25). The higher your score, the stronger your "self-monitoring" tendencies. A score of 20 and higher would be indicative of very strong self-monitoring, while a score of 5 or less would reflect extremely low self-monitoring.

Source: M. Snyder (1974). Self-monitoring of expressive behavior. *Journal of Personality and Social Psychology*, 30, no. 4, p. 531. Copyright 1974, American Psychological Association, Reprinted with permission.

## Reading 14

# Emergent Leadership and Social Influence

**E. P. Hollander**
State University of New York at Buffalo

The term *leader* is used so broadly that it is best to define our use of it at the outset. In general, leader denotes an individual with a status that permits him to exercise influence over certain other individuals. Specifically, our concern is directed toward leaders deriving status from followers who may accord or withdraw it, in an essentially free interchange within a group context. Group consent is therefore a central feature in the leader–follower relationships touched on here, although this limitation does not mean that we will totally neglect the possible implications for all kinds of groups, from the simple dyad to the institutionally based formal group or society. . . .

## STATUS IN GENERAL

There are different bases for status and different expectations regarding its operational features. These defy ready cataloguing, but in our usage here, *status* refers to the placement of an individual along a dimension, or in a hierarchy, by virtue of some criterion of value. To say that an individual has "status" does not describe an intrinsic attribute or a stable pattern of his behavior; rather it describes the relationship of that individual to certain others and their attendant behavior toward him. Interpersonal perception is a necessary part of this process.

Who perceives what about whom is of central importance not just in terms of the literal case, but also in terms of expectancies. The behavior of the object person is not seen just by itself; it is also effectively *matched* against a standard of expectation held by the perceiver. Before a status distinction can arise, therefore, two things must hold: an arousal of a socially conditioned expectancy, and a flow of information regarding the object person. The perceiver will have had some exposure to the perceived through direct experience or through secondary sources; this leads to a perceptual differentiation which underlies a shift in "behavior toward."

**Source:** Edited and reprinted with permission from E. P. Hollander, *Leaders, Groups, & Influence* (New York: Oxford Univ. Press, 1964).

Granting, as an example, that a millionaire possesses a fairly uniform degree of higher status in our society, he operates without it if, unshaven, unkempt, and unknown, he moves about among strangers. Even though an economic criterion and an expectancy already exist for a status distinction, the relevant information is absent. In this instance, the emergence of status is linked to one kind of standard, though a wide variety of others could apply (Hyman, 1942). What the relative impact of these will be resides in complex issues of value. In any case, status is not a sole and stable function of some given feature of social interaction between two particular individuals. Cross-pressures of time and place affect the balance.

If leaders occupy a given status relative to followers, this is one function of the way the former are at some moment perceived and reacted to by the latter. Gibb (1954, p. 915) has made the point this way: Followers subordinate themselves, not to an individual whom they perceive as utterly different, but to a member of their group who has superiority at this time and whom they perceive to be fundamentally the same as they are, and who may, at other times, be prepared to follow. Being a follower is not inconsistent with being a leader, in time. This begs the question of the persisting dichotomy, so some history may be useful here.

## THE CHANGING APPROACH TO LEADERSHIP

The tradition of concern and controversy about leadership extends far back into the history of social philosophy. This was to stamp related empirical work with a decided bent toward enumerating qualities of the leader. While recent research has seen the leader displaced from this traditional position at center-stage, not very long ago it was typical to indulge in a quest for broad traits of leadership.

Though essentially a matter of emphasis, as in the work of Cowley (1931), traits were selected without regard for situational variants. Gradually a useful distinction between appointed leaders and those who emerged through the willing response of followers was recognized. This was partly a reaction to the burgeoning interest in informal groups with their self-generating status hierarchies, and partly a result of the accessibility of sociometric devices which provided means for studying the consensual choice patterns of various groups.

During this phase, popularity as a feature of group-emergent leadership was given disproportionate importance. Much of the earlier sociometric work equated choice as a roommate or study companion with choice as a leader, and several well-known and substantial studies gave credence to this presumed parity, though only within a limited context (for example, Jennings, 1943).

Eventually, both the trait and popularity emphases were subordinated to an approach which focused on the varying demands for leadership imposed by an immediate situation (Hemphill, 1949; Carter, Haythorn, Shriver, and Lanzetta, 1951). The literature survey by Stogdill (1948) on personal factors associated with leadership was quite decisive in pointing up the disordered state of the earlier viewpoint, which disregarded situations. It was not as though the situational view prevailed entirely, however; influential as it was, the literature reflected some dissent (Gibb, 1950; Bell and French, 1950). We have this appropriate comment by Gouldner (1950, p. 13):

> The group contexts of leadership must be specified if a formalism sterile of action utility is to be avoided. Leadership must be examined in specific kinds of situations, facing distinctive problems. The opposite shortcoming must also be detoured; in other words, the similarities among *some* leadership situations or problems must be emphasized. Failure to do so would enmesh our investigation in an infinite analysis of unique situations as devoid of practical potentiality as the formalist approach.

Still another refinement within the situational framework was an awareness that followers define a situation in responding to leadership; they are not passive creatures of a frozen social matrix. Of his research on the follower as an alert participant, F. H. Sanford (1950, p. 4) has said:

> There is some justification for regarding the follower as the most crucial factor in any leadership event and for arguing that research directed at the follower will eventually yield a handsome payoff. Not only is it the follower who accepts or rejects leadership, but it is the follower who *perceives* both the leader and the situation and who reacts in terms of what he perceives. And what he perceives may be, to an important degree, a function of his own motivations, frames of reference, and "readinesses."

Thus, it is seen, several viewpoints have been held concerning leadership and followership: first, a search for characteristics of the leader on the supposition that there is some universality among these; second, a concern with group-emergent leadership where popularity among followers may be of significance; third, a focus upon situational factors that determine, or program, the demands made upon leadership and for leadership; and finally, an interest in the more subtle interplay of motives and perceptions between followers and their leaders.

If any current leaning is discernible, it seems to be toward a focus upon the interaction between individuals and its relation to influence assertion and acceptance. In this way, we are becoming more acute in noting how interpersonal perception affects and is affected by status differentiation, as shown, for example, in the work of Jones and deCharms (1957), Dittes and Kelley (1957), and the research reported here.

While it is true that two individuals may bear a stable relationship to one another in a given situation, the demands made upon them in a changing situation could reasonably alter their interpersonal behavior, assuming the necessary volitional conditions; being a leader or follower through the course of time or within a given group setting is not then a fixed state. The context for study consequently becomes more than the immediate situation in which interactions occur, since it includes the past interactions of the parties involved and their impressions of each other as well. The development of newer sociometric approaches has abetted this focus. . . .

## SOME IMPLICATIONS OF EMERGENT STATUS

The findings amassed suggest that two things in particular are important in an individual's attainment of leadership. First, that he be seen as competent in the group's central task; and second, that broadly speaking he be perceived as a member of the group—what Brown (1936) has called "membership character."

Any group member is bound by certain expectancies—whether norms or roles—which prevail at a given time. To directly challenge these would very likely limit his upward mobility, unless a person were extremely competent and, what is more important, widely perceived as such. In most instances, adherence to the prevailing expectancies of the group is essential for the group member's acceptance. We are in effect speaking then of conformity, but not in the usual sense of fixed behavioral norms to which all group members are expected to display manifest allegiance. We conceive of conformity in terms of *group expectancies* which may be person-specific and fluid or more generally applicable and static. Thus, what may be perceived to be nonconforming behavior for one group member may not be so perceived for another. Moreover, this is a function of status accumulated from past interactions, and is taken up more fully where we present the construct *idiosyncrasy credit* to refer to status as a summative consequence of being perceived by others as contributing to the group's task and living up to expectancies applicable at any given time. These "credits" are in essence positively disposed impressions of a person held by others; operationally, they provide the basis for influence assertion and its acceptance. The apparent paradox that leaders are said to be at once innovators and also to be conformers to group norms may be seen therefore as a matter of sequence.

So long as the person does not lose credits by sharp breaks with a past record of competence and conformity to expectancies, he rises to a level of credit which permits deviation from, and even open challenge of, prevailing social patterns of the group. In attaining this level, however, the particular expectancies applicable to him will have undergone change, so that it may be less appropriate to behave in the same way.

Guided by this credit model, an experiment with problem-solving groups was conceived to test the effects upon influence acceptance produced by the nonconformity to procedural norms of a confederate of the experimenter who was very competent in the task.

The key manipulation in that experiment was nonconformity by the confederate, through various zones of five trials each, to procedures previously agreed upon by the group in a pretrial discussion. The 15 trials were considered as three zones—early, middle, and late—with the discussion taken to be part of the first zone. A group choice, whether by majority rule or otherwise (this determined by the group) was required for each trial, following the three minutes permitted for considering alternatives. At the conclusion of each trial, the experimenter announced the outcome, that is, a negative or positive sum of varying magnitudes representing funds won or lost.

Six treatments were used: nonconformity throughout; nonconformity for the first two zones; for just the first zone alone; for the last two zones; for just the last zone alone; and not at all, as a control condition. Each subject was heard to report his recommended choice at least once during every one of the trials. Had it been *accepted* by the group as its own, the choice recommended by the confederate would have yielded the higher payoffs on all but four trials.

In the zones calling for nonconformity, the confederate violated procedures by speaking out of prescribed turn, by questioning the utility of majority rule, and by unsupported—but not harsh—challenges to the recommendations made by others. He manifested such behaviors on an approximate frequency of at least one per trial with a mean of two per trial considered optimum. Thus, he would break in with his choice immediately after an earlier respondent had spoken and before the next in sequence could do so; when there were periods of silence during a trial, he would observe aloud that maybe majority rule didn't work so well; and he would show a lack of enthusiasm for the choice offered by various others on the matter of basis.

The findings revealed the ongoing effect of task competence in increasing influence acceptance over time, seen in the rising means across zones. While current nonconformity does not yield a significant effect, past nonconformity does. In those groups where the confederate began nonconforming after the first zone, both his suggestions and nonconformity were accepted with minimal challenge; by the third zone, his suggestion that majority rule was faulty typically netted a rubber-stamping of his choice. Again, if he had already accrued credit, the pattern of interrupting people out of turn was simply imitated by others. However, where he exhibited nonconformity from the outset, quite opposite effects were elicited from the others, notably with comments of censure.

## Summary

In this chapter we have considered variables yielding emergent status in terms of potential influence. It has been shown that social interaction gives rise to a kind of interpersonal assessment, and that this is made up of task-related elements and behaviors matched by the perceiver against some social standard, referred to here as an "expectancy."

Where an individual fulfills these conditions of competence and an adherence to group expectancies over time, he is said to have accumulated "idiosyncrasy credits" and, at some threshold, these credits permit innovation in the group as one evidence of social influence. Thus the task-competent follower who conforms to the common expectancies of the group at one stage may emerge as the leader at the next stage. Correspondingly, the leader who fails to fulfill the expectancies associated with his position of influence may lose credits among his followers and be replaced by one of them. Which person achieves and retains leadership will therefore depend upon the perceptions of others from ongoing social interaction.

# References

Bell, G. B., & French, R. L. Consistency of individual leadership position in small groups of varying membership. *J. Abnorm. Soc. Psychol.*, 1950, 45, 764–767.

Brown, J. F. *Psychology and the social order.* New York: McGraw-Hill, 1936.

Carter, L. F., Haythorn, W., Shriver, Beatrice, & Lanzetta, J. The behavior of leaders and other group members. *J. Abnorm. Soc. Psychol.*, 1951, 46, 589–595.

Cowley, W. H. The traits of face-to-face leaders. *J. Abnorm. Soc. Psychol.*, 1931, 26, 304–313.

Dittes, J. E., & Kelley, H. H. Effects of different conditions of acceptance upon conformity to group norms. *J. Abnorm. Soc. Psychol.*, 1956, 53, 100–107.

Gibb, C. A. The sociometry of leadership in temporary groups. *Sociometry,* 1950, 13, 226–243.

Gibb, C. A. Leadership. In G. Lindzey (ed.), *Handbook of social psychology.* Vol. II. Cambridge, Mass.: Addison-Wesley, 1954.

Hemphill, J. K. *Situational factors in leadership.* Columbus: Ohio State Univer., 1949.

Hyman, H. H. The psychology of status. *Arch. Psychol.,* 1942, No.269.

Jennings, Helen H. *Leadership and isolation.* New York: Longmans, Green, 1943 (Rev. ed., 1950).

Jones, E. E., & deCharms, R. Changes in social perception as a function of the personal relevance of behavior. *Sociometry,* 1957, 20, 75–85.

Sanford, F. H. *Authoritarianism and leadership.* Philadelphia: Institute for Research in Human Relations, 1950.

Stogdill, R. M. Personal factors associated with leadership: A survey of the literature. *J. Psychol.,* 1948, 25, 37–51.

**Reading 15**

# Who Gets Power—And How They Hold on to It:

## *A Strategic-Contingency Model of Power*

**Gerald R. Salancik**
University of Illinois

**Jeffrey Pfeffer**
University of California at Berkeley

Power is held by many people to be a dirty word or, as Warren Bennis has said, "It is the organization's last dirty secret."

This article will argue that traditional "political" power, far from being a dirty business, is, in its most naked form, one of the few mechanisms available for aligning an organization with its own reality. However, institutionalized forms of power—what we prefer to call the cleaner forms of power: authority, legitimization, centralized control, regulations, and the more modern "management information systems"—tend to buffer the organization from reality and obscure the demands of its environment. Most great states and institutions declined, not because they played politics, but because they failed to accommodate to the political realities they faced. Political processes, rather than being mechanisms for unfair and unjust allocations and appointments, tend toward the realistic resolution of conflicts among interests. And power, while it eludes definition, is easy enough to recognize by its consequences—the ability of those who possess power to bring about the outcomes they desire.

The model of power we advance is an elaboration of what has been called strategic-contingency theory, a view that sees power as something that accrues to organizational subunits (individuals, departments) that cope with critical organizational problems. Power is used by subunits, indeed, used by all who have it, to enhance their own survival through control of scarce critical resources, through the placement of allies in key positions, and through the definition of organizational problems and policies. . . .

## WHAT IS ORGANIZATIONAL POWER?

You can walk into most organizations and ask without fear of being misunderstood, "Which are the powerful groups or people in this organization?" Although many organizational informants may be *unwilling* to tell you, it is unlikely they will be *unable* to tell you. Most people do not require explicit definitions to know what power is.

Power is simply the ability to get things done the way one wants them to be done. For a manager who wants an increased budget to launch a project that he thinks is important, his power is measured by his ability to get that budget. For an executive vice president who wants to be chairman, his power is evidenced by his advancement toward his goal. . . .

## WHERE DOES ORGANIZATIONAL POWER COME FROM?

Earlier we stated that power helps organizations become aligned with their realities. This hopeful prospect follows from what we have dubbed the strategic-contingencies theory of organizational power. Briefly, those subunits most able to cope with the organization's critical problems and uncertainties acquire power. In its simplest form, the strategic-contingencies theory implies that when an organization faces a number of lawsuits that threaten its existence, the legal department will gain power and influence over organizational decisions. Somehow other organizational interest groups will recognize its critical importance and confer upon it a status and power never before enjoyed. This influence may extend beyond handling legal matters and into decisions about product design, advertising production, and so on.

Such extensions undoubtedly would be accompanied by appropriate, or acceptable, verbal justifications. In time, the head of the legal department may become the head of the corporation, just as in times past the vice president for marketing had become the president when market shares were a worrisome problem and, before him, the chief engineer, who had made the production line run as smooth as silk.

Stated in this way, the strategic-contingencies theory of power paints an appealing picture of power. To the extent that power is determined by the critical uncertainties and problems facing the organization and, in turn, influences decisions in the organization, the organization is aligned with the realities it faces. In short, power facilitates the organization's adaptation to its environment—or its problems.

We can cite many illustrations of how influence derives from a subunit's ability to deal with critical contingencies. Michael Crozier described a French cigarette factory in which the maintenance engineers had a considerable say in the plantwide operation. After some probing he discovered that the group possessed the solution to one of the major problems faced by the company, that of troubleshooting the elaborate, expensive, and irrascible automated machines that kept breaking down and dumbfounding everyone else. It was the one problem that the plant manager could in no way control. . . .

The engineers' strategic role in coping with breakdowns afforded them a considerable say on plant decisions. Schedules and production quotas were set in consultation with them. And the plant manager, while formally their boss, accepted their decisions about personnel in their operation. His submission was to his credit, for without their cooperation he would have had an even more difficult time in running the plant. . . .

## POWER SHARING IN ORGANIZATIONS

Power is shared in organizations; and it is shared out of necessity more than out of concern for principles of organizational development or participatory democracy. Power is shared because no one person controls all the desired activities in the organization. While the factory owner may hire people to operate his noisy machines, once hired they have some control over the use of the machinery. And thus they have power over him in the same way he has power over them. Who has more power over whom is a mooter point than that of recognizing the inherent nature of organizing as a sharing of power. . . .

Because power derives from activities rather than individuals, an individual's or subgroup's power is never absolute and derives ultimately from the context of the situation. The amount of power an individual has at any one time depends, not only on the activities he or she controls, but also on the existence of other persons or means by which the activities can be achieved and on those who determine what ends are desired and, hence, on what activities are desired and critical for the organization. One's own power always depends on other people for these two reasons. Other people, or groups or organizations, can determine the definition of what is a critical contingency for the organization and can also undercut the uniqueness of the individual's personal contribution to the critical contingencies of the organization.

Perhaps one can best appreciate how situationally dependent power is by examining how it is distributed. In most societies, power organizes around scarce and critical resources. Rarely does power organize around abundant resources. In the United States, a person doesn't become powerful because he or she can drive a car. There are simply too many others who can drive with equal facility. In certain villages in Mexico, on the other hand, a person with a car is accredited with enormous social status and plays a key role in the community. In addition to scarcity, power is also limited by the need for one's capacities in a social system. While a racer's ability to drive a car around a 90° turn at 80 mph may be sparsely distributed in a society, it is not likely to lend the driver much power in the society. The ability simply does not play a central role in the activities of the society.

The fact that power revolves around scarce and critical activities, of course, makes the control and organization of those activities a major battleground in struggles for power. Even relatively abundant or trivial resources can become the bases for power if one can organize and control their allocation and the definition of what is critical. Many occupational and professional groups attempt to do just this in modern economies. Lawyers organize themselves into associations, regulate the entrance requirements for novitiates, and then get laws passed specifying situations that require the services of an attorney. Workers had little power in the conduct of industrial affairs until they organized themselves into closed and controlled systems. In recent years, women and blacks have tried to define themselves as important and critical to the social system, using law to reify their status. . . .

## THE CRITICAL CONTINGENCIES

The critical contingencies facing most organizations derive from the environmental context within which they operate. This determines the available needed resources and thus determines the problems to be dealt with. That power organizes around handling these problems suggests an important mechanism by which organizations keep in tune with their external environments. The strategic-contingencies model implies that subunits that contribute to the critical resources of the organization will gain influence in the organization. Their influence presumably is then used to bend the organization's activities to the contingencies that determine its resources. This idea may strike one as obvious. But its obviousness in no way diminishes its importance. Indeed, despite its obviousness, it escapes the notice of many organizational analysts and managers, who all too frequently think of the organization in terms of a descending pyramid, in which all the departments in one tier hold equal power and status. This presumption denies the reality that departments differ in the contributions they are believed to make to the overall organization's resources, as well as to the fact that some are more equal than others. . . .

## THE IMPACT OF ORGANIZATIONAL POWER ON DECISION MAKING

. . . Will organizational decisions always reflect the distribution of power in the organization? Probably not. Using power for influence requires a certain expenditure of effort, time, and resources. Prudent and judicious persons are not likely to use their power needlessly or wastefully. And it is likely that power will be used to influence organizational decisions primarily under circumstances that both require and favor its use. We have examined three conditions that are likely to affect the use of power in organizations: scarcity, criticality, and uncertainty. The first

suggests that subunits will try to exert influence when the resources of the organization are scarce. If there is an abundance of resources, then a particular department or a particular individual has little need to attempt influence. With little effort, he can get all he wants anyway.

The second condition, criticality, suggests that a subunit will attempt to influence decisions to obtain resources that are critical to its own survival and activities. Criticality implies that one would not waste effort, or risk being labeled obstinate, by fighting over trivial decisions affecting one's operations.

An office manager would probably balk less about a threatened cutback in copying machine usage than about a reduction in typing staff. An advertising department head would probably worry less about losing his lettering artist than his illustrator. Criticality is difficult to define because what is critical depends on people's beliefs about what is critical. Such beliefs may or may not be based on experience and knowledge and may or may not be agreed upon by all. Scarcity, for instance, may itself affect conceptions of criticality. When slack resources drop off, cutbacks have to be made—those "hard decisions," as congressmen and resplendent administrators like to call them. Managers then find themselves scrapping projects they once held dear.

The third condition that we believe affects the use of power is uncertainty: When individuals do not agree about what the organization should do or how to do it, power and other social processes will affect decisions. The reason for this is simply that, if there are no clear-cut criteria available for resolving conflicts of interest, then the only means for resolution is some form of social process, including power, status, social ties, or some arbitrary process like flipping a coin or drawing straws. Under conditions of uncertainty, the powerful manager can argue his case on any grounds and usually win it. Since there is no real consensus, other contestants are not likely to develop counterarguments or amass sufficient opposition. Moreover, because of his power and their need for access to the resources he controls, they are more likely to defer to his arguments.

Although the evidence is slight, we have found that power will influence the allocations of scarce and critical resources. In the analysis of power in the university, for instance, one of the most critical resources needed by departments is the general budget. First granted by the state legislature, the general budget is later allocated to individual departments by the university administration in response to requests from the department heads. Our analysis of the factors that contribute to a department getting more or less of this budget indicated that subunit power was the major predictor, overriding such factors as student demand for courses, national reputations of departments, or even the size of a department's faculty. Moreover, other research has shown that when the general budget has been cut back or held below previous uninflated levels, leading to monies becoming more scarce, budget allocations mirror departmental powers even more closely. . . .

## CHANGING CONTINGENCIES AND ERODING POWER BASES

The critical contingencies facing the organization may change. When they do, it is reasonable to expect that the power of individuals and subgroups will change in turn. . . .

One implication of the idea that power shifts with changes in organizational environments is that the dominant coalition will tend to be that group that is most appropriate for the organization's environment, as also will the leaders of an organization. One can observe this historically in the top executives of industrial firms in the United States. Up until the early 1950s, many top corporations were headed by former production line managers or engineers who gained prominence because of their abilities to cope with the problems of production. Their success, however, only spelled their demise. As production became routinized and mechanized, the problem of most firms became one of selling all those goods they so efficiently produced. Marketing executives were more frequently found in corporate boardrooms. Success outdid itself again, for keeping markets and production steady and stable requires the kind of control that can only come from acquiring competitors and suppliers or the invention of more and more appealing products—ventures that typically require enormous amounts of capital. During the 1960s, financial executives assumed the seats of power. And they, too, will give way to others. Edging over the horizon are legal experts, as regulation and antitrust suits are becoming more and more frequent in the 1970s, suits that had their beginnings in the success of the expansion generated by prior executives. The more distant future, which is likely to be dominated by multinational corporations, may see former secretaries of state and their minions increasingly serving as corporate figureheads. . . .

## IMPLICATIONS FOR THE MANAGEMENT OF POWER IN ORGANIZATIONS

While we could derive numerous implications from this discussion of power, our selection would have to depend largely on whether one wanted to increase one's power, decrease the power of others, or merely maintain one's position. More important, the real implications depend on the particulars of an organizational situation. To understand power in an organization one must begin by looking outside it—into the environment—for those groups that mediate the organization's outcomes but are not themselves within its control.

Instead of ending with homilies, we will end with a reversal of where we began. Power, rather than being the dirty business it is often made out to be, is probably one of the few mechanisms for reality testing in organizations. And the cleaner forms of power, the institutional forms, rather than having the virtues they are often credited with, can lead the organization to become out of touch. The real trick to managing power in organizations is to ensure somehow that leaders cannot be unaware of the realities of their environments and cannot avoid changing to deal with those realities. That, however, would be like designing the "self-liquidating organization," an unlikely event since anyone capable of designing such an instrument would be obviously in control of the liquidations.

Management would do well to devote more attention to determining the critical contingencies of their environments. For if you conclude, as we do, that the environment sets most of the structure influencing organizational outcomes and problems, and that power derives from the organization's activities that deal with those contingencies, then it is the environment that needs managing, not power. The first step is to construct an accurate model of the environment, a process that is quite difficult for most organizations. We have recently started a project to aid administrators in systematically understanding their environments. From this experience, we have learned that the most critical blockage to perceiving an organization's reality accurately is a failure to incorporate those with the relevant expertise into the process. Most organizations have the requisite experts on hand but they are positioned so that they can be comfortably ignored.

One conclusion you can, and probably should, derive from our discussion is that power—because of the way it develops and the way it is used—will always result in the organization suboptimizing its performance. However, to this grim absolute, we add a comforting caveat: If any criteria other than power were the basis for determining an organization's decisions, the results would be even worse.

## References

The literature on power is at once both voluminous and frequently empty of content. Some is philosophical musing about the concept of power, while other writing contains popularized palliatives for acquiring and exercising influence. Machiavelli's *The Prince,* if read carefully, remains the single best prescriptive treatment of power and its use. Most social scientists have approached power descriptively, attempting to understand how it is acquired, how it is used, and what its effects are. Mayer Zald's edited collection *Power in Organizations* (Vanderbilt University Press, 1970) is one of the more useful sets of thoughts about power from a sociological perspective, while James Tedeschi's edited book, *The Social Influence Processes* (Aldine-Atherton, 1972), represents the social psychological approach to understanding power and influence. The strategic-contingencies approach, with its emphasis on the importance of uncertainty for understanding power in organizations, is described by David Hickson and his colleagues in "A Strategic Contingencies Theory of Intraorganizational Power" (*Administrative Science Quarterly,* December 1971, pp. 216–229).

Unfortunately, while many have written about power theoretically, there have been few empirical examinations of power and its use. Most of the work has taken the form of case studies. Michel Crozier's *The Bureaucratic Phenomenon* (University of Chicago Press, 1964) is important because it describes a group's source of power as control over critical activities and illustrates how power is not strictly derived from hierarchical position. J. Victor Baldridge's *Power and Conflict in the University* (John Wiley & Sons, 1971) and Andrew Pettigrew's study of computer purchase decisions in one English firm (*Politics of Organizational Decision-Making,* Tavistock, 1973) both present insights into the acquisition and use of power in specific instances. Our work has been more empirical and comparative, testing more explicitly the ideas presented in this article. The study of university decision making is reported in articles in the June 1974, pp. 135–151, and December 1974, pp. 453–473, issues of the *Administrative Science Quarterly,* the insurance firm study in J. G. Hunt and L. L. Larson's collection, *Leadership Frontiers* (Kent State University Press, 1975), and the study of hospital administrator succession will appear in 1977 in the *Academy of Management Journal.*

**Reading 16**

# The Role of Self-monitoring and Gender on Leader Emergence: A Laboratory and Field Study

**Gregory H. Dobbins**
**William S. Long**
**Esther J. Dedrick**
University of Tennessee

**Tayna Cheer Clemons**
Anheuser-Busch

## INTRODUCTION

A major distinction has been made in leadership research between individuals who are formally appointed to positions of leadership and individuals who emerge as leaders of formal groups (see Bass, 1981, for a review). The focus of the present research is on emergent leadership. Most of the research investigating emergent leadership has been directed by the trait approach, which assumes that leaders are endowed with certain characteristics that predispose them to be effective in a wide range of situations. Despite the intuitive appeal of the trait approach, strong and consistent empirical support has been lacking. Leader abilities, aptitudes, interests, and personality characteristics typically account for less than 10 percent of the variance in leader emergence. Such results have prompted numerous researchers to conclude that a leadership trait or constellation of traits does not exist (e.g., Jenkins, 1947).

Abandoning the search for personal traits associated with leadership emergence may be premature. Lord, De Vader, and Alliger (1986) conducted a meta-analysis and concluded that previous reviews were far too pessimistic and, in fact, some variance in leader emergence can be predicted by the dominance, intelligence, and masculinity–femininity of the leader. Kenny and Zaccaro (1983) reanalyzed several data sets and concluded that "leadership is much more stable across situations than our introductory texts would indicate" (683). Although not identifying *the* leadership trait, Kenny and Zaccaro proposed that persons who are consistently cast into leader-

ship positions possess the ability to perceive and predict variations in group situations and pattern their own behavior accordingly. Other researchers (e.g., House, 1988) have also called for renewed investigation of traits underlying leadership.

Kenny and Zaccaro's description of leadership is very similar to the social psychological construct of self-monitoring. Self-monitoring refers to the ability and willingness to read verbal and nonverbal social cues and alter one's behavior accordingly (Snyder, 1979). High self-monitors (HSMs) are adept both at reading social cues and at regulating their self-presentation to fit a particular situation. HSMs are typically good actors and are able to display unfelt emotions. They place a premium on impression management and adopt what they see as a pragmatic interpersonal orientation. In essence, HSMs rely more upon situational factors to determine behavioral appropriateness and less upon their inner feelings, attitudes, and dispositions. Low self-monitors (LSMs), on the other hand, lack either the motivation or ability to regulate their self-presentation. They are less sensitive to external cues and do not alter their behavior to match the situation.

Associations have been revealed between self-monitoring and a myriad of criteria including cognitive, behavioral, and interpersonal functioning (see Snyder, 1986, for a review). For example, HSMs are better able than LSMs to communicate accurately an intended emotion through both vocal and facial channels of expression (Snyder, 1974). HSMs also spend more time and energy reviewing background information so that they accurately understand their audience (Elliot, 1979). Furthermore, the relationship between attitudes and behaviors is much weaker for HSMs than for LSMs (Ajzen, Timko, & White, 1982). HSMs also tend to use plural pronouns (e.g., *we, us*) more frequently and singular pronouns (e.g., *I, me*) less frequently than do LSMs. Although the origins of self-monitoring are not well understood, it appears to have both genetic and environmental precursors and is extremely difficult to alter in adults (Gangestad & Snyder, 1985). Thus, research indicates that HSMs are: (a) concerned about the appropriateness of social behavior; (b) attentive to social comparison information; (c) relatively adept at acting; and (d) able and willing to control behavior and optimize self-presentations, even if this means portraying themselves very differently across various contexts.

The above research suggests that self-monitoring may be related to leader emergence. Specifically, HSMs should be more attentive to the attitudes, needs, and desires of group members and better able to exhibit behavior patterns that match the interpersonal and situational specifications. In other words, HSMs should accurately read the setting and the feelings of group members and subsequently exhibit behaviors that match group members' expectations. Hypothesis 1 is based upon this rationale and predicts that *HSMs will emerge as leaders more frequently than will LSMs.*

The above prediction was tested by Garland and Beard (1979). They found that self-monitoring predicted leader emergence only for women. However, because self-monitoring was measured after subjects had been assigned to groups, some groups undoubtedly contained multiple HSMs or LSMs. This would have attenuated the relationship between self-monitoring and emergence because self-monitoring cannot predict emergence when all group members are either high or low. A much more appropriate test of Hypothesis 1 is to manipulate self-monitoring by systematically assigning HSMs and LSMs to groups.

## GENDER EFFECTS

A large body of research indicates that men emerge as leaders much more frequently than do women. For example, in an often cited study, Megargee (1969) examined the effects of dominance on leader emergence and found that men emerged more frequently than women irrespective of dominance levels. Similarly, Nyquist and Spence (1986) found that 90 percent of high dominant men became leaders over low dominant women, and only 25 percent of high dominant women emerged as leaders over low dominant men. Wentworth and Anderson (1984) found that men emerged as leaders in 86 percent of mixed-sex groups.

The above findings are consistent with research in social cognition and stereotyping (e.g., Ashmore & Del Boca, 1979; Dobbins, Cardy,

& Truxillo, 1988). This orientation proposes that group members have preexisting beliefs or schemata that link each sex with common behaviors and characteristics. The observation, storage, and retrieval of behavior are subsequently biased toward the characteristics of schemata. Because the prototypical characteristics of men are more "leader-like" than are the prototypical characteristics of women (Ashmore & Del Boca, 1979), group members should be inclined to nominate men as leaders more frequently than they nominate women. Thus, Hypothesis 2 predicts that *men will emerge as leaders more frequently than will women.*

## INFLUENCE ON DECISIONS

The present study will also determine the effects of self-monitoring and gender on an individual's influence on group decisions. Because HSMs should more accurately perceive the thoughts and feelings of others, they should be able to present their ideas in a manner that maximally influences the group. LSMs, on the other hand, should be unable (or not motivated) to accurately perceive the thoughts and reactions of other group members and thus will not alter their presentation style to be maximally persuasive. Thus Hypothesis 3 predicts that *HSMs should exert more influence on group decisions than do LSMs.*

Several individuals (e.g., Megargee, 1969) have proposed that women may not exert as much influence on group decisions as do men because they are perceived as less competent and their opinions are not highly valued by group members. Thus, Hypothesis 4 predicts that *men will exert more influence on group decisions than will women.*

Two studies tested the four predictions. . . .

## STUDY I: DISCUSSION

The ANOVAs provide support for the notion that self-monitoring is an important determinant of leader emergence. Specifically, HSMs emerged as leaders, exerted more influence on group decisions, and initiated more structure than did LSMs. Although the results of the ANOVAs clearly demonstrate that self-monitoring affects leader emergence, the actual mechanisms through which self-monitoring operates are not very clear. The hierarchical regression analyses suggest that HSMs are more likely to emerge as leaders because they are perceived as initiating more structure than are LSMs. These findings imply that self-monitoring affects emergence *indirectly* through leader behavior. It should be emphasized, however, that this conclusion is based upon group members' ratings of leader behavior. A large body of research indicates that ratings of leader behavior may be biased by whether the individual is categorized as a leader or nonleader (e.g., Lord, 1985; Lord, Foti, & Phillips, 1982). Thus, HSMs may have emerged as leaders because (a) they initiated more structure than did LSMs, or (b) they were more sensitive to leadership prototypes of group members and exhibited those behaviors that caused observers to categorize them as leaders (which, in turn, inflated their ratings of initiating structure). Future research should be conducted to determine which of these two explanations best accounts for the effects of self-monitoring on emergence.

The second major finding in Study I was that men were more likely to emerge as leaders than were women. The hierarchical regression analyses indicated that women were less likely to emerge as leaders largely because they were not perceived as initiating as much structure as were men. The present research does not indicate whether group members' perceptions were accurate (i.e., women actually initiated less structure than did men) or whether raters' stereotypes caused women to be perceived as initiating less structure than their male counterparts (e.g., Dobbins et al., 1988). In addition, it should be emphasized that gender also had a direct effect on emergence: That is, women were less likely to emerge as leaders even when their behavior was perceived the same as men. These combined findings suggest that gender exerts a *direct* and *indirect* effect on emergence and that women will be at an unfair disadvantage in emerging as leaders in mixed-sex groups.

Study I was conducted in a laboratory setting so that the composition of groups could be controlled. We realize that several aspects of the procedures were quite different from groups in actual organizations. Most important, the length of group interaction was very brief, much shorter than the length of interactions that occur in actual work groups. It is unclear whether the influence of self-monitoring would continue to operate over longer periods of time. A second study was conducted to address this concern.

## STUDY II: METHOD

Study II was a partial replication of Study I in a field setting. Self-monitoring and leader emergence were assessed in nine social organizations (e.g., fraternities) at a large southeastern university. This sample was selected because individuals in these organizations emerge into leadership positions and are not appointed. In fact, all leaders in Study II were elected by group members. Based upon the findings of Study I, we expected self-monitoring to predict leader emergence. . . .

## CONCLUSION

The combined findings of the laboratory and field studies suggest that self-monitoring may be *the* leadership trait identified by Kenny and Zaccaro (1983). Now that such effects have been convincingly demonstrated, future research should more thoroughly investigate the actual behaviors that mediate the effects of self-monitoring on emergence. This work could be conducted by having naive raters observe behavior or by coding videotaped recordings of HSMs and LSMs in groups.

Future research should also examine the relationship between self-monitoring and leader effectiveness. One hypothesis that deserves examination is that subordinates may be more willing to exert extra effort to accomplish group goals, be more satisfied with supervision, and more committed to the organization when their leader is an HSM rather than an LSM. In addition, the power and influence strategies used by HSM and LSM leaders should be compared. One intriguing hypothesis is that HSM leaders are more inclined to use referent power than are LSM leaders.

The moderating effects of task characteristics on the relationship between self-monitoring and leader emergence should also be examined. It would appear that self-monitoring skills should be at a premium in unstructured situations in which the task is more abstract and specific behaviors required for good performance are difficult to define. As the group task becomes more structured, the importance of self-monitoring skills alone should diminish and be replaced by the need for specific, technical knowledge. Thus, self-monitoring may be more strongly related to leader emergence and effectiveness in unstructured tasks than it is in structured tasks.

## References

Ajzen, I., Timko, C., & White, J. B. 1982. Self-monitoring and the attitude–behavior relation. *Journal of Personality and Social Psychology,* 42: 426–435.

Ashmore, R. D., & Del Boca, F. K. 1979. Sex stereotypes and implicit personality theory: Toward a cognitive-social psychological conceptualization. *Sex Roles,* 5: 219–248.

Bass, B. 1981. *Stogdill's handbook of leadership.* New York: Free Press.

Beatty, R. W., & Schneier, C. E. 1981. *Personnel administration: An experiential/skill building approach.* Reading, MA: Addison-Wesley.

Briggs, S. R., & Cheek, J. M. 1988. On the nature of self-monitoring: Problems with assessment, problems with validity. *Journal of Personality and Social Psychology,* 54: 663–678.

Carver, C. S. 1989. How should multifaceted personality constructs be tested? *Journal of Personality and Social Psychology,* 56: 577–585.

Dobbins, G. H., Cardy, R. L., & Truxillo, D. 1988. The effects of individual differences in stereotypes of women and purpose of appraisal on sex differences in performance ratings: A laboratory and field study. *Journal of Applied Psychology,* 73: 551–558.

Elliot, G. C. 1979. Some effects of deception and level of self-monitoring on planning and reacting to self-presentation. *Journal of Personality and Social Psychology,* 37: 1282–1292.

Gangestad, S., & Snyder, M. 1985. To carve nature at its joints: On the existence of discrete classes in personality. *Psychological Review,* 92: 317–349.

Garland, H., & Beard, J. F. 1979. Relationship between self-monitoring and leader emergence across two task situations. *Journal of Applied Psychology,* 64: 72–76.

House, R. 1988. Leadership research: Some forgotten, ignored, or overlooked findings. In J. Hunt, B. Baliga, H. Dachler, & C. Schriesheim (eds.), *Emerging leadership vistas,* 245–260. Lexington, MA: Lexington Books.

Jenkins, W. O. 1947. A review of leadership studies with particular reference to military problems. *Psychological Bulletin,* 44: 54–79.

Kenny, D., & Zaccaro, S. 1983. An estimate of variance due to traits in leadership. *Journal of Applied Psychology,* 68: 678–685.

Lennox, R., & Wolfe, R. 1984. Revision of the self-monitoring scale. *Journal of Personality and Social Psychology,* 46: 1349–1364.

Lord, R. G. (1985). An information processing approach to social perceptions, leadership, and behavioral measurement in organizations. In B. M. Staw & L. L. Cummings (eds.), *Research in organizational behavior,* 7: 87–128. Greenwich, CT: JAI Press.

Lord, R. G., De Vader, C., & Alliger, G. M. 1986. A meta-analysis of the relation between personality traits and leadership perceptions: An application of validity generalization procedures. *Journal of Applied Psychology,* 71: 402–410.

Lord, R. G., Foti, R. J., & Phillips, J. S. 1982. A theory of leadership categorization. In J. G. Hunt, V. Sekaran, & C. Schriescheim, (eds.), *Leadership: Beyond establishment views.* Carbondale, IL: SIU Press.

Megargee, E. I. 1969. Influence of sex roles on the manifestation of leadership. *Journal of Applied Psychology,* 53: 377–382.

Nyquist, L. V., & Spence, J. T. 1986. Effects of dispositional dominance and sex role expectations on leadership behaviors. *Journal of Personality and Social Psychology,* 50: 87–93.

Snyder, M. 1974. The self-monitoring of expressive behavior. *Journal of Personality and Social Psychology,* 30: 526–537.

Snyder, M. 1979. Self-monitoring processes. In L. Berkowitz (ed.), *Advances in experimental social psychology,* 12: 86–128. New York: Academic Press.

Snyder, M. 1986. *Public appearances/Private realities.* New York: Freeman and Company.

Wentworth, D. K., & Anderson, L. R. 1984. Emergent leadership as a function of sex and task type. *Sex Roles,* 11: 513–524.

# Chapter Six

# Leadership
# as an Influence Process

Chapter One portrayed leadership as an interpersonal process that involves the exercise of influence. Leaders, for example, frame reality, provide direction, initiate structure, facilitate, induce compliance, support, remove barriers, and control the behavior(s) of others. This chapter asks, *How* do leaders influence others? and *What* are their sources of power? You can profile your own preferred influence tactics with the first Self-Assessment exercise presented at the end of this introduction.

The first reading in this chapter is John R. P. French and Bertram Raven's (1959) classic perspective on "the bases of social power." The authors seek to identify the major types of power and articulate the source from which each type of power stems. According to French and Raven, *power* is the ability to exercise influence, and *influence* is the ability to bring about change (i.e., a "change in behavior, opinions, attitudes, goals, needs, values, and all other aspects of the person's psychological field" [pp. 150–151]). Power, therefore, can be seen as the ability to induce change in one's environment.

The work of French and Raven suggests that part of the leadership process consists of the exercise of influence. A leader's ability to influence others stems from his or her ability (or perceived ability) to exercise reward, coercive, referent, expert, and/or legitimate power. The nature of each of these types of power is defined in their article. You can develop your own power profile by completing the second Self-Assessment exercise presented at the end of this introduction to Chapter 6.

A leader's power base is not the simple sum of the various sources of power that he or she is capable of exercising. There appears to be a synergistic effect that stems from some combinations of power. For example, referent power, because it stems from a valued and respected person, tends to magnify the impact of other sources of power, especially legitimate, resource, and expert power. The opposite effect can also be produced. High coercive power may well dilute the impact of referent power. As might be suspected, therefore, not all forms of power are equally effective. Hinkin and Schriesheim (1990) found that "rationality" was the most commonly used influence tactic by effective leaders and that rationality was positively related to referent, expert, and legitimate power.[1] According to Podsakoff and Schriesheim's (1985) literature review, follower performance and satisfaction are commonly associated with the leader's use of expert

---

[1] T. R. Hinkin and C. A. Schriesheim, "Relationships between Subordinate Perceptions of Supervisor Influence Tactics and Attributed Bases of Supervisory Power," *Human Relations* 43 (1990), pp. 221–237.

**FIGURE 6.1**
**The Leader Power-**
**Follower Response**
**Relationship**

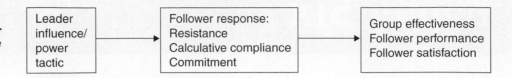

and referent power, while at times the use of legitimate, reward, and coercive power has a negative relationship with these two dimensions of leader effectiveness. These results suggest that effective leaders rely more upon some forms of power than others.[2] These observations are not surprising, according to sociologist Amitai Etzioni, who suggested that different forms of power produce different forms of compliance.[3] Coercive power commonly produces resistance, which eventually leads to alienation. Remunerative or reward power frequently produces an instrumental or calculative response. The level and type of subordinate compliance is based upon the attractiveness of the benefits offered relative to the cost incurred. Finally, reliance upon rationality, moralistic appeal, expert and/or referent power frequently elicits follower commitment. As illustrated in Figure 6.1, it is this level/type of compliance that mediates the impact of a leader's power upon the group's performance, member performance, and follower satisfaction with the leader.

As suggested by Hollander's (1961) idiosyncrasy credits theory, power does not automatically flow to just anyone, nor is one guaranteed that once one has power that one will be able to retain that power.[4] As the situation in which a leader and his or her followers are embedded changes, so too may the amount of power held by the leader change as well as the person in the leadership position.

As illustrated by Figure 6.2, the work of Salancik and Pfeffer (1977) suggests that critical contingencies play a role in defining the situation facing the group, which in turn influences "who will be the leader" (critical contingencies → situation → leader) and in part defines and shapes the leader's power. Also playing a role in giving definition to "who will be the leader" is who controls scarce resources (scarce resource control → leader) that are critical to helping the group overcome its most pressing issues. French and Raven's work suggests that a person's ability to administer rewards and coercion, for example, enables him or her to serve as a leader and provides further insight into the leader–follower, and the leader–situation relationship.

In the second reading in this chapter, Yukl and Tracey (1992) alert us to the fact that there are a number of different "influence tactics" that leaders employ in their relationship with their followers (downward influence) and as a part of their attempt to influence their boss and peers. Yukl and Tracey's work also provides us with insight into the effectiveness of these different tactics, highlighting the efficacy of rational persuasion, inspirational appeal, and consultation.

[2] P. M. Podsakoff and C. A. Schriesheim, "Field Studies of French and Raven's Bases of Power: Critique, Reanalysis, and Suggestions for Future Research," *Psychological Bulletin* 97 (1985), pp. 387–411.
[3] A. Etzioni, *A Comparative Analysis of Complex Organizations, on Power, Involvement, and Their Correlates* (New York: Free Press of Glencoe, 1961).
[4] E. P. Hollander, "Emergent Leadership and Social Influence." In L. Petrullo and J. C. Brengelmann, eds., *Leadership and Interpersonal Behavior* (New York: Holt, Rinehart, & Winston, 1961), pp. 30–47.

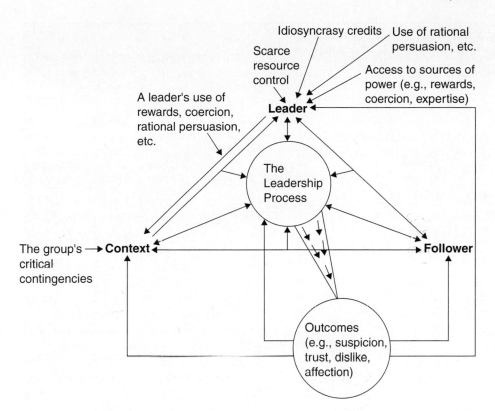

**FIGURE 6.2**
**The Expanded
Leadership Process**

**EXERCISE**
*Self-Assessment*

**Influence Tactics**

**Instructions:** The questions below ask you about the way in which you influence others. Read each statement carefully and indicate the degree to which you *agree* or *disagree* that this particular influence tactic is descriptive of your leadership style.

|  | Strongly Disagree | Disagree | Slightly Disagree | Neither Agree nor Disagree | Slightly Agree | Agree | Strongly Agree |
|---|---|---|---|---|---|---|---|
| 1. I would confront my follower(s) and demand that requested actions be carried out promptly. | ①) | 2 | 3 | 4 | 5 | 6 | ⑦ |
| 2. I would explain the reason for a request or proposal. | ①) | 2 | 3 | 4 | 5 | 6 | ⑦ |
| 3. I would make reference to a higher authority in order to get a requested action carried out. | 1 | 2 | 3 | 4 | 5 | ⑥ | 7 |
| 4. I would explain how the person would benefit from my proposal. | 1 | 2 | 3 | 4 | ⑤ | 6 | 7 |
| 5. I would indicate that I would do a favor in return for their carrying out a requested action. | 1 | ② | 3 | 4 | 5 | 6 | 7 |
| 6. I would provide evidence that a proposal is feasible. | 1 | ② | 3 | 4 | 5 | 6 | 7 |
| 7. I would compliment people on their past accomplishments before asking them to do another task. | 1 | 2 | 3 | ④ | 5 | 6 | 7 |
| 8. I would explain why my proposal is objectively better than competing ones. | 1 | 2 | 3 | 4 | ⑤ | 6 | 7 |
| 9. I would get other people to provide evidence in support of a plan or proposal that I was attempting to carry out. | 1 | 2 | 3 | 4 | ⑤ | 6 | 7 |
| 10. I would explain how likely problems or concerns should be handled. | 1 | 2 | 3 | 4 | ⑤ | 6 | 7 |
| 11. I would describe a proposed task or project with enthusiasm and conviction to convey that it is important and worthwhile. | 1 | 2 | 3 | 4 | ⑤ | 6 | 7 |
| 12. I would provide evidence that the requested action that I am proposing will lead to the successful completion of a task or project. | 1 | 2 | 3 | 4 | ⑤ | 6 | 7 |
| 13. I would tell others what it is that I am trying to accomplish and ask if they know a good way to do it. | 1 | 2 | 3 | 4 | ⑤ | 6 | 7 |

**Scoring:** This self-assessment is designed to reflect the extent to which the use of **rational persuasion** characterizes your leadership influence tactics. Sum your answers to questions 2, 4, 6, 8, 10, and 12 and divide by 6. This score reflects the extent to which you indicate that you rely upon rational persuasion as a way of influencing others while in a leadership situation. The other questions asked about other forms of influence: pressure (1), upward appeal (3), exchange (5), ingratiation (7), coalition (9), inspirational appeal (11), and consultation (13). (See Yukl, Lepsinger, & Lucia [1993] for a preliminary report on the development and validation of the Influence Behavior Questionnaire. See K. Clark and M. Clark, eds., *The Impact of Leadership* [Greensboro, NC: Center for Creative Leadership] for guidance on the measurement of these other forms [e.g., pressure, upward appeal] of leader influence.)

My rational persuasion score is: *4* .

My other influence tactic scores are:
Pressure _____
Upward appeal _____
Exchange _____
Ingratiation _____
Coalition _____
Inspirational appeal _____
Consultation _____

**Interpretation:** A score of 6 and greater on *rational persuasion* implies that you strongly prefer to influence others by employing rationality. Several leadership scholars (cf., Hinkin & Schriesheim, 1990) have observed that rationality is one of the more commonly used influence tactics. Indirect evidence suggests that rationality, as a form of influence, is positively associated with two dimensions of leader effectiveness—follower performance and satisfaction. You are also provided with a glimpse into your propensity to employ pressure, upward appeal, exchange, ingratiation, coalition building, inspirational appeal, and consultation as a part of your "influence repertoire."

Source: Items 2, 4, 6, 8, and 10 are patterned after items presented by G. Yukl, *Leadership in Organizations*, 4th edition (Englewood Cliffs, NJ: Prentice Hall), p. 219. The remaining items are patterned after items presented by G. Yukl and C. M. Falbe, "Influence Tactics and Objectives in Upward, Downward, and Lateral Influence Attempts," *Journal of Applied Psychology* 75, no. 2 (1990), p. 134.

## EXERCISE
*Self-Assessment*

**Personal Power Profile**

**Instructions:** Below is a list of statements that may be used in describing behaviors that supervisors (leaders) in work organizations can direct toward their subordinates (followers). First, carefully read each descriptive statement, thinking in terms of *how you prefer to influence others*. Mark the number that most closely represents how you feel. Use the following numbers for your answers.

7 = Strongly agree
6 = Agree
5 = Slightly agree
4 = Neither agree nor disagree
3 = Slightly disagree
2 = Disagree
1 = Strongly disagree

| To influence others, I would prefer to | Strongly Disagree | Disagree | Slightly Disagree | Neither Agree nor Disagree | Slightly Agree | Agree | Strongly Agree |
|---|---|---|---|---|---|---|---|
| 1.  Increase their pay level. | 1 | 2 | 3 | 4 | 5 | 6 | 7 |
| 2.  Make them feel valued. | 1 | 2 | 3 | 4 | 5 | 6 | 7 |
| 3.  Give undesirable job assignments. | 1 | 2 | 3 | 4 | 5 | 6 | 7 |
| 4.  Make them feel like I approve of them. | 1 | 2 | 3 | 4 | 5 | 6 | 7 |
| 5.  Make them feel that they have commitments to meet. | 1 | 2 | 3 | 4 | 5 | 6 | 7 |
| 6.  Make them feel personally accepted. | 1 | 2 | 3 | 4 | 5 | 6 | 7 |
| 7.  Make them feel important. | 1 | 2 | 3 | 4 | 5 | 6 | 7 |
| 8.  Give them good technical suggestions. | 1 | 2 | 3 | 4 | 5 | 6 | 7 |
| 9.  Make the work difficult for them. | 1 | 2 | 3 | 4 | 5 | 6 | 7 |
| 10.  Share my experience and/or training. | 1 | 2 | 3 | 4 | 5 | 6 | 7 |
| 11.  Make things unpleasant here. | 1 | 2 | 3 | 4 | 5 | 6 | 7 |
| 12.  Make being at work distasteful. | 1 | 2 | 3 | 4 | 5 | 6 | 7 |
| 13.  Influence their getting a pay increase. | 1 | 2 | 3 | 4 | 5 | 6 | 7 |
| 14.  Make them feel like they should satisfy their job requirements. | 1 | 2 | 3 | 4 | 5 | 6 | 7 |
| 15.  Provide them with sound job-related advice. | 1 | 2 | 3 | 4 | 5 | 6 | 7 |
| 16.  Provide them with special benefits. | 1 | 2 | 3 | 4 | 5 | 6 | 7 |
| 17.  Influence their getting a promotion. | 1 | 2 | 3 | 4 | 5 | 6 | 7 |
| 18.  Give them the feeling that they have responsibilities to fulfill. | 1 | 2 | 3 | 4 | 5 | 6 | 7 |
| 19.  Provide them with needed technical knowledge. | 1 | 2 | 3 | 4 | 5 | 6 | 7 |
| 20.  Make them recognize that they have tasks to accomplish. | 1 | 2 | 3 | 4 | 5 | 6 | 7 |

**Scoring:** Using the grid below, insert your scores from the 20 questions and proceed as follows: *Reward power*—sum your responses to items 1, 13, 16, and 17 and divide by 4. *Coercive power*—sum your responses to items 3, 9, 11, and 12 and divide by 4. *Legitimate power*—sum your responses to questions 5, 14, 18, and 20 and divide by 4. *Referent power*—sum your responses to questions 2, 4, 6, and 7 and divide by 4. *Expert power*—sum your responses to questions 8, 10, 15, and 19 and divide by 4.

| Reward | Coercive | Legitimate | Referent | Expert |
|---|---|---|---|---|
| 1 _____ | 3 _____ | 5 _____ | 2 _____ | 8 _____ |
| 13 _____ | 9 _____ | 14 _____ | 4 _____ | 10 _____ |
| 16 _____ | 11 _____ | 18 _____ | 6 _____ | 15 _____ |
| 17 _____ | 12 _____ | 20 _____ | 7 _____ | 19 _____ |
| Total _____ | _____ | _____ | _____ | _____ |
| Divide by 4 _____ | _____ | _____ | _____ | _____ |

**Interpretation:** A high score (6 and greater) on any of the five dimensions of power implies that you prefer to influence others by employing that particular form of power. A low score (2 and less) implies that you prefer not to employ this particular form of power to influence others. This represents your power profile. Your overall power position is not reflected by the simple sum of the power derived from each of the five sources. Instead, some combinations of power are synergistic in nature—they are greater than the simple sum of their parts. For example, *referent power* tends to magnify the impact of other power sources because these other influence attempts are coming from a "respected" person. *Reward power* often increases the impact of referent power, because people generally tend to like those who give them things that they desire. Some power combinations tend to produce the opposite of synergistic effects, such that the total is less than the sum of the parts. Power dilution frequently accompanies the use of (or threatened use of) *coercive power*.

Source: Modified version of T. R. Hinkin and C. A. Schriesheim, "Development and Application of New Scales to Measure the French and Raven (1959) Bases of Social Power," *Journal of Applied Psychology* 74 (1989), pp. 561–567. Copyright 1989, American Psychological Association, adapted and printed with permission.

## Reading 17

# The Bases of Social Power

**John R. P. French, Jr., and Bertram Raven**
University of Michigan

The processes of power are pervasive, complex, and often disguised in our society. Accordingly, one finds in political science, in sociology, and in social psychology a variety of distinctions among different types of social power or among qualitatively different processes of social influence (**1, 6, 14, 20, 23, 29, 30, 38, 41**). Our main purpose is to identify the major types of power and to define them systematically so that we may compare them according to the changes which they produce and the other effects which accompany the use of power. The phenomena of power and influence involve a dyadic relation between two agents which may be viewed from two points of view: (a) What determines the behavior of the agent who exerts power? (b) What determines the reactions of the recipient of this behavior? We take this second point of view and formulate our theory in terms of the life space of P, the person upon whom power is exerted. In this way we hope to define basic concepts of power which will be adequate to explain many of the phenomena of social influence, including some which have been described in other less genotypic terms.

Recent empirical work, especially on small groups, has demonstrated the necessity of distinguishing different types of power in order to account for the different effects found in studies of social influence. Yet there is no doubt that more empirical knowledge will be needed to make final decisions concerning the necessary differentiations, but this knowledge will be obtained only by research based on some preliminary theoretical distinctions. We present such preliminary concepts and some of the hypotheses they suggest.

## POWER, INFLUENCE, AND CHANGE

### PSYCHOLOGICAL CHANGE

Since we shall define power in terms of influence, and influence in terms of psychological change,

Source: Edited and reprinted with permission from D. Cartwright, *Studies in Social Power* (Ann Arbor, MI: Institute for Social Research, University of Michigan, 1959), pp. 150–67. Author affiliation may have changed since article was first published.

we begin with a discussion of change. We want to define change at a level of generality which includes changes in behavior, opinions, attitudes, goals, needs, values, and all other aspects of the person's psychological field. We shall use the word *system* to refer to any such part of the life space. Following Lewin (**26,** p. 305), the state of a system at time 1 will be denoted $s_1(a)$.

Psychological change is defined as any alteration of the state of some system $a$ over time. The amount of change is measured by the size of the difference between the states of the system *at* time 1 and at time 2: $ch(a) = s_2(a) - s_1(a)$.

Change in any psychological system may be conceptualized in terms of psychological forces. But it is important to note that the change must be coordinated to the resultant force of all the forces operating at the moment. Change in an opinion, for example, may be determined jointly by a driving force induced by another person, a restraining force corresponding to anchorage in a group opinion, and an own force stemming from the person's needs. . . .

## THE BASES OF POWER

By the basis of power, we mean the relationship between O and P, which is the source of that power. It is rare that we can say with certainty that a given empirical case of power is limited to one source. Normally, the relation between O and P will be characterized by several qualitatively different variables which are bases of power (**30,** Chapter 11). Although there are undoubtedly many possible bases of power which may be distinguished, we shall here define five which seem especially common and important. These five bases of O's power are: (1) *reward power,* based on P's perception that O has the ability to mediate rewards for him; (2) *coercive power,* based on P's perception that O has the ability to mediate punishments for him; (3) *legitimate power,* based on the perception by P that O has a legitimate right to prescribe behavior for him; (4) *referent power,* based on P's identification with O; and (5) *expert power,* based on the perception that O has some special knowledge or expertness. . . .

## REWARD POWER

Reward power is defined as power whose basis is the ability to reward. The strength of the reward power of O/P increases with the magnitude of the rewards which P perceives that O can mediate for him. Reward power depends on O's ability to administer positive valences and to remove or decrease negative valences. The strength of reward power also depends upon the probability that O can mediate the reward, as perceived by P. A common example of reward power is the addition of a piecework rate in the factory as an incentive to increase production.

The new state of the system induced by a promise of reward (for example the factory worker's increased level of production) will be highly dependent on O. Since O mediates the reward, he controls the probability that P will receive it. Thus P's new rate of production will be dependent on his subjective probability that O will reward him for conformity minus his subjective probability that O will reward him even if he returns to his old level. Both probabilities will be greatly affected by the level of observability of P's behavior. Incidentally, a piece rate often seems to have more effect on production than a merit rating system because it yields a higher probability of reward for conformity and a much lower probability of reward for nonconformity.

The utilization of actual rewards (instead of promises) by O will tend over time to increase the attraction of P toward O and therefore the referent power of O over P. As we shall note later, such referent power will permit O to induce changes which are relatively independent. Neither rewards nor promises will arouse resistance in P, provided P considers it legitimate for O to offer rewards.

The range of reward power is specific to those regions within which O can reward P for conforming. The use of rewards to change systems within the range of reward power tends to increase reward power by increasing the probability attached to future promises. However, unsuccessful attempts to exert reward power outside the range of power would tend to decrease the power; for example if O offers to reward P for performing an impossible act, this will reduce for P the probability of receiving future rewards promised by O.

## COERCIVE POWER

Coercive power is similar to reward power in that it also involves O's ability to manipulate the attainment of valences. Coercive power of O/P stems from the expectation on the part of P that he will be punished by O if he fails to conform to the influence attempt. Thus negative valences will exist in given regions of P's life space, corresponding to the threatened punishment by O. The strength of coercive power depends on the magnitude of the negative valence of the threatened punishment multiplied by the perceived probability that P can avoid the punishment by conformity, i.e., the probability of punishment for nonconformity minus the probability of punishment for conformity **(11)**. Just as an offer of a piece-rate bonus in a factory can serve as a basis for reward power, so the ability to fire a worker if he falls below a given level of production will result in coercive power.

Coercive power leads to dependent change also; and the degree of dependence varies with the level of observability of P's conformity. An excellent illustration of coercive power leading to dependent change is provided by a clothes presser in a factory observed by Coch and French **(3)**. As her efficiency rating climbed above average for the group the other workers began to "scapegoat" her. That the resulting plateau in her production was not independent of the group was evident once she was removed from the presence of the other workers. Her production immediately climbed to new heights.[1]

At times, there is some difficulty in distinguishing between reward power and coercive power. Is the withholding of a reward really equivalent to a punishment? Is the withdrawal of punishment equivalent to a reward? The answer must be a psychological one—it depends upon the situation as it exists for P. But ordinarily we would answer these questions in the affirmative; for P, receiving a reward is a positive valence as is the relief of suffering. There is some evidence that conformity to group norms in order to gain acceptance (reward power) should be distinguished from conformity as a means of forestalling rejection (coercive power) **(5)**.

The distinction between these two types of power is important because the dynamics are different. The concept of "sanctions" sometimes lumps the two together despite their opposite effects. While reward power may eventually result in an independent system, the effects of coercive power will continue to be dependent. Reward power will tend to increase the attraction of P toward O; coercive power will decrease this attraction **(11, 12)**. The valence of the region of behavior will become more negative, acquiring some negative valence from the threatened punishment. The negative valence of punishment would also spread to other regions of the life space. Lewin (25) has pointed out this distinction between the effects of rewards and punishment. In the case of threatened punishment, there will be a resultant force on P to leave the field entirely. Thus, to achieve conformity, O must not only place a strong negative valence in certain regions through threat of punishment, but O must also introduce restraining forces, or other strong valences, so as to prevent P from withdrawing completely from O's range of coercive power. Otherwise the probability of receiving the punishment, if P does not conform, will be too low to be effective.

## LEGITIMATE POWER

Legitimate power is probably the most complex of those treated here, embodying notions from the structural sociologist, the group-norm and role-oriented social psychologist, and the clinical psychologist.

There have been considerable investigation and speculation about socially prescribed behavior, particularly that which is specific to a given role or position. Linton (29) distinguishes group norms according to whether they are universals for everyone in the culture, alternatives (the individual having a choice as to whether or not to accept them), or specialties (specific to given positions). Whether we speak of internalized norms, role prescriptions and expectations (34), or internalized pressures (15), the fact remains that each individual sees certain regions toward which he should locomote, some regions toward which he should not locomote, and some regions toward which he may locomote if they are generally attractive for him. This applies to specific behaviors in which he may, should, or should not engage; it applies to certain attitudes or beliefs which he may, should, or should not hold. The feeling of "oughtness" may be an internalization from his parents, from his teachers, from his religion, or may have been logically developed from some idiosyncratic system of ethics. He will speak of such behaviors with expressions like "should," "ought to," or "has a right to." In many cases, the original source of the requirement is not recalled.

Though we have oversimplified such evaluations of behavior with a positive-neutral-negative trichotomy, the evaluation of behaviors by the person is really more one of degree. This dimension of evaluation, we shall call "legitimacy." Conceptually, we may think of legitimacy as a valence in a region which is induced by some internalized norm or value. This value has the same conceptual property as power, namely an ability to induce force fields (26, p. 40–41). It may or may not be correct that values (or the super-ego) are internalized parents, but at least they can set up force fields which have a phenomenal "oughtness" similar to a parent's prescription. Like a value, a need can also induce valences (i.e., force fields) in P's psychological environment, but these valences have more the phenomenal character of noxious or attractive properties of the object or activity. When a need induces a valence in P—for example, when a need makes an object attractive to P—this attraction applies to P but not to other persons. When a value induces a valence, on the other hand, it not only sets up forces on P to engage in the activity, but P may feel that all others ought to behave in the same way. Among other things, this evaluation applies to the legitimate right of some other individual or group to prescribe behavior or beliefs for a person even though the other cannot apply sanctions.

Legitimate power of O/P is here defined as that power which stems from internalized values in P which dictate that O has a legitimate right to influence P and that P has an obligation to accept this influence. We note that legitimate power is very similar to the notion of legitimacy of authority, which has long been explored by sociologists, particularly by Weber (42), and more recently by Goldhammer and Shils (14). However, legitimate power is not always a role relation: P may accept an induction from O simply because he had previously promised to help O and he values his word too much to break the promise. In all cases, the notion of legitimacy involves some sort of code or standard accepted by the individual by virtue of which the external agent can assert his power. We shall attempt to describe a few of these values here.

### Bases for Legitimate Power

Cultural values constitute one common basis for the legitimate power of one individual over another. O has characteristics which are specified by the culture as giving him the right to prescribe behavior for P, who may not have these characteristics. These bases, which Weber (42) has called the authority of the "eternal yesterday," include some things as age, intelligence, caste, and physical characteristics. In some cultures, the aged are granted the right to prescribe behavior for others in practically all behavior areas. In most cultures, there are certain areas of behavior in which a person of one sex is granted the right to prescribe behavior for the other sex.

Acceptance of the social structure is another basis for legitimate power. If P accepts as right the social structure of his group, organization, or society, especially the social structure involving a hierarchy of authority, P will accept the legitimate authority of O who occupies a superior office in the hierarchy. Thus legitimate power in a formal organization is largely a relationship between offices rather than between persons. And the acceptance of an office as *right* is a basis for legitimate power—a judge has a right to levy fines; a foreman should assign work; a priest is justified in prescribing religious beliefs; and it is the management's prerogative to make certain decisions **(10).** However, legitimate power also involves the perceived right of the person to hold the office.

Designation by a legitimizing agent is a third basis for legitimate power. An influencer O may be seen as legitimate in prescribing behavior for P because he has been granted such power by a legitimizing agent whom P accepts. Thus, a department head may accept the authority of his vice president in a certain area because that authority has been specifically delegated by the president. An election is perhaps the most common example of a group's serving to legitimize the authority of one individual or office for other individuals in the group. The success of such legitimizing depends upon the acceptance of the legitimizing agent and procedure. In this case it depends ultimately on certain democratic values concerning election procedures. The election process is one of legitimizing a person's right to an office which already has a legitimate range of power associated with it.

### Range of Legitimate Power of O/P

The areas in which legitimate power may be exercised are generally specified along with the designation of that power. A job description, for example, usually specifies supervisory activities and also designates the person to whom the jobholder is responsible for the duties described. Some bases for legitimate authority carry with them a very broad range. Culturally derived bases for legitimate power are often especially broad. It is not uncommon to find cultures in which a member of a given caste can legitimately prescribe behavior for all members of lower castes in practically all regions. More common, however, are instances of legitimate power where the range is specifically and narrowly prescribed. A sergeant in the army is given a specific set of regions within which he can legitimately prescribe behavior for his men.

The attempted use of legitimate power which is outside of the range of legitimate power will decrease the legitimate power of the authority figure. Such use of power which is not legitimate will also decrease the attractiveness of O **(11, 12, 36).**

### Legitimate Power and Influence

The new state of the system which results from legitimate power usually has high dependence on O though it may become independent. Here, however, the degree of dependence is not related to the level of observability. Since legitimate power is based on P's values, the source of the forces induced by O include both these internal values and O. O's induction serves to activate the values and to relate them to the system which is influenced, but thereafter the new state of the system may become directly dependent on the values with no mediation by O. Accordingly, this new state will be relatively stable and consistent across varying environmental situations, since P's values are more stable than his psychological environment.

We have used the term *legitimate* not only as a basis for the power of an agent, but also to describe the general behaviors of a person. Thus, the individual P may also consider the legitimacy of the attempts to use other types of power by O. In certain cases, P will consider that O has a legitimate right to threaten punishment for nonconformity; in other cases, such use of coercion would not be seen as legitimate. P might change in response to coercive power of O, but it will make a considerable difference in his attitude and conformity if O is not seen as having a legitimate right to use such coercion. In such cases, the attraction of P for O will be particularly diminished, and the influence attempt will arouse more resistance **(11).** Similarly the utilization of reward power may vary in legitimacy; the word *bribe,* for example, denotes an illegitimate reward.

## REFERENT POWER

The referent power of O/P has its basis in the identification of P with O. By identification, we mean a feeling of oneness of P with O, or a desire for such an identity. If O is a person toward whom P is highly attracted, P will have a desire to become closely associated with O. If O is an attractive group, P will have a feeling of membership or a desire to join. If P is already closely associated with O, he will want to maintain this relationship **(39, 41).** P's identification with O can be established or maintained if P behaves, believes, and perceives as O does. Accordingly, O has the ability to influence P, even though P may be unaware of this referent power. A verbalization of such power by P might be, "I am like O, and therefore I shall behave or believe as O does," or "I want to be like O, and I will be more like O if I behave or believe as O does." The stronger the identification of P with O the greater the referent power of O/P.

Similar types of power have already been investigated under a number of different formulations. Festinger (7) points out that in an ambiguous situation, the individual seeks some sort of "social reality" and may adopt the cognitive structure of the individual or group with which he identifies. In such a case, the lack of clear structure may be threatening to the individual, and the agreement of his beliefs with those of a reference group will both satisfy his need for structure and give him added security through increased identification with his group (16, 19).

We must try to distinguish between referent power and other types of power which might be operative at the same time. If a member is attracted to a group and he conforms to its norms only because he fears ridicule or expulsion from the group for nonconformity, we would call this coercive power. On the other hand, if he conforms in order *to obtain praise* for conformity, it is a case of reward power. The basic criterion for distinguishing referent power from both coercive and reward power is the mediation of the punishment and the reward by O: To the extent that O mediates the sanctions (i.e., has means control over P), we are dealing with coercive and reward power; but to the extent that P avoids discomfort or gains satisfaction by conformity based on identification, regardless of O's responses, we are dealing with referent power. *Conformity with majority opinion* is sometimes based on a respect for the collective wisdom of the group, in which case it is expert power. It is important to distinguish these phenomena, all grouped together elsewhere as "pressures toward uniformity," since the type of change which occurs will be different for different bases of power.

The concepts of "reference group" (40) and "prestige suggestion" may be treated as instances of referent power. In this case, O, the prestigeful person or group, is valued by P; because P desires to be associated or identified with O, he will assume attitudes or beliefs held by O. Similarly a negative reference group which O dislikes and evaluates negatively may exert negative influence on P as a result of negative referent power.

It has been demonstrated that the power which we designate as referent power is espe-cially great when P is attracted to O (2, 7, 8, 9, 13, 23, 30). In our terms, this would mean that the greater the attraction, the greater the identification, and consequently the greater the referent power. In some cases, attraction or prestige may have a specific basis, and the range of referent power will be limited accordingly: A group of campers may have great referent power over a member regarding campcraft, but considerably less effect on other regions (30). However, we hypothesize that the greater the attraction of P toward O, the broader the range of referent power of O/P.

The new state of a system produced by referent power may be dependent on or independent of O; but the degree of dependence is not affected by the level of observability to O (6, 23). In fact, P is often not consciously aware of the referent power which O exerts over him. There is probably a tendency for some of these dependent changes to become independent of O quite rapidly.

## EXPERT POWER

The strength of the expert power of O/P varies with the extent of the knowledge or perception which P attributes to O within a given area. Probably P evaluates O's expertness in relation to his own knowledge as well as against an absolute standard. In any case expert power results in primary social influence on P's cognitive structure and probably not on other types of systems. Of course changes in the cognitive structure can change the direction of forces and hence of locomotion, but such a change of behavior is secondary social influence. Expert power has been demonstrated experimentally (8, 33). Accepting an attorney's advice in legal matters is a common example of expert influence; but there are many instances based on much less knowledge, such as the acceptance by a stranger of directions given by a native villager.

Expert power, where O need not be a member of P's group, is called "informational power" by Deutsch and Gerard (4). This type of expert power must be distinguished from influence based on the content of communication as described by Hovland et al. (17, 18, 23, 24). The influence of the content of a communication upon an opinion is presumably a secondary influence produced after the *primary* influence (i.e., the acceptance of the information). Since power is here defined in terms of the primary changes, the influence of the content on a related opinion is not a case of expert power as we have defined it, but the initial acceptance of the validity of the content does seem to be based on expert power or referent power. In other cases, however, so-called facts may be accepted as self-evident because they fit into P's cognitive structure; if this impersonal acceptance of the truth of the fact is independent of the more or less enduring relationship between O and P, then P's acceptance of the fact is not an actualization of expert power. Thus we distinguish between expert power based on the credibility of O and informational influence which is based on characteristics of the stimulus such as the logic of the argument or the "self-evident facts."

Wherever expert influence occurs, it seems to be necessary both for P to think that O knows and for P to trust that O is telling the truth (rather than trying to deceive him).

Expert power will produce a new cognitive structure which is initially relatively dependent on O, but informational influence will produce a more independent structure. The former is likely to become more independent with the passage of time. In both cases the degree of dependence on O is not affected by the level of observability.

The "sleeper effect" (18, 24) is an interesting case of a change in the degree of dependence of an opinion on O. An unreliable O (who probably had negative referent power but some positive expert power) presented "facts" which were accepted by the subjects and which would normally produce secondary influence on their opinions and beliefs. However, the negative referent power aroused resistance and resulted in negative social influence on their beliefs (i.e., set up a force in the direction opposite to the influence attempt), so that there was little change in the subjects' opinions. With the passage of time, however, the subjects tended to forget the identity of the negative communicator faster than they forgot the contents of his communication, so there was a weakening of the negative referent influence and a consequent delayed positive change in the subjects' beliefs in the direction of the influence attempt ("sleeper effect"). Later, when the identity of the negative communicator was experimentally reinstated, these resisting forces were reinstated, and there was another negative change in belief in a direction opposite to the influence attempt (24).

The range of expert power, we assume, is more delimited than that of referent power. Not only is it restricted to cognitive systems, but the expert is seen as having superior knowledge or ability in very specific areas, and his power will be limited to these areas, though some "halo effect" might occur. Recently, some of our renowned physical scientists have found quite painfully that their expert power in physical sciences does not extend to regions involving international politics. Indeed, there is some evidence that the attempted exertion of expert power outside of the range of expert power will reduce that expert power. An undermining of confidence seems to take place.

## Summary

We have distinguished five types of power: referent power, expert power, reward power, coercive power, and legitimate power. These distinctions led to the following hypotheses.

1. For all five types, the stronger the basis of power, the greater the power.

2. For any type of power, the size of the range may vary greatly, but, in general, referent power will have the broadest range.

3. Any attempt to utilize power outside the range of power will tend to reduce the power.

4. A new state of a system produced by reward power or coercive power will be highly dependent on O, and the more observable P's conformity, the more dependent the state. For the other three types of power, the new state is usually dependent, at least in the beginning, but in any case the level of observability has no effect on the degree of dependence.

5. Coercion results in decreased attraction of P toward O and high resistance; reward power results in increased attraction and low resistance.

6. The more legitimate the coercion, the less it will produce resistance and decreased attraction.

## Notes

1. Though the primary influence of coercive power is dependent, it often produces secondary changes which are independent. Brainwashing, for example, utilizes coercive power to produce many primary changes in the life space of the prisoner, but these dependent changes can lead to identification with the aggressor and hence to secondary changes in ideology which are independent.

## References

<sup>1</sup> Asch, S. E. *Social psychology.* New York: Prentice-Hall, 1952.

<sup>2</sup> Back, K. W. Influence through social communication. *J. Abnorm. Soc. Psychol.*, 1951, 46, 9–23.

[3] Coch, L., & French, J. R. P., Jr. Overcoming resistance to change. *Hum. Relat.,* 1948, 1, 512–32.

[4] Deutsch, M., & Gerard, H. B. A study of normative and informational influences upon individual judgment. *J. Abnorm. Soc. Psychol.,* 1955, 51, 629–36.

[5] Dittes, J. E., & Kelley, H. H. Effects of different conditions of acceptance upon conformity to group norms. *J. Abnorm. Soc. Psychol.,* 1956, 53, 100–107.

[6] Festinger, L. An analysis of compliant behavior. In Sherif, M., & Wilson, M. O., (Eds.). *Group relations at the crossroads.* New York: Harper, 1953, 232–56.

[7] Festinger, L. Informal social communication. *Psychol. Rev.,* 1950, 57, 271–82.

[8] Festinger, L., Gerard, H. B., Hymovitch, B., Kelley, H. H., & Raven, B. H. The influence process in the presence of extreme deviates. *Hum. Relat.,* 1952, 5, 327–346.

[9] Festinger, L., Schacter, S., & Back, K. The operation of group standards. In Cartwright, D., & Zander, A. *Group dynamics: research and theory.* Evanston: Row, Peterson, 1953, 204–23.

[10] French, J. R. P., Jr., Israel, Joachim, & Ås Dagfinn. "Arbeidernes medvirkning i industribedriften. En eksperimentell underøkelse." Institute for Social Research, Oslo, Norway, 1957.

[11] French, J. R. P., Jr., Levinger, G., & Morrison, H. W. The legitimacy of coercive power. In preparation.

[12] French, J. R. P., Jr., & Raven, B. H. An experiment in legitimate and coercive power. In preparation.

[13] Gerard, H. B. The anchorage of opinions in face-to-face groups. *Hum. Relat.,* 1954, 7, 313–325.

[14] Goldhammer, H., & Shils, E. A. Types of power and status. *Amer. J. Sociol.,* 1939, 45, 171–178.

[15] Herbst, P. G. Analysis and measurement of a situation. *Hum. Relat.,* 1953, 2, 113–140.

[16] Hochbaum, G. M. Self-confidence and reactions to group pressures. *Amer. Soc. Rev.,* 1954, 19, 678–687.

[17] Hovland, C. I., Lumsdaine, A. A., & Sheffield, F. D. *Experiments on mass communication.* Princeton: Princeton Univer. Press, 1949.

[18] Hovland, C. I., & Weiss, W. The influence of source credibility on communication effectiveness. *Publ. Opin. Quart.,* 1951, 15, 635–650.

[19] Jackson, J. M., & Saltzstein, H. D. The effect of person-group relationships on conformity processes. *J. Abnorm. Soc. Psychol.,* 1958, 57, 17–24.

[20] Jahoda, M. Psychological issues in civil liberties. *Amer. Psychologist,* 1956, 11, 234–240.

[21] Katz, D., & Schank, R. L. *Social psychology.* New York: Wiley, 1938.

[22] Kelley, H. H., & Volkart, E. H. The resistance to change of group-anchored attitudes. *Amer. Soc. Rev.,* 1952, 17, 453–465.

[23] Kelman, H. Three processes of acceptance of social influence: compliance, identification and internalization. Paper read at the meeting of the American Psychological Association, August 1956.

[24] Kelman, H., & Hovland, C. I. "Reinstatement" of the communicator in delayed measurement of opinion change. *J. Abnorm. Soc. Psychol.,* 1953, 48, 327–335.

[25] Lewin, K. *Dynamic theory of personality.* New York: McGraw-Hill, 1935, 114–170.

[26] Lewin, K. *Field theory in social science.* New York: Harper, 1951.

[27] Lewin, K., Lippitt, R., & White, R. K. Patterns of aggressive behavior in experimentally created social climates. *J. Soc. Psychol.,* 1939, 10, 271–301.

[28] Lasswell, H. D., & Kaplan, A. *Power and society: A framework for political inquiry.* New Haven: Yale Univer. Press, 1950.

[29] Linton, R. *The cultural background of personality.* New York: Appleton-Century-Crofts, 1945.

[30] Lippitt, R., Polansky, N., Redl, F., & Rosen, S. The dynamics of power. *Hum. Relat.,* 1952, 5, 37–64.

[31] March, J. G. An introduction to the theory and measurement of influence. *Amer. Polit. Sci. Rev.,* 1955, 49, 431–451.

[32] Miller, J. G. Toward a general theory for the behavioral sciences. *Amer. Psychologist,* 1955, 10, 513–531.

[33] Moore, H. T. The comparative influence of majority and expert opinion. *Amer. J. Psychol.,* 1921, 32, 16–20.

[34] Newcomb, T. M. *Social psychology.* New York: Dryden, 1950.

[35] Raven, B. H. The effect of group pressures on opinion, perception, and communication. Unpublished doctoral dissertation, University of Michigan, 1953.

[36] Raven, B. H., & French, J. R. P., Jr. Group support, legitimate power, and social influence. *J. Person.,* 1958, 26, 400–409.

[37] Rommetveit, R. *Social norms and roles.* Minneapolis: Univer. Minnesota Press, 1953.

[38] Russell, B. *Power: A new social analysis.* New York: Norton, 1938.

[39] Stotland, E., Zander, A., Burnstein, E., Wolfe, D., & Natsoulas, T. Studies on the effects of identification. University of Michigan, Institute for Social Research. Forthcoming.

[40] Swanson, G. E., Newcomb, T. M., & Hartley, E. L. *Readings in social psychology.* New York: Henry Holt, 1952.

[41] Torrance, E. P., & Mason, R. Instructor effort to influence: An experimental evaluation of six approaches. Paper presented at USAF-NRC Symposium on Personnel, Training, and Human Engineering. Washington, DC, 1956.

[42] Weber, M. *The theory of social and economic organization.* Oxford: Oxford Univer. Press, 1947.

**Reading 18**

# Consequences of Influence Tactics Used with Subordinates, Peers, and the Boss

**Gary Yukl and J. Bruce Tracey**
School of Business, State University of New York at Albany

One of the most important determinants of managerial effectiveness is success in influencing people and developing their commitment to task objectives (Yukl, 1989). Despite the obvious importance of this subject, there has not been much empirical research on the influence behavior of managers. Several studies have examined issues such as how often various influence tactics are used by managers with different targets and for different influence objectives (Ansari & Kapoor, 1987; Erez & Rim, 1982; Erez, Rim, & Keider, 1986; Kipnis, Schmidt, & Wilkinson, 1980; Schmidt & Kipnis, 1984; Yukl & Falbe, 1990). Only a handful of studies have considered the relative effectiveness of different influence tactics.

Mowday (1978) investigated the relationship between the self-rated use of five influence tactics by elementary school principals and ratings made by the immediate superior of each principal on the principal's overall effectiveness in exercising influence. Only one tactic (information distortion) discriminated significantly between more and less effective principals.

Kipnis and Schmidt (1988) used profiles of scale scores on their self-report influence questionnaire to cluster managers into four influencer types, which were then compared with regard to performance evaluations. Kipnis and Schmidt found that shotgun managers (with high scores on assertiveness, appeal to higher authority, and coalition) received the lowest performance ratings and that tacticians (who used rational persuasion more than other tactics) received the highest performance ratings; ingratiators (who used ingratiation more than other tactics) received only a moderate performance rating.

Schilit and Locke (1982) had students interview managers to obtain descriptions of successful or unsuccessful upward influence attempts, either from the perspective of the agent (subordinate) or

from the perspective of the target (boss). The influence tactics used in each incident were coded into 18 categories, and the frequency of use for each tactic was compared for successful and unsuccessful influence attempts. Few significant differences were found, and the results for these tactics were not consistent across the two samples. . . .

The current study had two research objectives. The primary objective was to investigate the effectiveness of different influence tactics for influencing subordinates, peers, and superiors. Our research attempts to overcome the limitations of earlier research on tactic effectiveness by examining all three directions of influence, by including task commitment as an immediate criterion of influence success in addition to performance ratings, and by comparing a wide variety of potentially relevant influence tactics in the same study.

A secondary objective was to clarify and extend what is known about directional differences in how often various influence tactics are used with subordinates, peers, and superiors. Three prior studies (Erez et al., 1986; Kipnis et al., 1980; Yukl & Falbe, 1990) examined directional differences in the use of influence tactics. Fairly consistent results were found for pressure and exchange, but results were inconsistent across studies for other tactics. In the current study, we used a matched design with a large number of respondents to provide a more powerful test of directional differences than was possible in the earlier research involving a random groups design. Directional differences in tactic effectiveness and frequency of use were examined together for the first time in the same study in an attempt to integrate these previously separate lines of research.

## TACTICS AND MODEL

The study reported in this article deals with the nine influence tactics defined in Table 1. . . . The nine tactics cover a wide variety of proactive influence behaviors likely to be relevant to a manager's effectiveness in influencing others. These

Source: Edited and reprinted with permission from *Journal of Applied Psychology* 77, no. 4 (1992), pp. 525–535. Copyright (1992), American Psychological Association.

**TABLE 1   Definition of Influence Tactics**

| Tactic | Definition |
|--------|------------|
| Rational persuasion | The person uses logical arguments and factual evidence to persuade you that a proposal or request is viable and likely to result in the attainment of task objectives. |
| Inspirational appeal | The person makes a request or proposal that arouses enthusiasm by appealing to your values, ideals, and aspirations or by increasing your confidence that you can do it. |
| Consultation | The person seeks your participation in planning a strategy, activity, or change for which your support and assistance are desired, or the person is willing to modify a proposal to deal with your concerns and suggestions. |
| Ingratiation | The person seeks to get you in a good mood or to think favorably of him or her before asking you to do something. |
| Exchange | The person offers an exchange of favors, indicates willingness to reciprocate at a later time, or promises you a share of the benefits if you help accomplish a task. |
| Personal appeal | The person appeals to your feelings of loyalty and friendship toward him or her before asking you to do something. |
| Coalition | The person seeks the aid of others to persuade you to do something or uses the support of others as a reason for you to agree also. |
| Legitimating | The person seeks to establish the legitimacy of a request by claiming the authority or right to make it or by verifying that it is consistent with organizational, policies, rules, practices, or traditions. |
| Pressure | The person uses demands, threats, or persistent reminders to influence you to do what he or she wants. |

influence tactics have been used in prior research on influence effectiveness, but none of the prior studies included all nine of the tactics. . . .

In our preliminary model, the following factors determine the effectiveness of an influence tactic used by a particular agent in a particular context: (a) consistency with prevailing social norms and role expectations about the use of the tactic in that context, (b) the agent's possession of an appropriate power base for use of the tactic in that context, (c) potential of the tactic to influence the target's attitudes about the desirability of the requested action, (d) the agent's skill in using the tactic, and (e) the amount of intrinsic resistance by the target due to the nature of the request. The underlying assumption is that a tactic is more likely to be successful if the target perceives it to be a socially acceptable form of influence behavior, if the agent has sufficient position and personal power to use the tactic, if the tactic has the capability to affect the target's attitudes about the desirability of the request, if the tactic is used in a skillful way, and if it is used for a request that is legitimate and consistent with the target's values and needs. The model is used to derive specific hypotheses about the effectiveness of the nine tactics for influencing target commitment in a downward, lateral, or upward direction. For example, according to Kelman's (1958) theory of influence processes, tactics that are likely to cause internalization of favorable attitudes about the request (e.g., consultation, inspirational appeal, and rational persuasion) ought to be more successful than tactics that cause behavioral compliance without changing the target's attitudes. Tactics involving coercion and manipulation (e.g., pressure, legitimating, and some forms of coalition) are less socially acceptable than tactics that appeal to the target's informed judgment or to the target's friendship and identification with the agent. This set of tactics is least likely to result in target commitment.

## HYPOTHESES

Hypotheses about the use and effectiveness of each tactic for influencing target task commitment are presented next, along with a rationale for each hypothesis that is based on our preliminary model and on prior research. Formal hypotheses were not made for ratings of a manager's overall effectiveness because this criterion can be affected by many things besides a manager's use of influence tactics.

*Hypothesis 1a.* Rational persuasion is used more in an upward direction than in a downward or lateral direction.

*Hypothesis 1b.* Rational persuasion increases task commitment in all three directions.

Rational persuasion involves the use of logical arguments and factual information to convince a target that the agent's request or proposal is feasible and consistent with shared objectives (Eagly & Chaiken, 1984). This is a flexible tactic that can be used for influence attempts in any direction. Nevertheless, rational persuasion is likely to be used more in an upward direction than in other directions, because in an upward direction a manager is limited by a weaker power base and role expectations that discourage the use of some tactics (see discussion of other hypotheses). Directional differences for the use of rational persuasion were not consistent in three prior studies conducted with questionnaires (Erez et al., 1986; Kipnis et al., 1980; Yukl & Falbe, 1990). Agents reported greater use of this tactic in upward influence attempts, but directional differences were not found for targets.

Results for the consequences of using rational persuasion have been inconsistent also. In the questionnaire study by Kipnis and Schmidt (1988), managers who received the highest performance ratings had a profile in which rational persuasion was the dominant tactic for upward influence attempts. However, rational persuasion was not related to successful upward influence in the questionnaire study by Mowday (1978). Likewise, tactics involving aspects of rational persuasion were not related to outcome success in the four critical incident studies described earlier.

*Hypothesis 2a.* Inspirational appeals are used more in a downward direction than in a lateral or upward direction.

*Hypothesis 2b.* Inspirational appeals increase task commitment in all three directions.

Inspirational appeals use the target's values, ideals, aspirations, and emotions as a basis for gaining commitment to a request or proposal (Yukl, 1990). Inspirational appeals appear feasible for influence attempts made in any direction, but this tactic is especially appropriate for gaining the commitment of someone to work on a new task or project. Influence attempts involving task assignments occur most often in a downward direction and least often in an upward direction (Erez et al., 1986; Kipnis et al., 1980; Yukl & Falbe, 1990). Thus, managers have more opportunity to use inspirational appeals with subordinates than with peers or superiors. In the only prior study to examine directional differences for inspirational appeals, Yukl and Falbe (1990) found that inspirational appeals were used more in downward influence attempts than in lateral or upward influence attempts.

There is little evidence about the likely effectiveness of inspirational appeals, and this research deals only with the downward influence of leaders over subordinates. Descriptive studies of charismatic and transformational leadership (Bass, 1985; Conger, 1989; Tichy & Devanna, 1986) have found that managers who motivate exceptional effort by subordinates present a clear and inspiring vision, which is one type of inspirational appeal.

*Hypothesis 3a.* Consultation is used more in a downward direction than in a lateral or upward direction.

*Hypothesis 3b.* Consultation increases task commitment in all three directions.

When people gain a sense of ownership of a project, strategy, or change after participating in planning how to implement it, they are likely to be more committed to making the project, strategy, or change successful (Yukl, 1989). This influence tactic can be used in any direction, but it appears especially appropriate in the situation in which an agent has the authority to plan a task or project but relies on the target to help implement the plans. Because authority to assign work and make changes in work procedures is mostly downward, a manager probably has more opportunity to use consultation to influence subordinates than to influence peers or superiors (Yukl & Falbe, 1990). Only one study examined directional differences in frequency of use for consultation (Yukl & Falbe, 1990), and results were mixed. Agents reported greater use of consultation in a downward direction, but directional differences were not significant for target reports.

Evidence on the likely effectiveness of consultation as an influence tactic is limited and inconsistent. Schilit and Locke (1982) found that a consultation tactic (using the target as a platform to present ideas) was likely to be effective in upward incidents reported by targets, but the results were not significant for upward incidents reported by agents in that study or in the study by Case et al. (1988). In the study by Dosier et al. (1988) of downward incidents reported by agents, results for consultation tactics (listening, soliciting ideas) were not significant. Indirect evidence comes from research on leadership, which finds that consultation with individual subordinates is effective for increasing decision acceptance in some situations but not in others (see Vroom & Jago, 1988).

*Hypothesis 4a.* Ingratiation is used more in a downward and lateral direction than in an upward direction.

*Hypothesis 4b.* Ingratiation has a stronger positive effect on task commitment in a downward and lateral direction than in an upward direction.

The basis for influence in ingratiation is an increase in the target's feeling of positive regard toward the agent. Flattery, praise, expression of acceptance, and expression of agreement are used to increase the agent's attractiveness to the target (Liden & Mitchell, 1988; Tedeschi & Melburg, 1984). A target is more likely to cooperate with an agent for whom the target has feelings of positive regard. Compliments and flattery are more credible when the status and power of the agent is greater than that of the target (Wortman & Linsenmeier, 1977). Thus, ingratiation is most likely to increase positive regard and influence target cooperation when the agent is a superior, and it is least likely to do so when the agent is a subordinate.

Findings on directional differences in the use of ingratiation are somewhat inconsistent. In the studies by Kipnis et al. (1980) and Yukl and Falbe (1990), agents reported that ingratiation was used more in downward and lateral influence attempts than in upward influence attempts. No significant directional differences were found for target reports in the study by Yukl and Falbe (1990), and no clear pattern emerged for agent and target reports in the study by Erez et al. (1986).

Only two studies have examined the consequences of using ingratiation as a proactive influence tactic. In their questionnaire study of upward influence, Kipnis and Schmidt (1988) found that male managers whose influence profile involved a relatively high use of ingratiation received only moderate performance ratings but that female ingratiators received higher performance ratings. Outcome success was not significantly affected by ingratiation tactics (using courtesy, kind manners, or friendliness) in lateral incidents described by agents in the study by Keys et al. (1987).

*Hypothesis 5a.* Exchange is used more in a downward and lateral direction than in an upward direction.

*Hypothesis 5b.* Exchange has a stronger positive effect on task commitment in a downward and lateral direction than in an upward direction.

Exchange tactics involve explicit or implicit offers by an agent to provide a favor or benefit to the target in return for doing what the agent requests. To be effective, the agent must offer something the target considers desirable and appropriate (Yukl, 1990). Managers usually have considerable control over resources and rewards desired by subordinates. The potential for exchange with peers depends on the amount of lateral task interdependence and a manager's control over resources desired by peers. Descriptive studies have found that exchange is often used to obtain support and assistance from peers (see A. Cohen & Bradford, 1989; Kaplan, 1986). Managers have little control over resources desired by superiors, and it is awkward to initiate an exchange of tangible benefits with them because it is not consistent with role expectations. Thus, there is more opportunity to use exchange with subordinates and peers than with superiors. Three prior studies (Erez et al., 1986; Kipnis et al., 1980; Yukl & Falbe, 1990) found that exchange was used more in downward and lateral influence attempts than in upward influence attempts.

Results for the consequences of using exchange are not as clear or consistent. Schilit and Locke (1982) found that exchange (trading job-related benefits) was more likely to be successful than unsuccessful in upward critical incidents described by targets, but results for this tactic were not significant in upward incidents described by agents. No significant effects of exchange tactics (offering to trade favors or concessions) were found in the study of upward incidents by Case et al. (1988), in the study of lateral incidents by Keys et al. (1987), or in the questionnaire study by Mowday (1978) of upward influence.

*Hypothesis 6a.* Personal appeals are used more in a lateral direction than in a downward or upward direction.

*Hypothesis 6b.* Personal appeals increase task commitment in all three directions.

Personal appeals are based on referent power already possessed by the agent (Yukl, 1990). When a target has strong feelings of friendship toward the agent, it is more likely that the agent can appeal successfully to the target to do something unusual or extra as a special favor (e.g., do some of my work, make a change to accommodate me, help me deal with a problem). This tactic appears to be most appropriate for influence attempts with peers, because managers often need to ask for favors from peers but lack the authority to ensure compliance with a formal request (Kotter, 1982). However, no prior research has been conducted on directional differences in the use of personal appeals.

Only three studies have directly examined the effectiveness of personal appeals as an influence tactic. In the critical incident study by Schilit and Locke (1982), personal appeals (asking for favors or pity) were not related to success in upward influence attempts. Likewise, in the critical incidents study by Case et al. (1988), personal appeals (pleading, begging, or asking favors) were not related to the success of upward influence attempts. In the critical incidents study by Keys et al. (1987), personal appeals (appealing to sympathy of target) were not related to the success of lateral influence attempts. Some indirect evidence is provided by a study that found a positive correlation between a manager's referent power and the task commitment of subordinates and peers (Yukl & Falbe, 1991). Other power studies (see Podsakoff & Schriesheim, 1985) have found a positive correlation between a manager's referent power and measures of subordinate satisfaction and performance.

*Hypothesis 7a.* Coalition tactics are used more in a lateral and upward direction than in a downward direction.

*Hypothesis 7b.* Coalition tactics are negatively related to task commitment in all three directions.

With coalition tactics, an agent enlists the aid or endorsement of other people to influence a target to do what the agent wants (Stevenson, Pearce, & Porter, 1985). There is evidence from descriptive research that managers use coalitions to influence peers and superiors to support changes, innovations, and new projects (Kanter, 1983; Kotter, 1982). Yukl and Falbe (1990) proposed that coalitions are less likely to be used in downward influence attempts, because managers usually have substantial power over subordinates, and having to ask for help to influence a subordinate may reflect unfavorably on the competence of the manager. In a study by Erez et al. (1986), agents reported that coalitions were used most often in a lateral direction. However, in two other studies with agent reports (Kipnis et al., 1980; Yukl & Falbe, 1990) and in two studies with target reports (Erez et al., 1986; Yukl & Falbe, 1990), no significant directional differences were found for use of coalition tactics.

Coalitions are used most often as a follow-up tactic after the target has already resisted a direct influence attempt by the agent (Yukl & Falbe, 1992). Thus, use of this tactic often indicates a type of request or proposal for which target commitment is especially difficult to attain. Moreover, this tactic is likely to be viewed as manipulative by a target who is aware that the agent is using it. The most offensive form of coalition may be an upward appeal to the target's superior to pressure the target to comply with the agent's request.

Studies on the consequences of using coalition tactics have yielded inconsistent results. In the questionnaire study by Kipnis and Schmidt (1988), self-reported use of coalitions in upward influence was part of the profile for managers who received the lowest performance ratings. Only one of four critical incident studies found evidence that coalition tactics are effective. In a study by Keys et al. (1987), a lateral influence attempt was more likely to be successful when the

agent used a coalition tactic (gain support of several peers to influence target). In the critical incident study by Schilit and Locke (1982), coalition tactics (using group or peer support) were not significantly related to outcome success in upward influence attempts. Likewise, outcome success was not significantly related to use of a coalition tactic (soliciting assistance of peers) in the study of downward incidents by Dosier et al. (1988) or to use of coalition tactics (developing and showing support of peers, subordinates, or outsiders) in the study of upward incidents by Case et al. (1988).

*Hypothesis 8a.* Legitimating tactics are used more in a lateral direction than in a downward or upward direction.

*Hypothesis 8b.* Legitimating tactics are negatively related to task commitment in all three directions.

Legitimating tactics involve efforts to verify the legitimacy of a request and the agent's authority or right to make it. This tactic is most appropriate for a request that is unusual and of doubtful legitimacy to the target person (Yukl, 1990). Legitimating tactics are needed most in a lateral direction because ambiguity about authority relationships and task responsibilities is greatest in this direction. Legitimating tactics are rarely needed in a downward direction, because most managers have considerable authority to direct the work activities of subordinates. Legitimating tactics are seldom needed in an upward direction, and they are difficult to use in this direction because of the limited basis for claiming a right to dictate the actions of a person with higher authority. Directional differences in use of legitimating tactics were not examined in prior research.

Legitimating tactics may induce the target to comply with a request if the target is convinced the request is within the agent's scope of authority and consistent with organizational rules and policies. Yukl and Falbe (1991) found that the most frequent reason reported by managers for complying with a request made by a superior or peer was the legitimacy of the request. However, there is little reason to expect legitimating tactics to increase task commitment, and a negative reaction by the target may occur if this kind of tactic is used in an arrogant and demanding manner (Yukl, 1989). Only a few studies have examined the consequences of using legitimating tactics. In Mowday's (1978) questionnaire study of upward influence, legitimating tactics were not correlated significantly with influence success. In the study by Schilit and Locke (1982), legitimating tactics (using organizational rules) were not related significantly to outcome success in upward influence incidents. In the study by Keys et al. (1987), legitimating tactics (calling on company policies, procedures, or rules) were not related significantly to outcome success in lateral influence incidents.

*Hypothesis 9a.* Pressure tactics are used more in a downward direction than in a lateral or upward direction.

*Hypothesis 9b.* Pressure tactics are negatively related to task commitment in all three directions.

Many pressure tactics involve the use of a manager's coercive power, which is greater in relation to subordinates than in relation to peers or superiors. Previous studies consistently find greater use of pressure in a downward direction (Erez et al., 1986; Kipnis et al., 1980; Yukl & Falbe, 1990). Pressure may elicit reluctant compliance from a target, but it is unlikely to result in commitment. Research with critical incidents indicates that pressure is used most often as a follow-up tactic after an initial influence attempt has already failed (Yukl, Falbe, & Youn, in press). Thus, use of this tactic often indicates a type of request or proposal for which target commitment or even compliance is difficult to attain. Moreover, in many situations pressure is viewed as an inappropriate form of influence behavior, and target resentment about an agent's use of coercion is likely to result in target resistance.

Most studies on the consequences of influence tactics have found either a negative or nonsignificant correlation between pressure and the success of an influence attempt. In the study by Kipnis and Schmidt (1988), self-reported use of pressure was a key part of the profile for managers who received the lowest performance ratings. In the study by Schilit and Locke (1982), targets reported that some pressure tactics used in upward influence attempts (threatening to go over target's head, challenging the power of the target) were likely to be unsuccessful. In the same study, agents reported that another pressure tactic (threatening to resign) was likely to be unsuccessful. In the study by Case et al. (1988), an upward influence attempt was likely to be unsuccessful when the agent used a pressure tactic (telling or arguing without support). In the study by Dosier et al, (1988) of downward critical incidents, there was a marginally significant ($p < .10$) negative relationship between pressure tactics (threatening, warning, reprimanding, or embarrassing) and the success of an influence attempt. In two other studies (Keys et al., 1987; Mowday, 1978) results for the effects of pressure were not significant. Research on the use of coercive power by managers (see Podsakoff & Schriesheim, 1985; Yukl & Falbe, 1991) provides indirect evidence that pressure tactics are unlikely to result in target commitment. . . .

## RESULTS

. . . Pairwise comparisons were assessed with Duncan's multiple-range test. Complete or partial support was found for all of the directional hypotheses except Hypothesis 3a (involving consultation). Consistent with Hypothesis 1a, rational persuasion was used most in an upward direction. Consistent with Hypotheses 2a and 9a, inspirational appeal and pressure were used most in a downward direction. Consistent with Hypothesis 4a, ingratiation was used less in an upward direction than in a lateral or downward direction. Partially consistent with Hypothesis 5a, exchange was used most in a lateral direction and least in an upward direction. Consistent with Hypothesis 7a, coalition was used least in a downward direction. The current study is the first to examine directional differences for personal appeal and legitimating tactics, and consistent with Hypotheses 6a and 8a, these tactics were used most in a lateral direction. . . .

## RELATION OF TACTICS TO TASK COMMITMENT

. . . Consistent with Hypotheses 1b, 2b, and 3b, rational persuasion, inspirational appeal, and consultation by the agent were correlated significantly with target's task commitment in all three directions. Consistent with Hypotheses 4b and 5b, agent ingratiation and exchange correlated significantly with task commitment for subordinates and peers, and each of these correlations was significantly larger ($p < .01$) than the corresponding (nonsignificant) correlation for upward influence. Hypothesis 6b was partially supported; personal appeal correlated significantly with task commitment for subordinates and peers but not for superiors. No directional differences were expected for personal appeal, and the pairwise differences among correlations were not significant for this tactic. Hypothesis 7b was not supported, but the results are consistent with the interpretation that coalition tactics were not effective for influencing task commitment in any direction. Partial support was found for Hypothesis 8b; legitimating tactics correlated negatively with task commitment for peers. Partial support was found for Hypothesis 9b; pressure was negatively correlated with task commitment for subordinates and peers. Directional differences were not expected for legitimating tactics or pressure, and the pairwise differences in correlations were not significant for these two tactics. . . .

The multiple regression analyses showed that even the most highly intercorrelated tactics may account for unique variance in target commitment, and this finding provides additional support for our assumption that the nine tactics are distinct forms of influence behavior. The results varied more across the three samples for the regression analyses than for the simple correlations, but in general the most effective tactics were still rational persuasion, inspirational appeal, and consultation, and the least effective tactics were still coalition, pressure, and legitimating. Compared with results from the correlational analyses, results in the multiple regression analyses were weaker for ingratiation, exchange, and personal appeal.

## RELATION OF TACTICS TO EFFECTIVENESS RATINGS

The correlations between influence tactics and the ratings of effectiveness made by a manager's boss were also analyzed. For analyses involving upward influence, data on influence tactics and managerial effectiveness were obtained from the same source, namely, the manager's boss. For downward influence, the group mean score on each influence tactic was computed for a manager's subordinates and correlated with the effectiveness rating made by the manager's boss. For lateral influence, the group mean score on each influence tactic was computed for a manager's peers and correlated with the effectiveness rating made by the manager's boss. Use of group-level analysis is consistent with the moderately high level of interrater agreement found for each tactic within the subordinate sample and the peer sample. Results for the correlations were similar in all three directions. Effectiveness ratings were correlated positively with a manager's use of rational persuasion, inspirational appeal, and consultation. Correlations for the remaining tactics were negative or nonsignificant.

As was done for task commitment, a multiple regression analysis was conducted for each sample. Only rational persuasion had a significant beta weight in the regression analyses for subordinates and peers. A manager's use of rational persuasion with subordinates accounted for 18 percent of the variance in boss ratings of the manager's effectiveness ($R = .43$), $F(9, 119) = 3.0$, $p < .01$. A manager's use of rational persuasion with peers accounted for 15 percent of the variance in effectiveness ratings made by the manager's boss ($R = .39$), $F(9, 119) = 2.4$, $p < .05$. For the sample of boss respondents, a manager's use of rational persuasion and inspirational appeals accounted for 34 percent of the variance in effectiveness ratings ($R = .59$), $F(9, 119) = 6.9$, $p < .01$.

## DISCUSSION

Previous research provides no clear indication of the tactics likely to be effective for influencing subordinates, peers, and managers. The current study yielded stronger results, and these results appear consistent with theory and behavioral research in other topic areas, such as leadership, motivation, attitude change, and conflict resolution. The results supported most of the hypotheses about the likely effectiveness of each tactic for influencing target task commitment.

In general, consultation, inspirational appeal, and rational persuasion were moderately effective for influencing task commitment, regardless of direction. These three tactics all involve an attempt to change the target's attitude about the desirability of the request, and the tactics are likely to be viewed as socially acceptable for influence attempts in all three directions.

Pressure, coalition, and legitimating were usually ineffective. The negative correlations between these tactics and target commitment probably reflects their frequent use in influence attempts when resistance is anticipated or has already occurred in an earlier influence attempt. In addition, these tactics are likely to be viewed as socially undesirable forms of influence behavior in many situations, and the target may become resentful or angry with the agent for trying to coerce or manipulate him or her.

Ingratiation and exchange were moderately effective for influencing subordinates and peers, but these two tactics were ineffective for influencing superiors. Agents have a weak power base from which to use these tactics in an upward direction, and they are likely to be viewed as manipulative in this context. Ingratiation is more effective when used as part of a long-term strategy for improving upward relations, rather than as a tactic for immediately influencing a superior.

Personal appeals also appeared to be moderately effective for influencing subordinates and peers, but the results for this tactic were weak and difficult to interpret. The weak results may reflect the relatively low reliability of this scale in the current study. The questionnaire will be revised in subsequent research to increase the number of items for personal appeals and ingratiation.

Fewer tactics were correlated significantly with ratings of managerial effectiveness than with task commitment, but the three tactics that correlated most strongly with task commitment also correlated consistently with effectiveness ratings. Regardless of direction, rational persuasion was clearly the best predictor of effectiveness ratings made by a manager's boss. The strong correlation between rational persuasion and effectiveness ratings may be due to a close association between a manager's skillful use of rational persuasion and rater perception of manager expertise. Because perception of a manager's expertise is a strong predictor of effectiveness ratings (Podsakoff & Schriesheim, 1985; Yukl & Falbe, 1991), it is not surprising that skillful use of rational persuasion (which requires considerable expertise) also correlated strongly with effectiveness ratings.

In general, the findings in the current study are consistent with the explanation proposed earlier for weak and inconsistent findings in the six prior studies, namely, the focus on upward influence and the use of weak criteria. Results for most tactics were weaker for upward influence attempts than for downward or lateral influence attempts. Likewise, most of our results were weaker when the criterion was a rating of managerial effectiveness rather than task commitment. We expected to find stronger results for target task commitment than for effectiveness ratings because the latter criterion is determined by many factors besides agent influence behavior. However, another possible explanation of stronger results for task commitment is use of the same respondent to provide information about the predictors and the criterion. The results for task commitment (and for effectiveness ratings in an upward direction) may be inflated somewhat by respondent biases or attributions.

Directional differences in frequency of use were found for all of the tactics except consultation. The directional differences were consistent with hypotheses based on an analysis of working relationships that exist in most organizations for managers and their subordinates, peers, and bosses. The greater number of significant directional differences found in this study than in the study by Yukl and Falbe (1990) is probably due to our use of large samples and a matched design in which the same focal managers were described by subordinates, peers, and bosses. In earlier studies on directional differences, each sample of respondents described a different set of focal managers, and only Kipnis et al. (1980) used a large sample.

Even though most directional differences were significant, they accounted for only a small proportion of the variance in the measure of tactics. As Yukl and Falbe (1990) found, the relative frequency of use for the tactics was similar in all three directions. Thus, direction does not appear to be a very important determinant of tactic selection in comparison with other factors. Overall, there was a moderate correspondence between effectiveness and frequency of use; effective tactics tended to be used more often in all directions. The reasons why managers select particular tactics should be examined more closely in future research. . . .

Our research findings have implications for improving managerial effectiveness because it is an advantage for a manager to know which tactics have the highest likelihood of success for influencing a subordinate, peer, or superior. However, because of the limitations of the study, caution is needed in offering guidelines until the results are verified in follow-up research with different methods and samples. The findings indicate that some tactics are more likely to be successful, but the results do not suggest that these tactics will always result in task commitment. The outcome of any particular influence attempt is determined by many factors besides influence tactics, and any tactic can result in target resistance if it is not appropriate for the situation or is used in an unskillful manner. . . .

## References

Ansari, M. A., & Kapoor, A. (1987). Organizational context and upward influence tactics. *Organizational Behavior and Human Decision Processes, 40,* 39–49.

Bass, B. M. (1985). *Leadership and performance beyond expectations.* New York: Free Press.

Case, T., Dosier, L., Murkinson, G., & Keys, B. (1988). How managers influence superiors: A study of upward influence tactics. *Leadership and Organizational Development Journal, 9*(4), *25–31.*

Cohen, A., & Bradford, D. (1989). Influence without authority: The use of alliances, reciprocity, and exchange to accomplish work. *Organizational Dynamics, 17,* 5–17.

Cohen, J., & Cohen, P. (1983). *Applied multiple regression/correlation analysis for the behavioral sciences.* Hillsdale, NJ: Erlbaum.

Conger, J. A. (1989). *The charismatic leader: Behind the mystique of exceptional leadership.* San Francisco, CA: Jossey-Bass.

Dosier, L., Case, T., & Keys, B. (1988). How managers influence subordinates: An empirical study of downward influence tactics. *Leadership and Organizational Development Journal, 9*(5), 22–28.

Eagly, A., & Chaiken, S. (1984). Cognitive theories of persuasion. In L. Berkowitz (Ed.), *Advances in experimental social psychology* (Vol. 17, pp. 267–359). San Diego, CA: Academic Press.

Erez, M., & Rim, Y. (1982). The relationship between goals, influence tactics, and personal and organizational variables. *Human Relations, 35,* 877–878.

Erez, M., Rim, Y., & Keider, I. (1986). The two sides of the tactics of influence: Agent vs. target. *Journal of Occupational Psychology, 59,* 25–39.

Kanter, R. M. (1983). *The change masters.* New York: Simon & Schuster.

Kaplan, R. E. (1986, Spring). Trade routes: The manager's network of relationships. *Organizational Dynamics,* pp. 37–52.

Kelman, H. C. (1958). Compliance, identification, and internalization: Three processes of attitude change. *Journal of Conflict Resolution, 2,* 51–60.

Keys, B., Case, T., Miller, T., Curran, K. E., & Jones, C. (1987). Lateral influence in organizations. *International Journal of Management, 4,* 425–431.

Kipnis, D., & Schmidt, S. M. (1988). Upward influence styles: Relationship with performance evaluations, salary, and stress. *Administrative Science Quarterly: 33,* 528–542.

Kipnis, D., Schmidt, S. M., & Wilkinson, I. (1980). Intraorganizational influence tactics: Explorations in getting one's way. *Journal of Applied Psychology: 65,* 440–452.

Kotter, J. P. (1982). *The general managers.* New York: Free Press.

Liden, R. C., & Mitchell, T. R. (1988). Ingratiatory behaviors in organizational settings. *Academy of Management Review, 13,* 572–587.

Mowday, R. T. (1978). The exercise of upward influence in organizations. *Administrative Science Quarterly: 23,* 137–156.

Podsakoff, P., & Schriesheim, C. (1985). Field studies of French and Raven's bases of power: Critique, re-analysis, and suggestions for future research. *Psychological Bulletin, 97,* 387–411.

Schilit, W. K., & Locke, E. (1982). A study of upward influence in organizations. *Administrative Science Quarterly, 27,* 304–316.

Schmidt, S. M., & Kipnis, D. L. (1984). Manager's pursuit of individual and organizational goals. *Human Relations, 37,* 781–794.

Schriesheim, C., & Hinkin, T. R. (1990). Influence tactics used by subordinates: A theoretical and empirical analysis and refinement of the Kipnis, Schmidt, and Wilkinson subscales. *Journal of Applied Psychology, 75,* 246–257.

Stevenson, W., Pearce, J., & Porter, L. (1985). The concept of "coalition" in organization theory and research. *Academy of Management Review, 10,* 256–268.

Tedeschi, J. T., & Melburg, V. (1984). Impression management and influence in the organization. In S. B. Bacharach & E. J. Lawler (Eds.), *Research in the sociology of organizations* (Vol. 3, pp. 31–58). Greenwich, CT: JAI Press.

Tichy, N. M., & Devanna, M. A. (1986). *The transformational leader.* New York: Wiley.

Vroom, V. H., & Jago, A. G. (1988). *The new leadership: Managing participation in organizations.* Englewood Cliffs, NJ: Prentice Hall.

Wortman, C. B., & Linsenmeier, J. A. (1977). Interpersonal attraction and techniques of ingratiation in organizational settings. In B. M. Staw & G. R. Salancik (Eds.), *New directions in organizational behavior* (pp. 133–178). Chicago: St. Clair Press.

Yukl, G. (1989). *Leadership in organizations.* Englewood Cliffs, NJ: Prentice-Hall.

Yukl, G. (1990). *Skills for managers and leaders.* Englewood Cliffs, NJ: Prentice-Hall.

Yukl, G., & Falbe, C. M. (1990). Influence tactics in upward, downward, and lateral influence attempts. *Journal of Applied Psychology, 75,* 132–140.

Yukl, G., & Falbe, C. M. (1991). The importance of different power sources in downward and lateral relations. *Journal of Applied Psychology, 76,* 416–423.

Yukl, G., Falbe, C. M., & Youn, J. Y. (in press). Patterns of influence behavior for managers. *Group and Organization Management.*

Yukl, G., Lepsinger, R., Lucia, T. (in press). Preliminary report on the development and validation of the Influence Behavior Questionnaire. In K. Clark & M. Clark (Eds.), *The impact of leadership.* Greensboro, NC: Center for Creative Leadership.

# Chapter **Seven**

# Leadership and Leader Behaviors

The studies of leader traits reported in Chapter 3 successfully identified a number of personal attributes that endow an individual with the *potential* to be a successful leader. However, while there are important traits, the characteristics that an individual possesses do not provide a complete picture of "who is the effective leader," nor an answer to the question, What determines leadership success? In an earlier reading, Ralph Stogdill (1948) suggested that leadership consists of movement and getting work accomplished. He noted that the leader–follower relationship could be seen as a working relationship, one in which the leader orchestrates group activity. Kirkpatrick and Locke (1991) also suggested that leadership can be seen as an activity, noting that people who possess a key set of traits are more likely to engage in the behaviors associated with effective leadership.

Following the inability to explain the "totality" of leadership and effective leadership by employing the traits that individuals carry with them into leadership situations, an interest in understanding what it is that effective leaders actually "do" emerged. Students of leadership began to focus on the *behaviors* that leaders engage in, and whether or not effective leadership was a function of the actual behaviors engaged in by leaders. David G. Bowers and Stanley E. Seashore (1966) defined leadership as "organizationally useful behavior by one member of an organizational family toward another member or members of that same organizational family" (p. 240).

During the late 1940s, major research efforts looking into leader behavior were launched at the University of Michigan and The Ohio State University. These initiatives resulted in the identification of a number of different leader behaviors and accompanying categorization schemes.

Some of the more popular typologies employed to categorize leader behavior have focused on the amount of control exercised (or closeness of supervision), employee- versus job-orientation, as well as some very specific behaviors (e.g., communication, representation, fraternization, and organization[1]). Theoretically, it has been reasoned that leader behaviors have an impact upon follower attitudes (e.g., satisfaction with the leader and the job), motivation, work-related behaviors (e.g., performance), and group properties (e.g., group cohesiveness), each of which ultimately has an impact upon work group effectiveness.

---

[1] E. A. Fleishman, "The Description of Supervisory Behavior," *Journal of Applied Psychology* 37 (1953), pp. 1–6.

The first reading in this chapter by Bowers and Seashore (1966) highlights the fact that the work conducted at the University of Michigan resulted in the identification of a number of different leader behaviors and leader behavior classification schemes. Four dimensions of leader behavior (i.e., support, interaction facilitation, goal emphasis, and work facilitation) emerged as "the basic structure of what one may term 'leadership'" (Bowers and Seashore, p. 247). (The self-assessments appearing at the end of this chapter opener provide you with the opportunity to profile your own leadership style as it pertains to several important leader behaviors.) Accompanying their review of significant leader behaviors, Bowers and Seashore provide an interesting perspective on leadership. They note that effective work groups tend to require the presence of *each* of these four behaviors, yet they go on to note that *anyone* in a group may provide these behaviors and that they need not be directly infused into the group by the leader. The formal leader's role may be one of making sure that the necessary behaviors are present and in sufficient degree.

Under the direction of Ralph Stogdill, a group of researchers at The Ohio State University began an extensive and systematic study directed toward the identification of the behaviors that were associated with effective group performance. This work identified several behaviors engaged in by leaders (e.g., integration, production emphasis, evaluation, domination, initiation), which eventually resulted in an almost exclusive focus on two specific leader behaviors—consideration and initiating structure behaviors.

An early study conducted by Andrew W. Halpin (1957) examined the role of leader's initiating structure and consideration, and their relationship to leader effectiveness, the level of satisfaction of the leader's group members, and member ratings of confidence and proficiency, friendship and cooperation, and morale in association with their leader. While this study was conducted in a military context, findings similar to these have been observed in numerous settings. Halpin's work highlights leader behavior as an important part of the leadership process, making a difference in terms of morale, satisfaction, and effectiveness.

In the second reading, Edwin A. Fleishman (1962) and his colleague Edwin F. Harris investigated the effect of leader initiating structure and consideration behavior on member grievances, turnover, and group effectiveness. Their findings reinforce Halpin's observations suggesting the usefulness of employing these two behavioral dimensions in organization settings and across relatively divergent cultures (i.e., Japan, United States, and Israel).

Taken together, these studies provide a useful framework suggesting that leaders and leadership can be studied from the perspective of leader behaviors. In addition, their evidence suggests that what leaders do can make a difference. Meaningful effects of leader behavior have been found in the areas of employee behavior (e.g., grievances, turnover) and attitudes (e.g., satisfaction, morale, group culture), as well as assessments of leader performance and group effectiveness.

An overview of the leader behavior literature highlights the fact that the consequences associated with leader behaviors are not always consistent.[2] While consideration is commonly associated with follower satisfaction, the effects associated with initiating structure behavior are more volatile across situations. At times initiating structure is positively associated with satisfaction, while at other times its effects are negative. While leader consideration behavior is seldom associated with positive performance effects, the relationship between initiating structure and performance produces a mixed picture. Sometimes the

[2] A. K. Korman, "Consideration, Initiating Structure, and Organizational Criteria—A Review," *Personnel Psychology* 19 (1966), pp. 349–361; S. Kerr and C. Schriesheim, "Consideration, Initiating Structure, and Organizational Criteria—An Update of Korman's 1966 Review," *Personnel Psychology* 27 (1974), pp. 555–568.

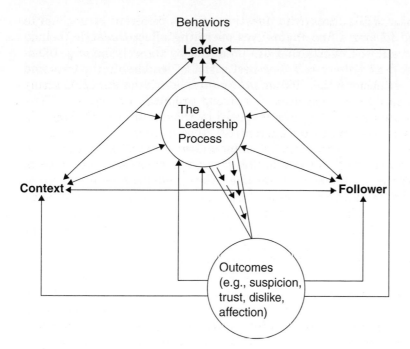

**FIGURE 7.1**
**The Leadership
Process: Leader
Behaviors**

effects are positive, sometimes there are no meaningful relationships, and at other times the effects are in fact negative.

It has been argued on numerous occasions, especially by Robert R. Blake and Jane S. Mouton in the presentation of their *managerial grid,*[3] that leaders who simultaneously display high degrees of both structuring and consideration behavior (high-high) are likely to be the most effective in terms of follower satisfaction and performance. Larson, Hunt, and Osborn (1976), after reviewing the literature, concluded that the "high-high paradigm" is still open to question.[4] While consideration and initiating structure are positively related, they observed support for the high-high paradigm in only 4 of 14 samples that examined the interactive effects of consideration and structure on satisfaction. There was no support found for the high-high paradigm in terms of its prediction of performance. Larson and his colleagues noted that in many situations, "models involving structure only or consideration only were found to predict satisfaction as well as the more complex models" (p. 628) reflecting the "high-high paradigm."

In the final reading in this chapter, Dean Tjosvold looks at the direct and interaction effects of a high-high model involving leader warmth and directiveness. His findings provide support for the coupling of warmth (consideration) with directiveness when performance and satisfaction are valued outcomes.

Figure 7.1 provides a perspective on where leader behavior fits into the model of the leadership process. This set of readings suggests strongly that *leader behavior is important.* It provides additional insight into leadership and the leadership process. Leader behaviors reflect part of the process of leadership—goals are set, roadblocks are removed, people are provided encouragement—and at the same time these behaviors have an impact upon the attitudes, motivation, and behaviors of the members of the group.

[3] R. R. Blake and J. S. Mouton, *The Managerial Grid* (Houston: Gulf, 1964); *The New Managerial Grid* (Houston: Gulf, 1978): *The Versatile Manager: A Grid Profile* (Homewood, IL: Dow Jones–Irwin, 1980); "Management by Grid Principles or Situationalism: Which?" *Group & Organization Studies* 6 (1981), no. 4, pp. 439–455.
[4] L. L. Larson, J. G. Hunt, and R. N. Osborn, "The Great Hi-Hi Leader Behavior Myth: A Lesson from Occam's Razor," *Academy of Management Journal* 19 (1976), pp. 628–641.

The next chapter will address the question of how different situations in which leaders and followers find themselves operating affect the style (behaviors) of the leader and the effects that are produced by these behaviors. Blake and Mouton suggest that there is a "one best style" of leadership that fits and works best in *all* situations (i.e., 9,9 or the team leader who simultaneously shows a strong regard for employees and a strong production emphasis). They envision a unique interaction that gets produced by the simultaneous display of a concern for people and production. By contrast, the readings presented in the next chapter will focus on situational demands and the shaping effects that these forces have on leader behaviors and leader effectiveness. Chapter 8, then, calls into question the argument that a single "best" model can be employed to define what it is that "effective leaders do."

**Leadership—Michigan Organizational Assessment**

**EXERCISE**
*Self-Assessment*

**Instructions:** This self-assessment asks about your leadership behaviors. The following statements describe the way you as a supervisor/leader might perform your job. Please indicate whether or not you AGREE with each of the statements as a description of YOUR leader behavior.

| As a leader (supervisor/manager) I would: | Strongly Disagree | Disagree | Slightly Disagree | Neither Agree nor Disagree | Slightly Agree | Agree | Strongly Agree |
|---|---|---|---|---|---|---|---|
| 1. Help subordinates with their personal problems. | 1 | 2 | 3 | 4 | 5 | 6 | 7 |
| 2. Make sure subordinates have clear goals to achieve. | 1 | 2 | 3 | 4 | 5 | 6 | 7 |
| 3. Keep people informed about the work which is being done. | 1 | 2 | 3 | 4 | 5 | 6 | 7 |
| 4. Make sure subordinates know what has to be done. | 1 | 2 | 3 | 4 | 5 | 6 | 7 |
| 5. Be concerned about them as people. | 1 | 2 | 3 | 4 | 5 | 6 | 7 |
| 6. Make it clear how they should do their job. | 1 | 2 | 3 | 4 | 5 | 6 | 7 |
| 7. Help them discover problems before they get too bad. | 1 | 2 | 3 | 4 | 5 | 6 | 7 |
| 8. Feel each subordinate is important as an individual. | 1 | 2 | 3 | 4 | 5 | 6 | 7 |
| 9. Help them solve work-related problems. | 1 | 2 | 3 | 4 | 5 | 6 | 7 |

**Scoring:** *Personal support*—Sum your answers to items 1, 5, and 8, and then divide by 3. *Goal emphasis*—Sum your responses to items 2, 4, and 6, and divide by 3. *Work facilitation*—Sum your responses to items 3, 7, and 9, and divide by 3.

Record your scores here:
Personal support        _____.
Goal emphasis           _____.
Work facilitation        _____.

**Interpretation:** This profile identifies the extent to which you perceive yourself engaging in three different behaviors as you carry out your leadership role: (1) *support*—you would likely engage in behaviors that enhance someone else's feelings of personal worth and importance; (2) *goal emphasis*—you would likely engage in behaviors that stimulate an enthusiasm for meeting the group's goal or achieving excellent performance; and (3) *work facilitation*—you would likely engage in behaviors that help achieve goal attainment by such activities as scheduling, coordinating, planning, and by providing resources such as tools, materials, and technical knowledge. A score of 6 and higher suggests that your leadership style would be strong on that particular dimension of leader behavior. A score of 2 and less suggests that your leadership style would not likely be characterized by this particular dimension of leader behavior.

**Source:** Institute for Social Research, *Michigan Assessment of Organizations II* (Ann Arbor, MI: Institute for Social Research, 1975).

**EXERCISE**
*Self-Assessment*

**Initiating Structure and Consideration**

**Instructions:** The questions below ask about your personal leadership orientation. Each item describes a specific kind of behavior but does not ask you to judge whether the behavior is desirable or undesirable.

READ each item carefully.

THINK about how frequently you engage in the behavior described by the item.

DRAW A CIRCLE around one of the five numerical response codes (1, 2, 3, 4, 5) following each question, which reflects the frequency of this behavior.

1. Put suggestions made by people in the work group into operation.

| **Always** | **Often** | **Occasionally** | **Seldom** | **Never** |
|---|---|---|---|---|
| 1 | 2 | 3 | 4 | 5 |

2. Treat all people in the work group as your equal.

| **Always** | **Often** | **Occasionally** | **Seldom** | **Never** |
|---|---|---|---|---|
| 1 | 2 | 3 | 4 | 5 |

3. Back up what people under you do.

| **Always** | **Often** | **Occasionally** | **Seldom** | **Never** |
|---|---|---|---|---|
| 1 | 2 | 3 | 4 | 5 |

4. Reject suggestions for change.

| **Always** | **Often** | **Occasionally** | **Seldom** | **Never** |
|---|---|---|---|---|
| 1 | 2 | 3 | 4 | 5 |

5. Talk about how much should be done.

| **A Great Deal** | **Fairly Much** | **To Some Degree** | **Comparatively Little** | **Not at All** |
|---|---|---|---|---|
| 1 | 2 | 3 | 4 | 5 |

6. Assign people in the work group to particular tasks.

| **Always** | **Often** | **Occasionally** | **Seldom** | **Never** |
|---|---|---|---|---|
| 1 | 2 | 3 | 4 | 5 |

7. Offer new approaches to problems.

| **Often** | **Fairly Often** | **Occasionally** | **Once in a While** | **Very Seldom** |
|---|---|---|---|---|
| 1 | 2 | 3 | 4 | 5 |

8. Emphasize meeting the deadlines.

| **A Great Deal** | **Fairly Much** | **To Some Degree** | **Comparatively Little** | **Not at All** |
|---|---|---|---|---|
| 1 | 2 | 3 | 4 | 5 |

**Scoring:** *Consideration* behavior—Subtract your score to questions 1, 2, and 3 from 6. Next, sum your adjusted response to questions 1, 2, 3, and 4 and divide by 4.

Enter your Consideration score here _____.

*Initiating Structure* behavior—Subtract your score to questions 5, 6, 7, and 8 from 6. Next, sum your adjusted response to questions 5, 6, 7, and 8, and divide by 4.

Enter your Initiating Structure score here _____.

**Interpretation:** A high score (4 and greater) suggests a relatively strong orientation toward consideration-oriented behavior by you as a leader. A low score (2 and less) suggests a relatively weak consideration orientation.

A high score (4 and greater) suggests a relatively strong orientation toward initiating structure-oriented behavior by you as a leader. A low score (2 and less) suggests a relatively weak orientation toward initiation of structure behavior.

**Source:** Sample items from and reprinted with permission: Edwin A. Fleishman's *Leadership Opinion Questionnaire.* (Copyright 1960, Science Research Associates, Inc., Chicago, IL).

**Reading 19**

# Predicting Organizational Effectiveness with a Four-Factor Theory of Leadership

**David G. Bowers and Stanley E. Seashore**
University of Michigan

For centuries writers have been intrigued with the idea of specifying predictable relationships between what an organization's leader does and how the organization fares. In our own time, behavioral science has looked extensively at this question, yet incongruities and contradictory or unrelated findings seem to crowd the literature. It is the intent in this paper to locate and integrate the consistencies, to explore some neglected issues, and, finally, to generate and use a network of variables for predicting outcomes of organizational effectiveness.

Leadership has been studied informally by observing the lives of great men and formally by attempting to identify the personality traits of acknowledged leaders through assessment techniques. Review of the research literature from these studies, however, reveals few consistent findings.[1] Since the Second World War, research emphasis has shifted from a search for personality traits to a search for behavior that makes a difference in the performance or satisfaction of the followers. The conceptual scheme to be outlined here is an example of this approach.

In this paper, the primary concern is with leadership in businesses or industrial enterprises, usually termed "supervision" or "management," although most of the constructs of leadership to be used here apply equally well to social groups, clubs, and voluntary associations.

Work situations in business organizations in a technologically advanced society typically involve a comparatively small number of persons who receive direction from one person. This is the basic unit of industrial society and has been called the "organizational family."[2] In this modern organizational family, there is usually task interdependence and there is frequently social interdependence as well. The ideal is that of a group of people working effectively together toward the accomplishment of some common aim.

**Source:** Edited and reprinted with permission from *Administrative Science Quarterly 2*, no. 2 (1966) pp. 238–263.

This paper presents a review of the conceptual structure resulting from several programs of research in leadership practices, followed by a reconceptualization that attempts to take into consideration all of these earlier findings. In an attempt to assess the usefulness of the reconceptualization, it is then applied to leadership and effectiveness data from a recent study.

## DIMENSIONS OF LEADERSHIP

It seems useful at the outset to isolate on a common-sense basis certain attributes of "leadership." First, the concept of leadership is meaningful only in the context of two or more people. Second, leadership consists of behavior; more specifically, it is behavior by one member of a group toward another member or members of the group, which advances some joint aim. Not all organizationally useful behavior in a work group is leadership; leadership behavior must be distinguished from the performance of noninterpersonal tasks that advance the goals of the organization. On a common-sense basis, then, leadership is organizationally useful behavior by one member of an organizational family toward another member or members of that same organizational family.

Defined in this manner, leadership amounts to a large aggregation of separate behaviors, which may be grouped or classified in a great variety of ways. Several classification systems from previous research have achieved considerable prominence and are briefly described here.

### OHIO STATE LEADERSHIP STUDIES

In 1945, the Bureau of Business Research at Ohio State University undertook the construction of an instrument for describing leadership. From extended conversations and discussions among staff members who represented various disciplines, a list of nine dimensions or categories of leadership behavior were postulated. Descriptive statements were then written and assigned to one or another of the nine dimensions, and after further refinement, 150 of these were selected as representing these nine dimensions and were incorporated into the Leader Behavior Description Questionnaire.

Two factor analyses attempted to simplify its conceptual framework further. Hemphill and Coons[3] intercorrelated and factor-analyzed group mean scores for 11 dimensions for a sample composed largely of educational groups,[4] and obtained three orthogonal factors.

1. *Maintenance of membership character*. Behavior of a leader which allows him to be considered a "good fellow" by his subordinates; behavior which is socially agreeable to group members.

2. *Objective attainment behavior*. Behavior related to the output of the group: for example, taking positive action in establishing goals or objectives, structuring group activities in a way that members may work toward an objective, or serving as a representative of group accomplishment in relation to outside groups, agencies, forces, and so on.

3. *Group interaction facilitation behavior*. Behavior that structures communication among group members, encouraging pleasant group atmosphere and reducing conflicts among members.

Halpin and Winer[5] made an analysis using data collected from air-force crews, revising the original measuring instrument to adapt it to the respondent group. Only 130 items were used, with appropriate rewording, and the number of dimensions was reduced to eight. Treatment of the data indicated that five of the eight were sufficient for describing the entire roster, and the correlation of the 130 items with these five dimensions was regarded as a matrix of oblique factor loadings. These item loadings were then factor analyzed and the results rotated, producing four orthogonal factors.

1. *Consideration*. Behavior indicative of friendship, mutual trust, respect, and warmth.

2. *Initiating structure*. Behavior that organizes and defines relationships or roles and establishes well-defined patterns of organization, channels of communication, and ways of getting jobs done.

3. *Production emphasis*. Behavior which makes up a manner of motivating the group to greater activity by emphasizing the mission or job to be done.

4. *Sensitivity (social awareness)*. Sensitivity of the leader to, and his awareness of, social interrelationships and pressures inside or outside the group.

The Halpin and Winer analysis has been the more widely known and used. Because the investigators dropped the third and fourth factors as accounting for too little common variance, "consideration" and "initiating structure" have become to some extent identified as "the Ohio State" dimensions of leadership.

## EARLY SURVEY RESEARCH CENTER STUDIES

Concurrent with the Ohio State studies was a similar program of research in human relations at the University of Michigan Survey Research Center. Approaching the problem of leadership or supervisory style by locating clusters of characteristics which *(a)* correlated positively among themselves and *(b)* correlated with criteria of effectiveness, this program developed two concepts called "employee-orientation" and "production-orientation."[6]

Employee-orientation is described as behavior by a supervisor, which indicates that he feels that the "human relations" aspect of the job is quite important; and that he considers the employees as human beings of intrinsic importance, takes an interest in them, and accepts their individuality and personal needs. Production-orientation stresses production and the technical aspects of the job, with employees as means for getting work done; it seems to combine the Ohio State dimensions of initiating structure and production emphasis. Originally conceived to be opposite poles of the same continuum, employee-orientation and production-orientation were later reconceptualized,[7] on the basis of further data, as representing independent dimensions.

Katz and Kahn,[8] writing from a greater accumulation of findings, presented another conceptual scheme, with four dimensions of leadership.

1. *Differentiation of supervisory role*. Behavior by a leader that reflects greater emphasis upon activities of planning and performing specialized skilled tasks; spending a greater proportion of time in actual supervision, rather than performing the men's own tasks himself or absorption in impersonal paperwork.

2. *Closeness of supervision*. Behavior that delegates authority, checks upon subordinates less frequently, provides more general, less fre-

quent instructions about the work, makes greater allowance for individuals to perform in their own ways and at their own paces.

3. *Employee-orientation.* Behavior that gives major emphasis to a supportive personal relationship and that reflects a personal interest in subordinates; being more understanding, less punitive, easy to talk to, and willing to help groom employees for advancement.

4. *Group relationships.* Behavior by the leader that results in group cohesiveness, pride by subordinates in their work group, a feeling of membership in the group, and mutual help on the part of those subordinates.

Differentiation of supervisory role corresponds in part to what the Ohio State studies refer to as initiating structure or objective attainment behavior, and clearly derives from the earlier concept of production-orientation. Closeness of supervision, on the other hand, has something in common with maintenance of membership character, consideration, and employee-orientation, but also with objective attainment behavior, initiating structure, and production-orientation. Employee-orientation clearly corresponds to the earlier concept by the same name, while group relationships is to some extent similar to the interaction facilitation behavior and social sensitivity of the Ohio State studies.

In still another conceptualization, combining theory with review of empirical data, Kahn[9] postulated four supervisory functions.

1. *Providing direct need satisfaction.* Behavior by a leader, not conditional upon behavior of the employee, which provides direct satisfaction of the employee's ego and affiliative needs.

2. *Structuring the path to goal attainment.* Behavior that cues subordinates toward filling personal needs through attaining organizational goals.

3. *Enabling goal achievement.* Behavior that removes barriers to goal achievement, such as eliminating bottlenecks or planning.

4. *Modifying employee goals.* Behavior that influences the actual personal goals of subordinates in organizationally useful directions.

Direct need satisfaction clearly resembles consideration and employee-orientation; enabling goal achievement seems similar to initiating structure or objective attainment behavior; structuring the path to goal attainment and modifying employee goals are probably closer to the Ohio State production emphasis factor.

## STUDIES AT THE RESEARCH CENTER FOR GROUP DYNAMICS

Cartwright and Zander,[10] at the Research Center for Group Dynamics, on the basis of accumulated findings, described leadership in terms of two sets of group functions.

1. *Group maintenance functions.* Behavior that keeps interpersonal relations pleasant, resolves disputes, provides encouragement, gives the minority a chance to be heard, stimulates self-direction, and increases interdependence among members.

2. *Goal achievement functions.* Behavior that initiates action, keeps members' attention on the goal, develops a procedural plan, evaluates the quality of work done, and makes expert information available.

These descriptive terms clearly refer to broader constructs than consideration or initiating structure. Group maintenance functions, for example, include what has been termed consideration, maintenance of membership character, or employee-orientation, but they also include functions concerned with relationships among group members not in formal authority positions. This concept is in some ways similar to group interaction facilitation behavior in the Ohio State factor analysis of Hemphill and Coons.[11] Goal achievement functions seem to encompass what the Ohio State studies referred to as initiating structure and production emphasis or objective attainment behavior, and what early Survey Research Center studies called production-orientation.

## MANN'S THREE SKILLS

In subsequent work at the Survey Research Center built upon earlier findings, a recent classification, proposed by several writers and developed and operationalized by Floyd Mann,[12] treats leadership in terms of a trilogy of skills required of supervisors or managers. Although behaviors requiring particular skills and those skills themselves are not necessarily perfectly parallel, it seems reasonable to assume at least an approximate correspondence between the two. The three skills are:

1. *Human relations skill.* Ability and judgment in working with and through people, including knowledge of principles of human behavior, interpersonal relations, and human motivation.

2. *Technical skill.* Ability to use knowledge, methods, techniques, and equipment necessary for the performance of specific tasks.

3. *Administrative skill.* Ability to understand and act according to the objectives of the total organization, rather than only on the basis of the goals and needs of one's own immediate group. It includes planning, organizing the work, assigning the right tasks to the right people, inspecting, following up, and coordinating the work.

## LIKERT'S NEW PATTERNS OF MANAGEMENT

Rensis Likert of the University of Michigan Institute for Social Research, building upon many of the findings of the Survey Research Center and the Research Center for Group Dynamics as well as upon his own early work in the same area for the Life Insurance Agency Management Association, describes five conditions for effective supervisory behavior.

1. *Principle of supportive relations.* The leadership and other processes of the organization must be such as to ensure a maximum probability that in his interactions and his relationships with the organization, each member will, in the light of his background, values, and expectations, view the experience as supportive, and as one that builds and maintains his sense of personal worth and importance.[13]

2. *Group methods of supervision.* Management will make full use of the potential capacities of its human resources only when each person in an organization is a member of one or more effectively functioning work groups that have a high degree of group loyalty, effective skills of interaction, and high performance goals.[14]

3. *High performance goals.* If a high level of performance is to be achieved, it appears to be necessary for a supervisor to be employee-centered, and at the same time to have high performance goals and a contagious enthusiasm as to the importance of achieving these goals.[15]

4. *Technical knowledge.* The (effective) leader has adequate competence to handle the technical problems faced by his group, or he sees that access to this technical knowledge is fully provided.[16]

5. *Coordinating, scheduling, planning.* The leader fully reflects and effectively represents the views, goals, values, and decisions of his group in those other groups where he is performing the function of linking his group to the rest of the organization. He brings to the group of which he is the leader the views, goals, and decisions of those other groups. In this way, he provides a linkage whereby communication and the exercise of influence can be performed in both directions.[17]

## COMPARISON AND INTEGRATION

These various research programs and writings make it clear that a great deal of conceptual content is held in common. In fact, four dimensions emerge from these studies, which seem to comprise the basic structure of what one may term "leadership":

1. *Support.* Behavior that enhances someone else's feeling of personal worth and importance.

2. *Interaction facilitation.* Behavior that encourages members of the group to develop close, mutually satisfying relationships.

3. *Goal emphasis.* Behavior that stimulates an enthusiasm for meeting the group's goal or achieving excellent performance.

4. *Work facilitation.* Behavior that helps achieve goal attainment by such activities as scheduling, coordinating, planning, and by providing resources such as tools, materials, and technical knowledge.

This formulation is obviously very close, except in terminology, to that expressed by Rensis Likert and was, in fact, stimulated by it. Table 1 indicates how concepts from the various research programs relate to these four basic concepts of leadership. More important, however, is the fact that each of these four concepts appears, sometimes separately, sometimes in combination, in all but two (Katz, et al., 1950; Kahn, 1958) of the previous formulations listed. These four dimensions are not considered indivisible, but capable of further subdivision according to some regularity of occurrence in social situations or according to the conceptual preferences of investigators.

## INDEPENDENCE OF LEADERSHIP AND POSITION

Traditional leadership research has focused upon the behavior of formally designated or recognized leaders. This is probably due, at least in part, to

**TABLE 1  Correspondence of Leadership Concepts of Different Investigators**

| Bowers and Seashore (1964) | Hemphill and Coons (1957) | Halpin and Winer (1957) | Katz et al. (1950) | Katz and Kahn (1951) | Kahn (1958) | Mann (1962) | Likert (1961) | Cartwright and Zander (1960) |
|---|---|---|---|---|---|---|---|---|
| Support | Maintenance of membership character | Consideration | Employee-orientation | Employee-orientation / Closeness of supervision | Providing direct need satisfaction | Human relations skills | Principle of supportive relationships | Group maintenance functions |
| Interaction facilitation | Group interaction facilitation behavior | Sensitivity | | Group relationships | | | Group methods of supervision | |
| Goal emphasis | Objective attainment behavior | Production emphasis | | | Structuring path to goal attainment / Modifying employee goals | Administrative skills | High-performance goals | Goal-achievement functions |
| Work facilitation | | Initiating structure | Production-orientation | Differentiation of supervisory role / Closeness of supervision | Enabling goal achievement | Technical skills | Technical knowledge, planning, scheduling | |

the historical influence of the hierarchical models of the church and the army. As a result, it has until recently been customary to study leadership either as an attribute of the person of someone who is authority-vested, or as an attribute of his behavior. More recently, attention has been paid to leadership in groups less formally structured, as illustrated by the work of Bass with leaderless group discussion, the work of Sherif, as well as some of the work of other researchers in the area of group dynamics.[18]

In the previous section, leadership was conceptualized in terms of four social-process functions, four kinds of behavior that must be present in work groups if they are to be effective. The performance of these functions was deliberately not limited to formally designated leaders. Instead, it was proposed that leadership, as described in terms of support, goal emphasis, work facilitation, and interaction facilitation, may be provided by anyone in a work group for anyone else in that work group. In this sense, leadership may be either "supervisory" or "mutual"; that is, a group's needs for support may be provided by a formally designated leader, by members for each other, or both; goals may be emphasized by the formal leader, by members to each other, or by both; and

similarly for work facilitation and interaction facilitation.

This does not imply that formally designated leaders are unnecessary or superfluous, for there are both common-sense and theoretical reasons for believing that a formally acknowledged leader through his supervisory leadership behavior sets the pattern of the mutual leadership which subordinates supply each other.

## LEADERSHIP AND ORGANIZATIONAL EFFECTIVENESS

Leadership in a work situation has been judged to be important because of its connection, to some extent assumed and to some extent demonstrated, to organizational effectiveness. Effectiveness, moreover, although it has been operationalized in a variety of ways, has often been assumed to be a unitary characteristic. These assumptions define a commonly accepted theorem that leadership (if not a unitary characteristic, then a limited roster of closely related ones) is always salutary in its effect and that it always enhances effectiveness. . . .

# RESULTS

## RELATION OF LEADERSHIP TO EFFECTIVENESS

Table 2 presents the correlation coefficients of leadership measures with measures of satisfaction. Table 3 presents similar correlations of leadership measures to performance factors. These data indicate first, that the incidence of significant relationships of leadership to effectiveness is well above the chance level. Of 40 satisfaction-leadership coefficients, 30 are significant beyond the 5 percent level of confidence. Of 56 performance-leadership coefficients, 13 are significant beyond the 5 percent level of confidence. Second, the significant coefficients are not uniformly distributed throughout the matrix; instead, certain effectiveness criteria (e.g., satisfaction with income) and certain leadership measures (e.g., peer work facil-

itation) have many significant relationships, whereas others have few or none (e.g., performance factor VI). Third, significant coefficients are as often found in relation to peer as to managerial leadership characteristics. . . .

## RELATION OF PEER TO MANAGERIAL LEADERSHIP

Before assessing the adequacy of leadership as a predictor of effectiveness, it seems advisable to answer the question posed earlier about the relationship between peer and managerial leadership. There is a close relationship between all managerial characteristics, on the one hand, and all peer characteristics on the other. Following the same method as that used for effectiveness, it appears that the best predictor of peer support is managerial support; of peer goal emphasis, managerial interaction facilitation; of peer work facili-

---

**TABLE 2   Correlation of Leadership with Satisfactions**

| Leadership Measure | Satisfaction with | | | | |
|---|---|---|---|---|---|
| | Company | Fellow Agents | Job | Income | Manager |
| *Peer* | | | | | |
| Support | .03* | .68 | .39 | .29* | .47 |
| Goal emphasis | .37 | .77 | .26* | .42 | .62 |
| Work facilitation | .29* | .68 | .34 | .51 | .45 |
| Interaction facilitation | .31 | .72 | .30* | .42 | .55 |
| *Manager* | | | | | |
| Support | .31 | .65 | .35 | .45 | .86 |
| Goal emphasis | .11* | .71 | .09* | .43 | .31 |
| Work facilitation | .31 | .61 | .24* | .36 | .41 |
| Interaction facilitation | .30* | .67 | .10* | .53 | .78 |

*All others significant beyond .05 level of confidence, 2-tail.

---

**TABLE 3   Correlation of Leadership with Performance Factors**

| Leadership Measure | Performance Factor | | | | | | |
|---|---|---|---|---|---|---|---|
| | I | II | III | IV | V | VI | VII |
| *Peer* | | | | | | | |
| Support | .26 | −.02 | −.27 | −.21 | .23 | −.12 | .27 |
| Goal emphasis | .49* | −.05 | −.45* | −.27 | .15 | .04 | .04 |
| Work facilitation | .33* | .14 | −.41* | −.41* | .18 | .00 | .04 |
| Interaction facilitation | .44* | −.13 | −.44* | −.24 | .11 | .14 | .05 |
| *Manager* | | | | | | | |
| Support | .28 | −.24 | −.26 | −.12 | .25 | .16 | .10 |
| Goal emphasis | .31* | .11 | −.27 | −.18 | .41* | .03 | −.19 |
| Work facilitation | .43* | .13 | −.37* | −.33* | .21 | .16 | −.12 |
| Interaction facilitation | .42* | −.29 | −.30 | −.21 | .13 | .20 | .01 |

*Significant beyond .05 level of confidence, 2-tail.

tation, managerial interaction facilitation. With one exception, therefore, the best predictor of the peer characteristic is its managerial opposite number. Table 4 indicates that three predictions are improved by related managerial characteristics.

Assuming causation, one may say that if a manager wishes to increase the extent to which his subordinates support one another, he must increase his own support and his own emphasis upon goals. If he wishes to increase the extent to which his subordinates emphasize goals to one another, he must first increase his own facilitation of interaction and his emphasis upon goals. By increasing his facilitation of the work, he will increase the extent to which his subordinates do likewise, and if, in addition, he increases his facilitation of interaction, his subordinates will in turn facilitate interaction among themselves.

These data appear to confirm that there is in fact a significant and strong relationship between managerial and peer leadership characteristics. In general, the statement may be made that a forerunner of each peer variable is its managerial opposite number, and that substantial improvement is in most cases made by combining with this another managerial characteristic. . . .

Figure 1a presents the relationships of leadership and nonleadership variables to satisfaction with the company and with income. This diagram indicates that supportive managers make more satisfactory arrangements about the office expenses of their agents and that these arrangements, in part, lead to greater satisfaction with the company as a whole. In addition, as managers facilitate the interaction of their agents, the goals of the company and needs or aspirations of the people who work for it come to be more compatible, which also leads to satisfaction with the company and with income.

Figure 1b presents a similar chain of relationships to satisfaction with the job itself. This diagram is interpreted to mean that as agents facilitate the work for each other, less time is spent by agents in paperwork for specific clients. When this happens, when agents behave more supportively toward each other, and when the agents are, on the whole, higher in need for affiliation, there is greater job satisfaction. Figure 1c presents relationships to two criteria: satisfaction with fellow agents and volume of business. When agents emphasize goals among themselves, they become more satisfied with each other; and when this condition exists, an agency does a greater volume of business. Figure 1d shows very succinctly that agents are satisfied with their manager if he is supportive and knowledgeable. Figure 1e presents relationship to business costs in diagram form. Earlier diagrams showed the network of relationships associated with satisfaction with the company and with the job; here, these two satisfaction states are associated with lower business costs. In addition, as agents facilitate the work for each other, they spend a smaller proportion of their time in miscellaneous activities. When this occurs, and when agents emphasize goals to one another, costs are also lower.

Figure 1f diagrams relationships to business growth. The relationships presented in this diagram are less reliable than those presented in earlier figures. They are, as a group, somewhat smaller in size than those found in relation to other criteria already described. With this caution in mind, however, they can be interpreted as follows: business growth is high when the agent force does *not* hold to a classical business ideology; when regional managers, by accepting the opinions and ideas of their agents, encourage professional development; and when managers reduce rivalries among agents by encouraging their interaction. Far from stressing growth attained by competitive effort, this paradigm presents a picture of growth through cooperative professionalism.

Two additional performance measures of effectiveness present one significant, reasonable "causal" relationship each: staff-clientele maturity is greater when agents have a higher level of aspiration, and more advanced underwriting occurs when agents have a higher level of education.

---

**TABLE 4    Improvement of Prediction of Peer Leadership Characteristics by Addition of Other Managerial Leadership Characteristics**

| Peer Measure | Managerial Best Predictor | Other Managerial Measures Improving Prediction |
|---|---|---|
| Support | Support | Goal emphasis |
| Goal emphasis | Interaction facilitation | Goal emphasis |
| Work facilitation | Work facilitation | None |
| Interaction facilitation | Interaction facilitation | Work facilitation |

**FIGURE 1** Predicted Measures: (*a*) Satisfaction with Company and with Income; (*b*) Satisfaction with Job; (*c*) Satisfaction with Fellow Agents; Business Volume; (*d*) Satisfaction with Manager; (*e*) Business Costs; (*f*) Business Growth

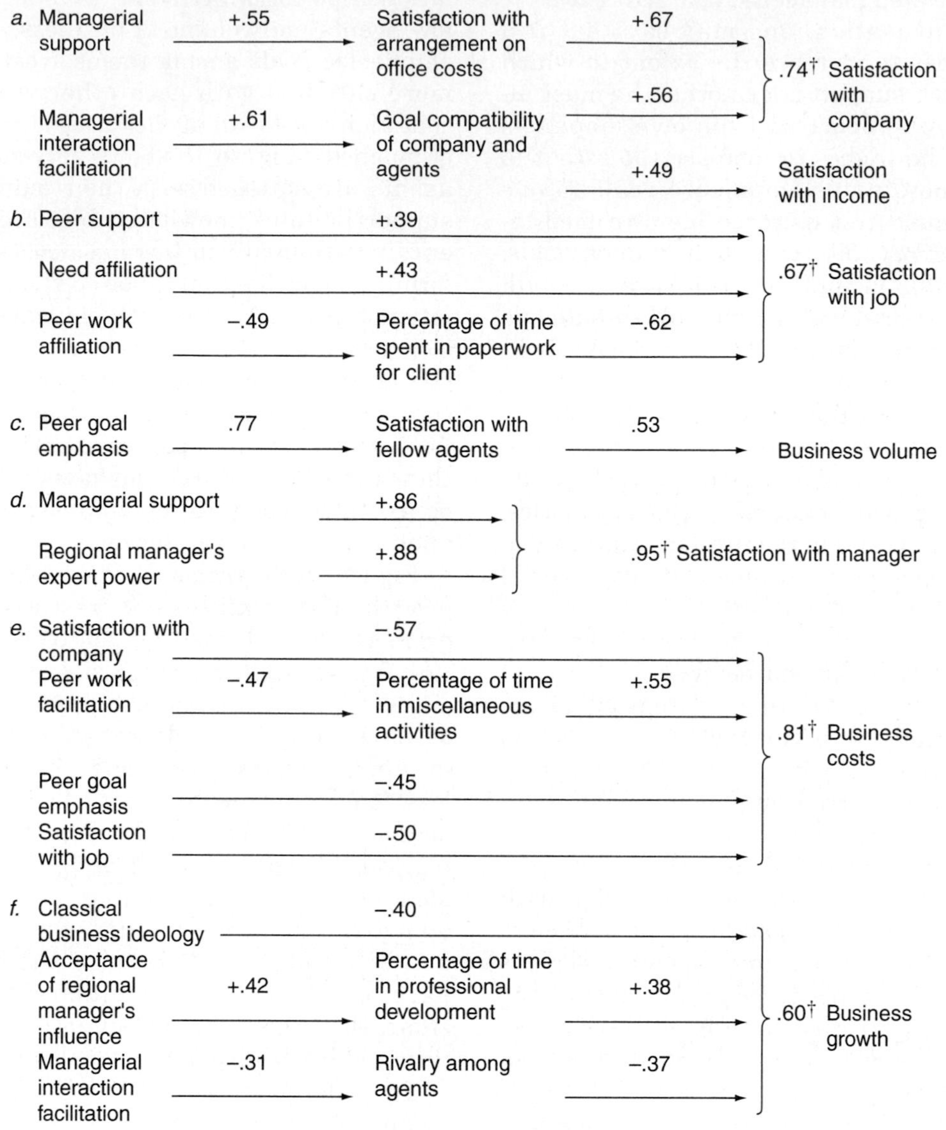

*a.* Managerial support — +.55 → Satisfaction with arrangement on office costs — +.67 →

.74[†] Satisfaction with company

Managerial interaction facilitation — +.61 → Goal compatibility of company and agents — +.56 →

— +.49 → Satisfaction with income

*b.* Peer support — +.39 →

Need affiliation — +.43 →

.67[†] Satisfaction with job

Peer work affiliation — −.49 → Percentage of time spent in paperwork for client — −.62 →

*c.* Peer goal emphasis — .77 → Satisfaction with fellow agents — .53 → Business volume

*d.* Managerial support — +.86 →

Regional manager's expert power — +.88 →

.95[†] Satisfaction with manager

*e.* Satisfaction with company — −.57 →

Peer work facilitation — −.47 → Percentage of time in miscellaneous activities — +.55 →

.81[†] Business costs

Peer goal emphasis — −.45 →

Satisfaction with job — −.50 →

*f.* Classical business ideology — −.40 →

Acceptance of regional manager's influence — +.42 → Percentage of time in professional development — +.38 →

.60[†] Business growth

Managerial interaction facilitation — −.31 → Rivalry among agents — −.37 →

[†] Multiple correlation of variables listed against the effectiveness measure.

Although significant correlations were presented earlier in relation to these two factors, the reasonable interpretation of them is that the leadership measures are either effects or coordinates, not causes, of these descriptive rather than evaluative performance factors.

That no reasonable, significant relationships to manpower turnover are to be found is extremely puzzling. In most investigations of the effect of social-psychological variables upon organizational behavior, it is assumed that performance measures which are more "person" than "production" oriented will show the highest relationships to questionnaire measurements. In the present case this assumption is not supported. No variations of analysis that were attempted produced any noticeable change. An attempt was made to assess curvilinear correlations, but no improvement over linear correlation resulted. It was also thought that the factorial measure of turnover might be too complicated and that a simpler measure of proportion of terminations might be more productive. This also produced no noticeable effect. Apparently, manpower turnover in this particular company or industry is related to forces in the individual, the environment, or perhaps the organizational situation not tapped by the questionnaire measurement used.

It is not surprising that no correlations are found with the regional manager's personal performance. It is, as explained earlier, the weakest factor, and differs from the other factors in being descriptive of a single individual rather than of the agency as a whole. It may well be affected more by variables such as the regional manager's distance from retirement than by factors assessed here.

## DISCUSSION AND CONCLUSIONS

To what extent have the data demonstrated the usefulness of the conceptualization presented at the beginning of this article? It seems reasonable to state the following:

1. Seven of the eight leadership characteristics outlined above in fact play some part in the predictive model generated from the data; only peer interaction facilitation seems to play no unique role.
2. Both managerial and peer leadership characteristics seem important.
3. There are plausible relationships of managerial to peer leadership characteristics.
4. The model is not a simple one of managerial leadership leading to peer leadership, which in turn leads to outcomes separately; instead, different aspects of performance are associated with different leadership characteristics, and, in some cases, satisfaction outcomes seem related to performance outcomes.
5. Some effectiveness measures are related to causal factors other than those tapped in this instrument.
6. The ability to predict outcomes with the variables selected varies from .95 to .00.
7. The role of leadership characteristics in this prediction varies in importance from strong, direct relationships in some cases (e.g., satisfaction with manager) to indirect relationships (e.g., business volume) to no relationship (e.g., advanced underwriting).
8. Leadership, as conceived and operationalized here, is not adequate alone to predict effectiveness; instead, additional and, in some cases, intervening constructs must be included to improve prediction. These "other" constructs are of several distinct types:
   a. *Leadership-related.* Regional manager's expert power, regional manager's influence acceptance, and rivalry among agents.
   b. *Work Patterns.* Percentage of time in miscellaneous activities, in paperwork for clients, and in professional development.
   c. *Personal and Motivational.* Education, level of aspiration, need for affiliation, goal compatibility of individual and organization, and classical business ideology.

## Notes

1. C. A. Gibb, "Leadership," in G. Lindzey, *Handbook of Social Psychology.* Cambridge, Mass.: Addison-Wesley Publishing Co., Inc. (1954), II, 877–917; R. M. Stogdill, Personal Factors Associated with Leadership: A Survey of the Literature, *Journal of Psychology,* 25 (1948), 35–71.

2. F. C. Mann, "Toward an Understanding of the Leadership Role in Formal Organization," in R. Dubin, G. C. Homans, F. C. Mann, and D. C. Miller, *Leadership and Productivity.* San Francisco, Calif.: Chandler Publishing Company (1965), pp. 68–103.

3. J. K. Hemphill and A. E. Coons, "Development of the Leader Behavior Description Questionnaire," in R. M. Stogdill and A. E. Coons (Eds.) *Leader Behavior: Its Description and Measurement.* Research Monograph No. 88, Columbus, Ohio: Bureau of Business Research, the Ohio State University (1957), pp. 6–38.

4. The 11 dimensions were made up of the original 9, one of which (communication) had been subdivided, plus an overall leadership evaluation.

5. A. W. Halpin and J. Winer, "A Factorial Study of the Leader Behavior Description Questionnaire," in R. M. Stogdill and A. E. Coons, *Leader Behavior, op. cit.,* pp. 39–51.

6. D. Katz, N. Maccoby, and Nancy C. Morse, *Productivity, Supervision, and Morale in an Office Situation.* Detroit, Mich.: The Darel Press, Inc. (1950); D. Katz, N. Maccoby, G. Gurin, and Lucretia G. Floor, *Productivity, Supervision, and Morale Among Railroad Workers.* Ann Arbor, Mich.: Survey Research Center (1951).

7. R. L. Kahn, The Prediction of Productivity, *Journal of Social Issues,* 12 (1956), 41–49.

8. D. Katz and R. L. Kahn, "Human Organization and Worker Motivation," in L. R. Tripp (Ed.), *Industrial Productivity.* Madison, Wisc.: Industrial Relations Research Association (1951), pp. 146–171.

9. R. L. Kahn, "Human Relations on the Shop Floor," in E. M. Hugh-Jones (Ed.), *Human Relations and Modern*

*Management.* Amsterdam, Holland: North-Holland Publishing Co. (1958), pp. 43–74.

10. D. Cartwright and A. Zander, *Group Dynamics Research and Theory.* Evanston, Ill.: Row, Peterson & Co. (1960).

11. Hemphill and Coons, *op. cit.*

12. Mann, *op. cit.*

13. R. Likert, *New Patterns of Management.* New York: McGraw-Hill Book Co. (1961), p. 103.

14. *Ibid.,* p. 104.

15. *Ibid.,* p. 8.

16. *Ibid.,* p. 171.

17. *Ibid.,* p. 171.

18. B. M. Bass, *Leadership, Psychology, and Organizational Behavior.* New York: Harper & Bros. (1960); Cartwright and Zander, *op. cit.;* M. and Carolyn W. Sherif, *An Outline of Social Psychology.* New York: Harper & Bros. (1956).

## Reading 20

# Patterns of Leadership Behavior Related to Employee Grievances and Turnover

**Edwin A. Fleishman**
Yale University

**Edwin F. Harris**
Chrysler Corporation

This study investigates some relationships between the leader behavior of industrial supervisors and the behavior of their group members. It represents an extension of earlier studies carried out at the International Harvester Company, while the authors were with the Ohio State University Leadership Studies.

Briefly, these previous studies involved three primary phases which have been described elsewhere (Fleishman, 1951, 1953a, 1953b, 1953c; Fleishman, Harris & Burtt, 1955; Harris & Fleishman, 1955). In the initial phase, independent leadership patterns were defined and a variety of behavioral and attitude instruments were developed to measure them. This phase confirmed the usefulness of the constructs "Consideration" and "Structure" for describing leader behavior in industry.

Since the present study, as well as the previous work, focused on these two leadership patterns, it may be well to redefine them here:

> *Consideration* includes behavior indicating mutual trust, respect, and a certain warmth and rapport between the supervisor and his group. This does not mean that this dimension reflects a superficial "pat-on-the-back," "first name calling" kind of human relations behavior. This dimension appears to emphasize a deeper concern for group members' needs and includes such behavior as allowing subordinates more participation in decision making and encouraging more two-way communication.
>
> *Structure* includes behavior in which the supervisor organizes and defines group activities and his relation to the group. Thus, he defines the role he expects each member to assume, assigns tasks, plans ahead, establishes ways of getting things done, and pushes for production. This

dimension seems to emphasize overt attempts to achieve organizational goals.

Since the dimensions are independent, a supervisor may score high on both dimensions, low on both, or high on one and low on the other.

The second phase of the original Harvester research utilized measures of these patterns to evaluate changes in foreman leadership attitudes and behavior resulting from a management training program. The amount of change was evaluated at three different times—once while the foremen were still in the training setting, again after they had returned to the plant environment, and still later in a "refresher" training course. The results showed that while still in the training situation there was a distinct increase in Consideration and an unexpected decrease in Structure attitudes. It was also found that leadership attitudes became more *dissimilar* rather than similar, despite the fact that all foremen had received the same training. Furthermore, when behavior and attitudes were evaluated back in the plant, the effects of the training largely disappeared. This pointed to the main finding, i.e., the overriding importance of the interaction of the training effects with certain aspects of the social setting in which the foremen had to operate in the plant. Most critical was the "leadership climate" supplied by the behavior and attitudes of the foreman's own boss. This was more related to the foreman's own Consideration and Structure behavior than was the fact that he had or had not received the leadership training.

The third phase may be termed the "criterion phase," in which the relationships between Consideration and Structure and indices of foremen proficiency were examined. One finding was that production supervisors rated high in "proficiency" by plant management turned out to have leadership patterns high in Structure and low in Consideration. (This relationship was accentuated in

**Source:** Edited and reprinted with permission from *Personnel Psychology* 15 (1962), pp. 43–56.

departments scoring high on a third variable, "perceived pressure of deadlines.") On the other hand, this same pattern of high Structure and low Consideration was found to be related to high labor turnover, union grievances, worker absences and accidents, and low worker satisfaction. There was some indication that these relationships might differ in "nonproduction" departments. An interesting sidelight was that foremen with low Consideration *and* low Structure were more often bypassed by subordinates in the informal organizational structure. In any case, it was evident that "what is an effective supervisor" is a complex question, depending on the proficiency criterion emphasized, management values, type of work, and other situational variables.

The present study examines some of the questions left unanswered by this previous work.

## PURPOSE

The present study focused on two main questions. First, what is the *form* of the relationship between leader behavior and indices of group behavior? Is it linear or curvilinear? As far as we know, no one has really examined this question. Rephrased, this question asks if there are critical levels of Consideration and/or Structure beyond which it does or does not make a difference in group behavior. Is an "average" amount of Structure better than a great deal or no Structure at all? Similarly, is there an optimum level of Consideration above and below which worker grievances and/or turnover rise sharply?

The second question concerns the interaction effects of different combinations of Consideration and Structure. Significant correlations have been found between each of these patterns and such indices as rated proficiency, grievances, turnover, departmental reputation, subordinate satisfactions, etc. (e.g., Fleishman, Harris & Burtt, 1955; Halpin, 1954; Hemphill, 1955; Stogdill & Coons, 1957). These studies present some evidence that scoring low on both dimensions is not desirable. They also indicate that some balance of Consideration and Structure may be optimal for satisfying both proficiency and morale criteria. The present study is a more intensive examination of possible optimum combinations of Consideration and Structure.

The present study investigates the relationships between foreman behavior and two primary indices of group behavior: labor grievances and employee turnover. Both of these may be considered as partial criteria of group effectiveness.

## PROCEDURE

### LEADER BEHAVIOR MEASURES

The study was conducted in a motor truck manufacturing plant. Fifty-seven production foremen and their work groups took part in the study. They represented such work operations as stamping, assembly, body assembly, body paint, machinery, and export. At least three workers, drawn randomly from each foreman's department, described the leader behavior of their foreman by means of the *Supervisory Behavior Description Questionnaire* (described elsewhere, Fleishman, 1953, 1957). Each questionnaire was scored on Consideration and Structure, and a mean Consideration score and a mean Structure score was computed for each foreman. The correlation between Consideration and Structure among foremen in this plant was found to be −.33. The correlation between these scales is usually around zero (Fleishman, 1957), but in this plant, foremen who are high in Structure are somewhat more likely to be seen as lower in Consideration and vice versa. However, the relationship is not high. . . .

## RESULTS

### LEADER BEHAVIOR AND GRIEVANCES

Figure 1 plots the average employee grievance rates for departments under foremen scoring at different levels of Consideration. From the curve fitted to these points, it can be seen clearly that the relationship between the foremen's behavior and grievances from their work groups is negative and curvilinear. For most of the range increased Consideration goes with reduced grievance rates. However, increased Consideration above a certain critical level (approximately 76 out of a possible 112) is not related to further decreases in grievances. Furthermore, the curve appears to be negatively accelerated. A given decrease in Consideration just below the critical point (76) is related to a small increase in grievances, but, as Consideration continues to drop, grievance rates rise sharply. Thus, a five-point drop on the Consideration scale, just below a score of 76, is related to a small grievance increase, but a five-point drop below 61 is related to a large rise in grievances. The correlation ratio (eta) represented by this curve is −.51.

Figure 2 plots grievances against the foremen's Structure scores. Here a similar curvilinear relationship is observed. In this case the correlation

**FIGURE 1    Relation between Consideration and Grievance Rates**

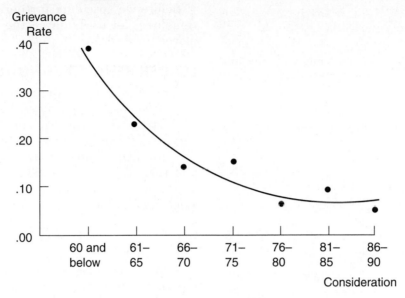

**FIGURE 2    Relation between Structure and Grievance Rates**

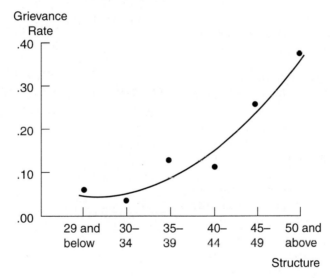

is positive (eta = .71). Below a certain level (approximately 36 out of a possible 80 on our scale), Structure is unrelated to grievances, but above this point increased Structure goes with increased grievances. Again we see that a given increase in Structure just above this critical level is accompanied by a small increase in grievances, but continued increases in Structure are associated with increasingly disproportionately large increases in grievances rates.

Both curves are hyperbolic rather than parabolic in form. Thus, it appears that for neither Consideration nor Structure is there an "optimum" point in the middle of the range below and above which grievances rise. Rather there seems to be a range within which increased Consideration or decreased Structure makes no difference. Of course, when one reaches these levels, grievances are already at a very low level and not much improvement can be expected. However, the important point is that this low grievance level is reached before one gets to the extremely high end of the Consideration scale or to the extremely low end of the Structure scale. It is also clear that extremely high Structure and extremely low Consideration are most related to high grievances.

**FIGURE 3**    **Combinations of Consideration and Structure Related to Grievances**

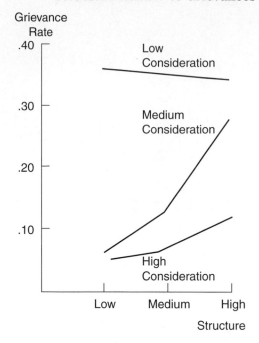

## DIFFERENT COMBINATIONS OF CONSIDERATION AND STRUCTURE RELATED TO GRIEVANCES

The curves described establish that a general relationship exists between each of these leadership patterns and the frequency of employee grievances. But how do *different combinations* of Consideration and Structure relate to grievances? Some foremen score high on both dimensions, some score low on both, etc.

Figure 3 plots the relation between Structure (low, medium, and high) and grievances for groups of foremen who were either low, medium, or high on Consideration. The curves show that grievances occur most frequently among groups whose foremen are low in Consideration, regardless of the amount of emphasis on Structure. The most interesting finding relates to the curve for the high Consideration foremen. This curve suggests that, for the high Consideration foremen, Structure could be increased without any appreciable increase in grievances. However, the reverse is not true; that is, foremen who were low in Consideration could not reduce grievances by easing up on Structure. For foremen average on Consideration, grievances were lowest where Structure was lowest and increased in an almost linear fashion as Structure increased. These data show a definite interaction between Consideration and Structure. Apparently, high Considera-

tion can compensate for high Structure. But low Structure will not offset low Consideration.

Before we speculate further about these relationships, let us examine the results with employee turnover.

## LEADER BEHAVIOR AND TURNOVER

Figures 4 and 5 plot the curves for the *Supervisory Behavior Description* scores of these foremen against the turnover criteria. Again, we see the curvilinear relationships. The correlation (eta) of Consideration and turnover is −.69; Structure and turnover correlate .63. As in the case with grievances, below a certain critical level of Consideration and above a certain level of Structure, turnover goes up. There is, however, an interesting difference in that the critical levels differ from those related to grievances. The flat portions of each of these curves are more extended and the rise in turnover beyond the point of inflection is steeper. The implication of this is quite sensible and indicates that "they gripe before they leave." In other words, a given increase in Structure (to approximately 39) or decrease in Consideration (to 66) may result in increased grievances, but not turnover. It takes higher Structure and lower Consideration before turnover occurs.

## DIFFERENT COMBINATIONS OF CONSIDERATION AND STRUCTURE RELATED TO TURNOVER

Figure 6 plots the relation between Structure (low, medium, and high) and turnover for groups of foremen who were also either low, medium, or high on Consideration. As with grievances, the curves show that turnover is highest for the work groups whose foremen combine low Consideration with high Structure; however, the amount of Consideration is the dominant factor. The curves show that turnover is highest among those work groups whose foremen are low in Consideration, regardless of the amount of emphasis these same foremen show on Structure. There is little distinction between the work groups of foremen who show medium and high Consideration since both of these groups have low turnover among their workers. Furthermore, increased Structure does not seem related to increased turnover in these two groups.[1]

---

[1] This, of course, is consistent with our earlier finding that for increased turnover it takes a bigger drop in Consideration and a bigger increase in Structure to make a difference. Thus, our high and medium Consideration groups separate for grievances, but overlap for turnover.

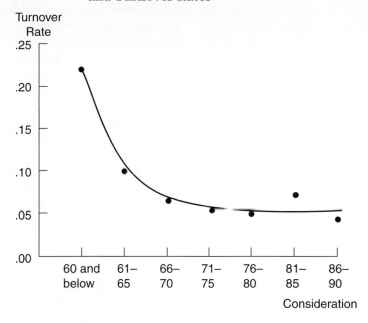

**FIGURE 4  Relations between Consideration and Turnover Rates**

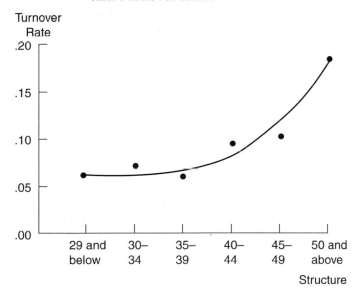

**FIGURE 5  Relation between Structure and Turnover Rates**

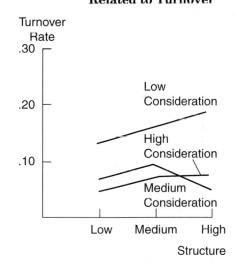

**FIGURE 6  Combination of Consideration and Structure Related to Turnover**

## CONCLUSIONS

1. This study indicates that there are significant relationships between the leader behavior of foremen and the labor grievances and employee turnover in their work groups. In general, low Consideration and high Structure go with high grievances and turnover.

2. There appear to be certain critical levels beyond which increased Consideration or de-

creased Structure have no effect on grievance or turnover rates. Similarly, grievances and turnover are shown to increase most markedly at the extreme ends of the Consideration (low end) and Structure (high end) scales. Thus, the relationship is curvilinear, not linear, and hyperbolic, not parabolic.

3. The critical points at which increased Structure and decreased Consideration begin to relate to group behavior are not the same for grievances and turnover. Increases in turnover

do not occur until lower on the Consideration scale and higher on the Structure scale, as compared with increases in grievances. For example, if Consideration is steadily reduced, higher grievances appear before increased turnover occurs. It appears that there may be different "threshold levels" of Consideration and Structure related to grievances and turnover.

4. Other principal findings concern the interaction effects found between different combinations of Consideration and Structure. Taken in combination, Consideration is the dominant factor. For example, both grievances and turnover were highest in groups having low Consideration foremen, regardless of the degree of Structuring behavior shown by these same foremen.

5. Grievances and turnover were lowest for groups with foremen showing medium to high Consideration together with low Structure. However, one of the most important results is the finding that high Consideration foremen could increase Structure with very little increase in grievances and no increase in turnover. High Consideration foremen had relatively low grievances and turnover, regardless of the amount of Structuring engaged in.

Thus, with regard to grievances and turnover, leader behavior characterized by low Consideration is more critical than behavior characterized by high Structure. Apparently, foremen can compensate for high Structure by increased Consideration, but low Consideration foremen cannot compensate by decreasing their Structuring behavior.

One interpretation is that workers under foremen who establish a climate of mutual trust, rapport, and tolerance for two-way communication with their work groups are more likely to accept higher levels of Structure. This might be because they perceive this Structure differently from employees in "low Consideration" climates. Thus, under "low Consideration" climates, high Structure is seen as threatening and restrictive, but under "high Consideration" climates, this same Structure is seen as supportive and helpful. A related interpretation is that foremen who establish such an atmosphere can more easily solve the problems resulting from high Structure. Thus, *grievances* may be solved at this level before they get into the official records. Similarly, *turnover* may reflect escape from a problem situation which cannot be resolved in the absence of mutual trust and two-way communication. In support of this interpretation, we do have evidence that leaders high in Consideration are also better at predicting subordinates' responses to problems (Fleishman & Salter, 1961).

One has to be careful in making cause and effect inferences here. A possible limitation is that our descriptions of foremen behavior came from the workers themselves. Those workers with many grievances may view their foremen as low in Consideration simply because they have a lot of grievances. However, the descriptions of foreman behavior were obtained from workers drawn randomly from each foreman's group; the odds are against our receiving descriptions from very many workers contributing a disproportionate share of grievances. In the case of turnover, of course, our descriptions could not have been obtained from people who had left during the previous 11 months. Yet substantial correlations were obtained between foremen descriptions, supplied by currently employed workers, with the turnover rates of their work groups. Furthermore, we do have evidence that leader behavior over a year period tends to be quite stable. Test-retest correlations for Consideration, as well as for Structure, tend to be high even when different workers do the describing on the retest (Harris & Fleishman, 1955). Our present preference is to favor the interpretation that high turnover and grievances result, at least in part, from the leader behavior patterns described.

The nonlinear relations between leader behavior and our criteria of effectiveness have more general implications for leadership research. For one thing, it points up the need for a more careful examination of the *form* of such relationships before computing correlation coefficients. Some previously obtained correlations with leadership variables may be underestimates because of linearity assumptions. Similarly, some previous negative or contradictory results may be "explained" by the fact that *(a)* inappropriate coefficients were used or *(b)* these studies were dealing with only the flat portions of these curves. If, for example, all the foremen in our study had scored over 76 on Consideration and under 36 on Structure, we would have concluded that there was no relation between these leadership patterns and grievances and turnover. Perhaps in comparing one study with another, we need to specify the range of leader behavior involved in each study.

There is, of course, a need to explore similar relationships with other criteria. There is no assurance that similar curvilinear patterns and interaction effects will hold for other indices (e.g., group productivity). Even the direction of these relationships may vary with the criterion used. We have evidence (Fleishman, Harris & Burtt, 1955), for example, that Consideration and Structure may relate quite differently to another effectiveness criterion: management's perceptions of foremen proficiency. However, research along these lines may make it possible to specify the particular leadership patterns which most nearly "optimize" these various effectiveness criteria in industrial organizations.

# References

Fleishman, E. A. *"Leadership Climate" and Supervisory Behavior.* Columbus, Ohio: Personnel Research Board, Ohio State University, 1951.

Fleishman, E. A. "Leadership Climate, Human Relations Training, and Supervisory Behavior." *Personnel Psychology,* VI (1953) 205–222. (a)

Fleishman, E. A. "The Description of Supervisory Behavior." *Journal of Applied Psychology,* XXXVII (1953) 1–6. (b).

Fleishman, E. A. "The Measurement of Leadership Attitudes in Industry." *Journal of Applied Psychology,* XXXVII (1953) 153–158. (c)

Fleishman, E. A. "A Leader Behavior Description for Industry." In Stogdill, R. M., and Coons, A. E. (Editors). *Leader Behavior: Its Description and Measurement.* Columbus, Ohio: Bureau of Business Research, 1957.

Fleishman, E. A., Harris, E. F., and Burtt, H. E. *Leadership and Supervision in Industry.* Columbus, Ohio: Bureau of Educational Research, Ohio State University, 1955.

Fleishman, E. A., and Salter, J. A. "The Relation between the Leader's Behavior and His Empathy toward Subordinates." *Advanced Management,* March, 1961, 18–20.

Harris, E. F., and Fleishman, E. A. "Human Relations Training and the Stability of Leadership Patterns." *Journal of Applied Psychology,* XXXIX (1955), 20–25.

Halpin, A. W. "The Leadership Behavior and Combat Performance of Airplane Commanders." *Journal of Abnormal and Social Psychology,* XLIX (1954), 19–22.

Hemphill, J. K. "Leadership Behavior Associated with the Administrative Reputation of College Departments." *Journal of Educational Psychology,* XLVI (1955), 385–401.

Stogdill, R. M., and Coons, A. E. (Editors). *Leader Behavior: Its Description and Measurement.* Columbus, Ohio: Bureau of Business Research, Ohio State University. 1957.

**Reading 21**

# Effects of Leader Warmth and Directiveness on Subordinate Performance on a Subsequent Task

**Dean Tjosvold**
Faculty of Administration, Simon Fraser University, Barnaby, British Columbia

When working with subordinates, organizational leaders typically have several objectives. The most evident, though not always the most important, is to complete the present task effectively. Leaders also want subordinates to become motivated to perform future tasks that they will not directly monitor. A related objective is for subordinates to believe that their leaders are competent and to feel open and positive towards them as people. These positive perceptions and attitudes are important in part because they may increase leader influence and encourage subordinates to complete future tasks successfully. Although there is extensive literature on the relationship between leadership and subordinate productivity and attitudes, little research has focused on how leader interaction with subordinates on a task affects their motivation and performance on subsequent projects. This study experimentally investigates the effect of warm or cold leaders who use a direct or nondirect approach to working with subordinates on a task on the subordinate's productivity on a subsequent task. It also investigates subordinates' perceptions of their leader as effective and helpful and their openness, attraction, and satisfaction with the leader.

Although a few recent analyses have tried to capture the complexity of leadership and the variety of behavioral options available to leaders (e.g., Yukl & Nemeroff, 1979), most research and thinking about leadership has concentrated on whether a leader is seen as initiating and structuring (production-oriented) or considerate (people-oriented). However, these distinctions have not been consistently related to subordinate productivity and satisfaction (Kerr & Schriesheim, 1974; Korman, 1966; Stogdill, 1974). Because subordinates typically provide both the predictor and criterion ratings, little is known about leader actions that cause subordinate outcomes (Kerr & Schriesheim, 1974; Korman, 1964; Luthans, 1979). Structure and consideration summarize subordinate perceptions but do not directly measure leader behavior (Schriesheim, Mowday, & Stogdill, 1979). Rather than try to measure or operationalize general classification, this study examines specific behaviors related to structure and consideration. The first independent variable is the extent the leader is direct in working on a task with subordinates. In the directive approach, leaders provide detailed direction and assistance to get the job completed; they give instructions and specific guidance to subordinates. In the nondirective approach, leaders give little direction but allow subordinates the autonomy to work on the task independently. The second independent variable involves leader interaction style, specifically, whether the leader demonstrates warmth or coldness to subordinates. Warmth conveys interest, openness, and friendliness, whereas coldness conveys distance and disinterest.

The consequences of a directive work approach are likely to depend in part on the warmth of the leader's interaction. Vertical Dyad Linkage Theory emphasizes that through interaction and exchange leaders and subordinates can develop quite different relationships (Dansereau, Graen, & Haga, 1975; Graen & Cashman, 1975). Through rewarding interaction, leaders and subordinates form strong relationships that allow leaders to influence subordinates effectively. However, rewarding interaction, strong relationships, and openness to influence are far from inevitable. Directive leaders may be influential and induce high productivity when they are present to direct, assist, and reward their subordinates. Indeed, a directive approach, and more generally, initiation of structure, has often been related to productivity (Stogdill, 1974). However, the directive leader's approach on future productivity when the leader is absent may be more problematic. A directive approach does communicate that the leader values and will reward productivity in the future. Subordinates believe that the leader will appreciate a strong effort to produce and disapprove of minimal effort; they realize that the situation calls for productivity. However, a directive approach may induce emotional reactions that decrease future motivation. Subordinates may resent the close supervision and become wary and suspicious of their leader (Kipnis, 1976). These feelings can undercut acceptance of the leader's production-oriented values and induce resistance to productivity.

Leader interaction style, in particular whether the leader is warm or cold, may alter the extent negative responses to the directive leader occur and the subordinate's openness and acceptance of the leader's production values (Valenzi & Dessler, 1978). Asch (1952) found that the perception of persons as warm or cold greatly affects responses to their other characteristics. Research in counseling and conflict suggests that warmth conveys acceptance of others as persons and thereby induces attraction and openness to the warm person's ideas and influence (Johnson, 1971; Rogers, 1965). Subordinates then with a warm, directive leader should incorporate the production-oriented values of their leader and as a result work diligently on a future assignment given to them by the leader. Warmth may have similar dynamics but a different outcome when coupled with a nondirective approach. Here subordinates are also open to the leader but their acceptance of the leader's values and orientation reduces their effort; they assume that the leader is relatively disinterested in production and see no compelling reason why they should be.

The impact on subsequent task performance when a leader is cold is not clear. The cold/directive leader may create negative feelings but does press for productivity. Subordinates with a cold/nondirective leader are not expected to be much influenced by the leader's orientation but also they are not expected to feel resentment for being pushed toward performance. On the basis of the above reasoning, it is hypothesized that a leader with a directive work approach when coupled with a warm interaction style, compared to a cold one, induces subordinates to be more productive on a subsequent task and to feel open and attracted to the leader. The analysis is expected to yield an interaction effect indicating that subordinates with the warm/directive leader are the most productive and subordinates with the warm/nondirective leader are the least productive.

## METHOD

### PARTICIPANTS

Fifty-six male and female undergraduates were recruited from courses at Simon Fraser University to participate in this study. Partly because no course credit was offered, students from several courses were approached, and approximately 20 percent of those contacted agreed to participate. They were randomly assigned to four conditions, 14 in each condition. The proportion of males and females was approximately the same for all conditions. Subsequent analysis yielded no significant findings attributable to sex of the participants. . . .

## DISCUSSION

This study, unlike most leadership research, documents effects of leader behavior on followers. In particular, a leader's approach to work and warmth of interaction were found to affect subordinates' perceptions, relationships, and task performance. Results suggest that subordinates feel open, want to work with, feel attracted to, and are satisfied with leaders who communicate warmth toward them. The impact of leader warmth and these positive attitudes on subordinate task performance depended on whether the leader was directive or nondirective. A warm leader who was directive and presumably clearly concerned about productivity had subordinates who themselves became work oriented and productive. A warm leader who was nondirective and less interested in task completion had the least productive subordinates. When the leader was cold toward subordinates, the leader's approach and values seemed to have little impact on subordinate task performance.

These results are consistent with the general conclusion based on considerable correlational evidence that leaders who are both high in structure and high in consideration facilitate productivity and satisfaction among subordinates. But this advice can be difficult to translate into specific action (Argyris, 1979; Gilmore, Beehr, & Richter, 1979). This study, in addition to providing experimental support for this argument, complements recent attempts to specify actions leaders can take to both initiate structure and be considerate (e.g., Yukl & Nemeroff, 1979). Leaders can convey a production orientation by giving specific instructions and help to subordinates as they complete their tasks. Warmth conveys acceptance and interest and seems to be strongly communicated nonverbally. An earlier experiment tried to operationalize consideration in terms of social talk, but the induction check indicated that participants did not clearly see that as demonstrating consideration (Gilmore et al., 1979). In addition, social talk will at times be distracting. Warmth can be demonstrated nonverbally as leaders and subordinates work on tasks.

Argyris (1970) has emphasized that organizational leaders should become more competent at expressing feelings. He argued that suppression of feeling greatly harms coordination and the organization's ability to make decisions and remain effective. This study demonstrates that leaders' expression of feelings can be examined experimentally and suggests that nonverbal communication is a useful way to operationalize expression of warmth, anger, success, and other important emotions. These operations can be used as a guide for leaders to learn to express their feelings.

This study focused on the subordinates' behavior following their interaction with their leader. Knowledge of the consequences of leader interaction on future tasks is important theoretically and practically because leaders seldom continuously interact with subordinates; they must attend to other subordinates, their own supervisor, and tasks. Experimentally, subsequent task performance can be measured without possible confounding with the leader's direct influence on task accomplishment. Because a directive work approach and warm interpersonal style were expected to enhance subordinates' acceptance of leader values and result in a desire to work on a task given by that leader, the particular task of business mathematical problems was selected because it was thought to measure motivation rather than ability. A task in which the leader works directly with and can monitor the subordinate may have yielded different results; in this situation subordinate acceptance of leader values may make less difference. A challenging task requiring originality and creativity may weaken any effects due to leader values because subordinates' interests and abilities may be the predominant causes of performance. Future research could explore the tasks that strengthen and weaken the effects of leader approach and style.

In addition to the task, operations of the independent and dependent variables, sample, and other aspects of the study further limit its results. Participants were undergraduates who took the role of a worker for a short time. Although employees in any organization take roles, their roles typically last much longer and have more substantial consequences than the participants in this study faced. The short interaction with the leader of this study is not atypical of organizations; indeed, many supervisors' interactions with employees are much shorter. However, this study only involves one interaction, and most subordinates and leaders interact repeatedly. It would seem reasonable to conclude that the impact of the leader's work approach and style would be accumulative; that is, subordinates would become progressively more accepting of the production-oriented values of the warm, directive leader (Graen & Cashman, 1975). But it can also be speculated that more subtle effects would also occur. Subordinates may accommodate their leader; perhaps they would realize that they cannot expect much support from the cold leader and consequently react less strongly to the leader. Research could explore the dynamics of repeated interactions between leaders and subordinates.

Although this study's results are limited, other previous research suggests that the results may generalize to actual organizational leader–subordinate relationships. Correlational evidence collected in many kinds of organizational settings indicates that high structure–high consideration is related to productive, satisfied employees. This study provides experimental support for this general finding and suggests ways leaders can behave in order to be seen as both concerned about production and people. Warmth of the leader's interaction was found to have a powerful impact on subordinates and, when coupled with a directive work approach, was found to aid productivity on a subsequent task.

# References

Argyris, C. (1970). *Intervention theory and method: A behavioral science view.* Reading, MA: Addison-Wesley.

Argyris, C. (1979). How normal science methodology makes leadership research less additive and less applicable. In J. G. Hunt & L. L. Larson (Eds.), *Crosscurrents in leadership* (pp. 47–63). Carbondale, IL: Southern Illinois University Press.

Asch, S. E. (1952). *Social psychology.* Englewood Cliffs, NJ: Prentice-Hall.

Dansereau, F., Jr., Graen, G., & Haga, W. J. (1975). A vertical dyad linkage approach to leadership within formal organizations: A longitudinal investigation of the role making process. *Organizational Behavior and Human Performance* 13, 46–78.

Gilmore, D. C., Beehr, T. A., & Richter, D. J. (1979). Effects of leader behaviors on subordinate performance and satisfaction: A laboratory experiment with student employees. *Journal of Applied Psychology,* 64, 166–172.

Graen, G., & Cashman, J. F. (1975). A role making model of leadership in formal organizations: A developmental approach. In J. G. Hunt & L. L. Larson (Eds.), *Leadership frontiers* (pp. 143–165). Kent, OII: Kent State University Press.

Johnson, D. W. (1971). Effects of warmth of interaction, accuracy of understanding and the proposal of compromises on listener's behavior. *Journal of Counseling Psychology,* 18, 207–216.

Johnson, D. W., & Johnson, F. P. (1982). *Joining together: Group theory and group skills.* Englewood Cliffs, NJ: Prentice-Hall.

Kerr, S., & Schriesheim, C. A. (1974). Consideration, initiating structure, and organizational criteria—An update of Korman's 1966 review. *Personnel Psychology,* 27, 555–568.

Kipnis, D. (1976). *The powerholders.* Chicago. University of Chicago Press.

Korman, A. K. (1966). "Consideration", "initiating structure", and organizational criteria. *Personnel Psychology,* 18, 349–360.

Luthans, F. (1979). Leadership: A proposal for a social learning theory base and observational and functional analysis techniques to measure leader behavior. In J. G. Hunt & L. L. Larson (Eds.), *Crosscurrents in leadership* (pp. 201–208). Carbondale: Southern Illinois University Press.

Mehrabian, A. (1968). Communication without words. *Psychology Today,* 2, 53–55.

Rogers, C. (1965). Dealing with psychological tensions. *Journal of Applied Behavioral Science,* 1, 6–25.

Schriesheim, C. A., Mowday, R. T., & Stogdill, R. M. (1979). Crucial dimensions of leader–group interactions. In J. G. Hunt and L. L. Larson (Eds.), *Crosscurrents in Leadership* (pp. 106–125). Carbondale, IL: Southern Illinois University Press.

Stogdill, R. M. (1974). *Handbook of leadership: A survey of theory and research.* New York: The Free Press.

Valenzi, E., & Dessler, G. (1978). Relationships of leader behavior, subordinate role ambiguity and subordinate job satisfaction. *Academy of Management Journal,* 21, 671–678.

Yukl, G. A., & Nemeroff, W. (1979). Identification and measurement of specific categories of leadership behavior. A progress report. In J. G. Hunt & L. L. Larson (Eds.), *Crosscurrents in leadership.* Carbondale, IL: Southern Illinois University Press.

# Chapter **Eight**

# Leadership and Situational Differences

This chapter addresses the *situation* in the leadership process. The evolving leadership model from the earlier chapters suggests that the situation in part defines the leadership process and that it influences the leader and interacts with the leader's attempts to influence his or her followers. Three key questions that will be addressed are:

- Does the situation in which the leader and follower are embedded make a difference?

- What leader behavior works and when?

- What is the process through which the situation produces its effects?

The importance of the situation has already been alluded to on numerous occasions through the first several chapters. Murphy (1941), for example, noted that situations in which people find themselves create needs, and it is the nature of these needs that defines the type of leadership that best serves the group. Accordingly, Murphy saw leadership as a function (interaction) of (a) what it is that an individual has to offer and (b) the nature of the demands placed upon followers by the situation in which they are embedded. In a similar fashion, Stogdill (1948) suggested that leadership is a working relationship—one in which different contexts create a unique set of group needs, and a group's emerging leader is that individual who is capable of making meaningful contributions to the group.

Leaders, according to Smircich and Morgan (1982), are those individuals who are capable of taking an ambiguous situation and framing it in a meaningful and acceptable way for the followers. Smircich and Morgan also defined leadership as a product of an interaction between the situation, the leader, and the followers.

In Salancik and Pfeffer's (1977) strategic contingencies model of leadership, the leader is a person who brings scarce resources to assist a group of individuals in overcoming a critical problem that they face. As the problems facing a group change, their leader may also change because of his or her access to critical and scarce resources. Thus, Salancik and Pfeffer's work also serves to highlight the importance of the situation in defining leadership and the leadership process.

Chapter 7's overview of the leader behavior literature highlighted the fact that there are inconsistent relationships between the behaviors that leaders engage in and the effects of these behaviors on member attitudes, behavior, and group effectiveness. While these inconsistent observations (e.g., the relationship between initiating structure and performance is sometimes positive, while at other times there is no significant relationship, or the relationship is negative in nature) can be frustrating, they underscore two very important facts. First, these behaviors (e.g., initiating structure and consideration) are *important* as witnessed by their occasionally significant relationship with follower attitudes and behavior. Second, the observation that these behaviors do not always produce significant and positive effects suggests that *something else is transpiring,* such that in one situation the particular leader behavior produces significant effects, and in another situation that behavior is relatively unimportant. The question that these observations raise is, What effects do situational differences produce in the leader–follower relationship?

Many decades ago Ralph Stogdill (1948) stated that "the qualities, characteristics, and skills required in a leader are determined to a large extent by the demands of the situation in which he [she] is to function as a leader" (p. 63). Chapter 8 provides an understanding of situational differences in the leadership process.

The simple theme of this chapter might well be "different strokes for different folks" and/or "different strokes for the same folks at different points in time." Put more directly, as conditions change, so do the leadership needs that are created and the leader behaviors that will prove effective. If team members know, for example, exactly what needs to be done, when, how, and why, it is unlikely that initiating structure will prove to be needed, or be effective if used. In contrast, when team members are operating under conditions of high levels of uncertainty—not knowing what, when, or how to execute the task—a leader who is capable of initiating some structure will make a meaningful contribution.

Influenced by Stogdill's (1948, 1974) reviews of the leader behavior literature and the emerging recognition of the importance of the leadership context, Steven Kerr, Chester A. Schriesheim, Charles J. Murphy, and Ralph M. Stogdill (1974), advanced a number of situational propositions linking leader initiation of structure and consideration to leader effectiveness.[1] They note that accumulated evidence suggests that leader effectiveness is not always associated with those who behave in a highly considerate and structuring manner. Among some of the situational factors that influence the effectiveness of leader consideration and initiating structure behavior are, for example, time urgency, amount of physical danger, presence of external stress, degree of autonomy, degree of job scope, importance, and meaningfulness of work.

Robert J. House (1971) contends that leader effectiveness is most appropriately examined in terms of the leader's *impact* upon the performance of his or her followers.[2] In the first reading in this chapter, House and Terence R. Mitchell (1974) assert that a leader's behavior will be motivational and subsequently have an impact upon the attitudes and performance behavior of the follower to the extent that it makes the satisfaction of a subordinate's needs contingent upon his or her performance. The strategic functions of a leader, according to House and Mitchell, consist of

> (1) recognizing and/or arousing subordinates' needs for outcomes over which the leader has some control, (2) increasing personal payoffs to subordinates for work-goal attainment, (3) making the path to those payoffs easier to travel by coaching and direction, (4) helping subordinates clarify expectancies, (5) reducing frustrating barriers, and (6) increasing the opportunities for personal satisfaction contingent on effective performance (p. 229).

---

[1] S. Kerr, C. A. Schriesheim, C. J. Murphy, and R. M. Stogdill, "Toward a Contingency Theory of Leadership Based upon the Consideration and Initiating Structure Literature," *Organizational Behavior and Human Performance* 12 (1974), pp. 62–82.
[2] R. J. House, "A Path-Goal Theory of Leader Effectiveness," *Administrative Science Quarterly* 16 (1971), pp. 321–38.

Characteristics of the follower and the situation in which the leader and follower are embedded tend to alter the nature of the leader–follower relationship. Thus, the effectiveness of a leader's behavior is a function of the influence that the leader exercises over the follower in interaction with attributes of the work environment.

According to House and Mitchell, there are four important dimensions to leader behavior—supportive (consideration), directive (initiating structure), participative, and achievement-oriented leadership—that are important under different situational (i.e., task-based) conditions. Their path-goal model addresses the leader's unique need to provide for follower satisfaction, motivation, and performance under four different task conditions: boring, ambiguous, unstructured, and lack of challenge. Role ambiguity, for example, calls for directive leadership to clarify the path to performance. The reduction of role ambiguity enables followers to see their way more clearly toward performance accomplishment. This role clarification, coupled with directive leadership, should prove to be motivating and satisfying for the employee, ultimately producing positive performance consequences.

The second reading in this section presents Fred E. Fiedler's (1974) contingency theory of leadership. Fiedler argues that situations vary in the degree to which they are favorable to the leader. Some situations are simply more favorable for a leader than other situations. Three factors that have a major influence on situation favorability are *leader–member relations* (i.e., the quality of the relationship between the leader and followers, as might be reflected by the degree to which the group accepts the leader and member loyalty to the leader); *task structure* (i.e., the degree of structure of the task to be performed, as might be reflected by the presence of a clear and unambiguous goal and a well-defined procedure that details how to proceed); and *position power* (i.e., the leader's ability to influence the followers, as might be achieved through the exercise of legitimate, reward, coercive, expert, and/or referent power).

An important part of the leadership process, according to Fiedler, is the interaction of the leader's orientation toward others and the favorability of the leadership situation. Some leaders have a strong interpersonal orientation. These individuals need to develop and maintain close interpersonal relationships. Task accomplishment is of secondary importance and becomes important only after their relationship needs have been reasonably well satisfied. Other leaders have a strong task orientation. Their first motivational concern centers on task accomplishment with the development of good interpersonal relationships being a secondary interest. According to the contingency theory of leadership, leaders' motivational orientation toward others can be captured by the attitudes they express about their *least preferred co-worker (LPC)*. (The self-assessment presented at the end of this chapter opener enables you to profile yourself according to your own "least preferred co-worker.")

Leaders with a high LPC score tend to see their least preferred co-workers in fairly favorable terms. These leaders tend to be relationship-oriented, and they are most effective as leaders in situations of intermediate favorability. Leaders with a low LPC score are more task-oriented, and they tend to evaluate their least preferred co-worker fairly negatively. These individuals and their directive leadership styles tend to be associated with effective group performance under highly favorable and unfavorable situations.

Paul Hersey and Kenneth Blanchard's (1976) situational leadership model has received a high level of visibility among management practitioners. Hersey and Blanchard tend to see both the situation facing the leader and follower, and the follower, as significant components of the context facing the leader and his or her choice as to the appropriate style of leadership. According to their situational theory of leadership, appropriate leader behavior is defined by (a) situational demands for direction (task behavior) and socio-emotional support (relationship behavior) and (b) the level of "maturity" of the follower or group relative to the task or objective that the leader is attempting to accomplish through the follower's efforts.

It should be noted that there are inconsistent views as to whether or not there is a "one best style" of leadership. Bass (1997) notes that there is very little empirical evidence that supports Hersey and Blanchard's (1969) model of situational leadership based upon follower maturity. In addition, Bass (1997) notes that, after several hundred investigations, controversy still surrounds Fiedler's (1983) contingency theory. Contingencies do, however, provide important insight into leadership. Bass (1997) contends that evidence supports the notion that "better leaders integrate a task-oriented and a relations-oriented approach" (p. 132).[3] In addition, effective leaders also "demonstrate the ability to clarify the path to the goals" (p. 132).[4] Blake and Mouton (1981) advocate (in their "managerial grid") that the "ideal" is a leader who exhibits high levels of task- and relationship-oriented behavior.[5] Several of the authors presented in this chapter, including Hersey and Blanchard, essentially argue that any one of a number of different styles of leadership is effective, so long as it is appropriately matched with the task (situation) facing the group.

In the final reading in this chapter, Robert Hooijberg (1996) notes that the significant changes that have come about in organizations during the past couple of decades have given birth to a number of new roles (e.g., leading cross-functional teams). Hooijberg suggests that accompanying these changes there is increasing pressure upon the leader to have a wide range of behaviors upon which to call as needs arise. He proposes that leaders with "behavioral complexity" will be more effective than those managers who are behaviorally restricted to a limited number of leadership functions. Hooijberg's work parallels the implicit call for a leader to possess the ability to shift between supportive, directive, participative, and achievement-oriented leadership, as outlined in House and Mitchell's path-goal theory of leadership. In addition, Hooijberg's behavioral complexity construct runs counter to the assumption in Fiedler's work, which suggests that it may be easier to match the leader with the situation or reengineer the situation—since changing leadership orientation is extremely difficult.

Figure 8.1 highlights several important components that now contribute to the leadership mosaic. Situational conditions (i.e., attributes of the task being performed) and follower attributes (e.g., task frustration, experienced ambiguity, expertise, ability to exercise self-direction and self-control) interact with the leader, shaping what might be effective leadership behavior.

[3] Bernard Bass. "Does the Transactional-Transformational Leadership Paradigm Transcend Organizational and National Boundaries?" *American Psychologist* 52, no. 2 (1997), pp. 130–139.
[4] Ibid.
[5] R. R. Blake & J. S. Mouton. 1981. *The versatile manager: A guide profile.* Homewood, IL: Dow-Jones/Irwin.

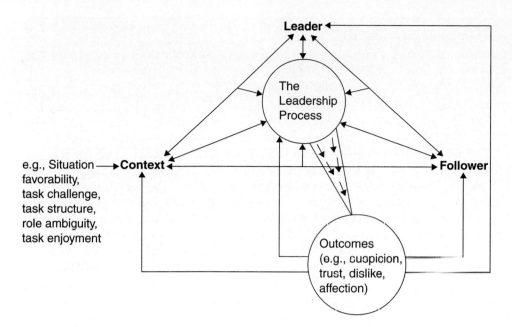

**FIGURE 8.1**
**The Leadership
Process: Critical
Contextual Factors**

**EXERCISE**
*Self-Assessment*

**Least Preferred Co-worker (LPC)**

**Instructions:** Think of the person with whom you can work least well. This may be someone you work with now or someone you knew in the past. It does not have to be the person you like least well, but it should be the person with whom you had the most difficulty in getting a job done. Describe this person as he or she appears to you, by circling a number for each scale.

| | | | | | | | | | |
|---|---|---|---|---|---|---|---|---|---|
| Pleasant | 8 | 7 | 6 | 5 | 4 | 3 | 2 | 1 | Unpleasant |
| Friendly | 8 | 7 | 6 | 5 | 4 | 3 | 2 | 1 | Unfriendly |
| Rejecting | 1 | 2 | 3 | 4 | 5 | 6 | 7 | 8 | Accepting |
| Helpful | 8 | 7 | 6 | 5 | 4 | 3 | 2 | 1 | Frustrating |
| Unenthusiastic | 1 | 2 | 3 | 4 | 5 | 6 | 7 | 8 | Enthusiastic |
| Tense | 1 | 2 | 3 | 4 | 5 | 6 | 7 | 8 | Relaxed |
| Distant | 1 | 2 | 3 | 4 | 5 | 6 | 7 | 8 | Close |
| Cold | 1 | 2 | 3 | 4 | 5 | 6 | 7 | 8 | Warm |
| Cooperative | 8 | 7 | 6 | 5 | 4 | 3 | 2 | 1 | Uncooperative |
| Supportive | 8 | 7 | 6 | 5 | 4 | 3 | 2 | 1 | Hostile |
| Boring | 1 | 2 | 3 | 4 | 5 | 6 | 7 | 8 | Interesting |
| Quarrelsome | 1 | 2 | 3 | 4 | 5 | 6 | 7 | 8 | Harmonious |
| Self-assured | 8 | 7 | 6 | 5 | 4 | 3 | 2 | 1 | Hesitant |
| Efficient | 8 | 7 | 6 | 5 | 4 | 3 | 2 | 1 | Inefficient |
| Gloomy | 1 | 2 | 3 | 4 | 5 | 6 | 7 | 8 | Cheerful |
| Open | 8 | 7 | 6 | 5 | 4 | 3 | 2 | 1 | Guarded |

**Scoring:** Your LPC score is the sum of the answers to these 16 questions. A high score (greater than 76) reflects a relationship-orientation, while a low score (less than 62) signals a task-orientation.

**Interpretation:** According to Fiedler's work, a person with a high LPC tends to be relationship-oriented. These leaders generally tend to perform best under conditions of intermediate favorability. Leaders with a low LPC score are more task-oriented, and they tend to function best under conditions of high and low favorability. Work by John K. Kennedy, Jr., (1982) indicates that "the performance of middle LPC leaders is generally superior to that of the high and low LPC leaders . . ." (p.1)[1]

**Source:** F. E. Fiedler and M. M. Chemers, *Leadership and Effective Management* (Glenview, IL: Scott, Foresman, 1974).

[1] J. K. Kennedy, Jr., "Middle LPC Leaders and the Contingency Model of Leadership Effectiveness," *Organizational Behavior and Human Performance* 31 (1982), pp. 1–14.

## Reading 22

# Path-Goal Theory of Leadership

**Robert J. House**
University of Toronto

**Terence R. Mitchell**
University of Washington

An integrated body of conjecture by students of leadership, referred to as the "path-goal theory of leadership," is currently emerging. According to this theory, leaders are effective because of their impact on subordinates' motivation, ability to perform effectively, and satisfactions. The theory is called path-goal because its major concern is how the leader influences the subordinates' perceptions of their work goals, personal goals, and paths to goal attainment. The theory suggests that a leader's behavior is motivating or satisfying to the degree that the behavior increases subordinate goal attainment and clarifies the paths to these goals.

## HISTORICAL FOUNDATIONS

The path-goal approach has its roots in a more general motivational theory called expectancy theory.[1] Briefly, expectancy theory states that an individual's attitudes (e.g., satisfaction with supervision or job satisfaction) or behavior (e.g., leader behavior or job effort) can be predicted from: (1) the degree to which the job, or behavior, is seen as leading to various outcomes (expectancy), and (2) the evaluation of these outcomes (valences). Thus, people are satisfied with their job if they think it leads to things that are highly valued, and they work hard if they believe that effort leads to things that are highly valued. This type of theoretical rationale can be used to predict a variety of phenomena related to leadership, such as why leaders behave the way they do, or how leader behavior influences subordinate motivation.[2]

This latter approach is the primary concern of this article. The implication for leadership is that subordinates are motivated by leader behavior to the extent that this behavior influ-

ences expectancies, e.g., goal paths and valences (goal attractiveness).

Several writers have advanced specific hypotheses concerning how the leader affects the paths and the goals of subordinates.[3] These writers focused on two issues: (1) how the leader affects subordinates' expectations that effort will lead to effective performance and valued rewards, and (2) how this expectation affects motivation to work hard and perform well.

While the state of theorizing about leadership in terms of subordinates' paths and goals is in its infancy, we believe it is promising for two reasons. First, it suggests effects of leader behavior that have not yet been investigated but which appear to be fruitful areas of inquiry. And, second, it suggests with some precision the situational factors on which the effects of leader behavior are contingent.

The initial theoretical work by Evans asserts that leaders will be effective by making rewards available to subordinates and by making these rewards contingent on the subordinates' accomplishment of specific goals.[4] Evans argued that one of the strategic functions of the leader is to clarify for subordinates the kind of behavior that leads to goal accomplishment and valued rewards. This function might be referred to as path clarification. Evans also argued that the leader increases the rewards available to subordinates by being supportive toward subordinates, i.e., by being concerned about their status, welfare, and comfort. Leader supportiveness is in itself a reward that the leader has at his or her disposal, and the judicious use of this reward increases the motivation of subordinates.

Evans studied the relationship between the behavior of leaders and the subordinates' expectations that effort leads to rewards and also studied the resulting impact on ratings of the subordinates' performance. He found that when subordinates viewed leaders as being supportive (considerate of their needs) and when these superiors provided directions and guidance to the subordinates, there

**Source:** Edited and reprinted with permission from *Journal of Contemporary Business* (Autumn, 1974), pp. 81–97.

was a positive relationship between leader behavior and subordinates' performance ratings.

However, leader behavior was only related to subordinates' performance when the leader's behavior also was related to the subordinates' expectations that their effort would result in desired rewards. Thus, Evans's findings suggest that the major impact of a leader on the performance of subordinates is clarifying the path to desired rewards and making such rewards contingent on effective performance.

Stimulated by this line of reasoning, House, and House and Dessler advanced a more complex theory of the effects of leader behavior on the motivation of subordinates.[5] The theory intends to explain the effects of four specific kinds of leader behavior on the following three subordinate attitudes or expectations: (1) the satisfaction of subordinates, (2) the subordinates' acceptance of the leader, and (3) the expectations of subordinates that effort will result in effective performance and that effective performance is the path to rewards. The four kinds of leader behavior included in the theory are: (1) directive leadership, (2) supportive leadership, (3) participative leadership, and (4) achievement-oriented leadership. Directive leadership is characterized by a leader who lets subordinates know what is expected of them, gives specific guidance as to what should be done and how it should be done, makes his or her part in the group understood, schedules work to be done, maintains definite standards of performance, and asks that group members follow standard rules and regulations. Supportive leadership is characterized by a friendly and approachable leader who shows concern for the status, well-being, and needs of subordinates. Such a leader does little things to make the work more pleasant, treats members as equals, and is friendly and approachable. Participative leadership is characterized by a leader who consults with subordinates, solicits their suggestions, and takes these suggestions seriously into consideration before making a decision. An achievement-oriented leader sets challenging goals, expects subordinates to perform at their highest level, continuously seeks improvement in performance, *and* shows a high degree of confidence that the subordinates will assume responsibility, put forth effort, and accomplish challenging goals. This kind of leader constantly emphasizes excellence in performance and simultaneously displays confidence that subordinates will meet high standards of excellence.

A number of studies suggest that these different leadership styles can be shown by the same leader in various situations.[6] For example, a leader may show directiveness toward subordinates in some instances and be participative or supportive in other instances.[7] Thus, the traditional method of characterizing a leader as either highly participative and supportive *or* highly directive is invalid; rather, it can be concluded that leaders vary in the particular fashion employed for supervising their subordinates. Also, the theory, in its present stage, is a tentative explanation of the effects of leader behavior—it is incomplete because it does not explain other kinds of leader behavior and does not explain the effects of the leader on factors other than subordinates' acceptance, satisfaction, and expectations. However, the theory is stated so that additional variables may be included in it as new knowledge is made available.

## PATH-GOAL THEORY

### GENERAL PROPOSITIONS

The first proposition of path-goal theory is that leader behavior is acceptable and satisfying to subordinates to the extent that the subordinates see such behavior as either an immediate source of satisfaction or as instrumental to future satisfaction.

The second proposition of this theory is that the leader's behavior will be motivational, i.e., increase effort, to the extent that (1) such behavior makes satisfaction of subordinates' needs contingent on effective performance, and (2) such behavior complements the environment of subordinates by providing the coaching, guidance, support, and rewards necessary for effective performance.

These two propositions suggest that the leader's strategic functions are to enhance subordinates' motivation to perform, satisfaction with the job, and acceptance of the leader. From previous research on expectancy theory of motivation, it can be inferred that the strategic functions of the leader consist of: (1) recognizing and/or arousing subordinates' needs for outcomes over which the leader has some control, (2) increasing personal payoffs to subordinates for work-goal attainment, (3) making the path to those payoffs easier to travel by coaching and direction, (4) helping subordinates clarify expectancies, (5) reducing frustrating barriers, and (6) increasing the opportunities for personal satisfaction contingent on effective performance.

Stated less formally, the motivational functions of the leader consist of increasing the number and kinds of personal payoffs to subordinates for work-goal attainment and making paths to these payoffs easier to travel by clarifying the paths, reducing road blocks and pitfalls, and increasing the opportunities for personal satisfaction en route.

# CONTINGENCY FACTORS

Two classes of situational variables are asserted to be contingency factors. A contingency factor is a variable which moderates the relationship between two other variables such as leader behavior and subordinate satisfaction. For example, we might suggest that the degree of structure in the task moderates the relationship between leaders' directive behavior and subordinates' job satisfaction. Figure 1 shows how such a relationship might look. Thus, subordinates are satisfied with directive behavior in an unstructured task and are satisfied with nondirective behavior in a structured task. Therefore, we say that the relationship between leader directiveness and subordinate satisfaction is contingent upon the structure of the task.

The two contingency variables are (a) personal characteristics of the subordinates and (b) the environmental pressures and demands with which subordinates must cope in order to accomplish the work goals and to satisfy their needs. While other situational factors also may operate to determine the effects of leader behavior, they are not presently known.

**FIGURE 1** **Hypothetical Relationship between Directive Leadership and Subordinate Satisfaction with Task Structure as a Contingency Factor**

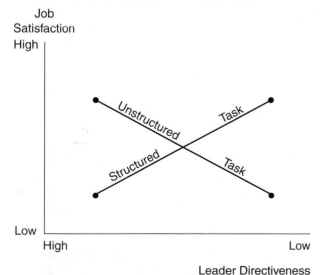

With respect to the first class of contingency factors, the characteristics of subordinates, path-goal theory asserts that leader behavior will be acceptable to subordinates to the extent that the subordinates see such behavior as either an immediate source of satisfaction or as instrumental to future satisfaction. Subordinates' characteristics are hypothesized to partially determine this perception. For example, Runyon[8] and Mitchell[9] show that the subordinate's source on a measure called Locus of Control moderates the relationship between participative leadership style and subordinate satisfaction. The Locus-of-Control measure reflects the degree to which an individual sees the environment as systematically responding to his or her behavior. People who believe that what happens to them occurs because of their behavior are called internals; people who believe that what happens to them occurs because of luck or chance are called externals. Mitchell's findings suggest that internals are more satisfied with a participative leadership style and externals are more satisfied with a directive style.

A second characteristic of subordinates on which the effects of leader behavior are contingent is subordinates' perception of their own ability with respect to their assigned tasks. The higher the degree of perceived ability relative to task demands, the less the subordinate will view leader directiveness and coaching behavior as acceptable. Where the subordinate's perceived ability is high, such behavior is likely to have little positive effect on the motivation of the subordinate and to be perceived as excessively close control. Thus, the acceptability of the leader's behavior is determined in part by the characteristics of the subordinates.

The second aspect of the situation, the environment of the subordinate, consists of those factors that are not within the control of the subordinate but which are important to need satisfaction or to ability to perform effectively. The theory asserts that effects of the leader's behavior on the psychological states of subordinates are contingent on other parts of the subordinates' environment that are relevant to subordinate motivation. Three broad classifications of contingency factors in the environment are: the subordinates' tasks, the formal authority system of the organization, and the primary work group.

Assessment of the environmental conditions makes it possible to predict the kind and amount of influence that specific leader behaviors will have on the motivation of subordinates. Any of the three environmental factors could act upon the subordinate in any of three ways: first, to serve as stimuli that motivate and direct the subordinate to perform necessary task operations; second, to constrain variability in behavior. Constraints may help the subordinate by clarifying expectancies that effort leads to rewards or by preventing the subordinates from experiencing conflict and confusion. Constraints also may be counterproductive to the extent that they restrict initiative or prevent increases in effort from being associated positively with rewards. Third, environmental factors may serve as rewards for achieving desired performance, e.g., it is possible for the subordinate to receive the necessary cues to do the job and the needed rewards for satisfaction from sources other than the leader, e.g., coworkers in the primary work group. Thus, the effect of the leader on subordinates' motivation will be a function of how deficient the environment is with respect to motivational stimuli, constraints, or rewards.

With respect to the environment, path-goal theory asserts that when goals and paths to desired goals are apparent because of the routine nature of the task, clear group norms, or objective controls of the formal authority systems, attempts by the leader to clarify paths and goals will be both redundant and seen by subordinates as imposing unnecessary, close control. Although such control may increase performance by preventing soldiering or malingering, it also will result in decreased satisfaction (see Figure 1). Also with respect to the work environment, the theory asserts that the more dissatisfying the task, the more the subordinates will resent leader behavior directed at increasing productivity or enforcing compliance to organizational rules and procedures.

Finally, with respect to environmental variables, the theory states that leader behavior will be motivational to the extent that it helps subordinates cope with environmental uncertainties, threats from others, or sources of frustration. Such leader behavior is predicted to increase subordinates' satisfaction with the job context and to be motivational to the extent that it increases the subordinates' expectations that their effort will lead to valued rewards.

These propositions and specification of situational contingencies provide a heuristic framework on which to base future research. Hopefully, this will lead to a more fully developed, explicitly formal theory of leadership.

Figure 2 presents a summary of the theory. It is hoped that these propositions, while admittedly tentative, will provide managers with some insights concerning the effects of their own leader behavior and that of others.

## EMPIRICAL SUPPORT

The theory has been tested in a limited number of studies which have generated considerable empirical support for our ideas and also suggest areas in which the theory requires revision. A brief review of these studies follows.

### LEADER DIRECTIVENESS

Leader directiveness has a positive correlation with satisfaction and expectancies of subordinates who are engaged in ambiguous tasks and has a negative correlation with satisfaction and expectancies of subordinates engaged in clear tasks. These findings were predicted by the theory and have been replicated in seven organiza-

**FIGURE 2   Summary of Path-Goal Relationships**

| Leader Behavior and | Contingency Factors | | Cause | Subordinate Attitudes and Behavior |
|---|---|---|---|---|
| 1 Directive | 1 Subordinate characteristics: | | | 1 Job satisfaction |
| 2 Supportive |   Authoritarianism | Influence → | Personal perceptions |   Job ⟶ Rewards |
| 3 Achievement-oriented |   Locus of Control | | | 2 Acceptance of leader |
| |   Ability | | |   Leader ⟶ Rewards |
| 4 Participative | 2 Environmental factors: | | Motivational stimuli | 3 Motivational behavior |
| |   The task | | |   Effort ⟶ Performance |
| |   Formal authority system | Influence → | Constraints |   Performance ⟶ Rewards |
| |   Primary work group | | Rewards | |

tions. They suggest that when task demands are ambiguous or when the organization procedures, rules, and policies are not clear, a leader behaving in a directive manner complements the tasks and the organization by providing the necessary guidance and psychological structure for subordinates.[10] However, when task demands are clear to subordinates, leader directiveness is seen more as a hindrance. . . .

## SUPPORTIVE LEADERSHIP

The theory hypothesizes that supportive leadership will have its most positive effect on subordinate satisfaction for subordinates who work on stressful, frustrating, or dissatisfying tasks. This hypothesis has been tested in 10 samples of employees,[11] and in only one of these studies was the hypothesis disconfirmed.[12] Despite some inconsistency in research on supportive leadership, the evidence is sufficiently positive to suggest that managers should be alert to the critical need for supportive leadership under conditions where tasks are dissatisfying, frustrating, or stressful to subordinates. . . .

## ACHIEVEMENT-ORIENTED LEADERSHIP

The theory hypothesizes that achievement-oriented leadership will cause subordinates to strive for higher standards of performance and to have more confidence in the ability to meet challenging goals. A recent study by House, Valency, and Van der Krabben provides a partial test on this hypothesis among white-collar employees in service organizations.[13] For subordinates performing ambiguous, nonrepetitive tasks, they found a positive relationship between the amount of achievement orientation of the leader and subordinates' expectancy that their effort would result in effective performance. Stated less technically, for subordinates performing ambiguous, nonrepetitive tasks, the higher the achievement orientation of the leader, the more the subordinates were confident that their efforts would pay off in effective performance. For subordinates performing moderately unambiguous, repetitive tasks, there was no significant relationship between achievement-oriented leadership and subordinate expectancies that their effort would lead to effective performance. This finding held in four separate organizations.

Two plausible interpretations may be used to explain these data. First, people who select ambiguous, nonrepetitive tasks may be different in personality from those who select a repetitive job and may, therefore, be more responsive to an achievement-oriented leader. A second explanation is that achievement orientation only affects expectancies in ambiguous situations because there is more flexibility and autonomy in such tasks. Therefore, subordinates in such tasks are more likely to be able to change in response to such leadership style. Neither of the above interpretations have been tested to date; however, additional research is currently under way to investigate these relationships.

## PARTICIPATIVE LEADERSHIP

In theorizing about the effects of participative leadership, it is necessary to ask about the specific characteristics of both the subordinates and their situation that would cause participative leadership to be viewed as satisfying and instrumental to effective performance.

Mitchell recently described at least four ways in which a participative leadership style would impact on subordinate attitudes and behavior as predicted by expectancy theory.[14] First, a participative climate should increase the clarity of organizational contingencies. Through participation in decision making, subordinates should learn what leads to what. From a path-goal viewpoint, participation would lead to greater clarity of the paths to various goals. A second impact of participation would be that subordinates, hopefully, should select goals they highly value. If one participates in decisions about various goals, it makes sense that this individual would select goals he or she wants. Thus, participation would increase the correspondence between organization and subordinate goals. Third, we can see how participation would increase the control the individual has over what happens on the job. If our motivation is higher (based on the preceding two points), then having greater autonomy and ability to carry out our intentions should lead to increased effort and performance. Finally, under a participative system, pressure towards high performance should come from sources other than the leader or the organization. More specifically, when people participate in the decision process, they become more ego-involved; the decisions made are in some part their own. Also, their peers know what is expected and the social pressure has a greater impact. Thus, motivation to perform well stems from internal and social factors as well as formal external ones.

A number of investigations prior to the above formulation supported the idea that participation appears to be helpful,[15] and Mitchell presents a number of recent studies that support the above four points.[16] However, it is also true that we would expect the relationship between a participative style and subordinate behavior to be moderated by both the personality characteristics of the subordinate and the situational demands. Studies by Tannenbaum and Allport and Vroom have shown that subordinates who prefer autonomy and self-control respond more positively to participative leadership in terms of both satisfaction and performance than subordinates who do not have such preferences.[17] Also, the studies mentioned by Runyon[18] and Mitchell[19] showed that subordinates who were external in orientation were less satisfied with a participative style of leadership than were internal subordinates.

House also has reviewed these studies in an attempt to explain the ways in which the situation or environment moderates the relationship between participation and subordinate attitudes and behavior.[20] His analysis suggests that where participative leadership is positively related to satisfaction, regardless of the predispositions of subordinates, the tasks of the subjects appear to be ambiguous and ego-involving. In the studies in which the subjects' personalities or predispositions moderate the effect of participative leadership, the tasks of the subjects are inferred to be highly routine and/or nonego-involving.

House reasoned from this analysis that the task may have an overriding effect on the relationship between leader participation and subordinate responses, and that individual predispositions or personality characteristics of subordinates may have an effect only under some tasks. It was assumed that when task demands are ambiguous, subordinates will have a need to reduce the ambiguity. Further, it was assumed that when task demands are ambiguous, participative problem solving between the leader and the subordinate will result in more effective decisions than when the task demands are unambiguous. Finally, it was assumed that when the subordinates are ego-involved in their tasks, they are more likely to want to have a say in the decisions that affect them. Given these assumptions, the following hypotheses were formulated to account for the conflicting findings reviewed above:

- When subjects are highly ego-involved in a decision or a task and the decision or task demands are ambiguous, participative leadership will have a positive effect on the satisfaction and motivation of the subordinate, *regardless* of the subordinate's predisposition toward self-control, authoritarianism, or need for independence.

- When subordinates are not ego-involved in their tasks and when task demands are clear, subordinates who are not authoritarian and who have high needs for independence and self-control will respond favorably to leader participation, and their opposite personality types will respond less favorably.

These hypotheses were derived on the basis of path-goal theorizing; i.e., the rationale guiding the analysis of prior studies was that both task characteristics and characteristics of subordinates interact to determine the effect of a specific kind of leader behavior on the satisfaction, expectancies, and performance of subordinates. To date, one major investigation has supported some of these predictions[21] in which personality variables, amount of participative leadership, task ambiguity, and job satisfaction were assessed for 324 employees of an industrial manufacturing organization. As expected, in nonrepetitive, ego-involving tasks, employees (regardless of their personality) were more satisfied under a participative style than a nonparticipative style. However, in repetitive tasks which were less ego-involving, the amount of authoritarianism of subordinates moderated the relationship between leadership style and satisfaction. Specifically, low authoritarian subordinates were *more satisfied* under a participative style. These findings are exactly as the theory would predict; thus, it has promise in reconciling a set of confusing and contradictory findings with respect to participative leadership.

## Summary and Conclusions

We have attempted to describe what we believe is a useful theoretical framework for understanding the effect of leadership behavior on subordinate satisfaction and motivation. Most theorists today have moved away from the simplistic notions that all effective leaders have a certain set of personality traits or that the situation completely determines performance. Some researchers have presented rather complex attempts at matching certain types of leaders with certain types of situations, e.g., the articles written by Vroom and Fiedler. But, we believe that a path-goal approach goes one step further. It not only suggests what type of style may be most effective in a given situation—it also attempts to explain *why* it is most effective.

We are optimistic about the future outlook of leadership research. With the guidance of path-goal theorizing, future research is expected to unravel many confusing puzzles about the reasons for and effects of leader behavior that have, heretofore, not been solved. However, we add a word of caution: The theory, and the research on it, are relatively new to the literature of organizational behavior. Consequently, path-goal theory is offered more as a tool for directing research and stimulating insight than as a proven guide for managerial action.

## Notes

1. T. R. Mitchell, "Expectancy Model of Job Satisfaction, Occupational Preference and Effort: A Theoretical, Methodological and Empirical Appraisal," *Psychological Bulletin* (1974, in press).

2. D. M. Nebeker and T. R. Mitchell, "Leader Behavior: An Expectancy Theory Approach," *Organizational Behavior and Human Performance*, Vol. 11 (1974), pp. 355–367.

3. M. G. Evans, "The Effects of Supervisory Behavior on the Path-Goal Relationship," *Organizational Behavior and Human Performance,* Vol. 55 (1970), pp. 277–298; T. H. Hammer and H. T. Dachler, "The Process of Supervision in the Context of Motivation Theory," Research Report No. 3 (University of Maryland, 1973); F. Dansereau, Jr., J. Cashman, and G. Graen, "Instrumentality Theory and Equity Theory as Complementary Approaches in Predicting the Relationship of Leadership and Turnover among Managers," *Organizational Behavior and Human Performance,* Vol. 10 (1973), pp. 184–200; R. J. House, "A Path-Goal Theory of Leader Effectiveness," *Administrative Science Quarterly,* Vol. 16, No. 3 (September 1971), pp. 321–338; T. R. Mitchell, "Motivation and Participation: An Integration," *Academy of Management Journal,* Vol. 16, No. 4(1973), pp. 160–179; G. Graen, F. Dansereau, Jr., and T. Minami, "Dysfunctional Leadership Styles," *Organizational Behavior and Human Performance,* Vol. 7(1972), pp. 216–236; "An Empirical Test of the Man-in-the-Middle Hypothesis among Executives in a Hierarchical Organization Employing a Unit Analysis," *Organizational Behavior and Human Performance,* Vol. 8(1972), pp. 262–285; R. J. House and G. Dessler, "The Path-Goal Theory of Leadership: Some Post Hoc and A Priori Tests," to appear in J. G. Hunt, ed., *Contingency Approaches to Leadership* (Carbondale, Ill.: Southern Illinois University Press, 1974).

4. M. G. Evans, "Effects of Supervisory Behavior"; "Extensions of a Path-Goal Theory of Motivation," *Journal of Applied Psychology,* Vol. 59(1974), pp. 172–178.

5. R. J. House, "A Path-Goal Theory"; R. J. House and G. Dessler, "Path-Goal Theory of Leadership."

6. R. J. House and G. Dessler, "Path-Goal Theory of Leadership"; R. M. Stogdill, *Managers, Employees, Organization* (Ohio State University, Bureau of Business Research, 1965); R. J. House, A. Valency, and R. Van der Krabben, "Some Tests and Extension of the Path-Goal Theory of Leadership" (in preparation).

7. W. A. Hill and D. Hughes, "Variations in Leader Behavior as a Function of Task Type," *Organizational Behavior and Human Performance* (1974, in press).

8. K. E. Runyon, "Some Interactions between Personality Variables and Management Styles," *Journal of Applied Psychology,* Vol. 57, No. 3(1973), pp. 288–294; T. R. Mitchell, C. R. Smyser, and S. E. Weed, "Locus of Control: Supervision and Work Satisfaction," *Academy of Management Journal* (in press).

9. T. R. Mitchell, "Locus of Control."

10. R. J. House, "A Path-Goal Theory"; and G. Dessler, "Path-Goal Theory of Leadership"; A. D. Szilagyi and H. P. Sims, "An Exploration of the Path-Goal Theory of Leadership in a Health Care Environment," *Academy of Management Journal* (in press); J. D. Dermer, "Supervisory Behavior and Budget Motivation" (Cambridge, Mass.: unpublished, MIT, Sloan School of Management, 1974); R. W. Smetana, "The Relationship between Managerial Behavior and Subordinate Attitudes and Motivation: A Contribution to a Behavioral Theory of Leadership" (Ph.D. diss., Wayne State University, 1974).

11. R. J. House, "A Path-Goal Theory"; and G. Dessler, "Path-Goal Theory of Leadership"; A.D. Szilagyi and H. P. Sims, "Exploration of Path-Goal"; J. E. Stinson and T. W. Johnson, "The Path-Goal Theory of Leadership: A Partial Test and Suggested Refinement," *Proceedings* (Kent, Ohio: 7th Annual Conference of the Midwest Academy of Management, April 1974), pp. 18–36; R. S. Schuler, "A Path-Goal Theory of Leadership: An Empirical Investigation" (Ph.D. diss., Michigan State University, 1973); H. K. Downey, J. E. Sheridan, and J. W. Slocum, Jr., "Analysis of Relationships Among Leader Behavior, Subordinate Job Performance and Satisfaction: A Path-Goal Approach (unpublished mimeograph, 1974); S. E. Weed, T. R. Mitchell, and C. R. Smyser, "A Test of House's Paths-Goal Theory of Leadership in an Organizational Setting" (paper presented at Western Psychological Assoc., 1974).

12. A. D. Szilagyi and H. P. Sims, "Exploration of Path-Goal."

13. R. J. House, A. Valency, and R. Van der Krabben, "Tests and Extensions of Path-Goal Theory of Leadership, II" (unpublished, in process).

14. T. R. Mitchell, "Motivation and Participation."

15. H. Tosi, "A Reexamination of Personality as a Determinant of the Effects of Participation," *Personnel Psychology,* Vol. 23(1970), pp. 91–99; J. Sadler, "Leadership

Style, Confidence in Management and Job Satisfaction," *Journal of Applied Behavioral Sciences,* Vol. 6(1970), pp. 3–19; K. N. Wexley, J. P. Singh, and J. A. Yukl, "Subordinate Personality as a Moderator of the Effects of Participation in Three Types of Appraisal Interviews," *Journal of Applied Psychology,* Vol. 83 (1973), pp. 54–59.

16. T. R. Mitchell, "Motivation and Participation."

17. A. S. Tannenbaum and F. H. Allport, "Personality Structure and Group Structure: An Interpretive Study of Their Relationship through an Event-Structure Hypothesis," *Journal of Abnormal and Social Psychology,* Vol. 53(1956), pp. 272–280; V. H. Vroom, "Some Personality Determinants of the Effects of Participation," *Journal of Abnormal and Social Psychology,* Vol. 59 (1959), pp. 322–327.

18. K. E. Runyon, "Some Interactions between Personality Variables and Management Styles," *Journal of Applied Psychology,* Vol. 57, No. 3(1973), pp. 288–294.

19. T. R. Mitchell, C. R. Smyser, and S. E. Weed, "Locus of Control."

20. R. J. House, "Notes on the Path-Goal Theory of Leadership" (University of Toronto, Faculty of Management Studies, May 1974).

21. R. S. Schuler, "Leader Participation, Task-Structure and Subordinate Authoritarianism" (unpublished mimeograph, Cleveland State University, 1974).

**Reading 23**

# How Do You Make Leaders More Effective?
# New Answers to an Old Puzzle

**Fred E. Fiedler**
University of Washington

Let's begin with a basic proposition: The organization that employs the leader is as responsible for his success or failure as the leader himself. Not that this is a new insight—far from it. Terman wrote in 1904 that leadership performance depends on the situation, as well as on the leader. Although this statement would not be questioned by anyone currently working in this area, it also has been widely ignored. Practically all formal training programs attempt to change the individual; many of them assume explicitly or implicitly that there is one style of leadership or one way of acting that will work best under all conditions. Most military academies, for example, attempt to mold the individual into a supposedly ideal leader personality. Others assume that the training should enable the individual to become more flexible or more sensitive to his environment so that he can adapt himself to it.

Before going further let's define a few terms. I will confine my discussion to *task groups* rather than the organization of which the group is a part. Furthermore, we will assume that anyone who is placed in a leadership position will have the requisite technical qualifications for the job. Just as the leader of a surgical team obviously has to have medical training, so a manager must know the essential administrative requirements of his job. We will here talk primarily about training *as a leader* rather than training as a specialist. The effectiveness of the leader will be defined in terms of how well his group or organization performs the primary tasks for which the group exists. We measure the effectiveness of a football coach by how many games his team wins and not by the character he builds, and the excellence of an orchestra conductor by how well his orchestra plays, not by the happiness of his musicians or his ability as a musicologist. Whether the musicians' job satisfaction or the conductor's mu-

sicological expertness do, in fact, contribute to the orchestra's excellence is an interesting question in its own right, but it is not what people pay to hear. Likewise, the performance of a manager is here measured in terms of his department's or group's effectiveness in doing its assigned job. Whether the accomplishment of this job is to be measured after a week or after five years depends, of course, upon the assignment the organization gives the group, and the accomplishments the organization considers important.

When we think of improving leadership, we almost automatically think of training the individual. This training frequently involves giving the man a new perspective on his supervisory responsibilities by means of role playing, discussions, detailed instructions on how to behave toward subordinates, as well as instruction in the technical and administrative skills he will need in his job. A training program might last a few days, a few months, or as in the case of college programs and military academies, as long as four years. What is the hard evidence that this type of training actually increases organizational performance?

Empirical studies to evaluate the effectiveness of various leadership training programs, executive development, and supervisory workshops have been generally disappointing. Certainly, the two field experiments and two studies of ongoing organizations conducted by my associates and me failed to show that training increases organizational performance. . . .

I repeat that these findings are by no means unusual. Empirical studies to determine whether or not leadership training improves organizational performance have generally come up with negative findings. Newport, after surveying 121 large companies, concluded that not *one* of the companies had obtained any scientifically acceptable evidence that the leadership training for their middle management had actually improved performance.

T-group and sensitivity training, which has become fashionable in business and industry, has yielded similarly unsatisfactory results. Reviews of the literature by Campbell and Dunnette and by House found no convincing evidence that this type of training increased organizational effectiveness, and a well-known study at the International Harvester Company by Fleishman, Harris, and Burtt on the effects of supervisory training concluded that the effects of supervisory training in modifying behavior were very short-lived and did not improve performance.

## EFFECT OF EXPERIENCE ON LEADERSHIP

Let us now ask whether supervisory experience improves performance. Actually, since leadership experience almost always involves on-the-job training, we are dealing with a closely related phenomenon.

Interestingly enough, the literature actually contains few, if any, studies which attempt to link leadership experience to organizational effectiveness. Yet, there seems to be a firmly held expectation that leadership experience makes a leader more effective. We simply have more trust in experienced leaders. We can infer this, for example, from the many regulations that require time in grade before promotion to the next higher level, as well as the many specifications of prior job in hiring executives for responsible positions.

We have already seen that the experienced petty officers and military academy officers did not perform more effectively than did the inexperienced enlisted men, nor did the more experienced officers or petty officers perform better than the less experienced.

In addition, we also analyzed data from various other groups and organizations. These included directors of research and development teams at a large physical research laboratory, foremen of craftshops, general foremen in a heavy machinery manufacturing company, managers of meat, and of grocery markets, in a large supermarket chain as well as post office supervisors and managers, and police sergeants. For all these managers we could obtain reliable performance ratings or objective group effectiveness criteria. None of the correlations was significant in the expected direction. The median correlation relating leadership experience to leadership performance for all groups and organizations was –.12— certainly not significant in the positive direction!

To summarize the findings, neither orthodox leadership training nor leadership experience nor sensitivity training appear to contribute across

the board to group or organizational effectiveness. It is, therefore, imperative first that we ask why this might be so, and second that we consider alternative methods for improving leadership performance.

## THE CONTINGENCY MODEL

The "Contingency Model," a recent theory of leadership, holds that the effectiveness of group performance is contingent upon (a) the leader's motivational pattern and (b) the degree to which the situation gives the leader power and influence. We have worked with a leadership motivation measure called the "Esteem for the Least Preferred Co-worker," or LPC for short. The subject is first asked to think of all the people with whom he has ever worked, and then given a simple scale on which he describes the one person in his life with whom he has been able to work *least well*. This "least preferred co-worker" may be someone he knows at the time or it may be someone he has known in the past. It does not have to be a member of his present work group.

In grossly oversimplified terms, the person who describes his least preferred co-worker in relatively favorable terms is basically motivated to have close interpersonal relations with others. By contrast, the person who rejects someone with whom he cannot work is basically motivated to accomplish or achieve on the task, and he derives satisfaction from being recognized as having performed well on the task. The task-motivated person thus uses the task to obtain a favorable position and good interpersonal relations.

## CLASSIFYING LEADERSHIP SITUATIONS

The statement that some leaders perform better in one kind of situation while some leaders perform better in different situations is begging a question, "What kinds of situations are best suited for which type of leader?" In other words, how can we best classify groups if we wish to predict leadership performance?

We can approach this problem by assuming that leadership is essentially a work relationship involving power and influence. It is easier to be a leader when you have complete control than when your control is weak and dependent on the good will of others. It is easier to be the captain of a ship than the chairman of a volunteer group organized to settle a school busing dispute. The *job* may be more complex for the navy captain, but *being in the leadership role* is easier for him than for the committee chairman. It is, therefore, not unreasonable to classify situations in terms of how much power and influence the situation gives the leader. We call this "situational favorableness." One simple categorization of groups on their situational favorableness classifies leadership situations on the basis of three major dimensions:

1. *Leader–member relations.* Leaders presumably have more power and influence if they have a good relationship with their members than if they have a poor relationship with them, if they are liked, respected, trusted, than if they are not. Research has shown that this is by far the most important single dimension.

2. *Task structure.* Tasks or assignments that are highly structured, spelled out, or programmed give the leader more influence than tasks that are vague, nebulous, and unstructured. It is easier, for example, to be a leader whose task it is to set up a sales display according to clearly delineated steps than it is to be a chairman of a committee preparing a new sales campaign.

3. *Position power.* Leaders will have more power and influence if their position is vested with such prerogatives as being able to hire and fire, being able to discipline, to reprimand, and so on. Position power, as it is here used, is determined by how much power the leader has over his subordinates. If the janitor foreman can hire and fire, he has more position power in his own group than the chairman of a board of directors who, frequently, cannot hire or fire—or even reprimand his board members.

Using this classification method we can now roughly order groups as being high or low on each of these three dimensions. This gives us an eight-celled classification (Figure 1). This scheme postulates that it is easier to be a leader in groups

that fall into Cell 1 since you are liked, have position power, and have a structured task. It is somewhat more difficult in Cell 2 since you are liked, have a structured task, but little position power, and so on to groups in Cell 8 where the leader is not liked, has a vague, unstructured task, and little position power. A good example of Cell 8 would be the disliked chairman of the volunteer committee we mentioned before.

The critical question is, "What kind of leadership does each of these different group situations call for?" Figure 2 summarizes the results of 63 analyses based on a total of 454 separate groups. These included bomber and tank crews, antiaircraft artillery units, managements of consumer cooperative companies, boards of directors, open-hearth shops, basketball and surveying teams, and various groups involved in creative and problem-solving tasks.

The horizontal axis of the graph indicates the "situational favorableness," namely, the leader's control and influence as defined by the eight-fold classification shown in Figure 1. The vertical axis indicates the relationship between the leader's motivational pattern, as measured by the LPC score, and his group's performance. A median correlation above the midline shows that the relationship-motivated leaders tended to perform better than the task-motivated leaders. A correlation below the midline indicates that the task-motivated leaders performed better than the relationship-motivated leaders. Figure 3 shows the predictions that the model would make in each of the eight cells.

These findings have two important implications for our understanding of what makes leaders effective. First, Figure 2 tells us that the task-motivated leaders tend to perform better than relationship-motivated leaders in situations that are very favorable and in those that are unfavorable. Relationship-motivated leaders tend to perform better than task-motivated leaders in situations that are intermediate in favorableness.

**FIGURE 1**   Cells or "Octants"

| | Very Favorable | | | Intermediate in Favorableness | | | Unfavorable | |
|---|---|---|---|---|---|---|---|---|
| | 1 | 2 | 3 | 4 | 5 | 6 | 7 | 8 |
| Leader–member relations | Good | Good | Good | Good | Poor | Poor | Poor | Poor |
| Task structure | High | High | Low | Low | High | High | Low | Low |
| Position power | Strong | Weak | Strong | Weak | Strong | Weak | Strong | Weak |

**FIGURE 2   Relationship between Leader LPC and Group Performance**

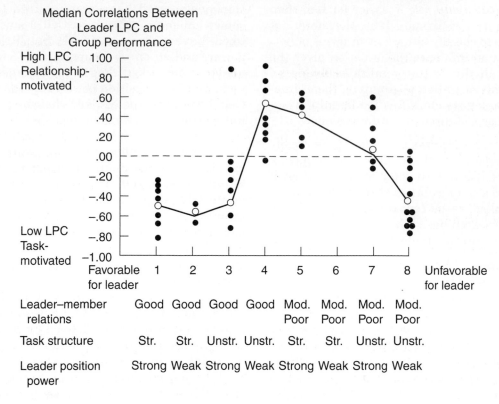

Median Correlations Between
Leader LPC and
Group Performance

| Leader–member relations | Good | Good | Good | Good | Mod. Poor | Mod. Poor | Mod. Poor | Mod. Poor |
|---|---|---|---|---|---|---|---|---|
| Task structure | Str. | Str. | Unstr. | Unstr. | Str. | Str. | Unstr. | Unstr. |
| Leader position power | Strong | Weak | Strong | Weak | Strong | Weak | Strong | Weak |

**FIGURE 3   Prediction of the Performance of Relationship- and Task-Motivated Leaders**

| | 1 | 2 | 3 | 4 | 5 | 6 | 7 | 8 |
|---|---|---|---|---|---|---|---|---|
| Relationship-motivated High LPC | | | | Good | Good | Some-what better | Some-what better | |
| Task-motivated Low LPC | Good | Good | Good | | | | | Good |

Hence, both the relationship- and the task-motivated leaders perform well under some conditions and not under others. It is, therefore, not correct to speak of any person as generally a good leader or generally a poor leader. Rather, a leader may perform well in one situation but not in another. This is also borne out by the repeated findings that we cannot predict a leader's performance on the basis of his personality traits, or even by knowing how well he performed on a previous task unless that task was similar in situational favorableness.

Second, the graph on Figure 2 shows that the performance of a leader depends as much on the situational favorableness as it does on the individual in the leadership position. Hence, the organi-

zation can change leadership performance either by trying to change the individual's personality and motivational pattern or by changing the favorableness of the leader's situation. As we shall see, this is really what training is all about.

Before we go further, we must ask how valid the Contingency Model is. How well does it predict in new situations? There have been at least 25 studies to date that have tested the theory. These validation studies included research on grocery and meat markets, a physical science laboratory, a machinery plant, a hospital, an electronics company, and teams of volunteer public health workers in Central America, as well as various experimentally assembled groups in the laboratory. Of particular importance is a large experiment that used cadets at West Point to test the entire eight cells of the model. This study almost completely reproduced the curve shown on Figure 2. In all studies that were recently reviewed, 35 of the 44 obtained correlations that were in the predicted direction—a finding that could have occurred by chance less than one time in 100. An exception is Cell 2, in which laboratory experiments—but not field studies—have yielded correlations showing the relationship-motivated leaders perform better than task-motivated leaders. . . .

## TO TRAIN OR NOT TO TRAIN

What does all this mean for improving managerial performance, and how can we apply the findings that we have described?

In sum, if we want to improve leadership performance, we can either change the leader by training, or we can change his leadership situation. Common sense suggests that it is much easier to change various aspects of a man's job than to change the man. When we talk about leadership behavior, we are talking about fairly deeply ingrained personality factors and habits of interacting with others. These cannot be changed easily, either in a few hours or in a few days. In fact, as we have seen, not even four years of military academy and 5 to 17 years of subsequent experience enable a leader to perform significantly better on different tasks than someone that has had neither training nor experience.

We have seen that a leader's performance depends not only on his personality, but also on the organizational factors that determine the leader's control and influence—that is, the "situational favorableness." As we have shown, appropriate training and experience improve situational favorableness. Whether or not they improve performance depends upon the match between the leader's motivational pattern and the favorableness of the situation. This means that a training program that improves the leader's control and influence may benefit the relationship-motivated managers, but it will be detrimental to the task-motivated managers, or vice versa, depending upon the situation.

The idea that we can improve a leader's performance by increasing the favorableness of his situation is, of course, far from new. A poorly performing manager may be given more authority, more explicit instructions, more congenial coworkers in the hope that it will help him do a better job. Moreover, decreasing the favorableness

of the situation in order to improve a manager's performance is also not quite as unusual as it might appear at first blush. If a man becomes bored, stale, or disinterested in his job, a frequent remedy is to transfer him to a more challenging job. As it turns out, "challenging" is just another way of saying that the job is less structured, has less position power, or requires working with difficult people. It is certainly well known that some men perform best under pressure and that they get into difficulty when life is too calm. These are the trouble shooters who are dispatched to branch offices or departments that need to be bailed out.

What, then, can an organization do to increase managerial performance? As a first step, it is necessary to determine which of the managers are task- and which are relationship-motivated. This can be accomplished by means of a short scale. Second, the organization needs to categorize carefully the situational favorableness of its managerial jobs. (Scales are available in Fiedler, F. E., *A Theory of Leadership Effectiveness,* McGraw-Hill, 1967.) Third, the organization can decide on a number of options in its management of executive personnel.

The least expensive and probably most efficient method is to develop a careful program of managerial rotation that moves some individuals from one job to another at a faster rate than it moves others. . . .

A second major option is management training. The problem here is whether to train only some people or all those who are eligible: Training a task-motivated manager who is accepted by his group and has a structured task is likely to improve his performance; training a relationship-motivated manager for the same job is likely to make him less effective. The organization would, therefore, be better off if it simply did not train relationship-motivated managers for these particular jobs. On the other hand, the relationship-motivated but not the task-motivated managers should be trained for jobs in which the situational favorableness is intermediate. . . .

## CONCLUSION

As a consequence of our research, we have both discredited some old myths and learned some new lessons.

The old myths:

• That there is one best leadership style, or that there are leaders who excel under all circumstances.

- That some men are born leaders, and that neither training, experience, nor conditions can materially affect leadership skills.

The lessons, while more pedestrian and less dogmatic, are more useful. We know that people differ in how they respond to management situations. Furthermore, we know that almost every manager in an organization can perform effectively, providing that we place him in a situation that matches his personality, providing we know how to match his training and experience to the available jobs—and providing that we take the trouble.

## Selected Bibliography

The interested reader may wish to consult Fiedler's *A Theory of Leadership Effectiveness* (McGraw-Hill, 1967), which presents a detailed summary of many of his studies as well as a fairly technical description of the theory. A more popular version of the theory is described in a *Harvard Business Review* article entitled, "Engineer the Job to Fit the Manager" (September 1965) and in *Psychology Today,* "Style or Circumstance: the Leadership Enigma" (March 1969). A more technical and extensive summary of the work on leadership training will appear shortly in a forthcoming issue of *Administrative Science Quarterly.*

# Reading 24
# Situational Leadership®

**Paul Hersey**
Center for Leadership Studies, Inc.

Situational Leadership is a practical model designed to help leaders be more effective in their interactions with people. It is based on an interplay among three factors:

1. The amount of guidance and direction a leader gives (similar to task behavior);

2. The amount of socio-emotional support a leader provides (similar to relationship behavior); and

3. The readiness level that followers exhibit in performing a specific task, function, or objective.

According to the Situational Leadership model, there is no one best style of leadership, or way to influence people. The style to be used depends on the readiness level of the people the leader is attempting to influence, as illustrated in Figure 1.

The model displays the interaction of two separate and distinct leadership orientations—task and relationships—appearing on the horizontal and vertical axes:

- *Task behavior* is defined as the extent to which the leader engages in spelling out the duties and responsibilities of an individual or group. These behaviors include telling people what to do, how to do it, when to do it, where to do it, and who is to do it. This is the guidance role of a leader.

- *Relationship behavior* is defined as the extent to which the leader engages in two-way or multiway communication. The behaviors include listening, facilitating, and supportive behaviors.

The products of this interaction are four leadership styles, one in each of the quadrants shown in Figure 1. Each behavior is plotted from low to high on its axis. This produces four distinct styles:

**FIGURE 1   Situational Leadership®**

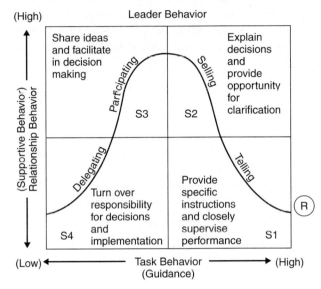

- Style 1 (Tell): This style demonstrates high degrees of task behavior and low degrees of relationship behavior.

- Style 2 (Sell): This style is characterized by high amounts of both task and relationship behavior.

- Style 3 (Participate): This style uses high amounts of relationship behavior and low amounts of task behavior.

- Style 4 (Delegate): In this style, low amounts of both task and relationship behavior are used.

Any one of the four styles may prove effective in a given situation. The key (independent) variable that is believed to affect its success lies in the concept of *follower readiness.* This is the extent to which a follower has the ability and willingness to accomplish a specific task. In contrast to personal characteristics (such as traits, values, or age), readiness is a measure of how ready a person is to perform a specific task, function, assignment, or objective that a leader views as important.

In assessing (and developing) follower readiness, a leader must consider two separate components:

- *Ability* (job readiness) is the knowledge, experience, and skill that an individual or group brings to a particular task or activity.

- *Willingness* (psychological readiness) is the extent to which an individual or group has the confidence, commitment, and motivation to accomplish a specific task. These components are interactive; willingness affects not only the use of present ability, but the extent to which competence and ability will grow. Similarly, one's current ability may impact self-assessments of competence, commitment, and motivation.

The combination of low or high levels of ability and willingness produces a continuum of follower readiness. For the sake of discussion and analysis, this continuum can be divided into four levels, each representing a different combination:

- Readiness Level One (R1): The follower is both unable to do the task, and lacks commitment, confidence, and willingness.

- Readiness Level Two (R2): The follower is motivated to make an effort and would try if the leader was there to provide guidance, but lacks current ability to perform well.

- Readiness Level Three (R3): The follower has the capacity to perform the function requested, but is insecure, apprehensive, or unwilling to use that ability.

- Readiness Level Four (R4): The follower has the requisite ability to perform successfully, and also demonstrates the necessary commitment and confidence to do it.

The leader's challenge is to identify follower readiness and then match it with the appropriate leadership style called for by the model. For example, a follower or group at Readiness Level 1 requires a leader to *tell* the person what to do. Guiding, directing, and structuring the work en-

vironment are all appropriate. Readiness Level 2 (willing but unable) calls for a *selling* approach—providing answers to the questions of what, how, when, where, and who. Although selling focuses on explaining, persuading, and clarifying, it also opens up the possibility of dialogue for the follower to ask questions and receive clarification.

Readiness Level 3 calls for a *participating* style. The leader encourages an able person through supportive communication, and engages in collaborative, facilitating, or committing behaviors, while accenting both task and relationship orientations. Readiness Level 4 needs a *delegating* style. The follower or group is able, confident, and willing, and only needs the opportunity to perform. Although some relationship behavior is still needed, followers need to take responsibility for the objective and implement action on their own. The leader may wish to observe, stand by to respond to requests for assistance, and monitor results.

In addition to specifying the high-probability leadership style for various readiness levels, Situational Leadership also attempts to indicate the probability of success of the other three options for each situation. In order of preference, they appear as follows for each level of follower readiness:

- R1: S1, S2, S3, S4.

- R2: S2, S1, S3, S4.

- R3: S3, S2, S4, S1.

- R4: S4, S3, S2, S1.

The Situational Leadership model has been used in a large number of U.S. companies for several decades, and therefore has considerable face validity. It is a prescriptive approach that tells leaders how to assess their followers and how to respond to that assessment of follower readiness with one of the four defined styles. It is flexible, with no hard and fast rules. It is based on subjective probabilities of success from using each style, in hopes of improving the odds for a productive outcome. Finally, the Situational Leadership model also recognizes that other situational variables may be of equal or greater importance, such as a crisis, time pressures, or the unique nature of the work.

**Reading 25**

# A Multidirectional Approach toward Leadership:
# An Extension of the Concept of Behavioral Complexity

**Robert Hooijberg**
Rutgers, The State University of New Jersey

## INTRODUCTION

Managerial jobs have changed from mainly supervising and giving orders to subordinates to, among other things, providing services to subordinates, forming cross-functional teams, shaping strategy, helping clients in the field, and leading cross-departmental and cross-company teams (Kanter, 1989). This means that managers "have to learn to manage in situations where [they] don't have command authority, where [they] are neither controlled nor controlling" (Drucker, interviewed by Harris, 1993, p. 115) and that they need to learn to manage upward and sideways in addition to managing downward (Conger, 1993). These changes have made the job of managers more complex.

Most leadership research continues to examine leadership as a purely downward-directed phenomenon of influencing subordinates and does not do justice to the complexity of the work environments of modern managerial activities. While leadership research has made great strides in better understanding what kind of leadership works best under specific circumstances, for the most part the target of the leadership behavior has remained unchanged. A few studies have explored different targets of leadership behaviors. For instance, research in the area of influence processes has looked at targets other than those in lower positions in the organizational hierarchy (e.g., Kipnis & Schmidt, 1988; Falbe & Yukl, 1992; Porter, Allen, & Angle, 1981; Yukl & Tracey, 1992). Also, research by Howell and Higgins (1990a,b) on champions of technology shows that there exists a need for downward, lateral, as well as upward leadership when introducing new technology in organizations. These literatures show that being influential and championing technology requires managers to affect people at lower, equal, and higher positions in the organizational hierarchy.

This paper makes a first attempt at better understanding the variations in the repertoire of leadership behaviors managers use in their interactions with their subordinates as well as their peers and superiors. The concept of behavioral complexity (Hooijberg & Quinn, 1992; Denison, Hooijberg, & Quinn, 1995) is used to refer to the need for managers to perform a wide array of leadership functions in the organizational arena. In contrast to more traditional approaches to leadership research, behavioral complexity reflects the idea that managers who perform multiple leadership functions[1] and tailor the performance of these leadership functions to the demands of their organizational role-set will be more effective than managers who perform only one leadership function and who do not vary the performance of their leadership functions. The concept of behavioral complexity will be discussed, followed by an examination of the relationships between behavioral complexity and managerial effectiveness. Data obtained from 282 managers from a *Fortune* 50 company and 252 managers from the public utility industry are used to examine the relationship between behavioral complexity and managerial effectiveness.

## BEHAVIORAL COMPLEXITY

Yukl (1989a) in his review of the leadership literature notes that "[a]lthough much of the leadership literature focuses on the relationship between leader and subordinates, the descriptive research has found that managers typically spend considerable time with persons other than direct subordinates or the manager's boss. Kotter (1982) found that the network of relationships for general managers often consisted of hundreds of people inside

---

[1] The concept of leadership function rather than leadership role is used here. Using leadership function rather than leadership role helps keep the text understandable because another important concept in this paper is organizational role.

and outside of their organization" (p. 56). The different members of a manager's network will place varying, even conflicting demands upon the manager. In order to address these concerns, Bass (1990) suggests that future research use "more sophisticated evaluations of the interactional processes of leaders, not only with subordinates, but also with peers [and] superiors" (p. 880).

The concept of behavioral complexity acknowledges and places at the center the idea that managers have to manage a network of relationships that includes superiors and peers as well as subordinates. As the size and differentiation of a leader's network grows, so does the potential for paradox and contradiction. The ability of a leader to match his/her behavioral repertoire to the demands of the situation thus becomes his/her distinctive competence. Thus, the concept of behavioral complexity is best understood in conjunction with the idea of requisite variety (Ashby, 1952). The combination of the concepts of behavioral complexity and requisite variety leads to a simple definition of effective leadership as *the ability to perform multiple roles and behaviors that circumscribe the requisite variety implied by an organizational or environmental context* (Denison, Hooijberg, & Quinn, 1995). However, behavioral complexity does not imply an extreme form of situationalism. Rather than defining an infinite set of contingencies, behavioral complexity suggests the development of a portfolio of leadership functions that allow a leader to respond to complex demands. This is consistent with Yukl's (1989b) observation that "the pendulum [in leadership research] appears to be swinging back from extreme situationalism to a more balanced theoretical perspective" (p. 279).

This paper distinguishes two dimensions of behavioral complexity: behavioral repertoire and behavioral differentiation. The concept of a behavioral repertoire refers to the portfolio of leadership functions a manager can perform. However, managers need more than the ability to perform multiple leadership functions, they also need to be able to perform these leadership functions when the situation calls for them and to not perform them when the situation does not call for them. The concept of behavioral differentiation refers to the extent to which a manager varies the performance of the leadership functions depending on the demands of the organizational situation. The concepts of behavioral repertoire and differentiation are discussed in more detail below.

## BEHAVIORAL REPERTOIRE

The argument is that the broader a manager's behavioral repertoire the more likely it is that the he/she can respond appropriately to the demands of the environment. The need for a broad behavioral repertoire becomes especially important as managerial jobs become more complex. Managerial jobs are becoming more complex in a variety of ways, including an increasingly global marketplace, more direct contact with clients, and organizational restructuring processes. For example, the leadership functions needed to manage a downsizing process will be varied and even contradictory. The people being squeezed out of the company will need to be managed very differently than those who "survive." If at the same time a manager also has to manage the relationship between his/her company and a foreign subsidiary the need for a broader portfolio of leadership skills becomes even greater.

The leadership literature has distinguished many leadership roles/styles/functions over the past decades. Yukl (1989a) in comparing leadership taxonomies by Mintzberg (1973), Morse and Wagner (1978), Stogdill (1948), Bowers and Seashore (1966), House and Mitchell (1974), Luthans and Lockwood (1984), Page (1985), and Yukl (1989a) distinguishes at least 11 leadership roles in his Integrating Taxonomy of Managerial Behavior. Most of the researchers Yukl (1989a) discusses argue that managers need to perform one of the leadership roles in their taxonomy depending on, for example, the characteristics of their subordinates, the task, and/or the organizational culture. This implies that these leadership researchers believe that managers who can perform all leadership roles in their taxonomy will have a higher likelihood of being effective in a wide variety of situations.

There exists some research that supports the idea that managers who perform multiple leadership functions are more effective than those who do not. Mintzberg (1973) observed that the executives in his study performed 10 leadership roles. Quinn and his colleagues (Quinn, 1988; Quinn, Spreitzer, & Hart, 1991; Hart & Quinn, 1993; Denison, Hooijberg, & Quinn, 1995) have found that managers who balance competing leadership functions well, tend to perform more successfully than managers who focus myopically upon a specific leadership function. Blake and Mouton (1964) also suggested that managers who performed both people-oriented and task-oriented leadership functions would be more effective than managers who emphasized one substantially more than the other. It seems clear from the literature that managers who perform multiple leadership functions are expected to be more effective than those who do not.

Few researchers, however, have gone beyond studying leader–follower relationships. The concept of behavioral repertoire expands the focus of the more traditional leader–follower relationships by suggesting that managers need to perform multiple leadership functions in their interactions with the other members of their network. For example, a manager may need to facilitate meetings with peers, obtain resources from superiors, develop innovative approaches, influence the perceptions of consumers, and communicate a vision to subordinates. To the degree a manager can perform all these different roles well, he/she is more likely to be effective.

The literature on influence attempts outlines a broad repertoire of tactics managers can draw upon. Yukl and Falbe (1990), for example, studied eight influence tactics managers might use to gain power: pressure, upward appeals, exchange, coalition, ingratiating, rational persuasion, inspirational appeals, and consultation tactics. Howell and Higgins (1990), in their study of champions of innovation, noted that champions "inspire and enthuse others with their vision of the potential of an innovation, . . . persist in promoting their vision despite strong opposition, . . . show extraordinary confidence in themselves and their mission, and . . . gain the commitment of others to support the innovation" (p. 320). Champions need to gain support from a wide variety of stakeholders, including top management, and when "multiple stakeholders must be convinced of the champion's vision, [the] literature suggests that *frequent* influence attempts and a variety of influence tactics will be required" (p. 320, emphasis added). Effective managerial leadership in today's organizations requires managers to have many of the characteristics and skills Howell and Higgins outline for their champions of technology.

In line with the presented research, then, it is proposed that managers who perform a variety of leadership functions, and who perform them frequently, in their interactions with the different members of their network will be more effective than managers who do not perform multiple leadership functions frequently. Therefore, it is hypothesized that:

*Hypothesis 1.* A broad behavioral repertoire of leadership functions and the frequent performance of these leadership functions is positively associated with managerial effectiveness.

## BEHAVIORAL DIFFERENTIATION

While Hooijberg and Quinn (1992) defined behavioral complexity as the ability of managers to perform multiple leadership functions, they did not indicate how managers achieve effective functioning across a variety of situations. Their approach is reflected mostly in what has been termed the behavioral repertoire. Being an effective leader across situations and time requires of managers not only the "ability to perceive the needs and goals of a constituency [but also the ability] to *adjust* one's personal approach to group action accordingly" (Kenny & Zaccaro, 1983, p. 678, emphasis added). The concept of behavioral differentiation refers to the ability of managers to perform the leadership functions they have in their behavioral repertoire differently (more adaptively, more flexibly, more appropriately, more individualized, and situation-specific) depending on the organizational situation.

Managers who, for example, can be directive and authoritarian as well as use persuasion in pushing their ideas are likely to be more effective than managers who can only be directive and authoritarian. A directive and authoritarian approach might work well with subordinates, but will likely be less effective when trying to get buy-in from one's peers and superiors. The need for behavioral differentiation becomes greater as a manager gets involved in cross-national management activities. While an American may be effective in managing his/her subordinates in the U.S. by being directive and authoritarian, this does not automatically lead to effectiveness if that same manager were to be put in charge of, for example, a Swedish subsidiary. The Swedish subordinates may not take well at all to being told what to do, rather than being consulted about what would be most appropriate to do.

Past research has emphasized the need for managers to take into consideration the characteristics of their subordinates and the structure and clarity of the task when performing their leadership functions (e.g., House, 1971; Hersey & Blanchard, 1982; Dansereau, Graen, & Haga, 1975; Fiedler, 1967; Vroom & Yetton, 1973). Those studies emphasize the need for managers to vary their leadership toward subordinates based on characteristics of the subordinates, the task, the culture, and other factors.

Several studies of influence attempts have assessed the variation in the use of influence tactics of managers in their interactions with their subordinates, peers, and superiors (e.g., Yukl & Falbe, 1990; Yukl & Tracey, 1992). Yukl and Tracey (1992) found that managers used different influence tactics depending on whether they interact with their subordinates, peers, or superiors. The managers in their study used inspirational appeal, ingratiation, and pressure most with subordinates; personal appeal, exchange, and legitimating most with peers; coalitions most with peers and superiors; and rational persuasion most with superiors.

Similar to the importance of choosing the right influence tactics, managers must carefully select the appropriate leadership role for their interactions with subordinates, peers, or superiors. The concept of behavioral differentiation suggests that managers who vary the performance of their leadership functions depending on the relationship they have with the people with whom they interact will function more effectively than those who do not. Therefore, it is hypothesized that:

*Hypothesis 2.* Behavioral differentiation is positively associated with managerial effectiveness.

To test the ideas implied by the behavioral complexity concept, a more complex study design is needed than those more commonly used in the study of leadership. Below a study design is presented that tests the hypotheses regarding the relationship between managerial effectiveness and behavioral differentiation and repertoire.

# METHODS

The context in which behavioral repertoire and differentiation are studied is a manager's organizational role-set. While behavioral complexity refers to the ability of individuals to adjust their behaviors to the demands of the situation in general, the focus here is on one particular type of situation, namely the immediate members of a manager's organizational role set. In this research, the relevant members of a manager's role-set are defined as the manager's subordinates, peers, and superiors. Subordinates, peers, and superiors are regarded as three groups of people who place distinctly different demands on managers and therefore provide an interesting point to start testing the concept of behavioral complexity. Data regarding managers' behavioral differentiation and repertoire were obtained from managers from a *Fortune* 50 company and from the public utility industry. . . .

# LEADERSHIP FUNCTIONS

The leadership functions specified in Quinn's (1988) competing values framework are used to measure the leadership behaviors of the managers in this study. The original model Quinn (1988) proposed contained eight leadership roles arranged in four quadrants with two leadership roles per quadrant. Denison, Hooijberg, and Quinn (1995) used confirmatory multidimensional scaling analyses to test the discriminant, convergent, and nomological validity[2] of the competing values framework. They found strong support for the quadrant structure of the competing values framework, but not necessarily for the individual leadership roles within the quadrants. Because the competing values model was demonstrated to be valid as far as its quadrant structure was concerned, four leadership functions will be assessed. For the purposes of this research, then, the original two leadership roles within each quadrant are aggregated into one leadership function (see Figure 1).

Quinn's (1988) competing values framework suits the purposes of this research well. The model distinguishes four major leadership functions and, therefore, the performance of four rather than one leadership function can be assessed. Quinn identifies two dimensions that indicate how the four leadership functions differ from each other theoretically: flexibility versus control, and internal focus versus external organizational focus. These dimensions define four distinct leadership functions that address different demands in the organizational arena. The *adaptive* leadership function is characterized by a flexible orientation and a focus on the environment external to the unit, and emphasizes developing innovations and obtaining resources for the unit. The *task* leadership function is characterized by a control orientation and a focus on the environment external to the unit, and emphasizes setting goals, clarifying goals, and making sure that goals are attained. The *stability* leadership function is characterized by a control orientation and a focus on the internal functioning of the unit, and emphasizes monitoring and coordinating the work of the unit. The *people* leadership function is characterized by a flexible orientation and a focus on the internal functioning of the unit, and emphasizes mentoring subordinates and facilitating group process in the unit. . . .

---

[2] Nomological validity refers to validity of the proposed relationships among constructs (Keser & Wollenberg, 1986). In the case of the Competing Values Framework it refers to the validity of the proposed relationships among the leadership roles.

**FIGURE 1** **Competing Values Framework**

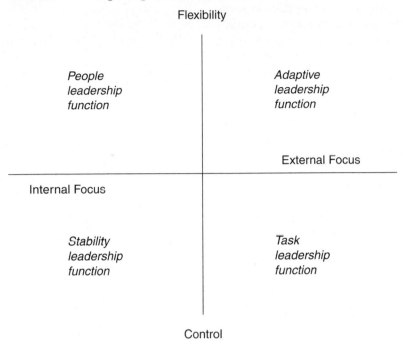

RESULTS

. . . Hypothesis 1 was strongly supported. Hypothesis 1 stated that behavioral repertoire is positively associated with managerial effectiveness. All models in both management samples showed that behavioral repertoire had a strong positive relationship with subordinates', peers', and superiors' perceptions of effectiveness. These results indicate that managers who were perceived to perform the four leadership functions frequently by all members of their organizational role-set were seen as more effective by their subordinates, peers, and superiors than managers who were not perceived to perform all four leadership functions frequently. In addition, behavioral repertoire clearly explained more variance in the dependent variables than any other variable.

The results provide only partial support for Hypothesis 2. Hypothesis 2 stated that perceptions of managerial effectiveness would be positively associated with behavioral differentiation. The results show that various measures of behavioral differentiation have a significant relationship with perceived effectiveness. The relationships between behavioral differentiation and perceptions of effectiveness are leadership-function specific and not all positive. Hypothesis 2 was supported for the positive relationship that behavioral differentiation of the people leader-

ship function has with superiors' perceptions of effectiveness in both management samples, for the positive relationship behavioral differentiation of the task leadership function has with peers' perceptions of effectiveness in the *Fortune* 50 company management sample, and for the positive relationship behavioral differentiation of the stability leadership function has with superiors' perceptions of effectiveness in the public utility management sample.

In contrast to what Hypothesis 2 predicted, the behavioral differentiation of some leadership functions was negatively associated with perceptions of effectiveness. Behavioral differentiation of the people leadership function had a negative association with subordinates' perceptions of effectiveness in both management samples and with peers' perceptions of effectiveness in the *Fortune* 50 company management sample. In addition, behavioral differentiation of the adaptive leadership function has a negative relationship with subordinates' and peers' perceptions of effectiveness in the *Fortune* 50 company management sample.

In addition to a review of the results in light of the hypotheses some other aspects of the results are noteworthy. First, the models explain substantial amounts of variance in subordinates', peers', and superiors' perceptions of effectiveness. The amount of explained variance ranges from 30 percent in peers' perceptions of effectiveness in the public utility management sample to 55 percent in subordinates' perceptions of effectiveness in the *Fortune* 50 company management sample.

The control variables do not have a significant impact on subordinates' perceptions of effectiveness in either the public utility or *Fortune* 50 company management sample. However, the older managers are the less likely they are to be perceived as effective by their peers and superiors in the *Fortune* 50 company management sample. In addition, the higher the level of education of the managers the more likely it is that their peers perceive them as effective. In the public utility management sample, women are less likely than men to be seen as effective by their peers and superiors. The managers with higher levels of education are more likely to be seen as effective by their superiors than people with lower levels of education.

## DISCUSSION

While leadership researchers have emphasized that managers need to vary the performance of their leadership functions depending on characteristics of their followers, the task, the organizational culture, their position power, and other factors, they have commonly equated followers with subordinates. The research presented in this paper has taken a distinctly different approach and examined the leadership behaviors of two groups of managers in their interactions with the members of their superiors and peers, in addition to their subordinates. The argument was made that in order for managers to be effective leaders in their interactions with their subordinates, peers, and superiors, they need to have a broad repertoire of leadership functions at their disposal as well the ability to vary the performance of these leadership functions depending on the organizational role of the person with whom they interact.

The results of this study show that behavioral repertoire has strong positive effects on subordinate, peer, and superior perceptions of effectiveness. These results indicate that to be effective it is important for managers to not only perform their leadership functions frequently in interactions with their subordinates, but also in their interactions with their peers and superiors. Having a broad portfolio of leadership functions at one's disposal will increase the likelihood that one can effectively meet the demands of the members of one's organizational role-set.

The results show that behavioral differentiation affects perceptions of effectiveness. Contrary to the hypothesis, the effects of the four measures of behavioral differentiation on perceptions of effectiveness are not all positive and not all significant. It is interesting that behavioral differentiation affects subordinates' and peers' perceptions of effectiveness negatively and superiors' perceptions of effectiveness positively. The univariate statistics show that the superiors give the managers higher scores on the performance of the leadership functions than the subordinates and the peers. That information might indicate that those managers who convey the impression that they perform their leadership functions frequently more convincingly to their superiors than to their subordinates and peers will be perceived to be more effective by their superiors and less effective by their subordinates and peers than those managers who convey the impression that they perform their leadership functions frequently equally well to their subordinates, peers, and superiors. Subordinates tend to be aware of how their bosses act toward their superiors and they may feel that their boss is "kissing-up," which in turn may negatively affect how effective they think their boss is.

An alternative explanation may lie in people's need for consistency. Staw and Ross (1980) asked psychology undergraduates and practicing administrators to rate the effectiveness of administrators described in various case scenarios. They found that administrators were rated highest when they followed consistent courses of action. This effect was strongest among the practicing administrators and weakest among psychology undergraduates. Extrapolating from Staw and Ross's findings, it might be argued that the subordinates of the managers in the current study interpreted the variation in their manager's behavior to reflect inconsistent behavior which, in turn, affected their impressions of their manager's effectiveness negatively. The superiors of the managers, on the other hand, might consider the variation of their managers to be consistent with the demands of the situation.

While the notion of impression management tactics does help us understand the observed differences in relationships between the behavioral differentiation of the people leadership function and subordinates', peers', and superiors' perceptions of effectiveness, the concept of behavioral differentiation was intended to refer to meeting the needs of the environment rather than impression management. Conceptually behavioral differentiation does not refer to the performance of actions that convey the most positive self-image of the performer but rather it refers to the performance of actions that meet needs of subordinates, team members, peers and superiors, and task requirements. Currently, however, the measure of behavioral differentiation may not be sensitive to that distinction.

## IMPLICATIONS FOR THEORY

The concept of behavioral complexity implies that a more holistic examination of a manager's leadership performance should be conducted than is done in more traditional leadership research approaches. Future leadership research needs to take serious Van Fleet and Yukl's (1986) assertion that upward and lateral influence can be as important as downward influence to the accomplishment of an organization's mission (in Bass, 1990, p. 908). In addition, future leadership research should not only use "more sophisticated evaluations of the interactional processes of leaders . . . with subordinates, . . . peers [and] superiors" (Bass, 1990, p. 880), but also more sophisticated evaluations of the interactional processes of leaders as members of cross-functional, cross-departmental, cross-company, and cross-national teams.

Katz and Kahn (1978) considered "the influential increment over and above mechanical compliance with the routine directives of the organization" to be the essence of leadership. Their definition does not limit the study of leadership to superior–subordinate relationships. Managers can exert leadership in their interactions with different types of followers, including peers and superiors. The changing nature of organizational work (Kanter, 1989; Conger, 1993) requires us to take a broader perspective of leader–follower relationships. . . .

## References

Ashby, W. R. *Design for a brain.* New York: Wiley, 1952.

Bagozzi, R. P., & Yi, Y. On the evaluation of structural equation models. *Journal of the Academy of Marketing Science,* 1988, *16*(1), 74–94.

Bass, B. M. *Stogdill's handbook of leadership: A survey of theory in research.* New York: Free Press, 1981.

Bass, B. M. *Bass and Stogdill's handbook of leadership. Theory, research, and managerial application* (3rd ed.). New York: Free Press, 1990.

Blake, R. R., & Mouton, J. S. *The managerial grid.* Houston, TX: Gulf, 1964.

Bowers, D. G., & Seashore, S. E. Predicting organizational effectiveness with a four-factor theory of leadership. *Administrative Science Quarterly,* 1966, *11,* 238–263.

Carmines, E. G., & MacIver, J. P. Analyzing models with unobserved variables: Analysis of covariance structures. In G. W. Bohrstedt and E. F. Borgatta (Eds.), *Social measurement: current issues.* Newbury Park, CA: Sage, 1981.

Conger, J. A. The dark side of leadership. *Organizational Dynamics,* 1993, *21,* 46–58.

Dansereau, F., Graen, G., & Haga, W. J. A vertical dyad linkage approach to leadership within formal organizations: A longitudinal investigation of the function-making process. *Organizational Behavior and Human Performance.* 1975, *13*(1), 46–78.

Denison, D. R., Hooijberg, R., & Quinn, R. E. Paradox and performance: A theory of behavioral complexity in managerial leadership. *Organization Science.* 6(5), 524–540.

Dobbins, G. H., & Platz, S. J. Sex differences in leadership: How real are they? *Academy of Management Review,* 1986, *11*(1), 118–127.

Falbe, C. M., & Yukl, G. Consequences for managers of using single influence tactics and combinations of tactics. *Academy of Management Journal,* 1992, *35*(3), 638–652.

Fiedler, F. E. *A theory of leadership effectiveness.* New York: McGraw-Hill, 1967.

Gillespie, H. R. An investigation of current management/leadership styles of manufacturing executives in American industry. *Dissertation Abstracts International,* 1980, *41*(7A), 3177.

Harris, T. G. The post-capitalist executive: An interview with Peter F. Drucker. *Harvard Business Review,* 1993, *71,* 114–122.

Hart, S. L., & Quinn, R. E. Roles executives play: CEOs, behavioral complexity, and firm performance. *Human Relations,* 1993, *46*(5), 543–574.

Hersey, P., & Blanchard, K. H. *Management of organizational behavior: Utilizing human resources* (4th, ed). Englewood Cliffs, NJ: Prentice-Hall, 1982.

Hooijberg, R., & Quinn, R. E. Behavioral complexity and the development of effective managers. In R. L. Phillips and J. G. Hunt (Eds.), *Strategic management: A multiorganizational-level perspective.* New York: Quorum, 1992.

House, R. J. A path-goal theory of leader effectiveness. *Administrative Science Quarterly,* 1971, *16,* 321–338.

House, R. J., & Mitchell, T. R. Path-goal theory of leadership. *Contemporary Business,* 1974, *3*(Fall), 81–98.

Howell, J. M., & Higgins, C. A. Champions of technology. *Administrative Science Quarterly,* 1990, *35,* 317–341.

Joreskog, K. G., & Sorbom, D. *Lisrel 7: User's reference guide.* Mooresville, IN: Scientific Software, 1989.

Kanter, R. M. The new managerial work. *Harvard Business Review,* 1989 (November–December).

Katz, D., & Kahn, R. L. *The social psychology of organizations* (2nd ed.). New York, NY; John Wiley & Sons, 1978.

Kenny, D. A., & Zaccaro, S. J. An estimate of variance due to traits in leadership. *Journal of Applied Psychology,* 1983, *68*(4), 678–685.

Keser, F., & Wollenberg, A. L. van den. *Modulair systeem methodenleer Quasi experimenteel design.* Vakgroep Mathematische Psychologie, Psychologisch Laboratorium, Nijmegen, 1986.

Kipnis, D., & Schmidt, S. Upward influence styles: Relationship with performance evaluations, salary, and stress. *Administrative Science Quarterly,* 1988, *33,* 528–542.

Kotter, J. P. *The General Managers.* New York: Free Press, 1982.

Lieberman, S. The effects of changes in roles on the attitudes of role occupants. *Human Relations,* 1956, *9,* 385–402.

Luthans, F., & Lockwood, D. L. Toward an observation system for measuring leader behavior in natural settings. In J. G. Hunt, D. Hosking, C. A. Schriesheim, and R. Steward (Eds.), *Leaders and managers: International perspectives on managerial behavior and leadership.* New York: Pergamon Press, 1984.

Mintzberg, H. *The nature of managerial work.* New York: Harper and Row, 1973.

Morse, J. J., & Wagner, F. R. Measuring the process of managerial effectiveness. *Academy of Management Journal,* 1978, *21,* 23–35.

Page, R. The Position Description Questionnaire. Unpublished paper, Control Data Business Advisors, Minneapolis, 1985.

Park, R. E. Behind our masks. *Survey,* 1926, *56,* 135–139.

Pinder, C., Pinto, P. R., & England, G. W. Behavioral Style and Personal Characteristics of Managers. Technical report, University of Minnesota, Center for the Study of Organizational Performance and Human Effectiveness, Minneapolis, 1973.

Porter, L. W., Allen, R. W., & Angle, H. L. The politics of upward influence in organizations. In B. M. Staw and L. L. Cummings (Eds.), *Research in Organizational Behavior* (Vol. 3). Greenwich, CT: JAI, 1981, pp. 109–149.

Quinn, R. E. *Beyond rational management: Mastering the paradoxes and competing demands of high performance.* San Francisco: Jossey-Bass, 1988.

Quinn, R. E., Spreitzer, G. M., & Hart, S. Challenging the assumptions of bipolarity: Interpenetration and managerial effectiveness. In S. Srivastva and R. Fry (Eds.), *Executive continuity.* San Francisco, CA: Jossey-Bass, 1991.

Schlenker, B. R. *Impression management: The self-concept, social identity, and interpersonal relations.* Monterey, CA: Brooks/Cole Publishing Company, 1980.

Staw, B. M., & Ross, J. *Journal of Applied Psychology,* 1980, *65*(3), 249–260.

Stogdill, R. M. Personal factors associated with leadership: A survey of the literature. *Journal of Psychology,* 1948, *25,* 35–71.

Van Fleet, D. D., & Yukl, G. A. *Military leadership: An organizational behavior perspective.* Greenwich, CT: JAI Press, 1986.

Vroom, V. H., & Yetton, E. W. *Leadership and decision making.* Pittsburgh: Pittsburgh University Press, 1973.

Wheaton, B. Assessment of fit in overidentified models with latent variables. In J. S. Long (Ed.), *Common problems/proper solutions: Avoiding error in quantitative research.* Beverly Hills, CA: Sage, 1988.

Wheaton, B., Muthen, B., Alwin, D. A., & Summers, G. F. Assessing reliability and stability in panel models. In D. R. Heise (Ed.), *Sociological methodology.* San Francisco: Jossey-Bass, 1977.

Yukl, G. A. A New Taxonomy for Integrating Diverse Perspectives on Managerial Behavior. Paper presented at the American Psychological Association Meeting, New York, 1987.

Yukl, G. A. *Leadership in organizations* (2nd ed.). Englewood Cliffs, NJ: Prentice-Hall, 1989. (a)

Yukl, G. A. Managerial leadership: A review of theory and research. *Journal of Management,* 1989, *15*(2), 251–289. (b)

Yukl, G. A., & Falbe, C. M. Influence tactics and objectives in upward, downward, and lateral influence attempts. *Journal of Applied Psychology,* 1990, *75*(2), 132–140.

Yukl, G. A., & Tracey, J. B. Consequences of influence tactics used with subordinates, peers, and the boss. *Journal of Applied Psychology,* 1992, *77*(4), 525–535.

Zaccaro, S. J., Foti, R. J., & Kenny, D. A. Self-monitoring and trait-based variance in leadership: An investigation of leader flexibility across multiple team situations. *Journal of Applied Psychology,* 1991, *76*(2), 308–315.

# Chapter **Nine**

# Leadership in the Cross-cultural Context

The vast majority of the contemporary scholarship directed toward leaders and the leadership process has been conducted in North America and Western Europe. Observing the volume of theory and research that has emerged around the concept of leadership over the past several decades led James R. Meindl and his colleagues (Sanford B. Ehrlich and Janet M. Dukerich, 1985)[1] to suggest that "we may have developed a highly romanticized, heroic view of leadership" (pp. 30–31). Leaders have come to occupy center stage in organizational life. We use leaders in our attempts to make sense of organizational behavior. They are seen as the key to organizational success and profitability, they are credited for organizational competitiveness, and they are the focus of blame in the face of organizational failure. This larger-than-life role ascribed to leaders and the Western romanticized affair with successful leaders raises questions as to how representative our understanding of leadership is across other cultures. That is, do leadership theory and research results generalize from one culture to the next?

Research into culture has generally addressed two questions. First, there has been an interest in whether or not there are significant leadership differences across cultures. Thus, it might be asked whether culture gives rise to leadership differences. The second question treats culture as a key contextual variable. A driving question in this stream of inquiry asks whether or not the effectiveness of leadership (e.g., leader behavior) is culture-specific.

Geert Hofstede's (1993, 1980) work provides a useful framework for the identification and classification of cultural differences. Hofstede's work spans 18 years, involving more than 150,000 people and cutting across 60 countries.[2] He identified five value dimensions that can be employed to explain differences in leadership (i.e., leader traits and behaviors) that might cut across cultures. These value frameworks consist of:

- Individualism–Collectivism

  Individualism is a mental set in which people see themselves first as individuals and believe their own interests and values take priority (Canada, Great Britain, and the United States).

[1] J. R. Meindl, S. B. Ehrlich, and J. M. Dukerich, "The Romance of Leadership," *Administrative Science Quarterly* 30 (1985), pp. 78–102.
[2] G. Hofstede, *Cultural Consequences: International Differences in Work-related Values* (Beverly Hills, CA: Sage, 1980). See also *Organizational Dynamics* (Spring 1993), pp. 53–61, for an interview with G. Hofstede by R. Hodgetts.

Collectivism reflects the feeling that the group or society should receive top priority (Hong Kong, Greece, Japan, and Mexico).

The self-assessment appearing at the end of this chapter opener provides you with the opportunity to profile yourself in terms of your individualistic/collectivistic values (general guiding principles for behavior).

- Power Distance

Power distance reflects the extent to which members of a social system accept the notion that members have different levels of power.

High power distance suggests that leaders make decisions simply because they are the leader (France, Japan, Spain, and Mexico).

Low power distance suggests that social system members do not automatically acknowledge the power of a hierarchy (Germany, Israel, Ireland, and the United States).

- Uncertainty Avoidance

Low uncertainty avoidance is reflected by people who accept the unknown and tolerate risk and unconventional behavior (Australia, Canada, and the United States).

High uncertainty avoidance is characterized by people who want predictable and certain futures (Argentina, Israel, Japan, and Italy).

- Masculinity–Femininity

Masculinity refers to an emphasis that gets placed on assertiveness and the acquisition of money and material objects, coupled with a deemphasis on caring for others (Italy and Japan).

Femininity places an emphasis upon personal relationships, a concern for others, and a high quality of life (Denmark and Sweden).

- Time Orientation

Long-term orientation is characterized by a long-range perspective coupled with a concern for thrift and weak expectations for quick returns on investments (Pacific Rim countries).

Short-term orientation is characterized by demands for immediate results and a low propensity to save (Canada and the United States).

The first reading in this chapter was written by Geert Hofstede. In this reading, Hofstede discusses differences in management as they exist around the globe. His writings provide us with insight into cross-cultural leadership differences as they relate to his value profile.

In the second reading in this chapter, Peter W. Dorfman and his colleagues Jon P. Howell, Shozo Hibino, Jin K. Lee, Uday Tate, and Arnoldo Bautista (1997) look at commonalities and differences in effective leadership processes across a set of Western and Asian countries. Dorfman et al. find that three leader behaviors (i.e., supportive, contingent reward, and charismatic) appear across different cultural settings, while three behaviors (i.e., directive, participative, and contingent punishment) appear to be culturally specific in terms of their linkage with leader effectiveness. The effects of contingent punishment are unique in that this behavior has a desirable effect in only one of the Western countries (the United States) and in neither of the two Asian countries studied. Leaders who demonstrate supportive kindness and concern for followers are val-

**FIGURE 9.1**
**The Leadership**
**Process: Critical**
**Contextual Factors**

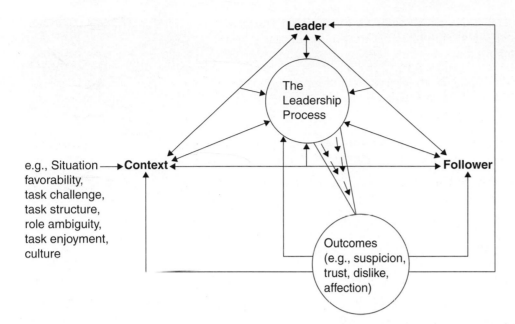

ued and effective in each of the countries studied. Leader contingent reward behavior is highly effective in the more collectivistic Asian cultures—as it often is in Western countries.

The readings in this and the preceding chapter sensitize us to the contextual factors with which leaders need to contend. Specifically, Hofstede (1993) and Dorfman et al. (1997) alert us to the fact that not all followers will have the same belief and value orientation. These differences clearly have leader and leadership implications. Our earlier reading by Murphy (1941) suggested that leadership is a function of an interaction between the leader, the situation, and the follower. In the next chapter, we will focus on the follower in the leadership process. We will want to carry into those readings an understanding of the individual differences that are produced by cultures and differential belief/value systems.

Figure 9.1 adds to our evolving mosaic yet another significant component that adds to the complexity of the different contexts (situations) creating follower demands and demands upon the leader. The two readings in this chapter illuminate the importance of culture-imposed values, expectations, and demands.

**EXERCISE**
*Self-Assessment*

**Individualism-Collectivism**

**Instructions:** Different social groups (e.g., family, friends, colleagues, and strangers) surround us. Focus upon those individuals whom you consider to be *your colleagues* (e.g., team/group members, coworkers, classmates). Then consider each of the following 25 statements and indicate its degree of importance.

| How Important Is It: | Not at All Important 0 | 1 | 2 | 3 | 4 | 5 | Very Important 6 |
|---|---|---|---|---|---|---|---|
| 1. To comply with direct requests from your colleagues? | 0 | 1 | 2 | 3 | 4 | 5 | 6 |
| 2. To maintain self-control toward your colleagues? | 0 | 1 | 2 | 3 | 4 | 5 | 6 |
| 3. To maintain status differences between you and your colleagues? | 0 | 1 | 2 | 3 | 4 | 5 | 6 |
| 4. To share credit for accomplishments of your colleagues? | 0 | 1 | 2 | 3 | 4 | 5 | 6 |
| 5. To share blame for failures of your colleagues? | 0 | 1 | 2 | 3 | 4 | 5 | 6 |
| 6. To respect and honor traditions and customs among your colleagues? | 0 | 1 | 2 | 3 | 4 | 5 | 6 |
| 7. To be loyal to your colleagues? | 0 | 1 | 2 | 3 | 4 | 5 | 6 |
| 8. To sacrifice your goals for your colleagues? | 0 | 1 | 2 | 3 | 4 | 5 | 6 |
| 9. To sacrifice your possessions for your colleagues? | 0 | 1 | 2 | 3 | 4 | 5 | 6 |
| 10. To respect elder colleagues? | 0 | 1 | 2 | 3 | 4 | 5 | 6 |
| 11. To compromise your wishes to act together with your colleagues? | 0 | 1 | 2 | 3 | 4 | 5 | 6 |
| 12. To maintain harmonious relationships among your colleagues? | 0 | 1 | 2 | 3 | 4 | 5 | 6 |
| 13. To nurture or help your colleagues? | | | | | | | |
| 14. To maintain a stable environment (e.g., maintain the status quo) among your colleagues? | 0 | 1 | 2 | 3 | 4 | 5 | 6 |
| 15. To accept your position or role among your colleagues? | 0 | 1 | 2 | 3 | 4 | 5 | 6 |
| 16. To follow advice regarding major decisions from your colleagues? | 0 | 1 | 2 | 3 | 4 | 5 | 6 |
| 17. To exhibit "correct" behaviors (i.e., proper manners and etiquette), regardless of how you really feel, toward your colleagues? | 0 | 1 | 2 | 3 | 4 | 5 | 6 |
| 18. To exhibit "correct" emotions, regardless of how you really feel, toward your colleagues? | 0 | 1 | 2 | 3 | 4 | 5 | 6 |
| 19. To be like or similar to your colleagues? | 0 | 1 | 2 | 3 | 4 | 5 | 6 |
| 20. To accept awards or recognition based only on age or position rather than merit from your colleagues? | 0 | 1 | 2 | 3 | 4 | 5 | 6 |
| 21. To cooperate with your colleagues? | 0 | 1 | 2 | 3 | 4 | 5 | 6 |
| 22. To communicate verbally with members of your colleagues? | 0 | 1 | 2 | 3 | 4 | 5 | 6 |
| 23. To "save face" of the members of your colleagues? | 0 | 1 | 2 | 3 | 4 | 5 | 6 |
| 24. To follow norms established by your colleagues? | 0 | 1 | 2 | 3 | 4 | 5 | 6 |
| 25. To identify yourself as a member of your colleagues? | 0 | 1 | 2 | 3 | 4 | 5 | 6 |

**Scoring:** Sum your answers to questions 1 through 25 and divide by 25. A low score (1 and less) reflects an individualistic orientation within this particular context. A high score (5 and greater) reflects a collectivistic orientation as it pertains to the set of colleagues upon whom you focused your attention.

My individualism/collectivism score is: _____

**Interpretation:** Individualism–collectivism (IC) is one of the most popular dimensions employed by cross-cultural psychologists to explain and predict differences across cultures. At the cultural level of analysis, IC refers to the degree to which a culture "encourages, fosters, and facilitates the needs, wishes, desires, and values of an autonomous and unique self over those of a group" (Matsumoto et al., 1997, p. 744). Individuals within an individualistic culture tend to see themselves as separate and autonomous individuals, while their counterparts in a collectivistic culture see themselves as fundamentally connected to others. Individual needs and goals take precedence in individualistic cultures, whereas they are sacrificed to satisfy the needs of the group in a collectivistic culture.

It should be noted that many cross-cultural psychology scholars (e.g., Triandis, McCusker, and Hui, 1990)[1] have suggested that an individual's IC should manifest differently in different contexts. Thus, an individual could have a collectivistic orientation at home and with close friends (in-group) and an individualistic orientation within the work context (out-group).

Individualism/collectivism has been linked to a number of factors important to leader and group behavior. Earley (1989), for example, hypothesized and observed that social loafing (i.e., the reduced performance displayed by individuals when they act as a part of a group rather than when they are acting alone) is more likely to occur among individuals who hold individualistic rather than collectivistic beliefs.[2] "Social loafing should not appear in a collective society, however, since an individual is motivated by in-group goals rather than self-interest" (p. 568). Based upon these tendencies it might be hypothesized that leaders with collectivistic beliefs might be more likely to take an in-group self-orientation.

**Source:** D. Matsumoto, M. D. Weissman, K. Preston, B. R. Brown, and C. Kupperbausch, "Context-specific Measurement of Individualism–Collectivism on the Individual Level: The Individualism–Collectivism Interpersonal Assessment Inventory," *Journal of Cross-Cultural Psychology* 28, no. 6 (1997), pp. 743–767. Copyright 1997, Sage Publications, Inc. Reprinted by permission of Sage Publications, Inc.

[1] Triandis, H. C., C. M. McCusker & C. H. Hui. Multi-method probes of individualism and collectivism. *Journal of Personality and Social Psychology,* 1990, 59, 1006–1020.

[2] Earley, P. C., "Social Loafing and Collectivism: A Comparison of the United States and the People's Republic of China," *Administrative Science Quarterly* 34 (1989), pp. 565–581.

## Reading 26

# Cultural Constraints in Management Theories

**Geert Hofstede**
University of Limburg, Maastricht, the Netherlands

. . . Diversity in management *practices* as we go around the world has been recognized in U.S. management literature for more than 30 years. The term "comparative management" has been used since the 1960s. However, it has taken much longer for the U.S. academic community to accept that not only practices but also the validity of *theories* may stop at national borders, and I wonder whether even today everybody would agree with this statement.

An article I published in *Organizational Dynamics* in 1980 entitled, "Do American Theories Apply Abroad?" created more controversy than I expected. The article argued, with empirical support, that generally accepted U.S. theories like those of Maslow, Herzberg, McClelland, Vroom, McGregor, Likert, Blake, and Mouton may not or only very partly apply outside the borders of their country of origin—assuming they do apply within those borders. Among the requests for reprints, a larger number were from Canada than from the United States.

## MANAGEMENT THEORISTS ARE HUMAN

Employees and managers are human. Employees as humans was "discovered" in the 1930s, with the Human Relations school. Managers as humans was introduced in the late 40s by Herbert Simon's "bounded rationality" and elaborated in Richard Cyert and James March's *Behavioral Theory of the Firm* (1963, and recently republished in a second edition). My argument is that management scientists, theorists, and writers are human too: They grew up in a particular society in a particular period, and their ideas cannot help but reflect the constraints of their environment.

The idea that the validity of a theory is constrained by national borders is more obvious in Europe, with all its borders, than in a huge borderless country like the U.S. Already in the six-

**Source:** Edited and Reprinted With Permission from Copyright Clearance Center. *Academy of Management Executive* 7, no. 1 (1993), pp. 81–94. Copyright (1993) Academy of Management.

teenth century Michel de Montaigne, a Frenchman, wrote a statement which was made famous by Blaise Pascal about a century later: *"Vérite en deça des Pyrenées, erreur au-delà"*—There are truths on this side of the Pyrenées which are falsehoods on the other.

## FROM DON ARMADO'S LOVE TO TAYLOR'S SCIENCE

According to the comprehensive 10-volume Oxford English Dictionary (1971), the words "manage," "management," and "manager" appeared in the English language in the sixteenth century. The oldest recorded use of the word "manager" is in Shakespeare's *Love's Labour's Lost,* dating from 1588, in which Don Adriano de Armado, "a fantastical Spaniard," exclaims (Act I, scene ii, 188):

> Adieu, valour! rust, rapier! be still, drum! for your manager is in love; yea, he loveth.

The linguistic origin of the word is from Latin *manus,* hand, via the Italian *maneggiare,* which is the training of horses in the *manege;* subsequently its meaning was extended to skillful handling in general, like of arms and musical instruments, as Don Armado illustrates. However, the word also became associated with the French *menage,* household, as an equivalent of "husbandry" in its sense of the art of running a household. The theatre of present-day management contains elements of both *manege* and *menage* and different managers and cultures may use different accents.

The founder of the science of economics, the Scot Adam Smith, in his 1776 book *The Wealth of Nations,* used "manage," "management" (even "bad management") and "manager" when dealing with the process and the persons involved in operating joint stock companies (Smith, V.i.e.). British economist John Stuart Mill (1806–1873) followed Smith in this use and clearly expressed his distrust of such hired people who were not driven by ownership. Since the 1880s the word "management" appeared occasionally in writings by American engineers, until it was canonized as a modern science by Frederick W. Taylor in *Shop Management* in 1903 and in *The Principles of Scientific Management* in 1911.

While Smith and Mill used "management" to describe a process and "managers" for the persons involved, "management" in the American sense—which has since been taken back by the British—refers not only to the process but also to the managers as a class of people. This class (1) does not own a business but sells its skills to act on behalf of the owners, and (2) does not produce personally but is indispensable for making others produce, through motivation. Members of this class carry a high status and many American boys and girls aspire to the role. In the U.S., the manager is a cultural hero.

Let us now turn to other parts of the world. We will look at management in its context in other successful modern economies: Germany, Japan, France, Holland, and among the overseas Chinese. Then we will examine management in the much larger part of the world that is still poor, especially Southeast Asia and Africa, and in the new political configurations of Eastern Europe, and Russia in particular. We will then return to the U.S. via mainland China.

## GERMANY

The manager is not a cultural hero in Germany. If anybody, it is the engineer who fills the hero role. Frederick Taylor's *Scientific Management* was conceived in a society of immigrants—where large numbers of workers with diverse backgrounds and skills had to work together. In Germany this heterogeneity never existed.

Elements of the mediaeval guild system have survived in historical continuity in Germany until the present day. In particular, a very effective apprenticeship system exists both on the shop floor and in the office, which alternates practical work and classroom courses. At the end of the apprenticeship the worker receives a certificate, the *Facharbeiterbrief,* which is recognized throughout the country. About two-thirds of the German worker population hold such a certificate and a corresponding occupational pride. In fact, quite a few German company presidents have worked their way up from the ranks through an apprenticeship. In comparison, two-thirds of the worker population in Britain have no occupational qualification at all.

The highly skilled and responsible German workers do not necessarily need a manager, American-style, to "motivate" them. They expect their boss or *Meister* to assign their tasks and to be the expert in resolving technical problems. Comparisons of similar German, British, and French organizations show the Germans as having the highest rate of personnel in productive roles and the lowest both in leadership and staff roles.

Business schools are virtually unknown in Germany. Native German management theories concentrate on formal systems. The inapplicability of American concepts of management was quite apparent in 1973 when the U.S. consulting firm of Booz, Allen and Hamilton, commissioned by the German Ministry of Economic Affairs, wrote a study of German management from an American viewpoint. The report is highly critical and writes among other things that "Germans simply do not have a very strong concept of management." Since 1973, from my personal experience, the situation has not changed much. However, during this period the German economy has performed in a superior fashion to the U.S. in virtually all respects, so a strong concept of management might have been a liability rather than an asset.

## JAPAN

The American type of manager is also missing in Japan. In the United States, the core of the enterprise is the managerial class. The core of the Japanese enterprise is the permanent worker group; workers who for all practical purposes are tenured and who aspire at life-long employment. They are distinct from the nonpermanent employees—mostly women and subcontracted teams led by gang bosses, to be laid off in slack periods. University graduates in Japan first join the permanent worker group and subsequently fill various positions, moving from line to staff as the need occurs while paid according to seniority rather than position. They take part in Japanese-style group consultation sessions for important decisions, which extend the decision-making period but guarantee fast implementation afterwards. Japanese are to a large extent controlled by their peer group rather than by their manager.

Three researchers from the East–West Center of the University of Hawaii, Joseph Tobin, David Wu, and Dana Danielson, did an observation study of typical preschools in three countries: China, Japan, and the United States. Their results have been published both as a book and as a video. In the Japanese preschool, one teacher handled 28 four year olds. The video shows one particularly obnoxious boy, Hiroki, who fights with other children and throws teaching materials down from the balcony. When a little girl tries to alarm the teacher, the latter answers, "What are you calling me for? Do something about it!" In the U.S. preschool, there is one adult for every nine children. This class has its problem child too, Glen, who refuses to clear away his toys. One of the teachers has a long talk with him and isolates him in a corner, until he changes his mind. It doesn't take much imagination to realize that managing Hiroki 30 years later will be a different process from managing Glen.

American theories of leadership are ill-suited for the Japanese group-controlled situation. During the past two decades, the Japanese have developed their own "PM" theory of leadership, in which P stands for performance and M for maintenance. The latter is less a concern for individual employees than for maintaining social stability. In view of the amazing success of the Japanese economy in the past 30 years, many Americans have sought for the secrets of Japanese management hoping to copy them.

There are no secrets of Japanese management, however; it is even doubtful whether there is such a thing as management, in the American sense, in Japan at all. The secret is in Japanese society; and if any group in society should be singled out as carriers of the secret, it is the workers, not the managers.

## FRANCE

The manager, U.S. style, does not exist in France either. In a very enlightening book, unfortunately not yet translated into English, the French researcher Philippe d'Iribarne (1989) describes the results of in-depth observation and interview studies of management methods in three subsidiary plants of the same French multinational: in France, the United States, and Holland. He relates what he finds to information about the three societies in general. When necessary, he goes back in history to trace the roots of the strikingly different behaviors in the completion of the same tasks. He identifies three kinds of basic principles (*logiques*) of management. In the USA, the principle is the *fair contract* between employer and employee, which gives the manager considerable prerogatives, but within its limits. This is really a labor *market* in which the worker sells his or her labor for a price. In France, the principle is the *honor* of each class in a society which has always been and remains extremely stratified, in which superiors behave as superior beings and subordinates accept and expect this, conscious of their own lower level in the national hierarchy but also

of the honor of their own class. The French do not think in terms of managers versus nonmanagers but in terms of *cadres* versus *noncadres;* one becomes cadre by attending the proper schools and one remains it forever; regardless of their actual task, cadres have the privileges of a higher social class, and it is very rare for a noncadre to cross the ranks.

The conflict between French and American theories of management became apparent in the beginning of the twentieth century, in a criticism by the great French management pioneer Henri Fayol (1841–1925) on his U.S. colleague and contemporary Frederick W. Taylor (1856–1915). The difference in career paths of the two men is striking. Fayol was a French engineer whose career as a *cadre supérieur* culminated in the position of Président-Directeur-Général of a mining company. After his retirement he formulated his experiences in a pathbreaking text on organization: *Administration industrielle et générale,* in which he focused on the sources of authority. Taylor was an American engineer who started his career in industry as a worker and attained his academic qualifications through evening studies. From chief engineer in a steel company he became one of the first management consultants. Taylor was not really concerned with the issue of authority at all; his focus was on efficiency. He proposed to split the task of the first-line boss into eight specialties, each exercised by a different person; an idea which eventually led to the idea of a matrix organization.

Taylor's work appeared in a French translation in 1913, and Fayol read it and showed himself generally impressed but shocked by Taylor's "denial of the principle of the Unity of Command" in the case of the eight-boss system.

Seventy years later André Laurent, another of Fayol's compatriots, found that French managers in a survey reacted very strongly against a suggestion that one employee could report to two different bosses, while U.S. managers in the same survey showed fewer misgivings. Matrix organization has never become popular in France as it has in the United States.

## HOLLAND

In my own country, Holland, or as it is officially called, the Netherlands, the study by Philippe d'Iribarne found the management principle to be a need for *consensus* among all parties, neither predetermined by a contractual relationship nor by class distinctions, but based on an open-ended exchange of views and a balancing of interests. In terms of the different origins of the word "manager," the organization in Holland is more *menage* (household) while in the United States it is more *manege* (horse drill).

At my university, the University of Limburg at Maastricht, every semester we receive a class of American business students who take a program in European Studies. We asked both the Americans and a matched group of Dutch students to describe their ideal job after graduation, using a list of 22 job characteristics. The Americans attached significantly more importance than the Dutch to earnings, advancement, benefits, a good working relationship with their boss, and security of employment. The Dutch attached more importance to freedom to adopt their own approach to the job, being consulted by their boss in his or her decisions, training opportunities, contributing to the success of their organization, fully using their skills and abilities, and helping others. This list confirms d'Iribarne's findings of a contractual employment relationship in the United States, based on earnings and career opportunities, against a consensual relationship in Holland. The latter has centuries-old roots; the Netherlands were the first republic in Western Europe (1609–1810), and a model for the American republic. The country has been and still is governed by a careful balancing of interests in a multiparty system.

In terms of management theories, both motivation and leadership in Holland are different from what they are in the United States. Leadership in Holland presupposes modesty, as opposed to assertiveness in the United States. No U.S. leadership theory has room for that. Working in Holland is not a constant feast, however. There is a built-in premium on mediocrity and jealousy, as well as time-consuming ritual consultations to maintain the appearance of consensus and the pretense of modesty. There is unfortunately another side to every coin.

## THE OVERSEAS CHINESE

Among the champions of economic development in the past 30 years we find three countries mainly populated by Chinese living outside the Chinese mainland: Taiwan, Hong Kong, and Singapore. Moreover, overseas Chinese play a very important role in the economies of Indonesia, Malaysia, the Philippines, and Thailand, where they form an ethnic minority. If anything, the little dragons— Taiwan, Hong Kong, and Singapore—have been more economically successful than Japan, mov-

ing from rags to riches and now counted among the world's wealthy industrial countries. Yet very little attention has been paid to the way in which their enterprises have been managed. *The Spirit of Chinese Capitalism* by Gordon Redding (1990), the British dean of the Hong Kong Business School, is an excellent book about Chinese business. He bases his insights on personal acquaintance and in-depth discussions with a large number of overseas Chinese businesspeople.

Overseas Chinese American enterprises lack almost all characteristics of modern management. They tend to be small, cooperating for essential functions with other small organizations through networks based on personal relations. They are family-owned, without the separation between ownership and management typical in the West, or even in Japan and Korea. They normally focus on one product or market, with growth by opportunistic diversification; in this, they are extremely flexible. Decision making is centralized in the hands of one dominant family member, but other family members may be given new ventures to try their skills on. They are low-profile and extremely cost-conscious, applying Confucian virtues of thrift and persistence. Their size is kept small by the assumed lack of loyalty of nonfamily employees, who, if they are any good, will just wait and save until they can start their own family business.

Overseas Chinese prefer economic activities in which great gains can be made with little manpower, like commodity trading and real estate. They employ few professional managers, except their sons and sometimes daughters who have been sent to prestigious business schools abroad, but who upon return continue to run the family business the Chinese way.

The origin of this system, or—in the Western view—this lack of system, is found in the history of Chinese society, in which there were no formal laws, only formal networks of powerful people guided by general principles of Confucian virtue. The favors of the authorities could change daily, so nobody could be trusted except one's kinfolk— of whom, fortunately, there used to be many, in an extended family structure. The overseas Chinese way of doing business is also very well adapted to their position in the countries in which they form ethnic minorities, often envied and threatened by ethnic violence.

Overseas Chinese businesses following this unprofessional approach command a collective gross national product of some 200 to 300 billion U.S. dollars, exceeding the GNP of Australia. There is no denying that it works.

# MANAGEMENT TRANSFER TO POOR COUNTRIES

Four-fifths of the world population live in countries that are not rich but poor. After World War II and decolonization, the stated purpose of the United Nations and the World Bank has been to promote the development of all the world's countries in a war on poverty. After 40 years it looks very much like we are losing this war. If one thing has become clear, it is that the export of Western—mostly American—management practices *and* theories to poor countries has contributed little to nothing to their development. There has been no lack of effort and money spent for this purpose: students from poor countries have been trained in this country, and teachers and Peace Corps workers have been sent to the poor countries. If nothing else, the general lack of success in economic development of other countries should be sufficient argument to doubt the validity of Western management theories in non-Western environments.

If we examine different parts of the world, the development picture is not equally bleak, and history is often a better predictor than economic factors for what happens today. There is a broad regional pecking order with East Asia leading. The little dragons have passed into the camp of the wealthy; then follow Southeast Asia (with its overseas Chinese minorities), Latin America (in spite of the debt crisis), South Asia, and Africa always trails behind. Several African countries have only become poorer since decolonization.

Regions of the world with a history of large-scale political integration and civilization generally have done better than regions in which no large-scale political and cultural infrastructure existed, even if the old civilizations had decayed or been suppressed by colonizers. It has become painfully clear that development cannot be pressure-cooked; it presumes a cultural infrastructure that takes time to grow. Local management is part of this infrastructure; it cannot be imported in package form. Assuming that with so-called modern management techniques and theories outsiders can develop a country has proven a deplorable arrogance. At best, one can hope for a dialogue between equals with the locals, in which the Western partner acts as the expert in Western technology and the local partner as the expert in local culture, habits, and feelings.

## RUSSIA AND CHINA

The crumbling of the former Eastern bloc has left us with a scattering of states and would-be states of which the political and economic future is extremely uncertain. The best predictions are those based on a knowledge of history, because historical trends have taken revenge on the arrogance of the Soviet rulers who believed they could turn them around by brute power. One obvious fact is that the former bloc is extremely heterogeneous, including countries traditionally closely linked with the West by trade and travel, like Czechia, Hungary, Slovenia, and the Baltic states, as well as others with a Byzantine or Turkish past; some having been prosperous, others always extremely poor.

The industrialized Western world and the World Bank seem committed to helping the ex-Eastern bloc countries develop, but with the same technocratic neglect for local cultural factors that proved so unsuccessful in the development assistance to other poor countries. Free market capitalism, introduced by Western-style management, is supposed to be the answer from Albania to Russia.

Let me limit myself to the Russian republic, a huge territory with some 140 million inhabitants, mainly Russians. We know quite a bit about the Russians as their country was a world power for several hundreds of years before communism, and in the nineteenth century it has produced some of the greatest writers in world literature. If I want to understand the Russians—including how they could so long support the Soviet regime—I tend to re-read Lev Nikolayevich Tolstoy. In his most famous novel *Anna Karenina* (1876) one of the main characters is a landowner, Levin, whom Tolstoy uses to express his own views and convictions about his people. Russian peasants used to be serfs; serfdom had been abolished in 1861, but the peasants, now tenants, remained as passive as before. Levin wanted to break this passivity by dividing the land among his peasants in exchange for a share of the crops; but the peasants only let the land deteriorate further. Here follows a quote:

> (Levin) read political economy and socialistic works . . . but, as he had expected, found nothing in them related to his undertaking. In the political economy books—in (John Stuart) Mill, for instance, whom he studied first and with great ardour, hoping every minute to find an answer to the questions that were engrossing him—he found

only certain laws deduced from the state of agriculture in Europe; but he could not for the life of him see why these laws, which did not apply to Russia, should be considered universal. . . Political economy told him that the laws by which Europe had developed and was developing her wealth were universal and absolute. Socialist teaching told him that development along those lines leads to ruin. And neither of them offered the smallest enlightenment as to what he, Levin, and all the Russian peasants and landowners were to do with their millions of hands and millions of acres, to make them as productive as possible for the common good.

In the summer of 1991, the Russian lands yielded a record harvest, but a large share of it rotted in the fields because no people were to be found for harvesting. The passivity is still there, and not only among the peasants. And the heirs of John Stuart Mill (whom we met before as one of the early analysts of "management") again present their universal recipes which simply do not apply.

Citing Tolstoy, I implicitly suggest that management theorists cannot neglect the great literature of the countries they want their ideas to apply to. The greatest novel in the Chinese literature is considered Cao Xueqin's *The Story of the Stone,* also known as *The Dream of the Red Chamber* which appeared around 1760. It describes the rise and fall of two branches of an aristocratic family in Beijing, who live in adjacent plots in the capital. Their plots are joined by a magnificent garden with several pavilions in it, and the young, mostly female members of both families are allowed to live in them. One day the management of the garden is taken over by a young woman, Tan-Chun, who states:

> I think we ought to pick out a few experienced trust-worthy old women from among the ones who work in the Garden—women who know something about gardening already—and put the upkeep of the Garden into their hands. We needn't ask them to pay us rent; all we need ask them for is an annual share of the produce. There would be four advantages in this arrangement. In the first place, if we have people whose sole occupation is to look after trees and flowers and so on, the condition of the Garden will improve gradually year after year and there will be no more of those long periods of neglect followed by bursts of feverish activity when things have been allowed to get out of hand. Secondly there won't be the spoiling and wastage we get at present. Thirdly the women themselves will gain a little extra to add to their incomes which will compensate them for the hard work they put in throughout the year. And fourthly, there's no

reason why we shouldn't use the money we should otherwise have spent on nurserymen, rockery specialists, horticultural cleaners and so on for other purposes.

As the story goes on, the capitalist privatization—because that is what it is—of the Garden is carried through, and it works. When in the 1980s Deng Xiaoping allowed privatization in the Chinese villages, it also worked. It worked so well that its effects started to be felt in politics and threatened the existing political order; hence the knockdown at Tienanmen Square of June 1989. But it seems that the forces of privatization are getting the upper hand again in China. If we remember what Chinese entrepreneurs are able to do once they have become overseas Chinese, we shouldn't be too surprised. But what works in China—and worked two centuries ago—does not have to work in Russia, not in Tolstoy's days and not today. I am not offering a solution; I only protest against a naive universalism that knows only one recipe for development, the one supposed to have worked in the United States.

## A THEORY OF CULTURE IN MANAGEMENT

Our trip around the world is over and we are back in the United States. What have we learned? There is something in all countries called "management," but its meaning differs to a larger or smaller extent from one country to the other, and it takes considerable historical and cultural insight into local conditions to understand its processes, philosophies, and problems. If already the word may mean so many different things, how can we expect one country's theories of management to apply abroad? One should be extremely careful in making this assumption, and test it before considering it proven. Management is not a phenomenon that can be isolated from other processes taking place in a society. During our trip around the world we saw that it interacts with what happens in the family, at school, in politics, and government. It is obviously also related to religion and to beliefs about science. Theories of management always had to be interdisciplinary, but if we cross national borders they should become more interdisciplinary than ever.

Cultural differences between nations can be, to some extent, described using first four, and now five, bipolar *dimensions*. The position of a country on these dimensions allows us to make some predictions on the way their society operates, including their management processes and the kind of theories applicable to their management.

As the word culture plays such an important role in my theory, let me give you my definition, which differs from some other very respectable definitions. *Culture* to me is *the collective programming of the mind which distinguishes one group or category of people from another.* In the part of my work I am referring to now, the category of people is the nation.

Culture is a *construct,* that means it is "not directly accessible to observation but inferable from verbal statements and other behaviors and useful in predicting still other observable and measurable verbal and nonverbal behavior." It should not be reified; it is an auxiliary concept that should be used as long as it proves useful but bypassed where we can predict behaviors without it.

The same applies to the *dimensions* I introduced. They are constructs too that should not be reified. They do not "exist"; they are tools for analysis which may or may not clarify a situation. In my statistical analysis of empirical data the first four dimensions together explain 49 percent of the variance in the data. The other 51 percent remain specific to individual countries.

The first four dimensions were initially detected through a comparison of the values of similar people (employees and managers) in 64 national subsidiaries of the IBM Corporation. People working for the same multinational, but in different countries, represent very well-matched samples from the populations of their countries, similar in all respects except nationality.

The first dimension is labelled *Power Distance,* and it can be defined as the degree of inequality among people which the population of a country considers as normal: from relatively equal (that is, small power distance) to extremely unequal (large power distance). All societies are unequal, but some are more unequal than others.

The second dimension is labelled *Individualism,* and it is the degree to which people in a country prefer to act as individuals rather than as members of groups. The opposite of individualism can be called *Collectivism,* so collectivism is low individualism. The way I use the word it has no political connotations. In collectivist societies a child learns to respect the group to which it belongs, usually the family, and to differentiate between in-group members and out-group members (that is, all other people). When children grow up they remain members of their group, and they expect the group to protect them when they are in trouble. In return, they have to remain loyal to their group throughout life. In individualist societies, a child learns very early to think of itself as "I" instead of as part of "we". It expects one day to have to stand on its own feet and not to get protection from its group any more; and therefore it also does not feel a need for strong loyalty.

The third dimension is called *Masculinity* and its opposite pole *Femininity.* It is the degree to which tough values like assertiveness, performance, success and competition, which in nearly all societies are associated with the role of men, prevail over tender values like the quality of life, maintaining warm personal relationships, service, care for the weak, and solidarity, which in nearly all societies are more associated with women's roles. Women's roles differ from men's roles in all countries; but in tough societies, the differences are larger than in tender ones.

The fourth dimension is labelled *Uncertainty Avoidance,* and it can be defined as the degree to which people in a country prefer structured over unstructured situations. Structured situations are those in which there are clear rules as to how one should behave. These rules can be written down, but they can also be unwritten and imposed by tradition. In countries which score high on uncertainty avoidance, people tend to show more nervous energy, while in countries which score low, people are more easy-going. A (national) society with strong uncertainty avoidance can be called rigid; one with weak uncertainty avoidance, flexible. In countries where uncertainty avoidance is strong a feeling prevails of "what is different, is dangerous." In weak uncertainty avoidance societies, the feeling would rather be "what is different, is curious."

The fifth dimension was added on the basis of a study of the values of students in 23 countries carried out by Michael Harris Bond, a Canadian working in Hong Kong. He and I had cooperated in another study of students' values which had yielded the same four dimensions as the IBM data. However, we wondered to what extent our common findings in two studies could be the effect of a Western bias introduced by the common Western background of the researchers. . . . Michael Bond resolved this dilemma by deliberately introducing an Eastern bias. He used a questionnaire prepared at his request by his Chinese colleagues, the *Chinese Value Survey (CVS),* which was translated from Chinese into different languages and answered by 50 male and 50 female students in each of 23 countries in all five continents. Analysis of the CVS data produced three dimensions significantly correlated with the three IBM dimensions of power distance, individualism, and masculinity. There was also a fourth dimension, but it did not resemble uncertainty avoidance. It was composed, both on the positive and on the negative side, from items that had not been included in the IBM studies but were present in the Chinese Value Survey because they were rooted in the teachings of Confucius. I labelled this dimension: *Long-term* versus *Short-term Orientation*. On the long-term side one finds values oriented towards the future, like thrift (saving) and persistence. On the short-term side one finds values rather oriented towards the past and present, like respect for tradition and fulfilling social obligations.

Table 1 lists the scores on all five dimensions for the United States and for the other countries we just discussed. The table shows that each country has its own configuration on the five dimensions. Some of the values in the table have been estimated based on imperfect replications or personal impressions. The different dimension scores do not "explain" all the differences in management I described earlier. To understand management in a country, one should have both knowledge of and empathy with the entire local scene. However, the scores should make us aware that people in other countries may think, feel, and act very differently from us when confronted with basic problems of society.

## IDIOSYNCRACIES OF AMERICAN MANAGEMENT THEORIES

In comparison to other countries, the U.S. culture profile presents itself as below average on power distance and uncertainty avoidance, highly individualistic, fairly masculine, and short-term oriented. The Germans show a stronger uncertainty avoidance and less extreme individualism; the Japanese are different on all dimensions, least on power distance; the French show larger power distance and uncertainty avoidance, but are less individualistic and somewhat feminine; the Dutch resemble the Americans on the first three dimensions, but score extremely feminine and relatively long-term oriented; Hong Kong Chinese combine large power distance with weak uncertainty avoidance, collectivism, and are very long-term oriented; and so on. . . .

## CONCLUSION

. . . In fact, the management theorist who ventures outside his or her own country into other parts of the world is like Alice in Wonderland. He or she will meet strange beings, customs, ways of organizing or disorganizing, and theories that are clearly stupid, old-fashioned, or even immoral—yet they may work, or at least they may not fail more frequently than corresponding theories do at home. Then, after the first culture shock, the traveller to Wonderland will feel enlightened, and may be able to take his or her experiences home and use them advantageously. All great ideas in science, politics, and management have travelled from one country to another, and been enriched by foreign influences. The roots of American management theories are mainly in Europe: with Adam Smith, John Stuart Mill, Lev Tolstoy, Max Weber, Henri Fayol, Sigmund Freud, Kurt Lewin, and many others. These theories were replanted here and they developed and bore fruit. The same may happen again. The last thing we need is a Monroe doctrine for management ideas.

| TABLE 1 | Culture Dimension Scores for Ten Countries | | | | | | | | |
|---|---|---|---|---|---|---|---|---|---|
| | **PD** | | **ID** | | **MA** | | **UA** | | **LT** |
| USA | 40 | L | 91 | H | 62 | H | 46 | L | 29 | L |
| Germany | 35 | L | 67 | H | 66 | H | 65 | M | 31 | M |
| Japan | 54 | M | 46 | M | 95 | H | 92 | H | 80 | H |
| France | 68 | H | 71 | H | 43 | M | 86 | H | 30* | L |
| Netherlands | 38 | L | 80 | H | 14 | L | 53 | M | 44 | M |
| Hong Kong | 68 | H | 25 | L | 57 | H | 29 | L | 96 | H |
| Indonesia | 78 | H | 14 | L | 46 | M | 48 | L | 25* | L |
| West Africa | 77 | H | 20 | L | 46 | M | 54 | M | 16 | L |
| Russia | 95* | H | 50* | M | 40* | L | 90* | H | 10* | L |
| China | 80* | H | 20* | L | 50* | M | 60* | M | 118 | H |

*estimated
PD = Power Distance; ID = Individualism; MA = Masculinity; UA = Uncertainty Avoidance; LT = Long-Term Orientation
H = top third, M = medium third, L = bottom third (among 53 countries and regions for the first four dimensions; among 23 countries for the fifth)

## Reading 27

# Leadership in Western and Asian Countries: Commonalities and Differences in Effective Leadership Processes across Cultures

**Peter W. Dorfman**
**Jon P. Howell**
New Mexico State University

**Shozo Hibino**
Chukyo University

**Jin K. Lee**
Korea University

**Uday Tate**
Southeastern Louisiana University

**Arnoldo Bautista**
Rural Development Directorship

## INTRODUCTION

It has become an axiom among international researchers that effective management and leadership processes must reflect the culture in which they are found (Ayman, 1993; Smith & Peterson, 1988). Unique cultural characteristics such as language, beliefs, values, religion, and social organization are generally presumed to necessitate distinct leadership approaches in different groups of nations—popularly known as culture clusters (Hofstede, 1993; Jackofsky, Slocum, & McQuaid, 1988; Ronen & Shenkar, 1985; Triandis, 1993a). Researchers who adhere to this culture-specific position often cite the individualistic nature of the United States as support for the argument that leadership theories developed in the United States are limited in their applicability to different cultures (Adler, 1991; Hofstede, 1980, 1993; Smith & Peterson, 1988; Triandis, 1993b). Some recent writers have pointed out, however, that universal tendencies in leadership processes *also* exist—the culture universal position (Bass & Avolio, 1993; Dorfman & Ronen, 1991; Fahr, Podsakoff, & Cheng, 1987; Wakabayashi & Graen, 1984).

Bass (1990) has shown that both of these two perspectives—culture-specific versus culture-universal—have demonstrated validity for practitioners and researchers alike. Construct development and research methods employed, however, often differ between those researchers who subscribe more to the culture-specific approach than those who acknowledge the possibility of culture universals. The culture-specific perspective, which is consistent with an "emic" or insider approach to construct development (Berry, 1980), reflects the view that certain leadership constructs and behaviors are likely to be unique to a given culture. In-depth emic studies that are culture-specific provide descriptively rich information about how leadership constructs are enacted in those cultures. In support of this position, Smith et al. (1989) found that the specific expression or enactment of basic leader functions of midlevel managers vary according to cultural constraints. At the executive level, research also indicates that successful CEOs often employ leadership styles consistent with society's cultural values (Jackofsky, Slocum, & McQuade, 1988).

The culture-universal position, in contrast, is consistent with an "etic" or outside imposed perspective that certain leadership constructs are comparable across cultures. In order to explore the universalist position, an etic methodology is employed whereby comparative studies are carried out among various cultures to empirically test potentially generalizable leadership hypotheses. In support of this "universalist" position, researchers have reported findings that show commonalities in leadership patterns across widely varying cultures. For instance, a literature review by Smith and Peterson (1988) showed the general leader behavior patterns of task- and relationship-oriented behaviors, which have been prominent in many U.S. leadership models, were effective in studies of collectivist cultures. *Our approach in this study employed both the emic and etic perspectives—emic culture-based predictions were developed regarding the incidence and impact of etic dimensions of leaders' behavior within a theoretically sound contingency model of leadership.* Thus the overall thrust of the research project reported here was to extend contingency theories of leadership to include national culture as an important situational variable.

## LEADERSHIP THEORY

Until recently, the major focus of leadership research in the United States has been on contingency theories that have attempted to specify the organizational circumstances under which particular leader behavior patterns are most effective (cf., Fiedler & Garcia, 1987; Indvik, 1986; Vroom & Jago, 1988). A careful reading of the leadership literature and recent summaries demonstrates that much has been learned by contingency theory researchers (Fiedler & House, 1988; Indvik, 1986; Yukl & Van Fleet, 1992). These researchers have shown that situational factors play a critical role in determining when a particular leader behavior is most effective. Contingency leadership theories thus provide an appropriate theoretical framework for this study because they were designed primarily to test leadership impacts in different situations and contexts. The primary contextual variable in this study is national culture.

We attempted to avoid the universalist bias of simply testing a specific U.S.-made theory abroad (Boyacigiller & Adler, 1991). Instead, we chose two well-known contingency models—House's path-goal theory and Yukl's multiple linkage model—and we created a syncretic model of leadership based on these two theories. Behling and McFillan (1993) have described syncretic models as combining and integrating similarities among existing models. Admittedly, our syncretic model was developed within a "Western" context. Yet the leadership constructs employed in our model

have been employed in leadership models by non-Western researchers (e.g., Misumi & Peterson, 1985b; Sinha, 1980) and have been studied in some cross-cultural contexts (reviewed by Dorfman, 1996). Our objective at this stage was to develop a model with variables and processes that had sound theoretical and research bases as well as potentially wide application across cultures.

House's path-goal theory of leadership is a midrange theory designed to predict subordinates' motivation, satisfactions, and performance (House, 1971). In addition to an extensive research base in the United States (Indvik, 1988), it has been found useful in leadership research in different cultures (Al-Gattan, 1985; Dorfman & Howell, 1988). Yukl's multiple linkage model (1994) is a metatheory that is designed to predict work group performance. Although the complexity of the multiple linkage model makes it difficult to test in its entirety, it is probably the most comprehensive contingency theory developed to date (Yukl & Van Fleet, 1992). In addition to being carefully developed by excellent scholars, these two models possess several characteristics that make them attractive as the basis for a model of leadership behaviors in different cultures. First, both models include etic leader behaviors that can be identified and described in all the cultures studied. Second, the leader behaviors have been widely researched in the United States and to some degree in other cultures. Third, both models incorporate mediator variables to help track the causal impacts of leadership behaviors on outcomes. Fourth, these models systematically incorporate situational moderator variables in their predictions. A weakness of these and other contingency models is that they neglect to include culture as a key type of moderator variable. Figure 1 describes the syncretic leadership model used in this study. This model is briefly described, followed by a justification of the relationships depicted in the model.

Figure 1 shows the leadership process as a set of causal leader behavior variables that impact followers' job satisfaction and role ambiguity—representing mediators in this model. The mediators are the most immediate results of a leader's behavior. Organizational commitment and job performance are outcome variables in the model. Job satisfaction and role ambiguity are shown affecting organizational commitment (Williams & Hazer, 1986) as well as job performance. Although the satisfaction-performance relationship in the U.S. literature is not strong, recent meta-analysis research indicates that the relationship is positive, and when

**FIGURE 1**   **Theoretical Model of Leadership Processes**

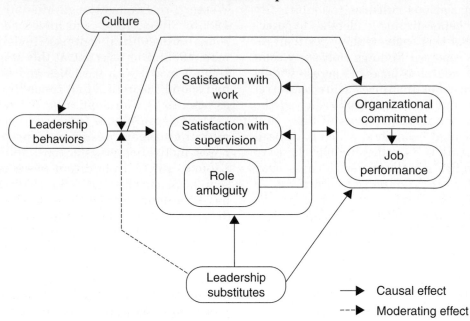

using the best satisfaction measures (e.g., Job Descriptive Index), correlations are approximately in the .30 range (Iaffaldano & Muchinsky, 1985; Ostroff, 1992).

To our knowledge, the link between satisfaction and performance has not been investigated systematically in non-Western countries. Job performance and commitment are also directly affected by leader behaviors (because this model does not attempt to include an exhaustive list of mediators). Finally, job performance is influenced by organizational commitment. Leadership substitutes moderate leadership effects and have direct effects on mediators and outcome variables. (We have chosen not to test for "substitutes for leadership" in this project because of the complexity of our study due to the multiplicity of data sets.) Culture is also an overall moderator of leadership effects and is shown to have a direct effect on the behaviors exhibited by leaders.

Viewing leader behaviors as causal variables is consistent with contingency leadership theories and most cross-cultural leadership research (Misumi & Peterson, 1985a, 1985b; Smith & Peterson, 1988). The actual leader behaviors used in this study are *directive, supportive, participative, contingent reward and punishment,* and *charismatic* behaviors. Each of these has shown potential importance in cross-cultural research, has been claimed by researchers to be universally important across cultures, and/or is used by managers and management trainers abroad (Al-Gattan, 1985;

Ayman & Chemers, 1983; Bass & Avolio, 1993; Bass & Yokochi, 1991; Bond & Hwang, 1986; Dorfman, 1996; Dorfman & Ronen, 1991; Dorfman & Howell, 1988; Fahr, Podsakoff, & Cheng, 1987; House, 1991; Misumi & Peterson, 1985b; Sinha, 1980). Showing culture as a causal variable affecting the level of leader behaviors is consistent with existing models of cross-cultural management (Bass, 1990; Negandhi & Prasad, 1971), and its role as a moderator in Figure 1 is implicit in much cross-cultural leadership research (Misumi & Peterson, 1985b; Smith, Peterson, Bond, & Misumi, 1992). . . .

## FIVE COUNTRIES

Five countries in the Asian-Pacific Basin were studied—Japan, South Korea, Taiwan, Mexico, and the United States. The five countries were chosen for two reasons. First, they are major players in a growing economic bloc called the Asian-Pacific Basin. Second, they represent considerable cultural variation on numerous dimensions such as individualism/collectivism, uncertainty avoidance, power distance, degree of industrialization, paternalism, and Eastern versus Western attitudes toward work and authority (Hofstede, 1991; Ronen & Shenkar, 1985). Our goal was to obtain two samples of respondents from North America (the United States and Mexico) and match these samples with the three major ethnic cultures in the Asian-Pacific Rim. Because of their cultural variation and the current interest in business issues in the Pacific Rim, we believe these cultures are theoretically and practically valuable contexts in which to test the transferability of general dimensions of leadership behavior.

## LEADERSHIP IN JAPAN

Japan is the second largest trading partner with the United States, and it may be a unique culture within the Pacific Rim, being higher in masculinity and uncertainty avoidance and only medium on collectivism in comparison to South Korea and Taiwan (Dorfman & Howell, 1994; Hofstede, 1991). Confucianism in Japan requires respect and obedience to leaders who have historically responded with highly paternalistic attitudes toward their subordinates, expressed by *mendou* ("I think about you; I will take care of you"). Japanese organizations are extremely hierarchical and are rigidly organized (Chen, 1995), yet helping and caring for followers and being involved in their personal lives is expected of Japanese managers (Whitehall & Takezawa, 1968; Bass, Burger, et al., 1979). The Japanese *sempai-kohai* mentor relationship system reinforces a close personal bond between supervisors and subordinates (Chen, 1995).

The ideal leadership model in Japan comes from early village leaders who were skillfully unassertive and who led by implicit consensus, nonverbal communication, and indirect discussions ("Too much talk was bad"). Japanese managers typically outline general objectives, make vague group assignments, and generally let subordinates use their own approaches to achieve overall objectives. The phrase *omakase* ("I trust you, you can do it") reflects this approach. Although only medium on collectivism, Asian scholars describe the Japanese as placing strong emphasis on group harmony and collective (not individual) responsibility (e.g., Hayashi, 1988). The Japanese tendency for collective decision making and extensive consultation through the *ringi* system of decision making is also well noted (Chen, 1995). We expect these complex forces to cause *supportive and participative* leadership to be highly impactful, and *directive* leadership to be impactful to some extent in Japan.

An emphasis by managers on equality of all group members also supports group harmony, which is usually considered more important than making money or overall productivity (Bass,

1990). Individuals are not singled out in Japan for praise or criticism ("The nail which sticks out gets pounded down"). Compliments and criticism are usually directed at the group; individual criticism is not conveyed openly, but may be directed at the individual after the workday is over. *Leader contingent punishment* behavior is therefore predicted to have no positive impact and may have a negative impact in Japan. However, since leader contingent reward behavior has been found impactful in other Asian cultures (Fahr, et al., 1987) and since Japanese leaders do control recognition and symbolic exchanges with followers (often shown over long periods through promotions and/or added responsibilities), *leader contingent reward* behavior is predicted to have a positive impact on followers in Japan.

Charisma is important for top-level managers in Japan, who represent a symbol of respected authority and may be called "mini-emperors." The main functions of senior management in Japan include establishing an overall theme, developing strategy, and engaging in high-level external relations (Morgan & Morgan, 1991). Other managers in Japanese organizations are considered part of their group, not separate from the group as is often the case with charismatics. Japanese managers also do not view themselves as risk-takers, another characteristic often attributed to charismatic leaders (Bass, 1985). We therefore expect *charismatic leader behaviors* to have little or no impact in this Japanese sample of middle managers and professionals. Based on the considerations discussed above, we present the following hypothesis:

**Hypothesis 1.** In Japan, directive, supportive, contingent reward and participative leader behaviors will positively affect mediators and/or outcome measures; contingent punishment will have no positive impact, and may have a negative impact on the same criteria. Charismatic leader behaviors will have no significant effects.

## LEADERSHIP IN SOUTH KOREA

South Korea continues to develop rapidly and represents an important manufacturing competitor to the United States and Japan. Its high collectivism and medium/high uncertainty avoidance make it culturally akin to Taiwan (Dorfman & Howell, 1994; Hofstede, 1991). South Korea is perhaps more heavily influenced by Confucianism than other Asian countries. The Confucian code of ethical behavior includes maintenance of harmonious relationships and trust as the basis of business activities. A social order emphasizes respect and obedience to senior individuals, who, in turn, assume responsibility for the well being and future of the young. Absolute loyalty to the ruler (or company president) is required (Steers, Shin, & Ungson, 1989). These factors result in leaders who assume a personal interest in the welfare and development of followers and who emphasize group harmony and smooth, conflict-free interpersonal relations (Steers, et al., 1989). While harmony (*inhwa*) is desirable, it is based on inequality among those of differing rank, power, and prestige (Alston, 1989). Thus, followers' responsiveness to their leaders is heavily reinforced by strong Confucian mandates of respect and obedience to leaders who maintain and care for their followers. Combining these values with generally vague job descriptions and training results in leaders with considerable power to direct activities. Based on these observations, we predict *supportive and directive leadership* to be highly impactful in South Korea.

Centralized planning and control and strong directiveness are clearly evident in the *chaebols,* which are large diversified companies, primarily owned and managed by founders and/or family members, which dominate South Korean business. Perhaps because of highly centralized and formalized organizational structures, key information is normally concentrated at the top organizational levels in South Korea. Top-down decision making style is typical with subordinates taking a passive role in communications (Chen, 1995). Although a recent survey reported South Korean executives expressing the importance of an "environment for voluntary participation," subordinates have difficulty in expressing views contrary to those of their supervisors. We predict, therefore, that *participative leadership* will have little or no impact in South Korea.

There is a clear emphasis on collective, rather than individual, achievement in South Korea (Hofstede, 1980; Steers, et al., 1989) and differentiating rewards among individuals is believed to disturb the needed harmony. These factors argue against leader contingent reward behavior in South Korea. However, the contingent reward scale used in this study measures social rewards only (e.g., compliments and recognition). A survey of executives showed that South Koreans prefer recognition to tangible rewards (Hayashi, 1988), and leader contingent reward behaviors have been found impactful in other cultures characterized by Confucianism (Fahr, et al., 1987). We therefore expect *leaders' contingent reward behavior* to have a positive impact in South Korea. In contrast, because negative feedback may undermine harmonious relations, managers often evaluate subordinates leniently and will temper criticism if the individual puts forth reasonable effort (Chen, 1995). The combination of trying to preserve the internal peace and harmony of others (*kibun*) and not conveying bad news or news someone does not wish to hear leads us to predict that *leaders' contingent punishment behavior* will have no impact in South Korea.

South Korean corporations are highly entrepreneurial in spirit. Successful South Korean entrepreneurs enunciate a clear and convincing vision of their business goals to obtain government-assisted loans and, like Chairman Kim of Daewoo, they aggressively pursue their vision. The charisma of Chairman Chung of Hyundai was evident when he personally inspired subordinates to believe in their new (and eventually successful) shipbuilding venture, in spite of expert opinion that it would fail. Family ownership, importance of personal loyalty, and combined ownership/management of South Korean companies suggest that charismatic leadership should be impactful in South Korea. We offer the following summary hypothesis for South Korea:

> **Hypothesis 2.** In South Korea, directive, supportive, charismatic, and contingent reward leader behaviors will positively affect mediators and/or outcome measures; contingent punishment and participative leader behaviors will have no significant impacts.

## LEADERSHIP IN TAIWAN

Taiwan reflects the prosperous "overseas" Chinese culture found in many areas of the Pacific Rim. Hofstede (1980) also reported the Chinese to be very high on collectivism and Dorfman and Howell (1988) found them high on both collectivism and paternalism. The Confucian norm of deference to rank (*wu-lun*) is strong, with followers preferring clear-cut directions from kind, "human-hearted" leaders (*jen*) who care about followers (Redding, 1990; Hsu, 1982). Most overseas Chinese business and management practices are based on the family business model—even large-scale business operations usually follow this cultural norm. According to Redding (1990), the managerial philosophy can be summarized by the word "patromonialism"—indicating themes such as paternalism, hierarchy, familialism, mutual obligation, personalism, and connections. Ingratiation of leaders (providing compliments, conformity in opinions and behavior, gift-giving) is common by followers and is called *enhancing others' face*. Hsu (1982) found that Chinese subordinates prefer a leadership style where the leader maintains a harmonious considerate relationship with followers while being directive. Hsu (1982) found that leader initiating structure correlated positively with Chinese followers' job satisfaction and that subordinates preferred leaders who define clear-cut tasks for each member of the group. We therefore expect *supportive and directive leadership* to be highly impactful among the Taiwanese workers sampled.

In a comparative study of beliefs about management behavior, Redding and Casey (1976) found Chinese managers distinctly more authoritarian and autocratic than Western managers, especially regarding sharing information with subordinates and allowing them to participate in decision making. Open discussion about decision-making processes tends to be viewed as a challenge to the leader's authority and is therefore not done (Redding & Casey, 1976). Subordinates typically assume the leader has considered all relevant factors prior to making a decision. A large power distance is maintained by the boss (Chen, 1995). One Chinese executive pointed out a weakness in Chinese organizations that very little input is obtained from employees. We therefore expect *participative leadership* to have no positive impact in Taiwan.

In Chinese organizations, control is achieved through conformity, nepotism, and obligation networks (*guanxi*), not through performance contingent rewards and punishments (Redding & Wong, 1986). Judgment of a person's worth is based on loyalty rather than ability or performance against objective criteria (Chen, 1995). Chinese culture urges avoidance of confrontation which is sometimes considered uncivilized behavior. Preserving others' face in social encounters is important so supervisors usually do not point out others' mistakes directly. They typically use vague or moderate language to protect the face of those being criticized. Fahr, Podsakoff, and Cheng (1987) found that punishment behavior of any kind has significant dysfunctional effects on subordinate performance in Taiwan. In contrast to punishing behaviors, recent studies of overseas Chinese (Fahr, Podsakoff, & Cheng, 1987) indicate that performance contingent rewards may play a positive role in Chinese organizations. We therefore expect *leaders' contingent punishment behavior* to have a negative impact in our Taiwanese sample, but *leaders' contingent reward behavior* will have a positive impact.

Redding (1990) has pointed out that managerial leadership among overseas Chinese is primarily transactional, not charismatic. Subordinates are expected to exhibit loyalty, diligence, conformity, and behaviors that enhance the superiors' face. This psychological contract governing the superior–subordinate relationship is a direct reflection of the Confucian family social structure which is based on filial piety (*hsiao*). The loyalty and devotion of subordinates derives from cultural dictates, not from an inspirational, charismatic leader. However, leaders at the very top of an organization may create a vision that inspires followers. One example was Mao Tse-tung, who also endeavored to replace the Confucian social structure with a socialistic structure, but overseas Chinese have not generally accepted the socialistic structure. And the individuals in our Taiwanese sample are supervisors, middle managers, and professional workers—not top level managers. We therefore expect that *charismatic leadership* will have no significant impact on followers in the Taiwanese sample. The following hypothesis summarizes our predictions for Taiwan:

> **Hypothesis 3.** In Taiwan, directive, supportive, and contingent reward leader behaviors will positively affect mediators and/or outcome measures; contingent punishment will have a negative impact on mediators and/or outcome measures. Participative and charismatic leader behaviors will have no significant effects.

## LEADERSHIP IN MEXICO

Mexico's high collectivism, paternalism, power distance, and masculinity seems to resemble the Asian culture cluster more than its neighbor the United States (Dorfman & Howell, 1988; Hofstede, 1991). Its Spanish/Indian history of authoritarian and omnipotent leaders has been enacted via the autocratic *patrón* and compliant follower roles which pervade Mexican society (Riding, 1985). Mexican society today still functions through relationships of power where status differences predominate. Mexico is also highly paternalistic (Dorfman & Howell, 1988; Farmer & Richman, 1965), and the compliant role of subordinates reinforces the strong directive leader. High collectivism and paternalism in Mexico encourages a caring, supportive type of leadership. Kakar (1971) and Ayman and Chemers (1983) found supportive leadership to have positive impacts on the attitudes of Mexican workers. We thus expect both *directive and supportive leadership* to be highly impactful in Mexico.

The authoritarian tradition in Mexico still resists incursions of Western liberalism, including seeking input from all levels for decision making. Participative leadership, as practiced in Western Europe and North America, requires individualistic followers, trusting relationships between managers and followers, and a firm structure for participation (Hofstede, 1980; Riding, 1985). None of these conditions are present in Mexican culture which is highly collectivist, nontrusting, and elitist without a history or framework for wide participation in organizational processes. Marrow (1964) reported that participative leaders in Latin America were viewed as weak and caused increased turnover as followers deserted a leader they deemed destined to fail. We therefore predict that *participative leadership* will not be impactful in Mexico.

Leaders' contingent reward and punishment behaviors seem well suited for individualistic cultures like the United States, not collectivist cultures like Mexico. However, recall that Mexican society functions through relationships of power and influence. In organizations, control of rewards and punishments are major reflections of one's power. Bass (1990) concluded that leaders' contingent punishment behavior was impactful in high power distance cultures. However, qualitative research with focus groups in Mexico (conducted as part of GLOBE leadership project; House, et al., 1994) revealed that the prototypical "good leader" will not offend or embarrass others but will maintain respect and interact with others in a culturally sensitive manner (*simpatico*). These limited, and somewhat contradictory observations, lead us to expect *leaders' contingent reward behavior* to have positive impacts but *contingent punishment behaviors* to have no significant impact on followers in Mexico.

Mexican history is filled with revolutionary charismatic leaders whose names are continuously honored and celebrated. Current political leaders often adopt key Mexican charismatics from the past as "spiritual" advisors (Riding, 1985). These historical figures are strongly masculine and possess a high degree of power. Bass (1990) predicted that charismatic leadership would be especially impactful in collectivist cultures. We therefore expect *charismatic leadership* to have a strong impact on Mexican followers. The following hypothesis is based on the information presented above:

> **Hypothesis 4.** In Mexico, directive, supportive, contingent reward, and charismatic leader behaviors will positively affect mediators and/or outcome measures. Participative leadership and contingent punishment will have no significant effects.

## LEADERSHIP IN THE UNITED STATES

The United States is culturally unique in comparison to the other countries sampled in this study. Hofstede (1980) described the United States as highly individualistic, low on power distance and uncertainty avoidance, and medium on masculinity. Dorfman and Howell (1988) reported the United States as medium on paternalism. These cultural factors make the expected leadership impacts somewhat distinct for the U.S. sample. Also, in contrast to the other cultures sampled for this study, there are clearer lines of leadership research in the United States from which to make predictions.

Supportive leadership has shown consistently strong positive relationships with followers' satisfaction and organizational commitment as well as moderate to strong relationships with followers' role ambiguity and performance in the United States (Indvik, 1986). These findings may reflect the moderate masculinity and low power distance scores for the U.S. culture. Directive leadership has also been important in U.S. organizations, with meta-analyses reporting strong positive relationships with measures of follower satisfaction and role ambiguity and moderate positive relationships with follower performance (Podsakoff, Tudor, & Schuler, 1983). Yet, these impacts are heavily moderated by many organizational and individual follower characteristics (Yukl, 1994). Kerr and Jermier (1978) suggested that workers who are highly experienced, educated, and professional will have less need for traditional directive leader behaviors in carrying our their job tasks. This may be particularly true of the managerial/professional sample in this study. Smith and Peterson (1988) and Hofstede (1980) pointed out that the extremely high individualism in the United States strongly supports participative management processes. For these reasons, we expect *supportive and participative leadership* to have a high degree of impact, but *directive leadership* to have no significant impact on followers in the U.S. sample.

Rewards and punishments contingent on individual performance also reflect the high individualism and high achievement motivation that characterizes U.S. workers (McClelland & Boyatzis, 1982). Podsakoff and his associates (1992) have consistently demonstrated positive effects for contingent reward behavior in the United States. Leaders' contingent punishment behavior has also demonstrated positive impacts on follower attitudes in several U.S. samples. *Leader contingent reward and punishment behaviors* are therefore expected to have positive impacts in the U.S. sample, although contingent reward behavior will likely have the strongest impact.

Much of the leadership research conducted in the United States in the last decade has focused on charismatic leadership. Numerous books and empirical studies have demonstrated its importance and prevalence at all levels in U.S. organizations (Bass, 1990). The high achievement orientation of U.S. workers, especially managers and professionals, will also likely cause followers to respond well to charismatic leader behaviors. We thus expect *charismatic leader behavior* to be highly impactful in the U.S. sample. The following hypothesis summarizes our predictions for the United States.

> **Hypothesis 5.** In the United States, supportive, contingent reward, contingent punishment, participative, and charismatic leadership will positively affect mediators and/or outcome measures. Directive leadership will have no significant effects. . . .

## METHOD

Field studies were conducted in each of the five countries to test the hypotheses. The research samples consisted of a total of 1,598 managers and professionals of large multinational or national companies located in the United States, Mexico, and the Asian-Pacific Basin. The United States, Mexican, and Taiwanese samples consisted entirely of managers and professionals working in electronics manufacturing operations. Large manufacturing organizations were studied because they represent the primary avenue for economic growth for the Asian-Pacific countries, and they provide intense market competition for U.S. manufacturers. Focusing on managers and professionals allowed us to provide some control for job duties and responsibilities across the cultures. The organizations were matched closely in terms of technological sophistication, organizational goals, and structure. The majority of the Japanese and South Korean samples were also engaged in complex manufacturing operations. All respondents were highly skilled and educated, with the majority of each sample having college degrees. . . .

## MEASURES

### Predictors—Leadership Behaviors

The following six patterns of leadership behavior were measured:

1. Directive—Clarifying performance expectations and assigning tasks. This was a modified version of the scale developed by Schriesheim (1978) for use in path-goal theory testing.

2. Supportive—Indicating a concern for the welfare of subordinates; showing warmth, respect, and trust. This scale was also developed by Schriesheim (1978).

3. Contingent reward—Developed by Podsakoff and Skov (1980), this scale assesses the degree to which leaders provide praise, positive feedback, and recognition contingent on high performance.

4. Contingent punishment—Voicing displeasure and providing negative feedback contingent on poor performance. This scale was also developed by Podsakoff and Skov (1980).

5. Charisma—Inspiring and developing confidence among followers, setting challenging goals, and encouraging high expectations. This scale was modified from scales developed by House (personal communication, 1987) and Yukl (1982) to encompass many of the dimensions in current models of charismatic leadership.

6. Participation—Consulting with, asking for suggestions, and obtaining information from subordinates for important decisions. This scale was also modified from scales developed by Yukl and House and reflects common interpretations of participative leadership in the management literature. . . .

### Results in Japan

Two of the four predictions of significant positive effects were supported—*supportive leadership* increased satisfaction with supervision and satisfaction with work; *contingent reward behavior* increased satisfaction with supervision and organizational commitment. Also as predicted, *contingent punishment* had a negative impact on satisfaction with supervision. *Participative and direct leadership* were not impactful in the Japanese sample (counter to our predictions). Also counter to our prediction, *charismatic leadership* did significantly reduce subordinates' role ambiguity. Note that supportive leadership and contingent reward behaviors both had multiple significant paths and strong effect sizes. . . .

### Results in South Korea

*Hypothesis 2 for South Korea was supported for three of four predictions of significant effects. Contingent reward behavior* improved satisfaction with work; *supportive leadership* increased satisfaction with supervision and reduced role ambiguity. *Charismatic leadership* improved satisfaction with supervision and organizational commitment. Also as predicted, *contingent punishment* had no effects. Counter to our predictions, *participative leadership* slightly improved satisfaction with work and *directive leadership* had no effects. Charismatic and supportive leadership both had multiple significant paths and strong effect sizes.

### Results in Taiwan

All six leader behaviors had significant effects in Taiwan, although the three leader behaviors predicted to be significant in Hypothesis 3 were among the strongest impacts. *Leader directiveness* increased satisfaction with supervision and organizational commitment and decreased role ambiguity; *contingent reward behavior* increased satisfaction with work and supervision; and *supportive leadership* increased satisfaction with supervision and organizational commitment. Although *contingent punishment* had a negative impact on satisfaction with supervision (as predicted), it had a positive effect on organizational commitment (not as predicted). Contrary to expectations, *charismatic leadership* increased satisfaction with work and supervision and decreased role ambiguity. The effect of *participative leadership* was most interesting as it had a significant *negative* impact on organizational commitment. Perhaps also noteworthy, Taiwan was the only country where all leader behaviors were impactful.

### Results in Mexico

Results in Mexico supported predictions for the leader behaviors expected to have a positive effect. *Directive leadership* increased organizational commitment and decreased role ambiguity; *contingent reward behavior* increased organizational commitment; *supportive leadership* increased satisfaction with supervision, organizational commitment, and decreased role ambiguity. *Charismatic leadership* increased satisfaction with supervision. Directive and supportive leadership had strong impacts as did charismatic leadership

and contingent reward. The effect of *participative leadership* was nonsignificant as predicted. *Contingent punishment* yielded a significant negative effect (on satisfaction with supervision) when we predicted no effect. Hypothesis 4 was thus supported for 5 of the 6 leader behaviors.

### Results in the United States

The predictions for hypothesis 5 were supported for five of the six leader behaviors, providing strong support for this hypothesis in the United States. *Contingent reward behavior* increased organizational commitment and satisfaction with work and supervision; *contingent punishment behavior* decreased role ambiguity; *supportive leadership* increased satisfaction with supervision and decreased role ambiguity; and *charismatic leadership* increased satisfaction with supervision. As expected, *directive leadership* had no impact. *Participative leadership* also had no impact, contrary to predictions. Supportive, charismatic, contingent reward, and leaders' contingent punishment all had strong effects. Note that contingent punishment significantly decreased subordinates' role ambiguity without the negative effects found in several other countries. . . .

## DISCUSSION

### LEADERSHIP ACROSS CULTURES

The results of this study in two Western and three Asian cultures support Bass's (1990) contention regarding the validity of both the "universal" and the "culture-specific" perspectives in the study of leadership across cultures. *Of six leader behaviors derived from popular contingency-based leadership theories, three behaviors (leader supportiveness, contingent reward, and charismatic) showed universally positive impacts in all five cultures; and three leader behaviors (participativeness, directiveness, and contingent punishment) had positive impacts in only two cultures.* The impact of contingent punishment was most unique among leader behaviors as it had a completely desirable effect only in the United States, but equivocal or undesirable effects in other countries. Overall, results from the independent and simultaneous tests supported our original "syncretic leadership model" which guided this study of individuals in different cultures.

The universality of leader supportiveness and contingent reward behavior are not surprising when one considers their specific content. Supportive leaders show concern for followers and are considerate and available to listen to followers' problems. Contingent rewarding leaders show appreciation for followers' good performance and provide recognition and compliments. The correlation between these two behaviors was .65 or above in all five cultures (leaders who are concerned and considerate are also often seen as appreciative and complimentary), and there was overlap between these two behavior patterns in the factor analyses for the three Asian cultures. A leader who demonstrates supportive kindness and concern for followers is clearly valued and impactful in all the cultures (Bennett, 1977; Misumi & Peterson, 1985A; Yukl, 1994). Reward systems in collectivist cultures are usually described as group-oriented (Hofstede, 1980; Bond & Hwang, 1986), but apparently performance contingent social rewards by the leader are individualized even in collectivist cultures with very positive results. These findings support the results by Fahr, Podsakoff, and Cheng (1987) that leader contingent reward behavior is a highly culture-free leadership pattern.

The universality of charismatic leadership was not expected. This leader behavior is emotional in nature and had its most consistent effects on subordinate satisfaction measures across cultures. It appears that charismatic leadership results in positive subordinate attitudes among midlevel managers and professionals in all the cultures studied. We should note that charismatic leadership *did not* affect follower performance in the three countries where performance data was available.

The impacts of leaders' directive, participative, and contingent punishment behaviors were culture-specific. Directive leadership had no impact in the United States, Japan, and South Korea. We expected the extremely high individualism and low/medium power distance of the U.S. culture, combined with the participative climate common among highly educated professionals and managers in U.S. organizations, to at least partially *neutralize* the effects of leaders' directiveness. This apparently occurred, making directiveness the only leader behavior that was not impactful in the U.S. sample. Although the lack of impact of leader directiveness in Japan is not consistent with findings by Misumi and Peterson (1985b), it might be explained by tendencies of Japanese managers to outline general objectives and to allow subordinates to use their own approaches to achieve those objectives. We have no explanation for the lack of impact of directiveness in South Korea. For Taiwan, the results showing a

high impact of directive leadership . . . are mirrored when examining the high *level* of directive leadership displayed. This leader behavior had the highest level of all leader behaviors (i.e., mean scale score) in Taiwan, and it was considerably higher than in any other country in our sample. These findings are consistent with the review of leadership studies in Taiwan by Bond and Hwang (1986). As expected, leader directiveness was a very important leader behavior in the status conscious and high power distance culture of Mexico.

Participative leadership had positive effects in the United States and South Korea. Our participation scale included items such as asking followers for suggestions, giving consideration to followers' inputs, and modifying proposals in light of follower objections. These items resulted in predictable positive responses in the United States. In fact, participative leadership in the U.S. sample was the strongest predictor of follower performance in the entire study. In addition, the *level* of participation displayed by supervisors in the United States was the highest of all samples. Although not predicted, a positive impact of participation on subordinate satisfaction was found in South Korea. This may be explained by the increasing tendency of South Korean managers to make decisions with the consultation of subordinates (Chen, 1995). This process involves informal consensus formation (*sajeonhyupui*) and is similar to *nemawashi* in Japan. We should note, however, that openly sharing information and expressing opinions in a work environment is difficult for many South Koreans.

Participation was also predicted to have no positive impacts in Taiwan and Mexico due to their military histories emphasizing strong central leadership and their low individualism (high collectivism) which discourages individual desires to impact organizational processes. These predictions were supported. Taiwanese managers tend to carefully control information, use authoritarian decision styles, and maintain power distances with their subordinates. In Mexico, the lack of a firm structure for participation, high collectivism, and lack of trust make participative leadership ineffective.

We did predict participation to be impactful in Japan which is known for high worker involvement (*nemawashi*) and group decision making (*ringi seido*) (Chen, 1995; Ronen, 1986). In hindsight, perhaps we should have expected that, because the type of worker involvement practiced in Japan is different from the type of participative leadership practiced in the United States, results would also differ. In our discussions with Japanese managers, they pointed out that in Japan managers turn problems over to their groups and let the group solve them. The leader will ask to hear the group's solution before implementation, but the problem belongs to the group. The leader facilitates the group's efforts. In the United States, problems are typically the responsibility of a manager who may solicit input and suggestions from followers to help him/her solve it. In the United States, the group's input may be used at the discretion of the leader; in Japan the leader's input may be used at the discretion of the group. We believe these widely different cultural perspectives on worker involvement are responsible for the nonsignificant finding for our participation measure in Japan. Not only did our measure of leader participation have no impact on worker attitudes or perceptions in Japan, the *level* of participative leader behaviors shown by Japanese managers was also low. We expect that this topic of participation/worker involvement will be a particularly interesting area for cross-cultural management research in the future. The Vroom-Yetton-Jago model of participative decision making (Vroom & Jago, 1988) may be a useful theoretic approach to guide an exploration of different styles of participative leadership in Western and Asian cultures.

The significant positive impact of leaders' contingent punishment behavior was predicted in the United States, where giving feedback to individual followers (positive and negative) is emphasized in management training. The negative impact of this leader behavior on subordinate satisfaction in Mexico and Japan gives empirical support to Riding's (1985) opinion that Mexicans are more Asian than Western in philosophy—Mexico's high collectivism is comparable to that of many Asian cultures (Hofstede, 1980). The negative effect of contingent punishment also conforms to what we expected in Japan. In Japanese organizations, individualized negative feedback is usually withheld or done with much subtlety to maintain group harmony and face saving. Japanese managers describe "by the window people" who are slowly shunted toward increasingly menial tasks if they continue to perform poorly. The Japanese stood out in their low *level* of contingent punishment behavior—the lowest of all samples and the lowest of all leader behaviors in Japan. . . .

## CROSS-CULTURAL ISSUES FOR THEORY BUILDING

In comparing the impacts of leadership behaviors in Asian versus Western culture clusters, one is struck by the fact that the United States is as different from Mexico as it is from the Asian cultures. *While there clearly are universal leader behavior patterns found in this study, the United States is unique in two respects.* It is the *only* culture where participative leadership had a positive effect on subordinate performance, and it is the *only* culture where leaders' contingent punishment behavior had a uniformly positive effect on subordinates. The following factors likely contributed toward the culturally unique results regarding leadership behaviors in the United States: uniquely high individualism (Dorfman & Howell, 1988; Hofstede, 1991), egalitarian management climate, changing attitudes towards formal authority, movements toward increased professionalism, team processes, and employee empowerment (Yukl, 1994). These national and cultural characteristics may play important roles in cross-cultural models of leadership.

A particularly important issue in contemporary cross-cultural research is construct equivalence (Singh, 1995). As usually conceived, construct equivalence consists of three aspects: functional, conceptual, and measurement equivalence. Our research speaks to each of these aspects. Three of our leader behaviors demonstrated functional equivalence by consistently predicting follower attitudes and perceptions in all five countries. The multisample confirmatory factor analysis showing similar factor structures and loadings across all cultures provides some evidence both to conceptual and measurement equivalence. Thus, this study has produced one piece of evidence supporting the construct equivalence of these six leadership behaviors across cultures. Clearly, additional studies are needed to confirm the value of these and other leadership behaviors in cross-cultural contexts.

Returning to our initial discussion of the controversy between the cultural-specific versus cultural-universal aspects of leadership, it might be useful to heed the following recent suggestion by Bond and Smith (1996): "The search for universals and an emphasis upon indigenous culture-specifics are often cast as contradictory enterprises that exemplify contrasting etic and emic approaches. Yet these concepts are no more separable than nature and nurture" (p. 226). Our results indicate that the similarities and differences between cultures can be meaningfully integrated within contemporary theoretical frameworks and simultaneously make sense for the specific cultures under study. Perhaps paradoxically, it is through hybrid research designs (Earley & Singh, 1995) such as this project that both cross-cultural generalities and cultural differences can be understood. . . .

## References

Adler, N. J. (1991). *International dimensions of organizational behavior,* 2nd ed. Boston: PWS-KENT.

Al-Gattan, A. R. A. (1985). Test of the path-goal theory of leadership in the multi-national domain. *Group and Organization Studies, 10*(4), 429–445.

Alston, J. P. (1989). *Wa, Guanxi* and *Inhwa:* Managerial principles in Japan, China, and Korea. *Business Horizons, March–April,* 26–31.

Ayman, R. (1993). Leadership perception: The role of gender and culture. In M. M. Chemers & R. Ayman (Eds.), *Leadership theory and research* (pp. 137–166). San Diego: Academic Press.

Ayman, R., & Chemers, M. M. (1983). Relationship of supervisory behavior ratings to work group effectiveness and subordinate satisfaction among Iranian managers. *Journal of Applied Psychology, 68*(2), 338–341.

Bass, B. M. (1985). *Leadership and performance beyond expectations.* New York: Free Press.

Bass, B. M. (1990). *Bass and Stogdill's handbook of leadership: Theory, research and managerial applications,* 3rd ed. New York: Free Press.

Bass, B. M., & Avolio, B. J. (1993). Transformational leadership: A response to critiques. In M. M. Chemers & R. Ayman (Eds.), *Leadership theory and research* (pp. 49–80). San Diego: Academic Press.

Bass, B. M., Burger, P. C., Doktor, R., & Barrett, G. V. (1979). *Assessment of managers: An international comparison.* New York: Free Press.

Bass, B. M., & Yokochi, N. (1991). Charisma among senior executives and the special case of Japanese CEOs. *Consulting Psychology Bulletin, 1 (Winter/Spring),* 31–38.

Behling, O., & McFillan, J. (1993). A syncretical model of charismatic leadership. Paper presented at the Pan-Pacific Conference, Beijing.

Bennett, M. (1977). Testing management theories cross-culturally. *Journal of Applied Psychology, 62,* 578–581.

Bentler, P. M., & Bonnett, D. G. (1980). Significance tests and goodness of fit in the analysis of covariance structures. *Psychological Bulletin, 88,* 588–606.

Berry, J. W. (1980). Social and cultural change. *Handbook of Cross-Cultural Psychology, 5,* 211–279.

Bond, M., & Hwang, K. (1986). The social psychology of Chinese people. In M. H. Bond (Ed.), *The psychology of the Chinese people* (pp. 213–237). Hong Kong: Oxford University Press.

Bond, M. H., & Smith, P. B. (1996). Cross-cultural social and organizational psychology. *Annual Review of Psychology, 47,* 205–235.

Boyacigiller, N., & Adler, N. (1991). A parochial dinosaur: Organizational science in a global context. *Academy of Management Review, 16,* 262–290.

Chen, M. (1995). *Asian management systems: Chinese, Japanese, and Korean styles of business.* London: Routledge.

Dorfman, P. W. (1996). International and cross-cultural leadership research. In B. J. Punnett & O. Shenkar (Eds.), *Handbook for international management research* (pp. 267–349). Oxford, UK: Blackwell.

Dorfman, P. W., & Howell, J. P. (1988). Dimensions of national culture and effective leadership patterns: Hofstede revisited. In E. G. McGoun (Ed.), *Advances in International Comparative Management* (vol. 3, pp. 127–149). Greenwich, CT: JAI Press.

Dorfman, P. W., & Howell, J. P. (1994). *The construct validity of Hofstede's culture scales: Replication and extension to individualized measures.* [Research colloquium]. New Mexico State University.

Dorfman, P. W., & Ronen, S. (1991). The universality of leadership theories: Challenges and paradoxes. Paper presented at the National Academy of Management annual meeting, Miami, FL.

Earley, P. C., & Mosakowski, E. (1996). Experimental international management research. In B. J. Punnett & Shenkar (Eds.), *Handbook for international management research* (pp. 83–114). Oxford, UK: Blackwell.

Earley, P. C., & Singh, H. (1995). International and intercultural management research: What's next? *Academy of Management Journal, 38,* 327–340.

Fahr, J. L., Podsakoff, P. M., & Cheng, B. S. (1987). Culture-free leadership effectiveness versus moderators of leadership behaviors: An extension and test of Kerr and Jermier's "substitutes for leadership" model in Taiwan. *Journal of International Business Studies, 18,* 43–60.

Farmer, R., & Richman, B. M. (1965). *Comparative management and economic progress.* Homewood, IL: Irwin.

Fiedler, F. E., & Garcia, J. E. (1987). *New approaches to effective leadership: Cognitive resources and organizational performance.* New York: Wiley.

Fiedler, F. E., & House, R. J. (1988). Leadership: A report of progress. In C. L. Cooper (Ed.), *International review of industrial and organizational psychology.* Greenwich, CT: JAI Press.

Ganster, D. C., Hennessey, H. W., & Luthans, F. (1983). Social desirability response effects: Three alternative methods. *Academy of Management Journal, 36,* 321–331.

Gioia, D. A., & Sims, H. P. (1985). On avoiding the influence of implicit leadership theories in leader behavior descriptions. *Educational and Psychological Measurement, 45,* 217–232.

Gomez-Mejia, L. R., & Balkin, D. B. (1992). Determinants of faculty pay: An agency theory perspective. *Academy of Management Journal, 35*(5), 921–955.

Hayashi, S. (1988). *Culture and management in Japan.* University of Tokyo Press.

Hofstede, G. (1980). *Culture's consequences: International differences in work-related values.* Beverly Hills, CA: Sage.

Hofstede, G. (1991). Culture and organizations: *The software of the mind.* New York: McGraw-Hill.

Hofstede, G. (1993). Cultural constraints in management theories. *Academy of Management Executive, 7*(1), 81–94.

House, R. J. (1971). A path-goal theory of leader effectiveness. *Administrative Science Quarterly, 16,* 321–338.

House, R. J. (1991). Charismatic leadership across cultures. Paper presented at the Academy of Management Annual Meeting, Miami, FL.

House, R. J., Hanges, P., Agar, M., & Ruiz-Quintanilla, A. (1994). Conference on Global Leadership and Organizational Behavior (GLOBE). Calgary, Canada.

Hsu, F. L. K. (1982). *American and Chinese: Passage to differences.* Honolulu: University of Hawaii Press.

Iaffaldono, J. T., & Muchinsky, P. M. (1985). Job satisfaction and job performance: A meta-analysis. *Psychological Bulletin, 97*(2), 251–273.

Indvik, J. (1986). Path-goal theory of leadership: A meta-analysis. In Proceedings of the Academy of Management Annual Meeting (pp. 189–192), Chicago: AMA.

Indvik, J. (1988). A more complete testing of path-goal theory. Paper presented at the Academy of Management Annual Meeting, Anaheim, CA.

Jackofsky, E. F., Slocum, J. W., Jr., & McQuaid, S. J. (1988). Cultural values and the CEO: Alluring companions? *Academy of Management Executive, 2*(1), 39–49.

James, L. R., Mulaik, S. A., & Brett, J. M. (1982). *Causal analysis: Assumptions, models and data.* Beverly Hills, CA: Sage.

Janssens, M., Brett, J. M., & Smith, F. (1995). Confirmatory cross-cultural research: Testing the viability of a corporation-wide safety policy. *Academy of Management Journal, 2,* 364–382.

Jöreskog, K. G., & Sorbom, D. (1989). *LISREL VII: Analysis of linear structural relationships by the method of maximum likelihood.* Mooresville, IN: Scientific Software.

Jöreskog, K. G., & Sorbom, D. (1993). *LISREL 8 user's reference guide.* Chicago, IL: Scientific Software International.

Kakar, S. (1971). Authority patterns and subordinate behavior in Indian organizations. *Administrative Science Quarterly, 16,* 298–307.

Kerr, S., & Jermier, J. (1978). Substitutes for leadership: Their meaning and measurement. *Organizational Behavior and Human Performance, 22,* 374–403.

Lord, R., & Maher, K. J. (1991). *Leadership and information processing: Linking perceptions and performance.* Boston: Unwin-Everyman.

Marrow, A. J. (1964). Risks and uncertainties in action research. *Journal of Social Issues, 20,* 5–20.

McClelland, D., & Boyatzis, R. E. (1982). Leadership motive pattern and long term success in management. *Journal of Applied Psychology, 67*(6), 737–743.

Medsker, G. J., Williams, L. J., & Holohan, P. J. (1994). A review of current practices for evaluating causal models in organizational behavior and human resources management research. *Journal of Management, 20,* 439–464.

Misumi, J., & Peterson, M. F. (1985a). *The behavioral science of leadership: An interdisciplinary Japanese research program.* Ann Arbor, MI: University of Michigan Press.

Misumi, J., & Peterson, M. F. (1985b). The performance-maintenance theory of leadership: Review of a Japanese research program. *Administrative Science Quarterly, 30,* 198–223.

Morgan, J. C., & Morgan, J. J. (1991). *Cracking the Japanese market: Strategies for success in the new global market.* New York: The Free Press.

Mulaik, S. A., James, L. R., Van Alstine, J., Bennett, N., Lind, S., & Stillwell, C. D. (1989). An evaluation of goodness-of-fit indices for structural equation models. *Psychological Bulletin, 105,* 430–445.

Negandhi, A. R., & Prasad, S. B. (1971). *Comparative management.* New York: Appleton-Century-Croft.

Ostroff, C. (1992). The relationship between satisfaction, attitudes, and performance: An organizational level analysis. *Journal of Applied Psychology, 77,* 963–974.

Peng, T. K., Peterson, M. F., & Shyi, Y. P. (1991). Quantitative methods in cross-national organizational research: Trends and equivalence issues. *Journal of Organizational Behavior, 12,* 87–108.

Podsakoff, P. M., & Skov, R. (1980). Leader reward and punishment behavior scales. Unpublished research, Indiana University: Bloomington, IN.

Podsakoff, P. M., Tudor, W. D., & Schuler, R. S. (1983). Leader expertise as a moderator of the effects of instrumental and supportive leader behavior. *Journal of Management, 9*(2), 173–185.

Podsakoff, P. M., Niehoff, B. P., MacKenzie, S. B., & Williams, M. L. (1992). Do substitutes for leadership really substitute for leadership? An empirical examination of Kerr and Jermier's situational leadership model. *Organizational Behavior and Human Decision Processes, 54,* 1–44.

Porter, L. W., & Smith, F. J. (1970). The etiology of organizational commitment: A progress report. Unpublished manuscript, University of California, Irvine.

Randall, D. M., Huo, Y. P., & Pawelk, P. (1993). Social desirability bias in cross-cultural ethics research. *International Journal of Organizational Analysis, 1* (April), 185–202.

Redding, S. G. (1990). *The spirit of Chinese Capitalism.* New York: deGruyter.

Redding, S. G., & Casey, T. W. (1976). Managerial beliefs among Asian managers. In R. L. Taylor, M. J. O'Connell, R. A. Zawacki, & D. D. Warwick (Eds.), *Proceedings of the Academy of Management 36th Annual Meeting* (pp. 351–356). Kansas City: Academy of Management.

Redding, S. G., & Wong, G. Y. (1986). The psychology of Chinese organizational behavior. In M. H. Bond (Ed.), *The psychology of the Chinese people* (pp. 267–295). Hong Kong: Oxford University Press.

Riding, A. (1985). *Distant neighbors: A portrait of the Mexicans.* New York: Random House.

Riordan, C. M., & Vandenberg, R. J. (1994). A central question in cross-cultural research: Do employees of different cultures interpret work-related measures in an equivalent manner? *Journal of Management, 20*(3), 643–671.

Rizzo, J. R., House, R. J., & Lirtzman, S. I. (1970). Role conflict and ambiguity in complex organizations. *Administrative Science Quarterly, 15,* 150–163.

Ronen, S. (1986). *Comparative and international management.* New York: Wiley.

Ronen, S., & Shenkar, O. (1985). Clustering countries on attitudinal dimensions: A review and synthesis. *Academy of Management Review, 10,* 435–454.

Schaubroeck, J., Cotton, J. L., & Jennings, K. R. (1989). Antecedents and consequences of role stress: A covariance structure analysis. *Journal of Organizational Behavior, 10,* 35–58.

Schriesheim, C. A. (1978). *Development, validation and application of the new leader behavior and expectancy research instruments.* Unpublished doctoral dissertation, Ohio State University, Columbus, OH.

Schumacher, R. E., & Lomax, R. G. (1996). *A beginner's guide to structural equation modeling.* Mahwah, NJ: Lawrence Erlbaum.

Singh, J. (1995). Measurement issues in cross-national research. *Journal of International Business Studies,* 3rd quarter, 597–619.

Sinha, J. B. P. (1980). *The nurturant task leader.* New Delhi: Concept.

Smith, P. C., Kendall, L. M., & Hulin, C. L. (1969). *The measurement of satisfaction in work and retirement.* Chicago: Rand-McNally.

Smith, P. B., & Peterson, M. F. (1988). *Leadership, organizations and culture: An event management model.* Beverly Hills, CA: Sage.

Smith, P. B., Peterson, M. F., Bond, M., & Misumi, J. (1992). Leader style and leader behavior in individualist and collectivist cultures. In S. Iwawaki, Y. Kashima, & K. Leung (Eds.), *Innovations in cross-cultural psychology: Selected papers from the tenth international conference of the International Association for Cross-Cultural Psychology* (pp. 76–85). Amsterdam: Swets Zeitlinger.

Smith, P. B., Peterson, M. F., Misumi, J., & Tayeb, M. (1989). Testing leadership theory cross culturally. *Recent advances in social psychology: An international perspective* (pp. 383–391). Amsterdam: North-Holland.

Steers, R. M., Shin, Y. K., & Ungson, G. R. (1989). *The Chaebol: Korea's new industrial might.* New York: Harper.

Thurstone, L. L. (1947). *Multiple factor analysis.* Chicago: University of Chicago Press.

Triandis, H. C. (1993a). Cross-cultural industrial and organizational psychology. In M. Dunnette & L. Hough (Eds.), *Handbook of Industrial and Organizational Psychology, 4,* 103–172. Palo Alto, CA: Consulting Psychologists Press.

Triandis, H. C. (1993b). The contingency model in cross-cultural perspective. In M. Chemers & R. Ayman (Eds.), *Leadership theory and research: Perspectives and directions* (pp. 167–188). San Diego: Academic Press.

Vroom, V., & Jago, A. G. (1988). *The New leadership: Managing participation in organizations.* Englewood Cliffs, NJ: Prentice-Hall.

Wakabayashi, M., & Graen, G. (1984). The Japanese career progress study: A seven year follow-up. *Journal of Applied Psychology, 69,* 603–614.

Whitehall, A. M., & S. Takezawa (1968). *The other worker.* Honolulu: East-West Center Press.

Williams, L., & Hazer, J. T. (1986). Antecedents and consequences of satisfaction and commitment in turnover models: A reanalysis using latent variable structure equation methods. *Journal of Applied Psychology, 71,* 219–231.

Yukl, G. (1982). Managerial behavior survey. Questionnaire for assessing patterns of managers' leadership behavior.

Yukl, G. (1994). *Leadership in organizations,* 3rd ed. Englewood Cliffs, NJ: Prentice-Hall.

Yukl, G., & Van Fleet, D. D. (1992). Theory and research on leadership in organizations. In M. Dunnette & L. M. Hough (Eds.), *Handbook of industrial and organizational psychology,* 2nd ed. (pp. 147–197). Palo Alto, CA: Consulting Psychologists Press.

# Chapter Ten

# Followers and the Leadership Process

In the last few chapters several situational factors that might play a role in determining the effectiveness of a particular behavior were considered. For example, followers might find their role clouded by ambiguity, they may experience frustration and the lack of challenge in their work, and some individuals might be more or less capable of exercising self-direction and self-control (possibly as a function of task-based knowledge/expertise and/or personal motivation).

This chapter addresses the role of the follower in the leadership process. In general, there are two significant questions that have been posed by students of leadership: (1) To what extent do "attributes" of the follower serve to moderate the leader behavior-outcome (e.g., satisfaction, performance) relationship? and (2) How does the follower affect/influence the leader and the nature of the leader–follower relationship? The readings in this chapter will provide insight into this complex part of the leadership process.

As we have seen thus far, students of leadership have sought to understand leadership and the leadership process by focusing primarily on the leader and on how his or her behaviors influence, for example, follower attitudes, motivation, behavior, and group effectiveness. Charles N. Greene (1975) calls attention to the fact that the causal arrow between leader behavior and followers may run in the opposite direction, suggesting that *follower performance may shape the amount of consideration and initiating structure behavior exhibited by the leader.* Even if this is true, this observation does not negate the impact that leader behavior (e.g., initiating structure and consideration) has upon subordinate attitudes and performance, but it highlights the notion that *the relationship between leader and follower is a reciprocal relationship.* The idea of a reciprocal relationship (i.e., a two-way influence process) reinforces Murphy's (1941) suggestion that leadership is an interactive and dynamic process, whereby the leader influences the follower, the follower influences the leader, and both are influenced by the context surrounding this leader–follower relationship.

Fillmore H. Sanford (1952) observes that attributes of the follower serve to influence the leadership process. He calls our attention to the personality traits that the followers carry into the leadership context, suggesting that the followers' personalities shape their reactions to the leader's behaviors.

According to Sanford, leadership can be seen as a relationship between a leader and follower. Therefore, it is important to understand the role of the follower in this relationship if one hopes to understand the total process. Sanford suggests that *the follower's own unique personality* (e.g., needs, abilities, and attitudes) *defines his or her "readiness for leadership."* When placed into a leadership situation, these factors combine to determine the follower's receptivity to a particular leader and his or her personality and leadership style. Those followers with an authoritarian personality tend, for example, to accept leaders who exhibit a strong and directive style of leadership, while those with more of an equalitarian personality tend to accept leaders who exhibit a democratic style of leadership.

Gary Yukl (1971)[1] explores the role of the follower's personality in the leadership equation as he presents a behavioral theory of leadership. As a part of this process, Yukl identifies the conditions under which three different dimensions of leader behavior (i.e., initiating structure, consideration, and decision centralization) are associated with members' satisfaction with the leader and their level of productivity.

Yukl carefully presents these three leader behaviors as separate and distinct dimensions and suggests that variation in one dimension does not imply variation in the next. His observation parallels earlier contentions that a production and people emphasis, or initiating structure and consideration behaviors, are not opposite ends of the same continuum. Instead these behaviors are independent of one another, and it is therefore possible for a leader to display either one or both behaviors.

In Yukl's behavioral theory of leadership, consideration and initiating structure stem from the leadership work conducted at The Ohio State University. *Consideration* refers to the degree to which a leader expresses a positive, indifferent, or negative attitude toward a subordinate. A leader high in consideration is friendly, supportive, and considerate. *Initiating structure* is a task-oriented behavior reflecting the leader's concern for productivity (e.g., goal-orientation), making sure that task decisions are made, and exhibiting behaviors that are directed toward making sure that directives are carried out. *Decision centralization* builds upon Lewin, Lippitt, and White's work with democratic, autocratic, and laissez-faire leaders. Specifically, decision centralization refers to the manner in which decisions are made, highlighting the amount of influence exercised by the leader and followers. Thus, decision centralization can range from high subordinate influence to complete leader influence over decisions affecting the group.

The degree to which a particular leader behavior produces follower satisfaction is shaped by the follower's personal preferences for that behavior (see Figure 10.1). This statement suggests that not all followers will necessarily like or dislike any particular leader behavior (e.g., initiating structure, decision centralization). Instead, the relationship between leader behavior and follower satisfaction with the leader will be influenced (moderated) by the follower's preferences. Subordinate preferences tend to be shaped by their own personalities, the situation in which they find themselves, and what they believe their leader should be doing at a particular point in time.

Yukl's work, along with that of Vroom (1964),[2] suggests that leader behavior is unlikely to have a direct impact upon follower performance. Instead, if a leader's behavior is going to have an impact upon performance, it must lead to an increase in one or more of the following intermediate (mediating) conditions: the skills/abilities that the follower brings to task performance; follower task motivation (i.e., the effort put forth toward task performance); the accuracy of the perceptions that the followers have in terms of their role requirements; and/or by providing the group with needed information, resources, and cooperation from individuals/groups outside of the work group (see Figure 10.2).

---

[1] G. Yukl, "Toward a Behavioral Theory of Leadership," *Organizational Behavior and Human Performance* 6 (1971), pp. 414–440; and an expanded version in *Leadership in Organizations* (Prentice-Hall, 1994).
[2] V. H. Vroom, *Work and Motivation* (New York: John Wiley & Sons, 1964).

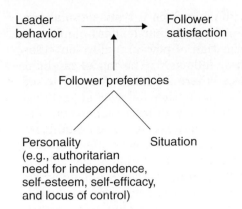

**FIGURE 10.1**
**The Leader Behavior–Follower Satisfaction Relationship**

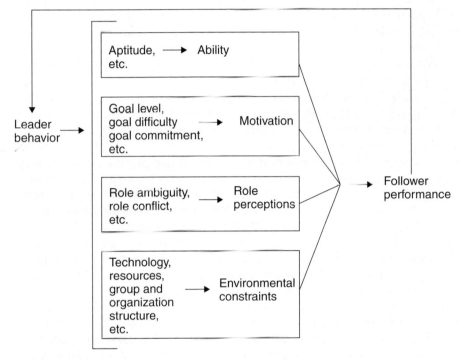

**FIGURE 10.2**
**The Leader Behavior–Follower Performance Relationship\***

\*This model depicts many of the arguments made by Wofford and Spinivaser (1983) in their leader-environment-follower theory of leadership. J. C. Wofford and T. N. Spinivaser, "Experimental Tests of the Leader-Environment-Follower Interaction Theory of Leadership," *Organizational Behavior and Human Performance* 32 (1983), pp. 35–54.

The concepts of social exchange (Blau, 1964)[3] and norms of reciprocity (Gouldner, 1960)[4] provide us with insight into the motivational forces encouraging followers to respond by "giving something back" when their leaders initiate transactional relationships. One of these leader–follower exchange relationships has been highlighted in leader–member exchange (LMX) theory. As noted in the introduction to Chapter 2, LMX theory, as presented by George Graen and his colleagues (cf., Dansereau, Graen, & Haga, 1975;[5] Graen & Cashman, 1975),[6]

[3] P. Blau, *Exchange and Power in Social Life* (New York: Wiley, 1964.)
[4] A. W. Gouldner, "The Norm of Reciprocity," *American Sociological Review* 25 (1960), pp. 165–167.
[5] F. Dansereau, G. Graen, and W. J. Haga, "A Vertical Dyad Linkage Approach to Leadership within Formal Organizations," *Organizational Behavior and Human Performance* 13 (1975), pp. 46–78.
[6] G. B. Graen and J. Cashman, "A Role-making Model of Leadership in Formal Organizations: A Developmental Approach." In J. G. Hunt and L. L. Larson (eds.), *Leadership Frontiers* (Kent, OH: Kent State University Press, 1975) pp. 143–165.

examines the follower–leader working relationship from a transactional perspective. Transactional models of leadership suggest that leaders employ resources that they have access to (i.e., their position of power) to develop different types of exchange relationships with their followers. The model might be seen as a quid pro quo approach to leadership, where a leader offers "x" to one follower in exchange for "z," while offering "w" to another follower in exchange for "y." Thus, different relationships are developed with different followers.

According to LMX, some of these relationships may become "high quality relationships" characterized by respect and mutual trust, whereas other relationships may be of low quality and based strictly upon a calculation of the value of that which is being exchanged. When a high level (quality) leader–member exchange relationship exists, followers perceive themselves as having a good working relationship with their leader. High leader–member exchange relationships have been associated with follower satisfaction and productivity (Graen, Novak, & Sommerkamp, 1982),[7] maintenance of group membership (Ferris, 1985),[8] and citizenship and in-role behavior (Setton, Bennett, & Liden, 1996).[9]

The LMX model suggests that we should not think strictly in terms of what the leader does, as though there is a single behavior or relationship that develops with his/her group. In fact, there may be many different behaviors engaged in by a leader with different behaviors directed toward different followers. The model also suggests to us that we need to look at the follower's personality and perceptions, as they will play an important role in explaining the leader–follower working relationship.

In the final reading, Edwin P. Hollander provides a perspective on leadership that is based upon the follower's role in reacting to leader qualities. He suggests that the leader–follower relationship is strongly affected by the "perceptions, misperceptions, and self-oriented biases" brought to the relationship by both the leader and the follower.

In summary, the literature focused on followers within the leadership context generates several observations that enhance our understanding of this complex mosaic called the leadership process (see Figure 10.3). First, we note that leaders influence followers and followers exercise an influence over the behavior of leaders. Second, this reciprocal relationship is dynamic in nature. Third, followers bring to the leadership situation their personality—skills/abilities, motives (e.g., needs, wants, preferences, expectations), biases, and personal histories. These follower attributes in part determine the effectiveness of a leader's influence attempts (i.e., characteristics of the follower will mediate the leader-outcome relationship).

---

[7] G. B. Graen, M. Novak, and P. Sommerkamp, "The Effects of Leader–Member Exchange and Job Design on Productivity and Job Satisfaction: Testing a Dual Attachment Model," *Organizational Behavior and Human Performance* 30 (1982), pp. 109–131.

[8] G. R. Ferris, "Role of Leadership in the Employee Withdrawal Process: A Constructive Replication," *Journal of Applied Psychology* 70 (1985), pp. 777–781.

[9] R. P. Setton, N. Bennett, and R. C. Liden, "Social Exchange in Organizations: Perceived Organizational Support, Leader–Member Exchange, and Employee Reciprocity," *Journal of Applied Psychology* 81 (1996), pp. 219–227.

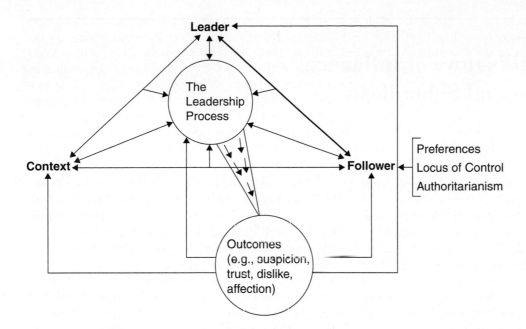

**FIGURE 10.3**
**The Leadership**
**Process: Followers**

## Reading 28

# The Reciprocal Nature of Influence between Leader and Subordinate

**Charles N. Greene**
Indiana University

Researchers and practitioners would agree that leader behavior is an important variable related to organizational effectiveness. Much of the empirical evidence on organizational leadership has come from the numerous field studies investigating the relationships between leadership styles (e.g., initiating structure and consideration) and subordinate performance and satisfaction (see Fleishman, 1973b). The majority of these studies have employed static correlational techniques or have contrasted the leader behavior of high- and low-productivity groups, which do not allow inferences of the direction of causality. To what extent does the leader influence the subordinate? To what extent does the subordinate influence the leader's behavior? Further, to what extent are there reciprocal effects? There is a need for more studies investigating such directional relationships between leader and group behavior (see e.g. Fleishman, 1973a).

Most often, the importance attributed to leader behavior stems from the presumed effect of the leader's behavior on his subordinates' performance and job satisfaction (Likert, 1961). There is evidence that leadership style affects subordinate performance and attitudes. For example, Day and Hamblin (1964) found subordinate performance varied according to the leader's use of punishment and closeness of supervision. More recently, Dawson, Messe, and Phillips (1972) have shown that experimental variation in the leader's consideration and structure produces changes in group behavior, and Jones, Gergen, Gumpert, and Thibaut (1965) have shown that leader attitudes do get translated into group attitudes.

Other studies investigating the possible effects of subordinate performance on leadership style have had mixed results. Jackson (1953) found that supervisors' leadership styles remained unchanged even though the performance characteristics of the different groups they managed varied substantially—thus indicating that subordinate performance did not affect subsequent leader behavior. In contrast, however, Hawthorne, Couch, Haefner, Langham, and Carter (1956), Lowin and Craig (1968), Farris and Lim (1969), and Crowe, Bochner, and Clark (1972) provided evidence that subordinate performance caused changes in leader behavior. . . .

There are sound theoretical bases (a number of which are reviewed by Lowin and Craig, 1968) from which one can argue that subordinate performance and, in addition, subordinate satisfaction can cause the leader to vary his style of leadership. For example, Katz and Stotland (1959) in their "functional view of attitudes" postulate that a person will develop positive attitudes toward objects which are instrumental to the satisfaction of his needs. This proposition can be applied to leader–subordinate relationships to the degree that the organization makes rewards bestowed on the leader contingent upon his subordinates' performance; in such an organization, the leader may develop more positive attitudes toward his high-performing subordinates. The expectation is that the person whose behavior causes another to be positively reinforced will in return be rewarded by the other. A further expectation is that low performance by a subordinate will cause the leader to restrict or to further specify the subordinate's work activities (both are forms of increased initiating structure) in attempting to improve his performance and, further, to express disapproval (a form of reduced consideration). Conversely, the leader would be expected to see little need for structure and thus engage in less structuring behavior with the high-performing subordinate and, further, to show greater approval and concern for the subordinate's own interests (both are forms of increased

**Source:** Edited and reprinted with permission from *Journal of Applied Psychology* 60 (1975), pp. 187–193. Copyright (1975) by the American Psychological Association.

This research was supported by a Graduate School of Business research grant, Indiana University.

The author wishes to thank Ralph M. Stogdill for the useful suggestions he provided during the formulation stage of this research.

consideration). Similar predictions can be made about the influence of subordinate satisfaction on leader behavior to the extent that a subordinate's expression of satisfaction with work is perceived as reinforcing to the leader. Of the few studies which have examined such causality questions, none were designed to examine the extent to which causation may be reciprocal. When longitudinal data are obtained, as an alternative to experimental designs, there are means for inferring the strength and direction of causality, without requiring the actual manipulation of variables. Two methods for longitudinal data collection are the cross-lagged panel correlational technique and dynamic correlational analysis.

The purpose of this research was to assess, by means of these two techniques, questions of the direction of causal influence in relationships between leader and follower variables. Does a manager's leadership style (in particular, consideration and structure) have greater effect on his subordinate's performance and satisfaction, or is the opposite direction of causality stronger? Further, to what extent are the relationships reciprocal?

## METHOD

### SAMPLE

The data were collected from 103 first-line managers and, for each manager, two of his immediate subordinates. The sample of first-line managers included: 42 department heads employed at either the corporate headquarters or a regional office of an insurance company; 31 project managers representing the research and engineering functions of a manufacturer of industrial and electronics equipment; and 30 first-line managers employed in the financial and marketing divisions of a chemical products firm. . . .

## CONSIDERATION AND SATISFACTION

. . . The "consideration-causes-subordinate satisfaction" coefficients were relatively strong (.40, .34, and .45, for the three respective time periods; all $p$'s < .001) and considerably stronger than the S → C cross-lagged coefficients. . . .

In addition, the significant but rather *moderate* dynamic correlations ($r$'s extended from .42 to .50, all $p$'s < .001) indicate that a third variable and, more likely, several additional variables may have contributed to the covariance between con-

sideration and satisfaction. This particular finding is not surprising, however, since there are other known causes of satisfaction with work. Thus, one interpretation that can be made from these results is that leader emphasis on consideration constitutes one of several likely causes of subordinate satisfaction.

## CONSIDERATION AND PERFORMANCE

The coefficients provided rather strong indications that subordinate performance *causes* leader emphasis on consideration. The only significant correlations were the P → C cross-lagged coefficients: $r$'s = .37, .45, and .33, respectively; all $p$'s < .001. All of the remaining correlations, including the C → P cross-lagged coefficients, were low and did not approach significance. These results help confirm the findings of Lowin and Craig's (1968) experiment and, further, can be interpreted as supporting the theoretical proposition that the leader's attitude toward his subordinates, and its expression, is contingent upon their performance. The leader may be expected, for example, to support and show his approval of those subordinates who have positively reinforced him by their good performance and to be less considerate of subordinates who negatively reinforce him by their low performance. . . .

## INITIATING STRUCTURE AND SATISFACTION

The correlations testing the relationships between leader initiating structure and subordinate work satisfaction . . . provide little evidence of causality. . . .

## INITIATING STRUCTURE AND PERFORMANCE

The only significant correlations obtained in the cross-lagged analysis of relationships between leader initiating structure and subordinate satisfaction were the moderate, though significant, P → IS cross-lagged coefficients (−.33, −.37, and −.36). Consistent with the theory discussed earlier, the most apparent explanation of these findings (given the negative signs of all of the coefficients) is that low performance by a subordinate caused the leader to engage in more structuring behavior. High subordinate performance, on the other hand, would appear to lead to reduced emphasis on initiating structure. The dynamic coefficients were significant but, as before, too low to exclude the possibility of additional variables affecting the relationships found.

The results concerning the proposition about the moderating effects of consideration were suggested earlier by Fleishman and Harris (1962) who did provide evidence of one such "additional variable." This earlier work by Fleishman and Harris demonstrated that leadership styles may interact so that high emphasis on consideration allows the leader to initiate more structure to achieve organizational objectives. Thus, high turnover and grievances were related to low consideration and high structure. However, supervisors with high consideration could increase structure without adverse effects on grievances and turnover. Supervisors with low structure had high turnover and grievances regardless. Thus, Fleishman and Harris (1962) found consideration to be an important moderator variable of the leader structure-group performance relationship. Cummins (1971) later replicated these results using "quality" as a group output measure. . . .

For leaders perceived to be high on consideration, the "initiating structure-causes-subordinate performance" cross-lagged coefficients were positive, significant, and substantially higher than the corresponding P → IS coefficients. Conversely, significant results in exactly the opposite direction were obtained when the leader was perceived as not emphasizing a high degree of consideration. Here, all of the correlations were negative and the patterns of coefficients rather strongly indicated that performance caused initiating structure, particularly in the low consideration group. While of substantially lesser magnitudes, the negative signs of the IS → P cross-lagged coefficients in the low consideration group are supportive of the contention that high emphasis on structure may be counterproductive when the leader shows little consideration. . . .

## Summary

The results of this investigation have provided indications that consideration causes subordinate satisfaction and, conversely, that subordinate performance causes both leader consideration and structure across conditions. However, when the relationship between initiating structure and subordinate performance was moderated by consideration, there was evidence of reciprocal causation. In particular, the results indicate how a leader might positively affect subordinate performance by increased emphasis on both consideration and structure. . . .

## References

Campbell, D. T. From description to experimentation: Interpreting trends as quasi-experiments. In C. W. Harris (Ed.), *Problems in measuring change.* Madison: University of Wisconsin Press, 1963.

Crowe, B. J., Bochner, S., & Clark, A. W. The effects of subordinates' behavior on managerial style. *Human Relations,* 1972, *25,* 215–237.

Cummins, R. C. Relationship of initiating structures and job performance as moderated by consideration. *Journal of Applied Psychology,* 1971, *55,* 489–490.

Dawson, J. E., Messe, L. A., & Phillips, J. L. Effect of instructor-leader behavior on student performance. *Journal of Applied Psychology,* 1972, *56,* 369–376.

Day, R. C., & Hamblin, R. L. Some effects of close and punitive styles of supervision. *American Journal of Sociology,* 1964, *69,* 499–510.

Farris, G. F., & Lim, G. F., Jr. Effects of performance on leadership cohesiveness, influence, satisfaction and subsequent performance. *Journal of Applied Psychology,* 1969, *53,* 490–497.

Fleishman, E. A. Overview. In E. A. Fleishman & J. G. Hunt (Eds.), *Current developments in the study of leadership.* Carbondale: Southern Illinois University Press, 1973. (a)

Fleishman, E. A. Twenty years of consideration and structure. In E. A. Fleishman & J. G. Hunt (Eds.), *Current developments in the study of leadership.* Carbondale: Southern Illinois University Press, 1973. (b)

Fleishman, E. A., & Harris, E. F. Patterns of leadership related to employee grievances and turnover. *Personnel Psychology,* 1962, *15,* 43–56.

Greene, C. N. Causal connections among managers' merit pay, satisfaction, and performance. *Journal of Applied Psychology,* 1973, *58,* 95–100.

Hawthorne, W. W., Couch, A., Haefner, D., Langham, P., & Carter, L. F. The effects of varying combinations of authoritarian and equalitarian leaders and followers. *Journal of Personality and Social Psychology,* 1956, *53,* 210–219.

Jackson, J. M. The effect of changing the leadership of small work groups. *Human Relations,* 1953, *6,* 25–44.

Jones, E. E., Gergen, K. J., Gumpert, P., & Thibaut, J. W. Some conditions affecting the use of ingratiation to influence performance evaluation. *Journal of Personality and Social Psychology,* 1965, *1,* 613–625.

Katz, D., & Stotland, E. A preliminary statement to a theory of attitude structure and change. In S. Koch (Ed.), *Psychology: A study of science* (Vol. 3). New York: McGraw-Hill, 1959.

Lawler, E. E., & Suttle, J. L. A causal correlational test of the need hierarchy concept. *Organizational Behavior and Human Performance,* 1972, *3,* 265–287.

Likert, R. *New patterns of management.* New York: McGraw-Hill, 1961.

Lowin, A., & Craig, J. R. The influence of level of performance on managerial style: An experimental object lesson in the ambiguity of correlational data. *Organizational Behavior and Human Performance,* 1968, *3,* 441–458.

Pelz, D. C., & Andrews, F. M. Detecting causal priorities in panel study data. *American Sociological Review,* 1964, *29,* 836–848.

Simon, H. A. Spurious correlation: A causal interpretation. *Journal of the American Statistical Association,* 1954, *49,* 467–479.

Stogdill, R. M. *Manual for job description and job expectation questionnaire—Form XII.* Columbus: Ohio State University, Bureau of Business Research, 1965. (a)

Stogdill, R. M. *Manual for job description and job expectation questionnaire.* Columbus: Ohio State University, College of Administrative Science, Program for Research in Leadership and Organization, 1965. (b)

Vroom, V. H. A comparison of static and dynamic correlation methods in the study of organizations. *Organizational Behavior and Human Performance,* 1966, *1,* 55–70.

Yee, A. H., & Gage, N. L. Techniques for estimating the source and direction of causal influence in panel data. *Psychological Bulletin,* 1968, *2,* 115–126.

## Reading 29

# The Follower's Role in Leadership Phenomena

**Fillmore H. Sanford**

Most psychological researches on leadership have been concerned with the traits of leaders. Psychologists, traditionally, have dealt with the characteristics of individuals and have made available many instruments, such as personality tests, to facilitate thinking in terms of traits. The search for "leadership traits," however, has not been very rewarding. Stogdill's review[1] strongly suggests that some new approach is needed if we are going to make sense out of leadership phenomena. The literature leads us to think either (a) that there are no general "leadership traits" or (b) that if there are, they do not come in such a form as to be properly described in terms of those personality variables which we now can most easily measure.

The present study departs rather drastically from the search for leadership traits. It looks instead at the follower. It starts off with the idea that leadership is a *relation* between leader and follower, as marriage is a relation between husband and wife and friendship a relation between two people. If we want to learn about marriage, we do not study only husbands or only wives. We have to study the relation that exists between them. The same thing holds for friendship or enmity or partnership or leadership. The present study, while based on the notion that leadership is a relation between leader and follower, does not succeed in studying the relation directly. It seeks to learn about the relation by looking at the follower—the heretofore neglected follower—and his role in the relationship.

The follower is always there when leadership occurs. It is he who accepts or rejects leadership. It is he who follows reluctantly or enthusiastically, obediently or creatively. In any situation where leadership occurs, he is there with all his psychological attributes. He brings with him his habits, attitudes, preferences, biases, and deep-lying psychological needs. If we know something about these psychological attributes, we know something about the follower's "readiness for leadership." We know something about the sort of relations he will be inclined to establish with what sort of leaders.

It is probably true, our general notion says, that every individual has his own unique pattern of readiness for leadership. He has learned both general and specific attitudes toward authority and the ways it is exercised. Perhaps he has learned to like strong and directive leadership, exercised by people with all the accoutrements of conventional status. Perhaps he dislikes leaders who are less than six feet tall and has a great antipathy for any female who tries to assume a leadership role. Another individual may have learned, by contrast, to reject any form of autocratic or directive leadership, preferring his leaders to be more human, more sympathetic, and more responsive to the follower.

In any group or in any society we may expect to find a wide variety of learned readinesses for leadership. But any group may have a modal pattern of readinesses that sets it off from other groups. Eventually we may be able to describe the southern or the middle class or the Jewish or the Protestant or the educated or uneducated orientation to leadership. Or we may be able to trace out the American as contrasted with the German or the Samoan pattern of attitudes toward authority in its various forms.

The present paper presents first some specimen data on what may be roughly called the American orientation to leadership. It analyzes

**Source:** Excerpts from "The Follower's Role in Leadership Phenomena," from *Readings in Social Psychology* by E. L. Hartley, Theodore M. Newcomb, and G. E. Swenson (copyright 1952 and renewed 1980 by Holt, Rinehart and Winston, Inc.), reprinted by permission of Wadsworth, an imprint of the Wadsworth Group, a division of Thomson Learning, fax 800 730-2215.

The present paper reports on some of the results from a large-scale study of leadership conducted at The Institute for Research in Human Relations. More detailed accounts appear in the author's book *Authoritarianism and Leadership* (Philadelphia: The Institute for Research in Human Relations, 1950), and in his report "Public Orientation to Roosevelt," *Public Opinion Quarterly* XV (1951), 189–216. Permission to reprint certain materials from these sources has been given by The Institute for Research in Human Relations and by Princeton University Press.

The project was supported by the Office of Naval Research, but the publication of assertions growing out of the study does not imply their endorsement by any branch of the Naval Service. John N. Patterson, Barney Korchin, Harry J. Older, Emily L. Ehle, Irwin Rosenstock, Doris M. Barnett, F. Loyal Greer, and Douglas Courtney were collaborators in the overall project and were direct or indirect contributors to the present report.

followers' responses to some interview items designed to elicit general attitudes about leadership, and it goes on to examine the public's orientation to F. D. Roosevelt as a leader. Then the paper talks about one personality factor in the individual which has something to do with his readiness to follow. . . .

## THE FOLLOWER'S PERSONALITY AS A FACTOR IN LEADERSHIP

The foregoing data bear on what we may eventually be able to describe as the "typical" American way of reacting to leadership. We have been working under the general background hypothesis that psychological needs or predispositions of the follower have an important hand in determining both how a leader is perceived and the degree to which he is accepted. The data so far presented tend to fall in line with this hypothesis and lead to tentative statements about some follower needs that are involved in the leader–follower relation. But we can come to closer grips with such matters if we can deal with the psychology of the individual follower rather than the psychology of masses of followers.

The plan of the project called for the intensive study of one personality variable which, on the basis of theory, ought to have a great deal to do with the individuals' reactions to leadership. The variable chosen was authoritarianism, and the instrument used to study it was an authoritarian–equalitarian(A–E) scale.[2] . . .

On the basis of theory and existing evidence, we expect that the people who score toward the authoritarian end of the A–E scale will want strong and directive leadership and will accept leadership that "pays off" in material terms. The authoritarian's "bargaining" orientation to authority, his respect for the strong and scorn for the weak, should lead him to accept Roosevelt as a good leader because Roosevelt was strong and because he produced.

The low scorers, on the other hand, tending toward a warmer—and perhaps more rational—relation with people and with authority, should emphasize Roosevelt's humanity or humanitarianism and should take a reasonably objective view of his ability to do his job. Being less deeply concerned with authority relationships, they should not be concerned with the strength-weakness dimension, unless they perceive strength as necessary for the achievement of a social goal, and

should judge Roosevelt against a relatively "democratic" frame of reference.

In order to test such hypotheses, the procedure was:

1. To select from our population 80 individuals who were in the B economic group ($5,000 to $10,000 annual income) and who had completed at least a high-school education.

2. To split the 80 into two groups with respect to A–E scores—40 "highs" and 40 "lows."

3. To classify the responses of all 80 individuals with respect to psychologically conceived variables.

4. To examine the tendency, if any, of "highs" and "lows" to respond in accordance with theoretical expectations.

The selection of 80 individuals of approximately the same income group and educational level should succeed in holding relatively constant these demographic variables so that personality variables can show through clearly.

Each response of these 80 individuals was classified according to the following variables:

1. *Emphasis on function.* The tendency of the respondent to think of Roosevelt's functioning as a leader of a democratic country. "Was an excellent administrator," "chose good advisers."

2. *Material dependency.* The respondent's emphasis on Roosevelt's "payoff," the material benefits he brought to his followers. "Looked out for the average man," "saved us from depression."

3. *Emphasis on power.* The emphasis on power and strength of the man; the suggestion that the follower wanted a powerful leader to keep him safe. "He was a pillar of strength in time of need."

4. *Personal warmth.* The emphasis on FDR's responsiveness to and fondness for people. "He liked people," "he was a great humanitarian."

The procedure was for three judges, two of whom were trained in psychology, to examine all 80 responses, to discuss each one, then to put in one pile all those agreed upon as clearly expressing the quality under consideration. This was done, of course, in ignorance of the A–E scores of the respondents. By this method all the 80 responses agreed upon as expressing a *concern with function* were separated out. Then the total 80 were shuffled, and those agreed upon as showing *material dependency* were separated, and so on for each of the four variables. It was then possible to compare with chance expectation the frequency of high scorers and low scorers in each pile.

Of the 80 responses, 25 were agreed upon as showing *concern with function*. Theory dictates that those who demonstate this relatively objective concern for the leader's function should be low scorers. The results showed 19 out of the 25 answers in this category were made by people in the low-scoring group. This result is different from chance expectation at the 2-percent level of significance. (The C.R. by the sign test is 2.40.)

Only 6 of these 80 respondents gave responses that were agreed upon as showing clear *material dependency*. (These 80 were all middle- or upper-middle-class people.) We expect from theory that high scorers will give this sort of response. The fact is that five out of the six expressing material dependency are high scorers. This difference is suggestive but by no means conclusive since the N is so small.

Thirty-one of the respondents gave responses agreed upon as *emphasizing the leader's power*. We would expect, theoretically, that our high scorers, with their respect for power, would be the ones responding in this category. Eighteen out of the 31 respondents here were high, 13 were low. This result does not differ significantly from chance. One gets the impression, however, that this may be because the low scorers, in a way consistent with personality structure, are regarding Roosevelt's strength as a *means* rather than as an end in itself. In time of stress the equalitarian is perfectly willing to accept the powerful leader whose emergency function is clear. There is reason to believe that while the equalitarian can take power or leave it alone, the authoritarian *needs* it—almost to a neurotic degree. In the reaction to Roosevelt, the low scorers may be expressing admiration for strength when strength was functionally necessary—during a war and a depression when democracy was threatened. The authoritarian may be admiring strength for its own sweet savor. But our present data cannot be used to test these hypotheses.

There were 13 of the 80 responses agreed upon by three judges as expressing admiration for Roosevelt's *warmth and humanitarian qualities*. We would expect our low scorers to predominate in this area. Twelve out of the 13 responses in this category were made by our equalitarians—a result that differs significantly (at better than the 1-percent level) from chance expectation.

These results show with reasonable clarity that personality factors in the follower play a role in determining the orientation to a leader. While authoritarians and equalitarians, as classified by the A–E scale, are almost equal in the frequency with which they express admiration for Roosevelt, they clearly differ in the reasons they give for accepting him as a leader. Authoritarians do not think of him in terms of his social function or in terms of his humanity and warmth. They tend to emphasize his materially beneficial accomplishments. The low scorers on the A–E scale— the so-called "equalitarians"—clearly see FDR's concern for people, observe his successful functioning, and show little concern for how he "paid off" in terms of beneficial accomplishments.

## DISCUSSION

The study of the follower and an emphasis on the leader–follower relation lead to a way of thinking about leadership that may overcome some of the limitations inherent in a trait approach and that someday may develop into a systematic theory of leadership. It may be worthwhile here to look at a summary sketch of this way of thinking.

Leadership is a relation. Psychological factors in the follower as well as psychological factors in the leader help determine this relation. The individual follower has his own unique pattern of needs and attitudes that constitute his readiness for leadership. He has problems which the leader must solve. He has learned certain standards whereby he judges the leader's effectiveness. All these factors are there in determining what sort of relation will be established with what sort of leader.

Because all Americans have more-or-less common learning experiences, American followers can be expected to have a more-or-less "typical" way of reacting to authority. And because the relevant learning differs somewhat from one group to another within American society, we might expect the ways of reacting to authority to differ somewhat from one demographic segment of the population to another.

In a concrete leadership situation, the follower's deep-lying attitudes and needs are present as background determiners of his reaction to the leader, but there are also *situationally determined needs* that arise. The need to achieve a group goal or the need to adjust to here-and-now demands is imposed on the more persistent patterns of needs, making new demands on the leader. In a life-or-death situation, the follower's need for warm approval is likely to be less important than his need to survive. He will thus be less likely to accept the "nice guy" as a leader, more likely to follow the man who appears able to help solve the immediate and pressing problem. It is possible to state this sort of observation as a definite hypothesis: The more psychologically significant the group goal, the greater the follower's emphasis on the leader's competence to assist in achieving that goal. A corollary to the hypothesis is as follows: The more *clearly perceived* the goal, and the more visible is progress toward it, the more follower emphasis there will be on the functional competence of the leader. The converse of each of these hypotheses will also be of interest. In groups where the goal is (a) not very important, and (b) not very visible, there will be a preference for leaders who meet those persistent psychological needs that are relatively independent of the immediate situation—e.g., the need for warm approval. Certainly in many everyday groups (fraternities, clubs, neighborhood or church organizations, etc.) the preferred leader often seems to be the one who is good at giving psychological structure and satisfaction to garden-variety individuals with standard American social needs. It sometimes happens in these groups, that "nice guy" leaders are bypassed or thrown out when the group comes down with a desire to do a specific and challenging job. Sometimes in such groups we also see "leadership by default." Where the role of the leader is neither very functionally significant nor clearly defined, the individual who desperately wants to be leader is allowed to assume the mantle, whether or not he is a "nice guy."

These are examples of the sort of hypotheses—testable hypotheses—that grow out of the present approach to leadership phenomena.

We can, with profit, start to think about leadership in terms of the follower's needs or problems and their variations from situation to situation. But we still cannot understand leadership without paying close attention to the leader and *his* problems. The leader is as much of an individual as is the follower. His needs, his abilities, obviously are involved in the leader–follower relation. We have built up a picture here of follower's needs creating a demand for leadership of a certain sort. In any situation there will be a pressure to put into the leader's role a person who fits the demand. Formal or informal candidates for the leader's role have their own pressures to exert also. Some people want to be leaders, sometimes desperately so. Some of these will be able, because of their own pattern of needs, to play the leader's role with only one style. Some people are very chronic "nice guys" and cannot meet situational demands for strong and directive authority. Others are chronic authoritarians who may desperately want to dominate others and would be a severe handicap to a group with a strong need for individual initiative and freedom of expression. There are individuals who seek responsibility but who clearly lack the abilities necessary to advance specific group goals. Others will have requisite abilities but do not particularly like to assume responsibility.

Who will become leader will depend on (a) the pattern of follower needs and (b) the pattern of leader needs and abilities. The leader–follower relation most likely to become established in a free situation—and most likely to persist in either a free situation or one in which leadership is determined from outside—is the relation that is reciprocally rewarding to both follower and leader.

## Notes

1. R. M. Stogdill, "Personal Factors Associated with Leadership: A Survey of the Literature," *J. Psychol.*, 1948, XXV, 35–71.

2. The most extensive studies of the variable are contained in W. Adorno, E. Frenkel-Brunswik, D. Levinson, and R. N. Sanford, *The Authoritarian Personality* (New York: Harpers, 1950). The A–E scale used in the present study is an adaptation of the F scale described in that volume.

## Reading 30

# Leadership, Followership, Self, and Others

**Edwin P. Hollander**
City University of New York Baruch College and University Graduate Center

Attempts to understand leadership as a function of leader qualities still represent a challenge in the field (see e.g., Kenny & Zaccaro, 1983; Lord, DeVader, & Alliger, 1986; Kirkpatrick & Locke, 1991). As a starting place, that venerable approach gained credence if only because the leader is usually seen as the major actor in leadership. It is easier to focus on one individual as the center of action, influence, and power than many in making attributions.

Another practical reason for attention to the leader is that leader action or inaction can have multiple effects on other people, not only in the success of the enterprise, but also in the "social health" of a group, organization, or larger entity, including a nation. Indeed, a reasonable question, not asked enough, is what are the *costs* of putting this person in a position of authority *and* responsibility? Another might be, how does he or she respond to disconfirming information from subordinates?

Despite the understandable focus on the leader, the concepts of leader and leadership do not exist in isolation. To be viable, both depend upon followership (see Hollander & Offermann, 1990a,b). Accordingly, this paper takes a relational approach to leader qualities, whose significance lies in how they are perceived and responded to by followers within the situation experienced with the leader. As Gibb (1947) long ago indicated, "Leadership is a concept applied to the personality-environment relation" (p. 267).

Although leaders are usually directors of activity, all initiatives need not come from the leader. Followers also have the potential for making significant contributions to successful leadership. Indeed, at every level in organizations, leaders are called upon to be responsive also as followers. Not least is the reality that leaders typically rise from among those who have shown ability in the follower role, and are thereby given a boost.

President Dwight D. Eisenhower's career presents a dramatic case in point. Long a junior staff officer before World War II, he was mentored by Generals MacArthur and Marshall. Promoted to colonel near the onset of war, 26 years after graduating from West Point, he was made a major general and commander of U.S. forces in Europe the very next year, elevated over 366 eligible officers. What were the qualities he displayed as a follower that eventually advanced him to supreme commander of Allied Forces and beyond? Without knowing them in detail, it is reasonable to surmise that they fit the task demands of the situation and that not just desire, nor geniality coupled with keen intelligence, could account alone for his dramatic rise and evident success.

## LEADER QUALITIES BY STAGES

Maccoby (1987) is among those who have made the essential point that the style that gets the leadership position is not the same as what is required for effectiveness later. There are even more distinctions, however, in addressing leader qualities needed at successive stages (cf., e.g., Howard & Bray, 1988; Kraut et al., 1989). Moreover, there are the more fundamental questions of who seeks the leader role? What motivates that quest? What features of leader style go with which motives?

Viewed sequentially, at least four distinctive, if partially overlapping, stages can be identified where certain qualities are more likely to be seen. Put briefly, these stages are definable as *wanting, getting, doing,* and *maintaining the job.* Motivational elements in seeking a leader role obviously take precedence, including needs for personalized power, achievement, and affiliation (see McClelland, 1975), as well as self-efficacy (Bandura, 1977), to touch on only some.

At the next stage come the qualities perceived to be important in securing it, such as self-presentation skills directed at seeming to fit legitimators' prototypes and perhaps serving their needs, which may involve self-monitoring (Snyder, 1979). Finally come those qualities involved in succeeding in leadership and maintaining the leader role, assessed by various, often indeterminant, performance

**Source:** Reprinted with permission from *Leadership Quarterly* 3, no.1 (1992), pp. 43–54. Copyright (1992) by Elsevier Science.

criteria. As noted, the latter stages may call forth manipulative skills aimed at impression management to achieve favorable outcomes for one's self, often at the expense of others and the broader enterprise (see e.g., Conger, 1990, on John DeLorean). In any case, leader qualities are more likely perceived by followers relevant to the present and future, in the context of the situation, rather than as desirable absolutely (see Hollander & Julian, 1968; Hollander, 1985, p. 493).

An illustration of this is provided by the characteristic known as Machiavellianism (Christie & Geis, 1970). Those high on this measure see the world in manipulative and power-oriented terms and look for situations where he or she can gain control, especially where there is low or less structure. An experiment by Gleason, Seaman, and Hollander (1978) was directed to precisely this point. Sixteen four-man task groups were constructed composed of one Hi Mach, one Lo Mach, and two middle Machs, based on pretesting introductory psychology students with the Machiavellianism Scale. As expected, the Hi Machs were observed to show greater ascendance than the others, especially under the low structure condition. Even more relevant in revealing the followers' perspective, their post-interaction ratings of those preferred as future leaders of the group showed the Middle Machs to be significantly more desired for the leader role than either the Hi's or Lo's. Without knowing precisely why these others were different, follower preferences clearly avoided those who scored at the extremes.

As leaders move through the stages of getting, to doing and maintaining the job, qualities like empathy, creativity, and flexibility loom larger as mediators of performance, beyond the drive to get the position. In general, this helps to account in part for why qualities that seemed appropriate at the wanting and getting stages fail to be satisfactory in the doing and maintaining stages. An obvious instance occurs when high expectations are created at the getting stage which are not sustained in doing the job. This phenomenon of heightened follower perceptions and expectations, which are disconfirmed, has been called "anticipointment."

## FOLLOWER PERCEPTIONS AND EXPECTATIONS

Recent developments in the study of leadership have made evident the practical importance of follower perceptions on the leader–follower relationship. The nature of this linkage increasingly is recognized as central to affecting the success or failure of leadership (Hollander & Offermann, 1990a,b). One instance of this is shown in the work on "derailment" (McCall, Lombardo, & Morrison, 1988), with 400 promising managers, seen to be on a fast track. Those failing to reach their expected potential were often perceived to lack interpersonal skills.

Other research by Kouzes and Posner (1987), with a sample of 2,600 top level managers, dealt with qualities they admired in their leaders. Among the most frequently chosen qualities were being honest and inspiring, in addition to being competent and forward looking. Again, the interpersonal or relational realm was perceived to play a significant role. Clearly, the followers' perspective is useful as an avenue to understanding leadership.

Hollander and Kelly (1990) gathered critical incidents and ratings of good and bad leadership from 81 respondents (40 men and 41 women) with organizational work experience, preponderantly of two years or more. Content analyses of the rewards in the situation described indicated that sensitivity to followers, support, and praise dominated good but were absent or negative in bad leadership. Respondents in good leadership reported increased participation/productivity, satisfaction, and a sense of being valued. This effect has been confirmed now with 120 more respondents.

## LEADER–FOLLOWER RELATIONSHIPS

This newer approach considers leadership to involve a set of relationships which includes the leader, follower, and their situation, most notably the task or function at hand. Especially now, the emergence of a diverse work force demands more attention to the complex interrelationships in the workplace that are vital to what comes out of the process. This reflects a growing recognition of leadership as a process, and not just a person.

The functions performed by leadership include the obvious one of directing activity, but also decision-making, goal-setting, communicating, adjudicating conflict, and otherwise maintaining the enterprise, among others. These dispersed functions often need some delegation to followers, which reveals the interlocking system of relationships between leaders and followers, and their commonly desired characteristics (Hollander & Webb, 1955; Kouzes & Posner, 1987).

Leadership also operates within constraints and opportunities that are presented by followers (Stewart, 1982). The constraints include the expectations and perceptions of followers which can influence leaders (Hollander, 1985, 1986; Lord & Maher, 1990). One early exponent of this general view, Fillmore Sanford (1950), asserted the proposition that followers are crucial to any leadership event. In addition, the repeated finding that follower behavior is affected by leader behavior is also shown to be reciprocal. Followers affect leaders in a variety of ways, not least as an audience to which leaders orient and address themselves (Hollander & Offermann, 1990a).

Given their need for mutual responsiveness, leadership and followership can be considered to be reciprocal systems requiring synchronization. Leadership is usually seen as the more active system, but followership can be proactive, not only reactive, as seen especially in social movements. Empowerment in some sectors of activity would be another instance of giving followership a more proactive role, as an accompaniment to leadership in the traditional directive mode.

## ROLE OF FOLLOWER ATTRIBUTIONS ABOUT LEADERS

Follower attributions about leaders affect followers' responses to and relations with their leader. These are affected by the leader's perceived attributes, including his or her competence, motivation, and personality characteristics, as related to followers and the prevailing situation. Lord and Maher (1990) consider these perceptions to be checked against prototypes held by followers of leader attributes, such as intelligence and expectations of how leaders should perform. In this feature of leadership, follower perceptions are seen as the key linking past performance and future performance, as part of the greater attention now to cognitive elements in leader–follower relations. This development is well represented by follower "implicit leadership theories" (ILTs), among other concepts (see Calder, 1977; Lord, DeVader, & Alliger, 1986; Rush, Thomas, & Lord, 1977). A precursor of this was the relating of followers' expectancies of leader attributes to perceptions of leader behavior (Hollander, 1964).

Indeed, the link between perceptions and behavior is the essence of the interest now in leader attributes *as perceived by followers,* and the response that ensues. For example, Calder (1977) and Pfeffer (1977) are among the proponents of a perceptual/attributional perspective which says that leaders are credited or blamed for outcomes over which they alone had little effect. Because positive or negative outcomes are more likely to be attributed to the leader, he or she is more readily faulted and even removed as a symbol when things go wrong, rather than firing the whole staff or team.

## SELF AND OTHER: DOMINANCE AND IDENTIFICATION MOTIFS

Fundamental to the leadership process is the way the leader perceives his or her social self relative to followers. A traditional view of the leader role associates it with authority as the basis for using power, which puts distance between the leader and followers (see Kipnis, 1976). Such a view sees followers as essentially compliant and manipulable, within a dominance motif. One expression of this is a quote from a corporate CEO that "leadership is confirmed when the ability to inflict pain is demonstrated" (Menzies, 1980).

An alternative view, more in keeping with a participative ethos, sees the leader–follower relationship within a mutual identification motif. This includes the prospect of two-way influence, and the perception and counterperception of leader and followers. Cantril (1958) has said that the leader must be able to perceive the reality worlds of followers and have sensitivity to guide intuitions, if a common consensus and mutual trust rather than "mere power, force, or cunning" are to develop and prevail (p. 129). In practical political terms, Kellerman (1984) has observed that presidential leadership has to be accomplished from "within the world of other people."

The identification with the leader motif is exemplified in Freud's (1921) concept of the leader as a shared "ego-ideal" with whom members of a group mutually identify. Fromm (1941) extended this contention in personality terms by writing that "the psychology of the leader and that of his followers, are, of course, closely linked with each other" (p. 65). Erikson (1975) made an associated point about this linkage in asserting that followers "join a leader and are joined together by him" (p. 153).

A good part of the imbalance in treating the leader–follower relationship arises from the lingering mythology that leaders simply exercise authority and power. Cowley (1928) called this "headship," rather than leadership, which by contrast engages followers in a concerted program of action. More recently, Kipnis (1976) has shown that assertions of power effectively undermine the goals of authentic leadership. Such assertions also are limited in creating positive identifications.

## LEGITIMACY AS A BASIS OF AUTHORITY

Followers' perceptions and identification with the leader begin with how he or she attained the role. This is the leader's basis of authority, which is the issue of legitimacy. Such perceptions also are a function of follower expectations, and of persisting "implicit theories" about leaders and how they are perceived to act or should act.

Election and appointment are two contrasting instances of legitimacy, which have been found to produce different effects on followers, insofar as they generate varying commitments to the leader. Election creates a heightened psychological identification with the leader, but also more vulnerability to criticism and the withdrawal of support by followers. The evidence indicates that a leader's legitimacy has a considerable effect in shaping followers' perceptions (e.g., Ben-Yoav, Hollander, & Carnevale, 1983), and on group performance and the leader's perception of followers (cf., Green & Mitchell, 1979).

The election case is, of course, a more obvious instance of leader emergence with the consent of followers. In that regard, election gives followers a greater sense of responsibility for and investment in the leader. But they also may have been found to have higher expectations about the leader, at least initially. Elected leaders who fail to perform to expectations have been found to be more vulnerable to criticism than appointed leaders, particularly if they were seen to be competent in the first place (Hollander & Julian, 1970, 1978). While election and appointment create different psychological climates between leaders and followers, organizational leaders *can* attain a "following" by doing more than exercising authority, as Katz and Kahn (1978) have observed.

One effect of the current attributional view is to make even more explicit the significance of followers' and others' perceptions of the leader as a constraint of check on leader behavior. There also are the related expectations about such leader characteristics as their requisite level of competence and motivation. The reverse perspective of the leader's perception of followers also is of significance (see Mitchell, Green, & Wood, 1981).

This is illustrated in the findings of an experiment by Elgie, Hollander, and Rice (1988).

Leader evaluations were studied of four types of followers, who provided either positive or negative feedback with either high or low task activity. The outcome measure was a score made up of their ratings of each follower on 10 semantic differential scales. An overall result showed that elected leaders gave more positive ratings generally than appointed leaders in ratings of their followers. A specific finding of interest was that elected and appointed leaders responded differently to high and low activity followers under the negative feedback condition, but similarly under the positive feedback condition. With the lower ratings they assigned, appointed leaders evidently viewed such negative feedback more critically, possibly as a greater threat to their status.

## TRANSACTIONAL MODELS OF LEADERSHIP

Process-oriented "transactional" models of leadership developed initially out of a social exchange perspective, emphasizing the implicit social exchange or transaction that exists between leader and followers as a feature of effectiveness (see Hollander, 1964, 1978; Hollander & Julian, 1969; Homans, 1961). In the transactional view, the leader gives benefits to followers, such as a definition of the situation and direction, which is reciprocated by followers in heightened esteem for and responsiveness to the leader. This transactional approach is part of the current organizational theme emphasizing a more active role for followers, and the potential for two-way influence (see Hollander & Offermann, 1990a). It also conveys the sense of the leader earning or deserving a following.

Followers' perceptions of and expectations about the leader's actions and motives are generated in accordance with an attributional process. Such interpersonal perceptions are seen in Heider's (1958) distinction between "can" and "will." When a leader is perceived to be able to achieve a favorable outcome, but does not because of a perceived failure of will, this causes a greater loss of following than the reverse, that is, an inability to achieve something desirable but still with an apparent try.

## IDIOSYNCRASY CREDIT

This attributional analysis is related to a social exchange concept, the "idiosyncrasy credit" (IC) model of innovative leadership (Hollander, 1958,

1964). The model deals with the latitude a leader has to bring about change as a function of followers' perceptions of that leader's competence and signs of loyalty that engender trust.

Credit is a term in common usage which emphasizes an interpersonal process long recognized. We give credit, take credit, and are discredited, as examples. It has its root in the word creed, referring to the belief, confidence, trust, and faith we have in another. In leadership it applies to attributions of a leader's intentions, and expectations of action, and likely consequences. An essential virtue of the credit perspective is to make plain the leader's need to establish himself or herself with followers as perceivers and evaluators who give or withhold credit.

In the IC model, leadership is viewed as a dynamic process of interpersonal evaluation in which credits are earned in the eyes of followers. These credits provide latitude for deviations that would be unacceptable for those without such credit. Credits come from perceived competence and conformity to group norms, as a sign of loyalty, and then can be used to take innovative actions expected as part of the leader's role.

Other factors may contribute to the accumulation of credits. Seniority is one of these that operates widely, though obviously not with uniform impact. A person may also benefit by having "derivative credit," in the form of a favorable reputation from another group, or from the society at large, as seen for example in high socioeconomic status. Most usually, however, a new member of a group is in a poor position to assert influence, especially in the direction of change, unless he or she has a unique qualification, such as an idea that helps deal with a major group problem, or a badly needed skill. In these circumstances their credit is gained by maximizing on the competence factor.

A benefit may also result from calling attention to oneself in a figure-ground sense, if the outcome for the group is positive. This is verified in the research by Sorrentino and Boutillier (1975) who found that initial quantity of participation in a group was viewed by others as a positive sign of a group member's motivation, while later participation was evaluated more as to quality. Relatedly, Ridgeway (1981) has contended that nonconformity may be a greater initial score of influence and has presented experimental evidence that appears contradictory to the IC model. Certainly it is true that within a brief time a person may call attention to himself or herself by

manifest nonconformity to prevailing norms. However, this will be evaluated in due course by the standard of the task contribution made, and a point of dysfunctionality may be reached where rejection may result.

An experiment pertinent to the expenditure of credits was conducted by Hollander, Julian, and Sorrentino (1969). They studied the effects on appointed or elected leaders of disagreements with their followers. Elected leaders who had been told they had strong group support in attaining that position were significantly more likely to make total reversals of their group's decision—indeed on about half the critical trials—than were those in the other conditions. In addition, elected leaders with strong support showed lower conciliation in their responses to group judgments, based on a content analysis of their messages to the group. Evidently, the elected leader in this condition felt freer to challenge group judgments, as a likely function of idiosyncrasy credit.

Unused credits can be lost by failing to fulfill follower expectations for that role, including inaction in the face of need. Also, the leader's self-serving and other negatively viewed behaviors can drain credits, as can perceptions of weak motivation, incompetence, and the responsibility for failure (see Alvarez, 1968).

Perceiving how and when credit is earned and expended therefore seems to be an essential interpersonal task. On the earning end, as one example, Porter (1985) says, "Managers are reluctant to spend the time and resources on interrelationship projects if they are uncertain to receive credit for them" (p. 389). On the expending end, situations may be perceived by a leader as risky to his or her status, and thereby cause restraint in taking action, especially for fear of a loss of personal power (see McClelland, 1975).

## SOCIAL SELF, SOCIAL PERCEPTIVENESS, AND SELF-MONITORING

As already noted, the study of leadership requires attention to the leader's self-concept. More pointedly, it is the social self that is pivotal to understanding the leader-follower relationship. If the leader's self-perception is inaccurate with respect to others' perceptions, the relationship is likely to be affected adversely. Misperception of others' perceptions and desires becomes magnified as a problem in leadership. It also accounts for a failure to know whether and when to use credit, as exemplified when a leader takes no action in the face of manifest need.

One quality that has been postulated as a significant ingredient in gaining and doing leadership successfully is social perceptiveness, that is, alertness to the surrounding environment and understanding of situations (see Stogdill, 1948; Hollander & Julian, 1968). A related feature of this quality is "self-monitoring," which Snyder (1979) identified as the ability to monitor and control one's expressive behaviors. Among the three characteristics included within this quality is "sensitivity to social cues." Recent research by Zaccaro, Foti, and Kenny (1991), using a rotation design, found that self-monitoring was stable as a characteristic correlating significantly with overall leader ranking.

## SELF-SERVING BIASES

More than the usual tendency, leaders may be given to self-serving biases that exist in many relationships. This is revealed in such everyday comments as "You are stubborn, but I am acting out of principle," or "I am only doing this for your own good." The role of leader may enhance this tendency, even in the absence of power over others, but especially with it (Kipnis, 1976). This brings about self-absorption and self-deception, which may readily be fed by followers, and result in what is commonly called an "ego-trip." More significantly, in executive suites, it can lead to calamitous results for the organizations involved (see, e.g., Conger, 1990; Byrne et al., 1991).

In an analysis of some psychological elements involved, Greenwald (1985) has presented an interpretation of how the leader's ego or self incorporates several distinctive cognitive biases. These include the self as the focus of knowledge, "beneffectance" as the perception of responsibility for desired, but not undesired, outcomes, and resistance to change.

A necessary corrective is to be aware of the perception, motives, and more about others. But the narcissism associated with leaders who draw on the affection of followers, as in "charismatic leadership," deprives them of this corrective (see Post, 1986). Followers, also, may be vulnerable to perceptual distortions as a feature of the self-serving bias and identification with the leader that can serve a need to bolster the self.

## CHARISMATIC AND TRANSFORMATIONAL LEADERSHIP

The concept of the "charismatic leader" (Weber, 1921) deals with leaders who have considerable emotional appeal to followers and a great hold over them through an identification process. While charisma refers to a quality usually seen to be possessed by a leader, it manifests itself in followers who accord it. Without their responsiveness, charisma is hollow.

More recently, from a political science perspective, Burns (1978) proposed a related concept of the "transformational leader." Burns' idea of the leader as an agent who may transform the outlook and behavior of followers has been applied to organizational leadership by Bass (1985) and Bennis and Nanus (1985). Their main point is that such leaders strive to go beyond the bounds of the usual to bring about a change in followers that will create a climate for exceptional performance (see Fiedler & House, 1988).

In one view, transformational leadership can be seen as an *extension* of transactional leadership, with greater leader intensity and follower arousal (Hollander & Offermann, 1990a). Research by Bass (1985) and Yammarino and Bass (1988) on transformational leadership in fact involves a measure with two transactional factors in addition to charisma, intellectual stimulation, and individual attention to followers. However, charisma also may be negative when primarily directed to the leader's self-serving ends, not least the manipulation of others primarily for the leader's ego gratification, as well as for other dubious causes, that can have disastrous effects for the broader good.

The potential for damage from a leader with charismatic appeal is evident. Such a leader is "mirror hungry" and has narcissistic needs for continual approval from others (Post, 1986). Coupled with personalized power needs, a charismatic appeal also can be destructive, as Hogan, Raskin, and Fazzini (1990) have observed in writing about "the dark side of charisma." Moreover, the charismatic leader fosters an atmosphere where imagery substitutes for, or is elevated above, performance (see Drucker, 1988).

All charismatic-transformational leaders do not provide problems in these ways, but their potential for affecting large numbers of others adversely requires attention, if only because appeals based on emotional arousal provide ample opportunities for abuse. It is not enough to say, for instance, that charismatic-transformational leaders transmit a vision—as if they were the only kind of leader who did so—without examining that vision and its probable or known consequences.

## CONCLUSIONS

Granted that the study of leadership has usually assumed the existence of followers, their role nonetheless has been seen as mainly passive. This is so despite the truth that followers are more likely to see and know the reality of the leader's day-to-day approach to leadership. Recent models and applications have increasingly sought to integrate followers more fully into the understanding of leadership phenomena. Building on the foundation provided by newer conceptions of leadership, such as the operation of attribution processes, leader–follower relations now have been examined with heightened attention.

A major implication of what has been presented here is to accord a more active role for those considered followers. In this newer view, leaders and their qualities are important particularly as they engage followers toward productive ends. Central to this process are the self–other perceptions, and misperceptions including self-serving biases, that can exist in leader–follower relations. The impact of these transcends the usual way of viewing leader qualities as personal possessions. Leader "charisma," for instance, needs to be seen as essentially interpersonal, since it depends upon the followers' recognizing the leader's special attributes. An essential question, therefore, is what leader qualities elicit a favorable response from particular followers, as well as generally. Some suggestions in that direction have been offered within a relational conception of leadership.

## References

Alvarez, R. (1968). Informal reactions to deviance in simulated work organizations: A laboratory experiment. *American Sociological Review* 33, 895–912.

Bandura, A. (1977). *Social learning theory.* Englewood Cliffs, NJ: Prentice-Hall.

Bass, B. M. (1985). *Leadership and performance beyond expectations.* New York: Free Press.

Bennis, W. G. & B. Nanus. (1985). *Leaders.* New York: Harper & Row.

Ben-Yoav, O., E. P. Hollander, & P. J. D. Carnevale. (1983). Leader legitimacy, leader-follower interaction, and followers' ratings of the leader. *Journal of Social Psychology* 121, 111–115.

Burns, J. M. (1978). *Leadership.* New York: Harper & Row.

Byrne, J. A., W. C. Symonds, & J. F. Siler. (1991). CEO Disease. *Business Week,* April 1, 52–60.

Calder, B. J. (1977). An attribution theory of leadership. In B. M. Staw & G. R. Salancik (Eds.), *New directions in organizational behavior.* Chicago: St. Clair Press.

Cantril, H. (1958). Effective democratic leadership: A psychological interpretation. *Journal of Individual Psychology* 14, 128–138.

Christie, R. & F. L. Geis. (1970). *Studies in Machiavellianism.* New York: Academic Press.

Conger, J. A. (1990). The dark side of leadership. *Organizational Dynamics* 19(2), 44–55.

Cowley, W. H. (1928). Three distinctions in the study of leaders. *Journal of Abnormal and Social Psychology* 23, 144–157.

Drucker, P. F. (1988). Leadership: More doing than dash. *Wall Street Journal,* January 6, p. 14.

Elgie, D. M., E. P. Hollander, & R. W. Rice. (1988). Appointed and elected leader responses to favorableness of feedback and level of task activity from followers. *Journal of Applied Social Psychology* 18, 1361–1370.

Erikson, E. H. (1975). *Life history and the historical moment.* New York: W.W. Norton.

Fiedler, F. E. & R. J. House. (1988). Leadership theory and research: A report of progress. In C. L. Cooper & I. Roberston (Eds.), *International review of industrial and organizational psychology* (pp. 73–92). London: Wiley.

Freud, S. ([1921]1960). *Group psychology and the analysis of the ego.* New York: Bantam. (Originally published in German in 1921.)

Fromm, E. (1941). *Escape from freedom.* New York: Rinehart.

Gibb, C. A. (1947). The principles and traits of leadership. *Journal of Abnormal and Social Psychology* 42, 267–284.

Gleason, J. M., F. J. Seaman, & E. P. Hollander. (1978). Emergent leadership processes as a function of task structure and Machiavellianism. *Social Behavior and Personality* 6, 33–36.

Green, S. G. & T. R. Mitchell. (1979). Attributional processes of leaders in leader-member interactions. *Organizational Behavior and Human Performance* 23, 429–458.

Greenwald, A. (1985). Totalitarian egos in the personalities of democratic leaders. Symposium Paper,

International Society of Political Psychology Annual Meeting, Washington, DC, June 20.

Heider, F. (1958). *The psychology of interpersonal relations.* New York: Wiley.

Hogan, R., R. Raskin, & D. Fazzini. (1990). The dark side of charisma. In K. E. Clark & M. B. Clark (Eds.), *Measures of leadership.* West Orange, NJ: Leadership Library of America.

Hollander, E. P. (1958). Conformity, status, and idiosyncrasy credit. *Psychological Review* 65, 117–127.

Hollander, E. P. (1964). *Leaders, groups, and influence.* New York: Oxford University Press.

Hollander, E. P. (1978). *Leadership dynamics: A practical guide to effective relationships.* New York: Free Press/Macmillan.

Hollander, E. P. (1985). Leadership and power. In G. Lindzey & E. Aronson (Eds.), *The handbook of social psychology* (3rd edition, pp. 485–537). New York: Random House.

Hollander, E. P. (1986). On the central role of leadership processes. *International Review of Applied Psychology* 35, 39–52.

Hollander, E. P. & J. W. Julian. (1968). Leadership. In E. F. Borgatta & W. W. Lambert (Eds.), *Handbook of personality theory and research* (pp. 890–899). Chicago: Rand McNally.

Hollander, E. P. & J. W. Julian. (1969). Contemporary trends in the analysis of leadership processes. *Psychological Bulletin* 71, 387–397.

Hollander, E. P. & J. W. Julian. (1970). Studies in leader legitimacy, influence, and innovation. In L. L. Berkowitz (Ed.), *Advances in experimental social psychology* (Volume 5, pp. 33–69). New York: Academic Press.

Hollander, E. P. & J. W. Julian. (1978). A further look at leader legitimacy, influence, and innovation. In L. Berkowitz (Ed.), *Group processes* (pp. 153–165). New York: Academic Press.

Hollander, E. P., J. W. Julian, & R. M. Sorrentino. (1969). The leader's sense of legitimacy as a source of constructive deviation. *ONR Technical Report No. 12.* Department of Psychology, State University of New York at Buffalo.

Hollander, E. P. & D. R. Kelly. (1990). Rewards from leaders as perceived by followers: Further use of critical incidents and rating scales. Eastern Psychological Association Annual Meeting, Philadelphia, March 30.

Hollander, E. P. & L. Offermann. (1990a). Power and leadership in organizations: Relationships in transition. *American Psychologist* 45, 179–189.

Hollander, E. P. & L. Offermann. (1990b). Relational features of organizational leadership and followership. In K. E. Clark & M. B. Clark (Eds.), *Measures of lead-ership* (pp. 83–97). West Orange, NJ: Leadership Library of America.

Hollander, E. P. & W. B. Webb. (1955). Leadership, followership, and friendship: An analysis of peer nominations. *Journal of Abnormal and Social Psychology* 50, 163–167.

Homans, G. C. (1961). *Social behavior: Its elementary forms.* New York: Harcourt, Brace and World.

Howard, A. & D. Bray. (1988). *Managerial lives in transition: Advancing age and changing times.* New York: Dorsey.

Katz, D. & R. L. Kahn. (1978). *The social psychology of organizations* (2nd edition). New York: Wiley.

Kenny, D. A. & S. J. Zaccaro. (1983). An estimate of variance due to traits in leadership. *Journal of Applied Psychology* 68, 678–685.

Kipnis, D. (1976). *The powerholders.* Chicago: University of Chicago Press.

Kirkpatrick, S. A. & E. A. Locke. (1991). Leadership: Do traits matter? *Academy of Management Executive* 5(2), 48–60.

Kouzes, J. M. & B. Z. Posner. (1987). *The leadership challenge: How to get extraordinary things done in organizations.* San Francisco: Jossey-Bass.

Kraut, A. I., P. R. Bedigo, D. D. McKenna, & M. D. Dunnette. (1989). The role of the manager: What's really important in different management jobs. *Academy of Management Executive* 3, 286–293.

Lord, R. G. & K. J. Maher. (1990). Leadership perceptions and leadership performance: Two distinct but interdependent processes. In J. Carroll (Ed.), *Advances in applied social psychology: Business settings* (Volume 4), pp. 129–154. Hillsdale, NJ: Erlbaum.

Lord, R. G., C. L. DeVader, & G. M. Alliger. (1986). A meta-analysis of the relation between personality traits and leadership perceptions: An application of validity generalization procedures. *Journal of Applied Psychology* 71, 402–409.

Maccoby, M. (1989). Leadership for our time. In L. Atwater & R. Penn (Eds.), *Military leadership: Traditions and future trends* (pp. 41–46). Annapolis: U.S. Naval Academy.

McCall, M. W., M. M. Lombardo, & A. M. Morrison. (1988). *The lessons of experience.* Lexington, MA: Lexington Books.

McClelland, D. (1975). *Power: The inner experience.* New York: Irvington.

Menzies, H. D. (1980). The ten toughest bosses. *Fortune* 101, 62–69.

Mitchell, T. R., S. G. Green, & R. E. Wood. (1981). An attributional model of leadership and the poor-performing subordinate: Development and validation.

In B. Shaw and L. Cummings (Eds.), *Research in Organizational behavior* (Volume 3, pp. 197–234). Greenwich, CT: JAI Press.

Pfeffer, J. (1977). The ambiguity of leadership. In M. W. McCall, Jr., & M. M. Lombardo (Eds.), *Leadership: Where else can we go?* Durham, NC: Duke University Press.

Porter, M. E. (1985). *Competitive advantage.* New York: Free Press.

Post, J. M. (1986). Narcissism and the charismatic leader–follower relationship. *Political Psychology* 7, 675–688.

Rush, M. C., J. C. Thomas, & R. G. Lord. (1977). Implicit leadership theory: A potential threat to the internal validity of leader behavior questionnaires. *Organizational Behavior and Human Performance* 20, 93–110.

Sanford, F. (1950). *Authoritarianism and leadership.* Philadelphia, PA: Institute for Research in Human Relations.

Snyder, M. (1979). Self-monitoring processes. In L. Berkowitz (Ed.), *Advances in Experimental Social Psychology* 12 (pp. 86–128). New York: Academic Press.

Sorrentino, R. M. & R. G. Boutillier. (1975). The effect of quantity and quality of verbal interaction on ratings of leadership ability. *Journal of Experimental Social Psychology* 11, 403–411.

Stewart, R. (1982). *Choices for the manager.* Englewood Cliffs, NJ: Prentice-Hall.

Stogdill, R. M. (1948). Personal factors associated with leadership. *Journal of Psychology* 25, 35–71.

Weber, M. (1921). The sociology of charismatic authority. Republished in translation (1946) in H. H. Gerth & C. W. Mills (Trans. and Eds.), *From Max Weber: Essays in Sociology* (pp. 245–252). New York: Oxford University Press.

Yammarino, R. & B. M. Bass. (1988). Long term forecasting of transformational leadership and its effects among Naval Officers: Some preliminary findings. In K. E. & M. B. Clark (Eds.), *Measures of Leadership* (pp. 151–169). West Orange, NJ: Leadership Library of America.

Zaccaro, S. J., R. J. Foti, & D. A. Kenny. (1991). Self-monitoring and trait-based variance in leadership: An investigation across multiple group situations. *Journal of Applied Psychology* 76, 308–315.

# Chapter **Eleven**

# Participative Leadership

The classic study of leader behavior conducted at the University of Michigan by Kurt Lewin and his students, Ronald Lippitt and Ralph K. White, during 1939 and 1940 stimulated an interest in looking at the relative effectiveness of three leadership styles—authoritarian, democratic, and laissez-faire—on group and individual behavior. Among some of the results from their investigation was the suggestion that leader behavior has a number of different effects on member reactions. Among some of their major observations are the following: (*a*) laissez-faire and democratic leadership are not the same; (*b*) democratic leadership can be efficient; (*c*) greater hostility, aggression, and discontent arise under autocratic than democratic leadership; (*d*) autocratic leadership produces more dependence and less individuality; (*e*) there is more group-mindedness and more friendliness under democratic leadership; and (*f*) groups with democratic leaders are more productive even when the leader is not present.[1]

Following the Hawthorne studies (1927–1933), the work of Lewin and his associates, Eric Trist and Fred Emery's work with sociotechnical systems, the onset of the human relations movement, and the development of the human resource model, there emerged a strong interest in participative leadership practices. This is evident by numerous participative management theories, a myriad of research investigations, the development of a number of employee-involvement strategies, and recent organizational efforts to create high-involvement organizations (cf., Lawler, 1992).[2]

The work of Lewin and his students contributed to our thinking about *leadership style* as it pertains to the use and location of power within the group. Different perspectives have been offered regarding leadership styles. One perspective positions the laissez-faire leadership style (i.e., do whatever you want) at one end of a continuum that becomes increasingly directive; laissez-faire leadership is followed by consensus, participative, consultative, benevolent autocratic, and, finally, autocratic (i.e., I will tell you what we are going to do because I am the leader/boss). This perspective has been contrasted with the use of a power (i.e., autocratic versus democratic) and involvement (i.e., active versus passive)

---

[1] R. White and R. Lippitt, "Leader Behavior and Member Reaction in Three 'Social Climates.'" In D. Cartwright and A. Zander, Eds., *Group Dynamics: Research and Theory* (New York: Harper & Row, 1968), pp. 318–35.
[2] E. E. Lawler III, *The Ultimate Advantage: Creating the High-Involvement Organization* (San Francisco: Jossey-Bass, 1992).

orientation to differentiate between leadership styles.[3] Accompanying this typology, the laissez-faire leader is positioned outside of the framework and is seen as employing a passive style of leadership (i.e., he or she is seen as not leading per se). In the first reading, Stephen M. Sales (1966) provides a review of the theory and empirical observations of the effects associated with authoritarian and democratic dimensions of leader behavior. Sales's observations, when coupled with those stemming from Lewin, Lippitt, and White's work, suggest that absenteeism and turnover may be higher under autocratic leaders than their democratic counterparts, and, as a result, productivity may be lower.

It has been suggested that leader behavior is determined by an interaction between attributes of the leader and characteristics of the situation in which the leadership process unfolds. Recognizing the role of situational differences and their impact upon the leadership process, the question has often been raised about when democratic/participative practices should be employed within the organizational context. In an earlier chapter, House and Mitchell (1974) provided insight into the appropriate conditions for participative management in their path-goal theory of leadership.

Victor H. Vroom and his associates have worked on the development of a model that addresses the use of participative decision making in the organizational context.[4] In the second reading in this chapter, Vroom (2000) presents a framework that is designed to help managers decide when to use a participative style of leadership vis à vis an autocratic style, and the amount of subordinate involvement that should be employed in a variety of situations. Instead of adopting a style of leadership that is "most comfortable," Vroom suggests that leaders should be flexible in their behavioral approach, analyze each leadership situation, and then select an approach that best fits the situation. This situationally driven decision tree model is designed to prescribe the "best" style of leadership for a given leadership situation. Vroom's work highlights the fact that neither the autocratic nor participative style of leadership is universally the most appropriate. (It is important to note that Vroom's work has been cast as both a leadership and decision-making model. His objective is to provide a model that details the type of leader behavior and the amount of subordinate participation that should be employed in different types of situations.)

Fueled by Frederick Herzberg's and Douglas McGregor's criticisms of scientific management, a number of different schools of thought (e.g., human relations, human resource) and theoretical models (e.g., cognitive, affective, contingency) have articulated the processes associated with efficacious participatory practices. While there has been a plethora of empirical studies that have examined participation, questions as to the effectiveness of participation remain.

In the face of the uncertainty surrounding the effectiveness of participative leadership practices (see the reviews conducted by Locke & Schweiger, 1979; Dachler & Wilpert, 1978; Strauss, 1982),[5] Cotton (1993) observes that the past several decades have been characterized by the adoption of a number of different employee involvement systems (e.g., employee ownership, self-directed work teams, job enrichment, representative participation, quality circles, and quality

---

[3] G. L. Steward and C. C. Manz, "Leadership for Self-managing Work Teams: A Typology and Integrative Model," *Organizational Dynamics* 19, no. 4 (1995), pp. 18–35.

[4] V. H. Vroom and P. H. Yetton, *Leadership and Decision Making* (Pittsburgh, PA: University of Pittsburgh Press, 1973); V. H. Vroom and A. G. Jago, *The New Leadership* (New York: Prentice-Hall, 1973).

[5] H. P. Dachler and B. Wilpert, "Conceptual Dimensions and Boundaries of Participation in Organizations," *Administrative Science Quarterly* 23 (1978), pp. 1–39; E. A. Locke and D. M. Schweiger, "Participation in Decision Making: One More Look," *Research in Organizational Behavior* 1 (1979), pp. 265–339; G. Strauss, "Workers' Participation in Management: An International Perspective," *Research in Organizational Behavior* 4 (1982), pp. 173–265.

of work life programs).[6] These involvement systems reflect organizational experimentation with different *forms* of participative leadership at different organizational *levels*—some operating at the team and department level, and others reflecting a top-management orientation toward organizational leadership.

In the third and final reading in this chapter, Katherine I. Miller and Peter R. Monge (1988) discuss the relationship of participation with satisfaction and productivity. They highlight three theoretical models—contingency, affective, and cognitive—to articulate how and why participation might have a favorable relationship with both of these outcomes. Miller and Monge conducted a statistical meta-analytic review of the participation literature, providing a test for each of these three models. They report finding strong support for the affective model, some support for the cognitive model, and no support for the contingency model. They suggest that "participation fulfills needs, fulfilled needs lead to satisfaction, satisfaction strengthens motivation, and increased motivation improves workers' productivity" (Miller & Monge, p. 731).

The self-assessment presented at the end of this chapter opener can provide you with insight into your human resource/human relations (i.e., Theory Y versus Theory X) orientation. Individuals with a strong Theory Y orientation are more predisposed to, and comfortable with, a participatory leadership orientation.

[6] J. L. Cotton, *Employee Involvement: Methods for Improving Performance and Work Attitudes* (Newbury Park, CA: Sage, 1993).

**EXERCISE**
*Self-Assessment*

**Participatory Leadership Attitudes**

**Instructions:** In the section below, you will see a series of statements. Please indicate your agreement or disagreement. Use the scale below for each statement.
For example: It is easier to work in cool weather than in hot.

| : _____ | : _____ | : _____ | : _____ | : _____ |
|---|---|---|---|---|
| Strongly Agree | Agree | Undecided | Disagree | Strongly Disagree |

If you think it is easier to work in cool weather, put an (X) above "agree"; if you think it is much easier to work in cool weather, put a mark above "strongly agree." If you think it doesn't matter, put a mark over "undecided" and so on. Put your mark in a space, not on the boundaries.

There is no right or wrong answer. It is only your opinion about the statements that follow that matters.

1. The average human being prefers to be directed, wishes to avoid responsibility, and has relatively little ambition.

| : _____ | : _____ | : _____ | : _____ | : _____ |
|---|---|---|---|---|
| Strongly Agree | Agree | Undecided | Disagree | Strongly Disagree |

2. Leadership skills can be acquired by most people regardless of their particular inborn traits and abilities.

| : _____ | : _____ | : _____ | : _____ | : _____ |
|---|---|---|---|---|
| Strongly Agree | Agree | Undecided | Disagree | Strongly Disagree |

3. The use of rewards (pay, promotion, etc.) and punishment (failure to promote, etc.) is not the best way to get subordinates to do their work.

| : _____ | : _____ | : _____ | : _____ | : _____ |
|---|---|---|---|---|
| Strongly Agree | Agree | Undecided | Disagree | Strongly Disagree |

4. In a work situation, if the subordinates cannot influence me, then I lose some influence on them.

| : _____ | : _____ | : _____ | : _____ | : _____ |
|---|---|---|---|---|
| Strongly Agree | Agree | Undecided | Disagree | Strongly Disagree |

5. A good leader should give detailed and complete instructions to his or her subordinates rather than merely giving them general directions and depending upon their initiative to work out the details.

| : _____ | : _____ | : _____ | : _____ | : _____ |
|---|---|---|---|---|
| Strongly Agree | Agree | Undecided | Disagree | Strongly Disagree |

6. Group goal setting offers advantages that cannot be obtained by individual goal setting.

| : _____ | : _____ | : _____ | : _____ | : _____ |
|---|---|---|---|---|
| Strongly Agree | Agree | Undecided | Disagree | Strongly Disagree |

7. A superior should give his or her subordinates only that information which is needed for them to do their immediate tasks.

| : _____ | : _____ | : _____ | : _____ | : _____ |
|---|---|---|---|---|
| Strongly Agree | Agree | Undecided | Disagree | Strongly Disagree |

8. The superior's authority over his or her subordinates in an organization is primarily economic.

| : _____ | : _____ | : _____ | : _____ | : _____ |
|---|---|---|---|---|
| Strongly Agree | Agree | Undecided | Disagree | Strongly Disagree |

**Scoring:** Four attitudes are being assessed by these 8 questions: (1) attitudes toward belief in the average person's capacities (questions 1 and 2); (2) attitudes toward sharing information (questions 5 and 7); (3) attitudes toward participation (questions 4 and 6); and (4) attitudes toward the nature of supervisory controls (questions 3 and 8).

For each of the 8 questions, assign:

  5 points for "strongly agree"
  4 points for "agree"
  3 points for "undecided"
  2 points for "disagree"
  1 point for "strongly disagree"

1. Rescore your answer to questions 1, 5, 7, and 8 by subtracting your score from 6.
2. Next, sum your scores for questions 1 and 2, and divide by 2.
3. Sum your scores for questions 5 and 7, and divide by 2.
4. Sum your scores for questions 4 and 6, and divide by 2.
5. Sum your scores for questions 3 and 8, and divide by 2.
6. Finally, sum your final scores as produced in steps 2, 3, 4, and 5 above and divide by 4.

My participatory attitude scores are:

  Person's capacity _____.
  Information sharing _____.
  Participation _____.
  Control _____.
  Overall score _____.

**Interpretation:** These questions on leadership, according to Haire, Ghiselli, and Porter (1966), are focused upon attitudes that pertain to a somewhat unilateral, autocratic approach to management at one extreme and a more group-oriented, team, participatory approach at the other. The questions are intended to capture beliefs in "the capacity of subordinates," and views on "the efficacy of participation, of sharing information, and of providing opportunities for internal self-control on the job" (p. 3).

A high score (4 and greater) for each of the four attitudes and in the aggregate would reflect a "favorable" disposition toward subordinates (followers), their capacities, and their involvement in organizational activities. A score of 2 and less might reflect a hesitancy toward the full and active involvement of followers in the leadership context (i.e., a propensity toward leader control as opposed to a participatory style of leadership). The high score might be reflective of McGregor's vision of the Theory Y leader, while the low score is reflective of Theory X.

**Source:** M. Haire, E. E. Ghiselli, and L. W. Porter, *Managerial Thinking: An International Study* (New York: John Wiley & Sons, 1966).

**Reading 31**

# Supervisory Style and Productivity

*Review and Theory*[1]

**Stephen M. Sales**
University of Michigan

It is widely assumed that employees will work harder for supervisors who employ given styles of supervision than they will for supervisors who use other styles. This supposition clearly underlies much of supervisory training; it is a basic tenet of the writings of Morse (1953), Likert (1961), and many others. However, the theoretical underpinnings of this assumption are often unclearly stated (when they are stated at all); furthermore, the wide variety of studies investigating the validity of this position are rarely fully described. The present article will sketch a theory which accounts for the predicted differential in productivity and will review and evaluate the literature relevant to this theory.

## AUTHORITARIANISM AND DEMOCRACY

The styles to be discussed are the authoritarian and democratic dimensions. The distinction between these orientations has often been made in the literature; it will not be extensively elaborated here. Rather, we shall discuss only the major differences between these styles.

Authoritarian supervision, in general, is characterized by the relatively high degree of power wielded by the supervisor over the work group. As contrasted with democratic supervision, both power and all decision-making functions are absolutely concentrated in the person of the authoritarian. Democratic supervision, on the other hand, is characterized by a sharing of power and by participative decision making. Under democratic supervision, the work group becomes in some ways co-equal with the supervisor; responsibility is spread rather than concentrated.

**Source:** Edited and reprinted with permission from *Personnel Psychology* 19 (1966), pp. 275–86.

## DIFFERENTIAL EFFECTIVENESS

It is commonly assumed that, with other conditions held constant, employees will produce more under democratic supervision than they would have produced under autocratic supervision. (Such an assumption, of course, lies behind the entire human relations movement.) There is at least one good reason for this prediction. Specifically, the reinforcing value of work performed under democratic supervision should be higher than that of work performed under autocratic supervision.

It is a basic tenet of experimental psychology that high levels of performance will be obtained in situations in which the reinforcement is large, whereas low performance levels will occur in those in which the reinforcement is small. In terms of industrial situations, the more reinforcement an employee receives for production, the higher his production should be. (This is, of course, the assumption which underlies incentive systems, although reinforcement is rather narrowly defined in such programs.) Vroom (1962, pp. 26–43) in particular has explored the ramifications of this argument.

The importance of this point for the present consideration is that production is attended by two different levels of need-satisfaction under the two styles of supervision sketched above. Democratic supervision, by allowing subordinates freedom in determining the specific form and content of their work, implicates the personalities of the employees in the tasks they perform. This means that production, under democratic supervision, becomes a means for satisfying the employees' ego-esteem and self-actualization needs (see Maslow, 1954; Argyris, 1957). That is, the "greater opportunity for regulating and controlling their own activities [provided by democratic supervision] . . . should increase the degree to which individuals could express their various and diverse needs and could move in the direction of fully exploiting their potential while on the job" (Morse & Reimer, 1956). Authoritarian supervision, inasmuch as it makes work merely the carrying out of the supervisor's will, reduces the degree to which such need-satisfaction can be derived from production. Therefore, since productivity is less satisfying under autocratic than under democratic supervision, one would expect that workers would be less productive in the former condition than in the latter. (This effect, of course, should be accentuated for those individuals for whom the needs in question are most important.)

It should be noted that the above considerations do not involve between-style differences which rest upon uncontrolled factors (even when such factors might themselves follow from the style variation). For instance, if turnover were higher under one supervisory style than under the other, one would expect that the method resulting in higher turnover would be accompanied by the lower productivity rate (because of lowered effectiveness during learning periods). Factors of this sort would lead to productivity differences between the supervisory styles; however, such differences would not truly bear upon the question of effectiveness as usually posed. That is, statements about supervisory style center in general about the proposition that employees will work harder for some supervisors than for others. This statement cannot be supported by dependent variable differences which may be shown to result from between-condition variations other than that of supervisory style. The present discussion is concerned solely with productivity differences which follow *directly* from the style of supervision. . . .

## EXPERIMENTAL INVESTIGATIONS

The original and best known study in this area is the experiment of Lewin, Lippitt, and White (e.g., Lippitt & White, 1958, pp. 496–510; White & Lippitt, 1962). These investigators employed as subjects 30 10-year-old boys who met in six groups which ostensibly were recreational clubs. These groups were supervised by adults who had been trained to act in either a democratic, autocratic, or laissez-faire manner. (The last condition is not considered in the present discussion.) Each club was exposed to each of the three styles for six weeks.

The results of this experiment, in terms of productivity, are extremely difficult to establish. When exposed to autocratic supervision[2] the boys spent more time at work than they did under democratic supervision (74 percent of the total time as opposed to 50 percent under democratic

supervision). However, the "work-mindedness" of the democratically supervised boys appeared to be somewhat higher since under democratic supervision the groups engaged in a slightly larger amount of "work-minded conversation." (There were 63 work-minded remarks per child under the democratic condition, whereas in the autocratic condition this figure fell to 52.) However, *no objective measure of productivity is reported by the authors, and therefore it is impossible to determine accurately which of the two styles evoked the higher production* (a factor often overlooked by reviewers of this study).

McCurdy and Eber (1953) examined supervisory style in an investigation on group problem-solving. In this experiment, three-man groups participated in a task in which the group determined the proper setting of three switches. In the authoritarian condition one subject was given the power to order the others at will, making him an "absolute" supervisor. The other subjects were instructed merely to obey orders. In the democratic condition the instructions emphasized equalitarianism, specifying that each subject could offer suggestions and that no individual could order the others in any way. No differences whatever appeared between the two conditions on a productivity criterion.

Shaw (1955), working with communication networks, also used problem-solving as a dependent variable in an investigation of supervisory style effects. Employing three different "nets," he instructed the subjects assigned to the position with the highest independence score within each structure[3] to behave either in an autocratic manner (e.g., by giving orders) or in a democratic manner (e.g., by making suggestions). Shaw found that the autocratically-supervised subjects (*a*) required less time to solve the problems, regardless of the communication net in which they were placed, and (*b*) made fewer errors.

Day and Hamblin (1964) trained a female student to employ "close" and "general" supervisory styles in leading groups of female subjects in an assembly-line task. These researchers found that subjects exposed to close supervision produced less than did subjects exposed to general supervision.

Sales (1964), like Day and Hamblin, replicated an industrial assembly-line setting in the laboratory. In Sales's experiment two male supervisors played democratic and autocratic roles over male and female groups. (Both role and sex of the subordinates were fully counterbalanced in this experiment.) Sales reports no differential effectiveness whatever between the two styles; the productivity means for the two conditions were virtually identical.

Spector and Suttell (1957) report a relevant laboratory study with naval trainees as subjects. These authors trained supervisors to use either "single leadership" or "leadership sharing" styles, patterns which seem to parallel the democratic–autocratic distinction. The task consisted of problems in which team members cooperated in receiving, processing, and recording information. No differences were detected in the productivity of the groups under the two styles.

In the most extensive of the investigations reported in this area, Morse and Reimer (1956) created groups exposed either to democratic or to autocratic supervision by altering the style of supervision used in an on-going industrial setting. In two divisions ("participative treatment") an attempt was made to push down the level of decision making. Supervisors were trained to employ more democratic supervisory methods, and they were given greater freedom of action than previously had been allowed. In two other divisions an "hierarchically controlled treatment" was established by an increase in the closeness of supervision and a movement upward in the level at which decisions were made. The treatments were administered for a year's time to approximately 500 employees.

Morse and Reimer found that both programs resulted in a significant increase in productivity. This increase was slightly higher for the hierarchically controlled divisions; however, the actual difference between the treatments was quite small.

On balance, then, the experimental studies reviewed above show no consistent superiority of one style over the other in terms of a productivity criterion. Of the six studies for which objective production data are available, one (Day & Hamblin, 1964) reports democratic supervision to be more effective and one (Shaw, 1955) reports authoritarian supervision to be more effective. The other four investigations note no differences of consequence between the two styles.

## SURVEY INVESTIGATIONS

Survey researches applied to the problem discussed herein follow a standard methodology. The supervisory style which exists in each of the work groups in the situation is determined (usually by means of questionnaires administered to the employees), and this variable is then related to productivity. Researchers using this methodology generally have found a clear relationship between style of supervision and work group productivity.

The extensive investigations performed by the Survey Research Center at the University of Michigan during the early 1950s (Katz, Maccoby, & Morse, 1950; Katz, Maccoby, Gurin, & Floor, 1951; Katz & Kahn, 1951, pp. 146–171) are representative of this approach. In a wide variety of industrial situations (including railway maintenance crews, insurance office staffs, and heavy industry production lines), these authors found (1) that general supervision was associated with high productivity whereas close supervision was associated with low productivity, and (2) that "employee-oriented" attitudes in the supervisor were associated with high productivity whereas "job-oriented" attitudes were associated with low productivity. It is unclear exactly what relationship these independent variables have to the democratic–autocratic dimension; however, it can certainly be assumed that employee-oriented attitudes and general supervision will tend to be associated with democracy (as here used) whereas job-oriented attitudes and close supervision will tend to be associated with authoritarianism. The data of Morse (1953) and Argyle, Gardner, and Cioffi (1957) support these assumptions.

Argyle et al. (1958) performed a successful replication of these earlier investigations in a British industrial situation. The authors report that foremen of high-producing work groups tended to use general rather than close supervision and were relatively more democratic in their behavior than were foremen of less productive work groups. Further, the attitudes of the more effective foremen tended to be more "employee-oriented" than those of the less effective foremen. In contrast to experimental findings, therefore, these survey data clearly seem to support the hypothesis that democratic supervision leads to higher production than does authoritarian supervision.

## DISCUSSION

The usual explanations offered for the failure of the experimental method to replicate survey findings rest upon either (*a*) the brevity of the experimental sessions or (*b*) the peripheral nature of the experimental tasks. It seems to the present author, however, that these explanations are respectively (*a*) too facile and (*b*) inadequately elaborated for proper handling of the problem.

Of the two, the "brevity" argument is the more open to attack. Experimental sessions are, of course, of relatively short duration. However, the entire science of experimental social psychology rests upon the assumption that experimental periods are sufficiently lengthy for treatments to "take," an assumption which is supported in every significant finding obtained in an experimental laboratory. To argue that the experiments reviewed here failed to demonstrate predicted productivity differences because of inadequate time periods (especially when these same time periods are sufficient to evoke morale differences—favoring the democratic supervisor—between the groups exposed to the two styles) seems somehow an unscientific and unsatisfactory way of explaining the findings. Furthermore, such an explanation fails to account for the quite small productivity differential which existed between the conditions created by Morse and Reimer in an experiment which continued over the course of an entire year.

It appears to the author that, rather than looking to brevity, one may best explain the equal experimental effectiveness of the two supervisory styles by concentrating upon the nature of the tasks involved. (This is, of course, the approach incompletely hinted at in the "peripheral nature" argument.) Specifically, it seems that no differences in effectiveness have been found between the two styles *because the tasks employed wholly fail to meet the conditions under which differential productivity was predicted.*

Democratic supervision, it will be remembered, was expected to be the more effective style because of the greater extent to which it makes productivity a means to need-satisfaction. This prediction rests upon the assumption that democratic supervision allows productivity to be a path to the satisfaction of self-actualization and ego-esteem needs, whereas autocratic supervision does not serve such a purpose.

These conditions do not seem to have been generated by the experimental investigations reported above. Democratic supervision, in these experiments, can hardly be seen as allowing the subjects to see production on the task involved as a path to self-actualization. *The thought is virtually absurd.* Regardless of the intent of the investigators, the decisions allowed by the democratic supervisors (e.g., suggesting possible solutions to simple problems) do not seem to implicate the unique personalities of the subjects in their tasks. This seems to have been true even in the Morse and Reimer investigation, for the authors report that "both groups of clerks indicated that their jobs throughout the course of the experiment did not give them a very high degree of self-actualization." To the extent that experimental studies fail to make productivity under democratic supervision a path to significantly greater need-satisfaction than it would be under autocratic supervision, there is no reason to suspect that they should demonstrate democratic supervision to be more effective. Such investigations simply fail to provide the conditions necessary for a test of the hypothesis in question.

It should not be inferred, however, that survey investigations provide a more adequate test of the hypothesis that workers will work harder for democratic supervisors, in spite of the satisfying direction of the findings. There are at least two reasons for approaching the results of these studies with caution, both of which rest upon the fact that spurious variables which clearly affect work group productivity accompany both these styles. To the extent that the effects of such variables cannot be discounted, survey methodology is incapable of offering convincing evidence concerning the relative effort expended by workers exposed to the styles in question.

In the first place, the supervisory styles discussed herein are accompanied by differential turnover and absenteeism (e.g., Mann & Baumgartel, 1953; Morse & Reimer, 1956; Argyle et al., 1958). These effects do contribute to productivity differences between groups exposed to these styles, since the higher absenteeism and turnover evoked by autocratic supervision would lead to a productivity difference favoring democratic supervision. However, such a difference would be irrelevant to the hypothesis that democratic supervision leads directly to more concerted effort on the part of the employees involved. The effects of absenteeism and/or turnover could be removed from the analysis by means of simple statistical techniques, although no survey research known to the author has as yet attempted to do so.

A second consideration lies in the fact that supervisors who naturally affect a democratic style of supervision cannot be assumed to be otherwise similar to those who affect an authoritarian style. In particular, the author feels that democratically oriented supervisors can be expected to be more intelligent than are autocratically oriented supervisors. There are no direct data drawn from industry which bear on this statement. However, the fact that intelligence has clearly been shown to be negatively correlated with measured ($F$-scale) authoritarianism (e.g., Titus & Hollander, 1957), which in turn has been shown to be highly correlated with authoritarian behavior (McGee, 1955), seems sufficient to make the point.

It may be assumed that the intelligence of the supervisor should be of some importance in determining the productivity of the employees under him. The more intelligent supervisor might be expected to diagnose production difficulties more quickly than the less intelligent supervisor, and he might also be expected to take more effective remedial action. Therefore, inasmuch as authoritarian and democratic supervisors are differentiated on intelligence, one might expect them to be differentiated on their skill in dealing with day-to-day production problems. The advantage, of course, would go to the democratic supervisors.

The effect of this predicted difference between the two supervisory populations would be to make the work groups under democratic supervision more productive than those under autocratic supervision. However, as in the case of the different levels of turnover evoked by the two styles, such a finding would *not* necessarily imply that employees worked harder for supervisors affecting the democratic style. Like the effect of absenteeism, the effect of supervisory intelligence could be removed from the analysis by means of proper statistical techniques, but again there has been no survey research which has done so.

Therefore, in neither experimental studies nor survey investigations has an adequate test of the theory sketched above been made. Experimental studies have not created the conditions necessary for such a test; survey research has introduced at least two contaminating variables which render proper interpretation of the observed relationship extremely difficult. Such studies have not *disproved* the theory in question. They simply have not offered the unambiguous evidence administrative science must have in order to evaluate plans of action (e.g., supervisory training) tacitly based on this theory.

This should not be interpreted to mean that such a test cannot be made. Experimental investigations of the sort attempted by Morse and Reimer (1956), *using a technology in which self-actualization could occur under democratic supervision,* would provide an adequate test, as would survey investigations in which the intelligence of the supervisors and the turnover (and/or absenteeism) levels existing in the various work groups were assessed and partialled out of the correlation between the style of the supervisor and the productivity of the subordinates. (Research now in progress is directed toward this latter objective.) Without such conditions, however, the hypothesis that democratic supervision will evoke greater effort from employees than will autocratic supervision cannot truly be either supported or rejected.

## Notes

1. The author wishes to express his appreciation to Dr. Ned A. Rosen of the New York State School of Industrial and Labor Relations, Cornell Unviversity, for his constant assistance and encouragement. A grant from the Foundation for Research on Human Behavior, Ann Arbor, Michigan, provided the time necessary for the preparation of this article.

2. Only the "submissive reaction" to autocracy will be here considered; the "aggressive reaction" is felt to be a function of the subjects and the situation employed by the investigators.

3. The research of Leavitt (1951) clearly suggests that these positions are the ones from which leadership is exercised.

## References

Argyle, Michael, Gardner, Godfrey, and Cioffi, Frank. "The Measurement of Supervisory Methods." *Human Relations,* X (1957), 295–313.

Argyle, Michael, Gardner, Godfrey, and Cioffi, Frank. "Supervisory Methods Related to Productivity, Absenteeism, and Labour Turnover." *Human Relations,* XI (1958), 23–40.

Argyris, Chris. *Personality and Organization.* New York: Harper & Brothers, 1957.

Coch, L. and French, J. R. P., Jr. "Overcoming Resistance to Change." *Human Relations,* I (1948), 512–532.

Day, R. C. and Hamblin, R. L. "Some Effects of Close and Punitive Styles of Supervision." *American Journal of Sociology,* LXIX (1964), 499–510.

Katz, D. and Kahn, R. L. "Human Organization and Worker Motivation." In Tripp, L. Reed (Editor), *Industrial Productivity.* Madison, Wisconsin: Industrial Relations Research Association, 1951.

Katz, D., Maccoby, N., Gurin, G., and Floor, Lucretia. *Productivity, Supervision, and Morale among Railroad Workers.* Ann Arbor, Michigan: Institute for Social Research, 1951.

Katz, D., Maccoby, N., and Morse, Nancy C. *Productivity, Supervision and Morale in an Office Situation.* Part 1. Ann Arbor, Michigan: Institute for Social Research, 1950.

Leavitt, Harold. "Some Effects of Certain Communication Patterns on Group Performance." *Journal of Abnormal and Social Psychology,* XLVI (1951), 16–30.

Likert, Rensis. *New Patterns of Management.* New York: McGraw-Hill, 1961.

Lippitt, R. and White, R. K. "An Experimental Study of Leadership and Group Life." In Maccoby, E. E., Newcomb, T. N., and Hartley, E. L. (Editors), *Readings in Social Psychology,* Third Edition. New York: Holt, Rinehart, & Winston, 1958.

Maslow, A. H. *Motivation and Personality.* New York: Harper & Brothers, 1954.

Mann, F. C. and Baumgartel, H. D. "Absences and Employee Attitudes in an Electric Power Company." Ann Arbor, Michigan: Institute for Social Research, 1953.

McCurdy, H. G. and Eber, H. W. "Democratic Versus Authoritarian: A Further Investigation of Group Problem-Solving." *Journal of Personality,* XXII (1953), 258–269.

McGee, H. M. "Measurement of Authoritarianism and Its Relation to Teacher Classroom Behavior." *Genetic Psychological Monographs,* LII (1955), 89–146.

Morse, Nancy C. *Satisfactions in the White-Collar Job.* Ann Arbor, Michigan: Institute for Social Research, 1953.

Morse, Nancy C. and Reimer, E. "The Experimental Change of a Major Organizational Variable." *Journal of Abnormal and Social Psychology,* LI (1956), 120–129.

Sales, Stephen M. "A Laboratory Investigation of the Effectiveness of Two Industrial Supervisory Dimensions." Unpublished MS Thesis, Cornell University, 1964.

Shaw, M. E. "A Comparison of Two Types of Leadership in Various Communication Nets." *Journal of Abnormal and Social Psychology,* L (1955), 127–134.

Spector, Paul, and Suttell, Barbara. *An Experimental Comparison of the Effectiveness of Three Patterns of Leadership Behavior.* Washington, DC: American Institute for Research, 1957.

Titus, H. E. and Hollander, E. P. "The California F-Scale in Psychological Research: 1950–1955." *Psychological Bulletin,* LIV (1957), 47–65.

Vroom, V. H. "Human Relations Research in Industry: Some Things Learned." In Baristow, Frances (Editor), *Research Frontiers in Industrial Relations Today.* Montreal: Industrial Relations Centre, 1962.

White, Ralph, and Lippitt, R. "Leader Behavior and Member Reaction in Three 'Social Climates.' " In Cartwright, Dorin, and Zander, Alvin (Editors), *Group Dynamics, Research and Theory,* Second Edition. Evanston, Illinois: Row, Peterson, 1962.

## Reading 32

# Leadership and the Decision-Making Process

**Victor H. Vroom**
Yale University

## THE BURNS DECISION

Jim Burns is an emergency response manager in a large company, specializing in ecological control systems. His work runs the gamut from removal and disposal of toxic waste to cleaning up spills of oil and other contaminants. Typically, his firm works on contracts with organizations both public and private, but occasionally Jim is called upon to deal with situations not covered by existing contracts.

This morning Jim received a phone call from the police in a nearby town. They asked for his firm's assistance in dealing with an oil spill that threatened a nearby river. Jim drove to the site with four of his associates, and within an hour the team of five had obtained the following picture of what happened.

While filling an oil tanker, the driver had gone into the cab and had fallen asleep. Before it was noticed, 10,000 gallons of crude oil had escaped and begun making its way five miles downstream and was within four hours of reaching a wildlife sanctuary.

Although the potential for environmental damage is clear, the liability is not. The driver was an employee of a small subcontractor who was uninsured and who would be forced into bankruptcy, if deemed liable. The oil company contacted its insurance company, which denied any responsibility for claims that might be made against it. Representatives of the State Environmental Protection Agency and Department of Fish and Game were contacted, and they offered their moral support, but neither had the half million dollars Jim estimated would be necessary to contain and clean up the spill.

A decision must be made soon about whether to risk the company's money in a matter in which reimbursement, if any, may have to be decided by the courts. The decision is Jim's to make, and he is experienced in making the difficult judgments that are called for. Although conscientious, the members of his team lack this experience and are likely to look to him for direction. Nonetheless, they will have to carry out any action, and Jim has found that their involvement in decisions helps them to work together as a team.

Jim Burns' challenge raises two general issues relevant to solving problems and making decisions in organizations. The first issue involves determining what solution or decision should be adopted. In this case should Jim begin the cleanup or defer any action pending resolution of the liability issues? It is this facet of decision making that is the focus of most business school curricula and of the optimization models developed by management scientists. (To be sure, the nature of this particular problem complicates matters further by the introduction of a potential conflict between organization goals and broader social concerns.)

The second issue revolves around not *what* should be decided but *how* and with *whom* it should be decided. Should Jim decide himself, or should he involve the team in some way in determining what decision would be made? In this second issue, theories of decision making intersect with theories of leadership style.

## LEADERSHIP STYLE

It is the latter perspective that has interested my colleagues and me and has become the focus of a large-scale program of research at Yale. We are interested in what happens between a leader and the leader's associates in decision-making situations. Our interest was inspired by an article by Bob Tannenbaum and Warren Schmidt. Their work distinguished seven different styles, varying in influence by the manager and the size of the area of freedom afforded subordinates.

Being a believer in parsimony, I have collapsed some of their alternatives, resulting in five styles that are labeled Decide, Consult Individually, Consult Group, Facilitate, and Delegate. Definitions of

**Source:** Edited and reprinted with permission from *Organizational Dynamic,* 28, 4 (2000), pp. 82–94. Copyright 2000. Elsevier Science.

**EXHIBIT 1    Vroom's Adaptation of Tannenbaum and Schmidt's Taxonomy**

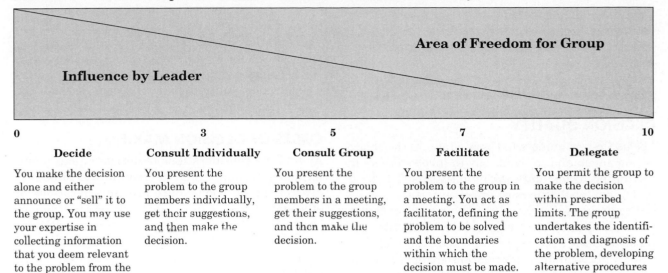

| Decide | Consult Individually | Consult Group | Facilitate | Delegate |
|---|---|---|---|---|
| 0 | 3 | 5 | 7 | 10 |
| You make the decision alone and either announce or "sell" it to the group. You may use your expertise in collecting information that you deem relevant to the problem from the group or others. | You present the problem to the group members individually, get their suggestions, and then make the decision. | You present the problem to the group members in a meeting, get their suggestions, and then make the decision. | You present the problem to the group in a meeting. You act as facilitator, defining the problem to be solved and the boundaries within which the decision must be made. Your objective is to get concurrence on a decision. Above all, you take care to ensure that your ideas are not given any greater weight than those of others simply because of your position. | You permit the group to make the decision within prescribed limits. The group undertakes the identification and diagnosis of the problem, developing alternative procedures for solving it, and deciding on one or more alternative solutions. While you play no direct role in the group's deliberations unless explicitly asked, your role is an important one behind the scenes, providing needed resources and encouragement. |

each of these styles were given to forty specialists in the field of organization development. The specialists were then asked to locate the styles on a 10-point scale, corresponding to the relative opportunities for influencing the decision that they were likely to provide to group or team members. The definitions of these five processes, adapted from Tannenbaum and Schmidt, and the mean-scale values assigned by the OD professionals, are shown in Exhibit 1.

This language for describing leadership styles can be used in two distinctly different ways. It can be the starting point for the development of a *normative* model that would help managers or leaders to select the style that best fits a given situation. Like our predecessors, we are convinced that each of the styles is appropriate to certain kinds of situations, and that an effective leader is one who explicitly tailors his or her style to demands of the immediate problem at hand.

The taxonomy of leadership styles in Exhibit 1 can also be used to describe what people do. A common vocabulary, independent of its normative uses, may be helpful in communication and set-

ting of expectations between leaders and their colleagues. Furthermore, these concepts can be used by social scientists in developing a descriptive model aimed at understanding how managers actually decide whether and when to share their decision-making power.

Over the last two decades, my colleagues and I at Yale have conducted a program of research designed to provide us with a normative model that can be used by managers in evaluating specific decisions that they face and in selecting the most effective leadership style of each. The result has been the development of an "expert system" that shows substantial promise in helping managers through the myriad of factors that need attention in deciding when and how to involve associates in making decisions. In addition, we have made progress in developing a descriptive model of what managers' decision-making practices actually do. Our studies, which now involve over 100,000 managers, have been aimed at understanding the factors that actually influence what managers do. Specifically, we have looked at such factors as organizational level, cultural influences, and the role of gender in leadership style. This article outlines the normative model first, and then examines our progress in understanding its similarities to, and differences from, what managers actually do.

## TOWARD A NORMATIVE MODEL

### DECISION QUALITY

Let us first examine what is at stake in the choice of how much and in what way to involve others in solving problems and making decisions. The first, and undoubtedly the most important, is the quality of the decision. Above all we want wise, well reasoned, and analytically sound decisions that are consistent with the goals to be achieved and with potentially available information about the consequences of alternative means of achieving them.

What happens to decision quality as one moves from the autocratic process to more participative processes? Undoubtedly the nature of the decision and its quality will change as we move across the scale. But will decision quality increase or decrease? A conservative answer, and one that we believe to be consistent with the available research evidence, is that the effects of participation on decision quality depend on certain observable features of the decision-making situation. It depends on where the relevant knowledge or expertise resides, that is, in the leader, in the group, or both. It depends on the goals of the potential participants, particularly on the extent to which group or team members support the organizational objectives embedded in the problem. Finally, the amount of synergy exhibited in team-based processes depends on the skills and abilities of team members in working together effectively in solving problems.

### DECISION IMPLEMENTATION

Although the quality of the decision may be the most important component of its effectiveness, it is not the only component. Many high-quality decisions have been ineffective because they were not effectively implemented. The effectiveness with which a group or team implements a decision can be shown to depend on the extent to which they are committed to its success. Here the evidence is clearer and less equivocal. People do support what they help to build. Under a wide range of conditions, increasing participation leads to greater "buy-in," commitment to decisions, and motivation to implement them effectively. To be sure, there are some situations in which the motivational benefits of greater commitment are non-existent or irrelevant to implementation. Sometimes the team may not be playing a role in implementation; in other situations, the team may view the leader as the expert or as a person with the legitimate right to make the decision and, as a result, may fully support whatever decision the leader might make.

### COSTS OF DECISION MAKING

Apart from considerations of decision quality and implementation, which determine the effectiveness of the decision, there are considerations of efficiency relevant to the decision process. Use of any decision-making process consumes resources. At the same time it can add to resources, albeit of a different kind. The resources consumed are costs and principally involve the time "used up" in the decision-making process. Increasing the amount of participation will increase the elapsed time to make the decision and, to an even greater degree, increase the number of hours consumed by the process. Both of these meanings of time constitute liabilities of participative leadership styles. Seeking consensus slows down the process and consumes substantially more hours than the directive or even consultative methods of decision making. The first of these costs, increasing the time interval between the occurrence of a problem and obtaining a solution, is most relevant in emergencies where a quick or immediate response is necessary. The second consideration, the hours consumed, is more generally relevant.

### DEVELOPMENT

Potentially offsetting these costs are developmental benefits of increased participation. Moving from the autocratic to highly participative styles increases the potential value of the group or team to the organization in three ways: (1) It develops the knowledge and competence of individual members by providing them with opportunities to work through problems and decisions typically occurring at higher organizational levels. (2) It increases teamwork and collaboration by providing opportunities to solve problems as part of a team. (3) It increases identification with organizational goals by giving people "a voice" in making significant decisions in *their* organizations. These developmental benefits may be negligible when the decision lacks significance, that is, when the issue being decided is trivial and lacks consequences to the organization. Furthermore, the development benefits may be of negligible value if the group or team members have a non-existent or tenuous future within the broader organization.

We term a style inefficient when it wastes time without a commensurate return in development. Conversely, it is efficient when it is used judiciously in precisely those situations in which sufficient developmental benefits are realized. It is interesting to note that costs (time) and development, the two components of efficiency, are realized at different points in time. The time costs are immediately realizable. The slowness of response and the number of hours consumed in a group meeting have immediate effects. In contrast, the growth and development of individuals and team may not pay off for a substantial period of time.

## PUTTING IT ALL TOGETHER

So far our inquiry has led us to identify four outcomes of participation, each of which is contingent on one or more situational factors. To be useful to leaders, we must supplement our analysis with a suitable tool for synthesizing the effects that we have postulated. Exhibits 2 and 3 depict decision matrices that constitute such a tool. In Exhibit 2 we show the Time-Driven Model. It is short-term in its orientation, being concerned with making effective decisions with minimum cost. No value is placed on employee development.

In contrast, Exhibit 3 shows the Development-Driven Model. It may be thought of as a long-term model, because it is concerned with making effective decisions with maximum developmental consequences. No value is placed on time.

To use one of these two models, you must have a decision problem in mind that has two properties. First, it must fall within your area of freedom or discretion, that is, it must be up to you to decide. Second, there must be some identifiable group of others who are potential participants in the decision.

One enters the matrix at the left-hand side, at "Problem Statement." Arranged along the top of the matrix are seven situational factors, each of which may be present (H for high) or absent (L for low) in that problem. To obtain the recommended process, you first ascertain whether the decision to be made is a significant one. If so, you select H and answer the second question, concerning the importance of gaining commitment from the group. Continuing this procedure (avoiding the crossing of any horizontal line) will bring you to a recommended process. Sometimes a con-

clusive determination can be made based on as few as two factors (e.g., L, L); others require three (e.g., L, H, H), four (e.g., H, H, H, H), or as many as seven factors (e.g., H, H, L, L, H, H, H).

Submitting the same problem to both the Time-Driven and Development-Driven Model can be instructive. Sometimes the two models yield identical recommendations. Where they differ, the Development-Driven Model recommends a higher level of participation. Occasionally, the difference may be greater than one position on the participation scale. For example, in the Jim Burns case with which this article began, the Time-Driven Model recommends Decide (H, H, H, H) and the Development-Driven Model recommends Consultation with the Group (H, H, H, H, L).

Although the situational factors that identify the columns in Exhibits 2 and 3 are sufficient for the experienced user of these matrices, a less experienced user may wish to refer to explanations of the situational factors in Exhibit 4. To practice using the models, read each of the four cases in Exhibit 5. Underneath each case, we have shown the recommended actions made by the two models, along with the path by which these recommended actions are obtained.

## WHERE DID THE MODEL COME FROM?

The model is an outgrowth of 25 years of research on leadership and decision-making processes. We began by collecting cases from managers of successful and unsuccessful decisions and ascertaining which decision process they used on each. If the decisions were unsuccessful, we wanted to find out why, whether it could have been avoided, and if so, how. Our goal was to build a model that would maximize the frequency of successful decisions, while avoiding as many of the unsuccessful ones as possible. Early on, we were joined by social scientists operating in various parts of the world, which helped us to test our concepts. We were somewhat encouraged by the findings (based on six separate studies conducted in three different countries): decisions made in accordance with a decision tree on which we were working at the time were almost twice as likely to be successful as were decisions that were inconsistent with the model.

But these investigations also made it clear that we had a long way to go, so we continued our efforts to extend and refine our early work. Now we have developed a complex set of equations that show great promise in forecasting the consequences of

**EXHIBIT 2**  **Time-Driven Model**

> Instructions: The matrix operates like a funnel. You start at the left with a specific decision problem in mind. The column headings denote situational factors which may or may not be present in that problem. You progress by selecting High or Low (H or L) for each relevant situational factor. Proceed down from the funnel judging only those situational factors for which a judgment is called for until you reach the recommended process.

| Decision Significance | Importance of Commitment | Leader Expertise | Likelihood of Commitment | Group Support | Group Expertise | Team Competence | |
|---|---|---|---|---|---|---|---|
| H | H | H | H | - | - | - | Decide |
| | | | L | H | H | H | Delegate |
| | | | | | | L | Consult (Group) |
| | | | | | L | - | Consult (Group) |
| | | | | L | - | - | Consult (Group) |
| | | L | H | H | H | H | Facilitate |
| | | | | | | L | Consult (Individually) |
| | | | | | L | - | Consult (Individually) |
| | | | | L | - | - | Consult (Individually) |
| | | | L | H | H | H | Facilitate |
| | | | | | | L | Consult (Group) |
| | | | | | L | - | Consult (Group) |
| | | | | L | - | - | Consult (Group) |
| | L | H | - | - | - | - | Decide |
| | | L | - | H | H | H | Facilitate |
| | | | | | | L | Consult (Individually) |
| | | | | | L | - | Consult (Individually) |
| | | | | L | - | - | Consult (Individually) |
| L | H | - | H | - | - | - | Decide |
| | | - | L | - | - | H | Delegate |
| | | | | | | L | Facilitate |
| | L | - | - | - | - | - | Decide |

participation on quality, implementation, cost, and development. The decision matrices shown in Exhibits 2 and 3 are derived from the use of these equations and are the simplest way in which the implications of the model can be shown *on paper*. However, the full power of the model is better revealed in a computer program that allows much more complexity and precision whereas, at the same time, is easier to use. Contained on a CD-ROM, the program has a number of features not possible in a decision matrix. These include: (1) using eleven situational factors, rather than the seven shown in the matri-

**EXHIBIT 3   Development-Driven Model**

| Decision Significance | Importance of Commitment | Leader Expertise | Likelihood of Commitment | Group Support | Group Expertise | Team Competence | |
|---|---|---|---|---|---|---|---|
| H | H | - | H | H | H | H | Delegate |
| | | | | | | L | Facilitate |
| | | | | | L | - | Consult (Group) |
| | | | | L | - | - | Consult (Group) |
| | | | L | H | H | H | Delegate |
| | | | | | | L | Facilitate |
| | | | | | L | - | Facilitate |
| | | | | L | - | - | Consult (Group) |
| | L | - | - | H | H | H | Delegate |
| | | | | | | L | Facilitate |
| | | | | | L | - | Consult (Group) |
| | | | | L | - | - | Consult (Group) |
| L | H | - | H | - | - | - | Decide |
| | | | L | - | - | - | Facilitate |
| | L | - | - | - | - | - | Decide |

(Left margin vertical label: PROBLEM STATEMENT)

**EXHIBIT 4   Situational Factors in the Normative Model**

| | |
|---|---|
| **DECISION SIGNIFICANCE:** | The significance of the decision to the success of the project or organization. |
| **IMPORTANCE OF COMMITMENT:** | The importance of team members' commitment to the decision. |
| **LEADER'S EXPERTISE:** | Your knowledge or expertise in relation to this problem. |
| **LIKELIHOOD OF COMMITMENT:** | The likelihood that the team would commit itself to a decision that you might make on your own. |
| **GROUP SUPPORT FOR OBJECTIVES:** | The degree to which the team supports the organization's objectives at stake in this problem. |
| **GROUP EXPERTISE:** | Team members' knowledge or expertise in relation to this problem. |
| **TEAM COMPETENCE:** | The ability of team members to work together in solving problems. |

ces, (2) permitting five possible responses, corresponding to the degree to which situational factors are present, (3) incorporating the Value of Time and Value of Development as situational factors, rather than portraying them as separate matrices, and (4) guiding managers through the process of analyzing the situations they face with definitions, examples, and other sources of help.

We have found by observing managers' use of the model on problems they are currently facing

# EXHIBIT 5   Applying the Matrices to the Sample Cases

| Setting: Banking; Your Position: President & Chief Executive Officer | Setting: Repertory Theater; Your Position: Executive Director | Setting: Auto Parts Manufacturer; Your Position: Country Manager | Setting: Manufacturer of Internal Combustion Engines; Your Position: Project Manager |
|---|---|---|---|

**Setting: Banking; Your Position: President & Chief Executive Officer**

The bank examiners have just left, insisting that many of your commercial real estate loans be written off, thereby depleting already low capital. Along with many other banks in your region, your bank is in serious danger of being closed by the regulators. As the financial problems surfaced, many of the top executives left to pursue other interests, but fortunately, you were able to replace them with three highly competent younger managers. While they had no prior acquaintance with one another, each is a product of a fine training program with one of the money center banks in which they rotated through positions in each of the banking functions.

Your extensive experience in the industry leads you to the inevitable conclusion that the only hope is a two-pronged approach involving reduction of all but the most critical expenses and the sale of assets to other banks. The task must be accomplished quickly since further deterioration of the quality of the loan portfolio could result in a negative capital position forcing regulators to close the bank.

The strategy is clear to you, but you have many details that will need to be worked out. You believe that you know what information will be needed in order to get the bank on a course for future prosperity. You are fortunate in having three young executives to help you out. While they have had little or no experience in working together you know that each is dedicated to the survival of the bank. Like you, they know what needs to be done and how to do it.

**ANALYSIS**
 TIME DRIVEN:
  H H H L H H L—CONSULT GROUP
 DVPT DRIVEN:
  H H L H H L—FACILITATE

**Setting: Repertory Theater; Your Position: Executive Director**

You are the executive director of a repertory theater affiliated with a major university. You are responsible for both financial and artistic direction of the theater. While you recognize that both of these responsibilities are important, you have focused your efforts where your own talents lie—on insuring the highest level of artistic quality to the theater's productions. Reporting to you is a group of four department heads responsible for production, marketing, development, and administration, along with an assistant dean who is responsible for the actors who are also students in the university. They are a talented set of individuals, and each is deeply committed to the theatre and experienced in working together as a team.

Last week you received a comprehensive report from an independent consulting firm commissioned to examine the financial health of the theatre. You were shocked by the major conclusion of the report. *"The expenses of operating the theater have been growing much more rapidly than income, and by year's end the theater will be operating in the red. Unless expenses can be reduced, the surplus will be consumed, and within five years the theater might have to be closed."*

You have distributed the report to your staff and are surprised at the variety of reactions that it has produced. Some dispute the report's conclusions criticizing its assumptions or methods. Others are more shaken, but even they seem divided about what steps ought to be taken and when. None of them or, in fact, anyone connected with the theater would want it to close. It has a long and important tradition both in the university and in its surrounding community.

**ANALYSIS**
 TIME DRIVEN:
  H H L L H H H—FACILITATE
 DVPT DRIVEN:
  H H L H H H—DELEGATE

**Setting: Auto Parts Manufacturer; Your Position: Country Manager**

Your firm has just acquired a small manufacturer of spare auto parts in Southeast Asia. The recent collapse in the economies in this region made values very attractive. Your senior management decided to acquire a foothold in this region. It was less interested in the particular acquired firm, which produces parts for the local market, than it was in using it as a base from which to produce parts at reduced cost for the worldwide market.

When you arrived at your new assignment two weeks ago, you were somewhat surprised by the less than enthusiastic reception that you received from the current management. You attribute the obvious strain in working relations not only to linguistic and cultural differences but also to a deep-seated resentment to their new foreign owners. Your top management team seem to get along very well with one another, but the atmosphere changes when you step into the room.

Nonetheless, you will need their help in navigating your way through this unfamiliar environment. Your immediate need is to develop a plan for land acquisition on which to construct new manufacturing and warehouse facilities. You and your administrative assistant, who accompanied you from your previous assignment, should be able to carry out the plan, but its development would be hazardous without local knowledge.

**ANALYSIS**
 TIME DRIVEN:
  H L L L—CONSULT INDIVIDUALLY
 DVPT DRIVEN:
  H L L—CONSULT GROUP

**Setting: Manufacturer of Internal Combustion Engines; Your Position: Project Manager**

Your firm has received a contract from one of the world's largest automobile manufacturers to produce an engine to power their "flagship" sports car. The engine is of Japanese design and is very complex not only by American but by world standards. As project manager, you have been involved in this venture from the outset, and you and your team of engineers have taken pride at the rave reviews the engine has received in the automotive press. Your firm had previously been known as a producer of outboard engines for marine use, and its image is now greatly enhanced as the manufacturer of the power plant of one of the world's fastest sports cars.

Your excitement at being a part of this project was dashed by a report of serious engine problems in cars delivered to customers. Seventeen owners of cars produced in the first month have experienced engine seizures—a circumstance which has caused the manufacturer to suspend sales, to put a halt to current production, and to notify owners of this year's production not to drive their cars! Needless to say, this situation is a disaster and unless solved immediately could expose your firm to extended litigation as well as terminate what had been a mutually beneficial relationship. As the person most informed about the engine, you have spent the last two weeks on the road inspecting several of the seized engines, the plant in which they are installed, and reviewing the practices in your own company's plant in which the engine is manufactured. As a result of this research, you have become convinced that the problem is due to operation of the engine at very high RPM's before it has warmed up to develop sufficient oil pressure. The solution would be to install an electronic control limiting engine RPM's until the engine has reached normal operating temperature.

**ANALYSIS**
 TIME DRIVEN:
  H H H H—DECIDE
 DVPT DRIVEN:
  H H H H L—CONSULT GROUP

on their jobs that the model's recommendations can be affected by the way in which the problem is framed. For example, if the problem is seen as a deficiency within the team, efforts to find a solution are less likely to be affected than if the problem is located in the situation. Accordingly, we have provided a help screen for "testing" a manager's framing of the problem, to make sure that it has been defined in a way that is likely to be productive. In addition, we have found in this rapidly changing world that groups defined by a common manager may not be the most effective for solution of organizational problems. Thus, the software provides a help screen called Team Formation, which provides advice on making up a group to solve a particular problem or make a particular decision.

## WHAT DETERMINES MANAGERS' STYLES?

### TOWARD A DESCRIPTIVE MODEL

To study managerial styles (as they are, rather than how our models say they should be), we have developed an innovative measuring device that we term a problem set. It consists of a set of 30 cases, each depicting a manager faced with a decision to make. Exhibit 5 gives examples of some of the shorter cases from a typical set. Cases are based on real situations. Each has been condensed to fit on a single page, providing information on the manager's role, the organizational context, the decision that has to be made, the group of persons that the manager is considering involving, and so on.

The set of cases covers the whole gamut of managerial decisions. Titles include "Saving a Savings Bank," "Trimming Expense Accounts," "Relocating the Head Office," and so forth. However, the cases are not randomly selected. Rather, they vary with respect to the critical factors that the model deems highly relevant to choice of leadership style. Each of the factors contained in the decision matrices shown in Exhibits 2 and 3 is varied across the set of cases, and each is varied independently of each other factor. This latter feature, which statisticians refer to as a multifactorial experimental design, is most important, because it permits determining which of the relevant factors influences each individual manager, in what way, and to what degree. Thus, the problem set becomes a powerful diagnostic tool capable of revealing "the manager's model," that is,

the way in which each individual manager responds to decision-making situations.

Although we originally developed the problem set as a research tool, we discovered early on that managers enjoyed and benefited from the experience of thinking through how they would deal with highly different situations, and attempting to make sense out of the different choices they made. To aid in the learning that was resulting from this measuring instrument, we have developed a Java-based computer program that could quickly analyze a manager's choices and produce a five-page individualized report comparing him or her with peers and with the models, both time-driven and development-driven. Furthermore, due to the power of the statistical design underlying the problem set, we are able to show each manager how his or her choices were influenced by each of the situational factors used in the decision matrices. Each manager's individualized analysis also shows how well his or her choices are likely to result in decisions that are (1) of high quality, (2) would be effectively implemented, (3) were economical in use of time, and (4) would have favorable developmental consequences on their team.

Here we will focus not on what *managers have learned* from having a mirror held up to them but rather what *we have learned from managers* about how they go about deciding when and where to share their decision-making power. In a world in which it is common to label managers with terms like autocratic or participative or Theory X or Theory Y, it was instructive to see that managers make different choices in different situations. In fact, it makes somewhat more sense to talk about autocratic and participative situations than autocratic or participative managers do. The differences in behavior among managers are about one-third of the size of the differences among situations.

Managers behave situationally. They adapt their behavior to the situations they face. Furthermore, the kinds of situations that evoke autocratic and participative styles are very similar to those in which the normative model would recommend such styles. Each of the seven situational factors shown at the top of Exhibits 2 and 3 affects the average manager in roughly the same way as they affect the behavior of the model. Managers make more participative choices on highly significant decisions, when they need the commitment of the group, when they lack the expertise, when the likelihood of commitment to *their* decision is low, when the group's expertise is high and when the group has a history of working together effectively.

But not all managers behave that way! Some are influenced by only one or two of these factors and seem to ignore the rest. Still others are affected by one of these factors, but in what we believe to be the wrong way. For example, one fifth of the U.S. managers that we have studied (and three quarters of all managers from Poland) are more likely to involve others in insignificant, trivial decisions.

One of the most important functions of the feedback is to draw each individual's attention to those aspects of the situation that they are overlooking. We should make it clear that the model not only responds to the seven situational factors, but also does so configurally. Thus, the effects of one factor depend on the level of certain other factors. For example, where the knowledge resides (in the leader or in the group or both or neither) has more effect on leadership style in highly significant decisions than in those of lesser significance.

Of great interest to us is the fact that managers also behave configurally. There is evidence in our data that managers attend to combinations of factors rather than being influenced by each factor separately. However, these effects are less strong among managers than in the model, suggesting that only a small number of managers behave that way or that, in the typical manager, the configural effects are small in relation to those that are linear.

We said earlier that the situational effects dwarfed the differences among individual managers. Although that statement is true, it does not imply that differences among managers in their typical or overall behavior are insignificant or inconsequential. If one averages the choices of a manager on the 30 cases, one obtains a mean score that reflects, on average, where he or she stands on the scale shown in Exhibit 1. We turn now to consider some of the things that we have found to correlate with differences in where people stand on our 10-point scale of participation.

The first factor is *when* people took the test! Our data have been collected over a 25-year period, and throughout most of that period we have observed an increase in the use of the more participative processes on that scale. Something seems to be producing a move toward higher involvement, more participation, greater empowerment, and more frequent use of teams over time. We do not know precisely what is producing this, but we suspect that it reflects changes in (1) the external environment of organizations (greater rates of change, greater complexity), (2) the flattening of the pyramid (greater spans of control resulting in difficulties in hierarchical control), (3) the growth of information technology, making it easier to get information closer to the occurrence of problems, and (4) the changing nature of the labor force (higher education, higher needs for independence, etc.). Of the demographic factors, the culture in which the organization functions accounts for the greatest variance. High involvement managers are more likely to be found in countries with high per capita GNP, with a strong democratic tradition and with a highly educated work force.

We have also investigated gender differences and have found women managers to be significantly more participative than their male counterparts. Supporting this conclusion, we have found sizeable differences in the reactions to autocratic men and autocratic women managers. In general, being participative is valued by direct reports, but this is truer for women than for men. Participative men and women are equally valued, but autocratic males are strongly preferred to autocratic women.

A third demographic factor that correlates with leadership style as measured by our problem sets is level in the organization. In each organization that we have studied in depth, the higher the level in the organizational ladder, the more participative the manager. To be sure, we have never carried our investigation up to the level of the CEO, where we cannot rely on sample size and the law of large numbers to cancel out chance factors due to personality or to measurement.

We should point out that our findings are restricted to what managers say they would do on a standardized set of cases. Although managers have no incentive to lie (because it will only decrease the accuracy of the computer feedback that they alone will receive), we have no guard against self-deception. As a possible check on such tendencies, we have given the same problem sets to both the manager and to his or her direct reports. The latter are asked to describe how their manager would respond to each case. The result is striking. Virtually all managers are seen by their direct reports as closer to the left side of that scale than they see themselves. We have referred to this difference as the autocratic shift. We do not know whether the biases are in managers' conceptions of themselves, the perceptions of them held by their direct reports, or both.

# CONCLUSION

Historically, the people dimension of management has been viewed as basically intuitive, clinical, and "touchy-feely." The kinds of analytical approaches that are customary in finance, operations, and to a lesser degree, strategy, have not been applied, or even viewed as applicable to issues of behavior. We have violated that norm and have sought to apply analytical methods to the development of better normative and descriptive tools for understanding leadership style. We will be the first to admit that our model is far from perfect. We ignore deliberately what style managers are "good at," what they are accustomed to practicing, and what they are encouraged to use in their "organizational culture." We do this because we believe that what worked in the past is not a guarantee of success in the future. We believe that leadership styles deserve a fresh look.

At Yale and in other environments, when I teach the model presented in this paper and provide people with computer feedback on their own leadership style, I stress that both are intended to stimulate reflection, and self-examination. They are not tools to be slavishly embraced and used in all decisions. I believe that much of the behavior that is currently driven by habits needs to be converted back into choices. The changing demands of today demand that we reexamine the styles we used in the past and reassess their appropriateness to today's environment.

## Selected Bibliography

The original inspiration for this body of work may be found in an article written in the *Harvard Business Review* by Bob Tannenbaum and Warren Schmidt ("How to Choose a Leadership Pattern," *Harvard Business Review,* 1958, 99–101.)

My initial work on leadership was done with Philip Yetton (*Leadership and Decision Making,* University of Pittsburgh Press: 1973). Subsequently I collaborated with Arthur G. Jago in writing *The New Leadership* (Prentice-Hall: 1988).

Those who wish to learn more about the specific findings cited, or the computer programs that are referred to in this article, may contact me at victor.vroom @yale.edu or at The Yale School of Management, 135 Prospect Street, P.O. Box 208200, New Haven, CT 06520-8200.

## Reading 33

# Participation, Satisfaction, and Productivity: A Meta-analytic Review

**Katherine I. Miller**
Michigan State University

**Peter R. Monge**
University of Southern California

I would not think of making a decision by going around the table and then deciding on the basis of how everyone felt. Of course, I like to hear everyone, but then I go off alone and decide. The decisions that are important must be made alone.

—*Richard M. Nixon (Schecter, 1972:18–19)*

Like Mr. Nixon, most people have strong feelings about the best way to make decisions. However, individuals often disagree about the proper decision-making procedure. Should subordinates be included in decision-making processes, or should managers stand alone as decision makers? Far from being limited to high national offices, the debate over the efficacy of participation in decision making exists throughout government, business, and many academic fields.

There are several reasons for the continuing disagreement on this topic. Moral reasoning regarding participation is often confounded with practical reasoning. Locke and Schweiger (1979) provided several examples of managers and academicians advocating the use of participation on moral grounds, regardless of whether or not it works. In addition, conflicting models of the mechanisms at work in the process of participation lead to confusion over the interpretation of research findings. Finally, in spite of the plethora of empirical research studies investigating participation, when reviewers of the literature draw conclusions on its effectiveness, they invariably still state that "it depends" (Locke & Schweiger; Lowin, 1968; Singer, 1974). Unfortunately, the question of what it depends on has never been clearly answered. To begin to answer this question, we carried out a meta-analytic review of

past research on the effects of participation in decision making on satisfaction and productivity.

## "ONE MORE LOOK" REVISITED

In recent years, several sets of scholars have done wide-ranging reviews of thinking and research on participation in the workplace. For example, Strauss (1982) took an international perspective on workers' participation, and Dachler and Wilpert (1978) looked at the dimensions and boundaries of the participation process. Perhaps the most comprehensive review of empirical research to date, however, is Locke and Schweiger's (1979) "one more look" at participation in decision making, which considered both moral and practical arguments for participation. They reviewed laboratory studies, correlational studies, multivariate field studies, and univariate field studies in which satisfaction and productivity were criterion variables. Locke and Schweiger concluded that little could be said about the effects of participation from multivariate field studies because too many other variables—differences in training, reward systems, education, and so forth—could account for effects often attributed to participation. They did, however, make generalizations based on correlational, laboratory, and univariate field studies.

Locke and Schweiger classified the conclusions of studies as "participation superior," "participation inferior," or "no difference or contextual" (1979: 317). Having found that the results in laboratory, correlational, and univariate field studies were remarkably consistent, they finally concluded:

(1) With respect to the productivity criterion, there is no trend in favor of participative leadership as compared to more directive styles; and (2) with respect to satisfaction, the results generally favor participative over directive methods, although nearly 40 percent of the studies did not find participation to be superior (Locke & Schweiger, 1979: 316).

Although Locke and Schweiger's review considered well over 50 empirical research reports on participation, their final conclusions seem somewhat anticlimatic—probably for several reasons. First, they used a very gross classification system in considering effects of participation. The categories of superior, inferior, and contextual, though certainly useful, tell us nothing about the strength of participation's effects on satisfaction and productivity. Second, many studies fell into the contextual category, 56 percent for the productivity criterion and 30 percent for the satisfaction criterion. They suggested a number of contextual factors to account for the effectiveness of participation, including two individual factors, knowledge and motivation, and several organizational factors, such as task attributes, group characteristics, and leaders' attributes, but did not go back to the studies reviewed to systematically sort out these contextual effects. Finally, no attempt was made to consider systematic patterns differentiating the studies concluding that participation was superior from those concluding that participation was inferior.

Meta-analysis (Hunter, Schmidt, & Jackson, 1982) can be employed to refine and extend Locke and Schweiger's findings. This method of cumulating results over studies allowed us to summarize numerically the effects of participation on satisfaction and productivity and to take into account artifactual and substantive sources of variance in the individual estimates of effects. Meta-analysis is an improvement over the review methods used by Locke and Schweiger on several counts. It considers the strength of effects between two variables rather than simply counting significant results or levels of probability, thus providing a more accurate representation of cumulated relationships between variables and eliminating the problem of giving a study with a strong effect the same consideration as one with a barely significant effect. Meta-analysis also provides methods for correcting for such systematic, artifactual sources of variance in the estimates of effects as measurement error and restriction in range. Finally, meta-analysis allows for the consideration of both substantive and methodological moderator variables that could account for unexplained variance in estimates of effects. . . .

Thus, we decided that a meta-analysis of this literature would be useful in resolving several of the problems of earlier reviews. In the next section, we discuss the relationships of participation with satisfaction and productivity through the

presentation of cognitive, affective, and contingency models of participation. Meta-analysis does not allow for direct tests of these models, but the models enable identification of substantive and methodological variables that could moderate the relationships of participation with satisfaction and productivity.

# PARTICIPATION, SATISFACTION, AND PRODUCTIVITY

Theorists have advanced a variety of models to account for participation's influence on satisfaction and productivity; each proposes mechanisms through which participation has its effects. We used three types of models—cognitive, affective, and contingency—to highlight differences in these propositions. Each of the three types emphasizes a different explanatory mechanism. The three are not mutually exclusive, however, as many theorists have proposed that cognitive, affect, and contingency variables all play important roles in the participative process.

## COGNITIVE MODELS OF PARTICIPATIVE EFFECTS

Cognitive models of participative effects suggest that participation in decision making is a viable strategy because it enhances the flow and use of important information in organizations. Theorists supporting such models (Anthony, 1978; Frost, Wakely, & Ruh, 1974) propose that workers typically have more complete knowledge of their work than management; hence, if workers participate in decision making, decisions will be made with better pools of information. In addition, cognitive models suggest that if employees participate in decision making, they will know more about implementing work procedures after decisions have been made (Maier, 1963; Melcher, 1976). Other scholars (Miles & Ritchie, 1971; Ritchie & Miles, 1970), designating cognitive models as the "human resources" theory of participation, note that such a model is "primarily concerned with the meaningful utilization of subordinates' capabilities and views satisfaction as a by-product of their participation in important organizational decisions" (Ritchie & Miles, 1970: 348).

Cognitive models predict a definite pattern of results in empirical research investigating participation, satisfaction, and productivity. First, because these models consider information to be crucial, increases in productivity are expected to be stronger where workers have good information about decisions to be made. For instance, such models would predict a stronger effect for participation in job design than for participation in companywide policy decisions or experimental discussions. Second, such models do not predict immediate increases in satisfaction as a result of participation in decision making, as it is essentially a knowledge of results that is hypothesized to lead to eventual increases in satisfaction. Third, they do not predict increases in workers' productivity and satisfaction simply from their working in participative work climates or for nondirective leaders. According to cognitive models, increases in productivity and satisfaction are attributable to specific inputs from subordinates on issues in which they are interested and knowledgeable.

## AFFECTIVE MODELS OF PARTICIPATIVE EFFECTS

There are several models linking participation to productivity and satisfaction through affective mechanisms. Followers of the "human relations"[1] school of management (Blake & Mouton, 1964; Likert, 1967; McGregor, 1960) adamantly espouse these models, in which the most crucial link is that between participation and workers' satisfaction. These theorists propose that participation will lead to greater attainment of high-order needs, such as self-expression, respect, independence, and equality, which will in turn increase morale and satisfaction. Ritchie and Miles stated that "managers who hold the human relations theory of participation believe simply in involvement for the sake of involvement, arguing that as long as subordinates feel they are participating and are being consulted, their ego needs will be satisfied and they will be more cooperative" (1970: 348).

The link between participation and productivity in affective models is less straightforward than that between participation and satisfaction. Essentially, this school proposes that participation will enhance productivity through intervening motivational processes: participation fulfills needs, fulfilled needs lead to satisfaction, satisfaction strengthens motivation, and increased motivation improves workers' productivity. According to French, Israel, and As (1960):

> One effect of a high degree of participation by workers in decisions concerning their own work will be to strengthen their motivation to carry out these decisions. This is the major rationale for expecting a relation between participation and pro-

duction. When management accords the workers participation in any important decision, it implies that workers are intelligent, competent, and valued partners. Thus, participation directly affects such aspects of worker-management relations as the perception of being valued, the perception of common goals, and cooperation. It satisfies such important social needs as the need for recognition and appreciation and the need for independence. These satisfactions and, in addition, the improvements in their jobs that are introduced through participation lead to higher job satisfaction (1960: 5).

Although several theorists (Locke & Schweiger, 1979; Ritchie & Miles, 1970) feel strongly that scholarly and practical emphasis should be placed on the cognitive effects of participation, researchers in the tradition of McGregor (1960), Likert (1967), and Coch and French (1948) still hold strongly to the importance of participation in providing affective changes in workers. Thus, it is important to consider the predictions of affective models as to the effects of participation on satisfaction and productivity. First, they predict that participation will affect satisfaction in a wide variety of situations. Participation need not be centered on issues of which employees are particularly knowledgeable, for it is the act, not the informational content, of participation that is the crucial mechanism. Second, such models do not predict increases in productivity without initial increases in workers' satisfaction. Finally, affective models suggest that participation will more strongly influence lower-level employees, because managers' higher-order ego needs may well be fulfilled by other aspects of their work.

## CONTINGENCY MODELS OF PARTICIPATIVE EFFECTS

Several theorists suggest that it is not possible to develop models of participative effects that will hold across a wide variety of individuals and situations. Rather, they suggest that participation will affect satisfaction and productivity differently for different people and situations. Scholars have offered a variety of contingency theories centering on personality, particular decision situations, relationships between superiors and subordinates, job levels, and values.

Vroom (1960) was the first to propose that personality might mediate the effects of participation on satisfaction and productivity. Specifically, he suggested that participation will positively influence only employees having personalities with low authoritarianism and high needs for independence. Vroom found some support for his hypotheses, and his work has stimulated other research. However, further studies have provided mixed support for his hypotheses (Abdel-Halim, 1983; Tosi, 1970; Vroom & Mann, 1960).

Vroom was also involved in the major theoretical statement of situational influences on the participation process. Vroom and Yetton (1973), building on the work of Tannenbaum and Schmidt (1958), considered different decision situations and provided rules for deciding the optimal level of participation in decision making. They proposed both rules to protect the quality of decisions and rules to protect their acceptance. Most of the research on this model has been descriptive, drawing on self-reports about how managers behave in different decision situations. However, several normative tests (Vroom & Jago, 1978) have indicated that decisions made within participative modes specified by these rules were more effective than other decisions. Vroom and Yetton's work moves toward an integration of cognitive and affective models of participation. Their contingency rules for protecting the quality of decisions deal with the cognitive portion of participation, and their rules for protecting the acceptance of decisions address its affective components.

Several other theorists have proposed additional variables as intervening in the process of participation. For example, Vroom and Deci (1960) suggested that the types of problems dealt with at various organizational levels influence the appropriateness of participation; it may be less appropriate at low levels, where jobs are routine, and more appropriate at high levels, where jobs involve addressing complex problems. Several scholars (Hulin, 1971; Singer, 1974) have suggested that values mediate the relationship between participation and outcomes, specifically, that many workers may not value participation to the extent that academicians do. Singer further commented, "While the necessity for determining a 'one best' leadership style for the 'composite worker' is understandable from a financial and expediency standpoint, to assume that *all* workers desire participation opportunities is to lack sensitivity to *individual* needs—the antithesis of the humanization that ardent proponents of participation advocate" (1974: 359). Thus, these scholars predicted that participation may only be effective for employees in certain types of organizations—such as research or service organizations, rather than manufacturing organizations—or only for middle- or upper-level employees.

## OVERVIEW

In sum, *cognitive* models of participation propose that participation leads to increases in productivity through bringing high-quality information to decisions and through increasing knowledge at times of implementation. Such models predict that: (1) The effects of participation on an individual's productivity will be the strongest for decisions that draw on the individual's expertise; (2) There will not be a direct influence of participation on job satisfaction. Rather, the effect of participation on productivity will mediate this effect. (3) Participation in specific decisions is necessary for increases in productivity and satisfaction; working in a participative climate is not adequate.

*Affective* models suggest that participation will satisfy higher-order needs of workers and that, as these needs are satisfied, workers will be more satisfied with their jobs. Such models predict that: (1) Working in a participative climate is adequate for increasing workers' productivity. It is not necessary that workers participate in decisions on which they have special knowledge. (2) There is no direct link between participation and productivity. Rather, improved attitudes reduce resistance to change and increase motivation through the satisfaction of needs. (3) Participation may provide more noticeable increases in satisfaction for employees who are not having higher-order needs fulfilled from other aspects of their jobs.

*Contingency* models of participation suggest that no single model of participation is appropriate for all employees in all organizations. Instead, various contingency models predict that: (1) Employees with high needs for independence and personalities with low authoritarianism will be the most positively influenced by participation. (2) Some decisions are more appropriate for participation than others. Appropriateness depends on requirements for the quality or acceptance of a decision (Vroom & Yetton, 1973), or on its complexity. (3) Employees who value participation will be the most positively influenced by it, and these are likely to be higher-level employees, or individuals working in research or service industries. . . .

## METHODS

Our literature search for relevant research on the effects of participation on satisfaction and productivity included journals in the areas of social psychology, management, organizational behavior, and communication, and several relevant social citation indices. We restricted it to the published literature and to English language journals and books, excluding dissertations and other unpublished research. It is possible that this led us to include more studies with significant results and fewer with nonsignificant results. However, Hunter, Schmidt, and Jackson (1982) did not see this as a serious problem, noting that it is likely that nonsignificant dissertation results may well be attenuated owing to methodological problems. They further stated that, typically, only a very large number of lost studies will make a substantive difference in a meta-analysis.

This literature search identified 106 articles and book chapters on participation. However, many of these were not appropriate for meta-analysis. We eliminated literature reviews and essays that were not based on data (12 articles), 13 data-based articles without quantifiable effect sizes, 5 studies in which participation was the dependent variable, 6 studies whose dependent variables were not appropriate for this meta-analysis, 15 studies lacking clear measures of participation, and 7 studies in which methodological problems[2] posed serious questions about an estimation of effects or whose data came from another study included in the meta-analysis. . . .

## RESULTS

### SATISFACTION

Forty-one estimates of the relationship between participation and satisfaction were considered. After cumulation of estimates of effects, the weighted mean correlation was .34, and the true variance was .0301. A chi-square test showed this variance to be statistically different from 0 ($x^2$ = 244.27, $df$ = 40, $p$ < .01), indicating that moderator variables would reduce the variance in estimates. We first looked at substantive moderators like organizational type, job level, and type of decision. None of these subgroupings proved useful in reducing variance or in differentiating among effect sizes. Hence, we considered methodological moderators. . . .

The organizational studies were divided into those that measured actual participation and those that measured perceived participation. The mean weighted correlation for studies of actual participation was .16; the variance among these estimates was .0035, which is not significantly different from 0 ($x^2$ = 8.19, $df$ = 10, $p$ > .05). However, the variance in studies investigating per-

ceived participation was still significant. We considered one additional moderator to eliminate the remaining variance: whether perceived participation was in reference to specific issues, such as goals, pay plans, or job redesign, or in reference to multiple issues or a general participative climate, evaluated by a question like "In general, how much do you participate in decision making on your job?" The mean weighted correlation for studies concerned with specific issues was .21; the variance among these estimates was .0009. This variance was not significant ($x^2$ = .78, $df$ = 4, $p$ > .05). The mean weighted correlation for studies concerned with multiple issues was .46. The variance among these effect size estimates was .0156. This variance is still significant ($x^2$ = 88.5, $df$ = 19, $p$ < .01). Several other variables (measurement, job level, and organizational type) were considered for further reducing the variance among effect sizes. However, no other moderator variables reduced the variance within subgroups, so the analysis of studies in which satisfaction was the dependent variable ended at this point.

. . . The satisfaction subgroups in which variance was reduced to the greatest extent possible . . . include (1) nonorganizational studies, (2) studies of actual participation, (3) studies of perceived participation in relation to specific issues, and (4) studies of perceived participation in relation to multiple issues. . . . Figure 1 is a tree diagram of analyses performed with satisfaction as the dependent variable.

All of the subgroup estimates for satisfaction differ significantly from 0, but there is substan-

**FIGURE 1**    **Tree Diagram of Studies in the Meta-analysis for Satisfaction as Dependent Variable**

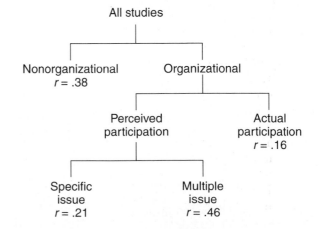

tial variation in the magnitudes of effects. The strongest effects of participation on satisfaction are found in studies of perceived participation focusing on multiple issues and in the nonorganizational studies. Much smaller effects are found in the studies of perceived participation focusing on single issues and in the studies of actual participation. In three out of four subgroups, the variance has been reduced to what would be expected from sampling error. Because of the reduction in variance and the sharp differences among subgroups in sizes of effects, it appears that the analyses were successful in partitioning the studies into appropriate subgroups.

## PRODUCTIVITY

Twenty-five studies containing estimates of the relationship between participation and productivity were analyzed. After cumulation of effect estimates the weighted mean correlation was .15, and the true variance was .0334. A chi-square test showed this variance differed significantly from 0 ($x^2$ = 69.47, $df$ = 25, $p$ < .01), so we considered moderator variables. Again, substantive moderator variables were considered first. Of these variables, the objects of participation proved to be useful for subgroup analysis. Seven studies investigated the effects of participation in goal setting on productivity. The cumulated mean weighted correlation for studies of goal setting was .11, and the variance among these estimates was 0. However, the variance among other studies was still significant, so we sought additional moderators. Because other substantive moderators did not prove useful, we evaluated methodological moderators. The first methodological moderator used was research setting. The mean weighted correlation for the nine field studies was .27; the variance among these estimates was 0. Hence, no further analyses were necessary on this subgroup. The variance among estimates for the laboratory studies was significant, so we analyzed these further.

The final moderator considered for studies in which productivity was the dependent variable was the manipulation used in the laboratory studies. Four of the studies manipulated leadership style; a research assistant or member of the experimental group had been instructed to be leader and to behave in an authoritarian or democratic style. The correlation between participation and productivity in the studies manipulating leadership style was −.33; the variance among these estimates was .014. This variance was not significant ($x^2$ = 3.73, $df$ = 3, $p$ > .05). The other four studies manipulated the nature of the tasks the groups performed, by placing subjects in assigned or participative task groups. The correlation between participation and productivity in these studies was −.01; the variance among the estimates was 0. . . .

The subgroups of studies investigating productivity in which variance was reduced to the greatest extent possible . . . are (1) studies concerned with participation in goal setting, (2) field studies, (3) laboratory studies in which leadership style was manipulated, and (4) laboratory studies in which the nature of a task was manipulated. . . . Figure 2 is a tree diagram of subgroup analyses performed with productivity as the dependent variable.

As with the satisfaction studies, the mean weighted correlations of the different subgroups differ substantially. The laboratory studies that manipulated the nature of a task show essentially no correlation, and the studies concerned with goal setting exhibit a significant, but small, positive correlation. The field studies show a relatively strong positive correlation, and the studies of leadership style exhibit a relatively strong negative correlation. The variance among estimates in these subgroups has been reduced to that attributable to sampling error. The substantially different effect sizes and the reduction in subgroup variance suggest that our partitioning efforts were appropriate and successful.

**FIGURE 2**  **Tree Diagram of Studies in the Meta-analysis for Productivity as Dependent Variable**

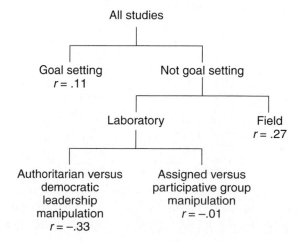

# DISCUSSION

## CONTINGENCY MODELS OF PARTICIPATION

This meta-analysis provided no support for any of the contingency predictions discussed. We considered both job type and organizational type as possible moderator variables at all stages of analysis, but there was no reduction of variance in effect sizes through subgroupings on the basis of these variables. Thus, it does not appear that participation is more effective for managers than for lower-level employees, or vice versa. There is also no evidence that research, service, and manufacturing organizations differ in terms of the effectiveness of participation. It was not possible to provide a test of contingency predictions referring to personality, because very few studies provided subgroup analyses considering individuals with different personality types. As mentioned earlier, studies that have considered authoritarianism and need for independence have provided conflicting conclusions.

Finally, it should be noted that the variance in studies of participation in goal setting was reduced to that accountable to sampling error. The correlation between participation in goal setting and productivity was significant, but small ($r = .11$). This result should come as little surprise to those researching goal setting, most of whom have now concluded (e.g., Latham & Marshall, 1982; Latham & Steele, 1983) that participation may have an effect on the levels of goals set, but that it has no effect on productivity if the levels of goals stay the same. Cumulating these results over a variety of research settings adds credence to the generalizability of this conclusion.

## COGNITIVE VERSUS AFFECTIVE MODELS OF PARTICIPATION

This meta-analysis provided several tests of the efficacy of cognitive and affective models of participation. First, the findings can be considered in terms of contrasting the effects of participation on satisfaction with the effects of participation on productivity. Affective models predict that participation will have a stronger effect on satisfaction than on productivity, and cognitive models predict the opposite. Second, cognitive models predict that participation will have a stronger influence on productivity and satisfaction for decisions about which employees have specific knowledge. In contrast, affective models predict that working in a participative climate will have the most beneficial effects on workers' attitudes and productivity.

The studies investigating effects of participation other than goal setting on *productivity* exhibited a stronger influence of participation ($r = .27$) than the studies of satisfaction investigating actual participation ($r = .16$) or perceived participation for a single variable ($r = .21$). Of course, comparisons of these effects for different dependent variables should be made with caution, and the differences here are not substantial. However, even the fact that there is a moderately strong effect size for field studies investigating the influence of participation on productivity indicates that cognitive models have some plausibility. Further, the relatively low, but significant, correlations between actual participation and satisfaction and between participation and satisfaction in studies of single issues might lessen confidence in affective models of participation.

However, the data seem more consistent with an affective explanation when we consider studies of participation involving multiple issues. These studies investigated perceived participation and typically used such items as "In general, how participative is your workplace?" or "How much do you generally share in decision making with your supervisor?" After subgroup analysis, some unexplained variance remained in this subgroup, but the mean weighted effect size was .46, much larger than the average correlations in other subgroups of field studies. It appears that working in a participative climate is strongly related to satisfaction at work. This result is in keeping with the human relations school of organizational behavior and with current interest in work climates. In particular, it supports the idea that microclimates (Schneider, 1981), such as a climate for variety, a climate for innovation, or a climate for participation, are related to individual attitudes. However, it is important to consider the structure of this relationship. Does a participative climate cause workers' satisfaction? Does workers' satisfaction help develop a participative climate? Or are these two variables redundant indicators of the same concept? LaFollette and Sims (1975), discussing Johannesson (1973), summarized this dilemma well:

> If it appears as if perceptual climate research is converging upon any domain, job satisfaction seems the likely candidate. Indeed it is hard to imagine how this possibly could have been avoided. Even if researchers had taken the pains to create new items and had adopted different

item formats (which they have not) there remains the psychological problem of divorcing description from feelings. Since descriptions of work situations have been operationally defined as indices of job satisfaction it seems redundant at best to also term such descriptions organizational climate (1975: 257).

Climate has traditionally been defined as a descriptive construct and satisfaction as an affective construct. However, these definitions get muddied operationally if satisfaction is measured through descriptors, as it is in the Job Descriptive Index (JDI), or if scales measuring climate include items on attitude. This problem probably is not crucial for the studies in this meta-analysis, because participation involves a specific microclimate, rather than omnibus organizational climate. Thus, it is not likely that measures of participative climate and overall work satisfaction are redundant. In addition, all of these studies considered descriptions of participation rather than attitudes toward participation as the independent variable. Finally, with the exception of studies using the JDI, measures of satisfaction were purely affective. Moreover, results of studies using the JDI were not systematically different from those of studies using other measures of satisfaction.

The question of causality remains: Does participation cause satisfaction or does satisfaction cause participation? All of the studies in the multiple-issue subgrouping were correlational, so we cannot answer this question with full confidence. However, we can bring evidence from the literature on climate to bear on this issue. Laboratory research investigating experimentally created social climates (Litwin & Stringer, 1968) found that manipulated climate had an effect on satisfaction. Hand, Richards, and Slocum (1973) found a positive relationship between initial perceptions of climate and subsequent acceptance of self and others. Taylor and Bowers's (1972)[3] cross-lagged panel study of over 284 work groups in 15 different organizations found that "organization climate shows evidence of being more the cause of, than caused by, satisfaction" (1972: 89).

Several concluding comments about the comparison between cognitive, affective, and contingency models of participation are in order. First, there was little support for contingency models of participation, though the lack of measures for several contingency variables could have affected findings. Second, this meta-analysis did not allow for a complete test of the models presented, as we lacked data on several intervening variables in these models, such as upward and downward sharing of information and satisfaction of higher-order ego needs. We would encourage researchers to measure these variables in future investigations of participation. Despite this limitation, some evidence to support both cognitive and affective models of participation emerged. The relatively large correlation between participation and productivity in field studies somewhat supports cognitive models. However, the largest subgroup correlation, between perceived participation and satisfaction, provides greater support for affective models of participation.

Estimates of the effect of participation on *both* satisfaction and productivity appeared in 13 studies. An examination of these studies sheds some light on the relative efficacy of cognitive and affective models: (1) the relationship between participation and satisfaction was stronger than that between participation and productivity in four studies (Katzell, Miller, Rotter, & Venet, 1970; Schuler & Kim, 1978; Shaw, 1955; and Vroom, 1960), (2) the relationship between participation and productivity was stronger in one study (Ivancevich, 1977), and (3) no significant difference emerged in the other eight studies. These studies provide somewhat stronger evidence for the relationship between participation and satisfaction than for that between participation and productivity. However, the large number of insignificant differences in this subset precludes our suggesting that this comparison provides strong evidence for either cognitive or affective models.

## RESEARCH SETTING AS A MODERATOR

Several of the strongest moderators were methodological variables; in particular, research setting and type of subject played important roles. For the studies concerned with satisfaction, the variance was zero among investigations involving nonorganizational subjects, all but one of which (Veen, 1972) had a laboratory setting. The weighted correlation for these studies was relatively high ($r = .38$). This effect size was considerably higher than that in studies involving actual participation in organizations ($r = .16$) or perceived participation in reference to a specific issue ($r = .21$).

There are two clear explanations for these results. First, an explanation in terms of internal validity suggests that the high degree of control in laboratories over extraneous variables would make the higher correlation a better indicator of the true relationship between participation and satisfaction. However, an explanation in terms of external validity suggests that college students and laboratory tasks have little in common with real organizational life; hence, field estimates of the effect between participation and satisfaction would be more meaningful. Both arguments undoubtedly have merit. This meta-analysis seems to indicate that there is a relatively high pure effect of participation on satisfaction, but that a host of other organizational influences dilute this effect in field studies investigating actual participation or perceived participation in relation to specific issues.

The effect of research setting in the productivity studies is also striking. Among studies not investigating goal setting, field studies showed a moderately high positive correlation ($r = .27$), and laboratory studies yielded either no correlation (assigned versus participative task manipulation, $r = -.01$) or negative correlations (authoritarian versus democratic leadership manipulation, $r = -.33$). The points of interest here are the sharp differences between laboratory and field studies and the differences in effect sizes for different manipulations.

The substantial difference between field and laboratory studies can probably be attributed to the tasks typically performed in these settings. The laboratory studies typically involved a simple and well-defined manipulated task like turning switches on a control panel or a game of 20 questions; the field studies typically involved participation in naturally occurring, more complex activities, such as pay incentive plans or job design, or participation over a wide gamut of organizational issues. In the laboratory, there usually was a correct answer; there are rarely such guarantees in organizations. Finally, organizational members in field studies had more at stake in the decisions that were made than students in a laboratory.

All of these factors contributed to a higher level of complexity for the organizational participative tasks than for the laboratory participative tasks. Research on small group behavior (Cartwright & Zander, 1960) has suggested that different types of leadership and structure are appropriate for different types of tasks; specifically, that authoritarian leadership and centralized group structure are most appropriate for simple tasks. The studies in this meta-analysis investigating leadership behavior bear this out. Most of the tasks were simple, and authoritarian leadership was more effective in eliciting high levels of productivity. In contrast, the field studies involv-

ing complex problems benefited more from participative processes. The lack of effects in the laboratory studies that manipulated the nature of a task is more difficult to interpret. It could be that in laboratory groups without defined leaders, such typical manipulations as assigned or participative groups are not strong enough to elicit effects on productivity. . . .

## CONCLUSIONS AND FUTURE DIRECTIONS

In spite of these limitations, this research supports some current wisdom about the effects of participation and extends our knowledge of the participative process in organizations in important ways. First, the meta-analysis provides some support for the conclusions reached by Locke and Schweiger (1979). Participation has an effect on both satisfaction and productivity, and its effect on satisfaction is somewhat stronger than its effect on productivity. This meta-analysis allowed us to be more explicit about these effects. As Figures 1 and 2 demonstrate, we can now make quite precise statements about the *magnitude* of the effect of participation on satisfaction and productivity. In addition, strong evidence exists for a consistent and substantial effect of research setting in these studies, because consideration of this methodological variable considerably reduces the variance among studies. Finally, our analysis indicates specific organizational factors that may enhance or constrain the effect of participation. For example, there is evidence that participative climate has a more substantial effect on workers' satisfaction than participation in specific decisions, and it appears that participation in goal setting does not have a strong effect on productivity.

These conclusions provide some clear avenues for future research. It is important for organizational scholars to conduct research that can specifically test the relationships in the cognitive and affective models. For instance, research contrasting the effects of both participative climate and participation in relation to specific issues on both satisfaction and productivity could lead to an important clarification of the cognitive and the affective processes at work in participative situations. Researchers should also extend our consideration of contingency variables to areas this meta-analysis highlights. For example, the contrast between studies of participative climate and studies of participation in relation to specific issues suggests that organizations with formal systems of participation may differ greatly from organizations in which participativeness is an informal managerial norm. Our investigation (Miller & Monge, 1986) of the Scanlon plan of participative management suggests that this might be the case. Future research could also usefully consider the development of participative systems and norms in organizations over time. Longitudinal research of this nature could help clarify the causal structure of the relationships among participation, satisfaction, and productivity. Finally, the meta-analytic procedure itself could be usefully extended to allow for the testing of relationships that go beyond the simple bivariate level.

## Notes

1. Ritchie and Miles (1970: 348) coined this term in regard to participation in decision making.

2. The category of methodological problems included a number of studies in which confounding variables or unusual methods made accurate estimation of effects impossible. For instance, the overtime study of Lawler and Hackman (1969) included an outlying data point that made interpretation difficult. In addition, the non-participative group in this study had much lower attendance than the participative group to begin with, limiting our confidence in the results. A second example of a methodological problem is Ivancevich's (1976) investigation of goal setting in which both participative and assigned groups went through extensive and active training sessions. In all ways except the actual goal setting, both groups had high levels of participation.

3. LaFollette and Sims (1975) cited this study.

## References

Abdel-Halim, A. A. 1983. Effects of task and personality characteristics on subordinate responses to participative decision making. *Academy of Management Journal,* 26: 477–484.

Abdel-Halim, A. A., & Rowland, K. M. 1976. Some personality determinants in the effects of participation: A further investigation. *Personnel Psychology,* 29: 41–55.

Alutto, J. A., & Acito, F. 1974. Decisional participation and sources of job satisfaction: A study of manufacturing personnel. *Academy of Management Journal,* 17: 160–167.

Alutto, J. A., & Vrenenburgh, D. J. 1977. Characteristics of decisional participation by nurses. *Academy of Management Journal,* 20: 341–347.

Anthony, W. P. 1978. *Participative management.* Reading, Mass.: Addison-Wesley.

Bartlem, C. S., & Locke, E. A. 1981. The Coch and French study: A critique and reinterpretation. *Human Relations,* 34: 555–566.

Baumgartel, H. 1956. Leadership, motivations, and attitudes in research laboratories. *Journal of Social Issues,* 12: 24–31.

Blake, R. R., & Mouton, J. S. 1964. *The managerial grid.* Houston: Gulf.

Carey, A. 1967. The Hawthorne studies: A radical criticism. *American Sociological Review,* 32: 403–416.

Cartwright, D., & Zander, A. 1960. *Group dynamics: Research and theory* (2nd ed.). Evanston, Ill.: Row, Peterson.

Coch, L., & French, J. R. P. 1948. Overcoming resistance to change. *Human Relations,* 1: 512–532.

Dachler, H. P., & Wilpert, B. 1978. Conceptual dimensions and boundaries of participation in organizations. *Administrative Science Quarterly,* 23: 1–39.

Dossett, D. L., Latham, G. P., & Mitchell, T. R. 1979. Effects of assigned versus participatively set goals, knowledge of results, and individual differences on employee behavior when goal difficulty is held constant. *Journal of Applied Psychology,* 64: 291–298.

Falcione, R. L. 1974. Credibility: Qualifier of subordinate participation. *Journal of Business Communication,* 11 (3): 43–54.

Fiman, B. G. 1973. An investigation of the relationships among supervisory attitudes, behaviors, and outputs: An examination of McGregor's Theory Y. *Personnel Psychology,* 26: 95–105.

Fox, W. M. 1957. Group reactions to two types of conference leadership. *Human Relations,* 10: 279–289.

French, J. R. P., Israel, J., & As, D. 1960. An experiment in a Norwegian factory: Interpersonal dimensions in decision-making. *Human Relations,* 13: 3–19.

French, J. R. P., Kay, E., & Meyer, H. H. 1966. Participation and the appraisal system. *Human Relations,* 19: 3–20.

Frost, C. H., Wakely, J. H., & Ruh, R. A. 1974. *The Scanlon Plan for organization development: Identity, participation, and equity.* East Lansing: Michigan State University Press.

Gibb, C. A. 1951. An experimental approach to the study of leadership. *Occupational Psychology,* 25: 233–248.

Glass, G. V., McGaw, B., & Smith, M. L. 1981. *Meta-analysis in social research.* Beverly Hills, Calif.: Sage Publications.

Hand, H. H., Richards, M. D., & Slocum, J. W. 1973. Organizational climate and the effectiveness of a human relations training program. *Academy of Management Journal,* 16: 185–195.

House, R. J., & Dessler, G. 1974. The path-goal theory of leadership: Some post hoc and a priori tests. In

J. Hunt & L. Larson (Eds.), *Contingency approaches to leadership:* 29–55. Carbondale: Southern Illinois University Press.

Hulin, C. L. 1971. Individual differences and job enrichment: The case against general treatment. In J. R. Maher (Ed.), *New perspectives in job enrichment:* 159–191. New York: Van Nostrand Reinhold Co.

Hunter, J. W., Schmidt, F. L., & Jackson, G. B. 1982. *Meta-analysis: Cumulating research findings across studies.* Beverly Hills, Calif.: Sage Publications.

Ivancevich, J. M. 1974. A study of a cognitive training program: Trainer styles and group development. *Academy of Management Journal,* 17: 428–439.

Ivancevich, J. M. 1976. Effects of goal setting on performance and job satisfaction. *Journal of Applied Psychology,* 61: 605–612.

Ivancevich, J. M. 1977. Different goal setting treatments and their effects on performance and job satisfaction. *Academy of Management Journal,* 20: 406–419.

Jenkins, G. D., & Lawler, E. E. 1981. Impact of employee participation in pay plan development. *Organizational Behavior and Human Performance,* 28: 111–128.

Johannesson, R. E. 1973. Some problems in the measurement of organizational climate. *Organizational Behavior and Human Performance,* 10: 118–144.

Katzell, R. A., Miller, C. E., Rotter, N. G., & Venet, T. G. 1970. Effects of leadership and other inputs on group processes and outputs. *Journal of Social Psychology,* 80: 157–169.

LaFollette, W. R., & Sims, H. P. 1975. Is satisfaction redundant with organizational climate? *Organizational Behavior and Human Performance,* 13: 257–278.

Lanzetta, J. T., & Roby, T. 1960. The relationship between certain group process variables and group problem-solving efficiency. *Journal of Social Psychology,* 52: 135–148.

Latham, G. P., & Marshall, H. A. 1982. The effects of self-set, participatively set, and assigned goals on the performance of government employees. *Personnel Psychology,* 35: 399–404.

Latham, G. P., Mitchell, T. R., & Dossett, D. L. 1978. Importance of participative goal setting and anticipated rewards on goal difficulty and job performance. *Journal of Applied Psychology,* 63: 163–171.

Latham, G. P., & Saari, L. M. 1979. The effects of holding goal difficulty constant on assigned and participatively set goals. *Academy of Management Journal,* 22: 163–168.

Latham, G. P., & Steele, T. P. 1983. The motivational effects of participation versus goal setting on performance. *Academy of Management Journal,* 26: 406–417.

Latham, G. P., & Yukl, G. A. 1976. Effects of assigned and participative goal setting on performance and job

satisfaction. *Journal of Applied Psychology,* 61: 166–171.

Lawler, E. E. 1975. Pay, participation and organizational change. In E. L. Cass & F. G. Zimmer (Eds.), *Man and work in society:* 137–149. New York: Van Nostrand Reinhold Co.

Lawler, E. E., & Hackman, J. R. 1969. Impact of employee participation in the development of pay-incentive plans: A field experiment. *Journal of Applied Psychology,* 53: 467–471.

Likert, R. L. 1967. *The human organization.* New York: McGraw-Hill Book Co.

Lischeron, J., & Wall, T. D. 1974. Attitudes towards participating among local authority employees. *Human Relations,* 28: 499–517.

Lischeron, J., & Wall, T. D. 1975. Employee participation: An experimental field study. *Human Relations,* 28: 863–884.

Litwin, G. H., & Stringer, R. A., Jr. 1968. *Motivation and organizational climate.* Boston: Harvard Business School, Division of Research.

Locke, E. A., & Schweiger, D. M. 1979. Participation in decision-making: One more look. *Research in Organizational Behavior,* 1: 265–339.

Lowin, A. 1968. Participative decision making: A model, literature critique, and prescriptions for research. *Organizational Behavior and Human Performance,* 3: 68–106.

Maier, N. R. F. 1963. *Problem solving discussions and conferences: Leadership methods and skills.* New York: McGraw-Hill Book Co.

McCurdy, H. G., & Lambert, W. E. 1952. The efficiency of small human groups in the solution of problems requiring genuine cooperation. *Journal of Personality,* 20: 478–494.

McGregor, D. 1960. *The human side of enterprise.* New York: McGraw-Hill Book Co.

Melcher, A. J. 1976. Participation: A critical review of research findings. *Human Resource Management,* 15 (2): 12–21.

Miles, R. E., & Ritchie, J. B. 1971. Participative management: Quality vs. quantity. *California Management Review,* 13 (4): 48–56.

Miller, K. I., & Monge, P. R. 1986. The development and test of a system of organizational participation and allocation. In M. McLaughlin (Ed.), *Communication yearbook 10:* in press. Beverly Hills, Calif.: Sage Publications.

Mitchell, T. R., Smyser, C. M., & Weed, S. E. 1975. Locus of control: Supervision and work satisfaction. *Academy of Management Journal,* 18: 623–631.

Morse, N. C., & Reimer, E. 1956. The experimental change of a major organizational variable. *Journal of Abnormal and Social Psychology,* 52: 120–129.

Neider, L. L. 1980. An experimental field investigation utilizing an expectancy theory view of participation. *Organizational Behavior and Human Performance, 26:* 425–442.

Obradovic, J. 1970. Participation and work attitudes in Yugoslavia. *Industrial Relations, 9:* 161–169.

Obradovic, J., French, J. R. P., & Rodgers, W. 1970. Workers' councils in Yugoslavia. *Human Relations, 23:* 459–471.

Ritchie, J. B., & Miles, R. E. 1970. An analysis of quantity and quality of participation as mediating variables in the participative decision making process. *Personnel Psychology, 23:* 347–359.

Roberts, K. H., Blankenship, L. V., & Miles, R. E. 1968. Organizational leadership, satisfaction, and productivity. *Academy of Management Journal, 11:* 401–422.

Roethlisberger, F. J., & Dickson, W. J. 1939. *Management and the worker.* Cambridge, Mass.: Harvard University Press.

Runyon, K. E. 1973. Some interactions between personality variables and management styles. *Journal of Applied Psychology, 57:* 288–294.

Schecter, J. 1972. The private world of Richard Nixon. *Time, 99* (1): 18–19.

Schneider, B. 1981. *Work climates: An interactionist perspective.* Research report No. 81-2, Department of Psychology, Michigan State University, East Lansing.

Schuler, R. S. 1976. Participation with supervisor and subordinate authoritarianism: A path-goal theory reconciliation. *Administrative Science Quarterly, 21:* 320–325.

Schuler, R. S. 1980. A role and expectancy perception model of participation in decision making. *Academy of Management Journal, 23:* 331–340.

Schuler, R. S., & Kim, J. S. 1978. Employees' expectancy perceptions as explanatory variables for effectiveness of participation in decision making. *Psychological Reports, 43:* 651–656.

Schweiger, D. M., & Leana, C. R. 1986. Participation in decision making. In E. A. Locke (Ed.), *Generalizing from laboratory to field settings:* 147–166. Lexington, Mass.: D. C. Heath Co.

Seeborg, I. S. 1978. The influence of employee participation in job redesign. *Journal of Applied Behavioral Science, 14:* 87–98.

Shaw, M. E. 1955. A comparison of two types of leadership in various communication nets. *Journal of Abnormal and Social Psychology, 50:* 127–134.

Singer, J. N. 1974. Participative decision-making about work: An overdue look at variables which mediate its effects. *Sociology of Work and Occupations, 1:* 347–371.

Smith, M. L., & Glass, G. V. 1977. Meta-analyses of psychotherapy outcome studies. *American Psychologist, 32:* 752–760.

Smith, P. C., Kendall, M., & Hulin, C. L. 1969. *The measurement of satisfaction in work and retirement.* Chicago: Rand McNally & Co.

Strauss, G. 1982. Workers' participation in management: An international perspective. *Research in Organizational Behavior, 4:* 173–265.

Tannenbaum, R., & Schmidt, W. 1958. How to choose a leadership pattern. *Harvard Business Review, 36* (2): 95–101.

Taylor, J. C., & Bowers, D. G. 1972. *Survey of organizations: A machine-scored standardized questionnaire instrument.* Ann Arbor, Mich.: Institute for Social Research.

Torrance, E. P. 1953. Methods of conducting critiques of group problem-solving performance. *Journal of Applied Psychology, 37:* 394–398.

Tosi, H. 1970. A reexamination of personality as a determinant of the effect of participation. *Personnel Psychology, 23:* 91–99.

Veen, P. 1972. Effects of participative decision-making in field hockey training: A field experiment. *Organizational Behavior and Human Performance, 7:* 288–307.

Vroom, V. H. 1960. *Some personality determinants of the effects of participation.* Englewood Cliffs, N.J.: Prentice-Hall.

Vroom, V. H., & Deci, E. L. (Eds.). 1960. *Management and motivation.* Baltimore: Penguin Books.

Vroom, V. H., & Jago, A. G. 1978. On the validity of the Vroom/Yetton model. *Journal of Applied Psychology, 63:* 151–162.

Vroom, V. H., & Mann, F. C. 1960. Leader authoritarianism and employee attitudes. *Personnel Psychology, 13:* 125–140.

Vroom, V. H., & Yetton, P. W. 1973. *Leadership and decision-making.* Pittsburgh, Pa.: University of Pittsburgh Press.

Wexley, K. E., Singh, J. P., & Yukl, G. A. 1973. Subordinate personality as a moderator of the effects of participation in three types of appraisal interviews. *Journal of Applied Psychology, 58:* 54–59.

Yukl, G. A., & Kanuk, L. 1979. Leadership behavior and the effectiveness of beauty salon managers. *Personnel Psychology, 32:* 663–675.

# Chapter Twelve

# Leadership: Substitutes, Neutralizers, and Enhancers

The previous two chapters suggested that the leadership-outcome relationship is not a simple and direct relationship. The path-goal (House & Mitchell, 1974), behavioral (Yukl, 1971), and contingency (Fiedler, 1974), theories of leadership, for example, suggest that there are a variety of situational factors that serve to mediate the leader-outcome relationship. As a consequence, the effectiveness of a particular leader behavior is influenced, for example, by characteristics of the task and the followers.

Influenced by his 1974[1] review of the literature on leader initiating structure and consideration, Steven Kerr concluded that existing evidence did not necessarily support a hypothesis that was implicitly embedded in most situational theories of leadership—namely, that in each and every situation some form of leadership will be effective. Instead, Kerr (1977) argued that there are many individual, task, and organizational factors that may serve as either *substitutes for* or *neutralizers of* a leader's behavior in terms of its impact upon follower satisfaction and performance.

There are two readings in this chapter. The first, by Steven Kerr and John M. Jermier (1978), and the second, by Jon P. Howell (1990) and his colleagues (David E. Bowen, Peter W. Dorfman, Steven Kerr, and Philip M. Podsakoff), both provide insight into the task, follower, and organizational factors that serve as substitutes and neutralizers of leadership. Both readings provide insight into the somewhat startling question, Is leadership necessary?

The concept "substitute for leadership" suggests that there are factors in the work environment that can take the place of the behavior of a leader. Attributes of the organization, technology, task, and follower can provide the motivation, guidance, reward, and satisfaction needed for effective performance to such a degree that the behaviors of the leader are rendered unimportant. The concept "neutralizer of leadership" suggests that there are work environment factors that *prevent* leaders from acting as they wish or which neutralize the effects of certain acts of leadership. (The first self-assessment at the end of this chapter opener provides you with an opportunity to assess the extent to which other factors in your work environment act as a substitute for leadership within your job.)

The organization literature suggests that there are a number of different forces within the work environment that structure the behavior and thinking of

---

[1] S. Kerr, C. Schriesheim, C. Murphy, and R. Stogdill, "Toward a Contingency Theory of Leadership Based upon the Consideration and Initiating Structure Literature," *Organizational Behavior and Human Performance* 12 (1974), pp. 62–82.

organizational members, as well as serve as sources of member motivation and satisfaction. For example, social system design (e.g., organization and work unit), technology, job design, and leader-initiating structure represent four sources of environmental structuring to which group and organizational members are exposed. Looking at the relative contributions of each of these sources of structure on employee attitudes (e.g., satisfaction, job involvement, identification), intrinsic motivation, and behaviors (e.g., performance and absenteeism), Pierce, Dunham, and Cummings (1984)[2] found that technology, job design, and work unit structure were substitutes for leader-initiating structure. Leader structure had little unique association with employee reactions except when the other sources of environmental structure were weak. In general, the most powerful substitute was found in the design of the member's job.

A study by Podsakoff (1993) and his associates revealed that the effects of a number of substitutes (i.e., subordinate, task, and organizational characteristics) had a substantial impact on employee attitudes, perceptions, and performance.[3] Commenting on their findings, they note, "The results of the present research provide strong support for Kerr and Jermier's (1978) suggestion that one reason why leader behaviors account for little variance in employee attitudes, perceptions, and behaviors is that the leader's context, defined in terms of subordinate, task, and organizational characteristics, also has an impact on such criterion measures" (p. 36). Based upon the findings of Podsakoff et al., three conclusions can be tentatively drawn: (*a*) the substitutes are more important than leader behavior in the determination of job satisfaction, commitment, and role ambiguity; (*b*) leader behaviors seem to be more important than the substitutes in terms of employee performance; and (*c*) for role conflict, altruism, attendance, and conscientiousness, the substitutes and leader behaviors are equally influential.

More recently, Podsakoff and his colleagues, MacKenzie and Bommer, conducted a meta-analysis of the substitutes for leadership that provides support for Kerr and Jermier's (1978) thesis.[4] Their findings (Podsakoff et al., 1996) reveal that "on average, substitutes for leadership uniquely account for more variance in criterion variables than do the leader behaviors" (p. 395). Across 10 employee response outcomes, the substitutes for leadership accounted for an average of 20.2 percent of the criterion variance. This is compared to the 7.2 percent accounted for by the leader behaviors. Podsakoff et al. note that this is not to suggest that leader behavior is unimportant, as it does influence follower attitudes, role perceptions, and behaviors.

Howell and his colleagues also suggest that there are certain attributes of the organization, task, and follower that actually serve to enhance (magnify) the leader and leadership effects. The concept "leadership enhancers" is similar to Fiedler's (1974) notion of situation favorableness. For example, directive leader behavior, coming from a relatively weak leader in a highly cohesive work group, is likely to be able to benefit from the presence of peer support, work facilitation, and clan control. (The second self-assessment at the end of this chapter opener provides you with an opportunity to assess the level of cohesiveness within a work group with which you are associated.)

[2] J. L. Pierce, R. B. Dunham, and L. L. Cummings, "Sources of Environmental Structuring and Participant Responses," *Organizational Behavior and Human Performance* 33 (1984), pp. 214–42.

[3] P. M. Podsakoff, B. P. Niehoff, S. B. MacKenzie, and M. L. Williams, "Do Substitutes for Leadership Really Substitute for Leadership? An Empirical Examination of Kerr and Jermier's Situational Leadership Model," *Organizational Behavior and Human Decision Processes* 54 (1993), pp. 1–44.

[4] P. M. Podsakoff, S. B. MacKenzie, and W. H. Bommer, "Meta-analysis of the Relationships between Kerr and Jermier's Substitutes for Leadership and Employee Job Attitudes, Role Perceptions, and Performance," *Journal of Applied Psychology* 81 (1996), pp. 380–99.

Charles C. Manz (1986) introduces the concept "self-leadership." The follower (subordinate) who exhibits self-leadership (e.g., self-direction and self-control) engages in behaviors that may render unnecessary the same behaviors stemming from the leader.[5] Building upon the work of Manz, it might be hypothesized that individuals with a strong sense of self (i.e., organization-based self-esteem and generalized self-efficacy) are more likely to have the capacity for self-leadership and serve as a substitute for directive leader behavior. (You can profile yourself with regard to the strength of your own organization-based self-esteem by turning to the third self-assessment at the end of this chapter opener.)

Bowers and Seashore (1966) suggest that there are certain behaviors that are important to effective group (team) functioning. In some instances, these behaviors (e.g., support, work and interaction facilitation, goal emphasis) need to be supplied by the leader. They go on to note, however, that it is not necessary that the leader supply these behaviors. These behaviors may find their substitute in one's peers, or one's self, as well as features of the organization, its technology, and the design of jobs. Figure 12.1 provides an expanded view of the leadership process, reflecting the central contributions of this chapter.

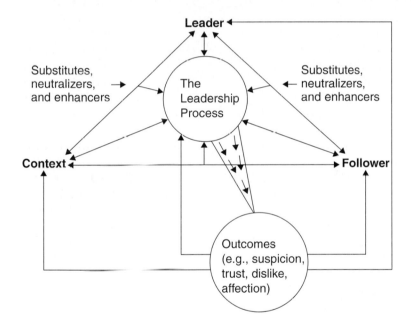

**FIGURE 12.1**
**The Role of the Leadership Process: Substitutes, Neutralizers, and Enhancers (S, N, E)**

---

[5] C. C. Manz, "Self-leadership: Toward an Expanded Theory of Self-influence Processes in Organizations," *Academy of Management Review* 11 (1986), pp. 585–600.

**EXERCISE**

*Self-Assessment*

**Substitutes for Leadership**

**Instructions:** Turn to Table 2 in the reading by Kerr and Jermier (1978), "Substitutes for Leadership: Their Meaning and Measurement." Thinking in terms of your current job, answer each of the questions posed in Table 2 by employing the following response scale:

5 = Almost always true, or almost completely true.
4 = Usually true, or true to a large extent.
3 = Sometimes true, sometimes untrue, or true to some extent.
2 = Usually untrue, or untrue to a large extent.
1 = Almost always untrue, or almost completely untrue.

**Scoring:** For each of the questions in Table 2 with an (R) following the items, subtract your response (i.e., 1–5) from 6. Next, sum your score to each of the items in category 1 and divide by 3. Following this procedure, move to the next category of questions, sum your score to each item and divide by the number of questions in that category. Complete this process for each of the 10 categories.

**Interpretation:** A high score (4 and greater) indicates a relatively strong presence of that "category" (e.g., ability, experience, training and knowledge; professional orientation; indifference toward organizational rewards; unambiguous, routine, and methodologically invariant tasks; and so on) acting as a substitute for leadership within your job.

**Group Cohesiveness**

**Instructions:** This questionnaire is concerned with work groups in an organization. Please think of your "work group" as the set of people with whom you work most closely on a day-to-day basis. If you are a member of only one work group, these questions will be easy to answer.

If you are not a member of a work group, think about the individual or set of individuals you deal with most frequently in the performance of your job.

If you are a member of two or more different groups, you will need to decide which one group is most important (for example, that you deal with most frequently). Think about one and only one group while answering these questions.

The following statements may or may not describe your work group. How much do you AGREE or DISAGREE with each statement?

|  | Strongly Disagree | Disagree | Slightly Disagree | Neither Agree nor Disagree | Slightly Agree | Agree | Strongly Agree |
|---|---|---|---|---|---|---|---|
| 1. I feel I am really part of my work group. | 1 | 2 | 3 | 4 | 5 | 6 | 7 |
| 2. There is confidence and trust among members of my work group. | 1 | 2 | 3 | 4 | 5 | 6 | 7 |
| 3. This group is extremely attractive to me. | 1 | 2 | 3 | 4 | 5 | 6 | 7 |
| 4. I look forward to being with the members of my work group each day. | 1 | 2 | 3 | 4 | 5 | 6 | 7 |
| 5. There is a strong bond holding members of this group together. | 1 | 2 | 3 | 4 | 5 | 6 | 7 |
| 6. There is a high level of tension among certain members of my work group. | 1 | 2 | 3 | 4 | 5 | 6 | 7 |

**Scoring:** Subtract your numeric answer to question 6 from 8. Next, add this adjusted score to your responses to questions 1 through 5, divide the total by 6, and enter your score here: _____.

**Interpretation:** A high score (6 and greater) suggests that you perceive a relatively high degree of group cohesiveness. A low score (2 and less) is indicative of a relatively low degree of group cohesiveness. As might be hypothesized from the material covered in this chapter, cohesive work groups are extremely likely to provide their members with personal and task support, thereby reducing the importance of (need for) certain leader behaviors.

**Source:** These are illustrative group cohesiveness items, constructed for this self-assessment. There is no prior validation evidence available.

**EXERCISE**

*Self-Assessment*

**Organization-Based Self-Esteem (OBSE)**

**Instructions:** The following questions ask about you and your relationship with an organization.

Please indicate the extent to which you believe in each of the following statements by expressing the level of your agreement or disagreement.

| I BELIEVE that: | Strongly Disagree | Disagree | Neither Agree nor Disagree | Agree | Strongly Agree |
|---|---|---|---|---|---|
| 1.  I COUNT around here. | 1 | 2 | 3 | 4 | 5 |
| 2.  I am TAKEN SERIOUSLY around here. | 1 | 2 | 3 | 4 | 5 |
| 3.  There is FAITH IN ME around here. | 1 | 2 | 3 | 4 | 5 |
| 4.  I am TRUSTED around here. | 1 | 2 | 3 | 4 | 5 |
| 5.  I am HELPFUL around here. | 1 | 2 | 3 | 4 | 5 |
| 6.  I am a VALUABLE PART of this place. | 1 | 2 | 3 | 4 | 5 |
| 7.  I am EFFICIENT around here. | 1 | 2 | 3 | 4 | 5 |
| 8.  I am an IMPORTANT PART of this place. | 1 | 2 | 3 | 4 | 5 |
| 9.  I MAKE A DIFFERENCE around here. | 1 | 2 | 3 | 4 | 5 |
| 10. I am COOPERATIVE around here. | 1 | 2 | 3 | 4 | 5 |

**Scoring:** Sum your scores to each of the 10 statements and then divide by 10.

My OBSE score is: _____.

**Interpretation:** A high score (4 and greater) suggests that you have a relatively high level of organization-based self-esteem. A low score (2 and less) suggests a relatively weak organization-based self-esteem.

It has been suggested that individuals who have a strong and positive sense of "self," as might be reflected by a high level of organization-based self-esteem and a strong generalized self-efficacy, (see your self-efficacy assessment from the Prologue), are more capable of functioning with less leadership support and direction than individuals whose sense of self within the work environment is relatively weak. This becomes particularly true as role conditions become increasingly difficult, conflict-laden, ambiguous, nonsupportive, and overloaded.

**Source:** Reprinted with permission from J. L. Pierce, D. G. Gardner, L. L. Cummings, and R. B. Dunham, "Organization-Based Self-Esteem: Construct Definition, Measurement, and Validation," *Academy of Management Journal* 32 (1989), pp. 622–48.

## Reading 34

# Substitutes for Leadership:

## *Their Meaning and Measurement*

**Steven Kerr**
University of Southern California

**John M. Jermier**
The Ohio State University

A number of theories and models of leadership exist, each seeking to most clearly identify and best explain the presumedly powerful effects of leader behavior or personality attributes upon the satisfaction and performance of hierarchical subordinates. These theories and models fail to agree in many respects, but have in common the fact that none of them systematically accounts for very much criterion variance. It is certainly true that data indicating strong superior–subordinate relationships have sometimes been reported. In numerous studies, however, conclusions have had to be based on statistical rather than practical significance, and hypothesis support has rested upon the researcher's ability to show that the trivially low correlations obtained were not the result of chance.

Current theories and models of leadership have something else in common: a conviction that hierarchical leadership is always important. Even situational approaches to leadership share the assumption that while the *style* of leadership likely to be effective will vary according to the situation, *some* leadership style will *always* be effective *regardless* of the situation. Of course, the extent to which this assumption is explicated varies greatly, as does the degree to which each theory is dependent upon the assumption. Fairly explicit is the vertical dyad linkage model developed by Graen and his associates (Graen, Dansereau, & Minami, 1972; Dansereau, Cashman, & Graen, 1973), which attributes importance to hierarchical leadership without concern for the situation. The Fiedler (1964, 1967) contingency model also makes the general assumption that hierarchical leadership is important in situations of low, medium, and high favorableness, though predictions about relationships between LPC [least preferred co-worker] and performance in Octants VI

**Source:** Edited and reprinted with permission from *Organizational Behavior and Human Performance* 22 (1978), pp. 375–403.

and VII are qualified (Fiedler & Chemers, 1974, p. 82). Most models of decision-centralization (e.g., Tannenbaum & Schmidt, 1958; Heller & Yukl, 1969; Vroom & Yetton, 1973; Bass & Valenzi, 1974) include among their leader decision-style alternatives one whereby subordinates attempt a solution by themselves, with minimal participation by the hierarchical superior. Even in such cases, however, the leader is responsible for initiating the method through delegation of the problem and is usually described as providing (structuring) information.

The approach to leadership which is least dependent upon the assumption articulated above, and which comes closest to the conceptualization to be proposed in this paper, is the path-goal theory (House, 1971; House & Mitchell, 1974). Under circumstances when both goals and paths to goals may be clear, House and Mitchell (1974) point out that "attempts by the leader to clarify paths and goals will be both redundant and seen by subordinates as imposing unnecessary close control." They go on to predict that "although such control may increase performance by preventing soldiering or malingering, it will also result in decreased satisfaction."

This prediction is supported in part by conclusions drawn by Kerr, Schriesheim, Murphy, and Stogdill (1974) from their review of the consideration-initiating structure literature and is at least somewhat consistent with results from a few recent studies. A most interesting and pertinent premise of the theory, however, is that even unnecessary and redundant leader behaviors will have an impact upon leadership satisfaction, morale, motivation, performance, and acceptance of the leader (House & Mitchell, 1974; House & Dessler, 1974). While leader attempts to clarify paths and goals are therefore recognized by path-goal theory to be unnecessary and redundant in certain situations, in no situation are they explicitly hypothesized by path-goal (or any other leadership theory) to be irrelevant.

This lack of recognition is unfortunate. As has already been mentioned, data from numerous studies collectively demonstrate that in many situations these leader behaviors *are* irrelevant, and hierarchical leadership (as operationalized in these studies) per se does not seem to matter. In fact, leadership variables so often account for very little criterion variance that a few writers have begun to argue that the leadership construct is sterile altogether, that "the concept of leadership itself has outlived its usefulness" (Miner, 1975, p. 200). This view is also unfortunate, however, and fails to take note of accurate predictions by leadership theorists even as such theorists fail to conceptually reconcile their inaccurate predictions.

What is clearly needed to resolve this dilemma is a conceptualization adequate to explain both the occasional successes and frequent failures of the various theories and models of leadership.

## SUBSTITUTES FOR LEADERSHIP

A wide variety of individual, task, and organizational characteristics have been found to influence relationships between leader behavior and subordinate satisfaction, morale, and performance. Some of these variables (for example, job pressure and subordinate expectations of leader behavior) act primarily to influence which leadership style will best permit the hierarchical superior to motivate, direct, and control subordinates. The effect of others, however, is to act as "substitutes for leadership," tending to negate the leader's ability to either improve or impair subordinate satisfaction and performance.

Substitutes for leadership are apparently prominent in many different organizational settings, but their existence is not explicated in any of the dominant leadership theories. As a result, data describing formal superior–subordinate relationships are often obtained in situations where important substitutes exist. These data logically ought to be, and usually are, insignificant and are useful primarily as a reminder that when leadership styles are studied in circumstances where the choice of style is irrelevant, the effect is to replace the potential power of the leadership construct with the unintentional comedy of the law of the instrument.[1]

What is needed, then, is a taxonomy of situations where we should not be studying "leadership" (in the formal hierarchical sense) at all. Development of such a taxonomy is still at an early stage, but Woodward (1973) and Miner (1975) have laid important groundwork through their classifications of control, and some effects of nonleader sources of clarity have been considered by Hunt (Note 2) and Hunt and Osborn (1975). Reviews of the leadership literature by House and Mitchell (1974) and Kerr et al. (1974) have also proved pertinent in this regard and suggest that individual, task, and organizational characteristics of the kind outlined in Table 1 will help to determine whether or not hierarchical leadership is likely to matter.

## CONCEPTUAL DOMAIN OF SUBSTITUTES FOR LEADERSHIP

Since Table 1 is derived from previously conducted studies, substitutes are only suggested for the two leader behavior styles which dominate the research literature. The substitutes construct probably has much wider applicability, however, perhaps to hierarchical leadership in general.

It is probably useful to clarify some of the characteristics listed in Table 1. "Professional orientation" is considered a potential substitute for leadership because employees with such an orientation typically cultivate horizontal rather than vertical relationships, give greater credence to peer review processes, however informal, than to hierarchical evaluations, and tend to develop important referents external to the employing organization (Filley, House, & Kerr, 1976). Clearly, such attitudes and behaviors can sharply reduce the influence of the hierarchical superior.

"Methodologically invariant" tasks may result from serial interdependence, from machine-paced operations, or from work methods which are highly standardized. In one study (House, Filley, & Kerr, 1971, p. 26), invariance was found to derive from a network of government contracts which "specified not only the performance requirements of the end product, but also many of the management practices and control techniques that the company must follow in carrying out the contract."

Invariant methodology relates to what Miner (1975) describes as the "push" of work. Tasks which are "intrinsically satisfying" (another potential substitute listed in Table 1) contribute in turn to the "pull" of work. Miner believes that for "task control" to be effective, a force comprised of both the push and pull of work must be developed. At least in theory, however, either type alone may act as a substitute for hierarchical leadership.

Performance feedback provided by the work itself is another characteristic of the task which potentially functions in place of the formal leader. It

**TABLE 1** **Substitutes for Leadership**

| | Will Tend to Neutralize | |
| --- | --- | --- |
| Characteristic | Relationship-Oriented, Supportive, People-Centered Leadership: Consideration, Support, and Interaction Facilitation | Task-Oriented, Instrumental, Job-Centered Leadership: Initiating Structure, Goal Emphasis, and Work Facilitation |
| *Of the Subordinate* | | |
| 1. Ability, experience, training, knowledge. | | X |
| 2. Need for independence. | X | X |
| 3. Professional orientation. | X | X |
| 4. Indifference toward organizational rewards. | X | X |
| *Of the Task* | | |
| 5. Unambiguous and routine. | | X |
| 6. Methodologically invariant. | | X |
| 7. Provides its own feedback concerning accomplishment. | | X |
| 8. Intrinsically satisfying. | X | |
| *Of the Organization* | | |
| 9. Formalization (explicit plans, goals, and areas of responsibility). | | X |
| 10. Inflexibility (rigid, unbending rules and procedures). | | X |
| 11. Highly-specified and active advisory and staff functions. | | X |
| 12. Closely-knit, cohesive work groups. | X | X |
| 13. Organizational rewards not within the leader's control. | X | X |
| 14. Spatial distance between superior and subordinates. | X | X |

has been reported that employees with high growth need strength in particular derive beneficial psychological states (internal motivation, general satisfaction, work effectiveness) from clear and direct knowledge of the results of performance (Hackman & Oldham, 1976; Oldham, 1976). Task-provided feedback is often: (1) the most immediate source of feedback given the infrequency of performance appraisal sessions (Hall & Lawler, 1969); (2) the most accurate source of feedback given the problems of measuring the performance of others (Campbell, Dunnette, Lawler, & Weick, 1970); and (3) the most self-evaluation evoking and intrinsically motivating source of feedback given the controlling and informational aspects of feedback from others (DeCharms, 1968; Deci, 1972, 1975; Greller & Herold, 1975). For these reasons, the formal leader's function as a provider of role structure through performance feedback may be insignificant by comparison.

Cohesive, interdependent work groups and active advisory and staff personnel also have the ability to render the formal leader's performance feedback function inconsequential. Inherent in mature group structures are stable performance norms and positional differentiation (Bales & Strodtbeck, 1951; Borgatta & Bales, 1953; Stogdill, 1959; Lott & Lott, 1965; Zander, 1968). Task-relevant guidance and feedback from others may be provided directly by the formal leader, indirectly by the formal leader through the primary work group members, directly by the primary work group members, by staff personnel, or by the client. If the latter four instances prevail, the formal leader's role may be quite trivial. Cohesive work groups are, of course, important sources of affiliative need satisfaction.

Programming through impersonal modes has been reported to be the most frequent type of coordination strategy employed under conditions of low-to-medium task uncertainty and low task interdependence (Van de Ven, Delbecq, & Koenig, 1976). Thus, the existence of written work goals, guidelines, and groundrules (organizational formalization) and rigid rules and procedures (organizational inflexibility) may serve as substitutes for leader-provided coordination under certain conditions. Personal and group coordination modes involving the formal leader may become important only when less costly impersonal strategies are not suitable. . . .

## ELABORATION OF THE CONSTRUCT

Table 1 was designed to capsulize our present knowledge with respect to possible substitutes for hierarchical leadership. Since present knowledge is the product of past research, and since past research was primarily unconcerned with the topic, the table is probably oversimplified and incomplete in a number of respects. Rigorous elaboration of the substitutes construct must necessarily await additional research, but we would speculate that such research would show the following refinements to be important.

### DISTINGUISHING BETWEEN "SUBSTITUTES" AND "NEUTRALIZERS"

A "neutralizer" is defined by Webster's as something which is able to "paralyze, destroy, or counteract the effectiveness of" something else. In the context of leadership, this term may be applied to characteristics which make it effectively *impossible* for relationship and/or task-oriented leadership to make a difference. Neutralizers are a type of moderator variable when uncorrelated with both predictors and the criterion and act as suppressor variables when correlated with predictors but not the criterion (Zedeck, 1971; Wherry, 1946).

A "substitute" is defined to be "a person or thing acting or used in place of another." In context, this term may be used to describe characteristics which render relationship and/or task-oriented leadership not only impossible but also *unnecessary.*[2] Substitutes may be correlated with both predictors and the criterion, but tend to improve the validity coefficient when included in the predictor set. That is, they will not only tend to affect which leader behaviors (if any) are influential, but will also tend to impact upon the criterion variable.

The consequences of neutralizers and substitutes for previous research have probably been similar, since both act to reduce the impact of leader behaviors upon subordinate attitudes and performance. For this reason it is not too important that such summaries of previous research as Table 1 distinguish between them. Nevertheless, an important theoretical distinction does exist. It is that substitutes do, but neutralizers do not, provide a "person or thing acting or used in place of" the formal leader's negated influence. The ef-

fect of neutralizers is therefore to create an "influence vacuum" from which a variety of dysfunctions may emerge.

As an illustration of this point, look again at the characteristics outlined in Table 1. Since each characteristic has the capacity to counteract leader influence, all 14 may clearly be termed neutralizers. It is *not* clear, however, that all 14 are substitutes. For example, subordinates' perceived "ability, experience, training, and knowledge" tend to impair the leader's influence, but may or may not act as substitutes for leadership. It is known that individuals who are high in task-related self-esteem place high value upon non-hierarchical control systems which are consistent with a belief in the competence of people (Korman, 1970). The problem is that subordinate perceptions concerning ability and knowledge may not be accurate. Actual ability and knowledge may therefore act as a substitute, while false perceptions of competence and unfounded self-esteem may produce simply a neutralizing effect.

"Spatial distance," "subordinate indifference toward organizational rewards," and "organizational rewards not within the leader's control" are other examples of characteristics which do not render formal leadership unnecessary, but merely create circumstances in which effective leadership may be impossible. If rewards are clearly within the control of some other person, this other person can probably act as a substitute for the formal leader, and no adverse consequences (except probably to the leader's morale) need result. When no one knows where control over rewards lies, however, or when rewards are linked rigidly to seniority or to other factors beyond anyone's control, or when rewards are perceived to be unattractive altogether, the resulting influence vacuum would almost inevitably be dysfunctional.

### DISTINGUISHING BETWEEN DIRECT AND INDIRECT LEADER BEHAVIOR EFFECTS

It is possible to conceptualize a *direct effect* of leadership as one which occurs when a subordinate is influenced by some leader behavior *in and of itself.* An *indirect effect* may be said to result when the subordinate is influenced by the *implications* of the behavior for some future consequence. Attempts by the leader to influence subordinates must always produce direct and/or indirect effects or, when strong substitutes for leadership exist, no effect.

**TABLE 2    Questionnaire Items for the Measurement of Substitutes for Leadership**

*(1) Ability, Experience, Training, and Knowledge*
—Because of my ability, experience, training, or job knowledge, I have the competence to act independently of my immediate superior in performing my day-to-day duties.
—Because of my ability, experience, training, or job knowledge, I have the competence to act independently of my immediate superior in performing unusual and unexpected job duties.
—Due to my lack of experience and training, I must depend upon my immediate superior to provide me with necessary data, information, and advice. (R)

*(2) Professional Orientation*
—For feedback about how well I am performing, I rely on people in my occupational specialty, whether or not they are members of my work unit or organization.
—I receive very useful information and guidance from people who share my occupational specialty, but who are not members of my employing organization.
—My job satisfaction depends to a considerable extent on people in my occupational specialty who are not members of my employing organization.

*(3) Indifference toward Organizational Rewards*
—I cannot get enthusiastic about the rewards offered in this organization, or about the opportunities available.
—This organization offers attractive payoffs to people it values. (R)
—In general, most of the things I seek and value in this world cannot be obtained from my job or my employing organization.

*(4) Unambiguous, Routine, and Methodologically Invariant Tasks*
—Because of the nature of the tasks I perform on my job, there is little doubt about the best way to get the work done.
—Because of the nature of the work I do, I am often required to perform nonroutine tasks. (R)
—Because of the nature of my work, at the beginning of each work day, I can predict with near certainty exactly what activities I will be performing that day.
—There is really only one correct way to perform most of my tasks.
—My job duties are so simple that almost anyone could perform them after a little bit of instruction and practice.
—It is so hard to figure out the correct approach to most of my work problems that second-guessers would have a field day. (R)

*(5) Task-provided Feedback Concerning Accomplishment*
—After I've done something on my job, I can tell right away from the results I get whether I've done it correctly.
—My job is the kind where you can make a mistake or an error and not be able to see that you've made it. (R)

—Because of the nature of the tasks I perform, it is easy for me to see when I've done something exceptionally well.

*(6) Intrinsically Satisfying Tasks*
—I get a great deal of personal satisfaction from the work I do.
—It is hard to imagine that anyone could enjoy performing the tasks that I perform on my job. (R)
—My job satisfaction depends to a considerable extent on the nature of the actual tasks I perform on the job.

*(7) Organizational Formalization*
—Clear, written goals and objectives exist for my job.
—My job responsibilities are clearly specified in writing.
—In this organization, performance appraisals are based on written standards.
—Written schedules, programs, and work specifications are available to guide me on my job.
—My duties, authority, and accountability are documented in policies, procedures, and job descriptions.
—Written rules and guidelines exist to direct work efforts.
—Written documents (such as budgets, schedules, and plans) are used as an essential part of my job.
—There are contradictions and inconsistencies among the written statements of goals and objectives. (R)
—There are contradictions and inconsistencies among the written guidelines and groundrules. (R)

*(8) Organizational Inflexibility*
—In this organization, the written rules are treated as a bible and are never violated.
—People in this organization consider the rulebooks and policy manuals as general guidelines, not as rigid and unbending. (R)
—In this organization, anytime there is a policy in writing that fits some situation, everybody has to follow that policy very strictly.

*(9) Advisory and Staff Functions*
—For feedback about how well I am performing, I rely on staff personnel inside the organization, based outside my work unit or department.
—In my job I must depend on staff personnel located outside of my work unit or department to provide me with data, reports, and informal advice necessary for my job performance.
—I receive very useful information and guidance from staff personnel who are based outside my work unit or department.

*(10) Closely Knit, Cohesive, Interdependent Work Groups*
—For feedback about how well I am performing, I rely on members of my work group other than my superior.
—The quantity of work I turn out depends largely on the performance of members of my work group other than my superior.

*(continued)*

## TABLE 2   *(Continued)*

—The quality of work I turn out depends largely on the performance of members of my work group other than my superior.

—I receive very useful information and advice from members of my work group other than my superior.

—I am dependent on members of my work group other than my superior for important organizational rewards.

—My job satisfaction depends to a considerable extent on members of my work group other than my superior.

### (11) Organizational Rewards Not within the Leader's Control

—On my job I must depend on my immediate superior to provide the necessary financial resources (such as budget and expense money). (R)

—On my job I must depend on my immediate superior to provide the necessary nonfinancial resources (such as file space and equipment). (R)

—My chances for a promotion depend on my immediate superior's recommendation. (R)

—My chances for a pay raise depend on my immediate superior's recommendation. (R)

—My immediate superior has little say or influence over which of his or her subordinates receives organizational rewards.

—The only performance feedback that matters to me is that given me by my immediate superior. (R)

—I am dependent on my immediate superior for important organizational rewards. (R)

### (12) Spatial Distance between Superior and Subordinates

—The nature of my job is such that my immediate superior is seldom around me when I'm working.

—On my job my most important tasks take place away from where my immediate superior is located.

—My immediate superior and I are seldom in actual contact or direct sight of one another.

### (13) Subordinate Need for Independence

—I like it when the person in charge of a group I am in tells me what to do. (R)

—When I have a problem, I like to think it through myself without help from others.

—It is important for me to be able to feel that I can run my life without depending on people older and more experienced than myself.

This distinction between direct and indirect effects of leader behavior has received very little attention, but its importance to any discussion of leadership substitutes is considerable. For example, in their review of path-goal theory, House and Dessler (1974, p. 31) state that "subordinates with high needs for affiliation and social approval would see friendly, considerate leader behavior as an immediate source of satisfaction" (direct effect). As Table 1 suggests, it is conceivable that fellow group members could supply such subordinates with enough affiliation and social approval to eliminate dependence on the leader. With other subordinates, however, the key "may be not so much in terms of what the leader does but may be in terms of how it is *interpreted* by his members" (Graen et al., 1972, p. 235). Graen et al. concluded from their data that "consideration is interpreted as the leader's evaluation of the member's role behavior . . ." (p. 233). For these subordinates, therefore, consideration seems to have been influential primarily because of its perceived implications for the likelihood of receiving future rewards. In this case the effect is an indirect one, for which group member approval and affiliation probably cannot substitute.

In the same vein, we are told by House and Dessler (1974, pp. 31–32) that:

Subordinates with high needs for achievement would be predicted to view leader behavior that clarifies path-goal relationships and provides goal-oriented feedback as satisfying. Subordinates with high needs for extrinsic rewards would be predicted to see leader directiveness or coaching behavior as instrumental to their satisfaction if such behavior helped them perform in such a manner as to gain recognition, promotion, security, or pay increases.

It is apparent from House and Dessler's remarks that the distinction between direct and indirect effects need not be limited to relationship-oriented behaviors. Such characteristics of the task as the fact that it "provides its own feedback" (listed in Table 1 as a potential substitute for task-oriented behavior) may provide achievement-oriented subordinates with immediate satisfaction (direct effect), but fail to negate the superior's ability to help subordinates perform so as to obtain future rewards (indirect effect). Conversely, subordinate experience and training may act as substitutes for the indirect effects of task-oriented leadership by preventing the leader from

**TABLE 3** Substitutes for Leadership: A Theoretical Extension

| Characteristic* | Relationship-Oriented, Supportive, People-Centered Leadership (Consideration, Support, and Interaction Facilitation): | | Task-Oriented, Instrumental, Job-Centered Leadership (Initiating Structure, Goal Emphasis, and Work Facilitation): | | (Other Leader Behaviors . . .) | |
|---|---|---|---|---|---|---|
| | Directly | Indirectly | Directly | Indirectly | Directly | Indirectly |
| **Substitutes** | | | | | | |
| *of the subordinate* | | | | | | |
| 1. ability | | | | X | ? | ? |
| 3. "professional" orientation | X | X | X | X | ? | ? |
| *of the task* | | | | | | |
| 5. unambiguous and routine | | | X | X | ? | ? |
| 7. provides its own feedback concerning accomplishment | | | X | | ? | ? |
| 8. intrinsically satisfying | X | | | | ? | ? |
| *of the organization* | | | | | | |
| 12. closely-knit, cohesive work groups | X | | X | X | ? | ? |
| **Neutralizers** | | | | | | |
| 4. indifference toward organizational rewards | | X | | X | ? | ? |
| 13. organizational rewards not within the leader's control | | X | | X | ? | ? |

\* Note: Identifying numbers for characteristics refer to item numbers in Table 1.

improving subordinate performance, but may not offset the direct effects.

## IDENTIFYING OTHER CHARACTERISTICS AND OTHER LEADER BEHAVIORS

Any elaboration of the substitutes construct must necessarily include the specification of other leader behaviors, and other characteristics which may act as substitutes for leader behaviors. As was mentioned earlier, most previous studies of leadership were concerned with only two of its dimensions. This approach is intuitively indefensible. Richer conceptualizations of the leadership process already exist and almost inevitably underscore the importance of additional leader activities. As these activities are delineated in future research, it is likely that substitutes for them will also be identified.

Table 3 is offered as a guide to research. It portrays a state of increased sophistication of the substitutes construct, assuming future development along lines suggested in this section. Substitutes would be differentiated from neutralizers, and direct effects of leadership empirically distinguished from indirect effects. The columns on the right are intended to represent as-yet-unexplored leader behaviors, and the dotted lines on the bottom indicate the presence of additional characteristics which may act either as neutralizers or as true substitutes for leadership.

## DISTINGUISHING BETWEEN CAUSE AND EFFECT IN LEADER BEHAVIOR

Another area where the substitutes construct appears to have implications for leadership research concerns the question of causality. It is now evident from a variety of laboratory experiments and longitudinal field studies that leader behavior may result from as well as cause subordinate attitudes and performance. It is possible to speculate upon the effect that leadership substitutes would have on the relative causal strength of superior- and subordinate-related variables. This paper has tried to show that such substitutes act to reduce changes in subordinates' attitudes and performance which are *caused* by leader behaviors. On the other hand, there seems no reason why leadership substitutes should prevent changes in leader behavior which *result* from different levels of subordinate performance, satisfaction, and morale. The substitutes for leadership construct may therefore help to explain why the direction of causality is sometimes predominantly from leader behavior to subordinate outcomes, while at other times the reverse is true.

## SPECIFICATION OF INTERACTION EFFECTS AMONG SUBSTITUTES AND NEUTRALIZERS

From the limited data obtained thus far, it is not possible to differentiate at all among leadership substitutes and neutralizers in terms of relative strength and predictive capability. We have received some indication that the strength of a substitute, as measured by its mean level, is not strongly related to its predictive power. Substitutes for leadership as theoretically important as intrinsic satisfaction, for example, apparently need only be present in moderate amounts . . . to have potent substituting effects. . . . Other, less important substitutes and neutralizers might have to be present to a tremendous degree before their effects might be felt. Clearly, the data reported in this study are insufficient to determine at what point a particular substitute becomes important, or at what point several substitutes, each fairly weak by itself, might combine to collectively impair hierarchical leader influence. Multiplicative functions involving information on the strength and predictive power of substitutes for leadership should be able to be specified as evidence accumulates.

## CONCLUSIONS

The research literature provides abundant evidence that for organization members to maximize organizational and personal outcomes, they must be able to obtain both guidance and good feelings from their work settings. Guidance is usually offered in the form of role or task structuring, while good feelings may stem from "stroking" behaviors,[3] or may be derived from intrinsic satisfaction associated with the task itself.

The research literature does *not* suggest that guidance and good feelings must be provided by the hierarchical superior; it is only necessary that they somehow be provided. Certainly the formal leader represents a potential source of structuring and stroking behaviors, but many other organization members do too, and impersonal equivalents also exist. To the extent that other potential sources are deficient, the hierarchical superior is clearly in a position to play a dominant role. In these situations the opportunity for leader downward influence is great, and formal leadership ought to be important. To the extent that other sources provide structure and stroking in abundance, the hierarchical leader will have little chance to exert downward influence. In such cases it is of small value to gain entree to the organization, distribute leader behavior questionnaires to anything that moves, and later debate about which leadership theory best accounts for the pitifully small percentage of variance explained, while remaining uncurious about the large percentage unexplained.

Of course, few organizations would be expected to have leadership substitutes so strong as to totally overwhelm the leader, or so weak as to require subordinates to rely entirely on him. In most organizations it is likely that, as was true here, substitutes exist for some leader activities but not for others. Effective leadership might therefore be described as the ability to supply subordinates with needed guidance and good feelings which are not being supplied by other sources. From this viewpoint it is inaccurate to inform leaders (say, in management development programs) that they are incompetent if they do not personally provide these things regardless of the situation. While it may (or may not) be necessary that the organization as a whole function in a "9–9" manner (Blake & Mouton, 1964), it clearly is unnecessary for the manager to behave in such a manner unless no substitutes for leader-provided guidance and good feelings exist.

Dubin (1976, p. 33) draws a nice distinction between "proving" and "improving" a theory and points out that "if the purpose is to prove the adequacy of the theoretical model . . . data are likely to be collected for values on only those units incorporated in the theoretical model. This usually means that, either experimentally or by discarding data, attention in the empirical research is focused solely upon values measured on units incorporated in the theory."

In Dubin's terms, if we are really interested in improving rather than proving our various theories and models of leadership, a logical first step is that we stop assuming what really needs to be demonstrated empirically. The criticality of the leader's role in supplying necessary structure and stroking should be evaluated in the broader organizational context. Data pertaining to both leadership and possible substitutes for leadership (Table 1) should be obtained, and both main and interaction effects examined. A somewhat different use of information about substitutes for leadership would be a "prescreen," to assess the appropriateness of a potential sample for a hierarchical leadership study.

What this all adds up to is that, if we really want to know more about the sources and consequences of guidance and good feelings in organizations, we should be prepared to study these things *whether or not* they happen to be provided through hierarchical leadership. For those not so catholic, whose interest lies in the derivation and refinement of theories of formal leadership, a commitment should be made to the importance of developing and operationalizing a *true* situational theory of leadership, one which will explicitly limit its propositions and restrict its predictions *to those situations* where hierarchical leadership theoretically ought to make a difference.

## Notes

1. Abraham Kaplan (1964, p. 28) has observed, "Give a small boy a hammer, and he will find that everything he encounters needs pounding."

2. This potentially important distinction was first pointed out by M. A. Von Glinow in a doctoral seminar.

3. "Stroking" is used here, as in transactional analysis, to describe "any type of physical, oral, or visual recognition of one person by another" (Huse, 1975, p. 288).

## References

Bales, R., & Strodtbeck, F. Phases in group problem solving. *Journal of Abnormal and Social Psychology,* 1951, 46, 485–495.

Bass, B., & Valenzi, E. Contingent aspects of effective management styles. In J. G. Hunt & L. L. Larson (Eds.), *Contingency approaches to leadership.* Carbondale: Southern Illinois Press, 1974.

Blake, R., & Mouton, J. *The managerial grid.* Houston: Gulf, 1964.

Bordua, D., & Reiss, A. Command, control, and charisma: Reflections on police bureaucracy. *American Journal of Sociology,* 1966, 72, 68–76.

Borgatta, E., & Bales, R. Task and accumulation of experience as factors in the interaction of small groups. *Sociometry,* 1953, 16, 239–252.

Campbell, J., Dunnette, E., Lawler, E., & Weick, K. *Managerial behavior, performance and effectiveness.* New York: McGraw-Hill, 1970.

Dansereau, F., Cashman, J., & Graen, G. Instrumentality theory and equity theory as complementary approaches in predicting the relationship of leadership and turnover among managers. *Organizational Behavior and Human Performance,* 1973, 10, 184–200.

DeCharms, R. *Personal causation.* New York: Academic Press, 1968.

Deci, E. Intrinsic motivation, extrinsic reinforcement, and inequity. *Journal of Personality and Social Psychology,* 1972, 22, 113–120.

Deci, E. *Intrinsic motivation.* New York: Plenum, 1975.

Dubin, R. Theory building in applied areas. In M. Dunnette (Ed.), *Handbook of industrial and organizational psychology.* Chicago: Rand-McNally, 1976.

Fiedler, F. E. A contingency model of leadership effectiveness. In L. Berkowitz (Ed.), *Advances in experimental social psychology.* New York: Academic Press, 1964.

Fiedler, F. E. *A theory of leadership effectiveness.* New York: McGraw-Hill, 1967.

Fiedler, F. E., & Chemers, M. M. *Leadership and effective management.* Glenview, IL: Scott, Foresman, 1974.

Filley, A. C., House, R. J., & Kerr, S. *Managerial process and organizational behavior* (2nd ed.). Glenview, IL: Scott, Foresman, 1976.

Graen, G., Dansereau, F., Jr., & Minami, T. Dysfunctional leadership styles. *Organizational Behavior and Human Performance,* 1972, 7, 216–236.

Greller, M., & Herold, D. Sources of feedback: A preliminary investigation. *Organizational Behavior and Human Performance,* 1975, 13, 244–256.

Hackman, R., & Oldham, G. Motivation through the design of work: Test of a theory. *Organizational Behavior and Human Performance,* 1976, 16, 250–279.

Hall, D., & Lawler, E. Unused potential in R and D labs. *Research Management,* 1969, 12, 339–354.

Heller, F. A., & Yukl, G. Participation, managerial decision-making, and situational variables. *Organizational Behavior and Human Performance,* 1969, 4, 227–234.

House, R. J. A path-goal theory of leader effectiveness. *Administrative Science Quarterly,* 1971, 16, 321–338.

House, R. J., & Dessler, G. The path-goal theory of leadership: Some post hoc and a priori tests. In J. G. Hunt & L. L. Larson (Eds.), *Contingency approaches to leadership.* Carbondale: Southern Illinois University Press, 1974.

House, R. J., Filley, A. C., & Kerr, S. Relation of leader consideration and initiating structure to R and D subordinates' satisfaction. *Administrative Science Quarterly,* 1971, 16, 19–30.

House, R. J., & Mitchell, T. R. Path-goal theory of leadership. *Journal of Contemporary Business,* 1974, 3, 81–97.

House, R. J., & Rizzo, J. R. Toward the measurement of organizational practices: Scale development and validation. *Journal of Applied Psychology,* 1972, 56, 288–296.

Hunt, J. G., & Osborn, R. N. An adaptive-reactive theory of leadership: The role of macro variables in leadership research. In J. G. Hunt & L. L. Larson (Eds.), *Leadership frontiers.* Carbondale: Southern Illinois University Press, 1975.

Huse, E. F. *Organization development and change.* St. Paul: West, 1975.

Kaplan, Abraham. *The conduct of inquiry.* San Francisco: Chandler, 1964.

Kerr, S., Schriesheim, C., Murphy, C. J., & Stogdill, R. M. Toward a contingency theory of leadership based upon the consideration and initiating structure literature. *Organizational Behavior and Human Performance,* 1974, 12, 62–82.

Korman, A. Toward a hypothesis of work behavior. *Journal of Applied Psychology,* 1970, 54, 31–41.

Lott, A., & Lott, B. Group cohesiveness as interpersonal attraction: A review of relationships with antecedent and consequent variables. *Psychological Bulletin,* 1965, 64, 259–302.

McNamara, J. Uncertainties in police work: The relevance of police recruits' backgrounds and training. In D. Bordua (Ed.), *The police: Six sociological essays.* New York: Wiley, 1967.

Miner, J. The uncertain future of the leadership concept: An overview. In J. G. Hunt & L. L. Larson (Eds.), *Leadership frontiers.* Carbondale: Southern Illinois Press, 1975.

Oldham, G. Job characteristics and internal motivation: The moderating effect of interpersonal and individual variables. *Human Relations,* 1976, 29, 559–570.

Ouchi, W. The relationship between organizational structure and organizational control. *Administrative Science Quarterly,* 1977, 22, 95–113.

Porter, L., Steers, R., Mowday, R., & Boulian, P. Organizational commitment, job satisfaction, and turnover among psychiatric technicians. *Journal of Applied Psychology,* 1974, 59, 603–609.

Rizzo, J. R., House, R. J., & Lirtzman, S. I. Role conflict and ambiguity in complex organizations. *Administrative Science Quarterly,* 1970, 15, 150–163.

Schuler, R., Aldag, R., & Brief, A. Role conflict and ambiguity: A scale analysis. *Organizational Behavior and Human Performance,* 1977, 20, 111–128.

Stogdill, R. *Individual behavior and group achievement.* New York: Oxford University Press, 1959.

Tannenbaum, R., & Schmidt, W. How to choose a leadership pattern. *Harvard Business Review,* 1958, 36, 95–101.

Van de Ven, A., Delbecq, A., & Koenig, R. Determinants of coordination modes within organizations. *American Sociological Review,* 1976, 41, 322–338.

Vroom, V., & Yetton, P. *Leadership and decision making.* Pittsburgh: University of Pittsburgh Press, 1973.

Wherry, R. Test selection and suppressor variables. *Psychometrika,* 1946, 11, 239–247.

Wilson, O., & McLaren, R. *Police administration* (3rd ed.). New York: McGraw-Hill, 1972.

Woodward, J. Technology, material control, and organizational behavior. In A. Negandhi (Ed.), *Modern organization theory.* Kent: Kent State University, 1973.

Zander, A. Group aspirations. In D. Cartwright & A. Zander (Eds.), *Group dynamics: Research and theory* (3rd ed.). New York: Harper & Row, 1968.

Zedeck, S. Problems with the use of "moderator" variables. *Psychological Bulletin,* 1971, 76, 295–310.

## Reference Notes

[1] Hunt, J. Paper presented at the Eastern Academy of Management Conference, 1975.

**Reading 35**

# Substitutes for Leadership:

*Effective Alternatives to Ineffective Leadership*

**Jon P. Howell**
New Mexico State University

**David E. Bowen**
University of Southern California

**Peter W. Dorfman**
New Mexico State University

**Steven Kerr**
University of Southern California

**Philip M. Podsakoff**
Indiana University

Leadership has been recognized through the ages as a primary means of influencing the behavior of others. Research into the keys to effective and ineffective leadership has also been going on for quite some time. The earliest assumption was that effective leaders possessed particular traits that distinguished them from ineffective leaders. Effective leaders were thought to be dynamic, intelligent, dependable, high-achieving individuals—so, since traits are hard to change, problems caused by poor leadership were considered best solved by *replacing the leader* with someone who possessed more of the key traits. Regrettably, researchers were unable to identify leader traits that systematically improved organizational effectiveness. Yet leader replacement continues to be a very popular tool in the executive toolkit.

Partly in response to the limitations of trait theory, research in the late 1940s began to focus on relationships between leader behaviors and employee performance, in search of behaviors exhibited by effective leaders that were not displayed by those less effective. With this approach, effective leaders need not possess magical traits but, instead, provide strong direction and support while encouraging subordinates to participate in important decisions. This emphasis on leader behaviors still permitted replacement of a weak leader but allowed an additional remedy as well:

namely, *changing the leader's behavior* through some form of training. Probably the most disappointing aspect of research on leader behaviors is that no strong, consistent relationships between particular leader behaviors and organizational effectiveness have ever been found. This has not prevented many off-the-shelf training programs from becoming popular, however, nor the marketers of such programs from becoming prosperous.

## SITUATIONAL THEORIES

By the late 1950s it became evident that an approach was needed that didn't depend on ideal traits and universal behaviors. One answer was "situational theory," which starts with the assumption that there are no traits, and no behaviors, that automatically constitute effective leadership. The key is the fit between a leader's style and the situation the leader faces; thus the leader who is highly effective in one situation may be totally ineffective in another. For instance, although General George Patton led the 3rd Army to outstanding performance in World War II, one could hardly imagine the effective use of his leadership style in Mahatma Gandhi's situation against the British in India.

According to situational theories, effective leaders must correctly identify the behaviors each situation requires and then be flexible enough to exhibit these behaviors. Leaders who are behaviorally inflexible, or who lack the necessary diagnostic skills, must be either trained or replaced—the same remedies identified by researchers of leader traits and behaviors. An alternative is to let the leader alone but *change the situation so that the fit is improved.*

Various situational leadership theories have spawned a large number of intervention strategies, many of them competent and some of them useful. However, an assumption underlies all these theories that is wholly unsupported by the research literature. This assumption is that, though different situations require different leadership styles, in *every* situation there is *some* leadership style that will be effective. It has been shown in numerous studies, however, that circumstances often counteract the potential power of leadership, making it virtually impossible in some situations for leaders to have much impact regardless of their style or how good the fit is between leader and situation.

## SUBSTITUTES FOR LEADERSHIP

Fortunately, additional remedies for problems stemming from weak leadership—remedies not articulated in any of the earlier trait, behavioral, or situational approaches—have been identified. Such remedies derive from acceptance of the conclusion, based on the research studies referenced earlier, that many organizations contain "substitutes for leadership"—attributes of subordinates, tasks, and organizations that provide task guidance and incentives to perform to such a degree that they virtually negate the leader's ability to either improve or impair subordinate performance. To the extent that powerful leadership substitutes exist, formal leadership, however displayed, tends to be unproductive and can even be counterproductive. In comparison with situational leadership approaches, research on leadership substitutes focuses on whether subordinates are receiving needed task guidance and incentives to perform without taking it for granted that the formal leader is the primary supplier.

### CLOSELY KNIT TEAMS OF HIGHLY TRAINED INDIVIDUALS

Consider the positive impact of substitutes in the following example. Todd LaPorte, Gene Rochlin, and Karlene Roberts are three researchers studying such highly stressful organizational situations as those involving pilots who land jet fighters on a nuclear carrier and air-traffic controllers who direct traffic into San Francisco. They have found that directive leadership is relatively unimportant compared with the work experience and training of individuals in closely knit work groups. This is particularly evident ". . . in the white heat of danger, when the whole system threatens to collapse. . . . The stress creates a need for competence among colleagues who by necessity develop close working relationships with each other." All such individuals are trained extensively and daily, regardless of their position in the hierarchy, to redirect operations or bring them to an abrupt halt. This can involve ignoring orders from managers who are removed from the front line of action. Here the experience and continuous training of individuals, along with the close relationships among members of a work force, substitute for the manager's directive leadership.

By creating alternate sources of task guidance and incentives to perform, substitutes for leadership may have a temporary negative effect on morale among leaders who perceive a loss of power. However, leadership substitutes can also serve as important remedies where there are organizational problems, particularly in situations where the leader is not the source of the problems or where, if the leader is the source, replacement, training, and improving the leader-situation fit are overly expensive, politically infeasible, or too time-consuming to be considered.

A principal advantage of the substitutes construct is that it identifies a remedy for problems stemming from weak leadership in addition to replacement, training, or situational engineering. The remedy is to intentionally, systematically *create substitutes for hierarchical leadership.* In fact, whereas weak, power-hungry leaders invariably regard substitutes as frustrating and necessarily dysfunctional (when they are aware of them at all), strong leaders understand and are comfortable with the idea that effective results can be achieved when task guidance and incentives to perform emanate from sources other than themselves. When other sources are deficient, the hierarchical superior is in a position to play a dominant role; when strong incentives and guidance derive from other sources, the hierarchical superior has less opportunity, but also less need, to exert his or her influence.

### INTRINSIC SATISFACTION

The degree of intrinsic satisfaction that employees derive from their work task is a strong leadership substitute in a large manufacturer of camping equipment in the western United States. The company produces sleeping bags that range from top-of-the-line light-weight backpackers to low-cost models filled with floor sweepings from a mattress factory. Manufacturing personnel are required to rotate among all the lines, so no one group gains a territorial claim to a particular product. Management reports that for workers on the top-quality down-filled bags, supervisory direction has become relatively unnecessary, yet output and quality typically exceed management expectations. Workers report pride in working on this line and usually solve production problems themselves or with coworkers.

The production of bottom-line bags is very different. Quality problems are commonplace, workers cooperate less to overcome the problems, and workers seem to care little about meeting output or quality standards. The constant supervision required to address these problems raises indirect costs. Consultants observing the various production lines during a typical day report that supervisors slowly gravitate away from high-quality lines toward the lowest-quality lines. Thus the workers' intrinsic satisfaction from producing a high-quality product alleviates the need for most supervisory leadership.

## COMPUTER TECHNOLOGY

Edward E. Lawler III has noticed that companies with computer-integrated manufacturing and networked computer systems rely on computers to take over many of the supervisor's leadership functions. Feedback is provided by computerized productivity and quality data; directions for certain tasks are entered into the information system; even error detection and goal setting are incorporated in some interactive systems. When individual workers have access to operating data and to a network that allows them to ask employees at other locations to help solve problems, they become more independent of their managers and arrive at solutions among themselves. Spans of control greater than 100 are not unheard of in these organizations. Computerized information technology is therefore providing a substitute for certain types of managerial leadership.

Effective leadership, then, depends upon a leader's ability to supply subordinates with task guidance and incentives to perform to the extent that these are not provided by other sources. The inverse of this assertion is equally valid. Leadership substitutes can contribute to organizational effectiveness by supplying subordinates with task guidance and incentives to perform that are not being provided by the hierarchical superior.

From this perspective it makes sense for a leader or someone above the leader to create substitutes when, for example, the leader must be frequently absent, has a large span of control, or is saddled with time-consuming nonmanagerial duties. Substitutes are also useful when a leader departs before a successor has been identified or there is a need to manage employees who are geographically dispersed or who, as in the following example, are culturally resistant to hierarchical supervision.

## EXTENSIVE PROFESSIONAL EDUCATION

Professional employees may come to their firms with so much formal education that they can perform most work assignments without relying upon technical guidance from their hierarchical superior. Their education also often includes a strong socialization component, instilling in them a desire for autonomous, self-controlling behavior. The result may be that they neither need nor will readily accept a leader's direction. In such instances, professional education and socialization can serve as substitutes for formal leadership. A 1981 study by Jeffrey Ford found that extensive subordinate education acted as a substitute for directive and supportive leadership in a book publishing firm, a branch bank, and a midwestern university.

## USING LEADERSHIP SUBSTITUTES TO SOLVE ORGANIZATIONAL PROBLEMS

The notion that professional education and socialization can substitute for traditional formal leadership identifies an important potential problem, but it can be turned to advantage if a leader is sensitive to the situation and builds collegial systems of task-related guidance and interpersonal support. This approach can be found in most well-run hospitals and universities, where deliberately designed substitutes for leadership abound.

Thus charges of medical malfeasance are often investigated by peer review teams, and university promotion and tenure decisions depend greatly on assessments by faculty colleagues who lack formal authority. Indeed, many a dean has learned that the same criticism that would be bitterly denied if it came from him or her is grudgingly accepted if the source is a peer-review committee. The trick is to develop norms and structures that consistently produce feedback when feedback is needed, rather than merely an occasional spontaneous outburst when circumstances become intolerable.

## TEAM APPROACHES

Tracy Kidder's *The Soul of a New Machine* provides an excellent account of how a key manager at Data General utilized subordinates' professional norms and standards as a substitute for leadership to produce a faster computer than the competition's. The company at that time was competitive, highly political, and resource-poor, but the computer-design engineers were young, creative, well-trained, and highly motivated. Recognizing the futility of relying on directive leadership and meager financial rewards, the leader obtained work space that encouraged considerable interaction among team members and discouraged interaction outside the team. He articulated key parameters and project deadlines, stayed out of members' personal disputes, obtained resources for the team, and buffered them from organization politics. Reflecting the attitude of team members, Kidder observes, "They were building the machine all by themselves, without any significant help from their leader."

Task guidance and incentives to perform may derive from a number of sources other than the leader, including organized staff groups, internal and external consultants, and competent peers at all organizational levels. In the Columbus, Ohio, police department, the creation of two-person patrol units and field-training officer positions effectively substituted for the guidance and support traditionally provided by hierarchical leaders, thus making time available for them to attend to other tasks. Where one-person patrols without field-training officers were utilized, leader guidance and support continued to be essential. (An ancillary benefit of substituting peer for hierarchical sources of task guidance is that it is often easier for subordinates to admit inadequacies to and request assistance from their coworkers than from their boss.)

## HIGH-ABILITY INDEPENDENT WORKERS

Even when subordinates haven't much formal education, ability combined with experience can serve as a substitute for hierarchical leadership. Cummins Engine Company, General Motors Corporation, and Procter and Gamble all have reduced supervisory personnel and managerial overhead by selecting and developing high-ability, independent workers who require little or no supervision. Paul Reeves, a key production foreman for Harmon Auto Parts, taught workers to take over his job by helping them increase their ability and experience so that their responsibilities could also be increased. Each worker voluntarily spent half-days with him—asking questions, discussing his responses and, eventually, helping him perform his duties. When Reeves was promoted, the group continued to operate effectively without a foreman.

## IN PLACE OF HIERARCHICAL FEEDBACK

Among the most important elements of task guidance is performance feedback. In the absence of feedback, ability to perform cannot be improved and motivation to perform cannot be sustained. Most organizations assign responsibility for feedback to the hierarchical superior, even in cases where the superior works at a physical distance from employees or doesn't know enough about their technical specialties to give them credible feedback.

However, many organizations have come to the realization that feedback from clients and peers, and feedback provided by the task itself, can serve as powerful substitutes for hierarchical feedback. Charles Manz and Hank Sims, two organizational researchers, described the operation of one such feedback system in a nonunion small-parts manufacturing plant. A subsidiary of a large U.S. corporation, the plant was organized around the concept of self-managed work teams from its inception in the early 1970s.

Each team of eight to twelve members is assigned a set of closely related production tasks, and the teams are buffered from each other by physical space and stores of in-process inventory. Each team prepares its own budgets, makes within-team job assignments, keeps track of quality control statistics and hours worked, and handles member absenteeism and discipline problems. Team members are trained in conducting meetings and in group problem solving. A hierarchical leader is responsible for each team, but this person is not supposed to supply either task guidance or interpersonal support, aside from encouraging self-observation, self-evaluation, and self-reinforcement. Manz and Sims found, in fact, that the most effective teams were those whose leaders did refrain from providing guidance and support. Leaders of effective teams spent much of their time representing the team to higher management, obtaining resources for the team, training new members, and coaching team members with respect to peer feedback and peer evaluation.

**TABLE 1  Eleven Managerial Leadership Problems and Effective Coping Strategies***

| Leadership Problems | Enhancer/Neutralizer | Substitutes |
|---|---|---|
| Leader doesn't keep on top of details in the department; coordination among subordinates is difficult. | Not useful. | Develop self-managed work teams; encourage team members to interact within and across departments |
| Competent leadership is resisted through noncompliance or passive resistance. | *Enhancers:* Increase employees' dependence on leader through greater leader control of rewards/resources; increase their perception of leader's influence outside of work group. | Develop collegial systems of guidance for decision making. |
| Leader doesn't provide support or recognition for jobs well done. | Not useful. | Develop a reward system that operates independently of the leader. Enrich jobs to make them inherently satisfying. |
| Leader doesn't set targets or goals, or clarify roles for employees. | Not useful. | Emphasize experience and ability in selecting subordinates. Establish group goal-setting. Develop an organizational culture that stresses high performance expectations. |
| A leader behaves inconsistently over time. | *Enhancers:* These are dysfunctional. *Neutralizer:* Remove rewards from leader's control. | Develop group goal-setting and group rewards. |
| An upper-level manager regularly bypasses a leader in dealing with employees, or countermands the leader's directions. | *Enhancers:* Increase leader's control over rewards and resources: build leader's image via in-house champion or visible "important" responsibilities. *Neutralizer:* Physically distance subordinates from upper-level manager. | Increase the professionalization of employees. |
| A unit is in disarray or out of control. | Not useful. | Develop highly formalized plans, goals, outines, and areas of responsibility. |
| Leadership is brutal, autocratic. | *Enhancers:* These are dysfunctional. *Neutralizers:* Physically distance subordinates; remove rewards from leader's control. | Establish group goal-setting and peer performance appraisal. |
| There is inconsistency across different organizational units. | Not useful. | Increase formalization. Set up a behaviorally focused reward system. |
| Leadership is unstable over time; leaders are rotated and/or leave office frequently. | Not useful. | Establish competent advisory staff units. Increase professionalism of employees. |
| Incumbent management is poor; there's no heir apparent. | *Enhancers:* These are dysfunctional. *Neutralizer:* Assign nonleader duties to problem managers. | Emphasize experience and ability in selecting employees. Give employees more training. |

* The suggested solutions are examples of many possibilities for each problem.

## SUBSTITUTES BY PROCEDURE

The detailed work rules, guidelines, policies, and procedures existing in many organizations also serve to some extent as substitutes for hierarchical leadership by providing important nonleader sources of task guidance. Researchers Jon Howell and Peter Dorfman found this to be the case in a medium-size hospital, as did Robert Miles and M. M. Petty in county-level social service agencies. This type of leadership substitute can be particularly useful in situations where consistent behavior is imperative. For example, units of a firm increase the firm's legal exposure by acting

**TABLE 2   Creative Strategies for Improving Leadership Effectiveness**

| Creating Substitutes for Leader Directiveness and Supportiveness | Creating Enhancers for Leader Directiveness and Supportiveness |
|---|---|
| Develop colleagial systems of guidance:<br>• Peer appraisals to increase acceptability of feedback by subordinates.<br>• Quality circles to increase workers' control over production quality.<br>• Peer support networks; mentor systems. | Increase subordinates' perceptions of leader's influence/expertise:<br>• Provide a visible champion of leader.<br>• Give leader important organizational responsibilities.<br>• Build leader's image through in-house publications and other means. |
| Improve performance-oriented organizational formalization:<br>• Automatic organization reward system (such as commissions or gainsharing).<br>• Group management-by-objectives (MBO) program.<br>• Company mission statements and codes of conduct (as at Johnson & Johnson). | Build organizational climate:<br>• Reward small wins to increase subordinates' confidence.<br>• Emphasize ceremony and myth to encourage team spirit.<br>• Develop superordinate goals to encourage cohesiveness and high performance norms. |
| Increase administrative staff availability:<br>• Specialized training personnel.<br>• Troubleshooters for human relations problems.<br>• Technical advisors to assist production operators. | Increase subordinates' dependence on leader:<br>• Create crises requiring immediate action.<br>• Increase leader centrality in providing information.<br>• Eliminate one-over-one approvals. |
| Increase professionalism of subordinates:<br>• Staffing based on employee professionalism.<br>• Development plans to increase employees' abilities and experience.<br>• Encourage active participation in professional associations. | Increase leader's position power:<br>• Change title to increase status.<br>• Increase reward power.<br>• Increase resource base. |
| Redesign jobs to increase:<br>• Performance feedback from the task.<br>• Ideological importance of jobs. | Create cohesive work groups with high performance norms:<br>• Provide physical setting conducive to teamwork.<br>• Encourage subordinates' participation in group problem solving.<br>• Increase group's status.<br>• Create intergroup competition. |
| Start team-building activities to develop group self-management skills such as:<br>• Solving work-related problems on their own.<br>• Resolving interpersonal conflicts among members.<br>• Providing interpersonal support to members. | |

inconsistently with respect to hiring, firing, leaves of absence, promotions, or other human resources actions. In other instances, such as pricing or purchasing activities, variation may be legal but cost-ineffective. It is quite common in these cases for organizations to install procedures, rules, and guidelines to replace or forestall managerial discretion.

## LEADERSHIP NEUTRALIZERS

Thus far we have discussed only leadership substitutes, whose effect is to make it both less possible and less necessary for leaders to influence subordinate satisfaction and performance, replacing the leader's impact with impact of their own. Leadership "neutralizers" are attributes of subordinates, tasks, and organizations that also inter-

fere with a leader's attempts to influence subordinates. Unlike leadership substitutes, however, neutralizers do not replace the leader's impact over subordinates, but rather create an "influence vacuum" that can have serious negative consequences.

## PHYSICAL DISTANCES

For example, when subordinates work at a physical distance from their leader, many recommended leadership practices have limited usefulness or are nearly impossible to perform. A case in point is found at Kinko's, which provides professional copying services at widely dispersed locations nationwide. Regional managers at Kinko's are continually frustrated by not being able to provide enough direction, guidance, and

**FIGURE 1** **A Decision Tree for Overcoming Ineffective Managerial Leadership**

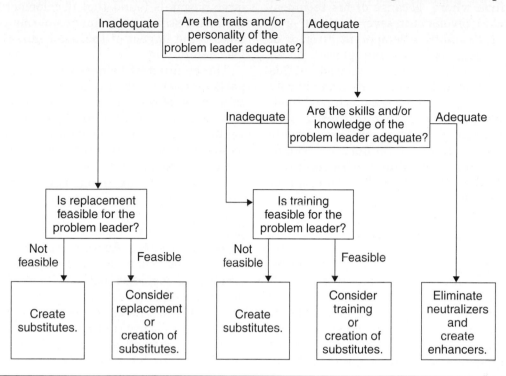

personal support for the new store managers because physical distances are too great for much personal interaction. In other organizations, subordinates and leaders may not share a common time zone; indeed, they may scarcely share the same work day.

Spatial distance will be increasingly important as a potential leadership neutralizer in the future because, as the number of firms with international operations continues to rise, managers will increasingly be required to supervise subordinates across great distances. Furthermore, the growing importance of the U.S. service sector means that more and more employees will be working at home or at their client's work site.

## REWARD SYSTEMS

Organizational reward systems can also be important neutralizers of the hierarchical leadership's effects. Rewards may be awarded strictly according to seniority, for example, or attractive rewards may be unavailable to subordinates. Leaders tend to have little influence on corporate "rebels" because, in part, the rebels are not attracted to the typical rewards available in corporate bureaucracies. Union contracts also may mandate that all employees within a given job classification be paid the same wage rate, and

civil service policies may require that promotions be based on objective examinations. In other cases, rewards may be controlled by higher management in ways that prevent the immediate supervisor from exerting influence. This occurs, for example, in firms requiring numerous one-over-one approvals before a salary recommendation takes effect. Other firms permit leaders to influence the amount of rewards, but their timing is wholly constrained by fiscal periods or employee anniversary dates.

## BYPASSING MANAGEMENT STRUCTURE

A very different type of neutralization occurs when someone at a higher level repeatedly bypasses a level of management to deal directly with that manager's subordinates. Another neutralizer is the continual countermanding by higher management of a leader's orders and instructions. These neutralizers often occur in instances where an organization's founder has finally, reluctantly, hired a subordinate manager to oversee operations and where a union's potential for mischief is so feared that supervisory efforts aimed at maintaining discipline are routinely reversed at higher levels.

Although normally dysfunctional, leadership neutralizers can occasionally be used to advantage.

One such occasion occurred in a petrochemical processing firm where, because of his technical expertise and involvement in several critical projects, an interpersonally incompetent director of design engineering could not be replaced. As an interim solution until he could be phased out, his day-to-day contact with employees was sharply curtailed, he was given numerous technical (non-leader) assignments, and his influence over salary and personnel decisions was considerably reduced. In this instance the "influence vacuum" caused by creating leadership neutralizers was deemed preferable to the state of leadership that previously existed.

## LEADERSHIP ENHANCERS

Leader "enhancers" are attributes of employees, tasks, and organizations that amplify a leader's impact on the employees. For example, cohesive work groups with strong norms in support of cooperation with management can crystallize ambiguous goals and role definitions, augment overly subtle leader-provided feedback, and otherwise increase the power of weak, inconsistent leaders—for better or for worse. A study of four large hospitals found that development of a culture with strong performance norms greatly enhanced the impact of the head nurse's directive leadership style.

The creation of leadership enhancers makes particular sense when a leader has both the skill to manage effectively and personal goals consonant with organizational objectives but is prevented by one or more neutralizers from being effective. One way to amplify such a leader's power is to alter the organization's reward system. For example, make additional resources available, grant more discretion concerning the distribution of existing resources, or increase subordinates' dependency on the leader for desired physical and financial resources. Another type of enhancement is to give the leader access to key information and prestigious people at high levels—for example, as a member of a visible, prestigious task force. Enhancement in this case derives from connecting the leader to sources of power and important information, as well as from signaling to others that the leader probably has considerable influence with those at the top.

# Chapter Thirteen

# Charismatic and Transformational Leadership

The last two decades of the twentieth century presented organizations with unparalleled levels of uncertainty, turbulence, rapid change, and intense competition. Many organizations are struggling with the need to manage chaos, to undergo internal cultural change, to reinvent their businesses, to restructure their organizations, to adopt or invent new technologies, to empower organizational members, to reduce organizational boundaries, to discover the path to continuous improvement, and to invent high involvement organization and management systems. In the face of such challenges, the transformational and charismatic leader represents a style of leadership that may be capable of navigating organizations through the chaos of the twenty-first century.

The current interest in charismatic and transformational leaders brings us back, in part, to a focus on the leader. It provides another perspective on traits of the leader and the "things" that leaders do. Yet, *charisma is relational* in nature. It is not something found solely in the leader as a psychological phenomenon, nor is it totally situationally determined. Instead, charisma is found in the interplay between the leader (his/her traits and behaviors) and the follower (his/her needs, beliefs, values, and perceptions).

Both transformational and charismatic forms of leadership are commonly discussed in terms of the effects that the leader has upon his/her followers and in terms of the relationship that exists between the leader and followers. It has been noted that transformational leaders move and change (fix) things "in a big way," not by offering tokens of inducement, but through the inspiration of others. They are individuals who through personal values, vision, passion, and a commitment to a mission energize and move others.[1]

The famous German sociologist, Max Weber, described the charismatic leader as one who reveals "a transcendent mission or course of action that may not be in itself appealing to the potential followers, but which is acted on because the followers believe their leader is extraordinarily gifted." He or she is described as "supernatural, superhuman or exceptional."[2]

Thus the charismatic leader is described as someone who by the sheer force of personality is capable of having profound effects upon followers. Charismatic leaders generate extremely intense loyalty, passion, and devotion. Followers are inspired and seem to enthusiastically and unquestionably give "blind" obedience

[1] J. M. Burns, *Leadership* (New York: Harper & Row, 1978).
[2] M. Weber, *The Theory of Social and Economic Organization,* A. M. Henderson and T. Parsons, ed. and trans. (New York: Oxford University Press, 1947), p. 358.

to the leader, heeding his or her word almost without hesitation. Their relationship is extremely emotional in nature, producing a profound effect upon the follower's commitment, motivation, and performance.

Not only is charismatic leadership seen in terms of the relationship between leader and follower and its effects, but there appear to be several traits possessed and behaviors engaged in by those individuals. Among the most defining characteristics of those leaders who have charisma are a strong sense of self-confidence, a strong conviction of the rightness of their own beliefs and ideals, and dominance (i.e., a strong need for power with a reliance upon referent power as their primary power base). In terms of behaviors, charismatic leaders role-model a set of values and beliefs that they want their followers to internalize, they set high goals and have demanding expectations, they demonstrate confidence in their followers' abilities, and they articulate exciting visions of the future.[3]

In the first two readings in this chapter, Robert J. House (1977), and Jay A. Conger and Rabindra N. Kanungo (1987) provide insight into charismatic leadership within the organizational context. House provides a theoretical explanation of charisma from a psychological perspective. His work gives us insight into how charismatic leadership emerges, and its effects in organizations. Building upon the assumption that charismatic leadership emerges from the behavior of the leader, Conger and Kanungo pursue the question, "What are the behavioral components that produce the experiences of a charismatic leader?"

While much of the literature on charismatic or transformational leadership demonstrates that such leadership has profound effects—especially in crisis situations—the processes involved are less clear. In the third reading, Boas Shamir, Robert J. House, and Michael B. Arthur (1993) offer a self-concept based motivational theory to explain the process by which charismatic behavior causes profound transformation effects on followers. In essence, they theorize that charismatic leadership produces its effects through an engagement of the followers' self-concept in the interest of the leader's vision.

The distinction between the charismatic and the transformational leader will not be readily apparent. Some authors make no distinction between the two while others conceptualize charisma as one of several attributes that may define the transformational leader. Thus, charismatic leaders by definition are transformational, but not all transformational leaders achieve their transforming effect through the charismatic effects produced by their personalities.

Bernard M. Bass has studied and written extensively about leaders and the leadership process.[4] He contrasts the transactional leader (i.e., that leadership style where something is offered by the leader in exchange for something wanted from the follower) with the transformational leader. Similar to the charismatic leader, the transformational leader, according to Bass, is one who is experienced as engaging in a particular set of behaviors—one who is a model of integrity and fairness, sets clear goals, has high expectations, encourages, provides support and recognition, stirs the emotions of people, and gets people to look beyond their self-interests and to reach for the improbable. Like the charismatic leader, Bass sees trust, loyalty, and respect as common by-products of this form of leadership. Transformational leaders achieve their results in one or more ways. They may inspire their followers through charisma, they may meet the emotional needs of their followers through individualized consideration, and/or they may intellectually stimulate their followers by stirring within them an awareness of problems, insight into solutions, and the passion to bring about

---

[3] R. J. House, "A 1976 Theory of Charismatic Leadership," in J. G. Hunt and K. Rowland, eds., *The Cutting Edge of Leadership* (Carbondale, IL: Southern Illinois University Press, 1976, pp. 189–207.

[4] See, for example, B. M. Bass, *Bass & Stogdill's Handbook of Leadership: Theory, Research & Managerial Implications* (New York: The Free Press, 1990).

resolution.[5] (We suggest that as a part of your reading and thinking about the role and influence of the transformational leader you reread Smircich and Morgan's [1982] discussion of the management of meaning, which was presented in Chapter 1.)

Ronald J. Deluga's (1988) study provides insight into a comparison of transformational and transactional leadership styles. His study suggests that the transformational leader is more effective and has stronger follower satisfaction than that produced by the transactional style of leadership. Philip W. Podsakoff, Scott B. MacKenzie, Robert H. Moorman, and Richard Fetter (1990) also provide empirical insight into transformational leaders, their behaviors, and the effects they produce. Specifically, they look at several consequences produced by six behaviors—articulating a vision, providing an appropriate model, fostering acceptance of group goals, high performance expectations, individualized support, and intellectual stimulation—commonly associated with transformational leadership. The self-assessment presented at the end of this chapter opener gives you the opportunity to profile yourself on several of the behavioral dimensions associated with transformational and transactional leader behaviors.

The research conducted by Podsakoff and his colleagues provides insight into the processes through which transformational leadership produces its effects. They observe that trust and satisfaction are common by-products of transformational leadership and that it is the simultaneous presence of transformational leadership, trust in the leader, and satisfaction that gives rise to the follower's engagement in acts of good organizational citizenship behaviors (i.e., going above and beyond the call of duty to assist the group and members of the group to achieve their goals).

The readings in this chapter provide yet another piece of understanding of the leadership phenomenon (see Figure 13.1). They remind the reader of the interactive nature of leadership and that a part of the leadership process is relational in nature. Followers see leaders as individuals and experience their acts of leadership. In some instances attributions are made, and some individuals emerge as charismatic leaders for some followers. In addition, some acts of leadership are extremely emotional in nature—powerful experiences—that tend to lift and energize followers, propelling them forward toward the achievement of some potentially tremendous feats. The results are not always positive, as might be witnessed through the acts of Adolf Hitler, James Jones, and, more recently, David Koresh. Each has been described as a leader with charismatic qualities but misguided values.

---

[5] B. Bass, "Leadership: Good, Better, Best," *Organizational Dynamics* 13 (1985), pp. 26–40.

**FIGURE 13.1**
**The Leadership**
**Process**

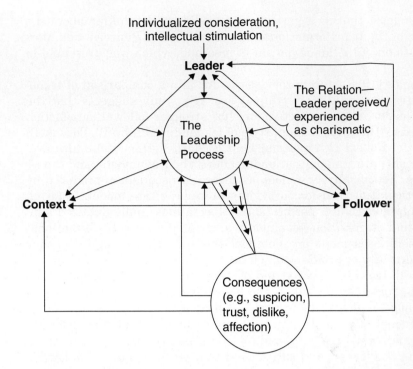

**EXERCISE**
*Self-Assessment*

**Transformational and Charismatic Leadership**

**Instructions:** Think about a situation in which you either assumed or were given a leadership role. Think about your own behaviors within this context. To what extent does each of the following statements characterize your leadership orientation?

| I: | | Very Little 1 | 2 | 3 | A Moderate Amount 4 | 5 | 6 | Very Much 7 |
|---|---|---|---|---|---|---|---|---|
| 1. | Have a clear understanding of where we are going. | 1 | 2 | 3 | 4 | 5 | 6 | 7 |
| 2. | Paint an interesting picture of the future for my group. | 1 | 2 | 3 | 4 | 5 | 6 | 7 |
| 3. | Am always seeking new opportunities for the organization/group. | 1 | 2 | 3 | 4 | 5 | 6 | 7 |
| 4. | Inspire others with my plans for the future. | 1 | 2 | 3 | 4 | 5 | 6 | 7 |
| 5. | Am able to get others to be committed to my dreams. | 1 | 2 | 3 | 4 | 5 | 6 | 7 |
| 6. | Lead by "doing," rather than simply by "telling." | 1 | 2 | 3 | 4 | 5 | 6 | 7 |
| 7. | Provide a good model for others to follow. | 1 | 2 | 3 | 4 | 5 | 6 | 7 |
| 8. | Lead by example. | 1 | 2 | 3 | 4 | 5 | 6 | 7 |
| 9. | Foster collaboration among group members. | 1 | 2 | 3 | 4 | 5 | 6 | 7 |
| 10. | Encourage employees to be "team players." | 1 | 2 | 3 | 4 | 5 | 6 | 7 |
| 11. | Get the group to work together for the same goal. | 1 | 2 | 3 | 4 | 5 | 6 | 7 |
| 12. | Develop a team attitude and spirit among employees. | 1 | 2 | 3 | 4 | 5 | 6 | 7 |
| 13. | Show that I expect a lot from others. | 1 | 2 | 3 | 4 | 5 | 6 | 7 |
| 14. | Insist on only the best performance. | 1 | 2 | 3 | 4 | 5 | 6 | 7 |
| 15. | Will not settle for second best. | 1 | 2 | 3 | 4 | 5 | 6 | 7 |
| 16. | Act without considering the feelings of others. | 1 | 2 | 3 | 4 | 5 | 6 | 7 |
| 17. | Show respect for the personal feelings of others. | 1 | 2 | 3 | 4 | 5 | 6 | 7 |
| 18. | Behave in a manner thoughtful of the personal needs of others. | 1 | 2 | 3 | 4 | 5 | 6 | 7 |
| 19. | Treat others without considering their personal feelings. | 1 | 2 | 3 | 4 | 5 | 6 | 7 |
| 20. | Challenge others to think about old problems in new ways. | 1 | 2 | 3 | 4 | 5 | 6 | 7 |
| 21. | Ask questions that prompt others to think. | 1 | 2 | 3 | 4 | 5 | 6 | 7 |
| 22. | Stimulate others to rethink the way they do things. | 1 | 2 | 3 | 4 | 5 | 6 | 7 |
| 23. | Have ideas that challenge others to reexamine some of their basic assumptions about work. | 1 | 2 | 3 | 4 | 5 | 6 | 7 |
| 24. | Always give positive feedback when others perform well. | 1 | 2 | 3 | 4 | 5 | 6 | 7 |
| 25. | Give special recognition when others' work is very good. | 1 | 2 | 3 | 4 | 5 | 6 | 7 |
| 26. | Commend others when they do a better-than-average job. | 1 | 2 | 3 | 4 | 5 | 6 | 7 |
| 27. | Personally compliment others when they do outstanding work. | 1 | 2 | 3 | 4 | 5 | 6 | 7 |
| 28. | Frequently do not acknowledge the good performance of others. | 1 | 2 | 3 | 4 | 5 | 6 | 7 |

*(continued)*

**Scoring:** Subtract your responses to questions 16, 19, and 28 from 8. There are seven dimension scores to be computed. *Articulate vision*—Sum your response to questions 1 through 5 and divide by 5. *Provide appropriate model*—Sum your responses to questions 6 through 8 and divide by 3. *Foster acceptance of goals*—Sum your responses to questions 9 through 12 and divide by 4. *High-performance expectations*—Sum your responses to questions 13 through 15 and divide by 3. *Individual support*—Sum your responses to questions 16 through 19 and divide by 4. *Intellectual stimulation*—Sum your responses to questions 20 through 23 and divide by 4. *Transactional leader behaviors*—Sum your responses to questions 24 through 28 and divide by 5.

My scores are:

Articulate vision _____.
Role model _____.
Foster goal acceptance _____.
Performance expectations _____.
Individual support _____.
Intellectual stimulation _____.
Transactional leader behavior _____.

**Interpretation:** Six basic dimensions of the *transformational* leader are profiled by this self-assessment: articulate vision, provide appropriate model, foster acceptance of goals, high-performance expectations, individual support, and intellectual stimulation. A high score (6 and greater) reflects a high behavioral orientation to engage in each of these behaviors. The seventh leadership dimension profiled here reflects your tendency to engage in behaviors characteristic of the transactional leader. A high score (6 and greater) reflects a strong behavioral orientation to give something to your followers in *exchange* for their giving something to you that as a leader you want (expect).

**Source:** Reprinted with permission. P. M. Podsakoff, S. B. MacKenzie, R.H . Moorman, and R. Fetter, "Transformational Leader Behaviors and Their Effects on Followers' Trust in Leader, Satisfaction, and Organizational Citizenship Behaviors," *Leadership Quarterly* 1, no. 2 (1990), pp. 107–42.

## Reading 36

# A 1976 Theory of Charismatic Leadership

**Robert J. House**
University of Toronto

Charisma is the term commonly used in the sociological and political science literature to describe leaders who by force of their personal abilities are capable of having profound and extraordinary effects on followers.[1] These effects include commanding loyalty and devotion to the leader and inspiring followers to accept and execute the will of the leader without hesitation or question or regard to one's self-interest. The term *charisma,* whose initial meaning was "gift," is usually reserved for leaders who by their influence are able to cause followers to accomplish outstanding feats. Frequently, such leaders represent a break with the established order, and through their leadership major social changes are accomplished.

Most writers concerned with charisma or charismatic leadership begin their discussion with Max Weber's conception of charisma. Weber describes as charismatic those leaders who "reveal a transcendent mission or course of action which may be in itself appealing to the potential followers, but which is acted on because the followers believe their leader is extraordinarily gifted" (Weber, 1947, p. 358). Transcendence is attributed implicitly to both the qualities of the leader and the content of his mission, the former being variously described as "supernatural, superhuman, or exceptional (Weber, 1947, p. 358).

Shils (1965) points out that Weber conceived of charismatic leadership as one of the processes through which routinized social processes, norms, and legal rules are changed. Weber distinguished innovators and creators from maintainers and attributed the "gift" of charisma in part to the creative or innovative quality of the leader's goals.

Several writers contend that charismatic leadership can and does exist in formal complex organizations (Dow, 1969; Oberg, 1972; Runciman, 1963; Shils, 1965). Yet despite the profound effects that charismatic leaders are presumed to have on followers' commitment, motivation, and performance, discussions of charisma have been speculative in nature and almost exclusively theoretical. To the knowledge of this writer none of the theoretical notions in the sociological or political science literature have been subjected to empirical test, despite the fact that many of these notions are implicitly testable.

In this chapter the sociological and political science literature on charisma will be reviewed and, where possible, the major assertions in this literature will be restated as propositions in an attempt to make them testable. In addition, selected literature from the discipline of social psychology will be reviewed and propositions which the writer believes are relevant to the concept of charisma will be inferred from the literature.

The outcome of this analysis is a speculative theoretical explanation of charisma from a psychological perspective rather than from a sociological or political science perspective. Hopefully, such an explanation will help us to have greater insight into how charismatic leadership emerges and its effects in modern organizations. Further, it is hoped that such an explanation will provide testable propositions with which to further leadership research.

In the remainder of this presentation the concept of charisma will be examined under the following topics: charismatic effects, characteristics of charismatic leaders, behavior of charismatic leaders, and situational factors associated with the emergence and effectiveness of charismatic leaders. While these topics will be addressed separately, they are necessarily intertwined. Thus, at times a discussion of one topic will have implications for the other topics, and reference will be made to such implications.

## THE EFFECTS OF CHARISMATIC LEADERSHIP

In the current literature the term charismatic leadership is generally defined and described in terms of the effects of the leader on followers, or in terms of the relationship between leaders and followers. For example, Oberg (1972) states that "the test for charisma . . . is the degree of devotion

**Source:** Edited and reprinted with permission from J. G. Hunt and K. Rowland (eds.), *The Cutting Edge of Leadership* (Carbondale, IL: Southern University Press). Note: For those interested in the references employed by House, please see the original publication.

and trust the object (charismatic leader) inspires and the degree to which it enables the individual to transcend his own finiteness and alienation and feel made whole" (p. 22). Tucker (1968) refers to both "charismatic following" and the "charismatic relationship":

> Often times, the relationship of the followers to the charismatic leader is that of disciples to a master, and in any event he is revered by them. They do not follow him out of fear or monetary inducement, but out of love, passionate devotion, enthusiasm. They are not as a rule concerned with career, promotion, salary, or benefice. The charismatic following is a nonbureaucratic group (p. 735).

It appears that most, if not all, writers agree that the effects of charismatic leadership are more emotional than calculative in that the follower is inspired enthusiastically to give unquestioned obedience, loyalty, commitment, and devotion to the leader and to the cause that the leader represents.

The charismatic leader is also implicitly assumed to be an object of identification by which the followers emulate the leader's values, goals, and behavior. Thus, one of the effects of the charismatic leader is to cause followers to model their behavior, feelings, and cognitions after the leader (Friedrich, 1961). Through the articulation of a transcendent goal the leader is assumed to clarify or specify a mission for the followers. By the leader's expression of self-confidence, and through the exhibition of confidence in followers, the leader is also assumed to inspire self-confidence in the followers. Thus the charismatic leader is asserted to clarify followers' goals, cause them to set or accept higher goals, and have greater confidence in their ability to contribute to the attainment of such goals.

Finally, according to the political science and sociological literature on charisma, the charismatic leader is assumed to have the effect of bringing about rather radical change by virtue of beliefs and values that are different from the established order. Thus Oberg (1972) speaks of the "change agent" function of the charismatic leader.

The above review of the effects of charismatic leadership suggests several dependent variables for a theory of charisma. Some of these effects are: follower trust in the correctness of the leader's beliefs, similarity of followers' beliefs to those of the leader, unquestioning acceptance of the leader, affection for the leader, willing obedience to the leader, identification with and emulation of the leader, emotional involvement of the follower in the mission, heightened goals of the follower, and the feeling on the part of followers that they will be able to accomplish, or contribute to the accomplishment of, the mission. This large number of charismatic effects is consistent with Etzioni's definition of charisma as "the ability of an actor to exercise diffuse and intensive influence over the normative (ideological) orientations of other actors" (Etzioni, 1961, p. 203).

The charismatic effects listed above constitute an *initial* list of variables that can be used as preliminary dependent variables for a theory of charisma. While this number of variables lacks parsimony as the defining criteria of a charismatic leader, this list of presumed "charismatic effects" provides a starting point for empiric research on charisma. If one were to identify a number of persons in a population (say military or industrial leaders in a given population) who informed observers (such as superiors or peers) could agree on as being clearly charismatic, it would be possible to identify these leaders' effects by measuring the degree to which their followers' responses to them were different from responses of followers of other leaders randomly selected from the same population. The major differences in follower responses could then be clustered into primary groups and scaled. The scores of the followers in these groups could then serve as the basis for a more accurate, complete, and parsimonious operational definition of charismatic effects. Leaders who have such effects on followers could be identified in subsequent samples. Such leaders could then be classified as charismatic leaders. Their personality characteristics and behaviors could be compared with those of other leaders (who do not have such effects) to identify characteristics and behaviors which differentiate the charismatic leaders from others. This process of operationally defining charismatic leadership permits one to identify leaders in a population who have the charismatic effects described in the political science and sociological literature and thereby specify an operational set of dependent variables for a theory of leadership.

Some of the above effects have also been the dependent variables in social-psychological research. Specifically, the ability of one person to arouse needs and enhance self-esteem of others, and the ability of one person to serve successfully as a behavioral model for another have been the subject of substantial empirical investigation by psychologists. Later in this chapter we will review this research in an attempt to identify and describe the specific situational factors and leader behaviors that result in such "charismatic" effects.

Defining charismatic leadership in terms of its effects permits one to identify charismatic leaders only after they have had an impact on followers. Such a definition says nothing about the personal characteristics, behaviors, or situational factors that bring about the charismatic effects. This is the scientific challenge that must be addressed if the mysterious quality of charismatic leadership is to be explained and charismatic effects are to be made predictable. We now turn to a discussion of these issues.

## DEFINITION OF CHARISMATIC LEADERSHIP

Throughout this chapter the term charismatic leadership will be used to refer to any leader who has the above "charismatic effects" on followers to an unusually high degree.[2] The operational definition of a given charismatic leader awaits research which will allow one to scale the above specific "charismatic effects." While it is not likely that all charismatic leaders have all of the above "charismatic effects," there are many possibilities that can be examined. For example, such effects may be present in a complex interacting manner. Alternatively, it may be the sum of, or some absolute level of, selected effects that do indeed differentiate charismatic leaders from others.

## CHARACTERISTICS OF THE CHARISMATIC LEADER

Both the literature concerning charismatic leadership and the opinion of laymen seem to agree that the charismatic leader can be described by a specific set of personal characteristics. According to Weber (1947), the charismatic leader is accepted by followers because both the leader and the follower perceive the leader as possessing a certain extraordinary gift. This "gift" of charisma is seldom specified and generally held to be some mysterious quality that defies definition. In actuality the "gift" is likely to be a complex interaction of personal characteristics, the behavior the leader employs, characteristics of followers, and certain situational factors prevailing at the time of the assumption of the leadership role.

The literature on charismatic leadership repeatedly attributes three personal characteristics to leaders who have charismatic effects, namely extremely high levels of self-confidence, dominance, and a strong conviction in the moral righ-

teousness of his/her beliefs.[3] It is interesting to note that three of these characteristics are also attributed to charismatic leaders by laymen as well as by scholars. As a classroom exercise I have on three occasions asked students to form into small groups and to discuss the characteristics of some charismatic leader that they have personally known or to whom they have been exposed. These groups repeatedly described the charismatic leaders that they selected for discussion as possessing dominance, self-confidence, and a strong conviction in their beliefs and ideals.

While the consensus of political science and sociological writers and the results of my own informal experiment are not evidence that leaders who have charismatic effects do indeed possess these characteristics, the argument is certainly subject to an empiric test with self-report measures of personality traits, beliefs, and values.

In addition to the characteristics discussed above it is hypothesized here that leaders who have charismatic effects have a high need to have influence over others. Such a need seems intuitively likely to characterize leaders who have such effects because without such a need they are unlikely to have developed the necessary persuasive skills to influence others and also are unlikely to obtain satisfaction from the leadership role. Uleman (1972) has developed a measure of the need for influence that can be used to test the above hypotheses.

The following proposition summarizes the above discussion:

**Proposition 1.** Characteristics that differentiate leaders who have charismatic effects on subordinates from leaders who do not have such charismatic effects are dominance and self-confidence, need for influence, and a strong conviction in the moral righteousness of their beliefs.[4]

## BEHAVIOR OF CHARISMATIC LEADERS

The sociological and political science literature offer some hints about the behavior of charismatic leaders.

### ROLE MODELING

First it is suggested that leaders who have charismatic effects express, by their actions, a set of values and beliefs to which they want their followers to subscribe. That is, the leader "role models" a value system for the followers. Gandhi constitutes an outstanding example of such systematic and intentional role modeling. He preached self-sacrifice, brotherly love, and nonviolent resistance to British rule. Repeatedly he engaged in self-sacrificing behaviors, such as giving up his lucrative law practice to live the life of a peasant, engaging in civil disobedience, fasting, and refusing to accept the ordinary conveniences offered to him by others.

The importance of the role modeling as a leadership strategy is illustrated by Gandhi's proposed leadership policies for the self-governance of India. "Most important for Gandhi was the example that leaders set for their followers . . . 'No leader of an independent India will hesitate to give an example by cleaning out his own toilet box'" (Collins & LaPierre, 1975, 234–35).

Concerning role modeling, a study by Joestling and Joestling (1972) is suggestive of the effects that a high status role model can have on the self-esteem of observers. Male and female students were asked to rate the value of being a woman. Half of the students were enrolled in the class taught by a qualified female instructor. Twenty-six percent of the women subjects in the class taught by a male thought there was nothing good about being a woman. In contrast only five percent of the women subjects in the class taught by a qualified female had similar negative attitudes toward being a woman.

While role modeling often proves successful, success does not always occur. The question then is what permits a leader to be a successful role model, i.e., to be emulated by the followers.

There is substantial evidence that a person is more likely to be modeled to the extent that that person is perceived as nurturant (i.e., helpful, sympathic, approving) and as being successful or possessing competence.

There is evidence that role modeling can have profound effects. Behavior resulting from modeling may be very specific such that the individual can be said to imitate or mimic the behavior of the model. Or, the behavior may be more general, taking the form of innovative behavior, generalized behavior orientations, and applications of principles for generating novel combinations of responses (Bandura, 1968).

Bandura (1968) reviews a substantial body of experimental evidence that shows that: (*a*) model's emotional responses to rewards or punishments elicit similar emotional responses in observers (p. 240); (*b*) stable changes in the valences (a measure of attractiveness) subjects assign to outcomes and changes in long-standing attitudes often result from the role modeling (pp. 243–44); and

(*c*) modeling is capable of developing generalized conceptual and behavioral properties of observers such as moral judgment orientations and delay-of-gratification patterns of behavior (p. 252).

Of particular significance for the study of leadership are the diverse kinds of attitudes, feelings, and behavior and the diversity of subjects involved in prior studies. Role modeling has been shown to influence the degree to which: (*a*) undergraduate females learn assertive behavior in assertiveness training programs (Young, Rimm & Kennedy, 1973); (*b*) mentally disturbed patients assume independence in their personal life (Goldstein, Martins, Hubben, Van Belle, Schaaf, Wiersma, & Goedhart, 1973); (*c*) undergraduates are willing to disclose unfavorable or favorable anxiety-related information to others (Sarason, Ganzer & Singer, 1972); (*d*) personal changes and learning outcomes result from adult *t*-groups (Pers, 1973); (*e*) individuals are willing to induce punishment (electric shock) to others (Baron, 1971); (*f*) nurses experience fear of tuberculosis (DeWolfe, 1967); and (*g*) subjects adopt biased attitudes toward minority ethnic groups (Kelman, 1958; Stotland and Patchen, 1961).

Many of the subjects in the above studies were either college students or adults. Thus, the findings are not limited to young children but are also relevant to persons in full-time occupations. Further, the dependent variables are all of significance for effective organizational or group performance. Feelings of fear, willingness to administer punishment, prejudicial attitudes, learning of interpersonal skills, and learning independence are relevant to interpersonal relations within organizations. Similarly, these cognitions and behaviors are relevant to the establishment of trust, to adequacy of communication, and to experiences that are satisfying in organizational life.

Thus it is argued here that role modeling is one of the processes by which leaders bring about charismatic effects. Furthermore, it is likely that the feelings, cognitions, and behavior that are modeled frequently determine subordinates' adjustment to organizational life, their job satisfaction, and their motivation to work. With respect to motivation, the above findings suggest that leaders can have an effect on the values (or valences) subordinates attach to the outcomes of their effort as well as their expectations. And, as will be discussed below, leaders can also have an effect on subordinates' self-esteem and their goal levels. Based on the above review of the literature concerned with role modeling, the following proposition is advanced:

**Proposition 2.** The more favorable the perceptions of the potential follower toward a leader, the more the follower will model: (*a*) the valences of the leader; (*b*) the expectations of the leader that effective performance will result in desired or undesired outcomes for the follower; (*c*) the emotional responses of the leader to work-related stimuli; and (*d*) the attitudes of the leader toward work and toward the organization. Here "favorable perceptions" is defined as the perceptions of the leader as attractive, nurturant, successful, or competent.

## IMAGE BUILDING

If proposition 2 is valid, then it can be speculated that leaders who have charismatic effects not only model the values and beliefs they want followers to adopt, but also that such leaders take actions consciously designed to be viewed favorably by followers. This speculation leads to the following proposition:

**Proposition 3.** Leaders who have charismatic effects are more likely to engage in behaviors designed to create the impression of competence and success than leaders who do not have such effects.

This proposition is consistent with the traditional literature on charismatic leadership. Weber (1947) speaks of the necessity of the charismatic leader to "prove" his extraordinary powers to the followers. Only as long as he can do so will he be recognized. While Weber and others have argued that such "proof" lies in actual accomplishments, the above proposition stresses the *appearance* of accomplishments and asserts that charismatic leaders engage in behaviors to gain such an appearance.

## GOAL ARTICULATION

In the traditional literature on charisma it is frequently asserted that charismatic leaders articulate a "transcendent" goal which becomes the basis of a movement or a cause. Such a goal is ideological rather than pragmatic and is laden with moral overtones. Alternatively, if a movement is already in effect, one behavior of the emergent leader is the articulation of the goal of the movement with conviction and exhortation of the moral rightness of the goal (Tucker, 1968, p. 738).

Examples of such goals are Martin Luther King's "I have a dream," Hitler's "Thousand-year Reich" and his "lebensraum," or Gandhi's vision of an India in which Hindus and Moslems would live in brotherly love independent from British rule.

Berlew (1974, p. 269) states:

> The first requirement for . . . charismatic leadership is a common or shared vision for what the future *could be*. To provide meaning and generate excitement, such a common vision must reflect goals or a future state of affairs that is valued by the organization's members and thus important to them to bring about. . . . All inspirational speeches or writings have the common element of some vision or dream of a better existence which will inspire or excite those who share the author's values. This basic wisdom too often has been ignored by managers.

Thus the following proposition is advanced:

**Proposition 4.** Leaders who have charismatic effects are more likely to articulate ideological goals than leaders who do not have such effects.

## EXHIBITING HIGH EXPECTATIONS AND SHOWING CONFIDENCE

Leaders who communicate high performance expectations for subordinates and exhibit confidence in their ability to meet such expectations are hypothesized to enhance subordinates' self-esteem and to affect the goals subordinates accept or set for themselves. Some examples of this kind of charismatic leader behavior are Churchill's statement that England's air defense in World War II was "England's finest hour," Hitler's claim that Aryans were "the master race," black leaders' exhortation that "Black is beautiful," and Martin Luther King's prediction that "We shall overcome." All of these statements imply high expectations and confidence in the followers.

There is substantial evidence that the expectation that one can accomplish one's goals is positively related to motivation and goal attainment. Persons with high self-esteem are more likely than persons with low self-esteem to seek higher personal rewards for performance (Pepitone, 1964) and to choose occupations that are congruent with self-perceived traits (Korman, 1966) and self-perceived ability level (Korman, 1967). Further, Korman (1968) has shown experimentally that for high self-esteem subjects there is a positive relationship between task performance and satisfaction, but that no such relationship exists for low self-esteem subjects. Raben and Klimoski (1973) have also shown experimentally that high self-esteem subjects are more likely than low self-esteem subjects to rise to the challenge of doing a task for which they believe they are not qualified. Thus, it is argued here that, to the extent the leader can affect the self-esteem of subordinates, leader behavior will have an effect on the kinds of rewards subordinates seek, their satisfaction with the rewards they obtain, and their motivation to perform effectively.

The effect of leader behavior on subordinate self-esteem has been given little attention in the leadership literature.[5] The assertion that leaders can affect subordinates' self-esteem is derived from two lines of research: research concerning the role-modeling effects and research concerned with reality testing.

We have already argued that through role modeling leaders can have a rather profound effect on subordinates' beliefs. One of these beliefs is self-esteem, which is defined by Lawler (1971, p. 107) as the belief that subordinates have with respect to their own general level of ability to cope with and control their environment. It is argued here that subordinates' self-perceptions are likely to be modeled after the leader's perceptions of the subordinates.[6] Thus if the leader communicates high performance expectations and shows confidence in subordinates, they will in turn set or accept a higher goal for themselves and have greater confidence in themselves.[7]

The second line of research suggesting that leaders affect subordinates' self-esteem is that research concerned with "reality testing." In social situations where interpersonal evaluation is highly subjective, individuals tend to "reality test," i.e., to test their notions of reality against the opinions of others (Deutsch & Gerard, 1955; Festinger, 1950). Consequently, to the extent that the leader shows followers that he/she believes them to be competent and personally responsible, the followers are hypothesized also to perceive themselves as competent. This self-perception is hypothesized to enhance motivation, performance, and satisfaction. Some indirect evidence in support of this line of reasoning is found in the results of studies by Berlew and Hall (1966), Stedry and Kay (1966), Korman (1971), Rosenthal and Jacobson (1968), Seaver (1973), and Meichenbaum, Bowers, and Ross (1969). Berlew and Hall (1966) and Stedry and Kay (1966) in field studies both found that individual performance increased as a function of the level of expectation superiors communicated to the individuals. Similarly, Korman (1971) showed in a laboratory study that the performance of students on creative tasks was a direct positive function of the expectations that other college students had for the laboratory subjects. Korman (1971) also showed that ratings of subordinates' performance in two field settings and self-ratings

of motivation in three field settings were all significantly correlated with the degree to which subordinates perceived their leaders' practices to reflect confidence in the subordinates.

These findings are consistent with those conducted in educational settings in which the expectations of teachers have been shown to be reflected in the performance of students (Meichenbaum, et al., 1969; Rosenthal & Jacobson, 1968; Seaver, 1973). In these studies teachers were induced to believe that certain students were more competent than others. This belief, or expectancy, on the part of the teacher was shown to be associated with higher student performance. However, there are also studies conducted in educational settings which have failed to demonstrate an effect of teachers' expectancies of students' performance (Anderson & Rosenthal, 1968; Collins, 1969; Conn, Edwards, Rosenthal, & Crowne, 1968; Evans & Rosenthal, 1969; Fiedler, Cohen & Finney, 1971). Seaver (1973) points out that in all of these disconfirming studies and also in the Rosenthal and Jacobson study, which is the subject of much controversy, the means of inducing teacher expectations were weak and thus "failure to find expectancy effects may be attributable solely to their failure to induce the desired expectancy in teachers" (p. 341).

If it is assumed that the leader's expectation of subordinates affects the subordinates' self-esteem and their self-esteem in turn affects their performance, then the above studies all provide indirect support for the assertion that leaders' expectations affect subordinates' performance.

The *combination* of a leader's confidence and high expectations, rather than high expectations alone, should be emphasized here. It is possible that leaders might set high performance standards, thus implying high expectations of subordinates, while at the same time showing low confidence in the subordinates' ability to meet such expectations. An example of this would be the leader who scores high on such questionnaire items as "he needles foremen for production."[8] While such leader behavior may motivate subordinates to strive for high performance in order to avoid punishment, it is also likely to induce fear of failure. Such a state in turn will likely be accompanied by efforts to avoid accountability on the part of the subordinates, strong feelings of dissatisfaction, low acceptance of the leader, and resistance to the leader's influence attempts in the long run.

Thus, while leader expectations are considered to have a significant effect on the reactions of subordinates, high expectations are hypothesized to have a positive effect *only* when subordinates perceive the superior to also have confidence in their (the subordinates') ability to meet such expectations.

## EFFECT ON FOLLOWERS' GOALS

In addition to affecting the self-esteem of subordinates, leader expectations and confidence are also hypothesized to affect several important characteristics of the subordinates' goals. In the following paragraphs we review the research concerned with goal characteristics.

In a series of laboratory studies, Locke and his associates (Bryan & Locke, 1967a, 1967b; Locke & Bryan, 1966a, 1966b) have demonstrated that when subjects are given specific goals by the experimenter they perform at significantly higher levels than those given the instruction to "do your best." Two field studies (Mace, 1935; Mendleson, 1971) also offer support for the generalizability of these laboratory findings to natural field settings. Thus, it is argued here that, if laboratory experimenters can influence the goal characteristics of experimental subjects, it seems reasonable that leaders can have similar influence on the goal characteristics of subordinates.

Specific and high expectations of leaders are hypothesized to clarify subordinates' performance goals. Further, it is hypothesized that the more the leader shows confidence in the subordinates' ability to meet goals, the more subordinates are likely to accept them as realistic and attainable.

Specific and high leader expectations are likely to provide a standard against which subordinates can evaluate their own performance. Accordingly, it is hypothesized here that leaders' expectations also serve as a basis on which subordinates may derive feedback. Finally, it is hypothesized that, when the leader's expectations are both high and clear to the subordinate and when the leader shows confidence in the subordinate's ability to meet such expectations, the subordinates will set and/or accept higher goals for themselves than would otherwise be the case, and will have more confidence that they will be able to meet the goals.

The above hypotheses concerning the leader's effect on followers' self-esteem and goals can be summarized in the following proposition:

**Proposition 5.** Leaders who simultaneously communicate high expectations of, and confidence in, followers are more likely to have followers who accept the goals of the leader and believe that they can contribute to goal accomplishment and are more likely to have followers who strive to meet specific and challenging performance standards.

## MOTIVE AROUSAL LEADER BEHAVIOR

One explanation for the emotional appeal of the charismatic leader may be the specific content of the messages he communicates to followers. It is speculated here that charismatic leaders communicate messages that arouse motives that are especially relevant to mission accomplishment. For example, Gandhi's exhortations of love and acceptance of one's fellow man likely aroused the need for affiliation, a need (or motive) especially relevant to the goal of uniting Hindus, Moslems, and Christians.

Military leaders often employ symbols of authoritarianism and evoke the image of the enemy, thus arousing the power motive, a motive especially relevant to effective combat performance. For example, Patton, when addressing infantry recruits, would do so against the background of a large American flag, dressed with medals of his accomplishments, and wearing a shining helmet displaying the four stars indicating the status of general.

Miner's research is relevant to defining some of the conditions under which the arousal of the need for power is associated with successful performance. Miner found that individuals who were high on a projective (sentence completion) measure of the power need were more likely to be successful in hierarchical bureaucratic organizations than individuals low on the power need. These findings did not hold true in egalitarian non-bureaucratic organizations, however (Miner, 1965).

Industrial leaders and leaders of scientists frequently stress excellence of performance as a measure of one's worth, thus arousing the need for achievement, a motive especially relevant to the assumption of personal responsibility, persistence, and pride in high-quality work performance. Varga (1975) has shown that the need for achievement is positively associated with economic and technical performance among research and development project leaders. He has also shown that the need for power is a strong factor contributing to such success when in conjunction with the need for achievement, but a factor making for failure when possessed by leaders low on the need for achievement.

There is some evidence that formally appointed leaders in a laboratory situation are capable of arousing subordinates' need for achievement (Litwin & Stringer, 1968). There is also a substantial amount of evidence that the achievement, affiliation, and power needs can be aroused from experimental inductions. For example the need for achievement has been aroused for males by suggesting to subjects that the experimental task is a measure of personal competence, or that the task is a standard against which one can measure his general level of ability (Heckhausen, 1967; McClelland, 1953; McClelland, Clarke, Roby, & Atkinson, 1958; Raynor, 1974).

The need for affiliation has been aroused by having fraternity members rate one another, while all were present, on a sociometric friendship index (Shipley & Veroff, 1952) while at the same time requiring each brother to stand and be rated by the other members of the fraternity on a list of trait adjectives.

The power need has been aroused experimentally by (a) evoking the image of, or reminding one of, an enemy, (b) having subjects observe the exercise of power by one person over another, or (c) allowing subjects to exercise power over another (Winter, 1973). Thus it is hypothesized that needs can be, and often are, similarly aroused by leaders in natural settings. By stressing the challenging aspects of tasks, making group members' acceptance of each other salient to performance appraisal, or talking about competition from others, it is hypothesized that leaders can and frequently do arouse the needs for achievement, affiliation, and power. Further it is hypothesized that, to the extent that such motives are associated with task-required performance, the arousal of these motives will result in increased effectiveness on the part of subordinates. Thus the performance consequence of motive arousal is contingent on the task contingencies. For example, when task demands of subordinates require assumption of calculated risks, achievement-oriented initiative, assumption of personal responsibility, and persistence toward challenging goals, the arousal of the need for achievement will facilitate task accomplishment. Further, there is evidence that when subordinates' need for achievement is high, task accomplishment will lead to satisfaction. When subordinates' need for achievement is low, task accomplishment will not be related to satisfaction (Steers, 1975).

When the task demands of subordinates require them to be persuasive, assert influence over or exercise control of others, or be highly competitive or combative, the arousal of the power motive is hypothesized to be related to effective performance and satisfaction. For example, on competitive tasks, or tasks requiring persuasion or aggression, the arousal of the power motive is hypothesized to lead to effective performance.

Finally, when task demands require affiliate behavior, as in the case of tasks requiring cohesiveness, team work, and peer support, the arousal of the affiliative motive becomes highly relevant to performance and satisfaction. An example of such tasks would be tasks that are enriched by assignment of major work goals to groups rather than individuals (Trist & Bamforth, 1951).

These speculations are summarized with the following proposition:

**Proposition 6.** Leaders who have charismatic effects are more likely to engage in behaviors that arouse motives relevant to the accomplishment of the mission than are leaders who do not have charismatic effects.[9]

## SOCIAL DETERMINANTS OF CHARISMATIC LEADERSHIP

The sociological literature (Weber, 1947) stresses that charismatic leadership is born out of stressful situations. It is argued that such leaders express sentiments deeply held by followers. These sentiments are different from the established order and thus their expression is likely to be hazardous to the leader (Friedland, 1964). Since their expression is hazardous, the leader is perceived as courageous. Because of other "gifts" attributed to the leader, such as extraordinary competence, the followers believe that the leader will bring about social change and will thus deliver them from their plight.

Thus it can be hypothesized that a strong feeling of distress on the part of followers is one situational factor that interacts with the characteristics and behavior of leaders to result in charismatic effects.

However Shils (1965) argues that charisma need not be born out of distress. Rather, according to Shils, charisma is dispersed throughout the formal institutions of society. Accordingly, persons holding positions of great power will be perceived as charismatic because of the "awe-inspiring" quality of power. Shils's only requirement is that the expression of power must appear to be integrated with a transcendent goal.

The above controversy suggests the hypothesis that leaders are more likely to have charismatic effects in situations stressful for followers than in nonstressful situations. Further it can be hypothesized that persons with the characteristics of dominance, self-confidence, need for influence, and strong convictions will be more likely to emerge as leaders under stressful conditions. Whether or not follower distress is a necessary condition for leaders to have charismatic effects or for persons with such characteristics to emerge as leaders is an empirical question that remains to be tested.

While there is lack of agreement as to whether or not leaders can have charismatic effects under nonstressful situations, all writers do seem to agree that charisma must be based on the articulation of an ideological goal. Opportunity to articulate such a goal, whether in stressful or nonstressful situations, thus can be hypothesized as one of the situational requirements for a person to have charismatic effects. This hypothesis suggests that, whenever the roles of followers can be defined as contributing to ideological values held by the follower, a leader can have some degree of charismatic effect by stressing such values and engaging in the specific behaviors described in the above propositions.

The question then is under what circumstances are roles definable in terms of ideological values. Clearly the roles of followers in political or religious movements can be defined in terms of ideological values. In addition, Berlew (1974) argues that since man seeks meaning in work there are many such ideological values to be stressed in modern formal organizations. Specifically he argues that any of the value-related opportunities listed in Table 1 can have a charismatic effect.

There are some work roles in society which do not lend themselves to ideological value orientation. These are generally the roles requiring highly routine, nonthinking effort in institutions directed exclusively to economic ends. It is hard to conceive of clerks or assembly-line workers in profit-making firms as perceiving their roles as ideologically oriented. However the same work when directed toward an ideological goal could lend itself to charismatic leadership. For example, in World War II, "Rosie the Riveter" expressed the ideological contribution of an assembly-line worker. And such menial efforts as stuffing envelopes frequently are directed toward ideological goals in political or religious organizations. The following proposition summarizes the above argument:

**Proposition 7.** A necessary condition for a leader to have charismatic effects is that the role

**TABLE 1   Sources of Meaning in Organizations: Opportunities and Related Values***

| Type of Opportunity | Related Need or Value |
|---|---|
| 1. A chance to be tested; to make it on one's own. | Self-reliance; self-actualization. |
| 2. A social experiment, to combine work, family, and play in some new way. | Community integration of life. |
| 3. A chance to do something *well*—e.g., return to real craftsmanship; to be really creative. | Excellence; unique accomplishment. |
| 4. A chance to do something *good*—e.g. ,run an honest, no rip-off business, or a youth counselling center. | Consideration; service. |
| 5. A chance to change the way things are—e.g., from Republican to Democrat or Socialist, from war to peace, from unjust to just. | Activism; social responsibility; citizenship. |

***Source:** Berlew, 1974, with permission by Prentice-Hall.

of followers be definable in ideological terms that appeal to the follower.

## SUMMARY AND OVERVIEW

Figure 1 presents a diagrammatic overview of the theory presented above. It is hypothesized that leaders who have charismatic effects are differentiated from others by some combination (possibly additive and possibly interactive) of the four personal characteristics shown in the upper right box: dominance, self-confidence, need for influence, and a strong conviction in the moral righteousness of his or her beliefs. Charismatic leaders are hypothesized to employ these characteristics with the following specific behaviors: goal articulation, role modeling, personal image-building, demonstration of confidence and high expectations for followers, and motive arousal behaviors. Goal articulation and personal image-building are hypothesized to result in favorable perceptions of the leader by followers. These favorable perceptions are asserted to enhance followers' trust, loyalty, and obedience to the leader and also to moderate the relationships between the remaining leader behaviors and the follower responses to the leader. The follower responses are

**FIGURE 1**   **A Model of Charismatic Leadership (Dotted lines indicate that favorable perceptions moderate the relationship between leader and follower responses)**

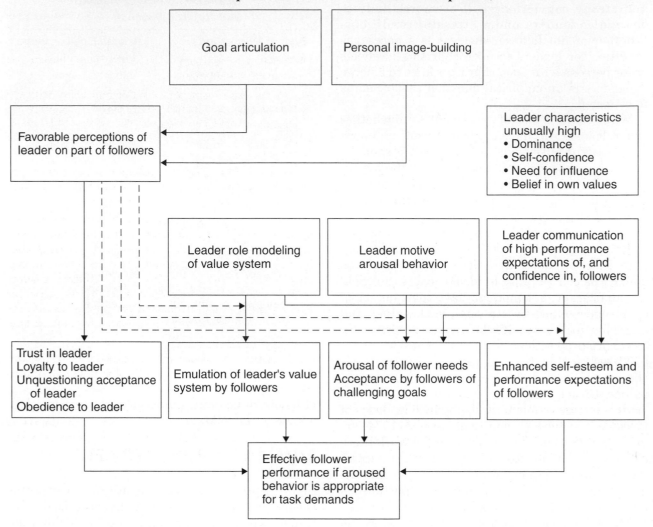

hypothesized to result in effective performance if the aroused behavior is appropriate for their task demands.

## CONCLUSION—WHY A 1976 THEORY

This chapter presents a "1976" theory of charismatic leadership. The date 1976 is attached to the title to reflect the philosophy of science of the writer. The theory is advanced for the purpose of guiding future research and not as a conclusive explanation of the charismatic phenomenon. As such it includes a set of propositions that are hopefully testable. Admittedly tests of the theory will require the development and valuation of several new scales. However it is hoped that the propositions are at least presently testable in principle. "A theory that can not be mortally endangered cannot be alive" (cited in Platt, 1964, from personal communication by W. A. H. Rustin).

The results of empiric tests of the theory will undoubtedly require revision of the theory. It is believed by the writer that theories, no matter how good at explaining a set of phenomena, are ultimately incorrect and consequently will undergo modification over time. Thus as MacKenzie and House (1975) have stated, "the fate of the better theories is to become explanations that hold for some phenomena in some limited condition." Or, as Hebb (1969, p. 21) asserts, "A good theory is one that holds together long enough to get you to a better theory."

Hopefully at some future date this theory will have led to a better theory.

# Notes

1. The author is indebted to Hugh J. Arnold, Martin G. Evans, Harvey Kolodny, Stephan J. Motowidlo, John A. Dearness, and William Cooper for their helpful critiques of this chapter. The literature review on which this chapter is based was conducted while the author was visiting professor at Florida International University, April–July, 1975.

2. This definition would be tautological if the "charismatic effects" were not operationally discovered using two independent operations. However, since the discovery of the "charismatic effects" involves having charismatic leaders identified by one set of observers (peers or superiors) and specification of their effects by an independent set of observers (namely their followers), such a definition avoids the tautological problem.

3. It is entirely possible that charismatic leaders present themselves as highly confident and as having a strong conviction in the moral righteousness of their beliefs but do not indeed believe in either themselves or their beliefs. Some leaders may thus have charismatic effects because of their ability to *act as though* they have such confidence and convictions. The writer is indebted to Ed Locke for pointing out this alternative hypothesis.

4. Sashkin, in his commentary on the present chapter, points out that earlier research has shown eminent leaders possess the traits of "intellectual fortitude and integrity of character" and speech fluency (or "capacity for ready communication"). While these traits were not specified in the earlier version of this presentation which Professor Sashkin reviewed, they are not in contradiction to the earlier literature on charismatic leadership and rather consistent with the general description of the charismatic personality advanced in this literature. Thus I would accept these characteristics, along with those in proposition 1, as possible characteristics that differentiate leaders who have charismatic effects from other leaders.

5. The argument that the enhancement of subordinate self-esteem is an important charismatic effect grew out of earlier conversations between the writer and David E. Berlew. See Berlew (1974) for further elaboration of this argument.

6. Such modeling, of course, will be a function of the degree to which the subordinate holds favorable perceptions of the leader, as specified in proposition 2.

7. It is possible that such leader behavior will have a positive effect on subordinates' task-related self-esteem only (i.e., on the subordinates' confidence in their ability to accomplish task goals). It is also possible that such leader behavior will result in enhanced chronic and generalized self-esteem of subordinates. Whether leaders can indeed have such a powerful effect on subordinates' self-perceptions is, of course, a question that requires empiric investigation.

8. Fleishman, E. A. *Manual for the Supervisory Behavior Description Questionnaire*. Washington, DC: American Institutes for Research, 1972.

9. The ability of the leader to arouse motives of subordinates is hypothesized to be a function of the degree to which subordinates hold favorable perceptions of the leader, as specified in proposition 2.

**Reading 37**

# Toward a Behavioral Theory of Charismatic Leadership in Organizational Settings

**Jay A. Conger and Rabindra N. Kanungo**
McGill University

Charismatic leadership has been largely overlooked by organizational theorists. In part, the problem can be attributed to the lack of a systematic conceptual framework. Drawing from political science, sociology, and social psychology, this paper addresses the problem by proposing a model linking organizational contexts to charismatic leadership. A series of research hypotheses is offered.

The term *charisma* often is used in political science and sociology to describe a subset of leaders who "by the force of their personal abilities are capable of having profound and extraordinary effects on followers" (House & Baetz, 1979, p. 399). Followers perceive the charismatic leader as one who possesses superhuman qualities and accept unconditionally the leader's mission and directives for action (Willner, 1984). These leaders represent revolutionary social forces, and they are responsible for significant social transformations (House & Baetz, 1979).

Certain writers contend that charismatic leaders can be found in business firms and other complex formal organizations (Bass, 1985; Berlew, 1974; Berger, 1963; Conger, 1985; Dow, 1969; Etzioni, 1961; House, 1977; Katz & Kahn, 1978; Oberg, 1972; Runciman, 1963; Shils, 1965; Zaleznik & Kets de Vries, 1975). Yet while examples of charismatic business leaders such as John De-Lorean and Lee Iacocca are well documented in the press and popular journals (Baker, 1983; Nicholson, 1983; Wright, 1979), they have received little attention as a subject of serious study. For example, only 12 of 5,000 citations reported in Bass's revision of *Stogdill's Handbook of Leadership* (1981) deal with charismatic leadership.

Several reasons are possible for the topic's conspicuous absence from the research literature. First, researchers have shied away from studying charismatic leadership because of its elusive nature and the mystical connotation of the term. Second, without a systematic conceptual framework, researchers often have found it difficult to define and operationalize charisma and to identify the variables that influence its development (Willner, 1984). Third, it is difficult to obtain access to charismatic business leaders.

This paper addresses the second of these problems, and by doing so, alleviates the first. It presents a model linking organizational contexts to charismatic leadership drawing upon research and theory from political science, sociology, social psychology, and existing theories of organizational leadership.

## THE LITERATURE

*Charisma* is a Greek word meaning gift. It is used in two letters of St. Paul—Romans, Chapter 12, and 1 Corinthians, Chapter 12—in the Christian Bible to describe the Holy Spirit. Prophecy, ruling, teaching, ministry, wisdom, and healing are among the charismatic gifts described. However, over time the word also came to signify the basis of ecclesiastical organization for the Church itself. The various roles played by members of the Church were determined by gifts of God, rather than by a set of rules or procedures designed by man.

Influenced by this use of charisma to describe a basis for legitimacy, the sociologist Max Weber expanded the concept to include any authority that derives its legitimacy not from rules, positions, or traditions, but from a "devotion to the specific and exceptional sanctity, heroism, or exemplary character of an individual person, and of the normative patterns or order revealed or ordained by him" (Eisenstadt, 1968, p. 46). In addition, Weber ascribed a revolutionary and counternormative quality to charismatic authority: "its attitude is revolutionary and transvalues everything; it makes a sovereign break with all traditional and rational norms" (Eisenstadt, 1968, p. 24).

Weber's conceptualization of charismatic authority, however, is limited by its lack of specificity. For

**Source:** Edited and reprinted with permission from Copyright Clearance Center. *Academy of Management Review* 12, no. 4 (1987), pp. 637–47. Author affiliation may have changed since the article was first published.

example, he used only generalities to describe a leader's qualities: "[they] comprise especially magical abilities, revelations of heroism, power of the mind and speech" (Etzioni, 1961, p. 12). He identified few behavioral dimensions that might distinguish these individuals from other leaders. Although he described charisma as "a certain quality of an individual personality," he also appears to acknowledge a relational basis for charisma: "It is recognition on the part of those subject to authority which is decisive for the validity of charisma" (Weber, 1947, p. 359).

Political scientists and sociologists have spent several decades examining the phenomenon. Although several have identified specific charismatic attributes such as a transcendent vision and/or ideology (Blau, 1963; Dow, 1969; Marcus, 1961; Willner, 1984), acts of heroism (Willner, 1984), an ability to inspire and build confidence (Dow, 1969; Friedrich, 1961; Marcus, 1961; Willner, 1984), the expression of revolutionary and often "hazardous" ideals (Berger, 1963; Dow, 1969; Friedland, 1964; Marcus, 1961), rhetorical ability (Willner, 1984), and a "powerful aura" (Willner, 1984), much of their work centered on determining the locus of charismatic leadership.

Some (Blau, 1963; Chinoy, 1961; Friedland, 1964; Wolpe, 1968) argued that social and historical contexts were the critical elements in the emergence of charismatic leadership, whereas others (Dow, 1969; Marcus, 1961; Willner, 1984) argued that attributes and relational dynamics between leaders and followers were responsible for the emergence of charisma:

> It involves a distinct social relationship between the leader and follower, in which the leader presents a revolutionary idea, a transcendent image or ideal which goes beyond the immediate . . . or the reasonable; while the follower accepts this course of action not because of its rational likelihood of success . . . but because of an effective belief in the extraordinary qualities of the leader (Dow, 1969, p. 315).

From in-depth case studies, Willner (1984) concluded that charismatic leadership was neither personality-based nor contextually-determined, but rather the phenomenon was largely relational and perceptual: "It is not what the leader is but what people see the leader as that counts in generating the charismatic relationship" (Willner, 1984, p. 14). Dow (1969) and Willner (1984) found that variations in individual personalities were too great to discern a single charismatic personality type and that the existence of a crisis—previously

argued to be necessary for the emergence of charismatic leadership (Chinoy, 1961; Devereux, 1955; Downtown, 1973; Hummel, 1975; Schiffer, 1973)—was "neither a necessary nor a sufficient cause" (Willner, 1984, p. 60).

Among organizational theorists, the topic of charismatic leadership was largely overlooked. Only a handful of theories of charismatic leadership in organizational or business settings have been proposed (Bass, 1985; Bennis & Nanus, 1985; Berlew, 1974; Conger, 1985; Etzioni, 1961; House, 1977; House & Baetz, 1979; Katz & Kahn, 1978; Zaleznik, 1977; Zaleznik & Kets de Vries, 1975). Generally these efforts have been conceptually less sophisticated than their counterparts in political science.

In addition to theoretical works, empirical studies of charismatic (and/or transformational) leadership have been reported by Avolio and Bass (1985), Bass (1985), Conger (1985), House (1985), Howell (1985), Smith (1982), Waldman, Bass, and Einstein (1985), and Yukl and Van Fleet (1982). These studies emphasized the behavioral and psychological attributes of charismatic leadership. Certain personal attributes of charismatic leaders that are identified consistently throughout this literature include vision or appealing ideological goals (Bass, 1985; Berlew, 1974; Conger, 1985; Katz & Kahn, 1978; House, 1977; Zaleznik & Kets de Vries, 1975), behavior that instills confidence (Bass, 1985; Berlew, 1974; House, 1977), an ability to inspire and/or create inspirational activities (Bass, 1985; Berlew, 1974; Conger, 1985; Zaleznik & Kets de Vries, 1975), self-confidence (Bass, 1985; House, 1977; Zaleznik & Kets de Vries, 1975), dominance (House, 1977; Zaleznik & Kets de Vries, 1975), a need for influence (House, 1977), rhetorical or articulation ability (Conger, 1985), and unconventional and/or counternormative behavior (Conger, 1985; Martin & Siehl, 1983).

In addition, House and Baetz (1979, p. 399) postulated a set of behavioral dimensions that distinguished the followers of charismatic leaders from others. These characteristics include an unquestioning acceptance of the leader by followers, followers' trust in the leader's beliefs, affection for the leader, willing obedience to the leader, emulation of and identification with the leader, similarity of followers' beliefs to those of the leader, emotional involvement of followers in the mission, heightened goals of the followers, and feelings on the part of the followers that they are able to accomplish or contribute to the leader's mission.

Unlike the political science and sociological literature, there appears to be little disagreement over the locus of charismatic leadership; a relational basis for charismatic leadership is widely accepted (Bass, 1985; Berlew, 1974; Conger, 1985; House, 1977; House & Baetz, 1979; Katz & Kahn, 1978; Zaleznik & Kets de Vries, 1975). It is believed that charisma per se is not found solely in the leader and his/her personal qualities but rather is found in the interplay between the leader's attributes and the needs, beliefs, values, and perceptions of his/her followers. Both Katz and Kahn (1978) and House and Baetz (1979) further contended that both the leader and his/her followers must share basic beliefs and values in order to validate the leader's charisma.

Unfortunately, a more unified conceptual framework for understanding the behavioral dimensions of the phenomenon has yet to be presented by organizational theorists. Instead, the literature provides a set of overlapping attributes that identify pieces of the puzzle but lack a structure to explain their relationships. Equally important, there is little or no empirical evidence to support conclusions.

## A BEHAVIORAL FRAMEWORK FOR STUDYING CHARISMA

If a deeper understanding of charismatic leadership within organizations is to be obtained, it is important to strip the aura of mysticism from charisma and to deal with it strictly as a behavioral process. Charismatic leadership, like any other form of leadership, should be considered to be an observable behavioral process that can be described and analyzed in terms of a formal model.

The model presented here builds on the idea that charisma is an attributional phenomenon. When members of a group work together to attain group objectives, observations of the influence process within the group help them determine their status. One who exerts maximum influence over other members is perceived as a leader. This role is consensually validated when followers recognize and identify the leader on the basis of interaction with him or her. Charismatic leadership is no exception to this process. Like other kinds of leadership, charisma must be viewed as an attribution made by followers who observe certain behaviors on the part of the leader within organizational contexts. The roles played by a person not only make the person, in the eyes of the followers, a task leader or a social leader, but they also

make him or her a charismatic leader or a noncharismatic leader. The leader's observed behavior within the organization can be interpreted by his/her followers as expressions of charismatic qualities. Such dispositional attributes are inferred from the leader's observed behavior in the same way that many personal styles of leadership have been observed previously (Blake & Mouton, 1964; Fiedler, 1967; Hersey & Blanchard, 1977; House, 1971). In this sense, charisma can be considered to be an additional inferred dimension of leadership behavior. As such, it is not an attribution made about an individual because of his or her rank in the organization, but rather it is an attribution made because of the behavior he or she exhibits. Charismatic disposition or leadership style should be subjected to the same empirical and behavioral analysis as participative, task, or people dimensions of leadership have been subjected to in the past.

## BEHAVIORAL COMPONENTS OF CHARISMA

If the follower's attribution of charisma depends on observed behavior of the leader, then what are the behavioral components responsible for such attributions? Can these attributions be identified and operationalized in order to develop charismatic qualities among organizational leaders? Table 1 includes a hypothesized description of what the present authors believe to be the essential and distinguishable behavioral components of charismatic leadership.

It is assumed that these components are interrelated and that they differ in presence and intensity among charismatic leaders. These ideas are represented in the following hypothesis.

**Hypothesis 1:** *The behavioral components of charismatic leadership are interrelated, and as such they form a constellation of components.*

Although all leadership roles involve charting a clear path for group members to achieve a common goal, attribution of charisma to leaders is believed to depend on four variables: the degree of discrepancy between the status quo and the future goal or vision advocated by the leader; the use of innovative and unconventional means for achieving the desired change; a realistic assessment of environmental resources and constraints for bringing about such change; and the nature of articulation and impression management employed to inspire subordinates in the pursuit of the vision. The role of these variables in the development of charisma is discussed on the next page.

**TABLE 1  Behavioral Components of Charismatic and Noncharismatic Leaders**

| | Noncharismatic Leader | Charismatic Leader |
|---|---|---|
| Relation to status quo | Essentially agrees with status quo and strives to maintain it. | Essentially opposed to status quo and strives to change it. |
| Future goal | Goal not too discrepant from status quo. | Idealized vision which is highly discrepant from status quo. |
| Likeableness | Shared perspective makes him/her likable. | Shared perspective and idealized vision makes him/her a likeable and honorable hero worthy of identification and imitation. |
| Trustworthiness | Disinterested advocacy in persuasion attempts. | Disinterested advocacy by incurring great personal risk and cost. |
| Expertise | Expert in using available means to achieve goals within the framework of the existing order. | Expert in using unconventional means to transcend the existing order. |
| Behavior | Conventional, conforming to existing norms. | Unconventional or counternormative. |
| Environmental sensitivity | Low need for environmental sensitivity to maintain status quo. | High need for environmental sensitivity for changing the status quo. |
| Articulation | Weak articulation of goals and motivation to lead. | Strong articulation of future vision and motivation to lead. |
| Power base | Position power and personal power (based on reward, expertise, and liking for a friend who is a similar other). | Personal power (based on expertise, respect, and admiration for a unique hero). |
| Leader–follower relationship | Egalitarian, consensus-seeking, or directive; nudges or orders people to share his/her views. | Elitist, entrepreneur, and exemplary; transforms people to share the radical changes advocated. |

### Charisma and the Future Vision

Many theorists see vision as a component of charismatic leadership (Bass, 1985; Berlew, 1974; Blau, 1963; Conger, 1985; Dow, 1969; Katz & Kahn, 1978; House, 1977; Marcus, 1961; Willner, 1984; Zaleznik & Kets de Vries, 1975). Here the word *vision* refers to some idealized goal that the leader wants the organization to achieve in the future. In this paper, it is hypothesized that the nature, formulation, articulation, and means of achieving this goal can be distinguished from those advocated by other kinds of leaders.

The more idealized or utopian the goal advocated by the leader, the more discrepant it is relative to the status quo. And, the greater the discrepancy of the goal from the status quo, the more likely followers will attribute extraordinary vision to the leader. By presenting an idealized goal to followers, a leader provides a challenge and a motivating force for change. The literature on change in attitude suggests that a maximum discrepant position within the latitude of acceptance puts the greatest amount of pressure on the followers to change their attitudes (Hovland &

Pritzker, 1957; Petty & Cacioppo, 1981). Since the idealized goal represents a perspective shared by the followers and promises to meet their hopes and aspirations, it tends to be within the latitude of acceptance in spite of the extreme discrepancy. A leader becomes charismatic when he/she succeeds in changing his/her followers' attitudes to accept the advocated vision. In religion, charisma stems from prophecy; in organizations, charisma stems from advocacy for the future. Failure of either prophecy or advocacy may change the attribution from charisma to madness.

What attributes of charismatic leaders make them successful advocates of their discrepant vision? Research on persuasive communication suggests that in order to be a successful advocate, one needs to be a credible communicator. A leader's credibility could result from projecting an image of being likable, trustworthy, and knowledgeable (Hovland, Janis, & Kelley, 1953; Sears, Freedman, & Peplau, 1985).

It is the shared perspective of the charismatic leader's idealized vision and its potential for satisfying followers' needs that makes the leader likable.

Both the perceived similarity between followers and their leader and the perceived potential of the leader to satisfy followers' needs form the basis of their interpersonal attraction (Byrne, 1977; Rubin, 1973). Through this idealized (and therefore discrepant) version of their vision, followers respect their leader and find him or her worthy of identifying with and imitating. Charismatic leaders are not just similar others who are generally liked (as one would find with popular, consensus-seeking leaders), but they are also holders of an idealized vision. Thus, the following hypothesis is advanced.

**Hypothesis 2:** *Leaders are charismatic when their vision is highly discrepant from the status quo yet remains within a latitude of acceptance for their followers.*

It is important for leaders to be trusted. Generally leaders are trusted when they advocate their position in a disinterested manner and demonstrate a concern for followers' needs rather than their own self-interest (Walster, Aronson, & Abrahams, 1966). However, charismatic leaders make these qualities appear extraordinary. They transform their concern for followers' needs into total dedication and commitment to the common cause they share with followers in a disinterested and selfless manner. They engage in exemplary acts that followers perceive as involving great personal risk, cost, and energy (Friedland, 1964). These personal risks might include: possible loss of finances or career success; the withdrawal of organizational resources; the potential for being fired or demoted; and the loss of formal or informal status, power, authority, and credibility. Lee Iacocca's reduction of his salary to one dollar during his first year at Chrysler (Iacocca & Novak, 1984) and John DeLorean's confrontations with senior management at GM (Martin & Siehl, 1983) are examples of personal risk. The higher the personal cost or sacrifice for the common good, the greater is the trustworthiness of leaders. The more leaders demonstrate that they are prepared to take high personal risks or incur high personal costs for achieving the shared vision, the more they are charismatic in the sense of being worthy of complete trust. This leads to the next hypothesis.

**Hypothesis 3:** *Charismatic leaders may take on high personal risks, incur high costs, and engage in self-sacrifice to achieve a shared vision.*

Finally, charismatic leaders appear to be experts in their area of influence. Past success may be a condition for the attribution of charisma (Weber, 1947)—for example, Iacocca's responsibility for the Ford Mustang. The attribution of charisma generally is influenced by leaders' expertise in two areas. First, charismatic leaders demonstrate the inadequacy of the traditional technology, rules, and regulations of the status quo as a means of achieving the shared vision (Weber, 1947). Second, the leaders devise effective but unconventional strategies and plans of action (Conger, 1985). Leaders are perceived as charismatic when they demonstrate expertise in transcending the existing order through the use of unconventional means. Iacocca's use of government-backed loans, money-back guarantees on cars, union representation on the board of directors, and advertisements featuring himself are examples of unconventional strategic actions in the automobile industry. Such phenomena lead to the following hypothesis.

**Hypothesis 4:** *Charismatic leaders demonstrate expertise in transcending the existing order through the use of unconventional or extraordinary means.*

### Charisma and Unconventional Behavior

Attribution of charisma to leaders depends on followers' perception of their revolutionary and unconventional qualities (Berger, 1963; Conger, 1985; Dow, 1969; Friedland, 1964; Marcus, 1961). The revolutionary qualities of leaders are manifested in part in their discrepant idealized visions. More important, charismatic leaders engage in innovative behaviors that run counter to the established norms of their organizations, industries, and/or societies while leading their followers toward the realization of their visions. Martin and Siehl (1983) demonstrated this in their analysis of John DeLorean's counternormative behavior at GM. Charismatic leaders are not group facilitators like consensual leaders, but they are active innovators. Their plans and the strategies they use to achieve change, their exemplary acts of heroism involving personal risks, and their self-sacrificing behaviors must be novel, unconventional, and out of the ordinary. Such behavior, when successful, evokes surprise and admiration in followers. Such uncommon behavior also leads to an attribution of charisma in the sense of the possession of superhuman abilities. Thus the following hypothesis is advanced.

**Hypothesis 5:** *Charismatic leaders engage in behaviors that are novel, unconventional, and counternormative, and as such, involve high personal risk or high probability of harming their own self-interest.*

## CHARISMA AND SENSITIVITY TO THE ENVIRONMENT

When a leader loses sight of reality and his or her unconventional behavior fails to achieve its objective, the leader may be degraded from charismatic to ineffective (Friedland, 1964). The knowledge, experience, and expertise of the leader become critical. Charismatic leaders realistically assess environmental resources and constraints affecting their ability to bring about change within their organizations. They are sensitive to both the abilities and emotional needs of followers, and they understand the resources and constraints of the physical and social environments in which they operate. Their innovative strategies and unconventional actions are based on realistic appraisals of environmental conditions. Instead of launching a course of action as soon as a vision is formulated, often leaders prepare the ground or will wait for an appropriate time, place, and the availability of resources. Charisma often fades due to a lack of sensitivity for the environment. The following hypothesis captures this idea.

**Hypothesis 6:** *Charismatic leaders engage in realistic assessments of the environmental resources and constraints affecting the realization of their visions. They implement innovative strategies when the environmental resource-constraint ratio is favorable to them.*

### Charisma and Articulation

Charismatic leaders articulate their visions and strategies for action through two processes. First, they articulate the context including: (*a*) the nature of the status quo; (*b*) the nature of the future vision; (*c*) the manner through which these future visions, if realized, remove sources of discontent and provide fulfillment of hopes and aspirations of the followers; and (*d*) plans of action for realizing the vision. In articulating the context, leaders' verbal messages paint positive pictures of the future vision and negative ones of the status quo. The status quo often is presented as intolerable, whereas the vision is presented as the most attractive and attainable alternative in clear, specific terms.

Second, charismatic leaders also communicate their own motivation to lead their followers. Through expressive modes of action, both verbal and nonverbal, the leaders communicate their convictions, self-confidence, and dedication in order to give credibility to what they advocate. Expression of high energy and persistence, unconventional and risky behavior, heroic deeds and personal sacrifices, all communicate the leaders' high motivation and enthusiasm, which then become contagious with their followers. In articulating their motivation to lead, charismatic leaders use a number of impression management techniques. For instance, they use rhetoric by selecting words to reflect assertiveness, confidence, expertise, and concern for followers' needs. These same qualities are also expressed through their dress, appearance, and other forms of body language. Unconventionality in the use of rhetoric and nonverbal forms of communication creates conditions for a dispositional attribution of charisma. These ideas about charismatic leaders' articulation of context and motivation are contained in the following two hypotheses.

**Hypothesis 7:** *Charismatic leaders portray the status quo as negative or intolerable and the future vision as the most attractive and attainable alternative.*

**Hypothesis 8:** *Charismatic leaders articulate their motivation to lead through assertive behavior and expression of self-confidence, expertise, unconventionality, and concern for followers' needs.*

### Charisma and the Use of Personal Power

Influence over followers can stem from different bases of power (French & Raven, 1968). Charismatic influence, however, stems from leaders' personal idiosyncratic power (referent and expert powers) rather than their position power (legal, coercive, and reward powers) legitimated by organizational rules and regulations. Participative consensual leaders also use personal power through consensus seeking. Some nonparticipative organizational leaders also use personal power through their benevolent but directive behavior. However, charismatic leaders differ from both consensual and directive leaders in the use of their personal power. Charismatic personal power stems from the elitist idealized vision, the entrepreneurial advocacy of radical changes, and the depth of knowledge and expertise to help achieve desired objectives. All these personal qualities appear extraordinary to their followers, and they form the basis of charisma. The following two hypotheses state this aspect of charismatic leadership.

**Hypothesis 9:** *Charismatic leaders' influence on their followers stems from the use of their personal idiosyncratic power (expert and referent) rather than the use of their position power (legal, coercive, and reward) within the organization.*

**Hypothesis 10:** *Charismatic leaders exert idiosyncratic personal power over their followers through elitist, entrepreneurial, and exemplary behavior rather than through consensus-seeking or directive behavior.*

### Charisma and the Reformer Role

A charismatic leader is seen as an organizational reformer. As Weber (1947) pointed out, charismatic authority is essentially unstable and transitory. Once a new order is institutionalized, charisma fades (Eisenstadt, 1968). Thus charisma is seen in leaders only when they act as agents bringing about radical changes. The attribution is made simply on the basis of actions taken to bring about change or reform. It is not a post facto attribution made after the outcomes of changes are known. Outcomes may, however, reinforce or diminish existing attributions.

From the perspective of change management, leaders should be distinguished from administrators (Zaleznik, 1977). Administrators act as caretakers responsible for the maintenance of the status quo. They influence others through their position power as legitimated by the organization. Leaders, as posed to administrators, direct or nudge their followers in the direction of an established goal. Charismatic leaders, however, transform their followers (instead of nudging them) and seek radical reforms in them in order to achieve the idealized goal. Thus, charisma can never be perceived either in an administrator (caretaker) role or in a leadership role designed only to nudge the system. This idea is contained in the following hypothesis.

**Hypothesis 11:** *Charismatic leaders act as reformers or agents of radical changes, and their charisma fades when they act as administrators (caretaker role) or managers (nudging role).*

### The Context for Emergence of Charisma

The preceding discussion implies that a need for major transition or change triggers the emergence of a charismatic leader. Sometimes contextual factors are so overwhelmingly in favor of a change that leaders take advantage of them. For instance, when a system is dysfunctional or when it faces a crisis, leaders find it to their advantage to advocate radical change, thereby creating a charismatic image for themselves. In periods of relative tranquility, leaders play a major role in creating the need for change in their followers. They anticipate future change and induce supportive conditions. In any case, context must be viewed as a precipitating factor, sometimes facilitating the emergence of certain behavior in leaders that forms the basis of charisma. As Willner (1984) pointed out regarding political leadership, "preconditions of exogenous social crisis and psychic distress are conducive to the emergence of charismatic political leadership, but they are not necessary" (p. 52). From the point of view of the leader, however, sensitivity to contextual factors is important if he or she is to develop appropriate strategies for change. The following two hypotheses deal with the role of context in the emergence of charisma.

**Hypothesis 12:** *Contextual factors that cause potential followers to be disenchanted with the prevailing social order, or that cause followers to experience psychological distress, although not a necessary condition for the emergence of charismatic leaders, facilitate such emergence.*

**Hypothesis 13:** *Under conditions of relative social tranquility and lack of psychological distress among followers, the actions by a leader that foster or support an attribution of charisma facilitate the emergence of that leader as a charismatic leader.*

## IMPLICATIONS

In order to demystify charisma, these tentative hypotheses for future testing have been presented. Existing evidence forms the basis of the model, but the specific predictions should be tested.

In the model, charisma is viewed both as a set of dispositional attributions by followers and as a set of leaders' manifest behaviors. The two are linked in the sense that the leaders' behaviors form the basis of followers' attributions. To validate such a framework, two steps are necessary. First, the behavioral and dispositional attributes of charismatic leaders suggested in this framework require independent empirical confirmation. To determine if convergent and discriminant validity exist, a behavioral attribute checklist or questionnaire could be developed including the attributes believed to characterize charismatic leaders as well as those cited in the literature for other forms of leadership. A group of test subjects could identify leaders they perceive as charismatic and as noncharismatic. Respondents then could describe the distinguishing attributes of charismatic and noncharismatic leaders using the checklist. With this format, it would be possible to test whether an attribution of charisma is associated with the attributes described. Second, the discriminant validity of the charismatic leadership construct as described in this paper could be tested by demonstrating that a dependent variable (e.g., followers' trust) is related to charisma in a different way than other leadership constructs.

The model also has direct implications for management. Specifically, if the behavioral components of charismatic leadership can be isolated, it may be possible to develop these attributes in managers. Assuming that charismatic leadership is important for organizational reforms, organizations may wish to select managers on the basis of charismatic characteristics that have been identified. Certain tests such as those already developed to test sensitivity to the environment (Kenny & Zaccaro, 1983) could be administered to potential managerial candidates. The need for such selection procedures may be particularly important for developing countries, where greater levels of organizational change would be necessary in order to adopt new technologies and to transform traditional ways of operating.

# References

Avolio, B. J., & Bass, B. M. (1985) *Charisma and beyond*. Paper presented at the annual meeting of the Academy of Management, San Diego.

Baker, R. (1983, March 27) Peripatetic pitchman. *New York Times Magazine*, p. 26.

Bass, B. M. (1981) *Stogdill's handbook of leadership*. New York: Free Press.

Bass, B. M. (1985) *Leadership performance beyond expectations*. New York: Academic Press.

Bennis, W. G., & Nanus, G. (1985) *Leaders*. New York: Harper & Row.

Berger, P. L. (1963) Charisma and religious innovation: The social location of Israelite prophecy. *American Sociological Review, 28*, 940–950.

Berlew, D. E. (1974) Leadership and organizational excitement. *California Management Review, 17*(2), 21–30.

Blake, R. R., & Mouton, J. S. (1964) *The managerial grid*. Houston: Gulf.

Blau, P. (1963) Critical remarks on Weber's theory of authority. *American Political Science Review, 57*, 305–315.

Byrne, D. (1977) *The attraction paradigm*. New York: Academic Press.

Chinoy, E. (1961) *Society*. New York: Random House.

Conger, J. (1985) *Charismatic leadership in business: An exploratory study*. Unpublished doctoral dissertation, Harvard Business School, Boston.

Devereux, G. (1955) Charismatic leadership and crisis. In W. Muensterberger & S. Axelrod (Eds.), *Psychoanalysis and the social sciences* (Vol. 4, pp. 145–157). New York: International University Press.

Dow, T. E., Jr. (1969) The theory of charisma. *Sociological Quarterly, 10*, 306–318.

Downtown, J. V., Jr. (1973) *Rebel leadership*. New York: Free Press.

Eisenstadt, S. N. (1968) *Max Weber: On charisma and institution building*. Chicago: University of Chicago Press.

Etzioni, A. (1961) *A comparative analysis of complex organizations*. New York: Free Press.

Fiedler, F. F. (1967) *A theory of leadership effectiveness*. New York: McGraw-Hill.

French, J. R., Jr., & Raven, B. H. (1968) The bases of social power. In D. Cartwright & A. Zander (Eds.), *Group dynamics* (pp. 259–269.) New York: Harper & Row.

Friedland, W. H. (1964) For a sociological concept of charisma. *Social Forces, 43*, 18–26.

Friedrich, C. J. (1961) Political leadership and the problem of the charismatic power. *Journal of Politics, 23*, 3–24.

Hersey, P., & Blanchard, K. H. (1977) *Management of organizational behavior: Utilizing human resources* (4th ed.). Englewood Cliffs, NJ: Prentice-Hall.

House, R. J. (1971) A path-goal theory of leadership effectiveness. *Administrative Science Quarterly*, 321–332.

House, R. J. (1977) A 1976 theory of charismatic leadership. In J. G. Hunt & L. L. Larson (Eds.), *Leadership: The cutting edge* (pp. 189–207). Carbondale, IL: Southern Illinois University press.

House, R. J. (1985) *Research contrasting the behavior and effects of reputed charismatic versus reputed noncharismatic*. Paper presented at the annual meeting of the Administrative Science Association, Montreal.

House, R. J., & Baetz, M. L. (1979) Leadership: Some empirical generalizations and new research directions. In B. M. Staw (Ed.), *Research in organizational behavior* (Vol. 1, pp. 399–401). Greenwich, CT: JAI Press.

Hovland, C. I., Janis, I. L., & Kelley, H. H. (1953) *Communication and persuasion*. New Haven, CT: Yale University Press.

Hovland, C. I., & Pritzker, H. A. (1957) Extent of opinion change as a function of amount of change advocated. *Journal of Abnormal Psychology,* 54, 257–261.

Howell, J. M. (1985) *A laboratory study of charismatic leadership.* Paper presented at the annual meeting of the Academy of Management, San Diego.

Hummel, R. P. (1975) Psychology of charismatic followers. *Psychological Reports,* 37, 759–770.

Iacocca, L., Novak, W. (1984) *Iacocca.* New York: Bantam Books.

Katz, D., & Kahn, R. L. (1978) *The social psychology of organizations.* New York: Wiley.

Kenny, D. A., & Zacarro, S. J. (1983) An estimate of variance due to traits in leadership. *Journal of Applied Psychology,* 68, 678–685.

Marcus, J. T. (1961), March Transcendence and charisma. *Western Political Quarterly,* 14, 236–241.

Martin, J., & Siehl, C. (1983) Organizational culture and counterculture: An uneasy symbiosis. *Organizational Dynamics,* 12(2), 52–64.

Nicholson, T. (1983, February 14) Iacocca shifts into high. *Newsweek,* pp. 101, 64.

Oberg, W. (1972) Charisma, commitment, and contemporary organization theory. *Business Topics,* 20(2), 18–32.

Petty, R. E., & Cacioppo, J. T. (1981) *Attitudes and persuasion: Classic and contemporary approaches.* Dubuque, IA: Brown.

Rubin, Z. (1973) *Liking and loving: An invitation to social psychology.* New York: Holt, Rinehart, & Winston.

Runciman, W. G. (1963) Charismatic legitimacy and one-party rule in Ghana. *Archives Eupreenes de Sociologie,* 4, 148–165.

Schiffer, I. (1973) *Charisma: A psychoanalytic look at mass society.* Toronto: University of Toronto Press.

Sears, D. O., Freedman, L., & Peplau, L. A. (1985) *Social psychology* (5th ed.) Englewood Cliffs, NJ: Prentice-Hall.

Shils, E. A. (1965) Charisma, order, and status. *American Sociological Review,* 30, 199–213.

Smith, B. J. (1982) *An initial test of a theory of charismatic leadership based on responses of subordinates.* Unpublished doctoral dissertation, University of Toronto.

Tucker, R. C. (1968) The theory of charismatic leadership. *Daedulus,* 97, 731–756.

Waldman, D. A., Bass, B. M., & Einstein, W. O. (1985) *Effort, performance and transformational leadership in industrial and military settings.* (Working Paper 85-80). State University of New York at Binghamton, School of Management.

Walster, E., Aronson, D., & Abrahams, D. (1966) On increasing the persuasiveness of a low prestige communicator. *Journal of Experimental Social Psychology,* 2, 325–342.

Weber, M. (1947) *The theory of social and economic organization.* (A. M. Henderson & T. Parsons, Trans.). New York: Oxford University Press.

Willner, A. R. (1968) *Charismatic political leadership: A theory.* Princeton, NJ: Princeton University, Center of International Studies.

Willner, A. R. (1984) *The spellbinders: Charismatic political leadership.* New Haven, CT: Yale University Press.

Wolpe, H. (1968) A critical analysis of some aspects of charisma. *Sociological Review,* 16, 305–318.

Wright, P. J. (1979) *On a clear day you can see General Motors.* New York: Avon Books.

Yukl, G. A. (1981) *Leadership in organizations.* Englewood Cliffs, NJ: Prentice-Hall.

Yukl, G. A., & Van Fleet, D. D. (1982) Cross-situational multimethod research on military leader effectiveness. *Organizational Behavior and Human Performance,* 30, 87–108.

Zaleznik, A. (1977) Managers and leaders: Are they different? *Harvard Business Review,* 55(3), 67–78.

Zaleznik, A., & Kets de Vries, M. F. R. (1975) *Power and the corporate mind.* Boston: Houghton Mifflin.

**Reading 38**

# The Motivational Effects of Charismatic Leadership: A Self-concept Based Theory

**Boas Shamir**
The Hebrew University

**Robert J. House**
University of Pennsylvania

**Michael B. Arthur**
Suffolk University

## INTRODUCTION

In the past 15 years a new genre of leadership theory, alternatively referred to as "charismatic," "transformational," "visionary," or "inspirational," has emerged in the organizational literature (House, 1977; Burns, 1978; Bass, 1985; Bennis and Nanus, 1985; Tichy and Devanna, 1986; Boal and Bryson, 1988; Conger and Kanungo, 1987; Kuhnert and Lewis, 1984; Sashkin, 1988).

These theories focus on exceptional leaders who have extraordinary effects on their followers and eventually on social systems. According to this new genre of leadership theory, such leaders transform the needs, values, preferences, and aspirations of followers from self-interests to collective interests. Further, they cause followers to become highly committed to the leader's mission, to make significant personal sacrifices in the interest of the mission, and to perform above and beyond the call of duty. We refer to this new genre of theories as charismatic because charisma is a central concept in all of them, either explicitly or implicitly.

Theories of charismatic leadership highlight such effects as emotional attachment to the leader on the part of the followers; emotional and motivational arousal of the followers; enhancement of follower valences with respect to the mission articulated by the leader; follower self-esteem, trust, and confidence in the leader; follower values; and follower intrinsic motivation.

**Source:** Edited and reprinted with permission from *Organization Science* 4, no. 4 (1993), pp. 577–594. Copyright (1993) The Institute of Management Science.

The leader behavior specified by charismatic theories is different from the behavior emphasized in earlier theories of organizational leadership. The earlier theories describe leader behavior in terms of leader/follower exchange relationships (Hollander, 1964; Graen and Cashman, 1975), providing direction and support (Evans, 1970; House, 1971), and reinforcement behaviors (Ashour, 1982; Podsakoff, Todor, and Skov, 1982). In contrast, the new leadership theories emphasize symbolic leader behavior, visionary and inspirational messages, nonverbal communication, appeal to ideological values, intellectual stimulation of followers by the leader, display of confidence in self and followers, and leader expectations for follower self-sacrifice and for performance beyond the call of duty. Such leadership is seen as giving meaningfulness to work by infusing work and organizations with moral purpose and commitment rather than by affecting the task environment of followers, or by offering material incentives and the threat of punishment.

Research based on these theories has yielded an impressive set of findings concerning the effects of charismatic leaders on follower attitudes, satisfaction, and performance. However, there is no motivational explanation to account for the profound effects of such leaders, some of which are difficult to explain within currently dominant models of motivation. The purpose of this paper is to offer a motivational theory to account for the effects of charismatic leaders on their followers.

## EMPIRICAL EVIDENCE

In the last decade, at least 35 empirical investigations of charismatic leadership in organizations have been conducted. . . .

These studies were conducted across a wide variety of samples. . . .

Space limitations prevent a detailed review of the findings of these studies (for reviews see Bass, 1990; House, Howell, Shamir, Smith and Spangler, 1991). While the studies were not guided by a unified theoretical perspective, there is a considerable convergence of the findings from studies concerned with charismatic leadership and those concerned with transformational and visionary leadership. Collectively, these findings indicate that leaders who engage in the theoretical charismatic behaviors produce the theoretical charismatic effects. In addition, they receive higher performance ratings, have more satisfied and more highly motivated followers, and are viewed as more effective leaders by their superiors and followers than others in positions of leadership. Further, the effect size of charismatic leader behavior on follower satisfaction and performance is consistently higher than prior field study findings concerning other leader behavior, generally ranging well below 0.01 probability of error due to chance, with correlations frequently ranging in the neighborhood of 0.50 or better.

## THE PROBLEM

Unfortunately, the literature on charismatic leadership does not provide an explanation of the process by which charismatic leadership has its profound effects. No motivational explanations are provided to explain how charismatic leaders bring about changes in followers' values, goals, needs, and aspirations.

Three types of changes that have been emphasized by previous theories present a particular theoretical challenge. First, Burns (1978) and Bass (1985) suggested that transformational or charismatic leaders are able to elevate followers' needs from lower to higher levels in the Maslow hierarchy. Second, Burns (1978) claimed that such leaders raise followers to higher levels of morality, to "more principled levels of judgment" (p. 455). Third, House (1977), Burns (1978), and Bass (1985) proposed that such leaders are successful in motivating followers to transcend their own self-interests for the sake of the team, the organization, or the larger polity. We shall refer to these effects as "the transformational effects of charismatic leadership." . . .

In the following sections of this paper, we first present some assumptions about the motivational significance of the self-concept. We then show how charismatic leaders activate self-concept related motivations, and how these motivations can explain the effects that are not well explained by current theories. Following, we specify leader behaviors that are likely to activate these processes. We derive from our motivational analysis testable propositions about the effects of these behaviors on followers' self-concepts, and their further effects on followers. We then discuss some follower attributes that moderate the hypothesized relationships. Finally, we specify organizational conditions under which charismatic leadership is likely to emerge and be effective. . . .

## THE THEORY

Our assumptions about the self-concept and its motivational implications allow us to propose a theory to explain the transformational effects of charismatic leadership. The theory has four main parts: (*a*) leader behaviors; (*b*) effects on followers' self-concepts; (*c*) further effects on followers; and (*d*) the motivational processes by which the leader behaviors produce the charismatic effects. These processes link the leader behaviors to their effects on followers' self-concepts, and the effects on followers' self-concepts to further effects on followers. The theory is outlined in Figure 1.

At the heart of our theory are five processes by which charismatic leaders motivate followers through implicating their self-concepts. These processes are presented first. We then derive from our motivational analysis a set of empirically observable leader behaviors that are hypothesized to activate the self-implicating processes, a set of effects on followers' self-concepts that are triggered by the leader behaviors, and a set of further effects on followers that are mediated by the self-concept effects.

We do not view the variables specified within each set as constituting exhaustive sets. Nor can we rule out the possibility that the variables within each set are intercorrelated and constitute syndromes (Meindl, 1990). At this stage, our propositions refer to the relationships between the sets of variables. Hopefully, empirical research guided by these propositions will enable a more parsimonious and more exact formulation of the relationships implied by the theory.

**FIGURE 1  An Outline of the Theory**

## THE SELF-IMPLICATING EFFECTS OF CHARISMATIC LEADERSHIP[1]

We suggest that charismatic leaders motivate their followers in the following manner:

[1] In the analysis that follows, we do not distinguish between "good" or "moral" and "evil" or "immoral" charismatic leadership. Indeed, our analysis suggests that the psychological mechanisms relied upon by the "Hitlers" and the "Gandhis" may be similar in certain respects. This means that the risks involved in following charismatic leaders are at least as large as the promises. The motivational processes and the creation of personal commitment described in this paper can lead to blind fanaticism in the service of megalomaniacs and dangerous values, no less than to heroic self-sacrifice in the service of a beneficial cause. An awareness of these risks is missing from most of the current literature on organizational charismatic or transformational leadership. We believe that these risks should not be neglected, but rather that we need more studies of the nature and effects of charismatic leadership and the conditions under which it produces

### (a) Increasing the Intrinsic Valence of Effort

This is accomplished by emphasizing the symbolic and expressive aspects of the effort—the fact that the effort itself reflects important values—that by making the effort, one makes a moral statement. Charismatic leadership is presumed to strengthen followers' belief in the necessity and propriety of "standing up and being counted."

The intrinsic valence of the effort may also be increased by making participation in the effort an

harmful versus beneficial effects for followers and collectives. "Beware Charisma! . . . But to beware does not necessarily mean or entail 'Avoid!' . . . Be aware! Then choose" (Hodgkinson, 1983). We hope that the analysis presented here will help lead to the awareness called for by Hodgkinson (1983). However, we do not endorse charismatic leadership as necessarily good or bad. For a theory that differentiates personalized authoritarian and exploitive charismatics from collective, egalitarian, and not exploitive, see House and Howell (1992).

expression of a collective identity, thus making the effort more meaningful for the follower. This implicates the self-concept of followers by increasing the salience of that identity in the follower's self-concept, thus increasing the likelihood of efforts and behaviors representing that identity. Charismatic leaders may use existing identities and emphasize their uniqueness or superiority ("Black is beautiful"), or they may create "new" desirable social categories for the followers ("the master race"). In both cases, the self-concepts of the followers are clearly engaged.

Meindl and Lerner (1983) have suggested that the salience of a shared identity can increase the "heroic motive" and the likelihood that self-interest oriented pursuits will voluntarily be abandoned for more altruistic or collectivistic endeavors. It follows that, when charismatic leaders increase the salience of collective identities in their followers' self-concepts, they also increase the likelihood of self-sacrificial, collective-oriented behavior on the part of followers.

It is important to note that, once followers choose to make the effort and through that effort identify themselves with certain values and with the leader and the collective, they are subject to considerable social and psychological forces that are likely to increase their commitment to that effort (Kanter, 1967; Salancik, 1977). We will return to this point in our discussion of personal commitment.

### (b) Increasing Effort-Accomplishment Expectancies

Charismatic leaders increase effort-accomplishment expectancies by enhancing the followers' self-esteem and self-worth. They enhance self-esteem by expressing high expectations of the followers and confidence in the followers' ability to meet such expectations (Yukl, 1989; Eden, 1990). By so doing, they enhance followers' perceived self-efficacy, defined as a judgment of one's capability to accomplish a certain level of performance. Self-efficacy is a strong source of motivation (Bandura, 1986, p. 351).

Charismatic leaders also increase followers' self-worth through emphasizing the relationships between efforts and important values. A general sense of self-worth increases general self-efficacy; a sense of moral correctness is a source of strength and confidence. Having complete faith in the moral correctness of one's convictions gives one the strength and confidence to behave accordingly.

Another aspect of charismatic leadership that is likely to increase effort-accomplishment ex-

pectancies is its emphasis on collective efficacy. "Perceived collective efficacy will influence what people choose to do as a group, how much effort they put into it, and their staying power when group efforts fail to produce results" (Bandura, 1986, p. 449). Thus, being a member of an efficacious collective enhances one's self-efficacy.

### (c) Increasing the Intrinsic Valence of Goal Accomplishment

This is one of the most import motivational mechanisms of charismatic leadership. Articulation of a vision and a mission by charismatic leaders presents goals in terms of the values they represent. Doing so makes action oriented toward the accomplishment of these goals more meaningful to the follower in the sense of being consistent with his or her self-concept.

Charismatic leadership also increases the meaningfulness of goals and related actions by showing how these goals are consistent with the collective past and its future and thus creating the sense of "evolving" which is central for self-consistency and a sense of meaningfulness (McHugh, 1968). In addition, such leadership stresses the importance of the goal as a basis for group identity and for distinguishing the group or collective from other groups. This brings meaning to the followers' lives and efforts by connecting them to larger entities and to concerns that transcend their own limited existence (Jahoda, 1981). By these leadership actions, certain identities are evoked and made more salient and therefore more likely to be implicated in action.

### (d) Instilling Faith in a Better Future

The "rewards" involved in the charismatic leadership process involve self-expression, self-efficacy, self-worth, and self-consistency, which emerge from the process and cannot be exchanged. In most cases, charismatic leadership de-emphasizes extrinsic rewards and their related expectancies in order to emphasize the intrinsic aspects of the effort. Refraining from providing pragmatic extrinsic justification for the required behavior increases the chances that followers will attribute their behavior to internal self-related causes and thus adds to followers' commitment to that course of action.

Note that while noncharismatic leadership emphasizes proximal, specific goals and increases the subjective likelihood that goal attainment would lead to specific outcomes (Locke and Latham, 1990; House, 1971), charismatic leadership tends to emphasize vague and distal goals and utopian outcomes. It is here that Bass refers to charismatic leaders' use of "symbolism, mysticism, imaging, and fantasy" (1985, p. 6). In order to understand the motivational impact of such messages (that contradict current motivational models which stress goal specificity and proximity), we have to resort to our assumption that having faith in a better future is a satisfying condition in itself. People would therefore follow leaders who provide hope (a vision) for a better future and faith in its attainment, even if such faith cannot be translated into specific proximal goals whose attainment is highly probable.

### (e) Creating Personal Commitment

Another important aspect of charismatic motivational influence is the creation of a high level of commitment on the part of the leader and the followers to a common vision, mission, or transcendent goal (Bennis and Nanus, 1985; House, 1977). "Their art is to manufacture ethics to give life through commitment to the spirit of the organization" (Hodgkinson, 1983, p. 218).

When we speak about commitment in the context of charismatic leadership, we refer to unconditional commitment—internalized "personal" or "moral" commitment (Johnson, 1982). This is a motivational disposition to continue a relationship, a role, or a course of action and to invest efforts regardless of the balance of external costs and benefits and their immediate gratifying properties.

We propose that such commitment is achieved when the relationship or role under consideration becomes a component of the individual's self-concept and when the course of action related to that relationship or role is consistent with and expressive of the individual's self-concept; in other words, when "action is not merely a means of doing but a way of being" (Strauss, 1969, p. 3).

Such a concept of commitment fits very well into our analysis of charismatic leadership. By recruiting the self-concept of followers, increasing the salience of certain identities and values, and linking behaviors and goals to those identities and values and to a mission that reflects them, charismatic leadership motivates followers through the creation of personal commitments.

These processes are self-reinforcing because the behavioral manifestations of such a commitment are likely to further bind the self-concept of the individual to the leader and the mission. Faced with their own voluntary and public action on behalf of the leader, the collective, or the mission, individuals are likely to integrate these relationships and values even further into their self-concepts as a result of self-attribution and self-justification processes and the need to reduce or avoid cognitive dissonance (Salancik, 1977; Staw, 1980). When the self is engaged in a situation, the need for self-justification and dissonance reduction is particularly strong.

Generated and reinforced in these ways, personal commitment is perhaps the most intrinsic of all intrinsic motivators since in the final analysis it is a commitment to one's own self-concept and evaluative standards, "to a conception of (oneself) as a certain kind or kinds of person who is expected and expects to act in a certain way in certain situations" (Strauss, 1969, p. 3).[2]

### Summary

To recapitulate, we have suggested that charismatic leaders achieve transformational effects through implicating the self-concept of followers. More specifically, we have argued that such leaders increase the intrinsic value of efforts and goals by linking them to valued aspects of the follower's self-concept, thus harnessing the motivational forces of self-expression, self-consistency, self-esteem, and self-worth. We have further argued that charismatic leaders change the salience hierarchy of values and identities within the follower's self-concept, thus increasing the probability that these values and identities will be implicated in action. Since values and identities are socially based, their control of behavior is likely to represent a shift from the instrumental to the moral and from concern with individual gains to concern with contributions to a collective. Finally, we have argued that charismatic leaders increase self-efficacy and collective efficacy through expressing positive evaluations, communicating higher performance expectations of followers, showing confidence in followers' ability to meet such expectations, and emphasizing the individual's ties to the collective. The differences between these processes and the motivational processes implied by more traditional leadership theories are outlined in Table 1.

---

[2] From an organizational perspective, however, commitment is a double-edged sword. To the extent that the leader's goals and values are congruent with the goals and values of the organization, charismatic leadership is likely to provide a strong link between organizational goals and member commitment to such goals. To the extent that the leader's goals and values are in conflict with those of the organization, such as when leaders represent a challenge to the status quo, charismatic leadership is likely to induce negative attitudes toward the organization and resistance to directives from management by organizational members. Thus, charismatic leadership represents a strong force for *or against* member commitment to organizational goals.

**TABLE 1   Summary of the Motivational Effects of Traditional and Charismatic Leadership Processes**

| Motivational Charismatic Component Processes | Traditional Leadership Processes | Charismatic Leadership |
|---|---|---|
| Intrinsic value of behavior | Making the task more interesting, varied, enjoyable, challenging, as in job enrichment | Linking behavior to followers' self-concepts, internalized values and cherished identities |
| Behavior-accomplishment expectancy | Coaching, training; providing material, instrumental and emotional support; clarifying goals | Increasing general self-efficacy (through increasing self-worth and communicating confidence and high expectations). Emphasizing collective efficacy |
| Intrinsic value of goal accomplishment | Setting goals, increasing task identity, providing feedback | Linking goals to the past and the present and to values in a framework of a "mission" which serves as a basis for identification |
| Accomplishment-reward expectancies | Establishing clear performance evaluation and tying rewards to performance | Generating faith by connecting behaviors and goals to a "dream" or a utopian ideal vision of a better future. |
| Valence of extrinsic rewards | Taken into consideration in rewarding performance | Not addressed |

## LEADER BEHAVIOR

The motivational processes described above are activated by two classes of leader behavior: (*a*) role modeling, and (*b*) frame alignment.

### (a) Role Modeling

Vicarious learning occurs when the relevant messages are inferred by followers from observation of leaders' behavior, life style, emotional reactions, values, aspirations, preferences, and the like. The leader becomes a "representative character" (Bellah et al., 1985)—a symbol which brings together in one concentrated image the way people in a given social environment organize and give meaning and direction to their lives. He or she becomes an image that helps define for the followers just what kinds of traits, values, beliefs, and behaviors it is good and legitimate to develop. Thus, the leader provides an ideal, a point of reference and focus for followers' emulation and vicarious learning.

This is sometimes exemplified by leaders' display of self-sacrificial behavior in the interest of the mission. By taking risks, making personal sacrifices, and engaging in unconventional ideological behavior (Conger and Kanungo, 1987; Sashkin, 1988), charismatic leaders demonstrate their own courage and conviction in the mission and thus both earn credibility and serve as a role model of the values of the vision and the mission.

### (b) Frame Alignment

[This term] (Snow et al., 1986) refers to the linkage of individual and leader interpretive orientations, such that some set of followers' interests, values, and beliefs and the leader's activities, goals, and ideology become congruent and complementary. The term "frame" denotes "schemata of interpretation" (Goffman, 1974) that enables individuals to locate, perceive, and label occurrences within their life and the world at large. By rendering events or occurrences meaningful, frames function to organize experience and guide action, whether individual or collective (see also Boal and Bryson, 1988).

Charismatic leaders engage in communicative processes that affect frame alignment and "mobilize" followers to action. They interpret the present and past. They link present behaviors to past events by citing historical examples (Willner, 1984). They articulate an ideology clearly, often using labels and slogans. They provide a vivid image of the future. Further, they amplify certain values and identities and suggest linkages between expected behaviors, amplified values and identities, and their vision of the future.

By articulating an ideological vision and recruiting a number of followers who share the values of the vision, charismatic leaders provide for followers a sense of identity with the collectivity and a sense of efficacy resulting from membership in the collectivity. Articulation of high performance expectations, together with display of confidence in followers, results in enhancing both follower self-esteem and self-worth.

By relating the vision to significant historical events and projecting it into the future, charismatic leaders provide for followers a sense of continuity.

These general behavioral principles can be translated into more specific and observable behaviors.

**Proposition 1.** *In order to implicate the followers' self-concepts, compared to noncharismatic leaders, the deliberate and nondeliberate messages of charismatic leaders will contain:*

(a) More references to values and moral justifications.

(b) More references to the collective and to collective identity.

(c) More references to history.

(d) More positive references to followers' worth and efficacy as individuals and as a collective.

(e) More expressions of high expectations from followers.

(f) More references to distal goals and less reference to proximal goals.

## EFFECTS ON FOLLOWERS' SELF-CONCEPT

Several effects on the followers' self-concept evolve directly from our preceding discussion. These are specified in the following proposition:

**Proposition 2.** *The more leaders exhibit the behaviors specified above, the more followers will have:*

(a) A high salience of the collective identity in their self-concept.

(b) A sense of consistency between their self-concept and their actions on behalf of the leader and the collective.

(c) A high level of self-esteem and self-worth.

(d) A similarity between their self-concept and their perception of the leader.

(e) A high sense of collective efficacy.

These effects on the self-concept represent three common processes of psychological attachment: personal identification, social identification, and value internalization. . . .

## SELF-CONCEPT AS AN INTERVENING VARIABLE AND FURTHER EFFECTS ON FOLLOWERS

The theory suggests that the above specified effects on followers' self-concepts mediate other effects of charismatic leaders on the followers. The changes in followers' self-concepts will produce these effects through the motivational mechanisms of self-expression, self-consistency, and the maintenance and enhancement of self-esteem and self-worth. These further effects are observable manifestations of the transformational effects of charismatic leadership.

First, it is proposed that the linkage formed by charismatic leaders between followers' self-concepts and the leader's mission will be evidenced by increased personal commitment of the followers to the leader and the mission. Second, increased social identification and value internalization will lead to a high willingness among followers to make personal sacrifices for the collective mission as articulated by the leader, and a high level of "extra role," organizational citizenship behaviors (O'Reilly and Chatman, 1986; Organ, 1988; Podsakoff et al., 1990). Such behaviors are of particular interest because they are the voluntary behavioral manifestations of performance beyond expectations—exertion of effort and self-sacrifice in the interest of the work team or the larger organization.

In addition, followers of charismatic leaders are expected to have a high sense of "meaningfulness" associated with the task. Such meaningfulness stems from a high sense of consistency between their self-concepts and their actions on behalf of the leader and the collective, and from the implications of these actions for their self-esteem and self-worth. Thus,

**Proposition 3.** *The more leaders exhibit the behaviors specified in the theory the more followers will demonstrate:*

(a) Personal commitment to the leader and the mission.

(b) A willingness to make sacrifices for the collective mission.

(c) Organizational citizenship behavior.

(d) Meaningfulness in their work and lives.

It is further proposed that the increased self-efficacy and collective efficacy, together with the high personal commitment to the mission and the sense of "meaningfulness" associated with the tasks, will produce heightened performance motivation among followers, which will in turn result in higher levels of performance. These final effects are not specified in our propositions because they are not unique to the proposed theory and may be produced by other leader behaviors triggering other motivational mechanisms. They are reinforced, however, by the self-processes outlined in our model.

## FOLLOWER ATTRIBUTES

Our theory implies that charismatic leaders will not have similar effects on all followers. We now turn to a discussion of some follower characteristics that may moderate the hypothesized relationships between leader behaviors and effects on followers.

### FOLLOWER VALUES AND IDENTITIES

The theory presented here implies that the leader, in order to have the transformational effects specified in the theory, must appeal to existing elements of the followers' self-concepts—namely, their values and identities. . . .

This line of reasoning leads to the following proposition:

**Proposition 4.** *A necessary condition for a leader's messages to have charismatic effects is that the message is congruent with the existing values and identities held by potential followers.*

### FOLLOWER ORIENTATIONS

Other follower characteristics may moderate the transformational effects of charismatic leadership. Organization members are known to differ on the dimension of having an "instrumental" or "expressive" orientation to work (Goldthorpe et al., 1968). Since charismatic leadership arouses expressive motivations, it can be hypothesized that it will have a higher appeal to people with an expressive orientation to work.

In addition, people differ in the extent to which they conceive of themselves as either pragmatic or principled in their relations with others (Snyder, 1979). We propose that people with a more principled orientation to social relations will be more susceptible to leadership messages that link their behaviors and actions to ideological values.

These considerations suggest the following propositions:

**Proposition 5.** *The more the potential followers have an expressive orientation toward work and life, the more susceptible they will be to the influence of charismatic leaders.*

**Proposition 6.** *The more the potential followers have a principled orientation to social relations, the more susceptible they will be to the influence of charismatic leaders.*

## ORGANIZATIONAL CONDITIONS FOR CHARISMATIC LEADERSHIP

Current enthusiasm about charismatic and transformational leadership in the organizational literature tends to give the impression that this type of leadership is equally applicable to all organizational situations. Our analysis leads us to qualify this enthusiasm and to theoretically specify the conditions under which charismatic leadership is more likely to emerge and to be effective.

First, the organizational task is a relevant consideration. Recall that charismatic leadership gives meaning to efforts and goals by connecting them to followers' values. These values are likely to reflect, at least in part, the dominant values of society or of the subculture of potential followers. Thus, it follows that charismatic leadership is more likely to emerge and be effective when the organizational task is closely related to dominant social values to which potential followers are exposed than when it is unrelated to such values or contradicts them. In the former case, it is easier to translate followers' dominant values into a mission.

To take an obvious example, at this time in the United States, charismatic leadership is more likely to emerge in high technology industries whose tasks can be easily linked to values such as scientific and economic progress and national pride, than in the production of tobacco, which may be perceived to contradict the dominant value of health. In other words, the situation has to offer at least some opportunities for "moral" involvement. Otherwise, charismatic leadership cannot emerge.

Second, charismatic leadership is more likely to be relevant under conditions that do not favor leadership based on the use of extrinsic rewards and punishments. The use of extrinsic incentives requires certain organizational conditions to be effective, among them the ability of the leader to specify and clarify goals, considerable available knowledge about the means for achieving them, objective or highly consensual ways of measuring performance, and a high degree of discretion in the allocation of rewards on the basis of performance. Under such conditions, the utilitarian and calculative logic of a leader who uses extrinsic motivation can be clarified to the followers and adhered to by the leader (House, 1971). We propose that charismatic leadership is more likely to emerge when performance goals cannot be easily specified and measured, and when leaders cannot link extrinsic rewards to individual performance.

Mischel (1973) describes such conditions as "weak psychological situations," which are not uniformly construed in the same way by all observers, do not generate uniform expectancies concerning desired behavior, do not provide sufficient performance incentives, or fail to provide the learning conditions required for successful construction of behavior. In such "weak" situations, followers' self-concepts, values, and identities can be more readily appealed to and engaged. Furthermore, in the absence of clear extrinsic justifications for behavior, followers are more likely to look for self-related justifications for their efforts (Bem 1982) and thus become more prone to the influence of charismatic leadership.

Third, charismatic leadership may be more appropriate under exceptional conditions, such as those requiring nonroutine and unusually high performance, in order to prevail and be effective, such as crises of high levels of uncertainty. When conditions change or when the situation requires exceptional efforts, behaviors, and sacrifices, extrinsically motivated leadership is not likely to be effective, since it is by definition "conditional" and these situations require "unconditional" commitment. Furthermore, in unstable conditions or when a new organization is being formed, there is more ambiguity and anxiety and a greater need for orientation on the part of organizational members. Under such conditions, members are more likely to look for charismatic leaders and to accept their definitions of the organization's identity and its mission.

Three related points are worth noting. First, exceptional circumstances are not a necessary condition for the emergence of charismatic leadership. Our analysis does not rule out the possibility of charismatic leadership in nonexceptional situations. For instance, members may be alienated from the existing organizational order under routine situations, and charismatic leadership may emerge to lead a movement to alleviate such alienating conditions (Boal and Bryson, 1988). Second, exceptional conditions do not necessarily imply crisis situations. They may include situations of exceptional opportunities as well. Crises are not necessary for the emergence of charismatic leaders (Willner, 1984; Conger and

Kanungo, 1987). Third, when crisis-handling leaders have charismatic effects, these effects will be short-term unless the leader can relate the handling of the crisis to a higher purpose that has intrinsic validity for the actors (Boal and Bryson, 1988, p. 17).

Based on the above reasoning, we suggest the following proposition:

**Proposition 7.** *The emergence and effectiveness of charismatic leaders will be facilitated to the extent to which:*

(a) There is an opportunity for substantial moral involvement on the part of the leader and the followers.

(b) Performance goals cannot be easily specified and measured.

(c) Extrinsic rewards cannot be made clearly contingent on individual performance.

(d) There are few situational cues, constraints and reinforcers to guide behavior and provide incentives for specific performance.

(e) Exceptional effort, behavior, and sacrifices are required of both the leaders and followers.

## CONCLUSION

In this paper, we have focused on certain fundamental effects of charismatic leaders on followers. We have argued that these effects are produced by leadership actions that implicate the self-concept of the followers, and engage the related motivations for self-expression, self-esteem, self-worth, and self-consistency. Our argument has resulted in a theory that links leader behavior and follower effects through follower self-concepts. According to this theory, leader behaviors activate self-concepts which in turn affect further motivational mechanisms. These intervening variables and processes in turn have a strong positive impact on the behaviors and psychological states of followers. Hopefully, our explanation helps to provide greater insights concerning the charismatic leadership phenomenon.

The outcome of our analysis is a theoretical extension of current theories of charismatic and transformational leadership. We recognize that the theory is speculative. However, we believe such speculation is warranted because it provides an explanation and accounts for the rather profound effects of charismatic leader behaviors demonstrated in prior research.

Some scholars have voiced skepticism concerning whether or not leaders can make a difference in organizational performance (Pfeffer, 1977; Salancik and Pfeffer, 1977; Meindl, Ehrlich, and Dukerich, 1985). This skepticism reflects the argument that people are biased toward over-attributing to leaders influence on events which are complex and difficult to understand. As a result, leadership in general, and charismatic leadership in particular, could be dismissed as an exaggerated perception on the part of the followers which does not have strong substantive effects on organizational outcomes, and is therefore not worthy of much attention by students of organizations.

Others, notably Meindl (1990), have criticized charismatic leadership theories for being much too "leader-centered." Meindl has offered a "follower-oriented" approach as an alternative to the conventional theories. In his view, the charismatic effects are a function of social psychological forces operating among followers, subordinates, and observers, rather than arising directly out of the interactions between followers and leaders. According to Meindl, these social-psychological forces are functionally autonomous from the traits and behaviors of the leaders per se. Therefore, according to this radical perspective, leader behavior and leader traits should be deleted from explanations of charismatic leadership.

Obviously, we do not accept this extreme position. We believe that the evidence for the effects of charismatic leadership is too strong to be dismissed. We view Meindl's (1990) ideas as complementary, rather than contradictory, to the theory presented here. The self-processes we have described can be influenced by inter-follower processes as well as by leader behaviors. Followers' self-concepts and the related motivations can be engaged by informal role models and other social influence processes that occur among peers. This does not rule out, however, the potentiality for self-engagement as a result of charismatic leader behaviors, nor does it rule out the possibility that leaders will be instrumental in the initiation or orchestration of such inter-follower processes.

We have presented our arguments in the form of testable propositions. The theory presented here also suggests the ways in which follower attributes and organizational conditions can moderate the charismatic leadership process. Our assumptions and theoretical propositions do not contradict existing models of motivation; rather, they suggest the existence of additional motivational mechanisms without which the transformational effects of charismatic leadership cannot be explained. Hopefully, the theory advanced here will be pruned, modified, and extended as a result of future empirical testing.

---

# References

Ashforth, B. E and F. Mael (1989), "Social Identity Theory and the Organization," *Academy of Management Review,* 14, 1, 20–39.

Ashour, A. S. (1982), "A Framework for a Cognitive Behavioral Theory of Leader Influence and Effectiveness," *Organizational Behavior and Human Performance,* 30, 407–430.

Avolio, B. J. and B. M. Bass (1987), "Charisma and Beyond," in J. G. Hunt, B. R. Baliga, H. P. Dachler, and C. A. Schreisheim (Eds.), *Emerging Leadership Vistas,* Lexington: MA: D.C. Heath and Company.

——, D. A. Waldman and W. O. Einstein (1988), "Transformational Leadership in Management Game Simulation," *Group and Organization Studies,* 13, 1, 59–80.

Bandura, A. (1986), *Social Foundations of Thought and Action: A Social Cognitive Theory,* Englewood Cliffs, NJ: Prentice-Hall.

Bass, B. M. (1985), *Leadership and Performance Beyond Expectations,* New York: The Free Press.

——, (1990) *Bass & Stogdill's Handbook of Leadership,* 3rd ed., New York: The Free Press.

——, B. J. Avolio and L. Goodheim (1987), "Biographical Assessment of Transformational Leadership at the World-Class Level," *Journal of Management,* 13, 7–19.

—— and F. J. Yammarino (1988), "Long Term Forecasting of Transformational Leadership and Its Effects among Naval Officers: Some Preliminary Findings," *Technical Report No. ONR-TR-2,* Arlington, VA: Office of Naval Research.

Bellah, R. N., R. Madsen, W. M. Sullivan, A. Swidler and S. M. Tipton (1985), *Habits of the Heart: Individualism and Commitment in American Life,* New York: Harper & Row.

Bem, D. J. (1982), "Self-Perception Theory," in L. Berkowitz (Ed.), *Advances in Experimental Social Psychology,* Vol. 6, New York: Academic Press.

Bennis, W. and B. Nanus (1985), *Leaders: The Strategies for Taking Charge,* New York: Harper & Row.

Boal, K. B. and J. M. Bryson (1988), "Charismatic Leadership: A Phenomenological and Structural Approach," in J. G. Hunt, B. R. Baliga, H. P. Dachler, and C. A. Schriesheim (Eds.) *Charismatic Leadership,* San Francisco: Jossey-Bass, 11–28.

Burns, J. M. (1978), *Leadership,* New York: Harper & Row.

Callero, P. J. (1985), "Role Identity Salience," *Social Psychology Quarterly,* 48, 3, 203–215.

Conger, J. A. and R. A. Kanungo (1987), "Towards a Behavioral Theory of Charismatic Leadership in Organizational Settings," *Academy of Management Review,* 12, 637–647.

Csikszentmihalyi, M. and E. Rochberg-Halton (1981). *The Meaning of Things: Domestic Symbols and the Self,* New York: Cambridge University Press.

Curphy, G. J. (1990), "An Empirical Study of Bass" (1985) *Theory of Transformational and Transactional Leadership,* Unpublished Doctoral Dissertation, The University of Minnesota.

Eden, D. (1990), *Pygmalion in Management,* Lexington, MA: D. C. Heath and Co.

Evans, G. (1970), "The Effects of Supervisory Behavior on the Path-Goal Relationship," *Organizational and Human Performance,* 5, 277–298.

Gecas, V. (1982), "The Self Concept," *Annual Review of Sociology,* 8, 1–33.

Goffman, E. (1974), *Frame Analysis,* Cambridge: Harvard University Press.

Goldthorpe, J. G., D. Lockwood, F. Beechofer and J. Platt (1968), *The Affluent Worker: Industrial Attitudes and Behavior,* Cambridge: Cambridge University Press.

Graen, G. and J. F. Cashman (1975), "A Role-Making Model of Leadership in Formal Organizations: A Developmental Approach," in J. G. Hunt, and L. L. Larson (Eds.), *Leadership Frontiers,* Kent, OH: Kent State University Press, 143–165.

Hater, J. J. and B. M. Bass (1988), "Supervisor's Evaluations and Subordinates' Perceptions of Transformational Leadership," *Journal of Applied Psychology,* 73, 695–702.

Hodgkinson, C. (1983), *The Philosophy of Leadership,* New York: St. Martin's Press.

Hollander, E. P. (1964), *Leaders, Groups, and Influence,* New York: Oxford University Press.

House, R. J. (1971), "A Path Goal Theory of Leader Effectiveness," *Administrative Science Quarterly,* 16, 3, 321–338.

——, (1977), "A 1976 Theory of Charismatic Leadership," in J. G. Hunt and L. L. Larson (Eds.), *Leadership: The Cutting Edge,* Carbondale: Southern Illinois University Press.

——, Howell, J. M., Shamir, B., Smith, B. J. and Spangler, W. D. (1991), "A 1991 Theory of Charismatic Leadership," Graduate School of Business Administration, University of Western Ontario, London, Ontario, Canada.

——, W. D. Spangler and J. Woycke (1991), Personality and Charisma in the U.S. Presidency: A Psychological

Theory of Leadership Effectiveness, *Administrative Science Quarterly* (in press).

Howell, J. M. (1988), "Two Faces of Charisma: Socialized and Personalized Leadership in Organizations," in J. A. Conger and R. N. Kanungo (Eds.), *Charismatic Leadership,* 213–236, San Francisco: Jossey-Bass.

—— and P. J. Frost (1989), "A Laboratory Study of Charismatic Leadership," *Organizational Behavior and Human Decision Process,* 43, 2, 243–269.

—— and C. Higgins (1990), "Champions of Technological Innovation," *Administrative Science Quarterly,* 35, 317–341.

Jahoda, M. (1981), "Work Employment and Unemployment: Values, Theories and Approaches in Social Research," *American Psychologist,* 36, 184–191.

Johnson, M. P. (1982), "Social and Cognitive Features of the Dissolution of a Commitment to a Relationship," in S. Duch (Ed.), *Personal Relationships,* London: Academic Press.

Kanter, R. M. (1967), "Commitment and Social Organization: A Study of Commitment Mechanisms in Utopian Communities," *American Sociological Review,* 33, 4, 499–517.

Kelman, H. C. (1958), "Compliance, Identification and Internalization: Three Processes of Attitude Change," *Journal of Conflict Resolution,* 2, 51–60.

Kinder, D. R. and D. O. Sears (1985), "Public Opinion and Political Action, in and G. Lindsey and E. Aronson (Eds.), *Handbook of Social Psychology,* 3rd ed., New York: Random House.

Kuhnert, K. W. and P. Lewis (1987), "Transactional and Transformational Leadership: A Constructive/Developmental Analysis," *Academy of Management Review,* 12, 648–657.

McCall, G. H. and J. T. Simmons (1978), *Identities and Interaction,* revised ed., New York: Free Press.

McHugh, P. (1968), *Defining the Situation: The Organization of Meaning in Social Interaction,* Indianapolis: Bobbs-Merril.

Meindl, J. R. (1990), "On Leadership: An Alternative to the Conventional Wisdom," in B. M. Straw and L. L. Cummings (Eds.), *Research in Organizational Behavior,* 12, Greenwich, CT: JAI Press, 159–203.

——, S. B. Ehrlich, and J. M. Dukerich (1985), "The Romance of Leadership," *Administrative Science Quarterly,* 30, 78–102.

—— and M. J. Lerner (1983), "The Heroic Motive: Some Experimental Demonstrations," *Journal of Experimental Social Psychology,* 19, 1–20.

Mischel, W. (1973), "Toward a Cognitive Social Learning Reconceptulization of Personality," *Psychological Review,* 80, 200–213.

O'Reilly and J. Chatman (1986), "Organizational Commitment and Psychological Attachment: The Effects of

Compliance, Identification and Internalization on Prosocial Behavior," *Journal of Applied Psychology,* 71, 3, 492–499.

Organ, D. W. (1988), *Organizational Citizenship Behavior,* Lexington, MA: Lexington Books.

Pereria, D. (1987), "Factors Associated with Transformational Leadership in an Indian Engineering Firm," Paper Presented at Administrative Science Association of Canada.

Pfeffer, J. (1977), "The Ambiguity of Leadership," *Academy of Management Review,* 2, 104–112.

Podsakoff, P. M., S. B. Mackenzie, R. H. Moorman and R. Fetter (1990), "Transformational Leader Behaviors and Their Effects on Followers' Trust in Leader, Satisfaction, and Organizational Citizenship Behaviors," *Leadership Quarterly,* 1, 2, 107–142.

Podsakoff, P. M., W. D. Todor and R. Skov (1982), "Effects of Leader Performance Contingent and Non-Contingent Reward and Punishment Behaviors on Subordinate Performance and Satisfaction," *Academy of Management Journal,* 25, 812–821.

Prentice, D. A. (1987), "Psychological Correspondence of Possessions, Attitudes and Values," *Journal of Personality and Social Psychology,* 53, 6, 993–1003.

Puffer, S. M. (1990), "Attributions of Charismatic Leadership: The Impact of Decision Style, Outcome, and Observer Characteristics," *Leadership Quarterly,* 1, 3, 177–192.

Roberts, N. (1985), "Transforming Leadership: A Process of Collective Action," *Human Relations,* 38, 1023–46.

Roberts, N. C. and R. T. Bradley (1988), "The Limits of Charisma," in J. A. Conger and R. N. Kanungo (Eds.), *Charismatic Leadership: The Elusive Factor in Organizational Effectiveness,* San Francisco: Jossey-Bass.

Salancik, G. R. (1977). "Commitment and the Control of Organizational Behavior and Belief," in B. M. Staw, and G. R. Salancik, (Eds.), *New Directions in Organizational Behavior,* Chicago: St. Clair, 1–54.

—— and J. Pfeffer (1977), "Constraints on Administrators' Discretion: The Limited Influence of Mayors on City Budgets," *Urban Affairs Quarterly,* June.

Santee, R. and S. Jackson (1979), "Commitment to Self-Identification: A Sociopsychological Approach to Personality," *Human Relations,* 32, 141–158.

Sashkin, M. (1988), "The Visionary Leader," in J. A Conger and R. A. Kanungo (Eds.), *Charismatic Leadership: The Elusive Factor in Organizational Effectiveness,* San Francisco: Jossey-Bass, 122–160.

Schlenker, B. R. (1985), "Identity and Self-Identification," in B. R. Schlenker (Ed.), *The Self and Social Life,* New York: McGraw-Hill.

Shamir, B. (1991) "Meaning, Self and Motivation in Organizations," *Organization Studies,* 12, 405–424.

Smith, B. J. (1982), *An Initial Test of a Theory of Charismatic Leadership Based on the Responses of Subordinates,* Unpublished Doctoral Dissertation, University of Toronto, Canada.

Snow, D. A., E. B. Rochford, S. K. Worden and R. D. Benford (1986), "Frame Alignment Processes, Micromobilization and Movement Participation," *American Sociological Review,* 51, August, 464–481.

Snyder, M. (1979) "Self Monitoring Processes," in L. Berkowitz (Ed.), *Advances in Experimental Social Psychology,* 12, New York: Academic Press, 85–128.

—— and W. Ickes (1985), "Personality and Social Behavior," in G. Lindzey, and E. Aronson, *Handbook of Social Psychology,* 3rd ed., New York: Random House.

Staw, B. M. (1980), "Rationality and Justification in Organizational Life," in B. M. Staw, and L. L. Cummings (Eds.), *Research in Organizational Behavior,* 2, Greenwich, CT: JAI Press, 45–80.

Strauss, A. L. (1969), *Mirrors and Masks,* London: M. Robertson.

Stryker, S. (1980), *Symbolic Interactionism: A Social Structural Version,* Menlo Park, CA: The Benjamin/Cummings Publishing Company.

Tajfel, H. and J. C. Turner (1985), "Social Identity Theory and Intergroup Behavior," in S. Worchel and W. G. Austin (Eds.), *Psychology of Intergroup Relations,* 2nd ed., Chicago: Nelson-Hall, 7–24.

Tichy, N. M. and M. A. Devanna (1986), *The Transformational Leader,* New York: Wiley.

Trice, H. M. and J. M. Beyer (1986), "Charisma and Its Routinization in Two Social Movement Organizations," in B. M. Staw and L. L. Cummings (Eds.), *Research in Organizational Behavior,* Greenwich, CT: JAI Press, 113–164.

Turner, R. H. (1968), "The Self Conception in Social Interaction," in G. Gordon and R. Gergen (Eds.), *The Self in Social Interaction,* New York: Wiley.

Waldman, D. A., B. M. Bass and W. O. Einstein (1987), "Leadership and Outcomes of Performance Appraisal Processes," *Journal of Occupational Psychology,* 60, 177–186.

Willner, A. R. (1984), *The Spellbinders: Charismatic Political Leadership,* New Haven, CT: Yale University Press.

Yukl, G. A. (1989), *Leadership in Organizations.* 2nd ed., Englewood Cliffs, NJ: Prentice-Hall.

—— and D. D. Van Fleet (1982) "Cross-Situational, Multimethod Research on Military Leader Effectiveness." *Organizational Behavior and Human Performance,* 30, 87–108.

## References Added in Proof

House, R. J. and J. M. Howell (1992), "Personality and Charismatic Leadership," *Leadership Quarterly,* 3, 2, 81–108.

Howell, J. M. and B. J. Avolio (1993), "Transformational Leadership, Transactional Leadership, Locus of Control and Support for Innovation: Key Predictors of Consolidated-business-unit Performance," *Journal of American Psychology,* 78, 6, in press.

Keller, R. T. (in press), "Transformational Leadership and the Performance of Research and Development Project Groups," *Journal of Management.*

Kirkpatrick, S. A. (1992), "Decomposing Charismatic Leadership: The Effects of Leader Content and Process on Follower Performance, Attitudes, and Perceptions," Unpublished Doctoral Dissertation, University of Maryland, College Park.

Koene, H., H. Pennings and M. Schreuder (1991), "Leadership, Culture, and Organizational Effectiveness," Paper Presented at the Center for Creative Leadership Conference, Boulder, Colorado.

Koh, W. L., J. R. Terborg, and R. M. Steers (1991), "The impact of Transformational Leaders on Organization Commitment, Organizational Citizenship Behavior, Teacher Satisfaction and Student Performance in Singapore," Academy of Management Meetings, August, 1991, Miami, FL.

Locke, E. A. and G. P. Latham (1990), *A Theory of Goal Setting and Task Performance,* Englewood Cliffs, NJ: Prentice-Hall.

Waldman, D. A. and Ramirez (1992), "CEO Leadership and Organizational Performance: The Moderating Effect of Environmental Uncertainty," Concordia University Working Paper 92-10-37, p. 59.

**Reading 39**

# Relationship of Transformational and Transactional Leadership with Employee Influencing Strategies

**Ronald J. Deluga**
Bryant College

Effective leadership implies an understanding of how managers and employees influence one another (Yates, 1985). Of particular importance to the practicing manager is the relationship of leadership style to employee influencing behavior. Could the manager's leadership style encourage constructive or destructive employee influencing? That is, in what ways could this interaction affect such critical organizational outcomes as manager effectiveness and employee satisfaction with the manager? The implications of these influencing dynamics on organizational productivity and employee developmental needs seem apparent. Thus the purpose of this study was to investigate the nature of managerial leadership and employee-influencing systems in a manufacturing environment. Transactional and transformational leadership have been two approaches offering an explanation as to how managers-employees influence one another (Bass, 1981, 1985a; Burns, 1978; Hollander, 1985).

Burns (1978) argues that leadership can be understood best as either a transactional or a transformational process. Transactional leadership suggests that most managers engage in a bargaining relationship with employees (Hollander, 1978). Bass (1981, 1985a) cites contingent reward and management-by-exception as two factors that emerge with transactional leadership. Contingent reward describes the familiar work-for-pay agreement. Employees are told what they need to do to obtain rewards. Management-by-exception characterizes how the manager reacts primarily to employee errors. The manager exerts corrective action only when employees fail to meet performance objectives.

On the other hand, transformational leadership differs from transactional leadership. The transformational manager cultivates employee acceptance of the work group mission. The manager–

employee relationship is one of mutual stimulation and is characterized by four factors, including (1) charisma, (2) inspiration, (3) individual consideration, and (4) intellectual stimulation (Bass, 1985a).

First, charisma is the fundamental factor in the transformational process. Charisma is the leader's ability to generate great symbolic power with which the employees want to identify. Employees idealize the leader and often develop a strong emotional attachment (Bass, 1985a).

Closely related to charisma is inspiration. Inspiration describes how the leader passionately communicates a future idealistic organization that can be shared. The leader uses visionary explanations to depict what the employee work group can accomplish. Excited employees are then motivated to achieve organizational objectives (Bass, 1985a).

Third, individual consideration characterizes how the leader serves as an employee mentor. He or she treats employees as individuals and uses a developmental orientation that responds to employee needs and concerns (Bass, 1985a).

Finally, intellectual stimulation describes how transformational leaders encourage employees to approach old and familiar problems in new ways. By stimulating novel employee thinking patterns, employees question their own beliefs and learn creatively to solve problems by themselves (Bass, 1985a).

Transformational and transactional leaders differ in another important respect. The typical manager is a transactional leader who analyzes employee lower-level needs and determines their goals (Zaleznik, 1983). That is, she or he attempts to satisfy the employee's basic wants and works to maintain the organizational status quo. However, the transactional leader also limits the employee's (1) effort toward goals, (2) job satisfaction, and (3) effectiveness toward contributing to organizational goals (Bass, 1985a). Bass (1986) suggests that transactional leadership is acceptable as far as it goes, but fundamentally is a prescription for organizational mediocrity.

**Source:** Edited and reprinted with permission from R. J. Deluga, *Group and Organization Studies* 13, no. 4. (1988), pp. 456–67. Copyright (1988) by Sage Publications. Author affiliation may have changed since article was first published.

Conversely, transformational leaders incorporate and amplify the impact of transactional leadership (Waldman, Bass, & Einstein, 1985). They recognize and exploit those employee higher-level needs that surpass immediate self-interests. By appealing to these elevated needs, the transformational leader motivates employees to perform beyond initial performance goals and objectives (Bass, 1985a); Burns, 1978; Tichy & Devanna, 1986).

## HYPOTHESES

Transactional and transformational leadership theories have contributed to the understanding of manager–employee influencing processes. However, just how manager–employee influencing networks interact has been cited as an under-developed research area requiring further methodological exploration (Ansari & Kapoor, 1987; Bass, 1985a; Crowe, Bochner & Clark, 1972; Kipnis, Schmidt, & Wilkinson, 1980; Tichy & Devanna, 1986). Thus the purpose of the study was to compare manager–employee influencing dynamics within the framework of the transformational and transactional leadership approaches.

As expressed in manager–employee influencing relationships, it seems reasonable that managers who have organizational support, multiple sources of power, and control resources valued by employees, and who are perceived to be in a position of dominance (French & Raven, 1959; Podsakoff & Schriesheim, 1985) would display stronger influencing patterns relative to employees. An accelerated managerial ability to influence would seemingly further diminish employees' influencing capability. Following the same mechanism, employees experiencing a favorable power position would likewise display an influencing advantage. Therefore:

**H1:** *Perceived transformational and transactional leadership (manager downward influencing behavior) will be inversely related to reported employee upward influencing behavior.*

Transactional leaders were described as engaging in an exchange relationship with employees. As such, it appears plausible that the flow of influencing behavior may constantly fluctuate in response to manager–employee comparative bargaining strength. Managers perceived as transactional would then seem to be more likely targets of employee influencing activity. Therefore:

**H2:** *Perceived transactional leadership will be more strongly inversely related to reported employee upward influencing behavior than transformational leadership.*

If in fact transactional leaders are subject to more employee influencing, the less volatile transformational manager–employee influencing behavior may minimize distractions and promote both leader effectiveness and employee satisfaction. Therefore:

**H3:** *Perceived transformational leadership will be more closely associated with reported leader effectiveness and employee satisfaction with the leader than transactional leadership.*

In terms of day-to-day managerial implications, the influencing activity predicted for transactional leadership may be organizationally detrimental. Managers and employees may take turns with the carrot and stick as their negotiating positions change. Lingering resentment could further escalate the game playing. For instance, an employee may feel he or she was unfairly denied a much-wanted promotion. At a later time, the relative power position could shift in favor of the employee. She or he may then feel compelled to seek revenge by withholding valued skills and knowledge.

On the other hand, the stability predicted for transformational leader–employee influencing behavior could be organizationally advantageous. Both the manager and employees would be jointly working toward shared group goals, rather than being diverted by the urge to repay past slights.

## METHOD

### PARTICIPANTS AND PROCEDURE

The target population was 400 exempt and nonexempt employees of a manufacturing firm located in a lower-middle-class multi-ethnic area of the Northeast. All were nonunion employees. After reading an explanatory page indicating company support and detailing instructions, volunteer employees completed a confidential self-report questionnaire. The questionnaire contained the leadership style and satisfaction with leadership instruments (Part I) as well as the upward influence strategy instrument (Part II). To encourage participation, all employees completing the questionnaire received a free coffee and donut. Also, participants had their names entered into a random drawing for the opportunity to win a day off with pay or a pair of state lottery ticks.

Over five working days, 117 usable questionnaires (29.3 percent) from 41 males and 76 females were anonymously returned to a box located in the factory cafeteria. Respondents included upper-level managers (23 percent), middle/entry-level managers (21 percent), manual laborers (36 percent), and "other" (20 percent) who represented the manufacturing (39.87 percent), international (28 percent), creative/marketing (31.5 percent), finance/administration (11.1 percent), and sales/merchandising (14.8 percent) departments. . . .

Strategies used by subordinates to influence their superiors were measured by Form M of the Profile of Organizational Influence Strategies (POIS-M) (Kipnis & Schmidt, 1982). The 27-item behavioral-based instruments assess how frequently an employee reports using each of six behavioral strategies directed as a first attempt and, when encountering resistance, as a second attempt toward influencing the manager. The strategies assessed by the POIS-M include:

(1) *Friendliness* is designed to create a favorable impression through flattering or "buttering up" the manager.

(2) *Bargaining* involves exchanging benefits and making deals.

(3) *Reason* is the use of facts and data to support the development of a logical argument.

(4) *Assertiveness* includes the use of a direct and forceful approach.

(5) *Higher authority* is "going over the boss's head" to gain support.

(6) *Coalition* is the mobilization of other employees to collectively influence the manager. . . .

## DISCUSSION

The findings appeared to support the hypotheses that perceived managerial downward influencing behavior would be inversely related to reported employee upward influencing behavior. Similarly, the data suggest that as compared to transformational leadership, transactional leadership does promote more influencing activity between managers and employees. Finally, transformational leadership was found to be more closely associated with leader effectiveness and employee satisfaction than was transactional leadership.

Therefore, further discussion of these findings seems warranted.

## TRANSACTIONAL LEADERSHIP

The transactional manager enters into an exchange relationship with employees and reacts primarily only when goals are not met (Bass, 1985a). It would appear that as employees fall short of expectations, the employee's bargaining position is eroded, while that of the manager is correspondingly strengthened. At the same time, alert employees aware of their own vulnerable position may conclude that influencing attempts would be futile or even professionally harmful. The manager subsequently can use her or his multiple sources of power (French & Raven, 1959; Podsakoff & Schriesheim, 1985), that is, reward and punishment, to control valued outcomes and influence employee performance. The process seems feasible, as previous studies have proposed that employee performance does appear to influence manager behavior (Greene, 1976; Sims, 1977; Sims & Szilagyi, 1978; Szilagyi, 1980).

The volatile process may also operate to the employee's advantage. Due to their own unique sources of power, such as expertise, effort, commitment, and access to valued facilities (Mechanic, 1962; Porter, Allen, & Angle, 1983), employees operating from a position of more relative strength may be able to obtain a greater flow of organizational benefits.

An example of this influencing process can occur when an employee has failed to meet recent sales goals. He or she is obviously in a weak negotiating position and is not likely to succeed in gaining the desired larger office, preferred vacation schedule, or a monetary bonus. In fact, the manager would probably use these desired benefits to influence the employee to reach the sales goals. However, employees may resent this carrot-and-stick approach and seek to retaliate as sales and bargaining strength improve. The retaliation may take the form of unreasonable demands to compensate for perceived slights or even through accepting a position with a competitor. As proposed above, the flow of power and influence may constantly fluctuate as a function of transactional manager–employee comparative power base potency. Associated dysfunctional "game playing" may result in marginal organizational performance.

# TRANSFORMATIONAL LEADERSHIP

The findings supported the prediction that relative to transactional manager–employee relationships, transformational manager–employee interactions would exhibit more stable influencing activity. This apparent equilibrium is indicated by these findings in two ways. First, the transformational manager–employee influencing patterns appear less volatile. Fewer and less severe inverse relationships are evident. Second, employees reported significantly greater satisfaction with transformational leadership and viewed the approach as more effective.

The transformational leader–employee interactions may be more balanced since the manager and satisfied employees both jointly and effectively work toward the organizational mission. Perhaps the vision of a common goal as articulated by the transformational leader has relegated harmful organizational game playing to a subordinate role.

For example, company sales may be plummeting due to the impact of a foreign competitor. The transformational leader emotionally arouses employees to collectively meet the foreign challenge and inspires them to extra effort and greater accomplishment. Employees are not occupied by what they may individually bargain for as a result of the crisis. Rather, employees are motivated to succeed beyond their immediate self-interests and to achieve the goals of organizational survival and prosperity.

## IMPLICATIONS

The battles among competing and mutually exclusive interests usually claim a high price in management attention; the focus of an entire organization may be adversely affected by turbulence in the internal balance of power (Selznick, 1957). The major point is that the transformational approach appears to alter destructive influencing networks created by fluctuating manager–employee power differences. In return, the organization will experience dividends in organizational productivity.

Implications for fostering transformationally oriented organizational cultures through training, job and organizational design, and human resource decisions seem clear. Bass (1986) has

suggested that training in mentoring and recognizing the varying development needs of employees can promote the transformational factor of individual consideration. Integrative problem-solving, rather than competitive (win-lose) relationships, would advance the transformational factor of intellectual stimulation. Both factors could be learned through the use of scenarios, videotapes of actual situations, and/or role playing. With appropriate feedback, work group productivity would increase. Similarly, organizations facing rapid environmental change would benefit from the flexibility nurtured by transformational leadership at all levels. For example, encouraging transformational leadership through recruiting programs, selection standards, and promotion policies seems likely to attract desirable prospects and retain valued employees.

Future studies might use longitudinal approaches examining how manager–employee influencing networks evolve over time. Perhaps the balance shifts as a function of organizational type, employee group, or internal/external environmental forces. Other investigations could systematically manipulate alternative leadership theories to further illuminate the dynamics of manager–employee influencing behavior.

## References

Ansari, M. A., & Kapoor, A. (1987). Organizational context and upward influence tactics. *Organizational Behavior and Human Decision Processes, 40,* 39–49.

Bass, B. M. (1981). *Stogdill's handbook of leadership: A survey of theory and research.* New York: Free Press.

Bass, B. M. (1985a). *Leadership and performance beyond expectations.* New York: Free Press.

Bass, B. M. (1985b). *Multifactor Leadership Questionnaire (Form 5).* Binghamton: University Center, State University of New York.

Bass, B. M. (1986). *Implications of a new leadership paradigm.* Binghamton: School of Management, State University of New York.

Burns, J. M. (1978). *Leadership.* New York: Harper.

Carmines, E. G., & Zeller, R. A. (1979). *Reliability and validity assessment.* Sage University Paper Series on Quantitative Applications in the Social Services, series no. 17. Beverly Hills, CA: Sage.

Crowe, B. J., Bochner, S., & Clark, A. W. (1972). The effects of subordinates' behavior on managerial style. *Human Relations, 25*(3), 215–237.

French, J., & Raven, B. H. (1959). The bases of social power. In D. Cartwright (Ed.), *Studies in social power* (pp. 150–167). Ann Arbor: Institute for Social Research.

Greene, C. N. (1976). A longitudinal investigation of performance-reinforcing behavior and subordinate satisfaction and performance. In S. Sikula & P. Hilgert (Eds.), *Proceedings: Midwest Division of the Academy of Management* (pp. 157–185). St. Louis: Washington University.

Hollander, E. P. (1978). *Leadership dynamics: A practical guide to effective relationships.* New York: Free Press.

Hollander, E. P. (1985). Leadership and Power. In G. Lindzey & E. Aronson (Eds.), *The handbook of social psychology: Vol. II.* (pp. 485–537). New York: Random House.

Kipnis, D., & Schmidt, S. M. (1982). *Profiles of organizational influence strategies (Form M).* San Diego: University Associates.

Kipnis, D., Schmidt, S. M., & Wilkinson, I. (1980). Intraorganizational influence tactics: Explorations in getting one's way. *Journal of Applied Psychology, 65*(4), 440–452.

Mechanic, D. (1962). Sources of power of lower participants in complex organizations. *Administrative Science Quarterly, 7*(3), 349–364.

Podsakoff, P. M., & Schriesheim, C. A. (1985). Field studies and Raven's bases of power: Critique, reanalysis, and suggestions for future research. *Psychological Bulletin, 97*(3), 387–411.

Porter, L. W., Allen, R. W., & Angle, H. L. (1983). The politics of upward influence in organizations. In L. W. Porter & R. W. Allen (Eds.), *Organizational influence processes* (pp. 408–422). Glenview, IL: Scott, Foresman.

Selznick, P. (1957). *Leadership in administration: A sociological interpretation.* Berkeley: University of California Press.

Sims, H. P. (1977). The leader as a manager of reinforcing contingencies: An empirical example and a model. In J. G. Hunt & L. L. Larson (Eds.), *Leadership: The cutting edge* (pp. 121–137). Carbondale: Southern Illinois University Press.

Sims, H. P., & Szilagyi, A. D. (1978). A causal analysis of leader behavior over three different time lags. *Proceedings: Eastern Academy of Management.*

Szilagyi, A. D. (1980). *Causal inferences in leadership: A three time period longitudinal analysis.* Working paper, University of Houston, Houston, TX.

Tichy, N. M., & Devanna, M. A. (1986). *The transformational leader.* New York: John Wiley.

Waldman, D. A., Bass, B. M., & Einstein, W. O. (1985). *Effort, performance, and transformational leadership in industrial and military service* (Working Paper 85–80). Binghamton: School of Management, State University of New York.

Yates, D. (1985). *The politics of management.* San Francisco: Jossey-Bass.

Zaleznik, A. (1983). The leadership gap. *Washington Quarterly, 6*(1), 32–39.

**Reading 40**

# Transformational Leader Behaviors and Their Effects on Followers' Trust in Leader, Satisfaction, and Organizational Citizenship Behaviors

**Philip M. Podsakoff and Scott B. MacKenzie**
Indiana University

**Robert H. Moorman**
West Virginia University

**Richard Fetter**
Indiana University

The search for and identification of those behaviors that increase a leader's effectiveness has been a major concern of practicing managers and leadership researchers alike for the past several decades (cf. Bass, 1981; House, 1971, 1988; House & Baetz, 1979; Stogdill, 1974; Yukl, 1989a, 1989b). Traditional views of leadership effectiveness have focused primarily, although not exclusively, on what Burns (1978) and Bass (1985) have called *transactional* leader behaviors. According to Burns (1978), transactional behaviors are founded on an exchange process in which the leader provides rewards in return for the subordinate's effort.

More recently, however, the focus of leadership research has shifted from one of examining the effects of transactional leadership to the identification and examination of those behaviors exhibited by the leader that make followers more aware of the importance and values of task outcomes, activate their higher-order needs, and induce them to transcend self-interests for the sake of the organization (Bass, 1985; Yukl, 1989a, 1989b). These *transformational* or *charismatic* behaviors[1] are believed to *augment* the impact of transactional leader behaviors on employee outcome variables, because "followers feel trust and respect toward the leader and they are motivated to do more than they are expected to do" (Yukl, 1989b, p. 272). Examples of this new focus on leadership include the work of House, Bass, and others (e.g., Avolio & Bass, 1988; Bass, 1985;

Bass, Avolio, & Goodheim, 1987; Bass, Waldman, Avolio, & Bebb, 1987; Bennis & Nanus, 1985; Boal & Bryson, 1988; House, 1977; House, Spangler, & Woycke, 1989; House, Woycke, & Fodor, 1988; Howell & Frost, 1989; Conger & Kanungo, 1987; Shamir, House, & Arthur, 1988; Tichy & DeVanna, 1986). While each of these approaches differs somewhat in the specific behaviors they associate with transformational leadership, all of them share the common perspective that effective leaders transform or change the basic values, beliefs, and attitudes of followers so that they are willing to perform beyond the minimum levels specified by the organization.

Preliminary research on transformational leadership has been rather promising. Some of this research (Bass, 1985; Bennis & Nanus, 1985; Boal & Bryson, 1988; Conger & Kanungo, 1987; House, 1977; House, Woycke, & Fodor, 1988; Howell & Frost, 1989; Kouzes & Posner, 1987; Tichy & DeVanna, 1986) has been primarily conceptual in nature, focusing on the identification of the key transformational behaviors, and the development of theories of their antecedents and consequences. The remainder of this research has focused on empirically testing these conceptual frameworks. Generally speaking, the empirical results have verified the impact of transformational leader behaviors on employee attitudes, effort, and "in-role" performance. For example, Bass (1985) cites a variety of field studies demonstrating that transformational leader behaviors are positively related to employees' satisfaction, self-reported effort, and job performance. Similar results have been reported by Howell and Frost (1989). They manipulated the behavior of leaders in a laboratory setting and found that charismatic leader behaviors

**Source:** Edited and reprinted with permission from *Leadership Quarterly* 1, no. 2 (1990), pp. 107–142. Copyright © 1990 by Elsevier Science. Author affiliation may have changed since article was first published.

produced better performance, greater satisfaction, and enhanced role perceptions (less role conflict) than directive leader behaviors.

Despite these encouraging results, it is important to note that the majority of the empirical research in this area has focused on the impact of transformational leader behaviors on in-role performance and follower satisfaction, rather than "extra-role" performance. While the effects of transformational behaviors on employee in-role performance are interesting, they do not capture the most important effects of transformational leader behaviors. The real essence of transformational leadership is that these leaders "lift ordinary people to extraordinary heights" (Boal & Bryson, 1988, p. 11) and cause followers to "do more than they are expected to do" (Yukl, 1989a, p. 272) and "perform beyond the level of expectations" (Bass, 1985). In other words, as noted by Graham (1988), the most important effects of transformational leaders should be on extra-role performance, rather than in-role performance. Transformational leaders should motivate followers to perform at a level "over and above mechanical compliance with the routine directives of the organization" (Katz & Kahn, 1978, p. 528).

Also surprising, given the theoretical discussions of Bennis and Nanus (1985), Boal and Bryson (1988), and Yukl (1989a, 1989b), is that a follower's *trust* in his or her leader has not been given more attention in empirical research as a potential mediator of the effects of transformational leader behaviors on criterion variables. Bennis and Nanus (1985), for example, have suggested that effective leaders are ones that earn the trust of their followers. Similarly, trust in and loyalty to the leader play a critical role in the transformational leadership model of Boal and Bryson (1988). Finally, as noted by Yukl (1989b), one of the key reasons why followers are motivated by transformational leaders to perform beyond expectations is that followers trust and respect them. Indeed, Kouzes and Posner (1987) cite several studies, all of which indicate that the leader characteristics most valued by followers are honesty, integrity, and truthfulness. Thus, trust is viewed as playing an important mediating role in the transformational leadership process.

Another potential mediator of the impact of transformational leader behaviors on extra-role performance, in addition to trust, is employee satisfaction. Organ (1988a, 1988b, in press) has reviewed empirical research which demonstrates that employee job satisfaction is an important determinant of extra-role (e.g., "organizational citizenship") behavior. Moreover, virtually all models of transformational leadership postulate that transformational leaders enhance followers' work attitudes and satisfaction. Thus, when Organ's research on the antecedents of organizational citizenship behaviors (OCBs) is combined with models of the effects of transformational leadership, satisfaction emerges as a potential mediator of the impact of transformational leader behavior on the extra-role performance of followers.

In summary, previous theoretical and empirical research suggests that there is good reason to believe that transformational leader behaviors influence extra-role or organizational citizenship behaviors. There are, however, several potential ways in which this might happen. As shown in Figure 1, one way is for transformational leader behaviors to *directly* influence organizational citizenship behaviors, much in the same way that transactional leader behaviors have been shown to influence in-role performance (e.g., Podsakoff, Todor, & Skov, 1982; Podsakoff, Todor, Grover, & Huber, 1984; Sims & Szilagyi, 1975). This is consistent with Smith, Organ, and Near's (1983) finding that a leader's individualized support behavior, one of the transformational leader behaviors identified by Bass (Avolio & Bass, 1988; Bass, 1985), has a direct effect on some forms of employee citizenship behavior (i.e., conscientiousness).

Another possibility, also depicted in Figure 1, is that transformational leader behaviors influence organizational citizenship behaviors *only indirectly,* through their effects on mediators like followers' trust in their leaders and satisfaction. For example, in addition to documenting the direct effects of leader supportiveness on conscientiousness, Smith et al. (1983) also found that employee satisfaction *mediated* the impact of leader supportiveness on employee altruism. Followers' trust in and loyalty to the leader also has been accorded a similar role in several recent discussions of the transformational leadership process (e.g., Boal & Bryson, 1988; Kouzes & Posner, 1987; Yukl, 1989b). Thus, both followers' trust and satisfaction have been identified as potential mediators of the impact of transformational leader behaviors on followers' citizenship behaviors.

Finally, it is possible that transformational leader behaviors influence followers' citizenship behaviors *both directly* and *indirectly.* Their total effects may, in other words, be due to a combination of direct (unmediated) effects, and indirect effects working through mediators like trust and satisfaction.

**FIGURE 1**   **Conceptual Relationship between Transformational Leader Behaviors, Potential Mediators, and Organizational Citizenship Behaviors**

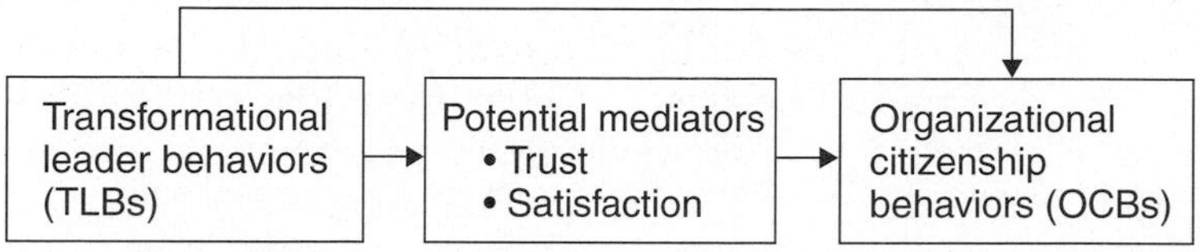

The purpose of the present study, therefore, is to examine the effects of transformational leader behaviors on organizational citizenship behaviors, and the potential mediating roles of trust and satisfaction in that process. Measures of transformational leader behaviors, trust, and satisfaction were obtained from 988 exempt employees of a large petrochemical company, and measures of these employees' citizenship behaviors were obtained from their leaders. Structural equation modeling then was used to examine the direct and indirect effects of these behaviors on trust, satisfaction, and citizenship behavior. Moreover, because Bass (Avolio & Bass, 1988; Bass, 1985) argues that the effects of transformational leadership behaviors *augment* or *supplement* the effects of transactional leadership behaviors, we examined the effects of the transformational behaviors in the empirical context of the effects of the principal transactional leader behavior identified by him—contingent reward behavior. . . .

## MEASURES

### TRANSFORMATIONAL LEADER BEHAVIORS

Although broadly speaking, the topic of transformational leadership has received a great deal of attention in recent years, our understanding of what is involved in transformational leadership still is somewhat unclear. The one thing that is clear, however, is that transformational leadership is multidimensional in nature. Our review of the extant literature suggests that there are at least six key behaviors associated with transformational leaders:

- *Identifying and articulating a vision*—Behavior on the part of the leader aimed at identifying new opportunities for his or her unit/division/ company, and developing, articulating, and inspiring others with his or her vision of the future.

- *Providing an appropriate model*—Behavior on the part of the leader that sets an example for employees to follow that is consistent with the values the leader espouses.

- *Fostering the acceptance of group goals*— Behavior on the part of the leader aimed at promoting cooperation among employees and getting them to work together toward a common goal.

- *High performance expectations*—Behavior that demonstrates the leader's expectations for excellence, quality, and/or high performance on the part of followers.

- *Providing individualized support*—Behavior on the part of the leader that indicates that he/she respects followers and is concerned about their personal feelings and needs.

- *Intellectual stimulation*—Behavior on the part of the leader that challenges followers to re-examine some of their assumptions about their work and rethink how it can be performed.

As shown in Table 1, each of these behaviors has been identified as an important element of the transformational leadership process. There is a great deal of consensus among the researchers on some of these behaviors, but not on others. For example, identifying and articulating a vision has been identified by virtually all of the authors as an important component of the transformational leadership process. Similarly, facilitating the acceptance of group goals and providing an appropriate model were identified by at least four different authors as elements of transformational leadership. In contrast, only Bass and his colleagues (Avolio & Bass, 1988; Bass, 1985) argue that intellectual stimulation should be considered an aspect of transformational leadership. However, in order to make certain that the domain of transformational leader behaviors was adequately tapped, and that our test of the impact of these behaviors was comprehensive, we chose to

**TABLE 1   Behavioral Components of Existing Models of Transformational Leadership**

| Behavioral Components | House (1977) | Bradford and Cohen (1984) | Bass (1985) | Bennis and Nanus (1985) | Tichy and DeVanna (1986) | Conger and Kanungo (1987) | Kouzes and Posner (1987) |
|---|---|---|---|---|---|---|---|
| Identify and articulate a vision | Provide an appealing vision | Determine and build a common vision | Charismatic leader behavior* | Management of attention through vision | Recognize a need for change and create a new vision | Advocate an appealing yet unconventional vision | Challenge the process and inspire a shared vision |
| Provide an appropriate model | Set an example for followers to imitate | | Charismatic leader behavior | | | Take a high personal risk to support the vision | Model the way |
| Foster the acceptance of group goals | | Build a shared responsibility team | | Work to develop commitment and trust | Team build to gain support for new vision | | Enable others to act |
| High performance expectations | Communicate high expectations of follower performance | | Inspirational leader behavior | | | | |
| Provide individualized support | | | Individualized consideration | | | Be sensitive to the needs of the followers | |
| Recognize accomplishments | | | | | | Behave with confidence and enthusiasm | Encourage the heart |
| Intellectual stimulation | | | Intellectual stimulation | | | | |
| Other | Behave to arouse individual motives | Continuously develop the skills of individuals | Charismatic leader behavior* | | | | |

Note: *Bass's (1985) conceptualization of charismatic leadership includes leader vision, as well as respect for the leader and the inspiration and encouragement provided by his or her presence.

include all six of the categories identified above in the present study. . . .

## AGGREGATE EFFECTS OF LEADER BEHAVIORS ON OCBS

An examination of the aggregate effects of the set of transformational leader behaviors on the set of organizational citizenship behaviors indicates that the effects of these leader behaviors on OCBs are *indirect,* rather than *direct,* in that they are mediated by followers' trust in their leaders. More specifically, our findings generally showed that: (*a*) transformational leader behaviors had no direct effects on OCBs, (*b*) transformational leader behaviors influenced both employee trust and satisfaction, and (*c*) trust influenced OCBs, but employee satisfaction did not. Moreover, it is important to note that these findings are completely independent of the effects of transactional leader behaviors, and also were relatively robust in comparison to the effects of common method biases.

In contrast, the effects of the transactional leader behavior (contingent rewards) on OCBs produced a markedly different pattern. Unlike the transformational leader behaviors, contingent reward behavior had a direct positive impact on both altruism and sportsmanship, but no effect at all on either trust or employee satisfaction. Thus, in contrast to the transformational behaviors, transactional leader behavior influenced OCBs *directly,* rather than indirectly. The fact that these two types of leader behavior appear to influence extra-role performance in very different ways emphasizes the importance of the distinction between transactional and transformational leader behaviors.

One possible explanation for why transactional leader behaviors have direct rather than indirect effects may have to do with the nature of the behaviors themselves. Transactional leader behaviors are ones which are founded on some sort of exchange, or give and take, between the leader and the subordinate. If, as shown by Jackson, Keith, and Schlacter (1983), managers consider both in-role and extra-role behaviors when evaluating employee performance, they may also recognize accomplishments in both of these areas as well. This may cause employees to see the performance of OCBs as a means of obtaining recognition and other forms of rewards, thus motivating them to engage in organizational citizenship behavior.

## INDIVIDUAL EFFECTS OF LEADER BEHAVIORS ON OCBs

An examination of the individual level results produced some interesting findings. The standardized estimates suggest that the "core" transformational leader behaviors, individualized support, and intellectual stimulation, were the key derminants of both trust and satisfaction. The "core" transformational behaviors and individualized support both had positive effects, as expected. However, intellectual stimulation was found to have a negative impact on both trust and satisfaction.

One possible explanation for this surprising finding may have to do with the effect of intellectual stimulation on role ambiguity, conflict, and stress. Although intellectual stimulation may produce desirable effects in the long run, it may be that in the short run, leaders who continually urge or exhort followers to search for new and better methods of doing things create ambiguity, conflict, or other forms of stress in the minds of those followers. If the increased task demands produced by a leader's intellectual stimulation behavior increase stress, ambiguity, and conflict, we might expect that followers will express less trust in the leader and engage in fewer OCBs. Indeed, this is consistent with recent research (cf., Cohen, 1980; Motowidlo, Packard, & Manning, 1986) that suggests that stress induced by increased task demands decreases interpersonal sensitivity and helping behavior.

Another possible reason why intellectual stimulation may reduce follower trust and satisfaction may have to do with the destabilizing nature of intellectual stimulation itself. According to Avolio and Bass (1988), intellectual stimulation causes a "cognitive reappraisal of current circumstances," thus possibly reversing an individual's "figure-ground" and leading to a questioning of "old" and perhaps comfortable assumptions.[2] It may be that this process is dissatisfying, and that leaders who continually do this are trusted less because they are perceived as being less predictable and/or dependable.

One additional finding of note is that high performance expectations reduced employee trust. Although it is not immediately obvious why this occurred, it may have to do with the way in which we measured high performance expectations. House (1977) suggests that two aspects of high performance expectations are important. One is that the leader must communicate those expectations to his/her subordinates. The other is that the leader must let them know that he/she is confident they can meet these expectations. In retrospect, our measure seems to do a good job of tapping the former component, but not the latter. It may be natural for an employee to distrust a leader who continually demands high levels of performance without ever expressing any confidence in the employee's ability to achieve those expectations. . . .

## Notes

1. Although there are differences between transformational and charismatic leader behaviors, they are similar in many respects. The principal reason we chose to use the term transformational leadership is that it is broader in the sense that it includes a wider variety of leader behaviors. Thus, unless otherwise indicated in our discussion, we will use the term transformational leadership throughout the paper. . . .

2. We would like to thank one anonymous reviewer for pointing out this possibility.

## References

Alexander, S., & Ruderman, M. (1987). The role of procedural and distributive justice in organizational behavior. *Social Justice Research, 1,* 177–198.

Avolio, B. J., & Bass, B. M. (1988). Transformational leadership, charisma, and beyond. In J. G. Hunt, B. R. Baliga, H. P. Dachler, & C. A. Schriesheim (Eds.), *Emerging leadership vistas* (pp. 29–49). Lexington, MA: Lexington Books.

Bagozzi, R. P. (1978). The construct validity of the affective, behavioral, and cognitive components of attitude by analysis of covariance structures. *Multivariate Behavioral Research, 13,* 9–31.

Bagozzi, R. P. (1980). *Causal models in marketing.* New York: Wiley.

Bass, B. M. (1981). *Stogdill's handbook of leadership* (rev. ed.). New York: Free Press.

Bass, B. M. (1985). *Leadership and performance beyond expectations.* New York: Free Press.

Bass, B. M., Avolio, B. J., & Goodheim, L. (1987). Biography and the assessment of transformational leadership at the world class level. *Journal of Management,* 13, 7–19.

Bass, B. M., Waldman, D. A., Avolio, B. J., & Bebb, M. (1987). Transformational leadership and the falling dominoes effect. *Group and Organization Studies,* 12, 73–87.

Batesman, T. S., & Organ, D. W. (1983). Job satisfaction and the good soldier: The relationship between affect and employee "citizenship." *Academy of Management Journal,* 26, 587–595.

Bennis, W., & Nanus, B. (1985) *Leaders: The strategies for taking charge.* New York: Harper & Row.

Bentler, P. M., & Bont, D. G. (1980). Significance tests and goodness of fit in the analysis of covariance structures. *Psychological Bulletin,* 88, 588–606.

Boal, K. B., & Bryson, J. M. (1988). Charismatic leadership: A phenomenological and structural approach. In J. G. Hunt, B. R. Baliga, H. P. Dachler, & C. A. Schriesheim (Eds.), *Emerging Leadership Vistas* (pp. 5–28). Lexington, MA: Lexington Books.

Bradford, D. L., & Cohen, A. R. (1984). *Managing for excellence: The guide to developing high performance in contemporary organizations.* New York: Wiley.

Burnkrant, R. E., & Page, T. J., Jr. (1982). An examination of the convergent, discriminant, and predictive validity of Fishbein's behavioral intention model. *Journal of Marketing Research, 19,* 550–561.

Burns, J. M. (1978). *Leadership.* New York: Harper & Row.

Churchill, G. A., Jr. (1979). A paradigm for developing better measures of marketing constructs. *Journal of Marketing Research, 16,* 64–73.

Cohen, S. (1980). Aftereffects of stress on human performance and social behavior: A review of research and theory. *Psychological Bulletin, 88,* 82–108.

Conger, J. A., & Kanungo, R. N. (1987). Toward a behavioral theory of charismatic leadership in organizational settings. *Academy of Management Review, 12,* 637–647.

Cook, J., & Wall, T. (1980). New work attitude measures of trust, organizational commitment and personal need non-fulfillment. *Journal of Occupational Psychology, 53,* 39–52.

Dansereau, F., Jr., Graen, G., & Haga, W. J. (1975). A vertical dyad linkage approach to leadership within formal organizations: A longitudinal investigation of the role-making process. *Organizational Behavior and Human Performance, 13,* 46–78.

Dunham, R. B., Smith, F. J., & Blackburn, R. S. (1977). Validation of the index of organizational reactions with the JDI, the MSQ, and the faces scales. *Academy of Management Journal, 20,* 420–432.

Folger, R. (1977). Distributive and procedural justice: Combined impact of "voice" and improvement on experienced inequity. *Journal of Personality and Psychology, 35,* 108–119.

Folger, R. (1986). Rethinking equity theory. In H. W. Bierhof, R. L. Cohen, & J. Greenberg, (Eds.), *Justice in Social Relations* (pp. 145–162). New York: Plenum.

Folger, R. (1987). Distributive and procedural justice in the workplace. *Social Justice Research, 1,* 143–159.

Folger, R., & Konovsky, M. A. (1989). Effects of procedural and distributive justice on reactions to pay raise decisions. *Academy of Management Journal, 32,* 115–130.

Giffin, K. (1967). The contribution of studies of source credibility to a theory of interpersonal trust in the communication process. *Psychological Bulletin, 68,* 104–120.

Gillet, B., & Schwab, D. P. (1975). Convergent and discriminant validities of corresponding Job Descriptive Index and Minnesota Satisfaction Questionnaire scales. *Journal of Applied Psychology, 60,* 629–631.

Graen, G. (1976). Role making processes within complex organizations. In M.D. Dunnette (Ed.), *Handbook of Industrial and Organizational Psychology* (pp. 1201–1245). Chicago: Rand McNally.

Graen, G., & Cashman, J. (1975). A role-making model of leadership in formal organizations: A developmental approach. J. G. Hunt & L. L. Larson (Eds.), *Leadership frontiers* (pp. 143–166). Kent, OH: Kent State University Press.

Graen, G., & Scandura, T. A. (1987). Toward a psychology of dynamic organizing. L. L. Cummings & B. M. Staw (Eds.), *Research in Organizational Behavior* (Vol. 9, pp. 175–208). Greenwich, CT: JAI.

Graham, J. W. (1988). Chapter 3 commentary: Transformational leadership: Fostering follower autonomy, not automatic followership. In J. G. Hunt, B. R. Baliga, H. P. Dachler, & C. A. Schriesheim (Eds.), *Emerging leadership vistas* (pp. 73–79). Lexington, MA: Lexington Books.

House, R. J. (1971). A path-goal theory of leader effectiveness. *Administrative Science Quarterly, 16,* 321–338.

House, R. J. (1977). A 1976 theory of charismatic leadership. In J. G. Hunt & L. L. Larson (Eds.), *Leadership: The cutting edge.* Carbondale, IL: Southern Illinois University Press.

House, R. J. (1988). Leadership research: Some forgotten, ignored, or overlooked findings. In J. G. Hunt, B. R. Baliga, H. P. Dachler, & C. A. Schriesheim (Eds.), *Emerging leadership vistas.* Lexington, MA: Lexington.

House, R. J., & Baetz, M. L. (1979). Leadership: Some empirical generalizations and new research directions. In B. M. Staw (Ed.), *Research in Organizational Behavior* (Vol. 1, pp. 341–423). Greenwich, CT: JAI Press.

House, R. J., Spangler, W. D., & Woycke, J. (1989). *Personality and charisma in the U.S. presidency: A psychological theory of leadership effectiveness.* Working paper, Wharton Business School, University of Pennsylvania.

House, R. J., Woycke, J., & Fodor, E. M. (1988). Perceived behavior and effectiveness of charismatic and non-charismatic U.S. presidents. In J. Conger, & R. Kanungo, (Eds.), *Charismatic Leadership and Management.* San Francisco: Jossey-Bass.

Howell, J. M., & Frost, P. J. (1989). A laboratory study of charismatic leadership. *Organizational Behavior and Human Decision Processes, 43,* 243–269.

Jackson, D. W., Keith, J. E., & Schlacter, J. L. (1983). Evaluation of selling performance: A study of current practices. *Journal of Personal Selling and Sales Management 3,* 43–51.

Joreskog, K. G., & Sorbom, D. (1986). *LISREL IV: Analysis of linear structural relationships by maximum likelihood, instrumental variables and least squares methods* (4th ed.). Mooresville, IN: Scientific Software.

Katz, D., & Kahn, R. L. (1978). *The social psychology of organizations* (2nd ed.). New York: Wiley.

Kouzes, J. M., & Posner, B. Z. (1987). *The Leadership Challenge.* San Francisco: Jossey-Bass.

Kuhnert, K. W., & Lewis, P. (1987). Transactional and transformational leadership: A constructive/developmental analysis. *Academy of Management Review, 12,* 648–657.

Lord, R. G. (1985). An information processing approach to social perceptions, leadership and behavioral measurement in organizations. In L. L. Cummings & B. M. Staw (Eds.), *Research in Organizational Behavior* (Vol. 7, pp. 87–128). Greenwich, CT: JAI Press.

Lord, R. G., Binning, J. F., Rush, M. C., & Thomas, J. C. (1978). The effect of performance cues and leader behavior on questionnaire ratings of leadership behavior. *Organizational Behavior and Human Performance, 21,* 27–39.

Marsh, H. W., Balla, J. R., & McDonald, R. P. (1988). Goodness-of-fit indexes in confirmatory factor analysis: The effect of sample size. *Psychological Bulletin, 103,* 391–410.

McCrae, R. R., & Costa, P. T. (1987). Validation of the five-factor model of personality across instruments and observers. *Journal of Personality and Social Psychology, 52,* 81–90.

Motowidlo, S. J. (1984). Does job satisfaction lead to consideration and personal sensitivity? *Academy of Management Journal, 27,* 910–915.

Motowidlo, S. J., Packard, J. S., & Manning, M. R. (1986). Occupational stress: Its causes and consequences for job performance. *Journal of Applied Psychology, 71,* 618–629.

Nunnally, J. C. (1978). *Psychometric Theory* (2nd ed.). New York: McGraw-Hill.

Organ, D. W. (1988a). *Organizational citizenship behavior: The good soldier syndrome.* Lexington, MA: Lexington Books.

Organ, D. W. (1988b). A restatement of the satisfaction-performance hypothesis. *Journal of Management, 14,* 547–557.

Organ, D. W. (in press). The motivational basis of organizational citizenship behavior. In B.M. Staw, & L. L. Cummings, (Eds.), *Research in organizational behavior* (Vol. 12). Greenwich, CT: JAI Press.

Phillips, J. S., & Lord, R. G. (1986). Notes on the practical and theoretical consequences of implicit leadership theories for the future of leadership measurement. *Journal of Management, 12,* 31–41.

Podsakoff, P. M., & Organ, D. W. (1986). Self-reports in organizational research: Problems and prospects, *Journal of Management, 13,* 419–441.

Podsakoff, P. M., Todor, W. D., Grover, R. A., & Huber, V. L. (1984). Situational moderators of leader reward and punishment behavior: Fact or fiction? *Organizational Behavior and Human Performance, 34,* 21–63.

Podsakoff, P. M., Todor, W. D., & Skov, R. (1982). Effects of leader performance contingent and noncontingent reward and punishment behaviors on subordinate performance and satisfaction. *Academy of Management Journal, 25,* 812–821.

Puffer, S. M. (1987). Prosocial behavior, noncompliant behavior, and work performance among commission salespeople. *Journal of Applied Psychology, 72,* 615–621.

Rotter, J. B. (1967). A new scale for the measurement of interpersonal trust. *Journal of Personality, 35,* 651–665.

Schmitt, N., & Stults, D. M. (1986). Methodology review: Analysis of multitrait-multimethod matrices. *Applied Psychological Measurement, 10,* 1–22.

Schwab, D. P. (1980). Construct validity in organizational behavior. In L. L. Cummings & B. M. Staw (Eds.), *Research in Organizational Behavior* (Vol. 2, pp. 3–43). Greenwich, CT: JAI Press.

Shamir, B., House, R. J., & Arthur, M. B. (1988). *The transformational effects of charismatic leadership: A motivational theory.* Unpublished Working Paper, The Hebrew University, Jerusalem.

Sims, H. P., Jr., & Szilagyi, A. D. (1975). Leader reward behavior and subordinate satisfaction and performance. *Organizational Behavior and Human Performance, 14,* 426–437.

Smith, C. A., Organ, D. W., & Near, J. P. (1983) Organizational citizenship behavior: Its nature and antecedents. *Journal of Applied Psychology, 68,* 653–663.

Stogdill, R. M. (1974). *Handbook of leadership.* New York: Free Press.

Tichy, N., & DeVanna, M. (1986). *The transformational leader.* New York: Wiley.

Tucker, L. R., & Lewis, C. (1973). The reliability coefficient for maximum likelihood factor analysis. *Psychometrika, 38,* 1–10.

Weiss, D. J., Dawis, R. V., England, G. W., & Lofquist, L. H. (1967). *Manual for the Minnesota Satisfaction Questionnaire* (Minnesota Studies in Vocational Rehabilitation: XXII). Minneapolis: University of Minnesota, Industrial Relations Center Work Adjustment Project.

Widaman, K. F. (1985). Hierarchically nested covariance structure models for multitrait-multimethod data. *Applied Psychological Measurement, 9,* 1–26.

Yukl, G. A. (1989a). *Leadership in organizations* (2nd ed.). Englewood Cliffs, NJ: Prentice-Hall.

Yukl, G. A. (1989b). Managerial leadership: A review of theory and research. *Yearly Review of Management, 15,* 251–289.

# Chapter **Fourteen**

# Dysfunctional Aspects of Leadership

It is common to think positively in terms of leaders and take for granted the positive (or presumed positive) effects associated with leadership. Examples include Lee Iacocca's turnaround of Chrysler, Steve Jobs's creation of Apple and the MacIntosh, Jack Welch's "reinvention" of General Electric, Norman Schwartzkopf and Colin Powell's victorious strategies during Operation Desert Storm, and George Mitchell's negotiated settlement in Northern Ireland and Richard Holbrooke's similar achievement in Bosnia. However, not all of our leadership stories are positive in nature. David Koresh's standoff with state and federal authorities at the Davidian Compound in Waco, Texas, Adolf Hitler's leadership of Germany in World War II, James Jones's leading of several hundred to commit mass suicide, Marshall Applewhite's similar encouragement of mass suicide among the members of Heaven's Gate, and Serbia's Slobodan Milosevic's ethnic cleansing of Kosovo serve to remind us that there can also be a negative (dysfunctional) side to leadership. At one extreme, some leaders' behaviors even become pathological (e.g., Saddam Hussein) once positions of power have been attained.

In one of our early readings, Smircich and Morgan (1982) alerted us to the fact that the leader–follower relationship can result in *learned helplessness*— that condition where individuals become dependent upon others to deal with uncertainty and ambiguity and are nearly incapable of problem-solving on their own. In the first reading in this chapter, Jay A. Conger (1990) addresses the dark side of leadership. He suggests that there are leaders who have lost touch with reality and who use their positions of leadership for their own personal gain. In both instances, negative consequences for the group and/or organization are common by-products. In this reading, Conger explores the dual question, How do leaders produce such negative outcomes, and why? Conger takes the position that leadership can make a significant difference. Unfortunately, this difference is not always positive.

In the second reading, Manfred F.R. Kets de Vries and Danny Miller (1985) note that leaders can be either extremely inspiring or pathologically destructive. They ask the question, What is it about leaders themselves that makes it so? (p. 586). In this reading, Kets de Vries and Miller explore the narcissistic personality and suggest that narcissism plays a central role in the personality of the pathologically destructive leader. Individuals whose personalities are characterized by a high degree of narcissism are driven by intense needs for power and prestige, leading them to seek out and attain leadership positions.

The self-assessment exercise presented at the end of this chapter opener provides you with an opportunity to construct your own Machiavellian profile. Machiavellianism, in general, reflects a person's general strategy for dealing with people. Individuals who have a strong Machiavellian orientation feel that people are manipulable in interpersonal situations; as leaders, these individuals tend to employ manipulation techniques as an influence tactic.

In another article, Manfred F. R. Kets de Vries[1] (1989) has written about leaders who "self-destruct." He suggests that the leadership position can be associated with loneliness and a disconnectedness that often result in self-defeating (destructive) behaviors. In addition to providing additional insight into how leaders sometimes unconsciously take steps that lead to their failure, he also offers a perspective on what might cure this problem.

The leadership dysfunctions identified in this chapter are by no means an exhaustive catalogue of the dark side of leadership. Small-group scholars, for example, have alerted us to a number of maladies that can impact groups, each of which can be related to the presence of a leader and which pose a challenge to leader effectiveness. Among them are: (*a*) *groupthink,* the condition in which a group has illusions of invulnerability and engages in single-minded thinking; (*b*) *risky shift (polarization),* the "presumed" tendency for a group to take a more extreme position than its members would have if acting alone; (*c*) *social loafing,* wherein group members fail to put forth their best efforts in the belief that their contributions (involvements) will essentially get lost in the group effort; and (*d*) *diffusion of responsibility,* a group dynamic or group process through which individuals fail to act in the belief or expectation that it is the job of others to act, or because the presence of others reduces feelings of accountability. Leaders concerned about the effectiveness of their groups will want to attempt to minimize the dysfunctional effects that stem from these group behaviors.

[1] Manfred F. R. Kets de Vries, "Leaders Who Self-destruct: The Causes and Cures," *Organizational Dynamics* 17, no. 4 (1989), pp. 4–17.

**Machiavellianism**

**Instructions:** Listed below are a number of statements. Each represents a commonly held opinion and there are no right or wrong answers. You will probably disagree with some items and agree with others. We are interested in the extent to which you *agree* or *disagree* with such matters of opinion.

Read each statement carefully. Then indicate the extent to which you agree or disagree by circling the number after each statement. The numbers and their meaning are indicated below.

If you *agree strongly*, circle +3.
If you *agree somewhat*, circle +2.
If you *agree slightly*, circle +1.

If you *disagree slightly*, circle –1.
If you *disagree somewhat*, circle –2.
If you *disagree strongly*, circle –3.

First impressions are usually best in such matters. Read each statement, decide if you agree or disagree and the strength of your opinion, and then circle the appropriate number after the statement. Give your opinion on every statement.

If you find that the numbers do not adequately indicate your own opinion, use the one which is closest to the way you feel.

| | Agree Strongly | Agree Somewhat | Agree Slightly | Disagree Slightly | Disagree Somewhat | Disagree Strongly |
|---|---|---|---|---|---|---|
| 1. Never tell anyone the real reason you did something unless it is useful to do so. | +3 | +2 | +1 | –1 | –2 | –3 |
| 2. The best way to handle people is to tell them what they want to hear. | +3 | +2 | +1 | –1 | –2 | –3 |
| 3. One should take action only when sure it is morally right. | +3 | +2 | +1 | –1 | –2 | –3 |
| 4. Most people are basically good and kind. | +3 | +2 | +1 | –1 | –2 | –3 |
| 5. It is safest to assume that all people have a vicious streak and it will come out when they are given a chance. | +3 | +2 | +1 | –1 | –2 | –3 |
| 6. Honesty is the best policy in all cases. | +3 | +2 | +1 | –1 | –2 | –3 |
| 7. There is no excuse for lying to someone else. | +3 | +2 | +1 | –1 | –2 | –3 |
| 8. Generally speaking, men won't work hard unless they're forced to do so. | +3 | +2 | +1 | –1 | –2 | –3 |
| 9. All in all, it is better to be humble and honest than to be important and dishonest. | +3 | +2 | +1 | –1 | –2 | –3 |
| 10. When you ask someone to do something for you, it is best to give the real reasons for wanting it rather than giving reasons which carry more weight. | +3 | +2 | +1 | –1 | –2 | –3 |
| 11. Most people who get ahead in the world lead clean, moral lives. | +3 | +2 | +1 | –1 | –2 | –3 |
| 12. Anyone who completely trusts anyone else is asking for trouble. | +3 | +2 | +1 | –1 | –2 | –3 |
| 13. The biggest difference between most criminals and other people is that the criminals are stupid enough to get caught. | +3 | +2 | +1 | –1 | –2 | –3 |

*(continued)*

| | Agree Strongly | Agree Somewhat | Agree Slightly | Disagree Slightly | Disagree Somewhat | Disagree Strongly |
|---|---|---|---|---|---|---|
| 14. Most men are brave. | +3 | +2 | +1 | −1 | −2 | −3 |
| 15. It is wise to flatter important people. | +3 | +2 | +1 | −1 | −2 | −3 |
| 16. It is possible to be good in all respects. | +3 | +2 | +1 | −1 | −2 | −3 |
| 17. Barnum was wrong when he said that there's a sucker born every minute. | +3 | +2 | +1 | −1 | −2 | −3 |
| 18. It is hard to get ahead without cutting corners here and there. | +3 | +2 | +1 | −1 | −2 | −3 |
| 19. People suffering from incurable diseases should have the choice of being put painlessly to death. | +3 | +2 | +1 | −1 | −2 | −3 |
| 20. Most men forget more easily the death of their father than the loss of their property. | +3 | +2 | +1 | −1 | −2 | −3 |

**Scoring:**

If you *agree strongly,* circling +3, give yourself 7 points.
If you *agree somewhat,* circling +2, give yourself 6 points.
If you *agree slightly,* circling +1, give yourself 5 points.

If you *disagree slightly,* circling −1, give yourself 3 points.
If you *disagree somewhat,* circling −2, give yourself 2 points.
If you *disagree strongly,* circling −3, give yourself 1 point.

Next, for each of the following questions (3, 4, 6, 7, 9, 10, 11, 14, 16, and 17) subtract your score from 8.

Now sum your scores across all of the 20 questions and add 20 points to that score.

My Machiavellian (Mach IV) score is: _____.

**Interpretation:** One hundred (100) points is normed as the neutral point. Your score will range between a low of 40 and a high of 160. The instrument is scaled such that the higher the score the stronger the Machiavellianism, the lower the score the weaker the Machiavellianism. A high Mach score might be reflected by 140 and more points, while a low Mach score might be reflected by 60 and fewer points.

According to Christie (1969), the Machiavellianism assessment attempts to tap into a person's general strategy for dealing with people. Machiavellianism reflects the degree to which an individual feels that other people are manipulable in interpersonal situations. Christie also notes that high Machs have a "'cool detachment,' which makes them less emotionally involved with other people, with sensitive issues, or with saving face in embarrassing situations."

An experimental study by Drory and Gluskinos (1980)[1] focusing on Machiavellianism and leadership reveals no performance differences between high Mach and low Mach groups. High Mach leaders did, however, give more orders and were less involved in reducing tension than their low Mach leader counterparts. Gemmill and Heisler (1972)[2] report that Machiavellianism was negatively related to job satisfaction and positively associated with job strain.

**Source:** R. Christie, unpublished manuscript (Department of Social Psychology, Columbia University, 1968). From R. Christie, *Studies in Machiavellianism* (New York: Academic Press, 1970). Copyright © 1970 by Academic Press, reproduced by permission of the publisher.

[1] A. Drory and U. M. Gluskinos, "Machiavellianism and Leadership," *Journal of Applied Psychology* 65 (1980), pp. 81–86.

[2] G. R. Gemmill and W. J. Heisler, "Machiavellianism as a Factor in Managerial Job Strain, Job Satisfaction, and Upward Mobility," *Academy of Management Journal* 15 (1972), pp. 51–62.

**Reading 41**

# The Dark Side of Leadership

**Jay A. Conger**
McGill University

In recent years, business leaders have gained great popularity: Lee Iacocca and Steven Jobs, for example, have stepped into the limelight as agents of change and entrepreneurship. But though we tend to think of the positive outcomes associated with leaders, certain risks or liabilities are also entailed. The very behaviors that distinguish leaders from managers also have the potential to produce problematic or even disastrous outcomes for their organizations. For example, when a leader's behaviors become exaggerated, lose touch with reality, or become vehicles for purely personal gain, they may harm the leader and the organization.

How do leaders produce such negative outcomes—and why? Three particular skill areas can contribute to such problems. These include leaders' strategic vision, their communications and impression-management skills, and their general management practices. We will examine each to discover its darker side.

## PROBLEMS WITH THE VISIONARY LEADER

As we know, the 1970s and 1980s brought tremendous changes in the world's competitive business environment. Previously successful organizations that had grown huge and bureaucratic were suddenly faced with pressures to innovate and alter their ways. Out of these turbulent times came a new breed of business leader: the strategic visionary. These men and women, like Ross Perot of Electronic Data Systems and Mary Kay Ash of Mary Kay Cosmetics, possessed a twofold ability: to foresee market opportunities and to craft organizational strategies that captured these opportunities in ways that were personally meaningful to employees. When their success stories spread, "vision" became the byword of the 1980s. Yet though many of these leaders led their organizations on to great successes, others

led their organizations on to great failures. The very qualities that distinguished the visionary leader contained the potential for disaster.

Generally speaking, unsuccessful strategic visions can often be traced to the inclusion of the leaders' personal aims that did not match their constituents' needs. For example, leaders might substitute personal goals for what should be shared organizational goals. They might construct an organizational vision that is essentially a monument to themselves and therefore something quite different from the actual wishes of their organizations or customers.

Moreover, the blind drive to create this very personal vision could result in an inability to see problems and opportunities in the environment. Thomas Edison, for example, so passionately believed in the future of direct electrical current (DC) for urban power grids that he failed to see the more rapid acceptance of alternating power (AC) systems by America's then-emerging utility companies. Thus the company started by Edison to produce DC power stations was soon doomed to failure. He became so enamoured of his own ideas that he failed to see competing and, ultimately, more successful ideas.

In addition, such personal visions encourage the leader to expend enormous amounts of energy, passion, and resources on getting them off the ground. The higher their commitment, the less willing they are to see the viability of competing approaches. Because of the leader's commitment, the organization's investment is also likely to be far greater in such cases. Failure therefore will have more serious consequences.

Fundamental errors in the leader's perceptions can also lead to a failed vision. Common problems include (1) an inability to detect important changes in markets (e.g., competitive, technological, or consumer needs); (2) a failure to accurately assess and obtain the necessary resources for the vision's accomplishment; and (3) a misreading or exaggerated sense of the needs of markets or constituents. For example, with a few exceptions like the Chrysler minivan, Lee Iacocca inaccurately believed that automobile style rather than engineering was the primary concern of automotive

| TABLE 1   The Sources of Failed Vision |
| --- |
| The vision reflects the internal needs of leaders rather than those of the market or constituents. |
| The resources needed to achieve the vision have been seriously miscalculated. |
| An unrealistic assessment or distorted perception of market and constituent needs holds sway. |
| A failure to recognize environmental changes prevents redirection of the vision. |

buyers. At Chrysler, he relied on new body styles and his charisma to market cars built on an aging chassis (the K car) developed in the late 1970s. The end result was that, after several initial years of successful sales, Chrysler's sales plunged 22.8 percent in 1987. Today, the future of Chrysler looks equally cloudy.

Ultimately, then, the success of a leader's strategic vision depends on a realistic assessment of both the opportunities and the constraints in the organization's environment and a sensitivity to constituents' needs. If the leader loses sight of reality or loses touch with constituents, the vision becomes a liability. Visions may fail for a wide variety of reasons; Table 1 outlines some of the more significant ones. We will examine several of these categories and illustrate them with the experiences of some prominent business leaders.

## MAKING THE LEADER'S PERSONAL NEEDS PARAMOUNT

As mentioned, one of the most serious liabilities of a visionary leader occurs when he or she projects purely personal needs and beliefs onto those of constituents. A common example is the inventor with a pet idea who acquires sufficient resources to initiate a venture that fails to meet the market's needs. When a leader's needs and wishes diverge from those of constituents, the consequences can be quite costly. . . .

## BECOMING A "PYRRHIC VICTOR"

In the quest to achieve a vision, a leader may be so driven as to ignore the costly implications of his strategic aims. Ambition and the miscalculation of necessary resources can lead to a "Pyrrhic victory" for the leader. The term "Pyrrhic victory" comes from an incident in Ancient Greece: Pyrrhus, the King of Epirus, sustained such heavy losses in defeating the Romans that despite his numerous victories over them, his entire empire was ultimately undermined. Thus the costs of a "Pyrrhic" victory deplete the resources that are needed for future success.

In this scenario, the leader is usually driven by a desire to expand or accelerate the realization of his vision. The initial vision appears correct, and early successes essentially delude or weaken the leader's ability to realistically assess his resources and marketplace realities. The costs that must be paid for acquisitions or market share ultimately become unsustainable and threaten the long-term viability of the leader's organization. . . .

## CHASING A VISION BEFORE ITS TIME

Sometimes a leader's perceptions of the market are so exaggerated or so significantly ahead of their time that the marketplace fails to sustain the leader's venture. The organization's resources are mobilized and spent on a mission that ultimately fails to produce the expected results. In this case, the leader is perhaps too visionary or too idealistic. He or she is unable to see that the time is not ripe, so the vision goes on to failure or, at best, a long dormancy. . . .

Two other factors may play important roles. In their own excitement over an idea, leaders may fail to adequately test-market a new product or service or fail to hear naysayers or overlook contrary signs from the environment. Again, because of successes in other projects . . . , they may delude themselves into believing they know their markets more accurately than they actually do. Or their spellbinding ability to lead may not be backed up by an adequate understanding of marketplace trends.

## HOW LEADERS COME TO DENY FLAWS IN THEIR VISIONS

All three of these cases share certain characteristics that cause leaders to deny the flaws in their visions. Often, for example, leaders will perceive that their course of action is producing negative results, yet they persist. Why this happens can be explained by a process called "cognitive dissonance," which prevents the leader from changing his course. Simply put, individuals act to keep the commitments they have made because failing to do so would damage their favorable perceptions of themselves. For example, studies have found that executives will sometimes persist in an ineffective course of action simply because they feel they have committed themselves to the decision. This same process, I suspect, occurs with leaders.

Others in the organization who tend to become dependent on a visionary leader may perpetuate the problem through their own actions. They may idealize their leader excessively and thus ignore negative aspects and exaggerate the good qualities. As a result, they may carry out their leader's orders unquestioningly—and leaders may in certain cases encourage such behavior because of their needs to dominate and be admired. The resulting sense of omnipotence encourages denial of market and organizational realities. The danger is that leaders will surround themselves with "yes people" and thus fail to receive information that might be important but challenging to the mission. Their excessive confidence and the desire for heroic recognition encourages them to undertake large, risky ventures—but because of their overreliance on themselves and their cadre of "yes people," strategic errors go unnoticed. Bold but poorly thought-out strategies will be designed and implemented. The leader's vision, in essence, becomes a vehicle for his or her own needs for attention and visibility.

Finally, problems with "group-think" can occur where the leader's advisors delude themselves into agreement with the leader or dominant others. In such a case, decision making becomes distorted, and a more thorough and objective review of possible alternatives to a problem are all but precluded. This is especially true of groups that are very cohesive, highly committed to their success, under pressure, and possessing favorable opinions of themselves—common characteristics in the organizations of powerful and charismatic leaders. When group-think occurs, the opinions of the leader and advisors with closely allied views come to dominate decision making. Doubts that others might have are kept hidden for fear of disapproval. It is more important "to go along to get along" rather than to consider contrary viewpoints. . . .

## MANIPULATION THROUGH IMPRESSION

### MANAGEMENT AND COMMUNICATION SKILLS

Because some leaders are gifted at communicating, it may be quite easy for them to misuse this ability. For instance, they may present information that makes their visions appear more realistic or more appealing than the visions actually are. They may also use their language skills to screen out problems in the larger environment or to foster an illusion of control when, in reality,

| TABLE 2 | Potential Liabilities in the Leader's Communications and Impression Management Skills |
|---|---|

Exaggerated self-descriptions.

Exaggerated claims for the vision.

A technique of fulfilling stereotypes and images of uniqueness to manipulate audiences.

A habit of gaining commitment by restricting negative information and maximizing positive information.

Use of anecdotes to distract attention away from negative statistical information.

Creation of an illusion of control through affirming information and attributing negative outcomes to external causes.

things are out of control. Table 2 highlights a number of these possible problem areas. . . .

When leaders rely greatly on their impression management skills in communicating, they do themselves a disservice. For instance, research in impression management indicates not only that one's self-descriptions are effective in deceiving an audience, but also that they may deceive the presenter as well. This is especially true when an audience reinforces and approves of the individual's image. Such positive responses encourage leaders to internalize their own self-enhancing descriptions. Especially when exaggeration is only moderate, leaders tend to internalize and believe such claims. So DeLorean may ultimately have come to believe in his own responsibility for the Pontiac GTO.

Considerable research has also been performed on people who are ingratiators—people who play to their audiences by telling them what they want to hear. Two particular tactics that I suspect charismatic leaders use to ingratiate themselves with their audiences are to (1) fulfill stereotypes and (2) create an image of uniqueness.

Research shows that if individuals behave in ways that fulfill the positive stereotypes of an audience they are more likely to interact successfully with them. This can be achieved by espousing the beliefs, values, and behaviors associated with the stereotype and appearing as the stereotype is expected to look. . . .

Anecdotal information may be used by the leader not only to influence decision makers' choices, but also to increase their confidence in a choice. The sheer amount of information the leader provides may act to build overconfidence. Various studies of decision making indicate that more information apparently permits people to generate more reasons for justifying their decisions and, in turn, increases the confidence of others in the decisions. Leaders might also create an illusion of control by selectively providing information that affirms they are in control and attribute failures or problems to external causes. All of these tactics may be used by leaders to mislead their direct reports and their investors.

## MANAGEMENT PRACTICES THAT BECOME LIABILITIES

The managerial practices of leaders also have certain inherent liabilities. Some leaders are known for their excessively impulsive, autocratic management style. Others become so disruptive through their unconventional behavior that their organizations mobilize against them. Moreover, leaders can at times be poor at managing their superiors and peers. In general, some of the very management practices that make leaders unique may also lead to their downfall.

Leaders' liabilities fall into several categories: (1) the way they manage relations with important others, (2) their management style with direct reports, and (3) their thoroughness and attention to certain administrative detail. Typical problems associated with each of these categories are shown in Table 3. We will start with the first category: managing relations with important others.

## MANAGING UPWARDS AND SIDEWAYS

Some leaders—particularly charismatic leaders in large organizations—seem to be very poor at managing upwards and sideways. Because they are usually unconventional advocates of radical reform, they may often alienate others in the organization, including their own bosses. The charismatic leader's unconventional actions may trigger the ire of forces within the organization which then act to immobilize him or her. Leaders' aggressive style may also alienate many potential supporters and ultimately leave them without sufficient political support for their ambitious plans. This problem is common when charismatic leaders are brought in from the outside; their radically different values and approaches may alienate the rest of the organization.

This kind of situation occurred at General Motors when Ross Perot was made a board member. Once on the board, Perot became one of the company's most outspoken critics. As an entrepreneur, he was quite naturally accustomed to running his own show, and after his company, Electronic Data Systems (EDS), merged with GM, he insisted that any changes made in EDS procedures be cleared through him. His style and outspokenness were so much at odds with the General Motors culture that the company offered Perot $700 million in stock to step down from the board—an offer he finally accepted.

A second problem related to managing relations within large organizations is the tendency of certain leaders to cultivate a feeling of being "special" among members of their operating units. This practice is often accompanied by a corresponding depreciation of other parts of the corporation. In short, the leader creates an "us versus them" attitude. Although this heightens the motivation of the leader's group, it further alienates other groups that may be important for resources or political support. Steven Jobs did this with the MacIntosh division at Apple Computer. Even though the company's Apple II Computer provided the profits, Jobs consistently downplayed that division's importance. He essentially divided the company into two rivals. He was fond of telling people in the MacIntosh division, "This is the cream of Apple. This is the future of Apple." He even went so far as telling marketing managers for Apple II that they worked for an outdated, clumsy organization. Jobs's later departure from Apple stemmed in part from morale problems he created within the company by using this tactic.

**TABLE 3    Potential Liabilities of a Leader's Management Practices**

Poor management of people networks, especially superiors and peers.

Unconventional behavior that alienates.

Creation of disruptive "in-group/out-group" rivalries.

An autocratic, controlling management style.

An informal/impulsive style that is disruptive and dysfunctional.

Alternation between idealizing and devaluing others, particularly direct reports.

Creation of excessive dependence in others.

Failure to manage details and effectively act as an administrator.

Attention to the superficial.

Absence from operations.

Failure to develop successors of equal ability.

In another case, the charismatic president of a division in a large corporation used as his group's emblem a mascot symbol of the TV cartoon character Roadrunner. (In the cartoons, Roadrunner was particularly adept at outwitting a wily coyote.) To him, his division managers were the "roadrunners" who were smarter and faster than the corporate "coyotes" who laid roadblocks in their path. He also had a habit of ignoring corporate staff requests for reports or information, and he returned their reports with "STUPID IDEA" stamped on the front cover. Although such behaviors and tactics fostered a sense of camaraderie and aggressiveness within the charismatic leader's division, they were ultimately detrimental both to the leader and to the organization. In this case, the executive eventually stepped down from the organization.

## RELATIONSHIPS WITH SUBORDINATES

Highly directive and visionary leaders are often described as autocratic. Jobs, for example, has been described as dictatorial. I suspect that in many cases the vision is such a personification of the leader that he or she becomes obsessed about its perfection or implementation. Leaders' natural impatience with the pace of the vision's achievement exacerbates the problem and encourages them to be more hands-on, more controlling.

There also appears to be, at times, an impulsive dynamic at work in the way leaders manage—and at such times they will override subordinates' suggestions or insights. Again, this occurs especially in relation to accomplishing the vision. DeLorean is described as increasing his production of the DeLorean car by 50 percent in the belief that his product would become an overnight sensation. Production went to an annual rate of 30,000 cars. This was done in spite of market research that showed total annual sales of between 4,000 and 10,000 cars. A company executive lamented, "Our figures showed that this was a viable company with half the production. If the extravagance had been cut out of New York, we could have broken even making just 6,000 cars a year. But that wasn't fast enough for John. First he had to build his paper empire in the stock market. A creditable success was not enough for him" (ibid., pg. 282).

Steven Jobs is known to have darted in and out of operations causing havoc: "He would leapfrog back and forth among various projects, dictating designs, with little or no knowledge of whether or not the technology even existed to

make his ideas work" (L. Butcher, *Accidental Millionaire,* Paragon House, 1988, pp. 140–141).

Another potential problem can arise from a style of informality when managing the hierarchy of an organization—this is especially true of charismatic leaders. Advantages of this style are that leaders are highly visible, approachable, and able to react quickly to issues and problems. The drawback is that they often violate the chain of command by going around direct reports and thus undercut their direct reports' authority. If a particular project or idea interests them, they do not hesitate to become involved, sometimes to the detriment of the project managers' responsibilities. DeLorean would drop in on his engineers to suggest what seemed trivial ideas. One company engineer said: "He came in one day to say we should hook into the cooling system and make a little ice-box for a six-pack of beer behind the driver's seat. Or, another time, he told us to work on a sixty-watt radio speaker that could be detached and hung outside the car for picnics" (H. Levin, ibid., pg. 267).

## ADMINISTRATIVE SKILLS

Some visionary leaders are so absorbed by the "big picture" that they fail to understand essential details—except for "pet" projects in which they become excessively involved. Iacocca, for instance, turned over most of the day-to-day operations to others as he became increasingly famous. As a result, he lost touch with new model planning. He himself admitted: "If I made one mistake, it was delegating all the product development and not going to a single meeting" (ibid., pg. 267). A DeLorean executive complained "He [John DeLorean] just didn't have time for the details of the project. But attention to detail is everything" (ibid., p. 267). Then, too, leaders may get so caught up in corporate stardom that they become absentee leaders. Again, Iacocca is an example. His success at Chrysler led to his becoming a best-selling author, a U.S. presidential prospect, and the head of the $277 million fundraising campaign for the Statue of Liberty—all of which distracted him from the important task of leading Chrysler.

Because these individuals are often excited by ideas, they may at times be poor implementors. Once an idea begins to appear as a tangible reality, I suspect they feel the need to move on to the next challenge, thereby leaving subordinates scrambling to pick up the pieces. Furthermore, because some leaders have high needs for visibility, they gravitate toward activities that afford them high people contact and recognition. Such activities are generally not performed at a desk while paying careful attention to the details.

## SUCCESSION PROBLEMS

A true leader is usually a strong figure and, as noted, often one upon whom subordinates develop dependencies. Thus it is difficult for others with leadership potential to develop fully in the shadow of such leaders. For while they may actively coach their subordinates, I suspect that it is extremely difficult for them to develop others to be leaders *of equal power.* Leaders simply enjoy the limelight too much to share it, so when they ultimately depart, a leadership vacuum is created. Moreover, under charismatic leadership authority may be highly centralized around the leader—and this is an arrangement that, unfortunately, weakens the authority structures that are normally dispersed throughout an organization.

It's clear that many of the qualities of a strong leader have both a positive and a negative face. That's why the presence of leaders entails risks for their direct reports, their organizations, and at times their societies. They must be managed with care. The negatives, however, must always be weighed in light of the positives. For companies and society, the need for organizational change and strategic vision may be so great that the risks of confrontation, unconventionality, and so on may seem a small price to pay. It is also possible that organizations and educational institutions can train, socialize, and manage future leaders in ways that will minimize their negative qualities.

---

## Selected Bibliography

For an in-depth look at the psychological dynamics of the dark side of leaders, we recommend *The Neurotic* *Organization* (Jossey-Bass, 1984) by Manfred Kets de Vries and Danny Miller and "Personality, Culture, and Organization" (*The Academy of Management Review,* April 1986), also by Manfred Kets de Vries and Danny Miller.

Works that provide an informative treatment on the topic of impression management include *The Presentation of Self in Everyday Life* (Doubleday-Anchor, 1959) by Erving Goffman and *Impression Management* (Brooks/Cole, 1980) by B. R. Schlenker. Books and articles that deal more systematically with the issue of commitment to a course of action as well as communicating information are *A Theory of Cognitive Dissonance* (Row, Peterson, 1957) by L. Festinger; Charles R. Schwenk's "Information, Cognitive Bias, and Commitment to a Course of Action" (*The Academy of Management Review,* April 1986); Barry Staw's "Knee Deep in the Big Muddy: A Study of Escalating Commitment to a Chosen Course of Action" (*Organizational Behavior and Human Performance,* June 1976); and "The Escalation of Commitment to a Course of Action" (*The Academy of Management Review,* October 1981). The definitive work on group-think is *Victims of Group Think* (Houghton Mifflin, 1972), by I. L. Janis.

Readers wishing more depth on the individual case studies of leaders should consult the following sources. For Edwin Land and the SX-70 camera, see G. W. Merry's Polaroid-Kodak Case Study (Harvard Business School, 1976) and P. C. Wensberg's *Land's Polaroid* (Houghton Mifflin, 1987). Several articles on Robert Campeau include "Buy-Out Bomb" (*Wall Street Journal,* Jan. 11, 1990), Kate Ballen's "Campeau Is on a Shopper's High" (*Fortune,* Aug. 15, 1988), and Eric Berg's "Is Campeau Himself Bankrupt?" (*New York Times,* Feb. 2, 1990). Two interesting sources on John DeLorean are Michael Daly's "The Real DeLorean Story" (*New York,* Nov. 8, 1982) and Hill Levin's *Grand Delusions* (Viking Press, 1983). *Accidental Millionaire* (Paragon House, 1988) by Lee Butcher presents a darker-side view of Steven Jobs. Two articles on the home banking industry and its slow takeoff are Efrem Sigel's "Is Home Banking for Real?" (*Datamation,* Sept. 15, 1986) and Laura Zinn's "Home Banking Is Here—If You Want It" (*Business Week,* Feb. 29, 1988).

## Reading 42

# Narcissism and Leadership: An Object Relations Perspective

**Manfred F. R. Kets de Vries**
European Institute of Business Administration (INSEAD), France

**Danny Miller**
École des Hautes Études Commerciales, Montreal and McGill University

If each of us were to confess his most secret desire, the one that inspires all his deeds and designs, he would say, "I want to be praised." Yet none will bring himself to do so, for it is less dishonorable to commit a crime than to announce such a pitiful and humiliating weakness arising from a sense of loneliness and insecurity, a feeling that afflicts both the fortunate and the unfortunate with equal intensity. No one is sure of who he is, or certain of what he does. Full as we may be of our own worth, we are gnawed by anxiety and, to overcome it, ask only to be mistaken in our doubt, to receive approval from no matter where or no matter whom . . .

　　　　—*Corian, Desir et honneur de la gloire*

## INTRODUCTION

When we think of leaders and leadership, a wide array of images come to mind, often conveying emotional reactions. Some leaders elicit thoughts of strength, power, and care, others recall the forces of terror, malevolence, and destructiveness. Our ubiquitous judgments of a leader's degree of "goodness" or evil are reflected in epithets such as Akbar the Great or Ivan the Terrible. We shall attempt in this paper to show that leadership effectiveness and dysfunction can often be explained by the narcissistic dispositions of the leader. We shall discuss and contrast three types of leaders and probe the etiology and consequences of their narcissistic orientations. The task will be to show the relationships between the intrapsychic development of the leader (using

**Source:** Edited and reprinted with permission from *Human Relations* 38, no. 6 (1985), pp. 583–601, Copyright 1985, Sage Publications, Inc.

an object relations perspective), his subsequent narcissistic orientation, and the concrete manifestations of this orientation in his leadership behavior. In no sense will our method be positivistic. We draw upon our experiences as practicing psychoanalysts, professors of management, and management consultants to demonstrate the linkages between early developmental experiences, types of narcissism, and leader behavior (Kets de Vries, 1980). The framework we shall employ is based on our clinical experiences with individuals who play a leadership role. It therefore goes without saying that our conclusions are to be viewed more as hypotheses than findings.

## LEADERS AND FOLLOWERS

The dynamics of leadership have remained very much a puzzle. We still know little about what makes a good leader. . . .

What most leaders seem to have in common is the ability to reawaken primitive emotions in their followers. Leaders, particularly those who are charismatic, are masters at manipulating certain symbols. Followers, when under the "spell" of certain types of leaders, often feel powerfully grandiose and proud, or helpless and acutely dependent. Max Weber (1947) used the term *charisma* to elucidate this strange influence of some leaders over followers which, for him, consisted of:

> a certain quality of an individual personality by virtue of which he is set apart from ordinary men and treated as endowed with supernatural, superhuman, or at least specifically exceptional powers or qualities. These are such as are not accessible to the ordinary person, but are regarded as of divine origin or as exemplary, and on the basis of them, the individual concerned is treated as a leader (pp. 358–359).

We don't have to go so far as Weber, but whatever strange "quality" leaders possess, some have the power to induce regressive behavior among their followers. They have the uncanny ability to exploit, not necessarily in full awareness, the unconscious feelings of their subordinates. In this process, some followers may try to embrace an idealized, "omnipotent" leader, one who will fulfill their dependency needs. This may lead to the destructive suspension of their own rational faculties. The mesmerizing influence of some leaders may also cause the common good to be sacrificed for personal folly. Rituals of adulation can supplant task-related activity. Form tends to dominate substance, as the followers become pawns to be manipulated, like the gullible spectators in Andersen's "The Emperor's New Clothes." Thus, functional requirements pertaining to common purposes or ideals may be neglected in favor of fleeting narcissistic gratifications.

In spite of the regressive potential of some leaders, there are others who transcend petty concerns, who are able to create a climate of constructiveness, involvement, and care, who engender initiative, and spur creative endeavors. This is the kind of person Zaleznik (1977) had in mind when he said:

> One often hears leaders referred to in adjectives rich in emotional content. Leaders attract strong feelings of identity and difference, or of love and hate. Human relations in leader-dominated structures often appear turbulent, intense, and at times even disorganized. Such an atmosphere intensifies individual motivation and often produces unanticipated outcomes (p. 74).

James MacGregor Burns (1978) probably had similar thoughts when he compared transactional with transforming leadership. While the first type of leader motivates followers by exchanging rewards for services rendered, whether economic, political, or psychological, the latter type of leader recognizes and exploits an existing need or demand of a potential follower. But, beyond that, the successful transforming leader looks for potential motives in followers, seeks to satisfy their higher needs, and engages their full potential. The result of the most adept transforming leadership is a relationship of mutual stimulation and elevation that converts followers into leaders and leaders into moral agents (Burns, 1978, p. 4).

To conclude, leadership can be pathologically destructive or most inspiring. But what is it about the leaders themselves that makes it so? What differentiates styles of leadership? Our theme will be that the degree of narcissism, and its genesis, stand central.

## THE NARCISSISTIC DISPOSITION

In studying leaders, we soon recognized that one critical component of their orientation is the quality and intensity of their narcissistic development. If there is one personality constellation to which leaders tend to gravitate it is the narcissistic one. Freud (1921, pp. 123–124), in his study of the relationship between leaders and followers already confirmed this, stating that "the leader himself need love no one else, he may be of a masterful nature, absolutely narcissistic, self-confident and independent." Later, he introduced a narcissistic libidinal personality, an individual whose main interest is self-preservation, who is independent and impossible to intimidate. Significant aggressiveness is possible, which sometimes manifests itself in a constant readiness for activity. People belonging to this type impress others as being strong personalities. They are especially suited to act as moral ideological bastions for others, in short, as true leaders (Freud, 1931, p. 21).

In a similar context, Wilhelm Reich referred to a phallic-narcissistic character which he portrayed as being "self-confident, often arrogant, elastic, vigorous and often impressive. . . The outspoken types tend to achieve leading positions in life and resent subordination. . . If their vanity is hurt, they react either with cold reserve, deep depression or lively aggression" (Reich, 1949, p. 201).

Narcissism became a particularly important topic for study when new developments in psychoanalytic theory occurred. The introduction of object relations theory and self-psychology was especially fruitful. The most important revisions concerning narcissism were formulated by clinicians such as Otto Kernberg (1975) and Heinz Kohut (1971).

For the purpose of this paper, we will not dwell on the theoretical controversies about whether narcissism is a result mainly of developmental arrest or regression, or whether it possesses its own developmental lines. Our aim is to explore the relationships between narcissism and leadership, a connection recognized by both Kernberg and Kohut. For example, Kernberg states that "because narcissistic personalities are often driven by intense needs for power and prestige to assume positions of authority and leadership, individuals with such characteristics are found rather frequently in top leadership positions" (Kernberg, 1979, p. 33). Kohut, in focusing on leaders as objects of identification, mentions that "certain types of narcissistically fixated personalities with their apparently absolute self-confidence and certainty lend themselves specifically to this role" (Kohut, 1971, p. 316).

Narcissism is often the driving force behind the desire to obtain a leadership position. Perhaps individuals with strong narcissistic personality features are more willing to undertake the arduous process of attaining a position of power. A central theme of our discussion will be that the kind of behavior we encounter in a leader will be likely to reflect the nature and degree of his narcissistic tendencies.

Although the narcissistic type of personality has long been recognized, only recently has it come under critical scrutiny. For example, the latest version of the Diagnostic and Statistical Manual of Mental Disorders (DSM III, American Psychiatric Association, 1980), lists a large number of criteria to describe narcissistic personality disorders. There are overtones of mental illness and impairment of functioning: symptoms include extremes of grandiosity, exploitativeness, exhibitionism, and so on. Many of these characteristics are also applicable, albeit in smaller measure, to narcissistic individuals who adopt a more "normal" mode of functioning.

Narcissists feel they must rely on themselves rather than on others for the gratification of life's needs. They live with the assumption that they cannot reliably depend on anyone's love or loyalty. They pretend to be self-sufficient, but in the depth of their beings they experience a sense of deprivation and emptiness. To cope with these feelings and, perhaps, as a cover for their insecurity, narcissists become preoccupied with establishing their adequacy, power, beauty, status, prestige, and superiority. At the same time, narcissists expect others to accept the high esteem in which they hold themselves, and to cater to their needs. What is striking in the behavior of these people is their interpersonal exploitativeness. Narcissists live under the illusion that they are entitled to be served, that their own wishes take precedence over those of others. They think that they deserve special consideration in life.

It must be emphasized, however, that these characteristics occur with different degrees of intensity. A certain dose of narcissism is necessary to function effectively. We all show signs of narcissistic behavior. Among individuals who possess only limited narcissistic tendencies, we find those who are very talented and capable of making great contributions to society. Those who gravitate toward the extremes, however, give narcis-

sism its pejorative reputation. Here we find excesses of rigidity, narrowness, resistance, and discomfort in dealing with the external environment. The managerial implications of narcissism can be both dramatic and crucial.

## THREE TYPES OF NARCISSISM: ETIOLOGY, DEFENSES, AND MANIFESTATIONS

We shall proceed to discuss three types of narcissistic orientations beginning with the most pernicious or pathological and proceeding toward the more adaptive or functional: these we shall call *reactive, self-deceptive,* and *constructive.* We will first discuss the general etiology and common defenses of these types, using an object relations perspective. We shall then present a discussion of the behavioral manifestations of the types in a leadership situation. Each type is based on examples from our clinical experiences which confirm how executives with different formative backgrounds manifest narcissistic behavior in various leadership situations. Table 1 summarizes our major findings for each of the three types.

### OBJECT RELATIONS AND THE ETIOLOGY OF NARCISSISM

Leaders may be said to occupy different positions on a spectrum ranging from healthy narcissism to pathology. We are by no means dealing with distinct categories. The factors that distinguish between health and dysfunction are the intrapsychic and interpersonal dynamics of the leader.

Over time, most people develop relatively stable ways of representing the experiences of themselves and others. These psychic representations in one's private inner world are known as *internal objects;* they are accumulated perceptions. They are composed of fantasies, ideals, thoughts, and images which create a kind of cognitive map of the world (Klein, 1948; Fairbairn, 1952; Jacobson, 1964; Guntrip, 1969; Mahler, Pine, & Bergman, 1975; Kernberg, 1976). The term "object relations" thus refers to theories, or aspects of theories, concerned with exploring the relationships between real, external people, the mental images retained of these people, and the significance of these mental residues for psychic functioning (Greenberg & Mitchell, 1983). Our interactions with actual people depend not only on how we view them, but also on our views of internal others. These psychic representations profoundly influence our affective

**TABLE 1   "Ideal" Varieties of Narcissism**

| Reactive | Self-deceptive | Constructive |
|---|---|---|
| Early object relations (etiology) | Overburdening parenting | "Good enough" care |
|    Rejecting, unresponsive parenting | Absence of secure attachment | Sense of acceptance |
|    Absence of secure attachment | | |
| Defensive reactions (splitting, projective identification, idealization/devaluation) | | |
|    Pervasive | Manifestation, frequency, and | Rare |
|    Severe |   intensity varies | Mild |
|    Frequent | | Infrequent |
|        Exploitativeness | | Manipulation |
| Symptomatology | | |
|    Exhibitionism | Lack of empathy | Sense of humor |
|    Grandiosity | Machiavellianism | Creativity |
|    Ruthlessness | Fear of failure | Self-confidence |
|    Coldness | "Ideal-hungry" | Ambition |
|    Entitlement | Preoccupation | Energy |
|    (want to dominate) | with own needs | Stubbornness |
| | (want to be loved) | Pride (want to achieve) |
| Manifestation in organizational functioning | | |
| 1. Leadership | | |
|    Transforming orientation | Transactional orientation | Transforming/transactional orientation |
|    Expelling mode | Binding mode | Reciprocal mode |
|    Tolerate only sycophants | Prefer noncritical subordinates | Meritocratic |
|    Cruel taskmaster | Diplomatic | Inspirational |
|    Ignore subordinates' needs | Instrumental consideration of subordinates | Mentor role |
|    Enraged by criticism | Hurt by criticism | Learns from criticism |
| 2. Decision-making | | |
|    Major, risk-laden, spectacular projects | Conservative, risk-averse, overcautious | Consultative in information-gathering, independent in decision-making |
|    Consults no one | Consults too many | Inner-directed |
|    Crushes opponents | Lacks resolve | |
|    Uses scapegoats | | |
|    Never admits defeat | | |

states as well as our behavior. Good internal objects have a generative and restorative function, and serve as a source of sustenance in dealing with life's adversities. They constitute the underpinnings of healthy functioning. But in the absence of good internal objects, various dysfunctions accrue. Therein lies the genesis of pathological narcissism. Naturally, the earliest "objects" are the parents whose nurturing gives rise to different kinds of "internal worlds." Since parents are not always consistent in dealing with their children, this world can be highly complex and turbulent. We shall proceed to discuss the etiology or early object relations of three types of narcissistic leaders.

### Reactive Narcissism

In describing messianic and charismatic leaders, Kohut (1971) argues that such leaders suffer from a pathology of narcissistic development. He attributes it to their failure during early childhood to integrate two important spheres of the self, namely, *the grandiose self* and *the idealized parental image* (Kohut, 1978, p. 826). The first construct refers to early feelings of grandiose omnipotence, when a child wishes to display his evolving capabilities and wants to be admired for it. The second construct applies to the equally illusory wishes about the idealized powers attributed to the parents, the desire to experience a sense of merger with an idealized person. Typically, the child's "I am perfect and you admire me," gradually changes into "you are perfect and I am part of you."

Clinical studies indicate that these early experiences which are a part of everyone's maturation, become mitigated and neutralized through phase-appropriate development (Winnicott, 1975). By this process, the child is gradually able to reduce frustration from the inevitable failures of parents to live up to his or her archaic expectations, and through experience, comes gradually to understand the difference between the ideal of perfection and just being good enough. He or she learns that the parent is neither completely good nor completely bad. A more balanced and integrated image of the parent is internalized to make for a more realistic appreciation. This fusion of originally split "good and bad" objects is said to be essential for the development of trust in the permanence, "constancy," or reliability of the parental figures (Klein, 1948). In turn, this early success in creating secure interpersonal attachments makes for confident self-esteem and for stable relationships. Kohut (1971) calls this a process of "transmuting internalization." He believes it to be the basis of the development of a permanent and durable psychic structure.

Unfortunately, phase-appropriate development does not always occur. Parental behavior may be experienced as cold and unempathic, even at the earliest stage of development. Parents might not be sufficiently sensitive to the needs of the growing child. In these cases, children acquire a defective sense of self and are unable to maintain a stable level of self-esteem. Consequently, childhood needs are not modified or neutralized, but continue to prevail. This, in turn, results in a persistent longing and a search for narcissistic recognition throughout adulthood. The stage is thus set for "reactive" narcissism. In a classic article, Kohut and Wolf (1978) refer to the understimulated and fragmented self that results from too few stimulating and integrating parental responses during childhood.

The legacy for the child of such deficient interactions may be a lingering sense of inadequacy. To cope with such feelings some individuals create for themselves a self-image of "specialness." This can be viewed as a compensatory, reactive refuge against an ever-present feeling of never having been loved by the parent. The illusion of uniqueness will vitally affect how the individual deals with his external environment. Any discrepancies between capacities and wants are likely to contribute to anxiety and to impaired re-

ality testing, the inability to distinguish wish from perception or, in other words, "inside" from "outside." Individuals with this "reactive" kind of orientation will frequently distort outside events to manage anxiety and to prevent a sense of loss and disappointment. If they are in a position of leadership this can have grave consequences. Reactive narcissism caused by emotionally unresponsive, rejecting parents is the severest type. This will become obvious from our discussion of defenses and symptoms.

In making these inferences, we should bear in mind that early experiences in themselves rarely have a direct impact on adult functioning. There are many mediating experiences during one's life. Early experiences do, however, play a substantial role in shaping the core personality which influences the kind of environment sought out by the individual. This has an effect on experience and, in turn, will influence personality. We are thus talking about an interactive cycle of personality, behavior, and situation (Erikson, 1963; McKinley Runyan, 1982).

### Self-deceptive Narcissism

We often find a second type of narcissistic leader with a very different type of early childhood development. These individuals were once led by one or both parents to believe that they were completely lovable and perfect, regardless of their actions and in spite of any basis in reality. Such self-deceptive leaders probably suffer from what Kohut and Wolf (1978) describe as an overstimulated or overburdened self. Because the responses of the figures of early childhood were inappropriate given the children's age, the latter never learn to moderate their grandiose self-images or their idealized parental images. Ideals of perfection have been too demanding to allow them to internalize soothing, stabilizing internal objects. These children become the proxies of their parents, entrusted with the mission to fulfill many unrealized parental hopes. What may appear as indulgence on the part of the parents is, in fact, exactly the opposite. The parents use their children to take care of their own needs, overburdening them with their implicit desires. When parents impose their unrealistic hopes onto their children, they engender delusions. They confuse the children about their true abilities.

Such unrealistic beliefs may sometimes be the original impetus which differentiates these individuals from others and makes them successful. Perhaps Freud (1917, p. 156) had this in mind when he noted that "if a man has been his mother's undisputed darling, he retains throughout life the triumphant feeling, the confidence in success, which not seldom brings actual success along with it." In those rare instances when such encouragements work out, the child may be sufficiently talented to live up to the parents' exaggerated expectations. A person who in more normal circumstances might have led an ordinary life, has used the expectations imposed on him as a child as a basis for excellence.

In general, however, the self-delusory quality of the unrealistic beliefs created by the parents will lead to problems. An exalted self-image is usually difficult to sustain in the light of external circumstances such as disappointment and failure. Thus, even though the early internalized objects are benign, disturbing interpersonal encounters when the child ventures forth from the protective family environment will give them an element of instability, of frailty. The overvalued image of the self that was garnered from an idealizing parent becomes more realistic after interactions with more honest and critical peers. Still, the traumas of early disappointments may have left a somewhat fragile and distorted concept of self. Self-deceiving narcissists are likely to suffer from interpersonal difficulties due to their desire to live up to the now internalized parental illusions of self-worth. They tend to demonstrate emotional superficiality and poverty of affect. Their behavior has an "ideal-hungry" quality resulting from difficulties in identity formation.

Conceptually, we have to be able to differentiate between the etiology of the reactive and self-defective modes of narcissism. In practice, however, a distinction is more difficult to make. Parents might each have responded differently toward the developing child. One parent might have taken a cold, hostile, rejecting attitude, while the other might have been supportive. Thus could have been created different gradations of benign and vicious internal objects, which accounts for mixtures of narcissistic styles. In addition, instead of being frustrated when ambitious parental expectations are incongruent with external reality, the child can sometimes strive successfully to bring his abilities up to his perceived capacity, as Freud notes so poignantly. Moreover, as we have pointed out, learning experiences later in life may also have buffering or mitigating effects.

### Constructive Narcissism

Miller (1981), in describing the childhood object relations of healthy or constructive narcissists, stated:

Aggressive impulses [were] neutralized because they did not upset the confidence and self-esteem of the parents.

Strivings toward autonomy were not experienced [by parents] as an attack.

The child was allowed to experience and express "ordinary" impulses (such as jealousy, rage, defiance) because his parents did not require him to be "special," for instance, to represent their own ethical attitudes.

There was no need to please anybody (under optimal conditions), and the child could develop and exhibit whatever was active in him during each developmental phase. . . .

Because the child was able to display ambivalent feelings, he could learn to regard both himself and the subject [the other] as "both good and bad," and did not need to split off the "good" from the "bad" object (pp. 33–34).

The constructive narcissists do not behave in a reactive or self-deceptive manner. They do not feel the same need to distort reality to deal with life's frustrations. Nor are they so prone to anxiety. They make less frequent use of primitive defenses, and are less estranged from their feelings, wishes, or thoughts. In fact, they often generate a sense of positive vitality that derives from confidence about their personal worth. Such people have internalized relatively stable and benign objects, which sustain them in the face of life's adversities. They are willing to express their wants and to stand behind their actions, irrespective of the reactions of others. When disappointed, they do not act spitefully, but are able to engage in reparative action. That is, they have the patience to wait, to search out the moment when their talents will be needed (Erikson, 1978). Boldness in action, introspection, and thoughtfulness are common.

## DEFENSE SYSTEMS

How do these three types of narcissistic leaders use their defensive systems? What struck us most in observing their behavior was how primitive the defenses of the first two types tend to be (Kernberg, 1975). At the core of the defensive systems is a mental process called *splitting*. All other defenses can be seen as derivatives of this very primitive mechanism.

What we mean by splitting is the tendency to see everything as either ideal (all good) or persecutory (all bad). When the individual has not sufficiently integrated or synthesized the opposite qualities of internal objects, these representations are kept separate to avoid contamination of "good" with "bad." Individuals with a tendency toward splitting possess affective and cognitive representations of themselves and others that are dramatically oversimplified. They fail to appreciate the real complexity and ambiguity of human relationships. Relationships are polarized between unbridled hatred, fear, or aggression on the one hand, and those of omnipotence and over-idealization on the other. Splitting thus avoids conflicts and preserves an illusory sense of being good. All evil is ascribed unto others. The price of maintaining this illusory sense of goodness is, of course, an impaired conception of reality.

Closely related to this defense are primitive *idealization* and *devaluation*. First, there is a need to create unrealistic, all-good, all-powerful representations of others. This process can be viewed as a protection against persecutory objects. A sense of intense helplessness and insignificance creates the need for all-powerful protectors. In the long run, however, no one can sustain these exaggerated expectations. A vengeful devaluation of the idealized figure then occurs when needs are not met.

Other derivatives of splitting are *projection* and *projective identification* (Ogden, 1982). These defense mechanisms serve to defend against persecution by bad internal objects. The person tries to get rid of unwanted aspects of the self. Consequently, internal representations of self and others are externalized and attributed (projected) to others. Blame is always placed on someone or something else. Never is there any sense of personal responsibility. Again, all this is associated with distortions of reality.

As we can see from Table 1, the frequency, severity, and intensity of these defensive mechanisms vary among the types of narcissism. The reactive type shows the highest frequency and intensity, the constructive type, the lowest.

## SYMPTOMS OF NARCISSISM

The most extreme symptoms of this developmental legacy and these defenses are summarized in the DSM III (American Psychiatric Association, 1980, p. 317), which lists the following diagnostic criteria for narcissistic personality disorders:

A. Grandiose sense of self-importance or uniqueness, for example, exaggeration of achievements and talents, focus on the special nature of one's problems.

B. Preoccupation with fantasies of unlimited success, power, brilliance, beauty, or ideal love.

C. Exhibitionism: the person requires constant attention and admiration.

D. Cool indifference or marked feelings of rage, inferiority, shame, humiliation, or emptiness in response to criticism, indifference of others, or defeat.

E. At least two of the following characteristics of disturbances in interpersonal relationships:

1. Entitlement: expectation of special favors without assuming reciprocal responsibilities, for example, surprise and anger that people will not do what one wants.

2. Interpersonal exploitativeness: taking advantage of others to indulge one's own desires or for self-aggrandizement, disregard for the personal integrity and rights of others.

3. Relationships that characteristically alternate between the extremes of over-idealization and devaluation.

4. Lack of empathy: inability to recognize how others feel, for example, one may be unable to appreciate the distress of someone who is seriously ill.

It is important once again to realize that particularly the first two types of narcissistic leaders will show many of these clinical indications, but each to a different extent. In our experience, reactive narcissists will be cold, ruthless, grandiose, and exhibitionistic. They will show a desire to dominate and control and will be extremely exploitative. Self-deceptive narcissists will be milder, they want to be liked and are much less tyrannical. Still, they lack empathy, are obsessed mainly with their own needs, and are given to being discreetly Machiavellian. Their behavior has an "as if" quality, because they lack a strong sense of inner conviction and identity (Deutsch, 1965). Finally, constructive narcissistic leaders are also quite ambitious and can be manipulative and hypersensitive to criticism. But they have enough self-confidence, adaptability, and humor to stress real achievements. They get on well with others because of their insights into relationships.

# ORGANIZATIONAL FUNCTIONING

## THE REACTIVE LEADER

We shall describe two managerial situations in which we have seen the reactive narcissistic (RN) personality in operation. The first is in *leadership* or interpersonal relations. The second relates to their efforts at *environmental scanning, analysis,* and *decision making*. The reactive narcissist can be an extremely demanding taskmaster. His grandiosity and exhibitionism cause him to gravitate toward subordinates who are sycophants. The arguments of others are ignored if they run counter to the ideas of the boss. Solicitous subordinates seem to be the only ones who are tolerated by a reactive narcissist, all others are "expelled." A strong Machiavellian streak runs through these situations: The leader cares little about hurting and exploiting others in the pursuit of his own advancement. The followers play politics simply to survive. The RN leader surpasses all other types in his total lack of empathy. He completely ignores the needs of subordinates and peers alike, reserving his attention to matters that concern him and him alone. The fluctuations in attitude toward his people will be extreme. Consequently, the level of employee turnover tends to be very high. Projects that require teamwork or subordinate initiative are seriously jeopardized.

The RN leader exhibits characteristic dysfunctions in making important decisions for his organization. He tends to do very little scanning or analysis of the internal and external environment before making decisions. The RN leader feels that he can manipulate and act upon his environment so that he need not study it very closely. The environment is somehow "beneath him," it is assumed to pose no challenges that cannot easily be met. The RN's grandiosity, exhibitionism, and preoccupation with fantasies of unlimited success cause him to undertake extremely bold and venturesome projects. The quality of his leadership style is transforming rather than transactional. He wishes to attract the attention of an invisible audience, to demonstrate his mastery and brilliance. Projects are undertaken on a grand scale, but they are often doomed to fail. First, their overblown scale reflects the desires of the leader more than the realities of the situation, too many resources are placed at risk for too little reason. Second, the leader doesn't listen to his advisors, peers, or subordinates. He feels that only he is sufficiently informed to make judgments. A potentially crucial forum is thereby lost. Third, even when it is clear that things are not going well with the project, the RN leader is reluctant to admit the evidence. He will not own up to having made any errors and he becomes especially rigid and sensitive to criticism. Thus, he initiates a momentum that is difficult to reverse (Miller & Friesen, 1980, 1984). When the leader finally realizes how fast the situation is deteriorating, his penchant for splitting causes him to blame others. He never sees himself as being responsible for anything that is at all negative.

## THE SELF-DECEPTIVE LEADER

These individuals have many of the traits of the reactive executives, but these are less evident in a managerial situation. We can again explore the categories of leadership, environmental scanning, and decision making. As leaders, self-deceptive (SD) executives are much more approachable than their RN counterparts. They care more about their subordinates, are more given to listening to the opinions of others, and are not nearly as exploitative as the RNs. However, they also show a hypersensitivity to criticism, extreme insecurity, and a strong need to be loved. SD leaders will be more tolerant of dissenting opinions in that they may seem to react sympathetically when the opinions are expressed. But they will tend to carry a grudge, to be less available to habitual critics and to promote weaker-willed subordinates over their vocal peers.

While the SD leader will often express interest in his subordinate's preoccupations, it will be out of a desire to appear sympathetic rather than out of a genuine sense of concern. He will want to do the right thing, but does not feel very enthusiastic about it. An exception to this pattern occurs in cases where the leader becomes attached to a subordinate that he has come to idealize. He will do all in his power to "bind" this person, to develop and bring him along in his own image. It is not surprising of course that this treasured subordinate generally idolizes the boss and is not usually a very strong or opinionated individual. If the subordinate were to show personal initiative, it would be interpreted as treason. The leader's idealization would then quickly change into devaluation, with predictable results for the subordinate's future in the organization.

The SD leader, in contrast to his RN counterpart, may be very eager to discover opportunities, and particularly threats, in his environment. He is insecure and therefore does a great deal of scanning of the internal and external environment to make sure that he will be able to neutralize threats and avoid costly mistakes. Competitors are watched, customers are interviewed, and information systems are established. A good deal of analysis and assessment takes place, so much so that it might sometimes paralyze action.

In making strategic decisions, the SD leader has a degree of performance anxiety. He wants to do the best job he possibly can so that he will be respected and admired, but he worries about his ability to do so. He is afraid of failure. This tends to make him much more conservative than the reactive executive. The SD executive studies the situation very thoroughly and solicits the opinions of others. Decision making is done in response to exchanges of various types, quite in contrast to the pernicious transforming style of the reactive leader. The SD leader's orientation is thus predominantly of a transactional nature. Of course, conservative (like-minded) managers are much more likely to get a receptive hearing than the more venturesome ones. They have a general tendency to procrastinate, to put things off just a bit too long, and their perfectionism and hesitancy can give rise to organizational stagnation. Note that the RN narcissist was working to impress the broader political or business community, to be revered, to fulfill bold, impossible, visionary dreams. The SD narcissist just wants to be loved and admired by the people he interacts with. Also his symptoms will wax and wane according to his degree of anxiety to a greater extent than those of the RN leader.

## THE CONSTRUCTIVE LEADER

These leaders are no strangers to manipulation and are not beyond occasional acts of opportunism. But they generally are able to get on fairly well with their subordinates. Constructive narcissists possess a high degree of confidence in their abilities and are highly task and goal oriented. Thus they may sometimes come across as lacking in warmth or consideration.

Although constructive leaders (CLs) enjoy being admired, they have a realistic appreciation of their abilities and limitations. Their attitude is one of give and take, and they recognize the competence of others. Constructive leaders are good listeners and appreciate the opinions of their subordinates, even though they are content to assume the ultimate responsibility for collective actions. They are willing to take a stand and stick to their decisions. This attitude may cause subordinates to complain that CLs are unsociable or uncooperative. In fact, constructive leaders sometimes do lack true empathy and may be prone to using others as mere instruments to accomplish their own objectives.

These leaders possess a sense of inner direction and self-determination that makes them confident. They have the ability to inspire others and to create a common cause, thereby transcending petty self-interests. Their inner directedness, however, can also be reflected by coldness, arrogance, or a stubborn insensitivity to the needs of others. Abstract concerns, such as "the good of

the company" or "helping the worker," may replace reciprocity in interpersonal relations and the building of a team. In general, however, constructive narcissists have a sense of humor that makes it possible for them to put things in perspective. Their independence can make for the creativity and vision necessary to energize subordinates to engage in ambitious endeavors. Since it lacks the rigidity of the other two types, the dominant leadership style has both a transforming and transactional quality.

The constructive leaders vary a good deal in their decision-making styles which are more reflections of the situation facing the firm than the personal foibles of the executive. Their flexibility allows them to do a good deal of analysis, environmental scanning, and consultation before making strategic decisions of far-reaching consequences. But it also enables them to handle more routine situations with dispatch, entrusting matters to subordinates. They also tend to avoid extremes of boldness and conservatism, operating more in "the middle range."

## ORGANIZATIONAL THERAPY

Constructive narcissistic leaders pose few organizational problems. But what can a firm's healthy managers do about the two more dysfunctional types of leaders? Where the organization is centralized and the narcissistic leader is dominant, poor performance and subsequent dismissal by a strong board of directors may be the only effective catalysts for change. And even these mutative influences are ruled out when a leader has strong financial control. But the outlook is much brighter where organizational power is more broadly distributed or where the narcissist occupies a less elevated position (Kets de Vries & Miller, 1984).

In fact, there are a number of organizational measures that can be taken to minimize the damage done by *lower level* narcissistic leaders. The first might be to try to become aware of their existence. In this pursuit, it may be useful to bear in mind that single indicators of each of the neurotic types are not sufficient to warrant a diagnosis of narcissism. But when these combine to form a syndrome this may indicate trouble.

It is very difficult to change a narcissist's personality. The primary emphasis must be to transfer the individual out of harm's way or to reduce his influence. A number of structural devices may be used to accomplish the latter. For example, power can be more broadly distributed in the organization so that many people get involved in strategic decisions, and lower level managers are induced to take responsibility for more routine concerns. Cross-functional committees, task forces, and executive committees can provide a useful forum in which a multitude of managers can express their viewpoint, providing opportunities for the narcissistic leaders (and especially their subordinates) to learn from and have their influence mitigated by others. Monolithic and unrealistic perspectives are thereby discouraged.

Regular leader appraisals in which subordinates have a chance to express their opinions to a third party about their boss may also be useful. Where a consensus of dissatisfaction emerges, particularly if it coincides with poor unit performance, it might be time to transfer or release the leader. Such an appraisal policy might inhibit overtly narcissistic exploitation.

When the top decision makers in an organization become aware of the narcissistic proclivities of some of the organization's managers, they can use this information in carrying out personnel policy. This is especially true when assigning subordinates to a narcissistic leader. One of the greatest dangers is to engage insecure, inexperienced managers to work for the narcissist. These employees will have too little strength or resolve to be able to cope, and still less potential to act as useful counterbalancing forces. In contrast, it might be useful to assign strong, confident, and secure personalities to work with the narcissistically inclined executive, those who are not afraid to express their opinions and can help to introduce more "reality" into the decision-making process.

It is particularly important, also, to look for signs of excessive narcissism in recruiting and making promotions. Psychological tests by trained clinicians and interviews with a candidate's previous superiors and subordinates might flag a narcissistic leader. There is no doubt that the easiest way to deal with these managers is to avoid hiring them, or failing that, to refrain from giving them much power.

# References

American Psychiatric Association. *DSM III: Diagnostic and statistical manual of mental disorders* (3rd ed.). Washington, 1980.

Bass, B. B. *Stogdill's handbook of leadership.* New York: The Free Press, 1981.

Burns, J. M. *Leadership.* New York: Harper and Row, 1978.

Deutsch, H. *Neuroses and character types.* New York: International Universities Press, 1965.

Erikson, E. H. *Childhood and society.* New York: W. W. Norton and Co., 1963.

Erikson, E. H. *Life history and the historical moment.* New York: W. W. Norton and Co., 1978.

Fairbairn, W. R. D. *An object-relations theory of personality.* New York: Basic Books, 1952.

Freud, S. *A childhood recollection from Dichtung und Wahrheit. The standard edition of the complete psychological works of Sigmund Freud* (Vol. XVII). London: The Hogarth Press and the Institute of Psychoanalysis, 1917.

Freud, S. *Group psychology and the analysis of the ego. The standard edition of the complete psychological works of Sigmund Freud* (Vol. XVIII). London: The Hogarth Press and the Institute of Psychoanalysis, 1921.

Freud, S. *Libidinal types, The standard edition of the complete psychological works of Sigmund Freud* (Vol. XXI). London: The Hogarth Press and the Institute of Psychoanalysis, 1931.

Greenberg, J. R., & Mitchell, S. A. *Object relations in psychoanalytic theory.* Cambridge, Massachusetts: Harvard University Press, 1983.

Guntrip, H. *Schizoid phenomena, object relations and the self.* New York: International Universities Press, 1969.

House, R. J., & Baetz, M. L. Leadership: Some empirical generalizations and new research directions. *Research in Organizational Behavior,* 1979, *1,* 341–423.

Jacobson, E. *The self and the object world.* New York: International Universities Press, 1964.

Kernberg, O. *Borderline conditions and pathological narcissism.* New York: Jason Aronson, 1975.

Kernberg, O. *Object relations theory and clinical psychoanalysis.* New York: Jason Aronson, 1976.

Kernberg, O. Regression in organizational leadership. *Psychiatry,* 1979, *42,* 29–39.

Kets de Vries, M. F. R. Leadership in a narcissistic age. Faculty of Management, *McGill University Working Paper,* 1980.

Kets de Vries, M. F. R., & Miller, D. *The neurotic organization: Diagnosing and changing counterproductive styles of management.* San Francisco: Jossey Bass, 1984.

Klein, M. *Contributions to psychoanalysis, 1921–1945.* London: The Hogarth Press, 1948.

Kohut, H. *The analysis of the self.* New York: International Universities Press, 1971.

Kohut, H. Creativeness, charisma, group psychology. In Paul H. Ornstein (Ed.), *The search for the self* (Vol. 2). New York: International Universities Press, 1978.

Kohut, H., & Wolf, E. S. The disorders of the self and their treatment: An outline. *The International Journal of Psychoanalysis,* 1978, *59,* 413–426.

Mahler, M. S., Pine, F., & Bergman, A. *The psychological birth of the human infant.* New York: Basic Books, 1975.

McKinley Runyan, W. *Life histories and psychobiography.* New York: Oxford University Press, 1982.

Miller, A. *Prisoners of childhood.* New York: Basic Books, 1981.

Miller, D., & Friesen, P. H. Momentum and revolution in organizational adaptation. *Academy of Management Journal,* 1980, *24,* 591–614.

Miller, D., & Friesen, P. H. *Organizations: A quantum view.* Englewood Cliffs, NJ: Prentice-Hall, 1984.

Mintzberg, H. If you're not serving Bill and Barbara, then you're not serving leadership. In J. G. Hunt, U. Sekaran, & C. A. Schriesheim (Eds.), *Leadership: Beyond establishment views.* Carbondale, Illinois: Southern Illinois University Press, 1981.

Ogden, T. H. *Projective identification and psychotherapeutic technique.* New York: Jason Aronson, 1982.

Reich, W. *Characteranalysis.* New York: Farrar, Strauss and Giroux, 1949.

Weber, M. *The theory of social and economic organizations.* New York: Oxford University Press, 1947.

Winnicott, D. W. *Through paediatrics to psychoanalysis.* New York: Basic Books, 1975.

Zaleznik, A. Managers and leaders: Are they different? *Harvard Business Review,* 1977, *55,* 67–78.

Zaleznik, A., & Kets de Vries, M. F. R. *Power and the corporate mind.* Boston: Houghton Mifflin, 1975.

# Chapter **Fifteen**

# Does Leadership Really Make a Difference?

There are few management and organization topics that have generated more interest and research activity, spanning nearly five decades, than the focus on leadership. Thousands of pages in academic books and journals have been devoted to the topic. During the past several years, the popular press has published and sold millions of copies of several dozen books written on the topic of leaders and leadership. Organizations frantically search for that magical leader who can pull the firm together and place it back onto the competitive path. We frequently hear stories about important historical leaders, we attribute organizational successes and failures to the things that our leaders did or failed to do, and at the national level we commonly resurrect dreams of the way it was when certain charismatic leaders were at the nation's helm.

Embedded in and reinforced by this attention is the implicit assumption that leadership is important, that leaders make a difference, and that positive group and organizational effects are produced by leaders and the leadership process. Our preoccupation with leaders and the leadership process makes the following question appear to hinge upon the absurd—Does leadership really make a difference? The readings contained in this chapter are intended, in part, to address and stimulate your thinking about this issue.

Not everyone agrees on the answer to this question. Instead it has produced a debate among a number of leadership scholars. James R. Meindl and his colleagues (Sanford B. Ehrlich and Janet M. Dukerich, 1985) have argued that as a society we have developed romantic notions about leaders and leadership.[1] In the process, observers make attributions that suggest that "the successful turnaround" was due to the new CEO and that the "losing season" was due to the coach's inability to bring out the talent of his or her team.

Joining the leadership debate are the contextualists and constructionists. The "contextualists" (e.g., Richard Hall, 1977; Jeffrey Pfeffer and Gerald R. Salancik, 1978) argue that situations generally place such strong constraints upon organizational leaders that it is virtually impossible for them to be able to significantly affect the behavior of the organization and its final level of performance.[2] The "social constructionists" contend that much of our understanding about

---

[1] J. R. Meindl, S. B. Ehrlich, and J. M. Dukerich, "The Romance of Leadership," *Administrative Science Quarterly* 30 (1985), pp. 78–102.

[2] R. H. Hall, *Organizations: Structure and Process,* 2nd ed. (Englewood Cliffs, NJ: Prentice-Hall 1977); J. Pfeffer and G. R. Salancik, *The External Control of Organizations: A Resource Dependence Perspective* (New York: Harper and Row, 1978).

leaders and leadership stems from socially provided information (e.g., Calder, 1977; Meindl, Ehrlich, and Dukerich, 1985; Meindl, 1990).[3] Echoing this debate, James Meindl and his colleagues note that "as observers of and as participants in organizations, we may have developed highly romanticized, heroic views of leadership" (p. 79). These heroic views paint unrealistic pictures about what leaders do, what they are able to accomplish, and the general effects they have on our lives.

Along with Chao C. Chen, Meindl (1991) has argued that much of what people have come to believe about leaders and leadership is the result of what others have told them. This romantic love affair with leaders results in stories that make effective leadership a socially constructed reality.[4] While these socially constructed and heroic views of leadership may be dramatically overestimated and removed from what is reality, Meindl and his colleagues note that this romantic relationship may be very important by helping to sustain followership— a phenomenon that produces significant contributions to the needs and goals of social systems, without which they would surely wither and die.

In an attempt to provide support for the argument that leadership does *not* make a difference, several scholars have looked at the leadership succession literature in an attempt to see if changes in organizational leadership are associated with significant gains (losses) in organizational performance. Two studies are frequently drawn upon in an attempt to support the view that leadership does not make a significant difference in terms of organizational performance. Stanley Lieberson and James F. O'Connor (1972) compared the impact of leadership relative to environmental and organizational influences in 167 organizations operating in 13 different industries. They concluded their study by suggesting that organizational performance was influenced more significantly by environmental factors than by those in top organizational leadership roles.[5] In addition, Gerald Salancik and Jeffrey Pfeffer (1977), in their study of the performance of city governments, concluded that changes from mayor to mayor were minor and unlikely to bring about major organizational changes.[6]

Others take the position that leadership *does* make a difference. In the popular press, management authors Tom Peters and Nancy Austin (1985) suggest that top-level leadership is an extremely important part of the process associated with the development and maintenance of excellent organizations.[7] There are also a number of organizational scholars who hold similar views (e.g., Robert J. House, 1988; Day and Lord, 1988).[8] Summarizing evidence from field-based longitudinal studies of the effects of lower organizational leadership and those conducted in the laboratory setting, House (1988) notes that there is an abundance of evidence demonstrating significant leadership effects in the areas of: level of effort expended, adaptability to change, performance under change conditions, level of group turnover, absenteeism, group member performance,

---

[3] B. J. Calder, "An Attribution Theory of Leadership," in B. M. Staw and G. R. Salancik, eds., *New Directions in Organizational Behavior* (Chicago: St. Clair, 1977) pp. 179–204; J. R. Meindl, "On Leadership: An Alternative to the Conventional Wisdom," *Research in Organizational Behavior 12* (1990), pp. 159–203.

[4] C. C. Chen and J. R. Meindl, "The Construction of Leadership Images in the Popular Press: The Case of Donald Burr and People Express," *Administrative Science Quarterly* 36 (1991), pp. 521–51.

[5] S. Lieberson and J. F. O'Connor, "Leadership and Organizational Performance: A Study of Large Corporations," *American Sociological Review* 37 (1972), pp. 117–30.

[6] G. R. Salancik and J. Pfeffer, "Constraints on Administrator Discretion: The Limited Influence of Mayors on City Budgets," *Urban Affairs Quarterly* 12 (1977), pp. 475–98.

[7] T. Peters and N. Austin, *A Passion for Excellence: The Leadership Difference* (New York: Random House 1985).

[8] R. J. House, "Leadership Research: Some Forgotten, Ignored, or Overlooked Findings," in J. G. Hunt, B. R. Baglia, H. P. Dachaler, and C. A. Schriesheim, eds., *Emerging Leadership Vistas* (Lexington, MA: D.C. Heath 1988); D. V. Day and R. G. Lord, "Executive Leadership and Organizational Performance: Suggestions for a New Theory and Methodology," *Journal of Management* 14 (1988), pp. 453–64.

decision acceptance, quality of decisions made, and the amount of follower learning from leadership training efforts (p. 347).

Very few scientific investigations have been conducted with a focus on the leadership effects produced by middle-level and upper-level organizational leaders. House cites evidence of leaders producing changes in organizational structure. In addition, House's interpretation of the evidence from the Lieberson and O'Connor study suggests that 31 percent of the variance in organizational net profit on sales over a 20-year time period could be directly attributed to changes in the top leadership of the companies participating in this study (pp. 347–48).

According to House, the research evidence, "when viewed collectively, demonstrates unequivocally that leadership can potentially influence significant variables related to organizational effectiveness and individual member satisfaction. However, there have also been longitudinal and experimental studies that show that leader behavior has little or no effect on subordinates' performance. Further, there are several studies that show that leader behavior is *caused* by the performance of subordinates" (p. 348).

The readings in this chapter focus attention on two important leadership issues. The first concerns the implicit notion that leadership does not make a difference in terms of organizational performance. The second issue concerns the implicit notion that the effects of leadership *are* essentially positive in nature.

## POINT: LEADERSHIP IS BUT A MIRAGE— IT REALLY *DOES NOT* MAKE A DIFFERENCE

In the first reading, Jeffrey Pfeffer (1977) questions the implicit assumption that leadership is causally related to the performance of organizations. He challenges common thinking about leadership by raising several significant questions. First, Pfeffer raises issues regarding the definition of leadership. He contends that there remains a great deal of ambiguity surrounding the meaning that is attached to the term, and that the concept of leadership is essentially redundant with other important organizational constructs such as influence, social power, and authority. As a result, it is difficult to know whether leadership is needed and whether it is leadership or other factors that account for the differences in organizational performance. Pfeffer also calls attention to the fact that there remains a considerable amount of confusion regarding the behaviors that leaders actually engage in and whether or not these behaviors have any significant and meaningful relationship with other organizational outcomes. While Pfeffer's first question focuses on the ambiguity of the leadership construct, his second question is concerned with whether or not leadership has any discernible effects on organizational outcomes. He suggests that there is very little evidence that the effects attributable to leadership are large in nature. He also argues that there are so many organizational constraints placed upon the behavior of all leaders that it should not be surprising that they are rendered incapable of producing any profound organizational effects. Third, Pfeffer argues that leadership is perceived to be an important and powerful force because we generally like to have a focus for the assignment of causal attributions. It is difficult, for example, to assign the functions of leadership—task accomplishment and group maintenance—to a large number of individuals whose interactions and relationships are left to chance. Instead, comfort is found in reducing causal uncertainty by directing cause and effect attributions toward a single point of focus—a leader. Thus, *leaders are important social constructions.* They are symbols, and, hence, targets for our attributions. They serve as scapegoats for our failures and heroes around which members of a group can rally in celebration of their collective accomplishments.

# COUNTERPOINT: LEADERSHIP REALLY *DOES* MAKE A DIFFERENCE

## The Positive Side of Leadership

Consistent with most of our thinking, as noted by Pfeffer (1977), leadership is generally cast as making a difference. In the last chapter, Conger (1990) provided insight into problems that can be associated with leadership. Now we turn to the positive difference that leadership can make in terms of organizational performance.

David V. Day and Robert G. Lord (1988) argue that there is ample evidence to indicate that top-level leadership is significantly related to organizational performance. There are instances where leadership has accounted for 45 percent of the variance in organizational performance. In one study of 167 corporations in 13 industries over a two-year time period, it was found that top-level leadership accounted for 7.5 percent of the variance in net income. While 7.5 percent might be seen as a relatively small proportion, 7.5 percent of several hundreds of millions of dollars translates into a very significant amount of money.

The effects of executive leadership may be *direct* in their impact upon both the external and internal environments of the organization. In addition, many of the effects of leadership are *indirect* in nature. In many instances, for example, top-level leaders create the culture of the organization, which in turn impacts the strength of commitment displayed by members throughout the organization. The philosophical orientation of top-level management has also been seen as indirectly affecting the success of employee involvement programs (e.g., management-by-objectives) and the degree to which employee ownership systems have resulted in the creation of psychological ownership and employee performance (e.g., citizenship) behaviors.[9]

In sum, a review and analysis of the research literature revolving around the question of whether leadership makes a difference to organizational performance led Alan Berkeley Thomas (1988) to conclude that "it is evident that it will require very considerable additional research before we can offer a general assessment of the impact of leadership on organizational performance."[10] In addition, the observations offered by House (1988) suggest that the contingency models of leadership best represent our understanding of whether or not leadership really makes a significant difference. It is clear that at times the answer to this question may well be yes—leaders and the leadership process make a difference (directly or indirectly). At other times the effects of leadership may be neutralized or substituted for by other forces operating within the organization (group) and/or its environment. Finally, it should be noted that the effects of leadership, when produced, are *not* always positive in nature.

[9] R. Rodgers and J. E. Hunter, "Impact of Management by Objectives on Organizational Productivity," *Journal of Applied Psychology* 76 (1991), pp. 322–36; L. Van Dyne, J. L. Pierce, and L. L. Cummings, "Employee Ownership: Empirical Support for Mediated Relationships." Presented at the eighth annual conference of the Society for Industrial and Organizational Psychology, Symposium on Psychological Ownership: Individual and Organizational Consequences, San Francisco, 1993.
[10] A. B. Thomas, "Does Leadership Make a Difference to Organizational Performance?" *Administrative Science Quarterly* 33 (1988), pp. 388–400.

**Reading 43**

# The Ambiguity of Leadership

**Jeffrey Pfeffer**
University of California, Berkeley

Leadership has for some time been a major topic in social and organizational psychology. Underlying much of this research has been the assumption that leadership is causally related to organizational performance. Through an analysis of leadership styles, behaviors, or characteristics (depending on the theoretical perspective chosen), the argument has been made that more effective leaders can be selected or trained or, alternatively, the situation can be configured to provide for enhanced leader and organizational effectiveness.

Three problems with emphasis on leadership as a concept can be posed: (*a*) ambiguity in definition and measurement of the concept itself; (*b*) the question of whether leadership has discernible effects on organizational outcomes; and (*c*) the selection process in succession to leadership positions, which frequently uses organizationally irrelevant criteria and which has implications for normative theories of leadership. The argument here is that leadership is of interest primarily as a phenomenological construct. Leaders serve as symbols for representing personal causation of social events. How and why are such attributions of personal effects made? Instead of focusing on leadership and its effects, how do people make inferences about and react to phenomena labelled as leadership (5)?

## THE AMBIGUITY OF THE CONCEPT

While there have been many studies of leadership, the dimensions and definition of the concept remain unclear. To treat leadership as a separate concept, it must be distinguished from other social influence phenomena. Hollander and Julian (24) and Bavelas (2) did not draw distinctions between leadership and other processes of social influence. A major point of the Hollander and Julian review was that leadership research might develop more rapidly if more general theories of

social influence were incorporated. Calder (5) also argued that there is no unique content to the construct of leadership that is not subsumed under other, more general models of behavior.

Kochan, Schmidt, and DeCotiis (33) attempted to distinguish leadership from related concepts of authority and social power. In leadership, influence rights are voluntarily conferred. Power does not require goal compatibility—merely dependence—but leadership implies some congruence between the objectives of the leader and the led. These distinctions depend on the ability to distinguish voluntary from involuntary compliance and to assess goal compatibility. Goal statements may be retrospective inferences from action (46, 53) and problems of distinguishing voluntary from involuntary compliance also exist (32). Apparently there are few meaningful distinctions between leadership and other concepts of social influence. Thus, an understanding of the phenomena subsumed under the rubric of leadership may not require the construct of leadership (5).

While there is some agreement that leadership is related to social influence, more disagreement concerns the basic dimensions of leader behavior. Some have argued that there are two tasks to be accomplished in groups—maintenance of the group and performance of some task or activity—and thus leader behavior might be described along these two dimensions (1, 6, 8, 25). The dimensions emerging from the Ohio State leadership studies—consideration and initiating structure—may be seen as similar to the two components of group maintenance and task accomplishment (18).

Other dimensions of leadership behavior have also been proposed (4). Day and Hamblin (10) analyzed leadership in terms of the closeness and punitiveness of the supervision. Several authors have conceptualized leadership behavior in terms of the authority and discretion subordinates are permitted (23, 36, 51). Fiedler (14) analyzed leadership in terms of the least preferred co-worker scale (LPC), but the meaning and behavioral attributes of this dimension of leadership behavior remain controversial.

**Source:** Edited and reprinted with permission from Copyright Clearance Center. *Academy of Management Review* 2, no. 1 (1977), pp. 104–12. Author affiliation may have changed since article was first published.

The proliferation of dimensions is partly a function of research strategies frequently employed. Factor analysis on a large number of items describing behavior has frequently been used. This procedure tends to produce as many factors as the analyst decides to find, and permits the development of a large number of possible factor structures. The resultant factors must be named and further impression is introduced. Deciding on a summative concept to represent a factor is inevitably a partly subjective process.

Literature assessing the effects of leadership tends to be equivocal. Sales (45) summarized leadership literature employing the authoritarian–democratic typology and concluded that effects on performance were small and inconsistent. Reviewing the literature on consideration and initiating structure dimensions, Korman (34) reported relatively small and inconsistent results, and Kerr and Schriesheim (30) reported more consistent effects of the two dimensions. Better results apparently emerge when moderating factors are taken into account, including subordinate personalities (50) and situational characteristics (23, 51). Kerr et al. (31) list many moderating effects grouped under the headings of subordinate considerations, supervisor considerations, and task considerations. Even if each set of considerations consisted of only one factor (which it does not), an attempt to account for the effects of leader behavior would necessitate considering four-way interactions. While social reality is complex and contingent, it seems desirable to attempt to find more parsimonious explanations for the phenomena under study.

# THE EFFECTS OF LEADERS

Hall asked a basic question about leadership: Is there any evidence on the magnitude of the effects of leadership? (17, p. 248). Surprisingly, he could find little evidence. Given the resources that have been spent studying, selecting, and training leaders, one might expect that the question of whether or not leaders matter would have been addressed earlier (12).

There are at least three reasons why it might be argued that the observed effects of leaders on organizational outcomes would be small. First, those obtaining leadership positions are selected, and perhaps only certain, limited styles of behavior may be chosen. Second, once in the leadership position, the discretion and behavior of the leader are constrained. And third, leaders can typically affect only a few of the variables that may impact organizational performance.

# HOMOGENEITY OF LEADERS

Persons are selected to leadership positions. As a consequence of this selection process, the range of behaviors or characteristics exhibited by leaders is reduced, making it more problematic to empirically discover an effect of leadership. There are many types of constraints on the selection process. The attraction literature suggests that there is a tendency for persons to like those they perceive as similar (3). In critical decisions such as the selection of persons for leadership positions, compatible styles of behavior probably will be chosen.

Selection of persons is also constrained by the internal system or influence in the organization. As Zald (56) noted, succession is a critical decision, affected by political influence and by environmental contingencies faced by the organization. As Thompson (49) noted, leaders may be selected for their capacity to deal with various organizational contingencies. In a study of characteristics of hospital administrators, Pfeffer and Salancik (42) found a relationship between the hospital's context and the characteristics and tenure of the administrators. To the extent that the contingencies and power distribution within the organization remain stable, the abilities and behaviors of those selected into leadership positions will also remain stable.

Finally, the selection of persons to leadership positions is affected by a self-selection process. Organizations and roles have images, providing information about their character. Persons are likely to select themselves into organizations and roles based upon their preferences for the dimensions of the organizational and role characteristics as perceived through these images. The self-selection of persons would tend to work along with organizational selection to limit the range of abilities and behaviors in a given organizational role.

Such selection processes would tend to increase homogeneity more within a single organization than across organizations. Yet many studies of leadership effect at the work group level have compared groups within a single organization. If there comes to be a widely shared, socially constructed definition of leadership behaviors or characteristics which guides the selection process, then leadership activity may come to be defined similarly in various organizations, leading to the selection of only those who match the constructed image of a leader.

## CONSTRAINTS ON LEADER BEHAVIOR

Analyses of leadership have frequently presumed that leadership style or leader behavior was an independent variable that could be selected or trained at will to conform to what research would find to be optimal. Even theorists who took a more contingent view of appropriate leadership behavior generally assumed that with proper training, appropriate behavior could be produced (51). Fiedler (13), noting how hard it was to change behavior, suggested changing the situational characteristics rather than the person, but this was an unusual suggestion in the context of prevailing literature, which suggested that leadership style was something to be strategically selected according to the variables of the particular leadership theory.

But the leader is embedded in a social system, which constrains behavior. The leader has a role set (27), in which members have expectations for appropriate behavior and persons make efforts to modify the leader's behavior. Pressures to conform to the expectations of peers, subordinates, and superiors are all relevant in determining actual behavior.

Leaders, even in high-level positions, have unilateral control over fewer resources and fewer policies than might be expected. Investment decisions may require approval of others, while hiring and promotion decisions may be accomplished by committees. Leader behavior is constrained by both the demands of others in the role set and by organizationally prescribed limitations on the sphere of activity and influence.

## EXTERNAL FACTORS

Many factors that may affect organizational performance are outside a leader's control, even if he or she were to have complete discretion over major areas of organizational decisions. For example, consider the executive in a construction firm. Costs are largely determined by operation of commodities and labor markets; and demand is largely affected by interest rates, availability of mortgage money, and economic conditions which are affected by governmental policies over which the executive has little control. School superintendents have little control over birth rates and community economic development, both of which profoundly affect school system budgets. While the leader may react to contingencies as they arise, or may be a better or worse forecaster, in accounting for variation in organizational outcomes, he or she may account for relatively little compared to external factors.

Second, the leader's success or failure may be partly due to circumstances unique to the organization but still outside his or her control. Leader positions in organizations vary in terms of the strength and position of the organization. The choice of a new executive does not fundamentally alter a market and financial position that has developed over years and affects the leader's ability to make strategic changes and the likelihood that the organization will do well or poorly. Organizations have relatively enduring strengths and weaknesses. The choice of a particular leader for a particular position has limited impact on these capabilities.

## EMPIRICAL EVIDENCE

Two studies have assessed the effects of leadership changes in major positions in organizations. Lieberson and O'Connor (35) examined 167 business firms in 13 industries over a 20-year period, allocating variance in sales, profits, and profit margins to one of four sources: year (general economic conditions), industry, company effects, and effects of changes in the top executive position. They concluded that compared to other factors, administration had a limited effect on organizational outcomes.

Using a similar analytical procedure, Salancik and Pfeffer (44) examined the effects of mayors on city budgets for 30 U.S. cities. Data on expenditures by budget category were collected for 1951–1968. Variance in amount and proportion of expenditures was apportioned for the year, the city, or the mayor. The mayoral effect was relatively small, with the city accounting for most of the variance, although the mayor effect was larger for expenditure categories that were not as directly connected to important interest groups. Salancik and Pfeffer argued that the effects of the mayor were limited both by absence of power to control many of the expenditures and tax sources, and by construction of politics in response to demands from interests in the environment.

If leadership is defined as a strictly interpersonal phenomenon, the relevance of these two studies for the issue of leadership effects becomes problematic. But such a conceptualization seems unduly restrictive and is certainly inconsistent with Selznick's (47) conceptualization of leadership as strategic management and decision making. If one cannot observe differences when leaders change, then what does it matter who occupies the positions or how they behave?

Pfeffer and Salancik (41) investigated the extent to which behaviors selected by first-line supervisors were constrained by expectations of others in their role set. Variance in task and social behaviors could be accounted for by role-set expectations, with adherence to various demands made by role-set participants a function of similarity and relative power. Lowin and Craig (37) experimentally demonstrated that leader behavior was determined by the subordinate's own behavior. Both studies illustrate that leader behaviors are responses to the demands of the social context.

The effect of leadership may vary depending upon level in the organizational hierarchy, while the appropriate activities and behaviors may also vary with organizational level (26, 40). For the most part, empirical studies of leadership have dealt with first-line supervisors or leaders with relatively low organizational status (17). If leadership has any impact, it should be more evident at higher organizational levels or where there is more discretion in decisions and activities. . . .

## THE ATTRIBUTION OF LEADERSHIP

Kelley conceptualized the layman as:

> [A]n applied scientist, that is, as a person concerned about applying his knowledge of causal relationships in order to *exercise control* of his world (29, p. 2).

Reviewing a series of studies dealing with the attributional process, he concluded that persons were not only interested in understanding their world correctly, but also in controlling it.

> The view here proposed is that attribution processes are to be understood not only as a means of providing the individual with a veridical view of his world, but as a means of encouraging and maintaining his effective exercise of control in that world (29, p. 22).

Controllable factors will have high salience as candidates for causal explanation, while a bias toward the more important causes may shift the attributional emphasis toward causes that are not controllable (29, p. 23). The study of attribution is a study of naive psychology—an examination of how persons make sense out of the events taking place around them.

If Kelley is correct that individuals will tend to develop attributions that give them a feeling of control, then emphasis on leadership may derive partially from a desire to believe in the effectiveness and importance of individual action, since individual action is more controllable than contextual variables. Lieberson and O'Connor (35) made essentially the same point in introducing their paper on the effects of top-management changes on organizational performance. Given the desire for control and a feeling of personal effectiveness, organizational outcomes are more likely to be attributed to individual actions, regardless of their actual causes.

Leadership is attributed by observers. Social action has meaning only through a phenomenological process (46). The identification of certain organizational roles as leadership positions guides the construction of meaning in the direction of attributing effects to the actions of those positions. While Bavelas (2) argued that the functions of leadership, such as task accomplishment and group maintenance, are shared throughout the group, this fact provides no simple and potentially controllable focus for attributing causality. Rather, the identification of leadership positions provides a simpler and more readily changeable model of reality. When causality is lodged in one or a few persons rather than being a function of a complex set of interactions among all group members, changes can be made by replacing or influencing the occupant of the leadership position. Causes of organizational actions are readily identified in this simple causal structure.

Even if, empirically, leadership has little effect, and even if succession to leadership positions is not predicated on ability or performance, the belief in leadership effects and meritocratic succession provides a simple causal framework and a justification for the structure of the social collectivity. More important, the beliefs interpret social actions in terms that indicate potential for effective individual intervention or control. The personification of social causality serves too many uses to be easily overcome. Whether or not leader behavior actually influences performance or effectiveness, it is important because people believe it does.

One consequence of the attribution of causality to leaders and leadership is that leaders come to be symbols. Mintzberg (39), in his discussion of the roles of managers, wrote of the symbolic role, but more in terms of attendance at formal events and formally representing the organization. The symbolic role of leadership is more important than implied in such a description. The leader as a symbol provides a target for action when difficulties occur, serving as a scapegoat when things go wrong. Gamson and Scotch (15) noted that in baseball, the firing of the manager served a scapegoating purpose. One cannot fire the whole team, yet when performance is poor, something must be done. The firing of the manager conveys to the world and to the actors involved that success is the result of personal actions, and that steps can and will be taken to enhance organizational performance.

The attribution of causality to leadership may be reinforced by organizational actions, such as the inauguration process, the choice process, and providing the leader with symbols and ceremony. If leaders are chosen by using a random number table, persons are less likely to believe in their effects than if there is an elaborate search or selection process followed by an elaborate ceremony signifying the changing of control, and if the leader then has a variety of perquisites and symbols that distinguish him or her from the rest of the organization. Construction of the importance of leadership in a given social context is the outcome of various social processes, which can be empirically examined.

Since belief in the leadership effect provides a feeling of personal control, one might argue that efforts to increase the attribution of causality to leaders would occur more when it is more necessary and more problematic to attribute causality to controllable factors. Such an argument would lead to the hypothesis that the more the *context* actually affects organizational outcomes, the more efforts will be made to ensure attribution to *leadership*. When leaders really do have effects, it is less necessary to engage in rituals indicating their effects. Such rituals are more likely when there is uncertainty and unpredictability associated with the organization's operations. This results both from the desire to feel control in uncertain situations and from the fact that in ambiguous contexts, it is easier to attribute consequences to leadership without facing possible disconfirmation.

The leader is, in part, an actor. Through statements and actions, the leader attempts to reinforce the operation of an attribution process which tends to vest causality in that position in the social structure. Successful leaders, as perceived by members of the social system, are those who can separate themselves from organizational failures and associate themselves with organizational successes. Since the meaning of action is socially constructed, this involves manipulation of symbols to reinforce the desired process of attribution. For instance, if a manager knows that business in his or her division is about to improve because of the economic cycle, the leader may, nevertheless, write recommendations and undertake actions and changes that are highly visible and that will tend to identify his or her behavior closely with the division. A manager who perceives impending failure will attempt to associate the division and its policies and decisions with others, particularly persons in higher organizational positions, and to disassociate himself or herself from the division's performance, occasionally even transferring or moving to another organization.

## CONCLUSION

The theme of this article has been that analysis of leadership and leadership processes must be contingent on the intent of the researcher. If the interest is in understanding the causality of social phenomena as reliably and accurately as possible, then the concept of leadership may be a poor place to begin. The issue of the effects of leadership is open to question. But examination of situational variables that accompany more or less leadership effect is a worthwhile task.

The more phenomenological analysis of leadership directs attention to the process by which social causality is attributed and focuses on the distinction between causality as perceived by group members and causality as assessed by an outside observer. Leadership is associated with a set of myths reinforcing a social construction of meaning which legitimates leadership role occupants, provides belief in potential mobility for those not in leadership roles, and attributes social causality to leadership roles, thereby providing a belief in the effectiveness of individual control. In analyzing leadership, this mythology and the process by which such mythology is created and supported should be separated from analysis of leadership as a social influence process, operating within constraints.

## References

[1] Bales, R. F. *Interaction Process Analysis: A Method for the Study of Small Groups* (Reading, Mass.: Addison-Wesley, 1950).

[2] Bavelas, Alex. "Leadership: Man and Function," *Administrative Science Quarterly* 4 (1960), pp. 491–98.

[3] Berscheid, Ellen, and Elaine Walster. *Interpersonal Attraction* (Reading, Mass.: Addison-Wesley, 1969).

[4] Bowers, David G., and Stanley E. Seashore. "Predicting Organizational Effectiveness with a Four-Factor

Theory of Leadership," *Administrative Science Quarterly* 11 (1966), pp. 238–63.

[5] Calder, Bobby J. "An Attribution Theory of Leadership," in *New Directions in Organizational Behavior,* ed. B. Staw and G. Salancik (Chicago: St. Clair Press, 1976).

[6] Cartwright, Dorwin C., and Alvin Zander. *Group Dynamics: Research and Theory,* 3d ed. (Evanston, Ill.: Row, Peterson, 1960).

[7] Cole, Jonathan R., and Stephen Cole. *Social Stratification in Science* (Chicago: University of Chicago Press, 1973).

[8] Collins, Barry E., and Harold Guetzkow. *A Social Psychology of Group Processes for Decision Making* (New York: Wiley, 1964).

[9] Collins, Randall. "Functional and Conflict Theories of Stratification," *American Sociological Review* 36 (1971), pp. 1002–19.

[10] Day, R. C., and R. L. Hamblin. "Some Effects of Close and Punitive Styles of Supervision," *American Journal of Sociology* 69 (1964), pp. 499–510.

[11] Domhoff, G. William. *Who Rules America?* (Englewood Cliffs, N.J.: Prentice-Hall, 1967).

[12] Dubin, Robert. "Supervision and Productivity: Empirical Findings and Theoretical Considerations," in *Leadership and Productivity,* ed. R. Dubin, G. C. Homans, F. C. Mann, and D.C. Miller (San Francisco: Chandler Publishing, 1965), pp. 1–50.

[13] Fiedler, Fred E. "Engineering the Job to Fit the Manager," *Harvard Business Review* 43 (1965), pp. 115–322.

[14] Fiedler, Fred E. *A Theory of Leadership Effectiveness* (New York: McGraw-Hill, 1967).

[15] Gamson, William A., and Norman A. Scotch, "Scapegoating in Baseball," *American Journal of Sociology* 70 (1964), pp. 69–72.

[16] Granovetter, Mark. *Getting a Job* (Cambridge, Mass.: Harvard University Press, 1974).

[17] Hall, Richard H. *Organizations: Structure and Process* (Englewood Cliffs, N.J.: Prentice-Hall, 1972).

[18] Halpin, A. W., and J. Winer. "A Factorial Study of the Leader Behavior Description Questionnaire," in *Leader Behavior: Its Description and Measurement,* ed. R. M. Stogdill and A. E. Coons (Columbus, Ohio: Bureau of Business Research, Ohio State University, 1957), pp. 39–51.

[19] Hargens, L. L. "Patterns of Mobility of New Ph.D.'s among American Academic Institutions," *Sociology of Education* 42 (1969), pp. 18–37.

[20] Hargens, L. L., and W. O. Hagstrom. "Sponsored and Contest Mobility of American Academic Scientists," *Sociology of Education* 40 (1967), pp. 24–38.

[21] Harrell, Thomas W. "High Earning MBA's," *Personnel Psychology* 25 (1972), pp. 523–30.

[22] Harrell, Thomas W., and Margaret S. Harrell. "Predictors of Management Success." *Stanford University Graduate School of Business, Technical Report No. 3 to the Office of Naval Research.*

[23] Heller, Frank, and Gary Yukl. "Participation, Managerial Decision Making, and Situational Variables," *Organizational Behavior and Human Performance* 4 (1969), pp. 227–41.

[24] Hollander, Edwin P., and James W. Julian. "Contemporary Trends in the Analysis of Leadership Processes," *Psychological Bulletin* 71 (1969), pp. 387–97.

[25] House, Robert J. "A Path-Goal Theory of Leader Effectiveness," *Administrative Science Quarterly* 16 (1971), pp. 321–38.

[26] Hunt, J. G. "Leadership-Style Effects at Two Managerial Levels in a Simulated Organization," *Administrative Science Quarterly* 16 (1971), pp. 476–85.

[27] Kahn, R. L., D. M. Wolfe, R. P. Quinn, and J. D. Snoek. *Organizational Stress: Studies in Role Conflict and Ambiguity* (New York: Wiley, 1964).

[28] Karabel, J., and A. W. Astin. "Social Class, Academic Ability, and College 'Quality'," *Social Forces* 53 (1975), pp. 381–98.

[29] Kelley, Harold H. *Attribution in Social Interaction* (Morristown, N.J.: General Learning Press, 1971).

[30] Kerr, Steven, and Chester Schriesheim. "Consideration, Initiating Structure and Organizational Criteria— An Update of Korman's 1966 Review," *Personnel Psychology* 27 (1974), pp. 555–68.

[31] Kerr, S., C. Schriesheim, C. J. Murphy, and R. M. Stogdill, "Toward a Contingency Theory of Leadership Based upon the Consideration and Initiating Structure Literature," *Organizational Behavior and Human Performance* 12 (1974), pp. 62–82.

[32] Kiesler, C., and S. Kiesler. *Conformity* (Reading, Mass.: Addison-Wesley, 1969).

[33] Kochan, T. A., S. M. Schmidt, and T. A. De-Cotiis. "Superior-Subordinate Relations: Leadership and Headship," *Human Relations* 28 (1975), pp. 279–94.

[34] Korman, A. K. "Consideration, Initiating Structure, and Organizational Criteria—A Review," *Personnel Psychology* 19 (1966), pp. 349–62.

[35] Lieberson, Stanley, and James F. O'Connor. "Leadership and Organizational Performance: A Study of Large Corporations," *American Sociological Review* 37 (1972), pp. 117–30.

[36] Lippitt, Ronald. "An Experimental Study of the Effect of Democratic and Authoritarian Group Atmospheres," *University of Iowa Studies in Child Welfare* 16 (1940), pp. 43–195.

[37] Lowin, A., and J. R. Craig. "The Influence of Level of Performance on Managerial Style: An Experimental Object-Lesson in the Ambiguity of Correlational Data,"

*Organizational Behavior and Human Performance* 3 (1968), pp. 440–58.

[38] Mills, C. Wright. "The American Business Elite: A Collective Portrait," in *Power, Politics, and People,* ed. C. W. Mills (New York: Oxford University Press, 1963), pp. 110–39.

[39] Mintzberg, Henry. *The Nature of Managerial Work* (New York: Harper and Row, 1973).

[40] Nealey, Stanley M., and Milton R. Blood. "Leadership Performance of Nursing Supervisors at Two Organizational Levels," *Journal of Applied Psychology* 52 (1968), pp. 414–42.

[41] Pfeffer, Jeffrey, and Gerald R. Salancik. "Determinants of Supervisory Behavior: A Role Set Analysis," *Human Relations* 28 (1975), pp. 139–54.

[42] Pfeffer, Jeffrey, and Gerald R. Salancik. "Organizational Context and the Characteristics and Tenure of Hospital Administrators," *Academy of Management Journal* 20 (1977).

[43] Reed, R. H., and H. P. Miller. "Some Determinants of the Variation in Earnings per College Men," *Journal of Human Resources* 5 (1970), pp. 117–90.

[44] Salancik, Gerald R., and Jeffrey Pfeffer. "Constraints on Administrator Discretion: The Limited Influence of Mayors on City Budgets," *Urban Affairs Quarterly,* in press.

[45] Sales, Stephen M. "Supervisory Style and Productivity: Review and Theory," *Personnel Psychology* 19 (1966), pp. 275–86.

[46] Schutz, Alfred. *The Phenomenology of the Social World* (Evanston, Ill.: Northwestern University Press, 1967).

[47] Selznick, P. *Leadership in Administration* (Evanston, Ill.: Row, Peterson, 1957).

[48] Spaeth, J. L., and A. M. Greeley. *Recent Alumni and Higher Education* (New York: McGraw-Hill, 1970).

[49] Thompson, James D. *Organizations in Action* (New York: McGraw-Hill, 1967).

[50] Vroom, Victor H. "Some Personality Determinants of the Effects of Participation," *Journal of Abnormal and Social Psychology* 59 (1959), pp. 322–27.

[51] Vroom, Victor H., and Phillip W. Yetton. *Leadership and Decision Making* (Pittsburgh: University of Pittsburgh Press, 1973).

[52] Warner, W. L., and J. C. Abbeglin. *Big Business Leaders in America* (New York: Harper and Row, 1955).

[53] Weick, Karl E. *The Social Psychology of Organizing* (Reading, Mass.: Addison-Wesley, 1969).

[54] Weinstein, Alan G., and V. Srinivasan. "Predicting Managerial Success of Master of Business Administration (MBA) Graduates," *Journal of Applied Psychology* 59 (1974), pp. 207–12

[55] Wolfle, Dael. *The Uses of Talent* (Princeton: Princeton University Press, 1971).

[56] Zald, Mayer N. "Who Shall Rule? A Political Analysis of Succession in a Large Welfare Organization," *Pacific Sociological Review* 8 (1965), pp. 52–60.

**Reading 44**

# Executive Leadership and Organizational Performance:

## *Suggestions for a New Theory and Methodology*

**David V. Day and Robert G. Lord**
University of Akron

The literature regarding executive leadership is paradoxical: Popular thinking (e.g., Peters & Austin, 1985) emphasizes the importance of top-level leadership in establishing "excellent" organizations, but many academic publications assert that executive leadership is an inconsequential determinant of organizational performance (e.g., Meindl & Ehrlich, 1987; Meindl, Ehrlich, & Dukerich, 1985; Pfeffer, 1977). These contrasting positions also have conflicting implications for practice and the development of leadership theory. The benefits of changing leaders or developing theories of executive leadership are bolstered by popular writers, but are undercut by the pessimistic conclusions of academic researchers. Both the popular and academic positions require more careful evaluation. We will scrutinize the arguments and data used by academicians to conclude that top-level leaders have minimal impact on performance. Others (Aupperle, Acar, & Booth, 1986) have recently evaluated the claims of popular writers such as Peters.

Succession studies have often been used by academicians to evaluate the impact of leadership on organizational performance. There are a number of factors that must be considered to interpret properly the results of succession studies. Neglecting these factors leads to erroneous conclusions, which is what has occurred with two widely cited succession studies, Lieberson and O'Connor (1972) and Salancik and Pfeffer (1977). Their misinterpreted results have been used as evidence by researchers arguing that leadership does not directly affect organizational outcomes (e.g., Meindl et al., 1985, p. 78). Even organizational scientists who have argued that leadership *substantially affects* performance have cited these two studies as providing contrary evidence (e.g., Gupta, 1986,

**Source:** Edited and reprinted with permission from *Journal of Management* 14 (1988), pp. 453–64. Copyright 1988. Author affiliation may have changed since article was first published.

A shorter version of this paper was presented at the Academy of Management 46th Annual Meeting, Chicago, 1986.

The authors wish to thank Ken Carson, Laura Kollar, Jim Phillips, and two anonymous reviewers for their helpful comments.

pp. 227–228). We believe, however, that proper interpretation of existing succession studies indicates that top-level leaders have a direct and significant effect on their company's performance.

Therefore, one goal of this paper is to assess comprehensively the problems in interpreting succession findings. Our purpose is to help determine whether leadership affects organizational performance and to emphasize the importance of top-level leadership as a topic worthy of its own theory and specific methodology. The plan of this paper is to (*a*) closely examine the conceptual and empirical basis of claims that leadership is not an important determinant of organizational performance, and (*b*) offer suggestions for developing a theory of executive leadership that is relevant to understanding *how* top-level leaders directly and significantly affect organizational performance.

## STUDIES OF EXECUTIVE SUCCESSION

Statements that top-level leaders have minimal effects on an organization's performance (e.g., Brown, 1982; Meindl et al., 1985; Tsui, 1984) are based on a very small database—usually entirely on the Lieberson and O'Connor (1972) and Salancik and Pfeffer (1977) studies and with occasional reference to studies of athletic teams. These studies have used succession as the methodology for showing the minimal impact of leadership. Because these are the principal sources of empirical support cited by researchers claiming that leaders have little effect on organizational performance, they are carefully evaluated in this section.

In a study of 167 corporations in 13 industries over a time-period of 20 years, Lieberson and O'Connor (1972) analyzed changes in sales, earnings, and profit margin associated with the succession of the president or chair of the board. They compared succession effects with year, industry, and company influences by apportioning performance variance to these sources. Their findings are summarized in Table 1. They found that leadership

**TABLE 1** Executive Succession Studies

**Lieberson & O'Connor (1972)**

| Variables | Variance Explained | | |
|---|---|---|---|
| | Sales | Net Income | Profit Margin |
| Year | .031 | .017 | .018 |
| Industry | .230 | .186 | .285 |
| Company | .648 | .677 | .226 |
| Administration | | | |
| (No lag) | .065 | .075 | .152 |
| (3-year lag) | .063 | .069 | .317 |

**Salancik & Pfeffer (1977)**

| Budget Category | Variance Explained | | |
|---|---|---|---|
| | City | Year | Mayor |
| Income | .908 | .025 | .056 |
| Property tax revenues | (.860) | (.018) | (.049) |
| General debt | .805 | .067 | .100 |
| | (.563) | (.035) | (.242) |
| Expenditures | .792 | .072 | .099 |
| Median for all expenditures | (.591) | (.025) | (.191) |

Note: Nonparenthesized figures computed in total dollars. Parenthesized figures computed as proportions of total city budget.

(administration) accounted for far less of the performance variance than either industry or company. With no lag time, the range of effect for leadership was from 6.5 percent of sales to 15.2 percent of profit margin. From these data, Lieberson and O'Connor, followed by a host of other researchers, have stressed the importance of environmental rather than leadership factors in explaining performance. However, even with no lag-time and size confounds, leadership accounted for 7.5 percent of the variance in net income. This translates into a substantial amount of money to most organizations, which makes leadership at upper organizational levels worthy of their (and our) consideration. If one looks at profit margins, which are not confounded with size, leadership explains 32 percent of the variance with a 3-year time lag. This latter result indicates a very dramatic effect of executive leadership on organizational performance.

The influence of mayors on two income and eight expenditure variables was the focus of Salancik and Pfeffer (1977). Thirty U.S. cities were examined during the years 1951–1968, with a total of 172 different mayors included in the analysis. They examined the relative effects of city, year, and mayor on the multiple dependent variables of property tax revenues; general debt; and eight expenditure variables (e.g., police, fire, highways, etc.). When the budget variables were computed in *total dollars,* the effects of the mayor variable was limited to around 10 percent (see Table 1); however, these results are misleading due to the large, but theoretically trivial, contribution of city size. When the budget variables were computed as *proportions of the total city budget* to control for size effects, the mayoral effect was over 24 percent. The mayoral effect on property tax revenues remained stable when size was controlled, decreasing a modest .7 percent. This is expected due to the direct influence that voters have over their taxes. Mayoral effects on median expenditures increased from 9.9 percent to 19.1 percent when city size was controlled.

Two other studies of executive succession are commendable for attempting to account for numerous methodological problems. Weiner and Mahoney (1981) examined the effects of CEO changes in a sample of 193 manufacturing companies over a 19-year period. By effectively controlling for size and order effects, they found that the CEO had substantial impact on some major organizational variables. For example, stewardship (i.e., leadership) explained 43.9 percent of the profitability (profit/assets) variance and also accounted for 47 percent of the variance in stock prices. In a study using a sample of Methodist ministers, Smith, Carson, and Alexander (1984) attempted to assess the impact of effective leaders on organizational performance. They differentiated effective from other leaders to determine whether leadership status had any incremental effect on organizational performance. Despite the large amount of variance accounted for by the control variable of the church's performance in the minister's first year of service (median $R^2$ = .701), the leadership status variable (effective/other) added significantly to the prediction for all five relevant performance variables. This study is also commendable for the attention given to potential confounds, such as ensuring the serial independence of all variables, correcting for inflation, and examining effects over extended time lags.

In short, with appropriate methodological corrections, these four studies indicate much larger leadership effects than implied by most of the literature. Although leadership does not explain all of the variance in organizational outcomes, such effects certainly are not trivial. . . .

# CONCLUSIONS FROM CURRENT LITERATURE

The results of research on the impact of changes in top-level leaders (e.g., Lieberson & O'Connor, 1972; Salancik & Pfeffer, 1977; Smith et al., 1984; Weiner & Mahoney, 1981), when properly interpreted and methodologically sound, show a consistent effect for leadership succession explaining 20 percent to 45 percent of the variance in relevant organizational outcomes. This finding has been largely overlooked in contemporary organizational theory on leadership.

Interestingly, this conclusion is consistent with much of the popular literature that stresses the importance of executive leadership in determining organizational performance. It underscores the practical and theoretical need for a systematic theory of executive leadership. Such a theory should address two main domains—individual differences in leadership ability and the mechanisms by which executive leaders impact on organizational performance. By individual differences we mean those dispositional factors that differentiate high ability leaders from low ability leaders. Such knowledge has obvious practical implications for selecting executive leaders; however, it goes beyond the scope of this study.

The second domain centers on the mechanisms by which executives affect organizational performance. We need a theory specifying what top-level leaders do that impacts on performance. Such a theory should also differentiate executive leadership from mere executive behavior. This type of theory would have profound implications for executive training, and it would also require that leadership be integrated with organizational theory.

We will focus on this need for a theory of executive leadership in the remainder of this article by discussing appropriate methodologies for investigating top-level leadership and by identifying some of the factors such a theory should address.

# IMPLICATIONS FOR A THEORY OF EXECUTIVE LEADERSHIP

Although the topic of executive leadership has been discussed extensively in the popular press and in historical accounts of specific organizations (e.g., Chandler, 1962), it has not been a major concern of leadership researchers or theorists. Their focus has been primarily lower-level leadership. We strongly urge researchers and theorists interested in leadership to consider upper levels of management as an important practical domain that needs theoretical and research attention. We believe the opportunity exists for the development of innovative and practically relevant leadership theory and research.

Commendably, some researchers have adopted a top-level focus. For example, Miller and Toulouse (1986) have investigated the effect of chief executive personality on corporate strategy and structure; Bourgeois (1985) reported that how accurately top-level management teams perceived the environment was positively related to the economic performance of their organization; and Donaldson and Lorsch (1983) undertook an in-depth study of executive decision making. Additional research using top-level executives is desired but, more importantly, an underlying theory that can integrate research findings would establish executive leadership as a distinct area of study. It is premature to say what a theory of executive leadership should be. We can, however, provide recommendations as to how such a theory should be developed.

## PROBLEMS TO AVOID

We think that the major problem to avoid is confusing levels or units of analysis in the development of leadership theory. Theories or empirical findings developed at lower levels do not necessarily apply to executive levels. In particular, there are two major problems in applying theories or results from studies of lower-level leadership to upper levels of an organization. First, leadership at lower levels is qualitatively different than upper-level leadership. Katz and Kahn (1978), Mintzberg (1973), and others have noted the qualitatively different nature of managerial and leader roles across levels.[1] According to Katz and Kahn (1978) leaders at the top echelons of organizations create organizational structure, formulate policy, and develop corporate strategies. Middle-level leaders interpret and elaborate structure, policy, and strategy, and lower-level leaders use technical knowledge, rewards, and sanctions to administer existing structure. Applying leadership theories developed at low levels to explain leadership at upper levels assumes a construct isomorphism across levels that is probably not true. Also, theories developed at lower levels may provide theoretical blinders (see Greenwald, Pratkanis, Leippe, & Baumgardner, 1986, for a general discussion of this issue), keeping researchers from discovering more appropriate perspectives when they focus on upper-level leadership.

A second problem to avoid centers around a predominant focus on style rather than substance in relation to leadership. Factors like the analytic and perceptual ability of leaders, their intelligence and experience, or the capacity to differentiate good from bad decisions are not incorporated into frameworks that focus only on style. For example, much leadership work has focused on the narrow question of how the dimensions of consideration and initiating structure relate to performance. A theory of executive leadership needs a much broader conceptual and methodological foundation. . . .

## WHERE TO LOOK FOR THEORY

We suspect that ideas relevant to theories of executive leadership will be found in very different sources or disciplines than are ideas relevant to lower-level leadership. Lower-level leadership theories seem to be based primarily on ideas borrowed from the social, motivational, and cognitive areas of psychology. We think more macro sources are appropriate for theories of executive-level leadership. In other words, leadership and organizational theory need to be integrated. Current developments in such areas as organizational culture, power and politics in organizations, systems theory, strategic management, and organizational evolution all interface with the problem of developing a theory of executive-level leadership.

An adequate coverage of all these topics is beyond the scope of this paper. As an illustration of this approach, however, we can provide a list of potential means by which executive leaders could impact on organizational performance. Table 2 is a list of such potential means that is organized within a systematic framework based on external/internal and direct/indirect dimensions.

## EXECUTIVE LEADERSHIP AND ORGANIZATIONAL PERFORMANCE

Many of the factors listed in Table 2 have obvious relations to the theoretical areas mentioned above. They are based on the general framework provided by open-systems theory (Katz & Kahn, 1978). Because open systems must interact with their environment, it follows that leaders can affect organizational performance by actions that operate on the *external* environment, such as exerting influence on government to change taxation or regulation policy, or they can operate on the *internal* environment to influence factors such as operating costs or product quality. Leadership theorists (Pfeffer, 1981) have also noted that leaders can impact on organizational outcomes through either *direct* means, such as formulating appropriate corporate level strategy, or by *indirect* means, such as effectively managing the symbols that help build commitment of employees to an organization. Direct means often involve the application of influence and/or political power applied either externally or internally. For example, changing regulatory policy requires substantial political influence in government or regulatory agencies. Similarly, reducing costs often involves tough decisions that require internal power to implement. Indirect means such as creating and maintaining a favorable public image often require that top executives be effective symbols or good communicators. Similar skills applied internally may be crucial in creating an organizational climate and culture that motivates and retains employees.

An issue that should be addressed is whether altering factors such as corporate strategy, internal organization, or production technology reflects top-level leadership or is better conceptualized simply as executive decision making. We believe the construct of leadership is crucial to changes affecting the above factors, for rarely does a single individual have the authority to unilaterally make such changes. Instead, changes require the agreement of management teams. Attaining such agreement often requires the application of social influence that goes beyond one's formal position. Such influence falls within common definitions of leadership as being an influence increment going beyond the formal powers associated with one's office (Katz & Kahn, 1978). Increments in influence are particularly necessary for implementing externally focused means to affect organizational performance.

The link between leadership and major changes in organizations is also underscored by recent work on organizational evolution. Tushman and Romanelli (1985) argue that organizations cycle through periods of relative stability and periods of radical reorientations and change. Though reorientations are often precipitated by external factors, they argue that executive leadership is often critical in both overcoming internal resistance to change and in guiding the reorientation. Moreover, how effectively top-level leaders manage such reorientations is a crucial determinant of organizational performance. Chandler's (1962) historical account of the development of organizations makes a similar point.

**TABLE 2   Potential Means by Which Top-level Leaders Can Affect Organizational Performance**

| Target | Objective | Tactics | |
| | | Direct | Indirect |
| --- | --- | --- | --- |
| **A. Influencing External Environments** | | | |
| 1. Government policy (e.g., regulation, taxation, trade). | Change policy to reduce uncertainty or increase resources. | Direct political influence. | Political influence via other groups (e.g., unions, suppliers). |
| 2. Acquiring resources and maintaining boundaries. | Increase stability. | Horizontal or vertical integration. | Create favorable public image or opinion. |
| | Reduce competition. | Promote entry barriers and noncompetitive pricing. | Enhance image of organization or product. |
| **B. Adapting to External Environments** | | | |
| 1. Choice of markets or environments. | Increased stability and munificence. | Strategic planning. | Influence top management's schemas; select those with similar schemas. |
| 2. Management and production system. | Fit with environment and strategy. | Organizational design. | Guide top management's labelling of environments. |
| **C. Internal Influence and Adaptation** | | | |
| 1. Subsystem organization and management. | Rationalization and integration. | Definition and functional specification of roles. | Shape top management's schemas of organizing; select those with similar schemas. |
| | Coordination and appraisal. | Design and implementation of management information systems. | Use information as sign and symbol. |
| 2. Productivity. | Increase organizational efficiency. | Reduce capital or personnel costs. | Strengthen productivity norms. |
| 3. Quality. | Increase product quality. | Increase quality control. | Strengthen quality norms. |
| 4. Organizational climate and culture. | Increase motivation and commitment of employees. | Determine or influence organizational politics. | Enhance participative decision making norms; symbolism of CEO. |

Note: For each objective there are additional tactics, however, space limitations prohibit their inclusion in this table.

He argues that executive leaders have a large impact in shaping strategic choices and notes that dramatic changes in strategies and structures often occur only when top executives also change.

A complement to theories of organizational evolution is the work done on the impact of executive leaders' problem-solving style and cognitive schemas. For example, Dutton and Jackson (1987) argue that the nature of leaders' cognitive categories helps them interpret trends in their organization or environment, thereby narrowing the range of actions they may consider. The same situation could be interpreted as a "threat" or as an "opportunity" depending on how it was categorized by leaders. These different interpretations affect leaders' processing of information as well as social processes involving communication and persuasion. Such work shows how the cognitive processes and schemas of executive leaders affect the more macro strategic choices they consider. Work in areas such as individual differences in decision making needs to be integrated with the more macro topics previously mentioned to explain how top-level leaders impact on organizational performance. Also, this cognitively oriented work could be developed to help explain many of the indirect effects noted in Table 2.

## CONCLUSIONS

We have argued that the academic literature on leadership has tended to neglect the topic of executive leadership largely because a few key articles have been widely misinterpreted.[2] We carefully reexamined those articles and the requirements to interpret succession studies. Based on this examination, we concluded that *executive* leaders do have a substantial impact on organizational performance. This conclusion illustrates the practical and theoretical need for more attention to the topic of executive-level leadership.

Although it is beyond the scope of this article to present such a theory, we provided several methodological recommendations pertinent to developing such a theory. Specifically, confusion over levels of analysis should be avoided, new methodologies should be seriously considered, and very different theoretical bases should be explored. We also offered some preliminary ideas on *macro*-level organizational theories that are relevant to executive leadership. Further, we suggested that such a theory could be organized along the internal/external and direct/indirect dimensions, and we used these dimensions to organize a list of potential means by which executive-level leaders could impact on organizational performance. Finally, we noted that these macro topics should be integrated with micro-level work demonstrating how the schemas and implicit theories of executives affect their strategic judgments and activities.

We think that such a theoretical area would have a natural link with work on leadership succession, for it specifies many potential means by which succession can impact on organizational performance, helping to explain why some changes in executive leaders have little impact on performance whereas other changes have profound and lasting ramifications. If developed further, such a theory would have practical importance as well, for it would have clear implications for training and selecting executive-level leaders. We think the topic of executive leadership offers a challenging and exciting opportunity for both leadership and management theorists. We hope that future researchers in these areas give this topic increased attention.

## Notes

1. We thank the anonymous reviewer who brought several of these studies to our attention.

2. This topic also may have been overlooked due to the inherent difficulties involved with research using executive samples as well as the micro-level orientation of most leadership researchers.

## References

Aupperle, K. E., Acar, W., & Booth, D. E. (1986). An empirical critique of "In search of excellence": How excellent are the excellent companies? *Journal of Management, 12,* 499–512.

Bourgeois, III, L. J. (1985). Strategic goals, perceived uncertainty, and economic performance in volatile environments. *Academy of Management Journal, 28,* 548–573.

Brown, M. C. (1982). Administrative succession and organizational performance: The succession effect. *Administrative Science Quarterly, 27,* 1–16.

Carroll, G. R. (1984). Dynamics of publisher succession in newspaper organizations. *Administrative Science Quarterly, 29,* 93–113.

Chandler Jr., A. D. (1962). *Strategy and structure: Chapters in the history of the industrial enterprise.* Cambridge, MA: M.I.T.

Donaldson, G., & Lorsch, J. W. (1983). *Decision making at the top: The shaping of strategic direction.* New York: Basic Books.

Dutton, J. E., & Jackson, S. E. (1987). The categorization of strategic issues by decision makers and its links to organizational action. *Academy of Management Review, 12,* 76–90.

Greenwald, A. G., Pratkanis, A. R., Leippe, M. R., & Baumgardner, M. H. (1986). Under what conditions does theory obstruct research progress? *Psychological Review, 93,* 216–229

Gupta, A. K. (1986). Matching managers to strategies: Point and counterpoint. *Human Resource Management, 25,* 215–234.

Jones, M. B. (1974). Regressing group on individual effectiveness. *Organizational Behavior and Human Performance, 11,* 426–451.

Katz, D., & Kahn, R. L. (1978). *The social psychology of organizations* (2nd ed.). New York: Wiley.

Lieberson, S., & O'Connor, J. F. (1972). Leadership and organizational performance: A study of large corporations. *American Sociological Review, 37,* 117–130.

Meindl, J. R., & Ehrlich, S. B. (1987). The romance of leadership and the evaluation of organizational performance. *Academy of Management Journal, 30,* 91–109.

Meindl, J. R., Ehrlich, S. B., & Dukerich, J. M. (1985). The romance of leadership. *Administrative Science Quarterly, 30,* 78–102.

Miller, D., & Toulouse, J. (1986). Chief executive personality and structure in small firms. *Management Science, 32,* 1389–1409.

Mintzberg, H. (1973). *The nature of managerial work.* New York: Harper & Row.

Peters, T., & Austin, N. (1985). *A passion for excellence: The leadership difference.* New York: Random House.

Pfeffer, J. (1981). Management as symbolic action: The creation and maintenance of organizational paradigms. In L. L. Cummings & B. M. Staw (Eds.), *Research in organizational behavior* (Vol. 3, pp. 1–52). Greenwich, CT: JAI Press.

Pfeffer, J. (1977). The ambiguity of leadership. *Academy of Management Review, 2,* 104–112.

Pfeffer, J., & Davis-Blake, A. (1986). Administrative succession and organizational performance: How administrator experience mediates the succession effect. *Academy of Management Journal, 29,* 72–83.

Salancik, G. R., & Pfeffer, J. (1977). Constraints on administrator discretion: The limited influence of mayors on city budgets. *Urban Affairs Quarterly, 12,* 475–498.

Smith, J. E., Carson, K. P., & Alexander, R. A. (1984). Leadership: It can make a difference. *Academy of Management Journal, 27,* 765–776.

Tsui, A. S. (1984). A role set analysis of managerial reputation. *Organizational Behavior and Human Performance, 34,* 64–96.

Tushman, M. L., & Romanelli, E. (1985). Organizational evolution: A metamorphosis model of convergence and reorientation. In L. L. Cummings & B. M. Staw (Eds.), *Research in organizational behavior* (Vol. 7, pp. 171–222). Greenwich, CT: JAI Press.

Weiner, N., & Mahoney, T. A. (1981). A model of corporate performance as a function of environmental, organizational, and leadership influences. *Academy of Management Journal, 24,* 453–470.

# Part Two

# Beyond the Theory and into the Practice of Leadership

The first 15 chapters have been devoted to a historical sampling of the empirical and conceptual literature on leadership and the leadership process. However, there are many other sources of learning about leadership, and these should not be overlooked. In particular, this section provides a glimpse into three domains that can be viewed as practitioner reflections and reports, analytical opportunities, and experiential exercises.

## PRACTITIONER REFLECTIONS AND REPORTS

A wide range of leaders (especially CEOs) have taken the initiative to think about, and report their insights into, what made them successful. Examples include Jack Welch at GE, Andy Grove at Intel, Max DePree at Herman Miller, Harvey Mackay at Mackay Envelope, Mary Kay Ash at Mary Kay Cosmetics, John Sculley at Apple, Ricardo Semler at Semco, Steven Jobs at NeXt, Harold Geneen at ITT, David Kearns at Xerox, and Donald Petersen at Ford Motor Company. (In other cases, independent authors have provided biographies of corporate leaders, such as Bill Gates at Microsoft, Jack Welch at GE, or Ted Turner at TBS and other ventures). In addition, scholars (such as Warren Bennis, John Kotter, Burt Nanus, John Gardner, and Noel Tichy) and consultants (such as William Byham and Stephen Covey) have observed leaders in action and shared their observations and conclusions in the form of books written for the practitioner market. These portraits are often rich in anecdotal information and contemporary illustrations, although sometimes lacking the broader data basis of well-designed studies. We encourage you to read some of these "contemporary and popular" leadership books, as they provide a different perspective on leading and the leadership phenomenon. Some of the more recent publications that you might find of interest are the following:

Anderson, *Transforming Leadership*

Blanchard, *Empowerment Takes More than a Minute*

Block, *Stewardship*

Bolman and Deal, *Leading with Soul*

Bradford and Cohen, *Power Up: Transforming Organizations through Shared Leadership*

Chaffee, *Accountable Leadership*

Crosby, *The Absolutes of Leadership*

Daft and Lengel, *Fusion Leadership*

DePree, *Leading without Power*

Fairholm, *Capturing the Heart of Leadership*

Fairhurst, *The Art of Framing: Managing the Language of Leadership*

Hesselbein, *The Leader of the Future*

Jaworski, *Synchronicity: The Inner Path of Leadership*

Kets de Vries, *Leaders, Fools, and Impostors*

Kotter, *Leading Change*

Manz, *The Leadership Wisdom of Jesus*

Mileham, *Transforming Corporate Leadership*

Miles, *Leading Corporate Transformation*

Murphy, *Leadership IQ*

Nair, *A Higher Standard of Leadership*

Nanus, *Visionary Leadership*

O'Toole, *Leading Change*

Pearce, *Leading Out Loud*

Pitcher, *The Drama of Leadership*

Pias, *Person-centered Leadership: An American Approach to Participatory Management*

Quinn, *Deep Change*

Spears, *Reflections on Leadership*

Taffinder, *The New Leaders*

Tichy and Cohen, *The Leadership Engine*

Wells, *From Sage to Artisan: The Nine Roles of the Value-driven Leader*

Wheatley, *The New Science of Leadership*

White, *The Future of Leadership*

## ANALYTICAL OPPORTUNITIES

It is a well-established fact that people learn in different ways. One fruitful approach is through the analysis of cases and (shorter) incidents. These provide opportunities to sift through information, identify key issues, determine the applicability of relevant theories, and suggest appropriate action plans. Cases and incidents, properly guided by a discussion leader, make it possible for the analyst to engage in both deductive (application of principles) and inductive (development of tentative generalizations) thinking. Also, because they are drawn from actual circumstances, they provide a sense of realism to the study of the leadership process. A number of cases and incidents are included to provide an opportunity for learning through the analysis and application of concepts.

## EXPERIENTIAL EXERCISES

An oft-quoted phrase (attributed to Confucius and others) suggests that "I hear and I forget, I see and I remember, I do and I understand." This forms the basic rationale for learning some things through experience. Structured experiential exercises typically involve the participants either in a physical activity or in generating some relevant individual or group data. The group is then invited to engage in a retrospective discussion of what took place or what the "data" mean (in the context of leadership theories). The process of active involvement serves as a powerful incentive to "see" abstract concepts take on meaning and shape realistic personal agendas for the future. Again, we have included a small sample of experiential exercises to stimulate such personalized learning.

# Applications

# Case Studies
# & Experiential Exercises

## Case

# Sam Perkins

Dr. Sam Perkins, a graduate of the Harvard University College of Medicine, was engaged in the private practice of internal medicine for 12 years. Fourteen months ago, he was persuaded by the governor to give up private practice to be director of the State Division of Human Services.

After one year as director, Perkins recognized he had made little progress in reducing the considerable inefficiency in the Division of Human Services. Employee morale and effectiveness seemed even lower than when he assumed the position. He realized his past training and experiences were of a clinical nature with little exposure to effective leadership techniques. Perkins decided to research literature published on the subject of leadership available to him at a local university.

Perkins soon realized that management scholars are divided on the question of what constitutes effective leadership. Some feel that leaders are born with certain identifiable personality traits that make them effective leaders. Others feel a leader can learn to be effective by treating subordinates with a personal and considerate approach and by giving particular attention to the subordinate's need for good working conditions. Still others emphasize the importance of developing a style of leadership characterized by either authoritarian, democratic, or laissez-faire approaches. Perkins was confused further when he learned there are a growing number of scholars who advocate that effective leadership is contin-

gent on the situation, and a proper response to the question of what constitutes effective leadership is that it "depends on the situation."

Since a state university was located nearby, Perkins contacted its College of Business Administration dean. The dean referred him to the director of the college's Management Center, Professor Joel McCann. Discussions between Perkins and McCann resulted in a tentative agreement that the Management Center would organize a series of leadership training sessions for the State Division of Human Services. Before agreeing on the price tag for the leadership conference, Perkins asked McCann to prepare a proposal reflecting his thoughts on the following:

## QUESTIONS

1. How will the question of what constitutes effective leadership be answered during the conference?

2. How will the lack of congruence among leadership researchers be resolved or reconciled?

3. What will be the specific subject content of the conference?

4. Who will the instructors be?

5. What will be the conference's duration?

6. How can the conference's effectiveness be evaluated?

7. What policies should the State Division of Human Services adopt regarding who the conference participants should be and how they should be selected? How can these policies be best implemented?

**Source:** Reprinted with permission from Champion/James, "Effective Leadership," *Critical Incidents in Management* (Homewood, IL: Richard D. Irwin, Inc.).

## Case

# A Different Style of Leadership

In my new position as Systems Engineer with BBG Industries, my initial assignment was in the Glass Research and Development Automations Section. My immediate supervisor, Al Sirroco, was given the mission of providing computer services for laboratory personnel and production, thus bridging the gap between data processing and process control. With a background in chemical engineering and computer sciences, Al was instrumental in pioneering the powerful and beneficial use of the computer as an aid to scientists and engineers. Utilizing a rented time-shared terminal, results were obtained that maximized calculation thruput and accuracy, thus providing concise historical records so vital in the research environment. Upper management was very impressed by Al's initial success in the realm of automation. The formation of the automation section was concrete evidence that management encouraged further growth in this field for BBG Industries.

Al faced the basic problem of obtaining group cohesiveness and coordination in order to build it into an effective organization. People in our group had diverse backgrounds, including a PhD in mathematics, computer operators with high-school diplomas, electrical engineers, and operations research personnel.

To overcome possible communications barriers among members of such a diverse unit, informal group meetings were held once a month. During such meetings each member could openly expound upon any problems requiring clarification, without any fear of retaliation. These staff meetings created an air of openness and relaxation of the status differences caused by differences in rank in our group. Each member had ample opportunity to make an informal presentation of what he or she was contributing to the group effort. Talk about work often spilled over to talk about personal life; the net effect was to produce a feeling of togetherness. After awhile one got the impression that any group member would help any other member with any kind of problem. One weekend, five of us helped bail out Tim, a computer operator, whose basement flooded in a rainstorm.

**Source:** Reprinted with permission from Andrew J. DuBrin (Robert E. Gmitter researched and wrote this case, with the exception of several editorial changes); *Casebook of Organizational Behavior,* Copyright 1977, Pergamon Press.

Our group obtained its first real surprise about Al's approach to managing people following a once-in-a-lifetime incident. An unfortunate situation occurred at the computer center which required the immediate dismissal of a key senior analyst. Although quiet and seemingly introverted, the analyst was held in high esteem because of his diligence and his record of accomplishment. Everyone in the group wondered what violation necessitated such drastic action on Al's part.

Rumors spread that perhaps the systems analyst had been engaged in sabotage, physical attack upon a fellow worker, criminal activity, drug abuse, or maybe a combination of several of these. The day after the incident, Al summoned the group into his office for an important announcement. He informed us that the extreme dedication to job performance shown by this systems analyst had caused him to suffer a nervous breakdown. Al maintained that it was necessary for his safety and the safety of the group for this man to be immediately separated from the company.

Evidence to corroborate Al's explanation was discovered when the individual's desk was cleaned out. A note was found buried beneath some papers in one of the drawers. His writings reflected several approaches to suicide. Al instigated efforts and received approval for the analyst to undergo psychiatric help immediately at the company's expense. In addition, severance pay of six month's salary was granted to him, and the company agreed to help him find future employment once his condition improved.

Al's explanation and the suicide note seemed to satisfy everyone's curiosity. However, several weeks later the real cause for the dismissal of the systems analyst surfaced via the company grapevine. One night when the analyst was working late, the only other employee in the building was a female computer operator. While she was walking down the aisle between the office and the computer equipment, he unzipped his pants, exposing himself. Upset by the incident, the computer operator reported the analyst's exhibitionism to her father, a manager in the laboratory. The father demanded retaliation and subsequent criminal prosecution.

Al's handling of the situation was unique and the termination of the systems analyst placated the father. By firing the analyst, the operator was spared the embarrassment of confronting him again at work. Yet, a couple of people in the group felt that Al's handling of the situation was bizarre. Irv, a mathematician, expressed it this way:

"Al sure is cool under pressure, but he's also quite a moralist. Sure, the poor guy exposed himself once that we know of. We cannot estimate the probability that he would expose himself again given the same circumstances. Maybe the father who complained so bitterly was really just jealous of the systems analyst. Worst of all, I question the value of Al making up a phony story just to bury the incident. If we fired everybody in this company who displayed a little deviant behavior once in their lives, we would probably have a pretty thin work force."

Al's approach to leadership can also be understood in his handling of overtime work. Many times crucial projects required extended periods of late hours in order to meet critical deadlines. For exempt professionals, the lab rule stipulated that no compensation would be given, regardless of the time expended in discharging one's responsibilities.

Al informally modified the rule for his group. The term "E-Time," for earned time, could be accumulated by each member for extra hours worked. This was an honor system with responsibility left entirely to the individual. Earned time could be cashed in by trading it for time off with pay when the project load lessened. Al's policy minimized the long, arduous hours of extended toil and promoted excellent group morale.

Al strived constantly to support individual accomplishments and to foster creativity in the glass industry. The director of research required a monthly meeting to discuss his group's progress, concepts, improvements, and future goals. Although key projects were mandatory in the agenda, voluntary participation and the initiation of topics were allowed at these important meetings. Each member of the group was encouraged by Al to make his contribution.

Al's impact upon people can be illustrated in his dealings with Kiwabi, a senior mathematician in the group. Kiwabi was advised to present a radical technique for the regression analysis of process data which reduced the time and amount of data, yet maintained qualitative accuracy. His brief presentation in the limelight impressed upper management and paved the way toward Kiwabi obtaining a fully paid leave of absence to obtain his PhD.

A study I had made of various computer systems for process control, as to their power and cost, was scheduled by Al for one of these meetings. My presentation led to future study of this same topic, which verified my findings. Not only was my career as a systems engineer brightened because of it, but the company benefited by obtaining more efficient computer systems with the latest technology at the maximum return upon investment. I honestly believe that without Al's prodding and guidance this study would not have come to fruition.

Supplementing our exposure at meetings, Al would circulate, via interlab memos, accomplishments and proposals of his personnel. By this mechanism, all pertinent managers and head scientists were made aware of the existence of group members. It also provided a first-rate opportunity for interface with groups requiring our supportive capabilities in the field of automation.

Al also scheduled trips to the plants to introduce us, explain our function, and relate our specialties. Plant associates could depend upon our expertise to assist them with problems. One such problem solved by our group was the correct depositing of raw materials, such as sand and dolomite, into holding bins. Predetermined amounts of raw material are required for each raw batch composition of glass before heating. The existing manual method had caused production upset due to the wrong ingredients in the bins. An automated, batch unloading protection system was designed, developed, and implemented by our group.

You can understand Al's comprehensive approach to managing people only by sampling the kind of things he did for people. Al would arrange trips for us to other companies, such as Mead Paper, to exchange technological applications and broaden our knowledge of automation. Al also encouraged a few of us to write articles for trade journals, and even provided help in this area. On the basis of these efforts a couple of us have achieved some national recognition.

Al had a keen sense of the ever-persistent technological changes taking place in the world of automation. To maintain the group's expertise, Al would submit a list of appropriate courses relevant to each individual's background. Participation and attendance at symposia and conferences were integrated into the work schedule. One of Al's pet projects was to get us involved in the Process Control Workshop at Purdue University.

The workshop consisted of international representation dedicated to standardization of the principles of process control automation.

For my money, Al is a top manager. But not everybody agrees with me. One of the skeptics in our groups said, "If Al walked into my office at 4:30 and reminded me to brush my teeth because it was good for me, I wouldn't be surprised. It would fit his leadership style."

## QUESTIONS

1. Evaluate Al Sirroco's handling of the systems analyst problem. What would you have done if you were the supervisor?

2. What style of leadership do you prefer? Would you want a leader like Al? Discuss the pros and cons.

## Case

# Donny Is My Leader

## BREAKING IN HARVEY

The first day I joined the team, Donny asked me how far I was going to run. The team had a goal of running two miles every Monday, Wednesday, and Friday morning, at a fair pace—about eight minutes a mile—on an inside track with 18 laps to the mile. I said I'd try for one mile and a half, a distance I had occasionally managed to complete jogging by myself. I ran at the tail end of the team and did, in fact, run the mile and a half. At the end of a mile and a half, Donny turned and shouted back to me from his place at the front of the group, "OK, Harvey, that's enough!" And I stopped.

When the others finished, Donny came over and congratulated me. He told me I'd run well. He suggested I try adding three more laps next time, stay at that level for a while, and then add another three until I reached the 36 laps or two-mile objective of the team.

The "team" is a very informal collection of people with no formally appointed leader. Donny, however, is referred to as the coach. The team has existed for a while with a small, hard core and with others who come and go. The regulars comprise Donny, who always runs on the right side of the "pacer," who is almost always "Choc," and Herb, who runs about fourth and takes over as leader when Donny is away. Barrie generally runs third and sometimes sets the pace but is sort of an irregular regular since he occasionally forsakes the group for a squash game or gets in late after a hard night. Harry and Larry are two recent regulars. Larry always runs last and

Harry runs just ahead of me. There are three or four others who occasionally join us. On some mornings we are as few as four running. On other mornings there are nine running.

My second day was a beautiful, warm morning and we ran outside. I quit after a mile and a quarter. Harry quit after a mile. No one said anything to us about the running—neither good nor bad.

My third day and my big mistake! I vowed to run one mile and 12 laps to myself, 3 better than my previous inside run. At the end of the 11th lap of the second mile, since I still had a little left in me, I sprinted the last lap, passing everyone. I'd noticed that all the finishers usually sprinted for the last one or two laps. However, when he was done, Donny came over and severely castigated me. How could I possibly have sprinted? If I could sprint, I must have had some strength left in me and therefore I could have gone for several more laps; in fact, I might even have been able to finish the two miles. He verbally lashed out at me several times both on the track and back down in the locker room. The others joined in, though in a more teasing mode. They said that next time I was not only going to run the two miles, but they would make me set the pace.

Soon after this occurrence, Harry became the culprit and the victim of Donny's wrath. We did each lap in about 28 seconds. Donny was the timekeeper. He shouted out the time for the first lap and for the first mile, and he counted out every second lap each time we passed the starting point (where a wall clock was mounted). Donny constantly encouraged us to keep going. Herb and Larry did so too. They called out milestones, "Three-quarters done!" or "Two-thirds done!" or "Five laps to go!" Near the end of the run, they kept up a steady stream of comments to urge those of us who were struggling to keep going and to try to finish the distance. On this particular day, at the end of the first lap, Harry said, "Hey, we're going too fast! We did it in 20 seconds." It was a bad day. Quite a few of us didn't finish. Donny was angry. He took it out on Harry repeatedly. He said that Harry's statement was incorrect and, furthermore, it had discouraged several of the team members, making them—including me—quit. He carried on all the way down to the locker room, in the showers, and even into the next running day.

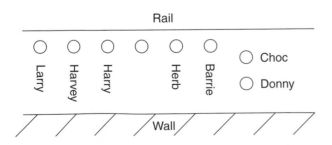

**Source:** Kolodny, H. F. & House, R. J., "Donny Is My Leader: A Case Study of Leadership," *The Organizational Behavior Teaching Journal* VI, no. 2 (1981), pp. 51–56. Copyright 1981 The Organizational Behavior Teaching Society. Reprinted by permission of Sage Publications, Inc.

# WEIGH-IN

Once a month, Donny had us weigh in. At that time, we set our objectives for how much weight we would lose by the next weigh-in. He made a big occasion out of it, talking about it several days before, advising us to begin to fast a few days before, and culminating with a rather ceremonious act on the day of the weigh-in.

Stepping out to the scale, he asked each person to announce his objective, then weighed him and made a large fanfare about those who had achieved their objective and those who hadn't. We were put into two groupings: those who'd reached target and those who had not. Each one who didn't was publicly castigated, in humour, and asked to reset goals for the next weigh-in. The successful ones were not pressed.

The next running day after the weigh-in, there was a great ceremony. Herb received a jersey on which was printed "Doctor D's Track Team." Choc had had them made up and kept them in his locker waiting for the appropriate occasion to have one handed out. Herb was the only one to be awarded. He had not only consistently run the distance, but he had also made his weight target. Donny let us all know that he wasn't going to be generous about giving the others out—even though they were all ready and printed. Only consistent demonstrations of performance across several fronts would merit a "Doctor D's Track Team" jersey.

# CHALLENGING THE LEADER

Larry usually ran in last place with the team. One summer he broke his ankle playing baseball, and he didn't run with us for most of the year. Then he started running again, sometimes joining us for short periods, sometimes running before or after us, sometimes faster for short spurts, though usually slower. He was slowly getting back in top shape.

Then one day he took his usual position at the rear as we were starting. After the first few laps, Donny had not called out the number of laps, and Larry chose to call them out loudly. Someone kibitzed and said that wasn't his job. I chipped in jokingly and said that I liked it when Larry called the laps. It was like old times again, I said, having Larry back. Larry kept calling the laps out as we completed them, and Donny, up front, said nothing.

Then Larry lost count somewhere around the eighth or ninth lap. I shouted to Donny, up front, to tell us where we were but he wouldn't answer. Because I feel lost when I don't know what I've run, I asked a few more times, "Would someone please say where we are?" Donny didn't answer. Then, after a while, in a loud voice, he said, "Strictly for Harvey, that was one mile we just passed." The next mile, he gave us two counts, one at the half mile and one at the end of the second mile. Normally he would count out every two laps (i.e., nine times a mile). In the third mile, he gave us three counts.

At the end of the run, he muttered something about "Teaching you guys respect the hard way."

**EXERCISE**
*What You See Is
(Not Necessarily)
What You Get:
Connecting
Observations of
Leadership
Figures to
Inferences*[1]

**Task:**

Class members, divided into three groups, are given one of three different objects (representing applicants for a top leadership position) to observe, touch, and assess.

**Group Size:**

Any number, as long as the group members can comfortably interact with each other (e.g., up to 10 or 15).

**Time Required:**

Approximately 45 minutes.

**Procedure:**

1. Divide the class into three groups, and present each group (preferably without the other groups seeing it) one of three objects—a ball of clay, a fancy bottle, or a tinkertoy figure. Tell them that their object represents a candidate for a leadership position in a for-profit firm.
2. Ask them to develop a comprehensive—but defensible—list of all the characteristics they can observe in their object.
3. After approximately 10 minutes, ask them to switch the focus of their efforts to generating a second list, which is an associated set of inferences about the leadership qualities (both positive and negative) that can be inferred from each characteristic.
4. Ask each group to briefly report (possibly using an overhead projector, flip chart paper, or the chalkboard), their group's conclusions (both lists).

**Discussion Questions:**

1. What similarities or differences do you see across the three candidates/objects?
2. Which "candidate" is most qualified for the position?
3. Under what conditions might the rejected candidates be effective in another context? Would it make any difference if the context was a not-for-profit organization?
4. What are the risks of relying on visual impressions and subsequent inferences to ascertain leadership traits? What other methods exist to identify leadership traits?
5. Which of the inferences made by another group are less defensible than others?
6. Which of the leader characteristics identified could be viewed as exactly the opposite in nature (desirable or undesirable)? Is this one of the "paradoxes" of leadership—that desirable leadership is in the eye of the beholder?
7. To what degree do we project our own characteristics (or valued characteristics) onto leadership "candidates"?
8. How does this exercise relate to the text's readings on "traits"?
9. If the groups now exchanged objects, would their observations of characteristics and the associated inferences be any different? If so, why?

[1] An interesting reading for reference in conjunction with this exercise is Robert Cunningham, "Meet Dr. Clay and Dr. Glass: A Leadership Exercise," *Journal of Management Education* (May 1997), pp. 262–64.

**EXERCISE**
*Tinkertoy
Construction*

A sighted group leader instructs blindfolded subordinates in putting together a Tinkertoy structure.

**Task:**

Groups of 4 to 6 persons.

**Group Size:**

One set of basic Tinkertoys for each group (or only one, if a demonstration group is to be used).
One blindfold for each participant.
One picture of the structure to be built for each leader.

**Materials Needed:**

Approximately one hour.

**Time Required:**

Divide the class into groups. Ask each group to designate a leader for the exercise. All other members—the subordinates—are then asked to put on blindfolds. Once all subordinates are blindfolded, a picture of the structure to be built is handed to the leader of each group (see Figure 1). Leaders are told that they may do anything they wish to get their subordinates to build the structure, except remove the blindfolds or touch the Tinkertoys themselves.

**Procedure:**

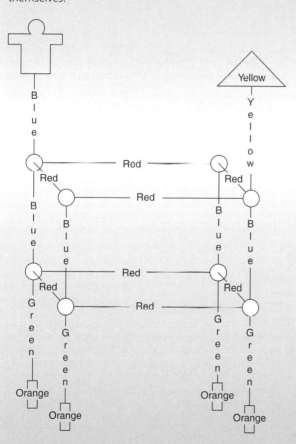

**FIGURE 1**
**Structure for
Blindfold
Leadership Exercise**

1. Does the structure look like you expected it to look? How is it different?
2. What did your leader do that was helpful?
3. What did your leader do that was not helpful?
4. What feelings did you have during, or following, this exercise?
5. What lessons for leadership can you derive from this experience?
6. What are the implications of, and relevant insights from, your readings about leadership?

**Discussion Questions:**

**Source:** Cindy P. Lindsay and Cathy A. Enz, "Resource Control and Visionary Leadership: Two Exercises," *Journal of Management Education* 15, no.1 (February 1991), pp. 127–35.

## EXERCISE
*Choosing a Leader*

| | |
|---|---|
| **Task:** | Class members select a leader and examine that person's life, significant contributing events, and leadership behaviors. |
| **Group Size:** | Members work as individuals initially, then combine their efforts in a group and all-class discussion. |
| **Materials Needed:** | None. |
| **Time Required:** | Approximately one hour in class. |
| **Procedure:** | Assign class members this task: |

"Examine the life of an individual whom you believe exemplifies the role of leader. This can be anyone, famous or not, past or present, industry or government, public or private, known to you personally or through the media. Some attention ought to be devoted to the chronology of events in the person's life. However, the bulk of your work should be directed at producing in-depth sociopsychological understanding. Pay attention to *how* the events and circumstances of the person's life affected the ultimate leadership self."

**Discussion Questions:**

1. Did your choice of leader come from:
   a. Public figures (current or historical)?
   b. Persons known from work?
   c. Family members?
   d. Personal acquaintances?
2. What factors do you think account for the class's observed distribution of choice from question 1?
3. Explore, in small groups, the leaders selected. What leadership qualities and characteristics are consistently represented there?
4. What can you learn about yourself as a leader from your choice of a leader to write about?

**Source:** David I. Sommers, "The Choice of a Leader to Write About Is Not a Random Event," *Journal of Management Education* (August 1991), pp. 359–61.

**Task:**

Rank-order a set of leader characteristics on an individual and group basis, comparing the results to those from a broad sample of top-level managers.

**Group Size:**

Groups of 3 to 5 persons.

**Materials Needed:**

One ranking sheet for each member.

**Time Required:**

Approximately one hour.

**Procedure:**

Distribute copies of the "Leader Characteristics" form to each class member (see Table 1). Ask them to rank-order the items from 1 to 10 according to which traits they most admire in leaders (1 being highest) and record their responses in column 2. Then form them into small discussion groups and have them develop a group-based ranking of the items from 1 to 10 and record their responses in column 4. Finally, allow them to score themselves (both individually and as a group) against the responses of 2,600 top-level managers (to be inserted in column 3).

**Discussion Questions:**

1. Which characteristics of leaders seem to be most admired by class members? Why?
2. What traits seem to be missing from this list?
3. How do these results compare to the research literature on leadership traits?
4. Why might your individual ranking differ from that of the top-level managers?
5. In a later book, Kouzes and Posner make a compelling argument that a leader's credibility is the most important ingredient contributing to his or her success (in the eyes of subordinates). Which factors in the list of 10 might be components of credibility?

**Source:** Data drawn from James M. Kouzes and Barry Z. Posner, *The Leadership Challenge* (San Francisco: Jossey-Bass, 1988), p. 17.

## TABLE 1   Leader Characteristics

| Trait | Columns | | | | |
| --- | --- | --- | --- | --- | --- |
| | 1 | 2 (Ind.) | 3 | 4 (Grp.) | 5 |
| Ambitious | | | | | |
| Caring | | | | | |
| Competent | | | | | |
| Determined | | | | | |
| Forward-looking | | | | | |
| Honest | | | | | |
| Imaginative | | | | | |
| Inspiring | | | | | |
| Loyal | | | | | |
| Self-controlled | | | | | |

**Source:** Data drawn from James M. Kouzes and Barry Z. Posner, *The Leadership Challenge* (San Francisco: Jossey-Bass, 1988), p. 17.

**EXERCISE**

*Leader–Subordinate Friendships (LSFs)*

| | |
|---|---|
| **Task:** | Participants complete the LSF questionnaire, share and tabulate results, and discuss their implications. |
| **Group Size:** | Groups of 3 to 5 persons. |
| **Materials Needed:** | One copy of the questionnaire for each participant (see Table 1). One transparency master for tabulating results (see Table 2). |
| **Time Required:** | Minimum of one hour, depending on depth of discussion desired. |
| **Procedure:** | Distribute a copy of the LSF questionnaire to each participant and allow a few minutes for its completion. Using a show of hands for each question and response category, tabulate the results (preferably using a visual display, such as the chalkboard or a transparency). Then lead the group in a discussion of the following questions. |
| **Discussion Questions:** | 1. What does *friendship* mean to you? |
| | 2. Can leaders and subordinates be friends on the job and still maintain an effective work environment? |
| | 3. What skills contribute to friendships? |
| | 4. What are the risks of these friendships? |
| | 5. Can LSFs substitute for other leader behaviors? |
| | 6. How friendly should a leader be with followers? |
| | 7. What are the organizationally desirable consequences of leader–subordinate friendships? |
| | 8. Is it possible that LSFs would prevent objective appraisal of subordinate performance? |
| | 9. How can one obtain the benefits of LSFs without incurring the drawbacks? |
| | 10. How does LSF relate to a leader's source of power? |

## TABLE 1   Leader–Subordinate Friendship Questionnaire

Please respond to the following statements according to your level of agreement: SA—Strongly agree; A—Agree; N—Neutral; D—Disagree; SD—Strongly disagree. Circle the appropriate letters.

1.  Managers should not try to maintain friendships with subordinates. — SA  A  N  D  SD
2.  It is possible to maintain friendships with subordinates without damaging one's effectiveness as a leader. — SA  A  N  D  SD
3.  As for myself, it works best if I do not try to be friends with my subordinates. — SA  A  N  D  SD
4.  Maintaining friendships with subordinates actually can make one a better leader. — SA  A  N  D  SD
5.  There is a certain skill associated with maintaining leader–subordinate friendships and still being an effective leader: Some managers have it and some don't. — SA  A  N  D  SD
6.  Friendships between leaders and subordinates are a natural consequence growing out of close physical proximity and considerable interpersonal contact. — SA  A  N  D  SD
7.  If a manager wants to maintain a friendship with one subordinate, then he or she must try to maintain friendship relationships with all subordinates. — SA  A  N  D  SD
8.  If a manager is going to maintain friendship relationships with subordinates at all, it might be a good idea to tie those relationships to performance (i.e., the better the performer, the more you encourage a friendship relationship with that subordinate). — SA  A  N  D  SD
9.  Maintaining friendships with subordinates gives a manager more information on which to base business decisions. — SA  A  N  D  SD
10.  Maintaining friendships with subordinates facilitates a manager's ability to motivate subordinates. — SA  A  N  D  SD
11.  The closer the leader–subordinate friendship, the greater the likelihood the subordinate will feel free to disagree with the boss. — SA  A  N  D  SD
12.  Maintaining leader–subordinate friendships gives the subordinate more power to influence the leader. — SA  A  N  D  SD
13.  It is generally not a good idea for subordinates to have the power to influence their bosses. — SA  A  N  D  SD
14.  The closer the friendship relationship between leader and subordinate, the greater the likelihood that the leader will feel free to give the negative performance feedback when a subordinate is doing poorly. — SA  A  N  D  SD
15.  The closer the leader–subordinate friendship, the less likely it is that a leader will give a subordinate a negative mark on a formal performance appraisal. — SA  A  N  D  SD
16.  Being a considerate manager or leader is the same as maintaining a friendship relationship with subordinates. — SA  A  N  D  SD
17.  It is easier for staff-area managers to maintain leader–subordinate friendships than it is for production or line-area managers. — SA  A  N  D  SD
18.  It is easier for an upper-level manager (a vice president for instance) to maintain leader–subordinate friendships with his or her immediate subordinates than it is for a lower-level manager or supervisor. — SA  A  N  D  SD
19.  What do you see as the major benefits, if any, of a manager maintaining friendships with subordinates?

    1.

    2.

    3.

    4.

20.  What do you see as the major drawbacks, if any, of a manager maintaining friendships with subordinates?

    1.

    2.

    3.

    4.

21.  In general, the benefits of maintaining leader–subordinate friendships outweigh the drawbacks. — SA  A  N  D  SD

**TABLE 2**   **Leader–Subordinate Friendship Tally**

| Question | Responses | | | | |
|---|---|---|---|---|---|
| | SA | A | N | D | SD |
| 1. | | | | | |
| 2. | | | | | |
| 3. | | | | | |
| 4. | | | | | |
| 5. | | | | | |
| 6. | | | | | |
| 7. | | | | | |
| 8. | | | | | |
| 9. | | | | | |
| 10. | | | | | |
| 11. | | | | | |
| 12. | | | | | |
| 13. | | | | | |
| 14. | | | | | |
| 15. | | | | | |
| 16. | | | | | |
| 17. | | | | | |
| 18. | | | | | |
| 21. | | | | | |

**Source:** Robert R. Taylor, Susan C. Hanlon, and Nancy G. Boyd, "Can Leaders and Subordinates Be Friends? A Classroom Approach for Addressing an Important Managerial Dilemma," *Journal of Management Education* (February 1992), pp. 39–55.

**EXERCISE**
*Leadership*
*(Locker-room)*
*Talks*

**Task:**

Class members are assigned a topic (see Table 1). Each member prepares and delivers a concise talk on the assigned topic, followed by class and instructor critiques of the effectiveness of the talk and the leadership dimensions demonstrated. The objective is to demonstrate the importance of, and develop, each student's confidence, willingness, and readiness to play an inspirational leadership role.

**Group Size:**

Any number (overlapping assignments to topics are possible).

**Time Required:**

Two minutes per student, plus critique time.

**Procedure:**

1. Explain the objectives of the exercise to the class.
2. Indicate the types of locker-room talk topics and how they fit into the classification scheme.
3. Assign topics and dates of presentations.
4. Cue the class members to act as real audiences, reacting as they might to the situation and the comments made by the speaker.
5. Call for two-minute talks, using a student timekeeper to cue the speaker when 15 seconds remain.
6. Call for comments from the class about the quality and effectiveness of the speeches, as well as the various dimensions of leadership displayed.

**Discussion Questions:**

1. What are the primary objectives of locker-room talks by leaders?
2. What are the primary abilities that need to be demonstrated by each speaker in these settings?
3. What characteristics of feedback to the speakers are most constructive?
4. How do you handle hostility? Distrust? Apathy?

*(continued)*

**TABLE 1    Topics for the Leadership Talks and a Classification of Each**

| Topic Number | Topic Description | Topic Number | Topic Description |
|---|---|---|---|
| 1. | Taking charge of an established group.<br>The speaker is a manager newly assigned to a group that has worked together under other managers for some time. | 7. | Reprimanding unacceptable behavior.<br>The speaker is calling to task certain individuals who have failed to perform up to required levels. |
| 2. | Announcing a new project.<br>The speaker is announcing a new undertaking to members of his or her department and is calling on all to rally behind the effort. | 8. | Calming a frightened group of people.<br>The speaker is endeavoring to restore peace and confidence to those who now panic in the face of distressing business developments. |
| 3. | Calling for better customer service.<br>The speaker is motivating all employees to be as attentive and responsive to the customer as possible. | 9. | Addressing a challenging opposition.<br>The speaker is presenting some heartfelt belief to a critical, even hostile, audience. |
| 4. | Calling for excellence and high-quality work.<br>The speaker is motivating all employees to perform their jobs with a commitment to meeting the highest possible standards. | 10. | Mediating opposing parties.<br>The speaker is calling for reconciliation between two groups bitterly opposed on some key issue. |
| 5. | Announcing the need for cost reductions.<br>The speaker is requesting that everyone look for ways to cut expenditures and immediately begin slashing spending. | 11. | Taking responsibility for error.<br>The speaker is the figurehead spokesman for an institution that has produced some unfortunate result affecting the audience. |
| 6. | Commending for a job well done.<br>The speaker is extolling a group of people who have worked very hard for an extended period to produce outstanding results. | 12. | Petitioning for special allowances.<br>The speaker is presenting the case for an institution seeking certain rights that must be authorized by some external body. |

|  | **Individual** | **Group** | **Institution** |
|---|---|---|---|
| ***Task-oriented*** | Taking responsibility:<br>Taking charge of an established group;<br>Introducing a new project;<br>Taking responsibility for error.[a] | Shaping behavior:<br>Commending for a job well done;<br>Reprimanding unacceptable behavior. | Forging a direction:<br>Calling for better customer service;<br>Calling for excellence and high-quality work;<br>Announcing the need for cost reductions. |
| ***Emotional-/values-/ oriented*** | Taking a stand:<br>Addressing a challenging opposition. | Building cohesion:<br>Calming a frightened group of people;<br>Mediating opposing parties. | Representing the firm:<br>Taking responsibility for error;[a]<br>Petitioning for special allowances. |

[a] This topic is suitable for both "taking responsibility" and "representing the firm."

**Source:** Richard G. Linowes, "Filling a Gap in Management Education: Giving Leadership Talks in the Classroom," *Journal of Management Education* (1992), pp. 6–24.

## EXERCISE
### *Follow the Leader*

**Task:**

Students are assigned to read biographical materials on well-known leaders and identify their relationship with their followers.

**Group Size:**

Any number.

**Time Required:**

Approximately one class session per leader studied.

**Procedure:**

Divide the class into study groups. Following prior reading, lecture, or discussion on "follow-ership" factors in leader effectiveness, assign (or allow choice in selection) one major leader (e.g., Lee Iacocca, Martin Luther King, Jr., Adolph Hitler, Eleanor Roosevelt, Mary Cunning-ham) per group. Provide the group with appropriate references documenting the leaders' lives, from which they may draw their analyses. Ask each group to identify:

1. The ways in which the leader they studied influenced his/her followers.
2. The influence of the followers on the leader studied.
3. How characteristics of their own and their followers' personalities affected the leader's success.

**Discussion Questions:**

1. Was your chosen leader successful?
2. Would you have willingly followed that leader?
3. What kinds of facts about the leader studied did you use to make your argument?
4. What kinds of facts about the leader studied did you omit in making your argument?
5. What leadership theories are relevant to your understanding of this leader, and how?
6. What characteristics of their followers' personalities (e.g., skills/abilities, needs, wants, preferences, expectations, biases, and personal histories) affected the leader's success?

## Suggested Leader References

Cunningham, M., and F. Schumer. *Powerplay: What Really Happened at Bendix.* New York: Fawcett Gold Medal, 1984.

Garrow, D. J. *Bearing the Cross: Martin Luther King, Jr., and the Southern Christian Leadership Conference.* New York: William Morrow, 1986.

Hitler, A. *Mein Kampf.* Boston: Houghton Mifflin, 1927.

Iacocca, L., with W. Novak. *Iacocca: An Autobiography.* New York: Bantam, 1984.

Laccy, R. *Ford: The Men and the Machine.* Boston: Little, Brown, 1986.

Langer, W. C. *The Mind of Adolf Hitler.* New York: New American Library, 1972.

Roosevelt, E. *The Autobiography of Eleanor Roosevelt.* Boston: G. K. Hall, 1984.

Sloan, A. *The Bendix–Martin Marietta War.* New York: Dow-Jones, 1977.

Youngs, J. W. T. *Eleanor Roosevelt: A Personal and Public Life.* Boston: Little Brown, 1985.

**Source:** Clayton P. Alderfer, "Teaching Personality and Leadership: A Course on Followership," *OBTR* 12, no.4 (1987–88), pp. 12–33.

**EXERCISE**
*Leadership
through Film:
Power and
Influence*

| | |
|---|---|
| **Task:** | Students view a "popular" video (full-length movie) and analyze it for illustrations of various sources and applications of power. This draws on Bandura's concept of vicarious (observational) learning. |
| **Group Size:** | Assignments can be made at three levels: total class, small group, or individual. |
| **Materials Needed:** | VCR/TV and selected video, if a single, common stimulus is desired for total-class discussion. |
| **Time Required:** | Approximately two hours to view an entire film, plus subsequent discussion time. |
| **Procedure:** | 1. Choose a video that is rich in demonstration of a leader's use of power and influence. Many prime examples exist, such as *Dead Poets' Society, Watership Down, Aliens, A Few Good Men,* and *The Magnificent Seven.* |
| | 2. Show the video to the class. (Alternatively, allow each class member to select the video of his or her choice and prepare a report.) |
| | 3. Ask each member to prepare a written paper that thoroughly discusses leadership and power. |
| **Discussion Questions:** | 1. *Who* has power in the video, *why* do they have that power, and *how* did they acquire it? |
| | 2. What was the *source* of that power (e.g., expert, legitimate, referent)? |
| | 3. How did they *use* their power (e.g., to make a legitimate request, to gain compliance, to persuade or inspire)? |
| | 4. What were the positive/negative *effects* of that power on the followers? |
| | 5. Alternatively, how could they have influenced their followers? |

**Sources:** Adapted from various reports by Timothy Serey, Claudia Harris, Kermith V. Harrington, and Ricky W. Griffin.

**EXERCISE**
*Deriving
Leadership
Lessons From*
The Lion King

Provide meaningful text-based responses to a variety of discussion questions.

**Task:**

Groups of 3–5 students.

**Group Size:**

Video of Disney's *The Lion King*.

**Materials Needed:**

Approximately one hour, plus viewing time.

**Time Required:**

Divide the class into small groups. Show the video to them (it's the story of Simba, heir to the throne of Pride Rock, who makes a bad decision and sends himself into exile as punishment. His power-crazed uncle Scar ascends to the throne as king, but eventually Simba is persuaded by friends Timon, Pumbaa, and Nala to forget his past and return to save his homeland). Assign them the first set of questions and give them 20 minutes to develop responses to them. Reconvene as a full class and facilitate a large-group discussion for 10 minutes. Repeat the process with the second set of questions in both small-group and large-group discussion.

**Procedure:**

1. According to French and Raven (1959), individuals have five sources of power by which they can induce others to behave in accordance with their wishes. Give examples of characters in *The Lion King* that have (a) reward power, (b) coercive power, (c) legitimate power, (d) expert power, and (e) referent power.

**Discussion
Questions (1):**

2. Katz (1955) discussed technical, human, and conceptual skills. Which of these three kinds of skills does an effective leader need? How do leaders acquire and develop these skills? Give examples from the movie.

3. Kirkpatrick and Locke (1991) asserted that certain key traits predispose individuals to lead effectively. Explain how (a) a personalized versus socialized power drive, (b) honesty and integrity, and (c) self-confidence affect the leadership of the three lion kings.

4. How do the behaviors of the three lion kings contribute to their effectiveness as leaders?

5. How did Timon and Pumbaa help their friend Simba become an effective leader? How did their motto "hakuna matata" impede Simba's development as a leader?

6. Compared with Scar, Mufasa and Simba shone as leaders. Nonetheless, neither one was perfect. Identify each one's leadership flaw.

1. How can a leader's enemies undermine the leader's effectiveness? How should an organizational leader view and deal with his or her enemies?

**Discussion
Questions (2):**

2. Simba took a personal physical risk when he battled Scar to reclaim Pride Rock. What risks do organizational leaders take when contending with their enemies?

3. What are the consequences, for both a leader and his or her group, of the leader's running away from a problem instead of confronting it?

4. Management educators have recently recognized the usefulness of the notion of spirituality (e.g., Bolman & Deal, 1995; Ferris, 1998; Neal, 1997). Rafiki persuaded Simba to reclaim the throne by helping him communicate with the spirit of his father, Mufasa. How can organizational leaders who do not necessarily subscribe to religion or to the supernatural use spirituality to lead more effectively?

5. It is not uncommon for organizational leaders to experience fear while facing stressful situations (Ferris, 1998). Simba had to confront his feelings of sadness, shame, guilt, and inadequacy before he could reclaim the throne. What lesson may be generalized to organizational leaders from Simba's process of overcoming his negative feelings about himself?

6. In the movie, effective leadership was associated with plentiful resources and a balanced ecosystem. Ineffective leadership was associated with depleted resources and a dysfunctional system. What analogous outcomes are associated with effective and ineffective leadership in business organizations?

*(continued)*

7. Identify a leader from history or fiction (or religious texts, which some view as history and others view as fiction) who faced experiences comparable to those Simba encountered. Elaborate on the parallels between this leader and Simba.

8. Before Simba reclaimed his throne, the inhabitants of the Pride Lands were in dire straits. Had Simba not returned to battle Scar, what, if anything, would the lionesses and other animals have done? Why do group members tend to look to a leader to rescue them from their problems? How can overdependence on a leader harm group members?

**Source:** Adapted from Debra R. Comer, "Not Just a Mickey Mouse Exercise: Using Disney's *The Lion King* to Teach Leadership," *Journal of Management Education,* 25, no. 4, pp. 430–436, copyright 2001 by Sage Publications. Reprinted by Permission of Sage Publications, Inc.

# Index